THE BODLEY HEAD
Bernard Shaw
VOLUME
IV

THE BODLEY HEAD

Bernard Shaw

COLLECTED PLAYS WITH

THEIR PREFACES

[VOLUME IV]

Misalliance, The Dark Lady of the Sonnets
Fanny's First Play, Androcles and the Lion
Pygmalion, Overruled, The Music-Cure
Great Catherine, The Inca of Perusalem
O'Flaherty, V.C.

MAX REINHARDT
THE BODLEY HEAD
LONDON SYDNEY
TORONTO

EDITORIAL SUPERVISOR

Dan H. Laurence

© 1972 The Trustees of the British Museum, The Governors
and Guardians of the National Gallery of Ireland, and the
Royal Academy of Dramatic Art
ISBN 0 370 01390 5
Printed and bound in Great Britain for
Max Reinhardt, The Bodley Head Ltd
9 Bow Street, London, WC2E 7AL
by William Clowes & Sons Ltd, Beccles
Set in Monotype Plantin Light
First published 1910, 1913, 1914, 1916, 1919, 1926
Revised and reprinted in the Collected Edition, 1930
Reprinted in the Standard Edition, 1931, 1932
This edition first published 1972

Publisher's Note

Bernard Shaw was, throughout his publishing career, an inveterate reviser. His most extensive revision of his plays was undertaken in 1930–32 for the Collected Edition. This text was subsequently reset and issued in 1931–32 as the Standard Edition: it contained corrections but no further textual revision. Shaw, however, did make further alterations in some of the plays and prefaces in the Standard Edition in later years. Accordingly, to ensure a definitive text, we have set type for the Bodley Head edition from the last printing of each volume of plays in the Standard Edition which was authorized for press by Shaw in his lifetime.

Shaw had strong personal opinions about style in printing, many of them highly idiosyncratic, and as he was his own publisher he had no difficulty implementing them. His spellings and contractions were often bizarre (*enterprize* and *wernt*], and sometimes archaic (*shew* for *show*, as in the title of his play *The Shewing-up of Blanco Posnet*). He had equally strong convictions about the superfluous use of punctuation, noting in *The Author* in April 1902:

"The apostrophes in ain't, don't, haven't, etc. look so ugly that the most careful printing cannot make a page of colloquial dialogue as handsome as a page of classical dialogue. Besides, shan't should be sha"n't, if the wretched pedantry of indicating the elision is to be carried out. I have written aint, dont, havnt, shant, shouldnt and wont for twenty years with perfect impunity, using the apostrophe only where its omission would suggest another word: for example, hell for he'll. There is not the faintest reason for persisting in the ugly and silly trick of peppering pages with these uncouth bacilli. I also write thats, whats, lets, for the colloquial forms of that is, what is, let us; and I have not yet been prosecuted."

Throughout this definitive edition we have undertaken to follow Shaw's dictates in all matters of spelling and punctuation. Except for a small number of corrections of obvious misprints, the texts are faithfully reproduced.

One additional technical matter must be noted here. Shaw's aesthetics of typography required that italics be reserved for stage directions. In all editions of Shaw's plays up to and including the Collected Edition emphasis within dialogue passages was obtained by letter-spacing. For technical reasons, however, Shaw's printer (William Maxwell, director of R. & R. Clark, Edinburgh) prevailed upon him to permit the setting of emphasised words in the Standard Edition in a slightly larger type. In the present edition the original spaced lettering has been restored. This move, we like to think, would have pleased Shaw.

CONTENTS

[7]

[8]

Misalliance

Misalliance

with

A Treatise on Parents and Children

Fanny's First Play

The Dark Lady of the Sonnets

Author's Note

Composition begun 8 September 1909;
completed 4 November 1909. First published
in German translation, as *Mesallianz*, 1910.
Published in *Misalliance, The Dark Lady of
the Sonnets, and Fanny's First Play*, 1914.
Revised text in Collected Edition, 1930. First
presented at the Duke of York's Theatre,
London, on 23 February 1910.

John Tarleton, Jun.   *Frederick Lloyd*
Bentley Summerhays   *Donald Calthrop*
Hypatia Tarleton   *Miriam Lewes*
Mrs Tarleton   *Florence Haydon*
Lord Summerhays   *Hubert Harben*
John Tarleton   *C. M. Lowne*
Joseph Percival   *Charles Bryant*
Lina Szczepanowska   *Lena Ashwell*
Julius Baker ("Gunner")   *O. P. Heggie*

Period—31 May 1909

Scene—*The House of John Tarleton, of Hindhead,
Surrey*

"As the debate is a long one [the play was originally sub-titled 'A Debate in One Sitting'], the
curtain will be lowered twice. The audience is
requested to excuse these interruptions, which are
made solely for its convenience."

Parents and Children

Contents

[13]

TRAILING CLOUDS OF GLORY

Childhood is a stage in the process of that continual remanufacture of the Life Stuff by which the human race is perpetuated. The Life Force either will not or cannot achieve immortality except in very low organisms: indeed it is by no means ascertained that even the amoeba is immortal. Human beings visibly wear out, though they last longer than their friends the dogs. Turtles, parrots, and elephants are believed to be capable of outliving the memory of the oldest human inhabitant. But the fact that new ones are born conclusively proves that they are not immortal. Do away with death and you do away with the need for birth: in fact if you went on breeding, you would finally have to kill old people to make room for young ones.

Now death is not necessarily a failure of energy on the part of the Life Force. People with no imagination try to make things which will last for ever, and even want to live for ever themselves. But the intelligently imaginative man knows very well that it is waste of labor to make a machine that will last ten years, because it will probably be superseded in half that time by an improved machine answering the same purpose. He also knows that if some devil were to convince us that our dream of personal immortality is no dream but a hard fact, such a shriek of despair would go up from the human race as no other conceivable horror could provoke. With all our perverse nonsense as to John Smith living for a thousand million eons and for ever after, we die voluntarily, knowing that it is time for us to be scrapped, to be remanufactured, to come back, as Wordsworth divined, trailing ever brightening clouds of glory. We must all be born again, and yet again and again. We

should like to live a little longer just as we should like
£50: that is, we should take it if we could get it for
nothing; but that sort of idle liking is not will. It is
amazing—considering the way we talk—how little a
man will do to get £50: all the £50 notes I have ever
known of have been more easily earned than a labori-
ous sixpence; but the difficulty of inducing a man to
make any serious effort to obtain £50 is nothing to
the difficulty of inducing him to make a serious effort
to keep alive. The moment he sees death approach,
he gets into bed and sends for a doctor. He knows
very well at the back of his conscience that he is
rather a poor job and had better be remanufactured.
He knows that his death will make room for a birth;
and he hopes that it will be a birth of something that
he aspired to be and fell short of. He knows that it is
through death and rebirth that this corruptible shall
become incorruptible, and this mortal put on immortality. Practise as you will on his ignorance, his fears,
and his imagination with bribes of paradises and
threats of hells, there is only one belief that can rob
death of its sting and the grave of its victory; and that
is the belief that we can lay down the burden of our
wretched little makeshift individualities for ever at
each lift towards the goal of evolution, which can only
be a being that cannot be improved upon. After all,
what man is capable of the insane self-conceit of
believing that an eternity of himself would be tolerable even to himself? Those who try to believe it
postulate that they shall be made perfect first. But if
you make me perfect I shall no longer be myself, nor
will it be possible for me to conceive my present
imperfections (and what I cannot conceive I cannot
remember); so that you may just as well give me a
new name and face the fact that I am a new person

and that the old Bernard Shaw is as dead as mutton. Thus, oddly enough, the conventional belief in the matter comes to this: that if you wish to live for ever you must be wicked enough to be irretrievably damned, since the saved are no longer what they were, and in hell alone do people retain their sinful nature: that is to say, their individuality. And this sort of hell, however convenient as a means of intimidating persons who have practically no honor and no conscience, is not a fact. Death is for many of us the gate of hell; but we are inside on the way out, not outside on the way in. Therefore let us give up telling one another idle stories, and rejoice in death as we rejoice in birth; for without death we cannot be born again; and the man who does not wish to be born again and born better is fit only to represent the City of London in Parliament, or perhaps the university of Oxford.

THE CHILD IS FATHER TO THE MAN

Is he? Then in the name of common sense why do we always treat children on the assumption that the man is father to the child? Oh, these fathers! And we are not content with fathers: we must have godfathers, forgetting that the child is godfather to the man. Has it ever struck you as curious that in a country where the first article of belief is that every child is born with a godfather whom we all call "our father which art in heaven," two very limited individual mortals should be allowed to appear at its baptism and explain that they are its godparents, and that they will look after its salvation until it is no longer a child. I had a godmother who made herself responsible in this way for me. She presented me with a Bible with a gilt clasp and edges, larger than the Bibles similarly presented to my sisters, because my sex entitled me to a heavier article. I must have seen that lady at least four times in the twenty years following. She never alluded to my salvation in any way. People occasionally ask me to act as godfather to their children with a levity which convinces me that they have not the faintest notion that it involves anything more than calling the helpless child George Bernard without regard to the possibility that it may grow up in the liveliest abhorrence of my notions.

A person with a turn for logic might argue that if God is the Father of all men, and if the child is father to the man, it follows that the true representative of God at the christening is the child itself. But such posers are unpopular, because they imply that our little customs, or, as we often call them, our religion, mean something, or must originally have meant something, and that we understand and believe that something.

However, my business is not to make confusion worse confounded, but to clear it up. Only, it is as well to begin by a sample of current thought and practice which shews that on the subject of children we are very deeply confused. On the whole, whatever our theory or no theory may be, our practice is to treat the child as the property of its immediate physical parents, and to allow them to do what they like with it as far as it will let them. It has no rights and no liberties: in short, its condition is that which adults recognize as the most miserable and dangerous politically possible for themselves: namely, the condition of slavery. For its alleviation we trust to the natural affection of the parties, and to public opinion. A father cannot for his own credit let his son go in rags. Also, in a very large section of the population, parents finally become dependent on their children. Thus there are checks on child slavery which do not exist, or are less powerful, in the case of manual and industrial slavery. Sensationally bad cases fall into two classes, which are really the same class: namely, the children whose parents are excessively addicted to the sensual luxury of petting children, and the children whose parents are excessively addicted to the sensual luxury of physically torturing them. There is a Society for the Prevention of Cruelty to Children which has effectually made an end of our belief that mothers are any more to be trusted than stepmothers, or fathers than slave-drivers. And there is a growing body of law designed to prevent parents from using their children ruthlessly to make money for the household. Such legislation has always been furiously resisted by the parents, even when the horrors of factory slavery were at their worst; and the extension of such legislation at present would be impossible if it were not that the parents affected by it cannot control a majority of votes in Parliament. In domestic life a great deal of service is done by children, the girls acting as nursemaids and general servants, and the lads as errand boys. In the country both boys and girls do a substantial share of farm labor. This is why it is necessary to coerce poor parents to send their children to school, though in the relatively small class which keeps plenty of servants it is impossible to induce parents to keep their children at home instead of paying schoolmasters to take them off their hands.

It appears then that the bond of affection between parents and children does not save children from the slavery that denial of rights involves in adult political relations. It sometimes intensifies it, sometimes mitigates it; but on the whole children and parents confront one another as two classes in which all the political power is on one side; and the results are not at all unlike what they would be if there were no immediate consanguinity between them, and one were white and the other black, or one enfranchised and the other disenfranchised, or one ranked as gentle and the other simple. Not that Nature counts for nothing in the case and political rights for everything. But a denial of political rights, and the resultant delivery of one class into the mastery of another, affects their relations so extensively and profoundly that it is impossible to ascertain what the real natural relations of the two classes are until this political relation is abolished.

WHAT IS A CHILD?

An experiment. A fresh attempt to produce the just man made perfect: that is, to make humanity divine. And you will vitiate the experiment if you make the slightest attempt to abort it into some fancy figure of your own: for example, your notion of a good man or a womanly woman. If you treat it as a little wild beast to be tamed, or as a pet to be played with, or even as a means to save you trouble and to make money for you (and these are our commonest ways), it may fight its way through in spite of you and save its soul alive; for all its instincts will resist you, and possibly be strengthened in the resistance; but if you begin with its own holiest aspirations, and suborn them for your own purposes, then there is hardly any limit to the mischief you may do. Swear at a child, throw your boots at it, send it flying from the room with a cuff or a kick; and the experience will be as instructive to the child as a difficulty with a short-tempered dog or a bull. Francis Place tells us that his father always struck his children when he found one within his reach. The effect on the young Places seems to have been simply to make them keep out of their father's way, which was no doubt what he desired, as far as he desired anything at all. Francis records the habit without bitterness, having reason to thank his stars that his father respected the inside of his head whilst cuffing the outside of it; and this made it easy for Francis to do yeoman's service to his country as that rare and admirable thing, a Freethinker: the only sort of thinker, I may remark, whose thoughts, and consequently whose religious convictions, command any respect.

Now Mr Place, senior, would be described by many as a bad father; and I do not contend that he was a conspicuously good one. But as compared with the conventional good father who deliberately imposes himself on his son as a god; who takes advantage of childish credulity and parent worship to persuade his son that what he approves of is right and what he disapproves of is wrong; who imposes a corresponding conduct on the child by a system of prohibitions and penalties, rewards and eulogies, for which he claims divine sanction: compared to this sort of abortionist and monster maker, I say, Place appears almost as a Providence. Not that it is possible to live with children any more than with grown-up people without imposing rules of conduct on them. There is a point at which every person with human nerves has to say to a child "Stop that noise." But suppose the child asks why! There are various answers in use. The simplest: "Because it irritates me," may fail; for it may strike the child as being rather amusing to irritate you; also the child, having comparatively no nerves, may be unable to conceive your meaning vividly enough. In any case it may want to make a noise more than to spare your feelings. You may therefore have to explain that the effect of the irritation will be that you will do something unpleasant if the noise continues. The something unpleasant may be only a look of suffering to rouse the child's affectionate sympathy (if it has any), or it may run to forcible expulsion from the room with plenty of unnecessary violence; but the principle is the same: there are no false pretences involved: the child learns in a straightforward way that it does not pay to be inconsiderate. Also, perhaps, that Mamma, who made the child learn the Sermon on the Mount, is not really a Christian.

THE SIN OF NADAB AND ABIHU

But there is another sort of answer in wide use which is neither straightforward, instructive, nor harmless. In its simplest form it substitutes for "Stop that noise," "Dont be naughty," which means that the child, instead of annoying you by a perfectly healthy and natural infantile procedure, is offending God. This is a blasphemous lie; and the fact that it is on the lips of every nurserymaid does not excuse it in the least. Dickens tells us of a nurserymaid who elaborated it into "If you do that, angels wont never love you." I remember a servant who used to tell me that if I were not good, by which she meant if I did not behave with a single eye to her personal convenience, the cock would come down the chimney. Less imaginative but equally dishonest people told me I should go to hell if I did not make myself agreeable to them. Bodily violence, provided it be the hasty expression of normal provoked resentment and not vicious cruelty, cannot harm a child as this sort of pious fraud harms it. There is a legal limit to physical cruelty; and there are also human limits to it. There is an active Society which brings to book a good many parents who starve and torture and overwork their children, and intimidates a good many more. When parents of this type are caught, they are treated as criminals; and not infrequently the police have some trouble to save them from being lynched. The people against whom children are wholly unprotected are those who devote themselves to the very mischievous and cruel sort of abortion which is called bringing up a child in the way it should go. Now nobody knows the way a child should go. All the ways discovered so far lead to the horrors of our existing civilizations, described quite justifiably by Ruskin as heaps of agonizing human maggots, struggling with one another for scraps of food. Pious fraud is an attempt to pervert that divine mystery called the child's conscience into an instrument of our own convenience, and to use that wonderful and terrible power called Shame to grind our own axe. It is the sin of stealing fire from the altar: a sin so impudently practised by popes, parents, and pedagogues, that one can hardly expect the nurserymaids to see any harm in stealing a few cinders when they are worried.

Into the blackest depths of this violation of children's souls one can hardly bear to look; for here we find pious fraud masking the violation of the body by obscene cruelty. Any parent or school teacher who takes a secret and abominable delight in torture is allowed to lay traps into which every child must fall, and then beat it to his or her heart's content. A gentleman once wrote to me and said, with an obvious conviction that he was being most reasonable and high-minded, that the only thing he beat his children for was failure in perfect obedience and perfect truthfulness. On these virtues, he said, he must insist. As one of them is not a virtue at all, and the other is the attribute of a god, one can imagine what the lives of this gentleman's children would have been if it had been possible for him to live down to his monstrous and foolish pretensions. And yet he might have written his letter to The Times (he very nearly did, by the way) without incurring any danger of being removed to an asylum, or even losing his reputation for taking a very proper view of his parental duties. And at least it was not a trivial view, nor an ill meant one. It was much more respectable than the general consensus of opinion that if a school teacher can devise a question a child cannot answer, or overhear it calling omega omeega, he or she may beat the child viciously. Only, the cruelty must be whitewashed by a moral excuse, and a pretence of reluctance. It must be for the child's good. The assailant must say "This hurts me more than it hurts you." There must be hypocrisy as well as cruelty. The injury to the child would be far less if the voluptuary said frankly "I beat you because I like beating you; and I shall do it whenever I can contrive an excuse for it." But to represent this detestable lust to the child as Divine wrath, and the cruelty as the beneficent act of God, which is exactly what all our floggers do, is to add to the torture of the body, out of which the flogger at least gets some pleasure, the maiming and blinding of the child's soul, which can bring nothing but horror to anyone.

THE MANUFACTURE OF MONSTERS

This industry is by no means peculiar to China. The Chinese (they say) make physical monsters. We revile them for it and proceed to make moral monsters of our own children. The most excusable parents are those who try to correct their own faults in their offspring. The parent who says to his child: "I am one of the successes of the Almighty: therefore imitate me in every particular or I will have the skin off your back" (a quite common attitude) is a much more absurd figure than the man who, with a pipe in his mouth, thrashes his boy for smoking. If you must hold yourself up to your children as an object lesson (which is not at all necessary), hold yourself up as a warning and not as an example. But you had much better let the child's character alone. If you once allow yourself to regard a child as so much material for you to manufacture into any shape that happens to suit your fancy you are defeating the experiment of the Life Force. You are assuming that the child does not know its own business, and that you do. In this you are sure to be wrong: the child feels the drive of the Life Force (often called the Will of God); and you cannot feel it for him. Handel's parents no doubt thought they knew better than their child when they tried to prevent his becoming a musician. They would have been equally wrong and equally unsuccessful if they had tried to prevent the child becoming a great rascal had its genius lain in that direction. Handel would have been Handel, and Napoleon and Peter of Russia *them*selves in spite of all the parents in creation, because, as often happens, they were stronger than their parents. But this does not happen always. Most children can be, and many are, hopelessly warped and wasted by parents who are ignorant and silly enough to suppose that they know what a human being ought to be, and who stick at nothing in their determination to force their children into their moulds. Every child has a right to its own bent. It has a right to be a Plymouth Brother though its parents be convinced atheists. It has a right to dislike its mother or father or sister or brother or uncle or aunt if they are antipathetic to it. It has a right to find its own way and go its own way, whether that way seems wise or foolish to others, exactly as an adult has. It has a right to privacy as to its own doings and its own affairs as much as if it were its own father.

SMALL AND LARGE FAMILIES

These rights have now become more important than they used to be, because the modern practice of limiting families enables them to be more effectually violated. In a family of ten, eight, six, or even four children, the rights of the younger ones to a great extent take care of themselves and of the rights of the elder ones too. Two adult parents, in spite of a house to keep and an income to earn, can still interfere to a disastrous extent with the rights and liberties of one child. But by the time a fourth child has arrived, they are not only outnumbered two to one, but are getting tired of the thankless and mischievous job of bringing up their children in the way they think they should go. The old observation that members of large families get on in the world holds good because in large families it is impossible for each child to receive what schoolmasters call "individual attention." The children may receive a good deal of individual attention from one another in the shape of outspoken reproach, ruthless ridicule, and violent resistance to their attempts at aggression; but the parental despots are compelled by the multitude of their subjects to resort to political rather than personal rule, and to spread their attempts at moral monster-making over so many children, that each child has enough freedom, and enough sport in the prophylactic process of laughing at its elders behind their backs, to escape with much less damage than the single child. In a large school the system may be bad; but the personal influence of the head master has to be exerted, when it is exerted at all, in a public way, because he has little more power of working on the affections of the individual scholar in the intimate way that, for example, the mother of a single child can, than the prime minister has of working on the affections of any individual voter.

CHILDREN AS NUISANCES

Experienced parents, when children's rights are preached to them, very naturally ask whether children are to be allowed to do what they like. The best reply is to ask whether adults are to be allowed to do what they like. The two cases are the same. The adult who is nasty is not allowed to do what he likes: neither can the child who likes to be nasty. There is no difference in principle between the rights of a child and those of an adult: the difference in their cases is one of circumstance. An adult is not supposed to be punished except by process of law; nor, when he is so punished, is the person whom he has injured allowed to act as judge, jury, and executioner. It is true that employers do act in this way every day to their workpeople; but this is not a justified and intended part of the situation: it is an abuse of Capitalism which nobody defends in principle. As between child and parent or nurse it is not argued about because it is inevitable. You cannot hold an impartial judicial inquiry every time a child misbehaves itself. To allow the child to misbehave without instantly making it unpleasantly conscious of the fact would be to spoil it. The adult has therefore to take some action of some sort with nothing but his conscience to shield the child from injustice or unkindness. The action may be a torrent of scolding culminating in a furious smack causing terror and pain, or it may be a remonstrance causing remorse, or it may be a sarcasm causing shame and humiliation, or it may be a sermon causing the child to believe that it is a little reprobate on the road to hell. The child has no defence in any case except the kindness and conscience of the adult; and the adult had better not forget this; for it involves a heavy responsibility.

And now comes our difficulty. The responsibility, being so heavy, cannot be discharged by persons of feeble character or intelligence. And yet people of high character and intelligence cannot be plagued with the care of children. A child is a restless, noisy little animal, with an insatiable appetite for knowledge, and consequently a maddening persistence in asking questions. If the child is to remain in the room with a highly intelligent and sensitive adult, it must be told, and if necessary forced, to sit still and not speak, which is injurious to its health, unnatural, unjust, and therefore cruel and selfish beyond toleration. Consequently the highly intelligent and sensitive adult hands the child over to a nurserymaid who has no nerves and can therefore stand more noise, but who has also no scruples, and may therefore be very bad company for the child.

Here we have come to the central fact of the question: a fact nobody avows, which is yet the true

explanation of the monstrous system of child imprisonment and torture which we disguise under such
hypocrisies as education, training, formation of
character and the rest of it. This fact is simply that a
child is a nuisance to a grown-up person. What is
more, the nuisance becomes more and more intolerable as the grown-up person becomes more cultivated,
more sensitive, and more deeply engaged in the
highest methods of adult work. The child at play is
noisy and ought to be noisy: Sir Isaac Newton at
work is quiet and ought to be quiet. And the child
should spend most of its time at play, whilst the
adult should spend most of his time at work. I am not
now writing on behalf of persons who coddle themselves into a ridiculous condition of nervous feeble-
ness, and at last imagine themselves unable to work
under conditions of bustle which to healthy people
are cheerful and stimulating. I am sure that if people
had to choose between living where the noise of
children never stopped and where it was never heard,
all the goodnatured and sound people would prefer
the incessant noise to the incessant silence. But that
choice is not thrust upon us by the nature of things.
There is no reason why children and adults should not
see just as much of one another as is good for them,
no more and no less. Even at present you are not compelled to choose between sending your child to a
boarding school (which means getting rid of it altogether on more or less hypocritical pretences) and
keeping it continually at home. Most working folk
today either send their children to day schools or turn
them out of doors. This solves the problem for the
parents. It does not solve it for the children, any
more than the tethering of a goat in a field or the
chasing of an unlicensed dog into the streets solves it

for the goat or the dog; but it shews that in no class are people willing to endure the society of their children, and consequently that it is an error to believe that the family provides children with edifying adult society, or that the family is a social unit. The family is in that, as in so many other respects, a humbug. Old people and young people cannot walk at the same pace without distress and final loss of health to one of the parties. When they are sitting indoors they cannot endure the same degrees of temperature and the same supplies of fresh air. Even if the main factors of noise, restlessness, and inquisitiveness are left out of account, children can stand with indifference sights, sounds, smells, and disorders that would make an adult of fifty utterly miserable; whilst on the other hand such adults find a tranquil happiness in conditions which to children mean unspeakable boredom. And since our system is nevertheless to pack them all into the same house and pretend that they are happy, and that this particular sort of happiness is the foundation of virtue, it is found that in discussing family life we never speak of actual adults or actual children, or of realities of any sort, but always of ideals such as The Home, a Mother's Influence, a Father's Care, Filial Piety, Duty, Affection, Family Life, etc. etc., which are no doubt very comforting phrases, but which beg the question of what a home and a mother's influence and a father's care and so forth really come to in practice. How many hours a week of the time when his children are out of bed does the ordinary breadwinning father spend in the company of his children or even in the same building with them? The home may be a thieves' kitchen, the mother a procuress, the father a violent drunkard; or the mother and father may be fashionable people who see their children three or four times a year during the holidays, and then not oftener than they can help, living meanwhile in daily and intimate contact with their valets and lady's-maids, whose influence and care are often dominant in the household. Affection, as distinguished from simple kindliness, may or may not exist: when it does it either depends on qualities in the parties that would produce it equally if they were of no kin to one another, or it is a more or less morbid survival of the nursing passion; for affection between adults (if they are really adult in mind and not merely grown-up children) and creatures so relatively selfish and cruel as children necessarily are without knowing it or meaning it, cannot be called natural: in fact the evidence shews that it is easier to love the company of a dog than of a commonplace child between the ages of six and the beginnings of controlled maturity; for women who cannot bear to be separated from their pet dogs send their children to boarding schools cheerfully. They may say and even believe that in allowing their children to leave home they are sacrificing themselves for their children's good; but there are very few pet dogs who would not be the better for a month or two spent elsewhere than in a lady's lap or roasting on a drawing-room hearthrug. Besides, to allege that children are better continually away from home is to give up the whole popular sentimental theory of the family; yet the dogs are kept and the children are banished.

CHILD FANCIERS

There is, however, a good deal of spurious family affection. There is the clannishness that will make a dozen brothers and sisters who quarrel furiously among themselves close up their ranks and make common cause against a brother-in-law or a sister-in-law. And there is a strong sense of property in children, which often makes mothers and fathers bitterly jealous of allowing anyone else to interfere with their children, whom they may none the less treat very badly. And there is an extremely dangerous craze for children which leads certain people to establish orphanages and baby farms and schools, seizing any pretext for filling their houses with children exactly as some eccentric old ladies and gentlemen fill theirs with cats. In such places the children are the victims of all the caprices of doting affection and all the excesses of lascivious cruelty. Yet the people who have this morbid craze seldom have any difficulty in finding victims. Parents and guardians are so worried by children and so anxious to get rid of them that anyone who is willing to take them off their hands is welcomed and whitewashed. The very people who read with indignation of Squeers and Creakle in the novels of Dickens are quite ready to hand over their own children to Squeers and Creakle, and to pretend that Squeers and Creakle are monsters of the past. But read the autobiography of Stanley the traveller, or sit in the company of men talking about their schooldays, and you will soon find that fiction, which must, if it is to be sold and read, stop short of being positively sickening, dare not tell the whole truth about the people to whom children are handed over on educational pretexts. Not very long ago a schoolmaster in Ireland was murdered by his boys; and for reasons which were never made public it was at first decided not to prosecute the murderers. Yet all these flogging schoolmasters and orphanage fiends and baby farmers are "lovers of children." They are really child fanciers (like bird fanciers or dog fanciers) by irresistible natural predilection, never happy unless they are surrounded by their victims, and always certain to make their living by accepting custody of children, no matter how many alternative occupations may be available. And bear in mind that they are only the extreme instances of what is commonly called natural affection, apparently because it is obviously unnatural.

The really natural feeling of adults for children in the long prosaic intervals between the moments of affectionate impulse is just that feeling that leads them to avoid their care and constant company as a burden beyond bearing, and to pretend that the places they send them to are well conducted, beneficial, and indispensable to the success of the children in after life. The true cry of the kind mother after her little rosary of kisses is "Run away, darling." It is nicer than "Hold your noise, you young devil; or it will be the worse for you;" but fundamentally it means the same thing: that if you compel an adult and a child to live in one another's company either the adult or the child will be miserable. There is nothing whatever unnatural or wrong or shocking in this fact; and there is no harm in it if only it be sensibly faced and provided for. The mischief that it does at present is produced by our efforts to ignore it, or to smother it under a heap of sentimental lies and false pretences.

CHILDHOOD AS A STATE OF SIN

Unfortunately all this nonsense tends to accumulate as we become more sympathetic. In many families it is still the custom to treat childhood frankly as a state of sin, and impudently proclaim the monstrous principle that little children should be seen and not heard, and to enforce a set of prison rules designed solely to make cohabitation with children as convenient as possible for adults without the smallest regard for the interests, either remote or immediate, of the children. This system tends to produce a tough, rather brutal, stupid, unscrupulous class, with a fixed idea that all enjoyment consists in undetected sinning; and in certain phases of civilization people of this kind are apt to get the upper hand of more amiable and conscientious races and classes. They have the ferocity of a chained dog, and are proud of it. But the end of it is that they are always in chains, even at the height of their military or political success; they win everything on condition that they are afraid to enjoy it. Their civilizations rest on intimidation, which is so necessary to them that when they cannot find anybody brave enough to intimidate them they intimidate themselves and live in a continual moral and political panic. In the end they get found out and bullied. But that is not the point that concerns us here, which is, that they are in some respects better brought up than the children of sentimental people who are always anxious and miserable about their duty to their children, and who end by neither making their children happy nor having a tolerable life for themselves. A selfish tyrant you know where to have, and he (or she) at least does not confuse your affections; but a conscientious and kindly meddler may literally worry you out of your senses. It is fortunate that only very few parents are capable of doing what they conceive their duty continually or even at all, and that still fewer are tough enough to ride roughshod over their children at home.

SCHOOL
But please observe the limitation "at home." What private amateur parental enterprise cannot do may be done very effectively by organized professional enterprise in large institutions established for the purpose. And it is to such professional enterprise that parents hand over their children when they can afford it. They send their children to school; and there is, on the whole, nothing on earth intended for innocent people so horrible as a school. To begin with, it is a prison. But it is in some respects more cruel than a prison. In a prison, for instance, you are not forced to read books written by the warders and the governor (who of course would not be warders and governors if they could write readable books), and beaten or otherwise tormented if you cannot remember their utterly unmemorable contents. In the prison you are not forced to sit listening to turnkeys discoursing without charm or interest on subjects that they dont understand and dont care about, and are therefore incapable of making you understand or care about. In a prison they may torture your body; but they do not torture your brains; and they protect you against violence and outrage from your fellow-prisoners. In a school you have none of these advantages. With the world's bookshelves loaded with fascinating and inspired books, the very manna sent down from Heaven to feed your souls, you are forced to read a hideous imposture called a school book, written by a man who cannot write: a book from which no human being can learn anything: a book which, though you may decipher it, you cannot in any fruitful sense read, though the enforced attempt will make you loathe the sight of a book all the rest of your life. With millions of acres of woods and valleys and hills and wind

[35]

and air and birds and streams and fishes and all sorts of instructive and healthy things easily accessible, or with streets and shop windows and crowds and vehicles and all sorts of city delights at the door, you are forced to sit, not in a room with some human grace and comfort of furniture and decoration, but in a stalled pound with a lot of other children, beaten if you talk, beaten if you move, beaten if you cannot prove by answering idiotic questions that even when you escaped from the pound and from the eye of your gaoler, you were still agonizing over his detestable sham books instead of daring to live. And your childish hatred of your gaoler and flogger is nothing to his adult hatred of you; for he is a slave forced to endure your society for his daily bread. You have not even the satisfaction of knowing how you are torturing him and how he loathes you; and you give yourself unnecessary pains to annoy him with furtive tricks and spiteful doing of forbidden things. No wonder he is sometimes provoked to fiendish outbursts of wrath. No wonder men of downright sense, like Dr Johnson, admit that under such circumstances children will not learn anything unless they are so cruelly beaten that they make desperate efforts to memorize words and phrases to escape flagellation. It is a ghastly business, quite beyond words, this schooling.

And now I hear cries of protest arising all round. First my own schoolmasters, or their ghosts, asking whether I was cruelly beaten at school? No; but then I did not learn anything at school. Dr Johnson's schoolmaster presumably did care enough whether Sam learned anything to beat him savagely enough to force him to lame his mind—for Johnson's great mind *was* lamed—by learning his lessons. None of my schoolmasters really cared a rap (or perhaps it would be fairer to them to say that their employers did not care a rap and therefore did not give them the necessary caning powers) whether I learnt my lessons or not, provided my father paid my schooling bill, the collection of which was the real object of the school. Consequently I did not learn my school lessons, having much more important ones in hand, with the result that I have not wasted my life trifling with literary fools in taverns as Johnson did when he should have been shaking England with the thunder of his spirit. My schooling did me a great deal of harm and no good whatever : it was simply dragging a child's soul through the dirt; but I escaped Squeers and Creakle just as I escaped Johnson and Carlyle. And this is what happens to most of us. We are not effectively coerced to learn: we stave off punishment as far as we can by lying and trickery and guessing and using our wits; and when this does not suffice we scribble impositions, or suffer extra imprisonments—"keeping in" was the phrase in my time—or let a master strike us with a cane and fall back on our pride at being able to bear it physically (he not being allowed to hit us too hard) to outface the dishonor we should have been taught to die rather than endure. And so idleness and worthlessness on the one hand and a pretence of coercion on the other became a despicable routine. If my schoolmasters had been really engaged in educating me instead of painfully earning their bread by keeping me from annoying my elders they would have turned me out of the school, telling me that I was thoroughly disloyal to it; that I had no intention of learning; that I was mocking and distracting the boys who did wish to learn; that I was a liar and a shirker and a seditious little nuisance; and

that nothing could injure me in character and degrade
their occupation more than allowing me (much less
forcing me) to remain in the school under such
conditions. But in order to get expelled, it was necessary to commit a crime of such atrocity that the parents
of the other boys would have threatened to remove
their sons sooner than allow them to be schoolfellows with the delinquent. I can remember only one
case in which such a penalty was threatened; and in
that case the culprit, a boarder, had kissed a housemaid, or possibly, being a handsome youth, been
kissed by her. She did not kiss me; and nobody ever
dreamt of expelling me. The truth was, a boy meant
just so much a year to the institution. That was why
he was kept there against his will. That was why he
was kept there when his expulsion would have been
an unspeakable relief and benefit both to his teachers
and himself.

It may be argued that if the uncommercial attitude
had been taken, and all the disloyal wasters and idlers
shewn sternly to the door, the school would not have
been emptied, but filled. But so honest an attitude was
impossible. The masters must have hated the school
much more than the boys did. Just as you cannot
imprison a man without imprisoning a warder to see
that he does not escape, the warder being tied to the
prison as effectually by the fear of unemployment and
starvation as the prisoner is by the bolts and bars,
so these poor schoolmasters, with their small salaries
and large classes, were as much prisoners as we were,
and much more responsible and anxious ones. They
could not impose the heroic attitude on their employers; nor would they have been able to obtain places
as schoolmasters if their habits had been heroic. For
the best of them their employment was provisional:

they looked forward to escaping from it into the pulpit. The ablest and most impatient of them were often so irritated by the awkward, slow-witted, slovenly boys: that is, the ones that required special consideration and patient treatment, that they vented their irritation on them ruthlessly, nothing being easier than to entrap or bewilder such a boy into giving a pretext for punishing him.

MY SCHOLASTIC ACQUIREMENTS

The results, as far as I was concerned, were what might have been expected. My school made only the thinnest pretence of teaching anything but Latin and Greek. When I went there as a very small boy I knew a good deal of Latin grammar which I had been taught in a few weeks privately by my uncle. When I had been several years at school this same uncle examined me and discovered that the net result of my schooling was that I had forgotten what he had taught me, and had learnt nothing else. To this day, though I can still decline a Latin noun and repeat some of the old paradigms in the old meaningless way, because their rhythm sticks to me, I have never yet seen a Latin inscription on a tomb that I could translate throughout. Of Greek I can decipher perhaps the greater part of the Greek alphabet. In short, I am, as to classical education, another Shakespear. I can read French as easily as English; and under pressure of necessity I can turn to account some scraps of German and a little operatic Italian; but these I was never taught at school. Instead, I was taught lying, dishonorable submission to tyranny, dirty stories, a blasphemous habit of treating love and maternity as obscene jokes, hopelessness, evasion, derision, cowardice, and all the blackguard's shifts by which the coward intimidates other cowards. And if I had been a boarder at an English public school instead of a day boy at an Irish one, I might have had to add to these, deeper shames still.

SCHOOLMASTERS OF GENIUS

And now, if I have reduced the ghosts of my schoolmasters to melancholy acquiescence in all this (which everybody who has been at an ordinary school will recognize as true), I have still to meet the much more sincere protests of the handful of people who have a natural genius for "bringing up" children. I shall be asked with kindly scorn whether I have heard of Froebel and Pestalozzi, whether I know the work that is being done by Miss Mason and the Dottoressa Montessori or, best of all as I think, the Eurythmics School of Jacques Dalcroze at Hellerau near Dresden. Jacques Dalcroze, like Plato, believes in saturating his pupils with music. They walk to music, play to music, work to music, obey drill commands that would bewilder a guardsman to music, think to music, live to music, get so clearheaded about music that they can move their several limbs each in a different metre until they become complicated living magazines of cross rhythms, and, what is more, make music for others to do all these things to. Stranger still, though Jacques Dalcroze, like all these great teachers, is the completest of tyrants, knowing what is right and that he must and will have the lesson just so or else break his heart (not somebody else's, observe), yet his school is so fascinating that every woman who sees it exclaims "Oh, why was I not taught like this!" and elderly gentlemen excitedly enrol themselves as students and distract classes of infants by their desperate endeavors to beat two in a bar with one hand and three with the other, and start off on earnest walks round the room, taking two steps backward whenever Monsieur Dalcroze calls out "Hop!" Oh yes: I know all about these wonderful schools that you cannot keep children or even adults out of, and these teachers whom their pupils not only obey without coercion, but adore. And if you will tell me roughly how many Masons and Montessoris and Dalcrozes you think you can pick up in Europe for salaries of from thirty shillings to five pounds a week, I will estimate your chances of converting your millions of little scholastic hells into little scholastic heavens. If you are a distressed gentlewoman starting to make a living, you can still open a little school: and you can easily buy a secondhand brass plate inscribed PESTALOZZIAN INSTITUTE and nail it to your door, though you have no more idea of who Pestalozzi was and what he advocated or how he did it than the manager of a hotel which began as a Hydropathic has of the water cure. Or you can buy a cheaper plate inscribed KINDERGARTEN, and imagine, or leave others to imagine, that Froebel is the governing genius of your little crèche. No doubt the new brass plates are being inscribed Montessori Institute, and will be used when the Dottoressa is no longer with us by all the Mrs Pipchins and Mrs Wilfers throughout this unhappy land.

I will go further, and admit that the brass plates may not all be frauds. I will tell you that one of my friends was led to genuine love and considerable knowledge of classical literature by an Irish schoolmaster whom you would call a hedge schoolmaster (he would not be allowed to teach anything now) and that it took four years of Harrow to obliterate that knowledge and change the love into loathing. Another friend of mine who keeps a school in the suburbs, and who deeply deplores my "prejudice against school-masters," has offered to accept my challenge to tell his pupils that they are as free to get up and go out of the school at any moment as their parents are to get up and go out of a theatre where my plays are being performed. Even among my own schoolmasters I can recollect a few whose classes interested me, and whom I should certainly have pestered for information and instruction if I could have got into any decent human relationship with them, and if they had not been compelled by their position to defend themselves as carefully against such advances as against furtive attempts to hurt them accidentally in the football field or smash their hats with a clod from behind a wall. But these rare cases actually do more harm than good; for they encourage us to pretend that all schoolmasters are like that. Of what use is it to us that there are always somewhere two or three teachers of children whose specific genius for their occupation triumphs over our tyrannous system and even finds in it its opportunity? For that matter, it is possible, if difficult, to find a solicitor, or even a judge, who has some notion of what law means, a doctor with a glimmering of science, an officer who understands duty and discipline, and a clergyman with an inkling of religion, though there are nothing like enough of them to go round. But even the few who, like Ibsen's Mrs Solness, have "a genius for nursing the souls of little children" are like angels forced to work in prisons instead of in heaven; and even at that they are mostly underpaid and despised. That friend of mine who went from the hedge schoolmaster to Harrow once saw a schoolmaster rush from an elementary school in pursuit of a boy and strike him. My friend, not considering that the unfortunate man was probably goaded beyond endurance, smote the schoolmaster and blackened his eye. The schoolmaster appealed to the law; and my friend found himself waiting nervously in the Hammersmith Police Court to answer for his breach of the peace. In his anxiety he asked a police officer what would happen to him. "What did you do?" said the officer. "I gave a man a black eye" said my friend. "Six pounds if he was a gentleman: two pounds if he wasnt," said the constable. "He was a schoolmaster" said my friend. "Two pounds" said the officer; and two pounds it was. The blood money was paid cheerfully; and I have ever since advised elementary schoolmasters to qualify themselves in the art of self-defence, as the British Constitution expresses our national estimate of them by allowing us to blacken three of their eyes for the same price as one of an ordinary professional man. How many Froebels and Pestalozzis and Miss Masons and Doctoress Montessoris would you be likely to get on these terms even if they occurred much more frequently in nature than they actually do?

No: I cannot be put off by the news that our system would be perfect if it were worked by angels. I do not admit it even at that, just as I do not admit that if the sky fell we should all catch larks. But I do not propose to bother about a supply of specific genius which does not exist, and which, if it did exist, could operate only by at once recognizing and establishing the rights of children.

WHAT WE DO NOT TEACH, AND WHY

To my mind, a glance at the subjects now taught in schools ought to convince any reasonable person that the object of the lessons is to keep children out of mischief, and not to qualify them for their part in life as responsible citizens of a free State. It is not possible to maintain freedom in any State, no matter how perfect its original constitution, unless its publicly active citizens know a good deal of constitutional history, law, and political science, with its basis of economics. If as much pains had been taken a century ago to make us all understand Ricardo's law of rent as to learn our catechisms, the face of the world would have been changed for the better. But for that very reason the greatest care is taken to keep such beneficially subversive knowledge from us, with the result that in public life we are either place-hunters, anarchists, or sheep shepherded by wolves.

But it will be observed that these are highly controversial subjects. Now no controversial subject can be taught dogmatically. He who knows only the official side of a controversy knows less than nothing of its nature. The abler a schoolmaster is, the more dangerous he is to his pupils unless they have the fullest opportunity of hearing another equally able person do his utmost to shake his authority and convict him of error.

At present such teaching is very unpopular. It does not exist in schools; but every adult who derives his knowledge of public affairs from the newspapers can take in, at the cost of an extra halfpenny, two papers of opposite politics. Yet the ordinary man so dislikes having his mind unsettled, as he calls it, that he angrily refuses to allow a paper which dissents from his views to be brought into his house. Even at his club he resents seeing it, and excludes it if it happens to run counter to the opinions of all the members. The result is that his opinions are not worth considering.

A churchman who never reads The Freethinker very soon has no more real religion than the atheist who never reads The Church Times. The attitude is the same in both cases: they want to hear nothing good of their enemies; consequently they remain enemies and suffer from bad blood all their lives; whereas men who know their opponents and understand their case, quite commonly respect and like them, and always learn something from them.

Here, again, as at so many points, we come up against the abuse of schools to keep people in ignorance and error, so that they may be incapable of successful revolt against their industrial slavery. The most important simple fundamental economic truth to impress on a child in complicated civilizations like ours is the truth that whoever consumes goods or services without producing by personal effort the equivalent of what he or she consumes, inflicts on the community precisely the same injury that a thief produces, and would, in any honest State, be treated as a thief, however full his or her pockets might be of money made by other people. The nation that first teaches its children that truth, instead of flogging them if they discover it for themselves, may have to fight all the slaves of all the other nations to begin with; but it will beat them as easily as an unburdened man with his hands free and with all his energies in full play can beat an invalid who has to carry another invalid on his back.

This, however, is not an evil produced by the denial of children's rights, nor is it inherent in the nature of schools. I mention it only because it would be folly to call for a reform of our schools without taking account of the corrupt resistance which awaits the reformer.

A word must also be said about the opposition to reform of the vested interest of the classical and coercive schoolmaster. He, poor wretch, has no other means of livelihood; and reform would leave him as a workman is now left when he is superseded by a machine. He had therefore better do what he can to get the workman compensated, so as to make the public familiar with the idea of compensation before his own turn comes.

TABOO IN SCHOOLS

The suppression of economic knowledge, disastrous as it is, is quite intelligible, its corrupt motive being as clear as the motive of a burglar for concealing his jemmy from a policeman. But the other great suppression in our schools, the suppression of the subject of sex, is a case of taboo. In mankind, the lower the type, and the less cultivated the mind, the less courage there is to face important subjects objectively. The ablest and most highly cultivated people continually discuss religion, politics, and sex: it is hardly an exaggeration to say that they discuss nothing else with fully-awakened interest. Commoner and less cultivated people, even when they form societies for discussion, make a rule that politics and religion are not to be mentioned, and take it for granted that no decent person would attempt to discuss sex. The three subjects are feared because they rouse the crude passions which call for furious gratification in murder and rapine at worst, and, at best, lead to quarrels and undesirable states of consciousness.

Even when this excuse of bad manners, ill temper, and brutishness (for that is what it comes to) compels us to accept it from those adults among whom political and theological discussion does as a matter of fact lead to the drawing of knives and pistols, and sex discussion leads to obscenity, it has no application to children except as an imperative reason for training them to respect other people's opinions, and to insist on respect for their own in these as in other important matters which are equally dangerous: for example, money. And in any case there are decisive reasons, superior, like the reasons for suspending conventional reticences between doctor and patient, to all considerations of mere decorum, for giving proper instruction in the facts of sex. Those who object to it (not counting coarse people who thoughtlessly seize every opportunity of affecting and parading a fictitious delicacy) are, in effect, advocating ignorance as a safeguard against precocity. If ignorance were practicable there would be something to be said for it up to the age at which ignorance is a danger instead of a safeguard. Even as it is, it seems undesirable that any special emphasis should be given to the subject, whether by way of delicacy and poetry or too impressive warning. But the plain fact is that in refusing to allow the child to be taught by qualified unrelated elders (the parents shrink from the lesson, even when they are otherwise qualified, because their own relation to the child makes the subject impossible between them) we are virtually arranging to have our children taught by other children in guilty secrets and unclean jests. And that settles the question for all sensible people.

The dogmatic objection, the sheer instinctive taboo which rules the subject out altogether as indecent, has no age limit. It means that at no matter what age a woman consents to a proposal of marriage, she should do so in ignorance of the relation she is undertaking. When this actually happens (and apparently it does happen oftener than would seem possible) a horrible fraud is being practised on both the man and the woman. He is led to believe that she knows what she is promising, and that he is in no danger of finding himself bound to a woman to whom he is eugenically antipathetic. She contemplates nothing but such affectionate relations as may exist between her and her nearest kinsmen, and has no knowledge of the condition which, if not foreseen, must come as an amazing revelation and a dangerous shock, ending possibly in the discovery that the marriage has been an irreparable mistake. Nothing can justify such a risk. There may be people incapable of understanding that the right to know all there is to know about oneself is a natural human right that sweeps away all the pretences of others to tamper with one's consciousness in order to produce what they choose to consider a good character. But they must here bow to the plain mischievousness of entrapping people into contracts on which the happiness of their whole lives depends without letting them know what they are undertaking.

ALLEGED NOVELTIES IN MODERN SCHOOLS

There is just one more nuisance to be disposed of before I come to the positive side of my case. I mean the person who tells me that my schooldays belong to a bygone order of educational ideas and institutions, and that schools are not now a bit like my old school. I reply, with Sir Walter Raleigh, by calling on my soul to give this statement the lie. Some years ago I lectured in Oxford on the subject of Education. A friend to whom I mentioned my intention said, "You know nothing of modern education: schools are not now what they were when you were a boy." I immediately procured the time sheets of half a dozen modern schools, and found, as I expected, that they might all have been my old school: there was no real difference. I may mention, too, that I have visited modern schools, and observed that there is a tendency to hang printed pictures in an untidy and soulless manner on the walls, and occasionally to display on the mantelshelf a deplorable glass case containing certain objects which might possibly, if placed in the hands of the pupils, give them some practical experience of the weight of a pound and the length of an inch. And sometimes a scoundrel who has rifled a bird's nest or killed a harmless snake encourages the children to go and do likewise by putting his victims into an imitation nest and bottling and exhibiting them as aids to "Nature study." A suggestion that Nature is worth study would certainly have staggered my schoolmasters; so perhaps I may admit a gleam of progress here. But as any child who attempted to handle these dusty objects would probably be caned, I do not attach any importance to such modernities in school furniture. The school remains what it was in my boyhood, because its real object remains what it was. And that object, I repeat, is to keep the children out of mischief: mischief meaning for the most part worrying the grown-ups.

WHAT IS TO BE DONE?

The practical question, then, is what to do with the children. Tolerate them at home we will not. Let them run loose in the streets we dare not until our streets become safe places for children, which, to our utter shame, they are not at present, though they can hardly be worse than some homes and some schools.

The grotesque difficulty of making even a beginning was brought home to me by the lady of the manor in the little village in Hertfordshire where I write these lines. She asked me very properly what I was going to do for the village school. I did not know what to reply. As the school kept the children quiet during my working hours, I did not for the sake of my own personal convenience want to blow it up with dynamite as I should like to blow up most schools. So I asked for guidance. "You ought to give a prize" said the lady. I asked if there was a prize for good conduct. As I expected, there was: one for the best-behaved boy and another for the best-behaved girl. On reflection I offered a handsome prize for the worst-behaved boy and girl on condition that a record should be kept of their subsequent careers and compared with the records of the best-behaved, in order to ascertain whether the school criterion of good conduct was valid out of school. My offer was refused because it would not have had the effect of encouraging the children to give as little trouble as possible, which is of course the real object of all conduct prizes in schools.

I must not pretend, then, that I have a system ready to replace all the other systems. Obstructing the way of the proper organization of childhood, as of everything else, lies our ridiculous misdistribution of the national income, with its accompanying class distinctions and imposition of snobbery on children as a necessary part of their social training. The result of our economic folly is that we are a nation of undesirable acquaintances; and the first object of all our institutions for children is segregation. If, for example, our children were set free to roam and play about as they pleased, they would have to be policed; and the first duty of the police in a State like ours would be to see that every child wore a badge indicating its class in society, and that every child seen speaking to another child with a lower-class badge, or any child wearing a higher badge than that allotted to it by, say, the College of Heralds, should immediately be skinned alive with a birch rod. It might even be insisted that girls with high-class badges should be attended by footmen, grooms, or even military escorts. In short, there is hardly any limit to the follies with which our Commercialism would infect any system that it would tolerate at all. But something like a change of heart is still possible; and since all the evils of snobbery and segregation are rampant in our schools at present we may as well make the best as the worst of them.

CHILDREN'S RIGHTS AND DUTIES

Now let us ask what are a child's rights, and what are the rights of society over the child. Its rights, being clearly those of any other human being, are summed up in the right to live: that is, to have all the conclusive arguments that prove that it would be better dead, that it is a child of wrath, that the population is already excessive, that the pains of life are greater than its pleasures, that its sacrifice in a hospital or laboratory experiment might save millions of lives, etc. etc. etc., put out of the question, and its existence accepted as necessary and sacred, all theories to the contrary notwithstanding, whether by Calvin or Schopenhauer or Pasteur or the nearest person with a taste for infanticide. And this right to live includes, and in fact is, the right to be what the child likes and can, to do what it likes and can, to make what it likes and can, to think what it likes and can, to smash what it dislikes and can, and generally to behave in an altogether unaccountable manner within the limits imposed by the similar rights of its neighbors. And the rights of society over it clearly extend to requiring it to qualify itself to live in society without wasting other people's time: that is, it must know the rules of the road, be able to read placards and proclamations, fill voting papers, compose and send letters and telegrams, purchase food and clothing and railway tickets for itself, count money and give and take change, and, generally, know how many beans make five. It must know some law, were it only a simple set of commandments, some political economy, agriculture enough to shut the gates of fields with cattle in them and not to trample on growing crops, sanitation enough not to defile its haunts, and religion enough to have some idea of why it is allowed its rights and why it must respect the rights of others. And the rest of its education must consist of anything else it can pick up; for beyond this society cannot go with any certainty, and indeed can only go this far rather apologetically and provisionally, as doing the best it can on very uncertain ground.

SHOULD CHILDREN EARN THEIR LIVING?

Now comes the question how far children should be asked to contribute to the support of the community. In approaching it we must put aside the considerations that now induce all humane and thoughtful political students to agitate for the uncompromising abolition of child labor under our capitalist system. It is not the least of the curses of that system that it will bequeath to future generations a mass of legislation to prevent capitalists from "using up nine generations of men in one generation," as they began by doing until they were restrained by law at the suggestion of

Robert Owen, the founder of English Socialism. Most of this legislation will become an insufferable restraint upon freedom and variety of action when Capitalism goes the way of Druidic human sacrifice (a much less slaughterous institution). There is every reason why a child should not be allowed to work for commercial profit or for the support of its parents at the expense of its own future; but there is no reason whatever why a child should not do some work for its own sake and that of the community if it can be shewn that both it and the community will be the better for it.

CHILDREN'S HAPPINESS

Also it is important to put the happiness of the children rather carefully in its place, which is really not a front place. The unsympathetic, selfish, hard people who regard happiness as a very exceptional indulgence to which children are by no means entitled, though they may be allowed a very little of it on their birthdays or at Christmas, are sometimes better parents in effect than those who imagine that children are as capable of happiness as adults. Adults habitually exaggerate their own capacity in that direction grossly; yet most adults can stand an allowance of happiness that would be quite thrown away on children. The secret of being miserable is to have leisure to bother about whether you are happy or not. The cure for it is occupation, because occupation means pre-occupation; and the pre-occupied person is neither happy nor unhappy, but simply alive and active, which is pleasanter than any happiness until you are tired of it. That is why it is necessary to happiness that one should be tired. Music after dinner is pleasant: music before breakfast is so unpleasant as to be clearly unnatural. To people who are not overworked holidays are a nuisance. To people who are, and who can afford them, they are a troublesome necessity. A perpetual holiday is a good working definition of hell.

THE HORROR OF THE PERPETUAL HOLIDAY

It will be said here that, on the contrary, heaven is always conceived as a perpetual holiday, and that whoever is not born to an independent income is striving for one or longing for one because it gives holidays for life. To which I reply, first, that heaven, as conventionally conceived, is a place so insane, so dull, so useless, so miserable, that nobody has ever ventured to describe a whole day in heaven, though plenty of people have described a day at the seaside; and that the genuine popular verdict on it is expressed in the proverb "Heaven for holiness and Hell for company." Second, I point out that the wretched people who have independent incomes and no useful occupation, do the most amazingly disagreeable and dangerous things to make themselves tired and hungry in the evening. When they are not involved in what they call sport, they are doing aimlessly what other people have to be paid to do: driving horses and motor cars; trying on dresses and walking up and down to shew them off; and acting as footmen and housemaids to royal personages. The sole and obvious cause of the notion that idleness is delightful and that heaven is a place where there is nothing to be done, is our school system and our industrial system. The school is a prison in which work is a punishment and a curse. In avowed prisons, hard labor, the only alleviation of a prisoner's lot, is treated as an aggravation of his punishment; and everything possible is done to intensify the prisoner's inculcated and unnatural notion that work is an evil. In industry we are over-worked and underfed prisoners. Under such absurd circumstances our judgment of things becomes as perverted as our habits. If we were habitually under-worked and overfed, our notion of heaven would be a place where everybody worked strenuously for twenty-four hours a day and never got anything to eat.

Once realize that a perpetual holiday is beyond human endurance, and that "Satan finds some mis-chief still for idle hands to do" and it will be seen that we have no right to impose a perpetual holiday on children. If we did, they would soon outdo the Labor Party in the claim for a Right to Work Bill.

In any case no child should be brought up to suppose that its food and clothes come down from heaven or are miraculously conjured from empty space by papa. Loathsome as we have made the idea of duty (like the idea of work) we must habituate children to a sense of repayable obligation to the community for what they consume and enjoy, and inculcate the repayment as a point of honor. If we did that today—and nothing but flat dishonesty prevents us from doing it—we should have no idle rich and indeed probably no rich, since there is no distinction in being rich if you have to pay scot and lot in personal effort like the working folk. Therefore, if for only half an hour a day, a child should do something service-able to the community.

Productive work for children has the advantage that its discipline is the discipline of impersonal necessity, not that of wanton personal coercion. The eagerness of children in our industrial districts to escape from school to the factory is not caused by lighter tasks or shorter hours in the factory, nor altogether by the temptation of wages, nor even by the desire for novelty, but by the dignity of adult work, the exchange of the humiliating liability to personal assault from the lawless schoolmaster, from which the grown-ups are free, for the stern but entirely dignified pressure of necessity to which all flesh is subject.

UNIVERSITY SCHOOLBOYISHNESS

Older children might do a good deal before beginning their collegiate education. What is the matter with our universities is that the students are school children, whereas it is of the very essence of university education that they should be adults. The function of a university is not to teach things that can now be taught as well or better by University Extension lectures or by private tutors or modern correspondence classes with gramophones. We go to them to be socialized: to acquire the hall mark of communal training; to become citizens of the world instead of inmates of the enlarged rabbit hutches we call homes; to learn manners and become unchallengeable ladies and gentlemen. The social pressure which effects these changes should be that of persons who have faced the full responsibilities of adults as working members of the general community, not that of a rowdy rabble of half emancipated school children and unemancipable pedants. It is true that in a reasonable state of society this outside experience would do for us very completely what the university does now so corruptly that we tolerate its bad manners only because they are better than no manners at all. But the university will always exist in some form as a community of persons desirous of pushing their culture to the highest pitch they are capable of, not as solitary students reading in seclusion, but as members of a body of individuals all pursuing culture, talking culture, thinking culture, above all, criticizing culture. If such persons are to read and talk and criticize to any purpose, they must know the world outside the university at least as well as the shopkeeper in the High Street does. And this is just what they do not know at present. You may say of them, paraphrasing Mr Kipling, "What do they know of Plato that only Plato know?" If our universities would exclude everybody who had not earned a living by his or her own exertions for at least a couple of years, their effect would be vastly improved.

THE NEW LAZINESS

The child of the future, then, if there is to be any future but one of decay, will work more or less for its living from an early age; and in doing so it will not shock anyone, provided there be no longer any reason to associate the conception of children working for their living with infants toiling in a factory for ten hours a day or boys drudging from nine to six under gas lamps in underground city offices. Lads and lasses in their teens will probably be able to produce as much as the most expensive person now costs in his own person (it is retinue that eats up the big income) without working too hard or too long for quite as much happiness as they can enjoy. The question to be balanced then will be, not how soon people should be put to work, but how soon they should be released from any obligation of the kind. A life's work is like a day's work: it can begin early and leave off early or begin late and leave off late, or, as with us, begin too early and never leave off at all, obviously the worst of all possible plans. In any event we must finally reckon work, not as the curse our schools and prisons and capitalist profit factories make it seem today, but as a prime necessity of a tolerable existence. And if we cannot devise fresh wants as fast as we shorten the process of supplying the old ones, there will come a scarcity of work simultaneously with an excess of leisure. Work may have to be shared out among people who want more of it. Our spurious substitute, exercise, will not serve. A new sort of laziness will become the bugbear of society: the laziness that refuses to face the mental toil and adventure of making work by inventing new ideas or extending the domain of knowledge, and insists on a ready-made routine. It may come to forcing people to retire before they are willing to make way for younger ones: that is, to driving all persons of a certain age out of industry, leaving them to find something experimental to occupy them on pain of perpetual holiday. Men will then try to spend twenty thousand a year for the sake of having to earn it. Instead of being what we are now, the cheapest and nastiest of the animals, we shall be the costliest, most fastidious, and best bred. In short, there is no end to the astonishing things that may happen when the curse of Adam becomes first a blessing and then an incurable habit. And in view of that day we must not grudge children their share of it.

THE INFINITE SCHOOL TASK

The question of children's work, however, is only a question of what the child ought to do for the community. How highly it should qualify itself is another matter. But most of the difficulty of inducing children to learn would disappear if our demands became not only definite but finite. When learning is only an excuse for imprisonment, it is an instrument of torture which becomes more painful the more progress is made. Thus when you have forced a child to learn the Church Catechism, a document profound beyond the comprehension of most adults, you are sometimes at a standstill for something else to teach; and you therefore keep the wretched child repeating its catechism again and again until you hit on the plan of making it learn instalments of Bible verses, preferably from the book of Numbers. But as it is less trouble to set a lesson that you know yourself, there is a tendency to keep repeating the already learnt lesson rather than break new ground. At school I began with a fairly complete knowledge of Latin grammar in the childish sense of being able to repeat all the paradigms; and I was kept at this, or rather kept in a class where the master never asked me to do it because he knew I could, and therefore devoted himself to trapping the boys who could not, until I finally forgot most of it. But when progress took place, what did it mean? First it meant Caesar, with the foreknowledge that to master Caesar meant only being set at Virgil, with the culminating horror of Greek and Homer in reserve at the end of that. I preferred Caesar, because his statement that Gaul is divided into three parts, though neither interesting nor true, was the only Latin sentence I could translate at sight: therefore the longer we stuck at Caesar the better I was pleased. Just so do less classically educated children see nothing in the mastery of addition but the beginning of subtraction, and so on through multiplication and division and fractions, with the black cloud of algebra on the horizon. And if a boy rushes through all that, there is always the calculus to fall back on, unless indeed you insist on his learning music, and proceed to hit him if he cannot tell you the year Beethoven was born.

A child has a right to finality as regards its compulsory lessons. Also as regards physical training. At present it is assumed that the schoolmaster has a right to force every child into an attempt to become Porson and Bentley, Leibnitz and Newton, all rolled into one. This is the tradition of the oldest grammar schools. In our times an even more horrible and cynical claim has been made for the right to drive boys through compulsory games in the playing fields until they are too much exhausted physically to do anything but drop off to sleep. This is supposed to protect them from vice; but as it also protects them from poetry, literature, music, meditation and prayer, it may be dismissed with the obvious remark that if boarding schools are places whose keepers are driven to such monstrous measures lest more abominable things should happen, then the sooner boarding schools are violently abolished the better. It is true that society may make physical claims on the child as well as mental ones: the child must learn to walk, to use a knife and fork, to swim, to ride a bicycle, to acquire sufficient power of self-defence to make an attack on it an arduous and uncertain enterprise, perhaps to fly. What as a matter of common sense it clearly has not a right to do is to make this an excuse for keeping the child slaving for ten hours at physical exercises on the ground that it is not yet as dexterous as Cinquevalli and as strong as Sandow.

THE REWARDS AND RISKS OF KNOWLEDGE

In a word, we cannot completely educate a child; for its education can end only with its life and will not even then be complete. Compulsory completion of education is the last folly of a rotten and desperate civilization. All we can fairly do is to prescribe definite acquirements and accomplishments as qualifications for citizenship in general, with further specific qualifications for professional employments; and to secure them, not by the ridiculous method of inflicting artificial injuries on the persons who have not yet mastered them, but by the natural co-operation of self-respect from within with social respect from without.

Most acquirements carry their own privileges with them. Thus a baby has to be pretty closely guarded and imprisoned because it cannot take care of itself. It has even to be carried about (the most complete conceivable infringement of its liberty) until it can walk. But nobody goes on carrying children after they can walk lest they should walk into mischief, though Arab boys make their sisters carry them, as our own spoiled children sometimes make their nurses, out of mere laziness, because sisters in the East and nurses in the West are kept in servitude. But in a society of equals (the only reasonable and permanently possible sort of society) children are in much greater danger of acquiring bandy legs through being left to walk before they are strong enough than of being carried when they are well able to walk. Anyhow, freedom of movement in a nursery is the reward of learning to walk; and in precisely the same way freedom of movement in a city is the reward of learning how to read public notices, and to count and use money. The consequences are of course much larger than the mere ability to read the name of a street or the number of a railway platform and the destination of a train. When you enable a child to read these, you also enable it to read this preface, to the utter destruction, you may

[61]

quite possibly think, of its morals (its docility). You also expose it to the danger of being run over by taxi-cabs and trains. The moral and physical risks of education are enormous: every new power a child acquires, from speaking, walking, and co-ordinating its vision, to conquering continents and founding religions, opens up immense new possibilities of mischief. Teach a child to write and you teach it how to forge: teach it to speak and you teach it how to lie: teach it to walk and you teach it how to kick its mother to death.

The great problem of slavery for those whose aim is to maintain it is the problem of reconciling the efficiency of the slave with the helplessness that keeps him in servitude; and this problem is fortunately not completely soluble; for it is not in fact found possible for a duke to treat his solicitor or his doctor as he treats his laborers, though they are all equally his slaves: the laborer being in fact less dependent on his favor than the professional man. Hence it is that men come to resent, of all things, protection, because it so often means restriction of their liberty lest they should make a bad use of it. If there are dangerous precipices about, it is much easier and cheaper to forbid people to walk near the edge than to put up an effective fence: that is why both legislators and parents and the paid deputies of parents are always inhibiting and prohibiting and punishing and scolding and laming and cramping and delaying progress and growth instead of making the dangerous places as safe as possible and then boldly taking and allowing others to take the irreducible minimum of risk.

ENGLISH PHYSICAL HARDIHOOD AND SPIRITUAL COWARDICE

It is easier to convert most people to the need for

allowing their children to run physical risks than moral ones. I can remember a relative of mine who, when I was a small child, unused to horses and very much afraid of them, insisted on putting me on a rather rumbustious pony with little spurs on my heels (knowing that in my agitation I would use them unconsciously), and being enormously amused at my terrors. Yet when that same lady discovered that I had found a copy of The Arabian Nights and was devouring it with avidity, she was horrified, and hid it away from me lest it should break my soul as the pony might have broken my neck. This way of producing hardy bodies and timid souls is so common in country-houses that you may spend hours in them listening to stories of broken collar bones, broken backs, and broken necks without coming upon a single spiritual adventure or daring thought.

But whether the risks to which liberty exposes us are moral or physical, our right to liberty involves the right to run them. A man who is not free to risk his neck as an aviator or his soul as a heretic is not free at all; and the right to liberty begins, not at the age of 21 years but of 21 seconds.

THE RISKS OF IGNORANCE AND WEAKNESS

The difficulty with children is that they need protection from risks they are too young to understand, and attacks they can neither avoid nor resist. You may on academic grounds allow a child to snatch glowing coals from the fire once. You will not do it twice. The risks of liberty we must let everyone take; but the risks of ignorance and self-helplessness are another matter. Not only children but adults need protection from them. At present adults are often exposed to risks outside their knowledge or beyond their comprehension or powers of resistance or foresight: for example, we have to look on every day at marriages or financial speculations that may involve far worse consequences than burnt fingers. And just as it is part of the business of adults to protect children, to feed them, clothe them, shelter them, and shift for them in all sorts of ways until they are able to shift for themselves, it is coming more and more to be seen that this is true not only of the relation between adults and children, but between adults and adults. We shall not always look on indifferently at foolish marriages and financial speculations, nor allow dead men to control live communities by ridiculous wills and living heirs to squander and ruin great estates, nor tolerate a hundred other absurd liberties that we allow today because we are too lazy to find out the proper way to interfere. But the interference must be regulated by some theory of the individual's rights. Though the right to live is absolute, it is not unconditional. If a man is unbearably mischievous, he must be killed. This is a mere matter of necessity, like the killing of a man-eating tiger in a nursery, a venomous snake in the garden, or a fox in the poultry yard. No society could be constructed on the assumption that such extermination is a violation of the creature's right to live, and therefore must not be allowed. And then at once arises the danger into which morality has led us: the danger of persecution. One Christian spreading his doctrines may seem more mischievous than a dozen thieves: throw him therefore to the lions. A lying or disobedient child may corrupt a whole generation and make human Society impossible: therefore thrash the vice out of him. And so on until our whole system of abortion, intimidation, tyranny, cruelty, and the rest is in full swing again.

[64]

THE COMMON SENSE OF TOLERATION

The real safeguard against this is the dogma of Toleration. I need not here repeat the compact treatise on it which I prepared for the Joint Committee on the Censorship of Stage Plays, and prefixed to The Shewing Up of Blanco Posnet. It must suffice now to say that the present must not attempt to schoolmaster the future by pretending to know good from evil in tendency, or protect citizens against shocks to their opinions and convictions, moral, political or religious: in other words it must not persecute doctrines of any kind, or what is called bad taste, and must insist on all persons facing such shocks as they face frosty weather or any of the other disagreeable, dangerous, or bracing incidents of freedom. The expediency of Toleration has been forced on us by the fact that progressive enlightenment depends on a fair hearing for doctrines which at first appear seditious, blasphemous, and immoral, and which deeply shock people who never think originally, thought being with them merely a habit and an echo. The deeper ground for Toleration is the nature of creation, which, as we now know, proceeds by evolution. Evolution finds its way by experiment; and this finding of the way varies according to the stage of development reached, from the blindest groping along the line of least resistance to conscious intellectual speculation, with its routine of hypothesis and verification, induction and deduction; or even into so rapid and intuitive an integration of all these processes in a single brain that we get the inspired guess of the man of genius and the fanatical resolution of the teacher of new truths who is first slain as a blasphemous apostate and then worshipped as a prophet.

Here the law for the child is the same as for the adult. The high priest must not rend his garments and cry "Crucify him" when he is shocked, nor the atheist clamor for the suppression of Law's Serious Call because it has for two centuries destroyed the natural happiness of innumerable children by persuading pious parents that it is a religious duty to make children miserable. It, and the Sermon on the Mount, and Machiavelli's Prince, and La Rochefoucauld's maxims, and Hymns Ancient and Modern, and De Glanville's apologue, and Dr. Watts's rhymes, and Nietzsche's Gay Science, and Ingersoll's Mistake of Moses, and the speeches and pamphlets of the people who want us to make war on Germany, and the Noodle's Orations and articles of our politicians and journalists, must all be tolerated not only because any of them may for all we know be on the right track but because it is in the conflict of opinion that we win knowledge and wisdom. However terrible the wounds suffered in that conflict, they are better than the barren peace of death that follows when all the combatants are slaughtered or bound hand and foot.

The difficulty at present is that though this necessity for Toleration is a law of political science as well established as the law of gravitation, our rulers are never taught political science: on the contrary, they are taught in school that the master tolerates nothing that is disagreeable to him; that ruling is simply being master; and that the master's method is the method of violent punishment. And our citizens, all school taught, are walking in the same darkness. As I write these lines the Home Secretary is explaining that he must not release a man who has been imprisoned for blasphemy, as his remarks were painful to the feelings of his pious fellow-townsmen. Now it happens that this very Home Secretary has driven many thousands of his fellow-citizens almost beside themselves by the crudity of his notions of government, and his simple inability to understand why he should not use and make laws to torment and subdue people who do not happen to agree with him. In a word, he is not a politician, but a grown-up schoolboy who has at last got a cane in his hand. And as all the rest of us are in the same condition (except as to command of the cane) the only objection made to his proceedings takes the shape of clamorous demands that *he* should be caned instead of being allowed to cane other people.

THE SIN OF ATHANASIUS

It seems hopeless. Anarchists are tempted to preach a violent and implacable resistance to all law as the only remedy; and the result of that speedily is that people welcome any tyranny that will rescue them from chaos. But there is really no need to choose between anarchy and tyranny. A quite reasonable state of things is practicable if we proceed on human assumptions and not on academic ones. If adults will frankly give up their claim to know better than children what the purposes of the Life Force are, and treat the child as an experiment like themselves, and possibly a more successful one, and at the same time relinquish their monstrous parental claims to personal private property in children, the rest may be left to common sense. It is our attitude, our religion, that is wrong. A good beginning might be made by enacting that any person dictating a piece of conduct to a child or to anyone else as the will of God, or as absolutely right, should be dealt with as a blasphemer: as, indeed, guilty of the unpardonable sin against the Holy

Ghost. If the penalty were death, it would rid us at once of that scourge of humanity, the amateur Pope. As an Irish Protestant, I raise the cry of No Popery with hereditary zest. We are overrun with Popes. From curates and governesses, who may claim a sort of professional standing, to parents and uncles and nurserymaids and school teachers and wiseacres generally, there are scores of thousands of human insects groping through our darkness by the feeble phosphorescence of their own tails, yet ready at a moment's notice to reveal the will of God on every possible subject; to explain how and why the universe was made (in my youth they added the exact date) and the circumstances under which it will cease to exist; to lay down precise rules of right and wrong conduct; to discriminate infallibly between virtuous and vicious character; and this with such certainty that they are prepared to visit all the rigors of the law, and all the ruinous penalties of social ostracism on those, however harmless their actions may be, who venture to laugh at their monstrous conceit or to pay their assumptions the extravagant compliment of criticizing them. As to children, who shall say what canings and birchings and terrifyings and threats of hell fire and impositions and humiliations and petty imprisonings and sendings to bed and standing in corners and the like they have suffered because their parents and guardians and teachers knew everything so much better than Socrates or Solon?

It is this ignorant uppishness that does the mischief. A stranger on the planet might expect that its grotesque absurdity would provoke enough ridicule to cure it; but unfortunately quite the contrary happens. Just as our ill health delivers us into the hands of medical quacks and creates a passionate demand for

impudent pretences that doctors can cure the diseases
they themselves die of daily, so our ignorance and
helplessness set us clamoring for spiritual and moral
quacks who pretend that they can save our souls from
their own damnation. If a doctor were to say to his
patients, "I am familiar with your symptoms, because
I have seen other people in your condition; and I will
bring the very little knowledge we have to your treatment; but except in that very shallow sense I dont
know what is the matter with you; and I cant undertake to cure you" he would be a lost man professionally; and if a clergyman, on being called on to award a
prize for good conduct in the village school, were to
say, "I am afraid I cannot say who is the best-behaved
child, because I really do not know what good conduct
is; but I will gladly take the teacher's word as to which
child has caused least inconvenience" he would
probably be unfrocked, if not excommunicated. And
yet no honest and intellectually capable doctor or
parson can say more. Clearly it would not be wise of
the doctor to say it, because optimistic lies have such
immense therapeutic value that a doctor who cannot
tell them convincingly has mistaken his profession.
And a clergyman who is not prepared to lay down the
law dogmatically will not be of much use in a village
school, though it behoves him all the more to be very
careful what law he lays down. But unless both the
clergyman and the doctor are in the attitude expressed
by these speeches they are not fit for their work. The
man who believes that he has more than a provisional
hypothesis to go upon is a born fool. He may have to
act vigorously on it. The world has no use for the
Agnostic who wont believe anything because anything might be false, and wont deny anything because
anything might be true. But there is a wide difference

between saying, "I believe this; and I am going to act on it," or, "I dont believe it; and I wont act on it," and saying, "It is true; and it is my duty and yours to act on it," or, "It is false; and it is my duty and yours to refuse to act on it." The difference is as great as that between the Apostles' Creed and the Athanasian Creed. When you repeat the Apostles' Creed you affirm that you believe certain things. There you are clearly within your rights. When you repeat the Athanasian Creed, you affirm that certain things are so, and that anybody who doubts that they are so cannot be saved. And this is simply a piece of impudence on your part, as you know nothing about it except that as good men as you have never heard of your creed. The apostolic attitude is a desire to convert others to our beliefs for the sake of sympathy and light: the Athanasian attitude is a desire to murder people who dont agree with us. I am sufficient of an Athanasian to advocate a law for the speedy execution of all Athanasians, because they violate the fundamental proposition of my creed, which is, I repeat, that all living creatures are experiments. The precise formula for the Superman, *ci-devant* The Just Man Made Perfect, has not yet been discovered. Until it is, every birth is an experiment in the Great Research which is being conducted by the Life Force to discover that formula.

THE EXPERIMENT EXPERIMENTING

And now all the modern schoolmaster abortionists will rise up beaming, and say, "We quite agree. We regard every child in our school as a subject for experiment. We are always experimenting with them. We challenge the experimental test for our system. We are continually guided by our experience in our great work of moulding the character of our future citizens, etc. etc. etc." I am sorry to seem irreconcilable; but it is the Life Force that has to make the experiment and not the schoolmaster; and the Life Force for the child's purpose is in the child and not in the schoolmaster. The schoolmaster is another experiment; and a laboratory in which all the experiments began experimenting on one another would not produce intelligible results. I admit, however, that if my schoolmasters had treated me as an experiment of the Life Force: that is, if they had set me free to do as I liked subject only to my political rights and theirs, they could not have watched the experiment very long, because the first result would have been a rapid movement on my part in the direction of the door, and my disappearance therethrough.

It may be worth inquiring where I should have gone to. I should say that practically every time I should have gone to a much more educational place. I should have gone into the country, or into the sea, or into the National Gallery, or to hear a band if there was one, or to any library where there were no schoolbooks. I should have read very dry and difficult books: for example, though nothing would have induced me to read the budget of stupid party lies that served as a text-book of history in school, I remember reading Robertson's Charles V. and his history of Scotland from end to end most laboriously. Once, stung by the airs of a schoolfellow who alleged that he had read Locke On The Human Understanding, I attempted to read the Bible straight through, and actually got to the Pauline Epistles before I broke down in disgust at what seemed to me their inveterate crookedness of mind. If there had been a school where children were really free, I should have had to be driven out of it for the sake of my health by the teachers; for the children to whom a literary education can be of any use are insatiable: they will read and study far more than is good for them. In fact the real difficulty is to prevent them from wasting their time by reading for the sake of reading and studying for the sake of studying, instead of taking some trouble to find out what they really like and are capable of doing some good at. Some silly person will probably interrupt me here with the remark that many children have no appetite for a literary education at all, and would never open a book if they were not forced to. I have known many such persons who have been forced to the point of obtaining university degrees. And for all the effect their literary exercises has left on them they might just as well have been put on the treadmill. In fact they are actually less literate than the treadmill would have left them; for they might now by chance pick up and dip into a volume of Shakespear or a translation of Homer if they had not been driven to loathe every famous name in literature. I should probably know as much Latin as French, if Latin had not been made the excuse for my school imprisonment and degradation.

WHY WE LOATHE LEARNING AND LOVE SPORT

If we are to discuss the importance of art, learning, and intellectual culture, the first thing we have to recognize is that we have very little of them at present; and that this little has not been produced by compulsory education: nay, that the scarcity is unnatural and has been produced by the violent exclusion of art and artists from schools. On the other hand we have quite a considerable degree of bodily culture: indeed there is a continual outcry against the sacrifice of mental accomplishments to athletics. In other words a sacrifice of the professed object of compulsory education to the real object of voluntary education. It is assumed that this means that people prefer bodily to mental culture; but may it not mean that they prefer liberty and satisfaction to coercion and privation. Why is it that people who have been taught Shakespear as a school subject loathe his plays and cannot by any means be persuaded ever to open his works after they escape from school, whereas there is still, 300 years after his death, a wide and steady sale for his works to people who regard his plays as plays, not as task work? If Shakespear, or for that matter, Newton and Leibnitz, are allowed to find their readers and students they will find them. If their works are annotated and paraphrased by dullards, and the annotations and paraphrases forced on all young people by imprisonment and flogging and scolding, there will not be a single man of letters or higher mathematician the more in the country: on the contrary there will be less, as so many potential lovers of literature and mathematics will have been incurably prejudiced against them. Everyone who is conversant with the class in which child imprisonment and compulsory schooling is carried out to the final extremity of the university degree knows that its scholastic culture is a sham; that it knows little about literature or art and a great deal about point-to-point races; and that the village cobbler, who has never read a page of Plato, and is admittedly a dangerously ignorant man politically, is nevertheless a Socrates compared to the classically educated gentlemen who discuss politics in country-houses at election time (and at no other time) after their day's earnest and skilful shooting. Think of the years and years of weary torment the women of the piano-possessing class have been forced to spend over the keyboard, fingering scales. How many of them could be bribed to attend a pianoforte recital by a great player, though they will rise from sick beds rather than miss Ascot or Goodwood ?

Another familiar fact that teaches the same lesson is that many women who have voluntarily attained a high degree of culture cannot add up their own house-keeping books, though their education in simple arithmetic was compulsory, whereas their higher education has been wholly voluntary. Everywhere we find the same result. The imprisonment, the beating, the taming and laming, the breaking of young spirits, the arrest of development, the atrophy of all inhibitive power except the power of fear, are real: the education is sham. Those who have been taught most know least.

ANTICHRIST

Among the worst effects of the unnatural segregation of children in schools and the equally unnatural constant association of them with adults in the family is the utter defeat of the vital element in Christianity. Christ stands in the world for that intuition of the highest humanity that we, being members one of another, must not complain, must not scold, must not strike, nor revile nor persecute nor revenge nor punish. Now family life and school life are, as far as the moral training of children is concerned, nothing but the deliberate inculcation of a routine of complaint, scolding, punishment, persecution, and revenge as the natural and only possible way of dealing with evil or inconvenience. "Aint nobody to be whopped for this

here?" exclaimed Sam Weller when he saw his employer's name written up on a stage coach, and conceived the phenomenon as an insult which reflected
on himself. This exclamation of Sam Weller is at once
the negation of Christianity and the beginning and the
end of current morality; and so it will remain as long
as the family and the school persist as we know them:
that is, as long as the rights of children are so utterly
denied that nobody will even take the trouble to ascertain what they are, and coming of age is like the turning of a convict into the streets after twenty-one years
penal servitude. Indeed it is worse; for the convict,
having learnt before his conviction how to live at large,
may remember how to set about it, however lamed his
power of initiative may have become through disuse;
but the child knows no other way of life than the
slave's way. Born free, as Rousseau says, he has been
laid hands on by slaves from the moment of his birth
and brought up as a slave. How is he, when he is at
last set free, to be anything else than the slave he
actually is, clamoring for war, for the lash, for police,
prisons, and scaffolds in a wild panic of delusion that
without these things he is lost. The grown-up Englishman is to the end of his days a badly brought-up child,
beyond belief quarrelsome, petulant, selfish, destructive, and cowardly: afraid that the Germans will come
and enslave him; that the burglar will come and rob
him; that the bicycle or motor car will run over him;
that the smallpox will attack him; and that the devil
will run away with him and empty him out like a sack
of coals on a blazing fire unless his nurse or his
parents or his schoolmaster or his bishop or his judge
or his army or his navy will do something to frighten
these bad things away. And this Englishman, without
the moral courage of a louse, will risk his neck for fun

fifty times every winter in the hunting field, and at Badajos sieges and the like will ram his head into a hole bristling with sword blades rather than be beaten in the one department in which he has been brought up to consult his own honor. As a Sportsman (and war is fundamentally the sport of hunting and fighting the most dangerous of the beasts of prey) he feels free. He will tell you himself that the true sportsman is never a snob, a coward, a duffer, a cheat, a thief, or a liar. Curious, is it not, that he has not the same confidence in other sorts of man?

And even sport is losing its freedom. Soon everybody will be schooled, mentally and physically, from the cradle to the end of the term of adult compulsory military service, and finally of compulsory civil service lasting until the age of superannuation. Always more schooling, more compulsion. We are to be cured by an excess of the dose that has poisoned us. Satan is to cast out Satan.

UNDER THE WHIP

Clearly this will not do. We must reconcile education with liberty. We must find out some means of making men workers and, if need be, warriors, without making them slaves. We must cultivate the noble virtues that have their root in pride. Now no schoolmaster will teach these any more than a prison governor will teach his prisoners how to mutiny and escape. Self-preservation forces him to break the spirit that revolts against him, and to inculcate submission, even to obscene assault, as a duty. A bishop once had the hardihood to say that he would rather see England free than England sober. Nobody has yet dared to say that he would rather see an England of ignoramuses than an England of cowards and slaves. And if anyone did, it would be necessary to point out that the antithesis is not a practical one, as we have at present an England of ignoramuses who are also cowards and slaves, and patriotically proud of it at that, because in school they are taught to submit, with what they ridiculously call Oriental fatalism (as if any Oriental has ever submitted more helplessly and sheepishly to robbery and oppression than we Occidentals do), to be driven day after day into compounds and set to the tasks they loathe by the men they hate and fear, as if this were the inevitable destiny of mankind. And naturally, when they grow up, they helplessly exchange the prison of the school for the prison of the mine or the workshop or the office, and drudge along stupidly and miserably, with just enough gregarious instinct to turn furiously on any intelligent person who proposes a change. It would be quite easy to make England a paradise, according to our present ideas, in a few years. There is no mystery about it: the way has been pointed out over and over again. The difficulty is not the way but the will. And we have no will because the first thing done with us in childhood was to break our will. Can anything be more disgusting than the spectacle of a nation reading the biography of Gladstone and gloating over the account of how he was flogged at Eton, two of his schoolfellows being compelled to hold him down whilst he was flogged. Not long ago a public body in England had to deal with the case of a schoolmaster who, conceiving himself insulted by the smoking of a cigaret against his orders by a pupil eighteen years old, proposed to flog him publicly as a satisfaction to what he called his honor and authority. I had intended to give the particulars of this case, but find the drudgery of raking over such stuff too sickening, and the effect unjust to a man who was doing only what others all over the country were doing as part of the established routine of what is called education. The astounding part of it was the manner in which the person to whom this outrage on decency seemed quite proper and natural claimed to be a functionary of high character, and had his claim allowed. In Japan he would hardly have been allowed the privilege of committing suicide. What is to be said of a profession in which such obscenities are made points of honor, or of institutions in which they are an accepted part of the daily routine? Wholesome people would not argue about the taste of such nastinesses: they would spit them out; but we are tainted with flagellomania from our childhood. When will we realize that the fact that we can become accustomed to anything, however disgusting at first, makes it necessary for us to examine carefully everything we have become accustomed to? Before motor cars became common, necessity had accustomed us to a foulness in our streets which would have horrified us had the street been our drawing-room carpet. Before long we shall be as particular about our streets as we now are about our carpets; and their condition in the nineteenth century will become as forgotten and incredible as the condition of the corridors of palaces and the courts of castles was as late as the eighteenth century. This foulness, we can plead, was imposed on us as a necessity by the use of horses and of huge retinues; but flogging has never been so imposed: it has always been a vice, craved for on any pretext by those depraved by it. Boys were flogged when criminals were hanged, to impress the awful warning on them. Boys were flogged at boundaries, to impress the boundaries on their memory. Other methods and other punishments were always available: the choice of this one betrayed the sensual impulse which makes the practice an abomination. But when its viciousness made it customary, it was practised and tolerated on all hands by people who were innocent of anything worse than stupidity, ill temper, and inability to discover other methods of maintaining order than those they had always seen practised and approved of. From children and animals it extended to slaves and criminals. In the days of Moses it was limited to 39 lashes. In the early nineteenth century it had become an open madness: soldiers were sentenced to a thousand lashes for trifling offences, with the result (among others less mentionable) that the Iron Duke of Wellington complained that it was impossible to get an order obeyed in the British army except in two or three crack regiments. Such frantic excesses of this disgusting neurosis provoked a reaction against it; but the clamor for it by depraved persons never ceased, and was tolerated by a nation trained to it from childhood in the schools until last year (1913) when, in what must be described as a paroxysm of sexual excitement provoked by the agitation concerning the White Slave Traffic (the purely commercial nature of which I was prevented from exposing on the stage by the Censorship twenty years ago), the Government yielded to an outcry for flagellation led by the Archbishop of Canterbury, and passed an Act under which a judge can sentence a man to be flogged to the utmost extremity with any instrument usable for such a purpose that he cares to prescribe. Such an Act is not a legislative phenomenon but a psychopathic one. Its effect on the White Slave Traffic was, of course, to distract public attention from its real cause and from the people who really profit by it to imaginary "foreign scoundrels," and to secure a monopoly of its organization for women.

And all this evil is made possible by the school-master with his cane and birch, by the parents getting rid as best they can of the nuisance of children making noise and mischief in the house, and by the denial to children of the elementary rights of human beings.

The first man who enslaved and "broke in" an animal with a whip would have invented the explosion engine instead could he have foreseen the curse he was laying on his race. For men and women learnt thereby to enslave and break in their children by the same means. These children, grown up, knew no other methods of training. Finally the evil that was done for gain by the greedy was refined on and done for pleasure by the lustful. Flogging has become a pleasure purchasable in our streets, and inhibition a grown-up habit that children play at. "Go and see what baby is doing; and tell him he mustnt" is the last word of the nursery; and the grimmest aspect of it is that it was first formulated by a comic paper as a capital joke.

TECHNICAL INSTRUCTION

Technical instruction tempts to violence (as a short cut) more than liberal education. The sailor in Mr Rudyard Kipling's Captains Courageous, teaching the boy the names of the ship's tackle with a rope's end, does not disgust us as our schoolmasters do, especially as the boy was a spoiled boy. But an unspoiled boy would not have needed that drastic medicine. Technical training may be as tedious as learning to skate or to play the piano or violin; but it is the price one must pay to achieve certain desirable results or necessary ends. It is a monstrous thing to force a child to learn Latin or Greek or mathematics on the ground that they are an indispensable gymnastic for the mental powers. It would be monstrous even if it were true; for there is no labor that might not be imposed on a child or an adult on the same pretext; but as a glance at the average products of our public school and university education shews that it is not true, it need not trouble us. But it is a fact that ignorance of Latin and Greek and mathematics closes certain careers to men (I do not mean artificial, unnecessary, noxious careers like those of the commercial schoolmaster). Languages, even dead ones, have their uses; and, as it seems to many of us, mathematics have their uses. They will always be learned by people who want to learn them; and people will always want to learn them as long as they are of any importance in life: indeed the want will survive their importance: superstition is nowhere stronger than in the field of obsolete acquirements. And they will never be learnt fruitfully by people who do not want to learn them either for their own sake or for use in necessary work. There is no harder schoolmaster than experience; and yet experience fails to teach where there is no desire to learn.

Still, one must not begin to apply this generalization too early. And this brings me to an important factor in the case: the factor of evolution.

DOCILITY AND DEPENDENCE

If anyone, impressed by my view that the rights of a child are precisely those of an adult, proceeds to treat a child as if it were an adult, he (or she) will find that though the plan will work much better at some points than the usual plan, at others it will not work at all; and this discovery may provoke him to turn back from the whole conception of children's rights with a jest at the expense of bachelors' and old maids' children. In dealing with children what is needed is not logic but sense. There is no logical reason why young persons should be allowed greater control of their property the day after they are twenty-one than the day before it. There is no logical reason why I, who strongly object to an adult standing over a boy of ten with a Latin grammar, and saying "You must learn this, whether you want to or not," should nevertheless be quite prepared to stand over a boy of five with the multiplication table or a copy book or a code of elementary good manners, and practise on his docility to make him learn them. And there is no logical reason why I should do for a child a great many little offices, some of them troublesome and disagreeable, which I should not do for a boy twice its age, or support a boy or girl when I would unhesitatingly throw an adult on his own resources. But there are practical reasons, and sensible reasons, and affectionate reasons for all these illogicalities. Children do not want to be treated altogether as adults: such treatment terrifies them and overburdens them with responsibility. In truth, very few adults care to be called on for independence and originality: they also are bewildered and terrified in the absence of precedents and precepts and commandments; but modern Democracy allows them a sanctioning and cancelling power if they are capable of using it, which children are not. To treat a child wholly as an adult would be to mock and destroy it. Infantile docility and juvenile dependence are, like death a product of Natural Selection; and though there is no viler crime than to abuse them, yet there is no greater cruelty than to ignore them. I have complained sufficiently of what I suffered through the process of assault, imprisonment, and compulsory lessons that taught me nothing, which are called my schooling. But I could say a good deal also about the things I was not taught and should have been taught, not to mention the things I was allowed to do which I should not have been allowed to do. I have no recollection of being taught to read or write; so I presume I was born with both faculties; but many people seem to have bitter recollections of being forced reluctantly to acquire them. And though I have the uttermost contempt for a teacher so ill-mannered and incompetent as to be unable to make a child learn to read and write without also making it cry, still I am prepared to admit that I had rather have been compelled to learn to read and write with tears by an incompetent and ill-mannered person than left in ignorance. Reading, writing, and enough arithmetic to use money honestly and accurately, together with the rudiments of law and order, become necessary conditions of a child's liberty before it can appreciate the importance of its liberty, or foresee that these accomplishments are worth acquiring. Nature has provided for this by evolving the instinct of docility. Children are very docile: they have a sound intuition that they must do what they are told or perish. And adults have an intuition, equally sound, that they must take advantage of this docility to teach children how to live properly or the children will not survive. The difficulty is to know where to stop. To illustrate this, let us consider the main danger of childish docility and parental officiousness.

THE ABUSE OF DOCILITY

Docility may survive as a lazy habit long after it has ceased to be a beneficial instinct. If you catch a child when it is young enough to be instinctively docile, and keep it in a condition of unremitted tutelage under the nurserymaid, the governess, the preparatory school, the secondary school, and the university, until it is an adult, you will produce, not a self-reliant, free, fully matured human being, but a grown-up schoolboy or schoolgirl, capable of nothing in the way of original or independent action except outbursts of naughtiness in the women and blackguardism in the men. That is exactly what we get at present in our rich and consequently governing classes: they pass from juvenility to senility without ever touching maturity except in body. The classes which cannot afford this sustained tutelage are notably more self-reliant and grown-up: an office boy of fifteen is often more of a man than a university student of twenty. Unfortunately this precocity is disabled by poverty, ignorance, narrowness, and a hideous power of living without art or love or beauty and being rather proud of it. The poor never escape from servitude: their docility is preserved by their slavery. And so all become the prey of the greedy, the selfish, the domineering, the unscrupulous, the predatory. If here and there an individual refuses to be docile, ten docile persons will beat him or lock him up or shoot him or hang him at the bidding of his oppressors and their own. The crux of the whole difficulty about parents, schoolmasters, priests, absolute monarchs, and despots of every sort, is the tendency to abuse natural docility. A nation should always be healthily rebellious; but rulers have yet to be found who will make trouble for themselves by cultivating that side of the national spirit. A child should begin to assert itself early, and shift for itself more and more not only in washing and dressing itself, but in opinions and conduct; yet as nothing is so exasperating and so unlovable as an uppish child, it is useless to expect parents and schoolmasters to inculcate this uppishness. Such unamiable precepts as Always contradict an authoritative statement, Always return a blow, Never lose a chance of a good fight, When you are scolded for a mistake ask the person who scolds you whether he or she supposes you did it on purpose, and follow the question with a blow or an insult or some other unmistakeable expression of resentment, Remember that the progress of the world depends on your knowing better than your elders, are just as important as those of the sermon on the mount; but no one has yet seen them written up in letters of gold in a schoolroom or nursery. The child is taught to be kind, to be respectful, to be quiet, not to answer back, to be truthful when its elders want to find out anything from it, to lie when the truth would shock or hurt its elders, to be above all things obedient, and to be seen and not heard. Here we have two sets of precepts, each of which will spoil an ordinary child if the other be omitted. Unfortunately we do not allow fair play between them. The rebellious, intractable, aggressive, selfish set provoke a corrective resistance, and do not pretend to high moral or religious sanctions; and they are never urged by grown-up people on young people. They are therefore more in danger of neglect or suppression than the other set, which have all the adults, all the laws, all the religions on their side. How is the child to be secured its due share of both bodies of doctrine?

THE SCHOOLBOY AND THE HOMEBOY

In practice what happens is that parents notice that boys brought up at home become mollycoddles, or prigs, or duffers, unable to take care of themselves. They see that boys should learn to rough it a little and to mix with children of their own age. This is natural enough. When you have preached at and punished a boy until he is a moral cripple, you are as much hampered by him as by a physical cripple; and as you do not intend to have him on your hands all your life, and are generally rather impatient for the day when he will earn his own living and leave you to attend to yourself, you sooner or later begin to talk to him about the need for self-reliance, learning to think, and so forth, with the result that your victim, bewildered by your inconsistency, concludes that there is no use trying to please you, and falls into an attitude of sulky resentment. Which is an additional inducement to pack him off to school.

In school, he finds himself in a dual world, under two dispensations. There is the world of the boys, where the point of honor is to be untameable, always ready to fight, ruthless in taking the conceit out of anyone who ventures to give himself airs of superior knowledge or taste, and generally to take Lucifer for one's model. And there is the world of the masters, the world of discipline, submission, diligence, obedience, and continual and shameless assumption of moral and intellectual authority. Thus the schoolboy hears both sides, and is so far better off than the home-bred boy who hears only one. But the two sides are not fairly presented. They are presented as good and evil, as vice and virtue, as villainy and heroism. The boy feels mean and cowardly when he obeys, and selfish and rascally when he disobeys. He loses his moral courage just as he comes to hate books and languages. In the end, John Ruskin, tied so closely to his mother's apron-string that he did not escape even when he went to Oxford, and John Stuart Mill, whose father ought to have been prosecuted for laying his son's childhood waste with lessons, were superior, as products of training, to our schoolboys. They were very conspicuously superior in moral courage; and though they did not distinguish themselves at cricket and football, they had quite as much physical hardihood as any civilized man needs. But it is to be observed that Ruskin's parents were wise people who gave John a full share in their own life, and put up with his presence both at home and abroad when they must sometimes have been very weary of him; and Mill, as it happens, was deliberately educated to challenge all the most sacred institutions of his country. The households they were brought up in were no more average households than a Montessori school is an average school.

THE COMINGS OF AGE OF CHILDREN

All this inculcated adult docility, which wrecks every civilization as it is wrecking ours, is inhuman and unnatural. We must reconsider our institution of the Coming of Age, which is too late for some purposes, and too early for others. There should be a series of Coming of Ages for every individual. The mammals have their first coming of age when they are weaned, and it is noteworthy that this rather cruel and selfish operation on the part of the parent has to be performed resolutely, with claws and teeth; for your little mammal does not want to be weaned, and yields only to a pretty rough assertion of the right of the parent to be relieved of the child as soon as the child is old enough to bear the separation. The same thing occurs with children: they hang on to the mother's apron-string and the father's coat tails as long as they can, often baffling those sensitive parents who know that children should think for themselves and fend for themselves, but are too kind to throw them on their own resources with the ferocity of the domestic cat. The child should have its first coming of age when it is weaned, another when it can talk, another when it can walk, another when it can dress itself without assistance; and when it can read, write, count money, and pass an examination in going a simple errand involving a purchase and a journey by rail or other public method of locomotion, it should have quite a majority. At present the children of laborers are soon mobile and able to shift for themselves, whereas it is possible to find grown-up women in the rich classes who are actually afraid to take a walk in the streets unattended and unprotected. It is true that this is a superstition from the time when a retinue was part of the state of persons of quality, and the unattended person was supposed to be a common person of no quality, earning a living; but this has now become so absurd that children and young women are no longer told why they are forbidden to go about alone, and have to be persuaded that the streets are dangerous places, which of course they are; but people who are not educated to live dangerously have only half a life, and are more likely to die miserably after all than those who have taken all the common risks of freedom from their childhood onward as matters of course.

THE CONFLICT OF WILLS

The world wags in spite of its schools and its families because both schools and families are mostly very largely anarchic: parents and schoolmasters are good-natured or weak or lazy; and children are docile and affectionate and very shortwinded in their fits of naughtiness; and so most families slummock along and muddle through until the children cease to be children. In the few cases when the parties are energetic and determined, the child is crushed or the parent is reduced to a cipher, as the case may be. When the opposed forces are neither of them strong enough to annihilate the other, there is serious trouble: that is how we get those feuds between parent and child which recur to our memory so ironically when we hear people sentimentalizing about natural affection. We even get tragedies; for there is nothing so tragic to contemplate or so devastating to suffer as the oppression of will without conscience; and the whole tendency of our family and school system is to set the will of the parent and the school despot above conscience as something that must be deferred to abjectly and absolutely for its own sake.

The strongest, fiercest force in nature is human will. It is the highest organization we know of the will that has created the whole universe. Now all honest civilization, religion, law, and convention is an attempt to keep this force within beneficent bounds. What corrupts civilization, religion, law, and convention (and they are at present pretty nearly as corrupt as they dare) is the constant attempts made by the wills of individuals and classes to thwart the wills and enslave the powers of other individuals and classes. The powers of the parent and the schoolmaster, and of their public analogues the lawgiver and the judge, become instruments of tyranny in the hands of those who are too narrow-minded to understand law and exercise judgment; and in their hands (with us they mostly fall into such hands) law becomes tyranny. And what is a tyrant? Quite simply a person who says to another person, young or old, "You shall do as I tell you; you shall make what I want; you shall profess my creed; you shall have no will of your own; and your powers shall be at the disposal of my will." It has come to this at last: that the phrase "she has a will of her own," or "he has a will of his own" has come to denote a person of exceptional obstinacy and self-assertion. And even persons of good natural disposition, if brought up to expect such deference, are roused to unreasoning fury, and sometimes to the commission of atrocious crimes, by the slightest challenge to their authority. Thus a laborer may be dirty, drunken, untruthful, slothful, untrustworthy in every way without exhausting the indulgence of the country-house. But let him dare to be "disrespectful" and he is a lost man, though he be the cleanest, soberest, most diligent, most veracious, most trustworthy man in the county. Dickens's instinct for detecting social cankers never served him better than when he shewed up Mrs Heep teaching her son to "be umble," knowing that if he carried out that precept he might be pretty well anything else he liked. The maintenance of deference to our wills becomes a mania which will carry the best of us to any extremity. We will allow a village of Egyptian fellaheen or Indian tribesmen to live the lowest life they please among themselves without molestation; but let one of them slay an Englishman or even strike him on the strongest provocation, and straightway we go stark mad, burning and destroying, shooting and shelling, flogging and hanging, if only such survivors as we may leave are thoroughly cowed in the presence of a man with a white face. In the committee room of a local council or city corporation, the humblest employees of the committee find defenders if they complain of harsh treatment.

Gratuities are voted, indulgences and holidays are pleaded for, delinquencies are excused in the most sentimental manner provided only the employee, however patent a hypocrite or incorrigible a slacker, is hat in hand. But let the most obvious measure of justice be demanded by the secretary of a Trade Union in terms which omit all expressions of subservience, and it is with the greatest difficulty that the cooler-headed can defeat angry motions that the letter be thrown into the waste-paper basket and the committee proceed to the next business.

THE DEMAGOGUE'S OPPORTUNITY

And the employee has in him the same fierce impulse to impose his will without respect for the will of others. Democracy is in practice nothing but a device for cajoling from him the vote he refuses to arbitrary authority. He will not vote for Coriolanus; but when an experienced demagogue comes along and says "Sir: *you* are the dictator: the voice of the people is the voice of God; and I am only your very humble servant" he says at once "All right: tell me what to dictate" and is presently enslaved more effectually with his own silly consent than Coriolanus would ever have enslaved him without asking his leave. And the trick by which the demagogue defeats Coriolanus is played on him in his turn by *his* inferiors. Everywhere we see the cunning succeeding in the world by seeking a rich or powerful master and practising on his lust for subservience. The political adventurer who gets into parliament by offering himself to the poor voter, not as his representative but as his will-less soulless "delegate," is himself the dupe of a clever wife who repudiates Votes for Women, knowing well that whilst the man is master, the man's mistress will rule. Uriah Heep may be a crawling creature; but his crawling takes him upstairs.

Thus does the selfishness of the will turn on itself, and obtain by flattery what it cannot seize by open force. Democracy becomes the latest trick of tyranny: "womanliness" becomes the latest wile of prostitution.

Between parent and child the same conflict wages and the same destruction of character ensues. Parents set themselves to bend the will of their children to their own—to break their stubborn spirit, as they call it—with the ruthlessness of Grand Inquisitors. Cunning, unscrupulous children learn all the arts of the sneak in circumventing tyranny: children of better character are cruelly distressed and more or less lamed for life by it.

OUR QUARRELSOMENESS

As between adults, we find a general quarrelsomeness which makes political reform as impossible to most Englishmen as to hogs. Certain sections of the nation get cured of this disability. University men, sailors, and politicians are comparatively free from it, because the communal life of the university, the fact that in a ship a man must either learn to consider others or else go overboard or into irons, and the habit of working on committees and ceasing to expect more of one's own way than is included in the greatest common measure of the committee, educate the will socially. But no one who has ever had to guide a committee of ordinary private Englishmen through their first attempts at collective action, in committee or otherwise, can retain any illusions as to the appalling effects on our national manners and character of the organization of the home and the school as petty tyrannies, and the absence of all teaching of self-respect and training in self-assertion. Bullied and ordered about, the Englishman obeys like a sheep, evades like a knave, or tries to murder his oppressor. Merely criticized or opposed in committee, or invited to consider anybody's views but his own, he feels personally insulted and wants to resign or leave the room unless he is apologized to. And his panic and bewilderment when he sees that the older hands at the work have no patience with him and do not intend to treat him as infallible, are pitiable as far as they are anything but ludicrous. That is what comes of not being taught to consider other people's wills, and left to submit to them or to override them as if they were the winds and the weather. Such a state of mind is incompatible not only with the democratic introduction of high civilization, but with the comprehension and maintenance of such civilized institutions as have been introduced by benevolent and intelligent despots and aristocrats.

WE MUST REFORM SOCIETY BEFORE WE CAN REFORM OURSELVES

When we come to the positive problem of what to do with children if we are to give up the established plan, we find the difficulties so great that we begin to understand why so many people who detest the system and look back with loathing on their own schooldays, must helplessly send their children to the very schools they themselves were sent to, because there is no alternative except abandoning the children to undisciplined vagabondism. Man in society must do as everybody else does in his class: only fools and romantic novices imagine that freedom is a mere matter of the readiness of the individual to snap his fingers at convention. It is true that most of us live in a condition of quite unnecessary inhibition, wearing ugly and uncomfortable clothes, making ourselves and other people miserable by the heathen horrors of mourning, staying away from the theatre because we cannot afford the stalls and are ashamed to go to the pit, and in dozens of other ways enslaving ourselves when there are comfortable alternatives open to us without any real drawbacks. The contemplation of these petty slaveries, and of the triumphant ease with which sensible people throw them off, creates an impression that if we only take Johnson's advice to free our minds from cant, we can achieve freedom. But if we all freed our minds from cant we should find that for the most part we should have to go on doing the necessary work of the world exactly as we did it before until we organized new and free methods of doing it. Many people believed in secondary co-education (boys and girls taught together) before schools like Bedales were founded: indeed the practice was common enough in elementary schools and in Scotland; but their belief did not help them until Bedales and St George's were organized; and there are still not nearly enough co-educational schools in existence to accommodate all the children of the parents who believe in co-education up to university age, even if they could always afford the fees of these exceptional schools. It may be edifying to tell a duke that our public schools are all wrong in their constitution and methods, or a costermonger that children should be treated as in Goethe's Wilhelm Meister instead of as they are treated at the elementary school at the corner of his street; but what are the duke and the coster to do? Neither of them has any effective choice in the matter: their children must either go to the schools that are, or to no school at all. And as the duke thinks with reason that his son will be a lout or a milksop or a prig if he does not go to school, and the coster knows that his son will become an illiterate hooligan if he is left to the streets, there is no real alternative for either of them. Child life must be socially organized: no parent, rich or poor, can choose institutions that do not exist; and the private enterprise of individual schoolmasters appealing to a group of well-to-do parents, though it may shew what can be done by enthusiasts with new methods, cannot touch the mass of our children. For the average parent or child nothing is really available except the established practice; and this is what makes it so important that the established practice should be a sound one, and so useless for clever individuals to disparage it unless they can organize an alternative practice and make it, too, general.

THE PURSUIT OF MANNERS

If you cross-examine the duke and the coster, you will find that they are not concerned for the scholastic attainments of their children. Ask the duke whether he could pass the standard examination of twelve-year-old children in elementary schools, and he will admit, with an entirely placid smile, that he would almost certainly be ignominiously plucked. And he is so little ashamed of or disadvantaged by his condition that he is not prepared to spend an hour in remedying it. The coster may resent the inquiry instead of being amused by it; but his answer, if true, will be the same. What they both want for their children is the communal training, the apprenticeship to society, the lessons in holding one's own among people of all sorts with whom one is not, as in the home, on privileged terms. These can be acquired only by "mixing with the world," no matter how wicked the world is. No parent cares twopence whether his children can write Latin hexameters or repeat the dates of the accession of all the English monarchs since the Conqueror; but all parents are earnestly anxious about the manners of their children. Better Claude Duval than Kaspar Hauser. Laborers who are contemptuously anti-clerical in their opinions will send their daughters to the convent school because the nuns teach them some sort of gentleness of speech and behavior. And peers who tell you that our public schools are rotten through and through, and that our universities ought to be razed to the foundations, send their sons to Eton and Oxford, Harrow and Cambridge, not only because there is nothing else to be done, but because these places, though they turn out blackguards and igno-ramuses and boobies galore, turn them out with the habits and manners of the society they belong to. Bad as those manners are in many respects, they are better than no manners at all. And no individual or family can possibly teach them. They can be acquired only by living in an organized community in which they are traditional.

Thus we see that there are reasons for the segrega-tion of children even in families where the great reason: namely, that children are nuisances to adults, does not press very hardly, as, for instance, in the houses of the very poor, who can send their children to play in the streets, or the houses of the very rich, which are so large that the children's quarters can be kept out of the parents' way like the servants' quarters.

NOT TOO MUCH WIND ON THE HEATH,
BROTHER

What, then, is to be done? For the present, unfortunately, little except propagating the conception of Children's Rights. Only the achievement of economic equality through Socialism can make it possible to deal thoroughly with the question from the point of view of the total interest of the community, which must always consist of grown-up children. Yet economic equality, like all simple and obvious arrangements, seems impossible to people brought up as children are now. Still, something can be done even within class limits. Large communities of children of the same class are possible today; and voluntary organization of outdoor life for children has already begun in Boy Scouting and excursions of one kind or another. The discovery that anything, even school life, is better for the child than home life, will become an over-ridden hobby; and we shall presently be told by our faddists that anything, even camp life, is better than school life. Some blundering beginnings of this are already perceptible. There is a movement for making our British children into priggish little barefooted vagabonds, all talking like that born fool George Borrow, and supposed to be splendidly healthy because they would die if they slept in rooms with the windows shut, or perhaps even with a roof over their heads. Still, this is a fairly healthy folly; and it may do something to establish Mr Harold Cox's claim of a Right to Roam as the basis of a much needed law compelling proprietors of land to provide plenty of gates in their fences, and to leave them unlocked when there are no growing crops to be damaged nor bulls to be encountered, instead of, as at present, imprisoning the human race in dusty or muddy thoroughfares between walls of barbed wire.

The reaction against vagabondage will come from the children themselves. For them freedom will not mean the expensive kind of savagery now called "the simple life." Their natural disgust with the visions of cockney book fanciers blowing themselves out with "the wind on the heath, brother," and of anarchists who are either too weak to understand that men are strong and free in proportion to the social pressure they can stand and the complexity of the obligations they are prepared to undertake, or too strong to realize that what is freedom to them may be terror and bewilderment to others, will drive them back to the home and the school if these have meanwhile learned the lesson that children are independent human beings and have rights.

WANTED: A CHILD'S MAGNA CHARTA

Whether we shall presently be discussing a Juvenile Magna Charta or Declaration of Rights by way of including children in the Constitution is a question on which I leave others to speculate. But if it could once be established that a child has an adult's Right of Egress from uncomfortable places and unpleasant company, and there were children's lawyers to sue pedagogues and others for assault and imprisonment, there would be an amazing change in the behavior of schoolmasters, the quality of school books, and the amenities of school life. That Consciousness of Consent which, even in its present delusive form, has enabled Democracy to oust tyrannical systems in spite of all its vulgarities and stupidities and rancors and ineptitudes and ignorances, would operate as power-fully among children as it does now among grown-ups. No doubt the pedagogue would promptly turn dema-gogue, and woo his scholars by all the arts of demagogy; but none of these arts can easily be so dis-honorable or mischievous as the art of caning. And, after all, if larger liberties are attached to the acquisi-tion of knowledge, and the child finds that it can no more go to the seaside without a knowledge of the multiplication and pence tables than it can be an astronomer without mathematics, it will learn the multiplication table, which is more than it always does at present, in spite of all the canings and keepings-in.

THE PURSUIT OF LEARNING

When the Pursuit of Learning comes to mean the pur-suit of learning by the child instead of the pursuit of the child by Learning, cane in hand, the danger will be precocity of the intellect, which is just as undesir-able as precocity of the emotions. We still have a silly habit of talking and thinking as if intellect were a mechanical process and not a passion; and in spite of the German tutors who confess openly that three out of every five of the young men they coach for exam-inations are lamed for life thereby; in spite of Dickens and his picture of little Paul Dombey dying of lessons, we persist in heaping on growing children and ado-lescent youths and maidens tasks Pythagoras would have declined out of common regard for his own health and common modesty as to his own capacity. And this overwork is not all the effect of compulsion; for the average schoolmaster does not compel his scholars to learn: he only scolds and punishes them if they do not, which is quite a different thing, the net effect being that the school prisoners need not learn unless they like. Nay, it is sometimes remarked that the school dunce—meaning the one who does not like—often turns out well afterwards, as if idleness were a sign of ability and character. A much more sensible explanation is that the so-called dunces are not exhausted before they begin the serious business of life. It is said that boys will be boys; and one can only add one wishes they would. Boys really want to be manly, and are unfortunately encouraged thoughtlessly in this very dangerous and overstraining aspiration. All the people who have really worked (Herbert Spencer for instance) warn us against work as earnestly as some people warn us against drink. When learning is placed on the voluntary footing of sport, the teacher will find himself saying every day "Run away and play: you have worked as much as is good for you." Trying to make children leave school will be like trying to make them go to bed; and it will be necessary to surprise them with the idea that teaching is work, and that the teacher is tired and must go play or rest or eat: possibilities always concealed by that infamous humbug the current schoolmaster, who achieves a spurious divinity and a witch doctor's authority by persuading children that he is not human, just as ladies used to persuade them that they have no legs.

CHILDREN AND GAME: A PROPOSAL

Of the many wild absurdities of our existing social order perhaps the most grotesque is the costly and strictly enforced reservation of large tracts of country as deer forests and breeding grounds for pheasants whilst there is so little provision of the kind made for children. I have more than once thought of trying to introduce the shooting of children as a sport, as the children would then be preserved very carefully for ten months in the year, thereby reducing their death rate far more than the fusillades of the sportsmen during the other two would raise it. At present the killing of a fox except by a pack of foxhounds is regarded with horror; but you may and do kill children in a hundred and fifty ways provided you do not shoot them or set a pack of dogs on them. It must be admitted that the foxes have the best of it; and indeed a glance at our pheasants, our deer, and our children will convince the most sceptical that the children have decidedly the worst of it.

This much hope, however, can be extracted from the present state of things. It is so fantastic, so mad, so apparently impossible, that no scheme of reform need ever henceforth be discredited on the ground that it is fantastic or mad or apparently impossible. It is the sensible schemes, unfortunately, that are hopeless in England. Therefore I have great hopes that my own views, though fundamentally sensible, can be made to appear fantastic enough to have a chance.

First, then, I lay it down as a prime condition of sane society, obvious as such to anyone but an idiot, that in any decent community, children should find in every part of their native country, food, clothing, lodging, instruction, and parental kindness for the asking. For the matter of that, so should adults; but the two cases differ in that as these commodities do not grow on the bushes, the adults cannot have them unless they themselves organize and provide the supply, whereas the children must have them as if by magic, with nothing to do but rub the lamp, like Aladdin, and have their needs satisfied.

THE PARENTS' INTOLERABLE BURDEN

There is nothing new in this: it is how children have always had and must always have their needs satisfied. The parent has to play the part of Aladdin's djinn; and many a parent has sunk beneath the burden of this service. All the novelty we need is to organize it so that instead of the individual child fastening like a parasite on its own particular parents, the whole body of children should be thrown not only upon the whole body of parents, but upon the celibates and childless as well, whose present exemption from a full share in the social burden of children is obviously unjust and unwholesome. Today it is easy to find a widow who has at great cost to herself in pain, danger, and disablement, borne six or eight children. In the same town you will find rich bachelors and old maids, and married couples with no children or with families voluntarily limited to two or three. The eight children do not belong to the woman in any real or legal sense. When she has reared them they pass away from her into the community as independent persons, marrying strangers, working for strangers, spending on the community the life that has been built up at her expense. No more monstrous injustice could be imagined than that the burden of rearing the children should fall on her alone and not on the celibates and the selfish as well.

This is so far recognized that already the child finds, wherever it goes, a school for it, and somebody to force it into the school; and more and more these schools are being driven by the mere logic of facts to provide the children with meals, with boots, with spectacles, with dentists and doctors. In fact, when the child's parents are destitute or not to be found, bread, lodging, and clothing are provided. It is true that they are provided grudgingly and on conditions infamous enough to draw down abundant fire from Heaven upon us every day in the shape of crime and disease and vice; but still the practice of keeping children barely alive at the charge of the community is established; and there is no need for me to argue about it. I propose only two extensions of the practice. One is to provide for all the child's reasonable human wants, on which point, if you differ from me, I shall take leave to say that you are socially a fool and personally an inhuman wretch. The other is that these wants should be supplied in complete freedom from compulsory schooling or compulsory anything except restraint from crime, though, as they can be supplied only by social organization, the child must be conscious of and subject to the conditions of that organization, which may involve such portions of adult responsibility and duty as a child may be able to bear according to its age, and which will in any case prevent it from forming the vagabond and anarchist habit of mind.

One more exception might be necessary: compulsory freedom. I am sure that a child should not be imprisoned in a school. I am not so sure that it should not sometimes be driven out into the open—imprisoned in the woods and on the mountains, as it were. For there are frowsty children, just as there are frowsty adults, who dont want freedom. This morbid result of over-domestication would, let us hope, soon disappear with its cause.

MOBILIZATION

Those who see no prospect held out to them by this except a country in which all the children shall be roaming savages, should consider, first, whether their condition would be any worse than that of the little caged savages of today; and second, whether either children or adults are so apt to run wild that it is necessary to tether them fast to one neighborhood to prevent a general dissolution of society. My own observation leads me to believe that we are not half mobilized enough. True, I cannot deny that we are more mobile than we were. You will still find in the home counties old men who have never been to London, and who tell you that they once went to Winchester or St Albans much as if they had been to the South Pole; but they are not so common as the clerk who has been to Paris or to Lovely Lucerne, and who "goes away somewhere" when he has a holiday. His grandfather never had a holiday, and, if he had, would no more have dreamed of crossing the Channel than of taking a box at the Opera. But with all allowance for the Polytechnic excursion and the tourist agency, our inertia is still appalling. I confess to having once spent nine years in London without putting my nose outside it; and though this was better, perhaps, than the restless globetrotting vagabondage of the idle rich, wandering from hotel to hotel and never really living anywhere, yet I should no more have done it if I had been properly mobilized in my childhood than I should have worn the same suit of clothes all that time (which, by the way, I very nearly did, my professional income not having as yet begun to sprout). There are masses of people who could afford at least a trip to Margate, and a good many who could afford a trip round the world, who are more immovable than Aldgate pump. To others, who would move if they knew how, travelling is surrounded with imaginary difficulties and terrors. In short, the difficulty is not to fix people, but to root them up. We keep repeating the silly proverb that a rolling stone gathers no moss, as if moss were a desirable parasite. What we mean is that a vagabond does not prosper. Even this is not true, if prosperity means enjoyment as well as responsibility and money. The real misery of vagabondage is the misery of having nothing to do and nowhere to go, the misery of being derelict of God and Man, the misery of the idle, poor or rich. And this is one of the miseries of unoccupied childhood. The unoccupied adult, thus afflicted, tries many distractions which are, to say the least, unsuited to children. But one of them, the distraction of seeing the world, is innocent and beneficial. Also it is childish, being a continuation of what nurses call "taking notice," by which a child becomes experienced. It is pitiable nowadays to see men and women doing after the age of 45 all the travelling and sightseeing they should have done before they were 15. Mere wondering and staring at things is an important part of a child's education: that is why children can be thoroughly mobilized without making vagabonds of them. A vagabond is at home nowhere because he wanders: a child should wander because it ought to be at home everywhere. And it has its papers and its passports, and gets what it requires not by begging and pilfering, but from responsible agents of the community as of right, and with some formal acknowledgment of the obligations it is incurring and a knowledge of the fact that these obligations are being recorded: if, further, certain qualifications are exacted before it is promoted from permission to go as far as its legs will carry it to using mechanical aids to locomotion, it can roam without much danger of gypsification.

Under such circumstances the boy or girl could

always run away, and never be lost; and on no other conditions can a child be free without being also a homeless outcast. Parents could also run away from disagreeable children or drive them out of doors or even drop their acquaintance, temporarily or permanently, without inhumanity. Thus both parties would be on their good behavior, and not, as at present, on their filial or parental behavior, which, like all unfree behavior, is mostly bad behavior.

As to what other results might follow, we had better wait and see; for nobody now alive can imagine what customs and institutions would grow up in societies of free children. Child laws and child fashions, child manners and child morals are now not tolerated; but among free children there would certainly be surprising developments in this direction. I do not think there would be any danger of free children behaving as badly as grown-up people do now because they have never been free. They could hardly behave worse, anyhow.

CHILDREN'S RIGHTS AND PARENTS' WRONGS

A very distinguished man once assured a mother of my acquaintance that she would never know what it meant to be hurt until she was hurt through her children. Children are extremely cruel without intending it; and in ninety-nine cases out of a hundred the reason is that they do not conceive their elders as having any human feelings. Serve the elders right, perhaps, for posing as superhuman! The penalty of the imposter is not that he is found out (he very seldom is) but that he is taken for what he pretends to be, and treated as such. And to be treated as anything but what you really are may seem pleasant to the imagination when the treatment is above your merits; but in actual experience it is often quite the reverse. When I was a very small boy, my romantic imagination, stimulated by early doses of fiction, led me to brag to a still smaller boy so outrageously that he, being a simple soul, really believed me to be an invincible hero. I cannot remember whether this pleased me much; but I do remember very distinctly that one day this admirer of mine, who had a pet goat, found the animal in the hands of a larger boy than either of us, who mocked him and refused to restore the animal to his rightful owner. Whereupon, naturally, he came weeping to me, and demanded that I should rescue the goat and annihilate the aggressor. My terror was beyond description: fortunately for me, it imparted such a ghastliness to my voice and aspect as I, under the eye of my poor little dupe, advanced on the enemy with that hideous extremity of cowardice which is called the courage of despair, and said "You let go that goat," that he abandoned his prey and fled, to my unforgettable, unspeakable relief. I have never since exaggerated my prowess in bodily combat.

Now what happened to me in the adventure of the goat happens very often to parents, and would happen to schoolmasters if the prison door of the school did not shut out the trials of life. I remember once, at school, the resident head master was brought down to earth by the sudden illness of his wife. In the confusion that ensued it became necessary to leave one of the schoolrooms without a master. I was in the class that occupied that schoolroom. To have sent us home would have been to break the fundamental bargain with our parents by which the school was bound to keep us out of their way for half the day at all hazards. Therefore an appeal had to be made to our better feelings: that is, to our common humanity, not to make a noise. But the head master had never admitted any common humanity with us. We had been carefully broken in to regard him as a being quite aloof from and above us: one not subject to error or suffering or death or illness or mortality. Consequently sympathy was impossible; and if the unfortunate lady did not perish, it was because, as I now comfort myself with guessing, she was too much preoccupied with her own pains, and possibly making too much noise herself, to be conscious of the pandemonium downstairs.

A great deal of the fiendishness of schoolboys and the cruelty of children to their elders is produced just in this way. Elders cannot be superhuman beings and suffering fellow-creatures at the same time. If you pose as a little god, you must pose for better for worse.

HOW LITTLE WE KNOW ABOUT OUR PARENTS

The relation between parent and child has cruel moments for the parent even when money is no object, and the material worries are delegated to servant and school teachers. The child and the parent are strangers to one another necessarily, because their ages must differ widely. Read Goethe's autobiography; and note that though he was happy in his parents and had exceptional powers of observation, divination, and story-telling, he knew less about his father and mother than about most of the other people he mentions. I myself was never on bad terms with my mother: we lived together until I was forty-two years old, absolutely without the smallest friction of any kind, yet when her death set me thinking curiously about our relations, I realized that I knew very little about her. Introduce me to a strange woman who was a child when I was a child, a girl when I was a boy, an adolescent when I was an adolescent; and if we take naturally to one another I will know more of her and she of me at the end of forty days (I had almost said of forty minutes) than I knew of my mother at the end of forty years. A contemporary stranger is a novelty and an enigma, also a possibility; but a mother is like a broomstick or like the sun in the heavens, it does not matter which as far as one's knowledge of her is concerned: the broomstick is there and the sun is there; and whether the child is beaten by it or warmed and enlightened by it, it accepts it as a fact in nature, and does not conceive it as having had youth, passions, and weaknesses, or as still growing, yearning, suffering, and learning. If I meet a widow I may ask her all about her marriage; but what son ever dreams of asking his mother about her marriage, or could endure to hear of it without violently breaking off the old sacred relationship between them, and ceasing to be her child or anything more to her than the first man in the street might be?

Yet though in this sense the child cannot realize its parent's humanity, the parent can realize the child's; for the parents with their experience of life have none of the illusions about the child that the child has about the parents; and the consequence is that the child can hurt its parents' feelings much more than its parents can hurt the child's, because the child, even when there has been none of the deliberate hypocrisy by which children are taken advantage of by their elders, cannot conceive the parent as a fellow-creature, whilst the parents know very well that the children are only themselves over again. The child cannot conceive that its blame or contempt or want of interest could possibly hurt its parent, and therefore expresses them all with an indifference which has given rise to the term *enfant terrible* (a tragic term in spite of the jests connected with it); whilst the parent can suffer from such slights and reproaches more from a child than from anyone else, even when the child is not beloved, because the child is so unmistakably sincere in them.

OUR ABANDONED MOTHERS

Take a very common instance of this agonizing incompatibility. A widow brings up her son to manhood. He meets a strange woman, and goes off with and marries her, leaving his mother desolate. It does not occur to him that this is at all hard on her: he does it as a matter of course, and actually expects his mother to receive, on terms of special affection, the woman for whom she has been abandoned. If he shewed any sense of what he was doing, any remorse; if he mingled his tears with hers and asked her not to think too hardly of him because he had obeyed the inevitable destiny of a man to leave his father and mother and cleave to his wife, she could give him her blessing and accept her bereavement with dignity and without reproach. But the man never dreams of such considerations. To him his mother's feeling in the matter, when she betrays it, is unreasonable, ridiculous, and even odious, as shewing a prejudice against his adorable bride.

I have taken the widow as an extreme and obvious case; but there are many husbands and wives who are tired of their consorts, or disappointed in them, or estranged from them by infidelities; and these parents, in losing a son or a daughter through marriage, may be losing everything they care for. No parent's love is as innocent as the love of a child: the exclusion of all conscious sexual feeling from it does not exclude the bitterness, jealousy, and despair at loss which characterize sexual passion: in fact, what is called a pure love may easily be more selfish and jealous than a carnal one. Anyhow, it is plain matter of fact that naïvely selfish people sometimes try with fierce jealousy to prevent their children marrying.

FAMILY AFFECTION

Until the family as we know it ceases to exist, nobody will dare to analyse parental affection as distinguished from that general human sympathy which has secured to many an orphan fonder care in a stranger's house than it would have received from its actual parents. Not even Tolstoy, in The Kreutzer Sonata, has said all that we suspect about it. When it persists beyond the period at which it ceases to be necessary to the child's welfare, it is apt to be morbid; and we are probably wrong to inculcate its deliberate cultivation. The natural course is for the parents and children to cast off the specific parental and filial relation when they are no longer necessary to one another. The child does this readily enough to form fresh ties, closer and more fascinating. Parents are not always excluded from such compensations: it happens sometimes that when the children go out at the door the lover comes in at the window. Indeed it happens now oftener than it used to, because people remain much longer in the sexual arena. The cultivated Jewess no longer cuts off her hair at her marriage. The British matron has discarded her cap and her conscientious ugliness; and a bishop's wife at fifty has more of the air of a *femme galante* than an actress had at thirty-five in her grandmother's time. But as people marry later, the facts of age and time still inexorably condemn most parents to comparative solitude when their children marry. This may be a privation and may be a relief: probably in healthy circumstances it is no worse than a salutary change of habit; but even at that it is, for the moment at least, a wrench. For though parents and children sometimes dislike one another, there is an experience of succor and a habit of dependence and expectation formed in infancy which naturally attaches a child to its parent or to its nurse (a foster parent) in a quite peculiar way. A benefit to the child may be a burden to the parent; but people become attached to their burdens sometimes more than the burdens are attached to them; and to "suffer little children" has become an affectionate impulse deep in our nature.

Now there is no such impulse to suffer our sisters and brothers, our aunts and uncles, much less our cousins. If we could choose our relatives, we might, by selecting congenial ones, mitigate the repulsive effect of the obligation to like them and to admit them to our intimacy. But to have a person imposed on us as a brother merely because he happens to have the same parents is unbearable when, as may easily happen, he is the sort of person we should carefully avoid if he were anyone else's brother. All Europe (except Scotland, which has clans instead of families) draws the line at second cousins. Protestantism draws it still closer by making the first cousin a marriageable stranger; and the only reason for not drawing it at sisters and brothers is that the institution of the family compels us to spend our childhood with them, and thus imposes on us a curious relation in which familiarity destroys romantic charm, and is yet expected to create a specially warm affection. Such a relation is dangerously factitious and unnatural; and the practical moral is that the less said at home about specific family affection the better. Children, like grown-up people, get on well enough together if they are not pushed down one another's throats; and grown-up relatives will get on together in proportion to their separation and their care not to presume on their blood relationship. We should let children's feelings take their natural course without prompting. I have seen a child scolded and called unfeeling because it did not occur to it to make a theatrical demonstration of affectionate delight when its mother returned after an absence: a typical example of the way in which spurious family sentiment is stoked up. We are, after all, sociable animals; and if we are let alone in the matter of our affections, and well brought up otherwise, we shall not get on any the worse with particular people because they happen to be our brothers and sisters and cousins. The danger lies in assuming that we shall get on any better.

The main point to grasp here is that families are not kept together at present by family feeling but by human feeling. The family cultivates sympathy and mutual help and consolation as any other form of kindly association cultivates them; but the addition of a dictated compulsory affection as an attribute of near kinship is not only unnecessary, but positively detrimental; and the alleged tendency of modern social development to break up the family need alarm nobody. We cannot break up the facts of kinship nor eradicate its natural emotional consequences. What we can do and ought to do is to set people free to behave naturally and to change their behavior as circumstances change. To impose on a citizen of London the family duties of a Highland cateran in the eighteenth century is as absurd as to compel him to carry a claymore and target instead of an umbrella. The civilized man has no special use for cousins; and he may presently find that he has no special use for brothers and sisters. The parent seems likely to remain indispensable; but there is no reason why that natural tie should be made the excuse for unnatural aggravations of it, as crushing to the parent as they are oppressive to the child. The mother and father will not always have to shoulder the burthen of maintenance which should fall on the Atlas shoulders of the fatherland and motherland. Pending such reforms and emancipations, a shattering break-up of the paternal home must remain one of normal incidents of marriage. The parent is left lonely and the child is not. Woe to the old if they have no impersonal interests, no convictions, no public causes to advance, no tastes or hobbies! It is well to be a mother but not to be a mother-in-law; and if men were cut off artificially from intellectual and public interests as women are, the father-in-law would be as deplorable a figure in popular tradition as the mother-in-law.

It is not to be wondered at that some people hold that blood relationship should be kept a secret from the persons related, and that the happiest condition in this respect is that of the foundling who, if he ever meets his parents or brothers or sisters, passes them by without knowing them. And for such a view there is this to be said: that our family system does unquestionably take the natural bond between members of the same family, which, like all natural bonds, is not too tight to be borne, and superimposes on it a painful burden of forced, inculcated, suggested, and altogether unnecessary affection and responsibility which we should do well to get rid of by making relatives as independent of one another as possible.

THE FATE OF THE FAMILY

The difficulty of inducing people to talk sensibly about the family is the same as that which I pointed out in a previous volume as confusing discussions of marriage. Marriage is not a single invariable institution: it changes from civilization to civilization, from religion to religion, from civil code to civil code, from frontier to frontier. The family is still more variable, because the number of persons constituting a family, unlike the number of persons constituting a marriage, varies from one to twenty: indeed, when a widower with a family marries a widow with a family, and the two produce a third family, even that very high number may be surpassed. And the conditions may vary between opposite extremes: for example, in a London or Paris slum every child adds to the burden of poverty and helps to starve the parents and all the other children, whereas in a settlement of pioneer colonists every child, from the moment it is big enough to lend a hand to the family industry, is an investment in which the only danger is that of temporary over-capitalization. Then there are the variations in family sentiment. Sometimes the family organization is as frankly political as the organization of an army or an industry: fathers being no more expected to be sentimental about their children than colonels about soldiers, or factory owners about their employees, though the mother may be allowed a little tenderness if her character is weak. The Roman father was a despot: the Chinese father is an object of worship: the sentimental modern western father is often a playfellow looked to for toys and pocket-money. The farmer sees his children constantly: the squire sees them only during the holidays, and not then oftener than he can help: the tram conductor, when employed by a joint stock company, sometimes never sees them at all.

Under such circumstances phrases like The Influence of Home Life, The Family, The Domestic Hearth, and so on, are no more specific than The Mammals, or The Man In The Street; and the pious generalizations founded so glibly on them by our sentimental moralists are unworkable. When households average twelve persons with the sexes about equally represented, the results may be fairly good. When they average three the results may be very bad indeed; and to lump the two together under the general term The Family is to confuse the question hopelessly. The modern small family is much too stuffy: children "brought up at home" in it are unfit for society.

But here again circumstances differ. If the parents live in what is called a garden suburb, where there is a good deal of social intercourse, and the family, instead of keeping itself to itself, as the evil old saying is, and glowering at the neighbors over the blinds of the long street in which nobody knows his neighbor and every-one wishes to deceive him as to his income and social importance, is in effect broken up by school life, by out-of-door habits, and by frank neighborly inter-course through dances and concerts and theatricals and excursions and the like, families of four may turn out much less barbarous citizens than families of ten which attain the Boer ideal of being out of sight of one another's chimney smoke.

All one can say is, roughly, that the homelier the home, and the more familiar the family, the worse for everybody concerned. The family ideal is a humbug and a nuisance: one might as reasonably talk of the barrack ideal, or the forecastle ideal, or any other substitution of the machinery of social organization for the end of it, which must always be the fullest and most capable life: in short, the most godly life. And this significant word reminds us that though the popular conception of heaven includes a Holy Family, it does not attach to that family the notion of a separate home, or a private nursery or kitchen or mother-in-law, or anything that constitutes the family as we know it. Even blood relationship is miraculously abstracted from it; and the Father is the father of all children, the mother the mother of all mothers and babies, and the Son the Son of Man and the Savior of his brothers: one whose chief utterance on the subject of the conventional family was an invitation to all of us to leave our families and follow him, and to leave the dead to bury the dead, and not debauch ourselves at that gloomy festival the family funeral, with its sequel of hideous mourning and grief which is either affected or morbid.

FAMILY MOURNING

I do not know how far this detestable custom of mourning is carried in France; but judging from the appearance of the French people I should say that a Frenchwoman goes into mourning for her cousins to the seventeenth degree. The result is that when I cross the Channel I seem to have reached a country devastated by war or pestilence. It is really suffering only from the family. Will anyone pretend that England has not the better of this striking difference? It is such senseless and unnatural conventions as this that make us so impatient of what we call family feeling. Even apart from its insufferable pretensions, the family needs hearty discrediting; for there is hardly any vulnerable part of it that could not be amputated with advantage.

ART TEACHING

By art teaching I hasten to say that I do not mean giving children lessons in freehand drawing and perspective. I am simply calling attention to the fact that fine art is the only teacher except torture. I have already pointed out that nobody, except under threat of torture, can read a school book. The reason is that a school book is not a work of art. Similarly, you cannot listen to a lesson or a sermon unless the teacher or the preacher is an artist. You cannot read the Bible if you have no sense of literary art. The reason why the continental European is, to the Englishman or American, so surprisingly ignorant of the Bible, is that the authorized English version is a great work of literary art, and the continental versions are comparatively artless. To read a dull book; to listen to a tedious play or prosy sermon or lecture; to stare at uninteresting pictures or ugly buildings: nothing, short of disease, is more dreadful than this. The violence done to our souls by it leaves injuries and produces subtle maladies which have never been properly studied by psychopathologists. Yet we are so inured to it in school, where practically all the teachers are bores trying to do the work of artists, and all the books art-

less, that we acquire a truly frightful power of enduring boredom. We even acquire the notion that fine art
is lascivious and destructive to the character. In
Church, in the House of Commons, at public meetings, we sit solemnly listening to bores and twaddlers
because from the time we could walk or speak we have
been snubbed, scolded, bullied, beaten and imprisoned whenever we dared to resent being bored or
twaddled at, or to express our natural impatience and
derision of bores and twaddlers. And when a man
arises with a soul of sufficient native strength to break
the bonds of this inculcated reverence and to expose
and deride and tweak the noses of our humbugs and
panjandrums, like Voltaire or Dickens, we are shocked
and scandalized, even when we cannot help laughing.
Worse, we dread and persecute those who can see and
declare the truth, because their sincerity and insight
reflects on our delusion and blindness. We are all
like Nell Gwynne's footman, who defended Nell's
reputation with his fists, not because he believed her
to be what he called an honest woman, but because he
objected to be scorned as the footman of one who was
no better than she should be.

This wretched power of allowing ourselves to be
bored may seem to give the fine arts a chance sometimes. People will sit through a performance of
Beethoven's ninth symphony or of Wagner's Ring
just as they will sit through a dull sermon or a front
bench politician saying nothing for two hours whilst
his unfortunate country is perishing through the delay
of its business in Parliament. But their endurance is
very bad for the ninth symphony, because they never
hiss when it is murdered. I have heard an Italian
conductor (no longer living) take the *adagio* of that
symphony at a lively *allegretto*, slowing down for the

warmer major sections into the speed and manner of the heroine's death song in a Verdi opera; and the listeners, far from relieving my excruciation by rising with yells of fury and hurling their programs and opera glasses at the miscreant, behaved just as they do when Richter conducts it. The mass of imposture that thrives on this combination of ignorance with despairing endurance is incalculable. Given a public trained from childhood to stand anything tedious, and so saturated with school discipline that even with the doors open and no schoolmasters to stop them they will sit there helplessly until the end of the concert or opera gives them leave to go home; and you will have in great capitals hundreds of thousands of pounds spent every night in the season on professedly artistic entertainments which have no other effect on fine art than to exacerbate the hatred in which it is already secretly held in England.

Fortunately, there are arts that cannot be cut off from the people by bad performances. We can read books for ourselves; and we can play a good deal of fine music for ourselves with the help of a pianola. Nothing stands between us and the actual handwork of the great masters of painting except distance; and modern photographic methods of reproduction are in some cases quite and in many nearly as effective in conveying the artist's message as a modern edition of Shakespear's plays is in conveying the message that first existed in his handwriting. The reproduction of great feats of musical execution is already on the way: the gramophone, for all its wheezing and snarling and braying, is steadily improving in its manners; and what with this improvement on the one hand, and on the other that blessed selective faculty which enables us to ignore a good deal of disagreeable noise if there is a thread of music in the middle of it (few critics of the gramophone seem to be conscious of the very considerable mechanical noise set up by choirs and orchestras) we have at last reached a point at which, for example, a person living in an English village where the church music is the only music, and that music is made by a few well-intentioned ladies with the help of a harmonium, can hear masses by Palestrina very passably executed, and can thereby be led to the discovery that Jackson in F and Hymns Ancient and Modern are not perhaps the last word of beauty and propriety in the praise of God.

In short, there is a vast body of art now within the reach of everybody. The difficulty is that this art, which alone can educate us in grace of body and soul, and which alone can make the history of the past live for us or the hope of the future shine for us, which alone can give delicacy and nobility to our crude lusts, which is the appointed vehicle of inspiration and the method of the communion of saints, is actually branded as sinful among us because, wherever it arises, there is resistance to tyranny, breaking of fetters, and the breath of freedom. The attempt to suppress art is not wholly successful: we might as well try to suppress oxygen. But it is carried far enough to inflict on huge numbers of people a most injurious art starvation, and to corrupt a great deal of the art that is tolerated. You will find in England plenty of rich families with little more culture than their dogs and horses. And you will find poor families, cut off by poverty and town life from the contemplation of the beauty of the earth, with its dresses of leaves, its scarves of cloud, and its contours of hill and valley, who would positively be happier as hogs, so little have they cultivated their humanity by the only effective instrument of culture: art. The dearth is artificially maintained even when there are the means of satisfying it. Story books are forbidden, picture post cards are forbidden, theatres are forbidden, operas are forbidden, circuses are forbidden, sweetmeats are forbidden, pretty colors are forbidden, all exactly as vice is forbidden. The Creator is explicitly prayed to, and implicitly convicted of indecency every day. An association of vice and sin with everything that is delightful and of goodness with everything that is wretched and detestable is set up. All the most perilous (and glorious) appetites and propensities are at once inflamed by starvation and uneducated by art. All the wholesome conditions which art imposes on appetite are waived: instead of cultivated men and women restrained by a thousand delicacies, repelled by ugliness, chilled by vulgarity, horrified by coarseness, deeply and sweetly moved by the graces that art has revealed to them and nursed in them, we get indiscriminate rapacity in pursuit of pleasure and a parade of the grossest stimulations in catering for it. We have a continual clamor for goodness, beauty, virtue, and sanctity, with such an appalling inability to recognize it or love it when it arrives that it is more dangerous to be a great prophet or poet than to promote twenty companies for swindling simple folk out of their savings. Do not for a moment suppose that uncultivated people are merely indifferent to high and noble qualities. They hate them malignantly. At best, such qualities are like rare and beautiful birds: when they appear the whole country takes down its guns; but the birds receive the statuary tribute of having their corpses stuffed.

And it really all comes from the habit of preventing children from being troublesome. You are so careful of your boy's morals, knowing how troublesome they may be, that you keep him away from the Venus of Milo only to find him in the arms of the scullery maid or someone much worse. You decide that the Hermes of Praxiteles and Wagner's Tristan are not suited for young girls; and your daughter marries somebody appallingly unlike either Hermes or Tristan solely to escape from your parental protection. You have not stifled a single passion nor averted a single danger: you have depraved the passions by starving them, and broken down all the defences which so effectively protect children brought up in freedom. You have men who imagine themselves to be ministers of religion openly declaring that when they pass through the streets they have to keep out in the wheeled traffic to avoid the temptations of the pavement. You have them organizing hunts of the women who tempt them—poor creatres whom no artist would touch without a shudder—and wildly clamoring for more clothes to disguise and conceal the body, and for the abolition of pictures, statues, theatres, and pretty colors. And incredible as it seems, these unhappy lunatics are left at large, unrebuked, even admired and revered, whilst artists have to struggle for toleration. To them an undraped human body is the most monstrous, the most blighting, the most obscene, the most unbearable spectacle in the universe. To an artist it is, at its best, the most admirable spectacle in nature, and, at its average, an object of indifference. If every rag of clothing miraculously dropped from the inhabitants of London at noon tomorrow (say as a preliminary to the Great Judgment), the artistic people would not turn a hair; but the artless people would go mad and call on the mountains to hide them. I submit that this indicates a thoroughly healthy state on the part of the artists, and a thoroughly morbid one on the part of the artless. And the healthy state is attainable in a cold country like ours only by familiarity with the undraped figure acquired through pictures, statues, and theatrical representations in which an illusion of natural clotheslessness is produced and made poetic.

In short, we all grow up stupid and mad to just the extent to which we have not been artistically educated; and the fact that this taint of stupidity and madness has to be tolerated because it is general, and is even boasted of as characteristically English, makes the situation all the worse. It is becoming exceedingly grave at present, because the last ray of art is being cut off from our schools by the discontinuance of religious education.

THE IMPOSSIBILITY OF SECULAR EDUCATION

Now children must be taught some sort of religion. Secular education is an impossibility. Secular education comes to this: that the only reason for ceasing to do evil and learning to do well is that if you do not you will be caned. This is worse than being taught in a church school that if you become a dissenter you will go to hell; for hell is presented as the instrument of something eternal, divine, and inevitable: you cannot evade it at the moment the schoolmaster's back is turned. What confuses this issue and leads even highly intelligent religious persons to advocate secular education as a means of rescuing children from the strife of rival proselytizers is the failure to distinguish between the child's personal subjective need for a religion and its right to an impartially communicated historical objective knowledge of all the creeds and Churches.

Just as a child, no matter what its race and color may be, should know that there are black men and brown men and yellow men, and, no matter what its political convictions may be, that there are Monarchists and Republicans and Positivists, Socialists and Unsocialists, so it should know that there are Christians and Mahometans and Buddhists and Shintoists and so forth, and that they are on the average just as honest and well-behaved as its own father. For example, it should not be told that Allah is a false god set up by the Turks and Arabs, who will all be damned for taking that liberty; but it should be told that many English people think so, and that many Turks and Arabs think the converse about English people. It should be taught that Allah is simply the name by which God is known to Turks and Arabs, who are just as eligible for salvation as any Christian. Further, that the practical reason why a Turkish child should pray in a mosque and an English child in a church is that as worship is organized in Turkey in mosques in the name of Mahomet and in England in churches in the name of Christ, a Turkish child joining the Church of England or an English child following Mahomet will find that it has no place for its worship and no organization of its religion within its reach. Any other teaching of the history and present facts of religion is false teaching, and is politically extremely dangerous in an empire in which a huge majority of the fellow-subjects of the governing island do not profess the religion of that island.

But this objectivity, though intellectually honest, tells the child only what other people believe. What it should itself believe is quite another matter. The sort of Rationalism which says to a child "You must suspend your judgment until you are old enough to choose your religion" is Rationalism gone mad. The child must have a conscience and a code of honor (which is the essence of religion) even if it be only a provisional one, to be revised at its confirmation. For confirmation is meant to signalize a spiritual coming of age, and may be a repudiation. Really active souls have many confirmations and repudiations as their life deepens and their knowledge widens. But what is to guide the child before its first confirmation? Not mere orders, because orders must have a sanction of some sort or why should the child obey them? If, as a Secularist, you refuse to teach any sanction, you must say "You will be punished if you disobey." "Yes," says the child to itself, "if I am found out; but wait until your back is turned and I will do as I like, and lie about it." There can be no objective punishment for successful fraud; and as no espionage can cover the whole range of a child's conduct, the upshot is that the child becomes a liar and schemer with an atrophied conscience. And a good many of the orders given to it are not obeyed after all. Thus the Secularist who is not a fool is forced to appeal to the child's vital impulse towards perfection, to the divine spark; and no resolution not to call this impulse an impulse of loyalty to the Fellowship of the Holy Ghost, or obedience to the Will of God, or any other standard theological term, can alter the fact that the Secularist has stepped outside Secularism and is educating the child religiously, even if he insists on repudiating that pious adverb and substituting the word metaphysically.

NATURAL SELECTION AS A RELIGION

We must make up our minds to it therefore that whatever measures we may be forced to take to prevent the recruiting sergeants of the Churches, free or established, from obtaining an exclusive right of entry to schools, we shall not be able to exclude religion from them. The most horrible of all religions: that which teaches us to regard ourselves as the helpless prey of a series of senseless accidents called Natural Selection, is allowed and even welcomed in so-called secular schools because it is, in a sense, the negation of all religion; but for school purposes a religion is a belief which affects conduct: and no belief affects conduct more radically and often so disastrously as the belief that the universe is a product of Natural Selection. What is more, the theory of Natural Selection cannot be kept out of schools, because many of the natural facts that present the most plausible appearance of design can be accounted for by Natural Selection; and it would be as absurd to keep a child in delusive ignorance of so potent a factor in evolution as to keep it in ignorance of radiation or capillary attraction. Even if you make a religion of Natural Selection, and teach the child to regard itself as the irresponsible prey of its circumstances and appetites (or its heredity as you will perhaps call them), you will none the less find that its appetites are stimulated by your encouragement and daunted by your discouragement; that one of its appetites is an appetite for perfection; that if you discourage this appetite and encourage the cruder acquisitive appetites the child will steal and lie and be a nuisance to you; and that if you encourage its appetite for perfection and teach it to attach a peculiar sacredness to it and place it before the other appetites, it will be a much nicer child and you will have a much easier job, at which point you will, in spite of your pseudo-scientific jargon, find yourself back in the old-fashioned religious teaching as deep as Dr Watts and in fact fathoms deeper.

MORAL INSTRUCTION LEAGUES

And now the voices of our Moral Instruction Leagues will be lifted, asking whether there is any reason why the appetite for perfection should not be cultivated in rationally scientific terms instead of being associated with the story of Jonah and the great fish and the thousand other tales that grow up round religions. Yes: there are many reasons; and one of them is that children all like the story of Jonah and the whale (they insist on its being a whale in spite of demonstrations by Bible smashers without any sense of humor that Jonah would not have fitted into a whale's gullet—as if the story would be credible of a whale with an enlarged throat) and that no child on earth can stand moral instruction books or catechisms or any other statement of the case for religion in abstract terms. The object of a moral instruction book is not to be rational, scientific, exact, proof against controversy, nor even credible: its object is to make children good. If it makes them sick instead its place is the waste-paper basket. And if it is to be read it must be readable.

Take for an illustration the story of Elisha and the bears. To the authors of the moral instruction books it is in the last degree reprehensible. It is obviously not true as a record of fact; and the picture it gives us of the temper of God (which is what interests an adult reader) is shocking and blasphemous. But it is a capital story for a child. It interests a child because it is about bears; and it leaves the child with an impression that children who poke fun at old gentlemen and make rude remarks about bald heads are not nice children, which is a highly desirable impression, and just as much as a child is capable of receiving from the story. When a story is about God and a child, children take God for granted and criticize the child. Adults do the opposite, and are thereby often led to talk great nonsense about the bad effect of Bible stories on infants.

But let no one think that a child or anyone else can learn religion from a teacher or a book or by any academic process whatever. It is only by an unfettered access to the whole body of Fine Art: that is, to the whole body of inspired revelation, that we can build up that conception of divinity to which all virtue is an aspiration. And to hope to find this body of art purified from all that is obsolete or dangerous or fierce or lusty, or to pick and choose what will be good for any particular child, much less for all children, is the shallowest of vanities. Such schoolmasterly selection is neither possible nor desirable. Ignorance of evil is not virtue but imbecility: admiring it is like giving a prize for honesty to a man who has not stolen your watch because he did not know you had one. Virtue chooses good from evil; and without knowledge there can be no choice. And even this is a dangerous simplification of what actually occurs. We are not choosing: we are growing. Were you to cut all of what you call the evil out of a child, it would drop dead. If you try to stretch it to full human stature when it is ten years old, you will simply pull it into two pieces and be hanged. And when you try to do this morally, which is what parents and schoolmasters are doing every day, you ought to be hanged; and some day, when we take a sensible view of the matter, you will be; and serve you right. The child does not stand between a good and a bad angel: what it has to deal with is a middling angel who, in normal healthy cases, wants to be a good angel as fast as it can without killing itself in the process, which is a dangerous one.

Therefore there is no question of providing the child with a carefully regulated access to good art. There is no good art, any more than there is good anything else in the absolute sense. Art that is too good for the child will either teach it nothing or drive it mad, as the Bible has driven many people mad who might have kept their sanity had they been allowed to read much lower forms of literature. The practical moral is that we must read whatever stories, see whatever pictures, hear whatever songs and symphonies, go to whatever plays we like. We shall not like those which have nothing to say to us; and though everyone has a right to bias our choice, no one has a right to deprive us of it by keeping us from any work of art or any work of art from us.

I may now say without danger of being misunderstood that the popular English compromise called Cowper-Templeism (unsectarian Bible education) is not so silly as it looks. It is true that the Bible inculcates half a dozen religions: some of them barbarous; some cynical and pessimistic; some amoristic and romantic; some sceptical and challenging; some kindly, simple, and intuitional; some sophistical and intellectual; none suited to the character and conditions of western civilization unless it be the Christianity which was finally suppressed by the Crucifixion, and has never been put into practice by any State before or since. But the Bible contains the ancient literature of a very remarkable Oriental race; and the imposition of this literature, on whatever false pretences, on our children left them more literate than if they knew no literature at all, which was the practical alternative. And as our Authorized Version is a great work of art as well, to know it was better than knowing no art, which also was the practical alternative. It is at least not a school book; and it is not a bad story book, horrible as some of the stories are. Therefore as between the Bible and the blank represented by secular education in its most matter-of-fact sense, the choice is with the Bible.

THE BIBLE

But the Bible is not sufficient. The real Bible of modern Europe is the whole body of great literature in which the inspiration and revelation of Hebrew Scripture has been continued to the present day. Nietzsche's Thus Spake Zoroaster is less comforting to the ill and unhappy than the Psalms; but it is much truer, subtler, and more edifying. The pleasure we get from the rhetoric of the book of Job and its tragic picture of a bewildered soul cannot disguise the ignoble irrelevance of the retort of God with which it closes, nor supply the need for such modern revelations as Shelley's Prometheus or The Niblung's Ring of Richard Wagner. There is nothing in the Bible greater in inspiration than Beethoven's ninth symphony; and the power of modern music to convey that inspiration to a modern man is far greater than that of Elizabethan English, which is, except for people steeped in the Bible from childhood like Sir Walter Scott and Ruskin, a dead language.

Besides, many who have no ear for literature or for music are accessible to architecture, to pictures, to statues, to dresses, and to the arts of the stage. Every device of art should be brought to bear on the young; so that they may discover some form of it that delights them naturally; for there will come to all of them that period between dawning adolescence and full maturity when the pleasures and emotions of art will have to satisfy cravings which, if starved or insulted, may become morbid and seek disgraceful satisfactions, and, if prematurely gratified otherwise than poetically, may destroy the stamina of the race. And it must be borne in mind that the most dangerous art for this necessary purpose is the art that presents itself as religious ecstasy. Young people are ripe for love long before they are ripe for religion. Only a very foolish person would substitute the Imitation of Christ for Treasure Island as a present for a boy or girl, or for Byron's Don Juan as a present for a swain or lass. Pickwick is the safest saint for us in our nonage. Flaubert's Temptation of St Anthony is an excellent book for a man of fifty, perhaps the best within reach as a healthy study of visionary ecstasy; but for the purposes of a boy of fifteen Ivanhoe and the Templar make a much better saint and devil. And the boy of fifteen will find this out for himself if he is allowed to wander in a well-stocked literary garden, and hear bands and see pictures and spend his pennies on cinematograph shows. His choice may often be rather disgusting to his elders when they want him to choose the best before he is ready for it. The greatest Protestant Manifesto ever written, as far as I know, is Houston Chamberlain's Foundations of the Nineteenth Century: everybody capable of it should read it. Probably the History of Maria Monk is at the opposite extreme of merit (this is a guess: I have never read it); but it is certain that a boy let loose in a library would go for Maria Monk and have no use whatever for Mr Chamberlain. I should probably have read Maria Monk myself if I had not had the Arabian Nights and their like to occupy me better. In art, children, like adults, will find their level if they are left free to find it, and not restricted to what adults

think good for them. Just at present our young people
are going mad over ragtimes, apparently because
syncopated rhythms are new to them. If they had
learnt what can be done with syncopation from
Beethoven's third Leonora overture, they would
enjoy the ragtimes all the more; but they would put
them in their proper place as amusing vulgarities.

ARTIST IDOLATRY

But there are more dangerous influences than ragtimes
waiting for people brought up in ignorance of fine art.
Nothing is more pitiably ridiculous than the wild
worship of artists by those who have never been
seasoned in youth to the enchantments of art. Tenors
and prima donnas, pianists and violinists, actors and
actresses enjoy powers of seduction which in the
middle ages would have exposed them to the risk of
being burnt for sorcery. But as they exercise this power
by singing, playing, and acting, no great harm is done
except perhaps to themselves. Far graver are the
powers enjoyed by brilliant persons who are also
connoisseurs in art. The influence they can exercise
on young people who have been brought up in the
darkness and wretchedness of a home without art,
and in whom a natural bent towards art has always
been baffled and snubbed, is incredible to those who
have not witnessed and understood it. He (or she)
who reveals the world of art to them opens heaven to
them. They become satellites, disciples, worshippers
of the apostle. Now the apostle may be a voluptuary
without much conscience. Nature may have given
him enough virtue to suffice in a reasonable environment. But this allowance may not be enough to defend
him against the temptation and demoralization of

finding himself a little god on the strength of what ought to be a quite ordinary culture. He may find adorers in all directions in our uncultivated society among people of stronger character than himself, not one of whom, if they had been artistically educated, would have had anything to learn from him or regarded him as in any way extraordinary apart from his actual achievements as an artist. Tartuffe is not always a priest. Indeed he is not always a rascal: he is often a weak man absurdly credited with omniscience and perfection, and taking unfair advantages only because they are offered to him and he is too weak to refuse. Give everyone his culture, and no one will offer him more than his due.

In thus delivering our children from the idolatry of the artist, we shall not destroy for them the enchantment of art: on the contrary, we shall teach them to demand art everywhere as a condition attainable by cultivating the body, mind, and heart. Art, said Morris, is the expression of pleasure in work. And certainly, when work is made detestable by slavery, there is no art. It is only when learning is made a slavery by tyrannical teachers that art becomes loathsome to the pupil.

"THE MACHINE"

When we set to work at a Constitution to secure freedom for children, we had better bear in mind that the children may not be at all obliged to us for our pains. Rousseau said that men are born free; and this dangerous saying, as Rousseau meant it, was and is a great and true saying; yet let it not lead us into the error of supposing that all men long for freedom and embrace it when it is offered to them. On the contrary, it has to be forced on them; and even then they will give it the slip if it is not religiously inculcated and strongly safe-guarded.

Besides, men are born docile, and must in the nature of things remain so with regard to everything they do not understand. Now political science and the art of government are among the things they do not understand, and indeed are not at present allowed to understand. They can be enslaved by a system, as we are at present, because it happens to be there, and nobody understands it. An intelligently worked Capitalist system, as Comte saw, would give us all that most of us are intelligent enough to want. What makes it produce such unspeakably vile results is that it is an automatic system which is as little understood by those who profit by it in money as by those who are starved and degraded by it: our millionaires and statesmen are manifestly no more "captains of industry" or scientific politicians than our bookmakers are mathematicians. For some time past a significant word has been coming into use as a substitute for Destiny, Fate, and Providence. It is "The Machine": the machine that has no god in it. Why do governments do nothing in spite of reports of Royal Commissions that establish the most frightful urgency? Why do our philanthropic millionaires do nothing, though they are ready to throw bucketfuls of gold into the streets? The Machine will not let them. Always The Machine. In short, they dont know how. They try to reform Society as an old lady might try to restore a broken down locomotive by prodding it with a knitting needle. And this is not at all because they are born fools, but because they have been educated, not into manhood and freedom, but into blindness and slavery by their parents and schoolmasters, themselves the

victims of a similar misdirection, and consequently of
The Machine. They do not want liberty. They have
not been educated to want it. They choose slavery
and inequality; and all the other evils are automatically added to them.

And yet we must have The Machine. It is only in
unskilled hands under ignorant direction that machinery is dangerous. We can no more govern modern
communities without political machinery than we can
feed and clothe them without industrial machinery.
Shatter The Machine, and you get Anarchy. And yet
The Machine works so detestably at present that we
have people who advocate anarchy and call themselves Anarchists.

THE PROVOCATION TO ANARCHISM

The Anarchists are right when they say that Governments, like schoolmasters, try to simplify their task by
destroying liberty and glorifying authority, especially
their own. But the difficulty of combining law and
order with free institutions is not a natural one. It is a
matter of inculcation. If people are brought up to be
slaves, it is useless and dangerous to let them loose at
the age of twenty-one and say "Now you are free."
No one with the tamed soul and broken spirit of a
slave can be free. It is like saying to a laborer brought
up on a family income of thirteen shillings a week,
"Here is one hundred thousand pounds: now you are
wealthy." Nothing can make such a man really
wealthy. Freedom and wealth are difficult and responsible conditions to which men must be accustomed
and socially trained from birth. A nation that is free at
twenty-one is not free at all; just as a man first en-
riched at fifty remains poor all his life, even if he does

not curtail it by drinking himself to death in the first wild ecstasy of being able to swallow as much as he likes for the first time. You cannot govern men brought up as slaves otherwise than as slaves are governed. You may pile Bills of Right and Habeas Corpus Acts on Great Charters; promulgate American Constitutions; burn the chateaux and guillotine the seigneurs; chop off the heads of kings and queens and set up Democracy on the ruins of feudalism: the end of it all for us is that already in the twentieth century there has been as much brute coercion and savage intolerance, as much flogging and hanging, as much impudent injustice on the bench and lustful rancor in the pulpit, as much naïve resort to torture, persecution, and suppression of free speech and freedom of the press, as much war, as much of the vilest excess of mutilation, rapine, and delirious indiscriminate slaughter of helpless non-combatants, old and young, as much prostitution of professional talent, literary and political, in defence of manifest wrong, as much cowardly sycophancy giving fine names to all this villainy or pretending that it is "greatly exaggerated," as we can find any record of from the days when the advocacy of liberty was a capital offence and Democracy was hardly thinkable. Democracy exhibits the vanity of Louis XIV, the savagery of Peter of Russia, the nepotism and provinciality of Napoleon, the fickleness of Catherine II: in short, all the childishness of all the despots without any of the qualities that enabled the greatest of them to fascinate and dominate their contemporaries.

And the flatterers of Democracy are as impudently servile to the successful, and insolent to common honest folk, as the flatterers of the monarchs. Democracy in America has led to the withdrawal of ordinary refined persons from politics; and the same result is coming in England as fast we make Democracy as democratic as it is in America. This is true also of popular religion: it is so horribly irreligious that nobody with the smallest pretence to culture, or the least inkling of what the great prophets vainly tried to make the world understand, will have anything to do with it except for purely secular reasons.

IMAGINATION

Before we can clearly understand how baleful is this condition of intimidation in which we live, it is necessary to clear up the confusion made by our use of the word imagination to denote two very different powers of mind. One is the power to imagine things as they are not: this I call the romantic imagination. The other is the power to imagine things as they are without actually sensing them; and this I will call the realistic imagination. Take for example marriage and war. One man has a vision of perpetual bliss with a domestic angel at home, and of flashing sabres, thundering guns, victorious cavalry charges, and routed enemies in the field. That is romantic imagination; and the mischief it does is incalculable. It begins in silly and selfish expectations of the impossible, and ends in spiteful disappointment, sour grievance, cynicism, and misanthropic resistance to any attempt to better a hopeless world. The wise man knows that imagination is not only a means of pleasing himself and beguiling tedious hours with romances and fairy tales and fools' paradises (a quite defensible and delightful amusement when you know exactly what you are doing and where fancy ends and facts begin), but also a means of foreseeing and being prepared for realities as yet unexperienced, and of testing the feasibility and desirability of serious Utopias. He does not expect his wife to be an angel; nor does he overlook the facts that war depends on the rousing of all the murderous blackguardism still latent in mankind; that every victory means a defeat; that fatigue, hunger, terror, and disease are the raw material which romancers work up into military glory; and that soldiers for the most part go to war as children go to school, because they are afraid not to. They are afraid even to say they are afraid, as such candor is punishable by death in the military code.

A very little realistic imagination gives an ambitious person enormous power over the multitudinous victims of the romantic imagination. For the romancer not only pleases himself with fictitious glories: he also terrifies himself with imaginary dangers. He does not even picture what these dangers are: he conceives the unknown as always dangerous. When you say to a realist "You must do this" or "You must not do that," he instantly asks what will happen to him if he does (or does not, as the case may be). Failing an unromantic convincing answer, he does just as he pleases unless he can find for himself a real reason for refraining. In short, though you can intimidate him, you cannot bluff him. But you can always bluff the romantic person: indeed his grasp of real considerations is so feeble that you find it necessary to bluff him even when you have solid considerations to offer him instead. The campaigns of Napoleon, with their atmosphere of glory, illustrate this. In the Russian campaign Napoleon's marshals achieved miracles of bluff, especially Ney, who, with a handful of men, monstrously outnumbered, repeatedly kept the Russian troops paralysed with terror by pure bounce.

Napoleon himself, much more a realist than Ney (that was why he dominated him), would probably have surrendered; for sometimes the bravest of the brave will achieve successes never attempted by the cleverest of the clever. Wellington was a completer realist than Napoleon. It was impossible to persuade Wellington that he was beaten until he actually was beaten. He was unbluffable; and if Napoleon had understood the nature of Wellington's strength instead of returning Wellington's snobbish contempt for him by an academic contempt for Wellington, he would not have left the attack at Waterloo to Ney and D'Erlon, who, on that field, did not know when they were beaten, whereas Wellington knew precisely when he was not beaten. The unbluffable would have triumphed anyhow, probably, because Napoleon was an academic soldier, doing the academic thing (the attack in columns and so forth) with superlative ability and energy; whilst Wellington was an original soldier who, instead of outdoing the terrible academic columns with still more terrible and academic columns, outwitted them with the thin red line, not of heroes, but, as this uncompromising realist never hesitated to testify, of the scum of the earth.

GOVERNMENT BY BULLIES

These picturesque martial incidents are being reproduced every day in our ordinary life. We are bluffed by hardy simpletons and headstrong bounders as the Russians were bluffed by Ney; and our Wellingtons are threadbound by slave-democracy as Gulliver was threadbound by the Lilliputians. We are a mass of people living in a submissive routine to which we have been drilled from our childhood. When you ask us to take the simplest step outside that routine, we say shyly, "Oh, I really couldnt," or "Oh, I shouldnt like to," without being able to point out the smallest harm that could possibly ensue: victims, not of a rational fear of real dangers, but of pure abstract fear, the quintessence of cowardice, the very negation of "the fear of God." Dotted about among us are a few spirits relatively free from this inculcated paralysis, sometimes because they are half-witted, sometimes because they are unscrupulously selfish, sometimes because they are realists as to money and unimaginative as to other things, sometimes even because they are exceptionally able, but always because they are not afraid of shadows nor oppressed with nightmares. And we see these few rising as if by magic into power and affluence, and forming, with the millionaires who have accidentally gained huge riches by the occasional windfalls of our commerce, the governing class. Now nothing is more disastrous than a governing class that does not know how to govern. And how can this rabble of the casual products of luck, cunning, and folly, be expected to know how to govern? The merely lucky ones and the hereditary ones do not owe their position to their qualifications at all. As to the rest, the realism which seems their essential qualification often consists not only in a lack of romantic imagination, which lack is a merit, but of the realistic, constructive, Utopian imagination, which lack is a ghastly defect. Freedom from imaginative illusion is therefore no guarantee whatever of nobility of character: that is why inculcated submissiveness makes us slaves to people much worse than ourselves, and why it is so important that submissiveness should no longer be inculcated.

And yet as long as you have the compulsory school as we know it, we shall have submissiveness inculcated.

What is more, until the active hours of child life are organized separately from the active hours of adult life, so that adults can enjoy the society of children in reason without being tormented, disturbed, harried, burdened, and hindered in their work by them as they would be now if there were no compulsory schools and no children hypnotized into the belief that they must tamely go to them and be imprisoned and beaten and over-tasked in them, we shall have schools under one pretext or another; and we shall have all the evil consequences and all the social hopelessness that result from turning a nation of potential freemen and freewomen into a nation of two-legged spoilt spaniels with everything crushed out of their nature except dread of the whip. Liberty is the breath of life to nations; and liberty is the one thing that parents, schoolmasters, and rulers spend their lives in extirpating for the sake of an immediately quiet and finally disastrous life.

Johnny Tarleton, an ordinary young business man of thirty or less, is taking his weekly Friday to Tuesday in the house of his father, John Tarleton, who has made a great deal of money out of Tarleton's Underwear. The house is in Surrey, on the slope of Hindhead; and Johnny, reclining, novel in hand, in a swinging chair with a little awning above it, is enshrined in a spacious half hemisphere of glass which forms a pavilion commanding the garden, and, beyond it, a barren but lovely landscape of hill profile with fir trees, commons of bracken and gorse, and wonderful cloud pictures.

The glass pavilion springs from a bridgelike arch in the wall of the house, through which one comes into a big hall with tiled flooring, which suggests that the proprietor's notion of domestic luxury is founded on the lounges of week-end hotels. The arch is not quite in the centre of the wall. There is more wall to Johnny's right than to his left; and this space is occupied by a hat rack and umbrella stand in which tennis rackets, white parasols, caps, Panama hats, and other summery articles are bestowed. Just through the arch at this corner stands a new portable Turkish bath, recently unpacked, with its crate beside it, and on the crate the drawn nails and the hammer used in unpacking. Near the crate are open boxes of garden games: bowls and croquet. Nearly in the middle of the glass wall of the pavilion is a door giving on the garden, with a couple of steps to surmount the hot-water pipes which skirt the glass. At intervals round the pavilion are marble pillars with specimens of Viennese pottery on them, very flamboyant in colour and florid in design. Between them are folded garden chairs flung anyhow against the pipes. In the side walls are two doors: one near the hat stand, leading to the interior of the house, the other on the opposite side and at the other end, leading to the vestibule.

There is no solid furniture except a sideboard which

stands against the wall between the vestibule door and the pavilion, a small writing table with blotter, rack for telegram forms and stationery, and a waste-paper basket, standing out in the hall near the sideboard, and a lady's worktable, with two chairs at it, towards the other side of the lounge. The writing table has also two chairs at it. On the sideboard there is a tantalus, liqueur bottles, a syphon, a glass jug of lemonade, tumblers, and every convenience for casual drinking. Also a plate of sponge-cakes, and a highly ornate punchbowl in the same style as the keramic display in the pavilion. Wicker chairs and little bamboo tables with ash trays and boxes of matches on them are scattered in all directions. In the pavilion, which is flooded with sunshine, is the elaborate patent swing seat and awning in which Johnny reclines with his novel. There are two wicker chairs right and left of him.

Bentley Summerhays, one of those smallish, thin-skinned youths, who from 17 to 70 retain unaltered the mental airs of the later and the physical appearance of the earlier age, appears in the garden and comes through the glass door into the pavilion. He is unmistakably a grade above Johnny socially; and though he looks sensitive enough, his assurance and his high voice are a little exasperating.

JOHNNY. Hallo! Wheres your luggage?

BENTLEY. I left it at the station. Ive walked up from Haslemere. [*He goes to the hat stand and hangs up his hat*].

JOHNNY [*shortly*] Oh! And whos to fetch it?

BENTLEY. Dont know. Dont care. Providence, probably. If not, your mother will have it fetched.

JOHNNY. Not her business, exactly, is it?

BENTLEY [*returning to the pavilion*] Of course not. Thats why one loves her for doing it. Look here:

chuck away your silly weekend novel, and talk to a chap. After a week in that filthy office my brain is simply blue-mouldy. Lets argue about something intellectual. [*He throws himself into the wicker chair on Johnny's right*].

JOHNNY [*straightening up in the swing with a yell of protest*] No. Now seriously, Bunny, Ive come down here to have a pleasant week-end; and I'm not going to stand your confounded arguments. If you want to argue, get out of this and go over to the Congregationalist minister's. He's a nailer at arguing. He likes it.

BENTLEY. You cant argue with a person when his livelihood depends on his not letting you convert him. And would you mind not calling me Bunny? My name is Bentley Summerhays, which you please.

JOHNNY. Whats the matter with Bunny?

BENTLEY. It puts me in a false position. Have you ever considered the fact that I was an afterthought?

JOHNNY. An afterthought? What do you mean by that?

BENTLEY. I—

JOHNNY. No, stop: I dont want to know. It's only a dodge to start an argument.

BENTLEY. Dont be afraid: it wont overtax your brain. My father was 44 when I was born. My mother was 41. There was twelve years between me and the next eldest. I was unexpected. I was probably unintentional. My brother and sisters are not the least like me. Theyre the regular thing that you always get in the first batch from young parents: quite pleasant, ordinary, do-the-regular-thing sort: all body and no brains, like you.

JOHNNY. Thank you.

BENTLEY. Dont mention it, old chap. Now I'm different. By the time I was born, the old couple knew something. So I came out all brains and no more body than is absolutely necessary. I am really a good deal older than you, though you were born ten years sooner. Everybody feels that when they hear us talk; consequently, though it's quite natural to hear me calling you Johnny, it sounds ridiculous and unbecoming for you to call me Bunny. [*He rises*].

JOHNNY. Does it, by George? You stop me doing it if you can: thats all.

BENTLEY. If you go on doing it after Ive asked you not, youll feel an awful swine [*He strolls away carelessly to the sideboard with his eye on the sponge-cakes*]. At least I should; but I suppose youre not so particular.

JOHNNY [*rising vengefully and following Bentley, who is forced to turn and listen*] I'll tell you what it is, my boy: you want a good talking to; and I'm going to give it to you. If you think that because your father's a K.C.B., and you want to marry my sister, you can make yourself as nasty as you please and say what you like, youre mistaken. Let me tell you that except Hypatia, not one person in this house is in favor of her marrying you; and I dont believe she's happy about it herself. The match isnt settled yet: dont forget that. Youre on trial in the office because the Governor isnt giving his daughter money for an idle man to live on her. Youre on trial here because my mother thinks a girl should know what a man is like in the house before she marries him. Thats been going on for two months now; and whats the result? Youve got yourself thoroughly disliked in the office; and youre getting yourself thoroughly disliked here, all through your bad manners and your conceit, and the damned impudence you think clever.

BENTLEY [*deeply wounded and trying hard to control himself*] Thats enough, thank you. You dont suppose,

I hope, that I should have come down if I had known that that was how you all feel about me. [*He makes for the vestibule door*].

JOHNNY [*collaring him*] No: you dont run away. I'm going to have this out with you. Sit down: d'y' hear? [*Bentley attempts to go with dignity. Johnny slings him into a chair at the writing table, where he sits, bitterly humiliated, but afraid to speak lest he should burst into tears*]. Thats the advantage to having more body than brains, you see: it enables me to teach you manners; and I'm going to do it too. Youre a spoilt young pup; and you need a jolly good licking. And if youre not careful youll get it: I'll see to that next time you call me a swine.

BENTLEY. I didnt call you a swine. But (*bursting into a fury of tears*] you are a swine: youre a beast: youre a brute: youre a cad: youre a liar: youre a bully: I should like to wring your damned neck for you.

JOHNNY [*with a derisive laugh*] Try it, my son. [*Bentley gives an inarticulate sob of rage*]. Fighting isnt in your line. Youre too small; and youre too childish. I always suspected that your cleverness wouldnt come to very much when it was brought up against something solid: some decent chap's fist, for instance.

BENTLEY. I hope your beastly fist may come up against a mad bull or a prizefighter's nose, or something solider than me. I dont care about your fist; but if everybody here dislikes me—[*he is checked by a sob*]. Well, I dont care. [*Trying to recover himself*] I'm sorry I intruded: I didnt know. [*Breaking down again*] Oh you beast! you pig! Swine, swine, swine, swine, swine! Now!

JOHNNY. All right, my lad, all right. Sling your mud as hard as you please: it wont stick to me. What I want to know is this. How is it that your father, who I suppose is the strongest man England has produced in our time—

BENTLEY. You got that out of your halfpenny paper. A lot you know about him!

JOHNNY. I dont set up to be able to do anything but admire him and appreciate him and be proud of him as an Englishman. If it wasnt for my respect for him, I wouldnt have stood your cheek for two days, let alone two months. But what I cant understand is why he didnt lick it out of you when you were a kid. For twenty-five years he kept a place twice as big as England in order: a place full of seditious coffee-colored heathens and pestilential white agitators in the middle of a lot of savage tribes. And yet he couldnt keep you in order. I dont set up to be half the man your father undoubtedly is; but, by George, it's lucky for you you were not my son. I dont hold with my own father's views about corporal punishment being wrong. It's necessary for some people; and I'd have tried it on you until you first learnt to howl and then to behave yourself.

BENTLEY [contemptuously] Yes: behavior wouldnt come naturally to your son, would it?

JOHNNY [stung into sudden violence] Now you keep a civil tongue in your head. I'll stand none of your snobbery. I'm just as proud of Tarleton's Underwear as you are of your father's title and his K.C.B., and all the rest of it. My father began in a little hole of a shop in Leeds no bigger than our pantry down the passage there. He—

BENTLEY. Oh yes: I know. Ive read it. "The Romance of Business, or The Story of Tarleton's Underwear. Please Take One!" I took one the day after I first met Hypatia. I went and bought half a dozen unshrinkable vests for her sake.

[148]

JOHNNY. Well: did they shrink?

BENTLEY. Oh, dont be a fool.

JOHNNY. Never mind whether I'm a fool or not. Did they shrink? Thats the point. Were they worth the money?

BENTLEY. I couldnt wear them: do you think my skin's as thick as your customers' hides? I'd as soon have dressed myself in a nutmeg grater.

JOHNNY. Pity your father didnt give your thin skin a jolly good lacing with a cane!

BENTLEY. Pity you havnt got more than one idea! If you want to know, they did try that on me once, when I was a small kid. A silly governess did it. I yelled fit to bring down the house, and went into convulsions and brain fever and that sort of thing for three weeks. So the old girl got the sack; and serve her right! After that, I was let do what I liked. My father didnt want me to grow up a broken-spirited spaniel, which is your idea of a man, I suppose.

JOHNNY. Jolly good thing for you that my father made you come into the office and shew what you were made of. And it didnt come to much: let me tell you that. When the Governor asked me where I thought we ought to put you, I said "Make him the Office Boy." The Governor said you were too green. And so you were.

BENTLEY. I daresay. So would you be pretty green if you were shoved into my father's set. I picked up your silly business in a fortnight. Youve been at it ten years; and you havnt picked it up yet.

JOHNNY. Dont talk rot, child. You know you simply make me pity you.

BENTLEY. "Romance of Business" indeed! The real romance of Tarleton's business is the story that you understand anything about it. You never could explain any mortal thing about it to me when I asked you. "See what was done the last time": that was the beginning and the end of your wisdom. Youre nothing but a turnspit.

JOHNNY. A what!

BENTLEY. A turnspit. If your father hadnt made a roasting jack for you to turn, youd be earning twenty-four shillings a week behind a counter.

JOHNNY. If you dont take that back and apologize for your bad manners, I'll give you as good a hiding as ever—

BENTLEY. Help! Johnny's beating me! Oh! Murder! [*He throws himself on the ground, uttering piercing yells*].

JOHNNY. Dont be a fool. Stop that noise, will you, I'm not going to touch you. Sh—Sh—

Hypatia rushes in through the inner door, followed by Mrs Tarleton, and throws herself on her knees by Bentley. Mrs Tarleton, whose knees are stiffer, bends over him and tries to lift him. Mrs Tarleton is a shrewd and motherly old lady who has been pretty in her time, and is still very pleasant and likeable and unaffected. Hypatia is a typical English girl of a sort never called typical: that is, she has an opaque white skin, black hair, large dark eyes with black brows and lashes, curved lips, swift glances and movements that flash out of a waiting stillness, boundless energy and audacity held in leash.

HYPATIA [*pouncing on Bentley with no very gentle hand*] Bentley: whats the matter? Dont cry like that: whats the use? Whats happened?

MRS TARLETON. Are you ill, child? [*They get him up*]. There, there, pet! It's all right: dont cry [*they put him into a chair*]: there! there! there! Johnny will go for the doctor; and he'll give you something nice to make it well.

HYPATIA. What has happened, Johnny?

MRS TARLETON. Was it a wasp?

BENTLEY [*impatiently*] Wasp be dashed!

MRS TARLETON. Oh Bunny! that was a naughty word.

BENTLEY. Yes, I know: I beg your pardon. [*He rises, and extricates himself from them*]. Thats all right. Johnny frightened me. You know how easy it is to hurt me; and I'm too small to defend myself against Johnny.

MRS TARLETON. Johnny: how often have I told you that you must not bully the little ones. I thought youd outgrown all that.

HYPATIA [*angrily*] I do declare, mamma, that Johnny's brutality makes it impossible to live in the house with him.

JOHNNY [*deeply hurt*] It's fourteen years, mother, since you had that row with me for licking Robert and giving Hypatia a black eye because she bit me. I promised you then that I'd never raise my hand to one of them again; and Ive never broken my word. And now because this young whelp begins to cry out before he's hurt, you treat me as if I were a brute and a savage.

MRS TARLETON. No dear, not a savage; but you know you mustnt call our visitor naughty names.

BENTLEY. Oh, let him alone——

JOHNNY [*fiercely*] Dont you interfere between my mother and me: d'y' hear?

HYPATIA. Johnny's lost his temper, mother. We'd better go. Come, Bentley.

MRS TARLETON. Yes: that will be best. [*To Bentley*] Johnny doesnt mean any harm, dear: he'll be himself presently. Come.

The two ladies go out through the inner door with Bentley, who turns derisively at the door to cock a snook at Johnny as he goes out.

Johnny, left alone, clenches his fists and grinds his teeth, but can find no relief in that way for his rage. After choking and stamping for a moment, he makes for the vestibule door. It opens before he reaches it; and Lord Summerhays comes in. Johnny glares at him, speechless. Lord Summerhays takes in the situation, and quickly takes the punchbowl from the sideboard and offers it to Johnny

LORD SUMMERHAYS. Smash it. Dont hesitate: it's an ugly thing. Smash it: hard. [*Johnny, with a stifled yell, dashes it in pieces, and then sits down and mops his brow*]. Feel better now? [*Johnny nods*]. I know only one person alive who could drive me to the point of having either to break china or commit murder; and that person is my son Bentley. Was it he? [*Johnny nods again, not yet able to speak*]. As the car stopped I heard a yell which is only too familiar to me. It generally means that some infuriated person is trying to thrash Bentley. Nobody has ever succeeded, though almost everybody has tried. [*He seats himself comfortably close to the writing table, and sets to work to collect the fragments of the punchbowl in the waste-paper basket whilst Johnny, with diminishing difficulty, collects himself*]. Bentley is a problem which I confess I have never been able to solve. He was born to be a great success at the age of fifty. Most Englishmen of his class seem to be born to be great successes at the age of twenty-four at most. The domestic problem for me is how to endure Bentley until he is fifty. The problem for the nation is how to get itself governed by men whose growth is arrested when they are little more than college lads. Bentley doesnt really mean to be offensive. You can always make him cry by telling him you dont like him. Only, he cries so loud that the experiment should be made in the open air: in the middle of Salisbury

Plain if possible. He has a hard and penetrating intellect and a remarkable power of looking facts in the face; but unfortunately, being very young, he has no idea of how very little of that sort of thing most of us can stand. On the other hand, he is frightfully sensitive and even affectionate; so that he probably gets as much as he gives in the way of hurt feelings. Youll excuse me rambling on like this about my son.

JOHNNY [*who has pulled himself together*] You did it on purpose. I wasnt quite myself: I needed a moment to pull round. Thank you.

LORD SUMMERHAYS. Not at all. Is your father at home?

JOHNNY. No: he's opening one of his free libraries. Thats another nice little penny gone. He's mad on reading. He promised another free library last week. It's ruinous. Itll hit you as well as me when Bunny marries Hypatia. When all Hypatia's money is thrown away on libraries, where will Bunny come in? Cant you stop him?

LORD SUMMERHAYS. I'm afraid not. He's a perfect whirlwind. Indefatigable at public work. Wonderful man, I think.

JOHNNY. Oh, public work! He does too much of it. It's really a sort of laziness, getting away from your own serious business to amuse yourself with other people's. Mind: I dont say there isnt another side to it. It has its value as an advertisement. It makes useful acquaintances and leads to valuable business connections. But it takes his mind off the main chance; and he overdoes it.

LORD SUMMERHAYS. The danger of public business is that it never ends. A man may kill himself at it.

JOHNNY. Or he can spend more on it than it brings him in: thats how I look at it. What I say is that everybody's business is nobody's business. I hope I'm not

[153]

a hard man, nor a narrow man, nor unwilling to pay reasonable taxes, and subscribe in reason to deserving charities, and even serve on a jury in my turn; and no man can say I ever refused to help a friend out of a difficulty when he was worth helping. But when you ask me to go beyond that, I tell you frankly I dont see it. I never did see it, even when I was only a boy, and had to pretend to take in all the ideas the Governor fed me up with, I didnt see it; and I dont see it.

LORD SUMMERHAYS. There is certainly no business reason why you should take more than your share of the world's work.

JOHNNY. So I say. It's really a great encouragement to me to find you agree with me. For of course if nobody agrees with you, how are you to know that youre not a fool?

LORD SUMMERHAYS. Quite so.

JOHNNY. I wish youd talk to him about it. It's no use my saying anything: I'm a child to him still: I have no influence. Besides, you know how to handle men. See how you handled me when I was making a fool of myself about Bunny!

LORD SUMMERHAYS. Not at all.

JOHNNY. Oh yes I was: I know I was. Well, if my blessed father had come in he'd have told me to control myself. As if I was losing my temper on purpose!

Bentley returns, newly washed. He beams when he sees his father, and comes affectionately behind him and pats him on the shoulders.

BENTLEY. He l-lo, commander! have you come? Ive been making a filthy silly ass of myself here. I'm awfully sorry, Johnny, old chap: I beg your pardon. Why dont you kick me when I go on like that?

LORD SUMMERHAYS. As we came through Godalming I thought I heard some yelling—

BENTLEY. I should think you did. Johnny was rather rough on me, though. He told me nobody here liked me; and I was silly enough to believe him.

LORD SUMMERHAYS. And all the women have been kissing you and pitying you ever since to stop your crying, I suppose. Baby!

BENTLEY. I did cry. But I always feel good after crying: it relieves my wretched nerves. I feel perfectly jolly now.

LORD SUMMERHAYS. Not at all ashamed of yourself, for instance?

BENTLEY. If I started being ashamed of myself I shouldnt have time for anything else all my life. I say: I feel very fit and spry. Lets all go down and meet the Grand Cham. [*He goes to the hat stand and takes down his hat*].

LORD SUMMERHAYS. Does Mr Tarleton like to be called the Grand Cham, do you think, Bentley?

BENTLEY. Well, he thinks he's too modest for it. He calls himself Plain John. But you cant call him that in his own office: besides, it doesnt suit him: it's not flamboyant enough.

JOHNNY. Flam what?

BENTLEY. Flamboyant. Lets go and meet him. He's telephoned from Guildford to say he's on the road. The dear old son is always telephoning or telegraphing: he thinks he's hustling along like anything when he's only sending unnecessary messages.

LORD SUMMERHAYS. Thank you: I should prefer a quiet afternoon.

BENTLEY. Righto! I shant press Johnny: he's had enough of me for one week-end. [*He goes out through the pavilion into the grounds*].

JOHNNY. Not a bad idea, that.

LORD SUMMERHAYS. What?

[155]

JOHNNY. Going to meet the Governor. You know you wouldnt think it; but the Governor likes Bunny rather. And Bunny is cultivating it. I shouldnt be surprised if he thought he could squeeze me out one of these days.

LORD SUMMERHAYS. You dont say so! Young rascal! I want to consult you about him, if you dont mind. Shall we stroll over to the Gibbet? Bentley is too fast for me as a walking companion; but I should like a short turn.

JOHNNY [*rising eagerly, highly flattered*] Right you are. Thatll suit me down to the ground. [*He takes a Panama and stick from the hat stand*].

Mrs Tarleton and Hypatia come back just as the two men are going out. Hypatia salutes Summerhays from a distance with an enigmatic lift of her eyelids in his direction and a demure nod before she sits down at the worktable and busies herself with her needle. Mrs Tarleton, hospitably fussy, goes over to him.

MRS TARLETON. Oh, Lord Summerhays, I didnt know you were here. Wont you have some tea?

LORD SUMMERHAYS. No, thank you: I'm not allowed tea. And I'm ashamed to say Ive knocked over your beautiful punchbowl. You must let me replace it.

MRS TARLETON. Oh, it doesnt matter: I'm only too glad to be rid of it. The shopman told me it was in the best taste; but when my poor old nurse Martha got cataract, Bunny said it was a merciful provision of Nature to prevent her seeing our china.

LORD SUMMERHAYS [*gravely*] That was exceedingly rude of Bentley, Mrs Tarleton. I hope you told him so.

MRS TARLETON. Oh, bless you! I dont care what he says; so long as he says it to me and not before visitors.

JOHNNY. We're going out for a stroll, mother.

MRS TARLETON. All right: dont let us keep you. Never mind about that crock: I'll get the girl to come and take the pieces away [*Recollecting herself*] There! Ive done it again!

JOHNNY. Done what?

MRS TARLETON. Called her the girl. You know, Lord Summerhays, it's a funny thing; but now I'm getting old, I'm dropping back into all the ways John and I had when we had barely a hundred a year. You should have known me when I was forty! I talked like a duchess; and if Johnny or Hypatia let slip a word that was like old times, I was down on them like anything. And now I'm beginning to do it myself at every turn.

LORD SUMMERHAYS. There comes a time when all that seems to matter so little. Even queens drop the mask when they reach our time of life.

MRS TARLETON. Let you alone for giving a thing a pretty turn! Youre a humbug, you know, Lord Summerhays. John doesnt know it; and Johnny doesnt know it; but you and I know it, dont we? Now thats something that even you cant answer; so be off with you for your walk without another word.

Lord Summerhays smiles; bows; and goes out through the vestibule door, followed by Johnny. Mrs Tarleton sits down at the worktable and takes out her darning materials and one of her husband's socks. Hypatia is at the other side of the table, on her mother's right. They chat as they work.

HYPATIA. I wonder whether they laugh at us when they are by themselves!

MRS TARLETON. Who?

HYPATIA. Bentley and his father and all the toffs in their set.

MRS TARLETON. Oh, thats only their way. I used to think that the aristocracy were a nasty sneering lot, and that they were laughing at me and John. Theyre always giggling and pretending not to care much about anything. But you get used to it: theyre the same to one another and to everybody. Besides, what does it matter what they think? It's far worse when theyre civil, because that always means that they want you to lend them money; and you must never do that, Hypatia, because they never pay. How can they? They dont make anything, you see. Of course, if you can make up your mind to regard it as a gift, thats different; but then they generally ask you again; and you may as well say no first as last. You neednt be afraid of the aristocracy, dear: theyre only human creatures like ourselves after all; and youll hold your own with them easy enough.

HYPATIA. Oh, I'm not a bit afraid of them, I assure you.

MRS TARLETON. Well, no, not afraid of them, exactly; but youve got to pick up their ways. You know, dear, I never quite agreed with your father's notion of keeping clear of them, and sending you to a school that was so expensive that they couldnt afford to send their daughters there; so that all the girls belonged to big business families like ourselves. It takes all sorts to make a world; and I wanted you to see a little of all sorts. When you marry Bunny, and go among the women of his father's set, theyll shock you at first.

HYPATIA [*incredulously*] How?

MRS TARLETON. Well, the things they talk about.

HYPATIA. Oh! scandalmongering?

MRS TARLETON. Oh no: we all do that: thats only human nature. But you know theyve no notion of decency. I shall never forget the first day I spent with a marchioness, two duchesses, and no end of Ladies This and That. Of course it was only a committee:

theyd put me on to get a big subscription out of John.
I'd never heard such talk in my life. The things they
mentioned! And it was the marchioness that started it.

HYPATIA. What sort of things?

MRS TARLETON. Drainage!! She'd tried three
systems in her castle; and she was going to do away
with them all and try another. I didnt know which
way to look when she began talking about it: I thought
theyd all have got up and gone out of the room. But
not a bit of it, if you please. They were all just as bad
as she. They all had systems; and each of them swore
by her own system. I sat there with my cheeks burning
until one of the duchesses, thinking I looked out of it,
I suppose, asked me what system I had. I said I was
sure I knew nothing about such things, and hadnt we
better change the subject. Then the fat was in the fire,
I can tell you. There was a regular terror of a countess
with an anaerobic system; and she told me, downright
brutally, that I'd better learn something about them
before my children died of diphtheria. That was just
two months after I'd buried poor little Bobby; and
that was the very thing he died of, poor little lamb!
I burst out crying: I couldnt help it. It was as good as
telling me I'd killed my own child. I had to go away;
but before I was out of the door one of the duchesses
—quite a young woman—began talking about what
sour milk did in her inside and how she expected to
live to be over a hundred if she took it regularly. And
me listening to her, that had never dared to think that
a duchess could have anything so common as an
inside! I shouldnt have minded if it had been children's
insides: we have to talk about them. But grown-up
people! I was glad to get away that time.

HYPATIA. There was a physiology and hygiene class
started at school; but of course none of our girls were
let attend it.

MRS TARLETON. If it had been an aristocratic school plenty would have attended it. Thats what theyre like: theyve nasty minds. With really nice good women a thing is either decent or indecent; and if it's indecent, we just dont mention it or pretend to know about it; and theres an end of it. But all the aristocracy cares about is whether it can get any good out of the thing. Theyre what Johnny calls cynical-like. And of course nobody can say a word to them for it. Theyre so high up that they can do and say what they like.

HYPATIA. Well, I think they might leave the drains to their husbands. I shouldnt think much of a man that left such things to me.

MRS TARLETON. Oh, dont think that, dear, whatever you do. I never let on about it to you; but it's me that takes care of the drainage here. After what that countess said to me I wasnt going to lose another child nor trust John. And I dont want my grandchildren to die any more than my children.

HYPATIA. Do you think Bentley will ever be as big a man as his father? I dont mean clever: I mean big and strong.

MRS TARLETON. Not he. He's overbred, like one of those expensive little dogs. I like a bit of a mongrel myself, whether it's a man or a dog; theyre the best for everyday. But we all have our tastes: whats one woman's meat is another woman's poison. Bunny's a dear little fellow; but I never could have fancied him for a husband when I was your age.

HYPATIA. Yes; but he has some brains. He's not like all the rest. One cant have everything.

MRS TARLETON. Oh, youre quite right, dear: quite right. It's a great thing to have brains: look what it's done for your father! Thats the reason I never said a word when you jilted poor Jerry Mackintosh.

HYPATIA [*excusing herself*] I really couldnt stick it out with Jerry, mother. I know you liked him, and nobody can deny that he's a splendid animal—

MRS TARLETON [*shocked*] Hypatia! How can you! The things that girls say nowadays!

HYPATIA. Well, what else can you call him? If I'd been deaf or he'd been dumb, I could have married him. But living with father, Ive got accustomed to cleverness. Jerry would drive me mad: you know very well he's a fool: even Johnny thinks him a fool.

MRS TARLETON [*up in arms at once in defence of her boy*] Now dont begin about my Johnny. You know it annoys me. Johnny's as clever as anybody else in his own way. I dont say he's as clever as you in some ways; but he's a man, at all events, and not a little squit of a thing like your Bunny.

HYPATIA. Oh, I say nothing against your darling: we all know Johnny's perfection.

MRS TARLETON. Dont be cross, dearie. You let Johnny alone; and I'll let Bunny alone. I'm just as bad as you. There!

HYPATIA. Oh, I dont mind your saying that about Bentley. It's true. He is a little squit of a thing. I wish he wasnt. But who else is there? Think of all the other chances Ive had! Not one of them has as much brains in his whole body as Bentley has in his little finger. Besides, theyve no distinction. It's as much as I can do to tell one from the other. They wouldnt even have money if they werent the sons of their fathers, like Johnny. Whats a girl to do? I never met anybody like Bentley before. He may be small; but he's the best of the bunch: you cant deny that.

MRS TARLETON [*with a sigh*] Well, my pet, if you fancy him, theres no more to be said.

A pause follows this remark: the two women sewing silently.

HYPATIA. Mother: do you think marriage is as much a question of fancy as it used to be in your time and father's?

MRS TARLETON. Oh, it wasnt much fancy with me, dear: your father just wouldnt take no for an answer; and I was only too glad to be his wife instead of his shop-girl. Still, it's curious; but I had more choice than you in a way, because, you see, I was poor; and there are so many more poor men than rich ones that I might have had more of a pick, as you might say, if John hadnt suited me.

HYPATIA. I can imagine all sorts of men I could fall in love with; but I never seem to meet them. The real ones are too small, like Bunny, or too silly, like Jerry. Of course one can get into a state about any man: fall in love with him if you like to call it that. But who would risk marrying a man for love? *I* shouldnt. I remember three girls at school who agreed that the one man you should never marry was the man you were in love with, because it would make a perfect slave of you. Theres a sort of instinct against it, I think, thats just as strong as the other instinct. One of them, to my certain knowledge, refused a man she was in love with, and married another who was in love with her, and it turned out very well.

MRS TARLETON. Does all that mean that youre not in love with Bunny?

HYPATIA. Oh, how could anybody be in love with Bunny? I like him to kiss me just as I like a baby to kiss me. I'm fond of him; and he never bores me; and I see that he's very clever; but I'm not what you call gone about him, if thats what you mean.

MRS TARLETON. Then why need you marry him?

HYPATIA. What better can I do? I must marry somebody, I suppose. Ive realized that since I was twenty-three. I always used to take it as a matter of course that I should be married before I was twenty.

BENTLEY'S VOICE [*in the garden*] Youve got to keep yourself fresh: to look at these things with an open mind.

JOHN TARLETON'S VOICE. Quite right, quite right: I always say so.

MRS TARLETON. Theres your father, and Bunny with him.

BENTLEY. Keep young. Keep your eye on me. Thats the tip for you.

Bentley and Mr Tarleton (an immense and genial veteran of trade) come into view and enter the pavilion.

JOHN TARLETON. You think youre young, do you? You think I'm old? [*energetically shaking off his motoring coat and hanging it up with his cap*].

BENTLEY [*helping him with the coat*] Of course youre old. Look at your face and look at mine. What you call your youth is nothing but your levity. Why do we get on so well together? Because I'm a young cub and youre an old josser. [*He throws a cushion at Hypatia's feet and sits down on it with his back against her knees*].

TARLETON. Old! Thats all you know about it, my lad. How do, Patsy! [*Hypatia kisses him*]. How is my Chickabiddy? [*He kisses Mrs Tarleton's hand and poses expansively in the middle of the picture*]. Look at me! Look at these wrinkles, these grey hairs, this repulsive mask that you call old age! What is it? [*Vehemently*] I ask you, what is it?

BENTLEY. Jolly nice and venerable, old man. Dont be discouraged.

TARLETON. Nice? Not a bit of it. Venerable? Venerable be blowed! Read your Darwin, my boy. Read your Weismann. [*He goes to the sideboard for a drink of lemonade*].

MRS TARLETON. For shame, John! Tell him to read his Bible.

TARLETON [*manipulating the syphon*] Whats the use of telling children to read the Bible when you know they wont. I was kept away from the Bible for forty years by being told to read it when I was young. Then I picked it up one evening in a hotel in Sunderland when I had left all my papers in the train; and I found its wasnt half bad. [*He drinks, and puts down the glass with a smack of enjoyment*]. Better than most halfpenny papers, anyhow, if only you could make people believe it. [*He sits down by the writing table, near his wife*]. But if you want to understand old age scientifically, read Darwin and Weismann. Of course if you want to understand it romantically, read about Solomon.

MRS TARLETON. Have you had tea, John?

TARLETON. Yes. Dont interrupt me when I'm improving the boy's mind. Where was I? This repulsive mask—yes. [*Explosively*] What is death?

MRS TARLETON. John!

HYPATIA. Death is a rather unpleasant subject, papa.

TARLETON. Not a bit. Not scientifically. Scientifically it's a delightful subject. You think death's natural. Well, it isnt. You read Weismann. There wasnt any death to start with. You go look in any ditch outside and youll find swimming about there as fresh as paint some of the identical little live cells that Adam christened in the Garden of Eden. But if big things like us didnt die, we'd crowd one another off the face of the globe. Nothing survived, sir, except the sort of people that had the sense and good manners to die and make room for the fresh supplies. And so death was introduced by Natural Selection. You get it out of your head, my lad, that I'm going to die because I'm wearing out or decaying. There no such thing as decay to a vital man. I shall clear out; but I shant decay.

BENTLEY. And what about the wrinkles and the almond tree and the grasshopper that becomes a burden and the desire that fails?

TARLETON. Does it? by George! No, sir: it spiritualizes. As to your grasshopper, I can carry an elephant.

MRS TARLETON. You do say such things, Bunny! What does he mean by the almond tree?

TARLETON. He means my white hairs: the repulsive mask. That, my boy, is another invention of Natural Selection to disgust young women with me, and give the lads a turn.

MRS TARLETON. John: I wont have it. Thats a forbidden subject.

TARLETON. They talk of the wickedness and vanity of women painting their faces and wearing auburn wigs at fifty. But why shouldnt they? Why should a woman allow Nature to put a false mask of age on her when she knows that she's as young as ever? Why should she look in the glass and see a wrinkled lie when a touch of fine art will shew her a glorious truth? The wrinkles are a dodge to repel young men. Suppose she doesnt want to repel young men! Suppose she likes them!

MRS TARLETON. Bunny: take Hypatia out into the grounds for a walk: theres a good boy. John has got one of his naughty fits this evening.

HYPATIA. Oh, never mind me. I'm used to him.

BENTLEY. I'm not. I never heard such conversation: I cant believe my ears. And mind you, this is the man who objected to my marrying his daughter on the ground that a marriage between a member of the great and good middle class with one of the vicious and corrupt aristocracy would be a misalliance. A misalliance, if you please! This is the man Ive adopted as a father!

TARLETON. Eh? Whats that? Adopted me as a father, have you?

BENTLEY. Yes. Thats an idea of mine, I knew a chap named Joey Percival at Oxford (you know I was two months at Balliol before I was sent down for telling the old woman who was head of that silly college what I jolly well thought of him. He would have been glad to have me back, too, at the end of six months; but I wouldnt go: I just let him want; and serve him right!) Well, Joey was a most awfully clever fellow, and so nice! I asked him what made such a difference between him and all the other pups—they were pups, if you like. He told me it was very simple: they had only one father apiece; and he had three.

MRS TARLETON. Dont talk nonsense, child. How could that be?

BENTLEY. Oh, very simple. His father—

TARLETON. Which father?

BENTLEY. The first one: the regulation natural chap. He kept a tame philosopher in the house; a sort of Coleridge or Herbert Spencer kind of card, you know. That was the second father. Then his mother was an Italian princess; and she had an Italian priest always about. He was supposed to take charge of her conscience; but from what I could make out she jolly well took charge of his. The whole three of them took charge of Joey's conscience. He used to hear them arguing like mad about everything. You see, the philosopher was a freethinker, and always believed the latest thing. The priest didnt believe anything, because it was sure to get him into trouble with someone or another. And the natural father kept an open mind and believed whatever paid him best. Between the lot of them Joey got cultivated no end. He said if he could only have had three mothers as well, he'd have backed himself against Napoleon.

TARLETON [*impressed*] Thats an idea. Thats a most interesting idea: a most important idea.

MRS TARLETON. You always were one for ideas, John.

TARLETON. Youre right, Chickabiddy. What do I tell Johnny when he brags about Tarleton's Underwear? It's not the underwear. The underwear be hanged! Anybody can make underwear. Anybody can sell underwear. Tarleton's Ideas: thats whats done it. Ive often thought of putting that up over the shop.

BENTLEY. Take me into partnership when you do, old man. I'm wasted on the underwear; but I shall come in strong on the ideas.

TARLETON. You be a good boy; and perhaps I will.

MRS TARLETON [*scenting a plot against her beloved Johnny*] Now, John. you promised—

TARLETON. Yes, yes, All right, Chickabiddy: dont fuss. Your precious Johnny shant be interfered with. [*Bouncing up, too energetic to sit still*] But I'm getting sick of that old shop. Thirty-five years Ive had of it: same blessed old stairs to go up and down every day: same old lot: same old game: sorry I ever started it now. I'll chuck it and try something else: something that will give a scope to all my faculties.

HYPATIA. Theres money in underwear: theres none in wild-cat ideas.

TARLETON. Theres money in me, madam, no matter what I go into.

MRS TARLETON. Dont boast, John. Dont tempt Providence.

TARLETON. Rats! You dont understand Providence. Providence likes to be tempted. Thats the secret of the successful man. Read Browning. Natural theology on an island, eh? Caliban was afraid to tempt Providence: that was why he was never able to get even with

Prospero. What did Prospero do? Prospero didnt even tempt Providence: he was Providence. Thats one of Tarleton's ideas; and dont you forget it.

BENTLEY. You are full of beef today, old man.

TARLETON. Beef be blowed! Joy of life. Read Ibsen. [*He goes into the pavilion to relieve his restlessness, and stares out with his hands thrust deep in his pockets*].

HYPATIA [*thoughtful*] Bentley: couldnt you invite your friend Mr Percival down here?

BENTLEY. Not if I know it. Youd throw me over the moment you set eyes on him.

MRS TARLETON. Oh, Bunny! For shame!

BENTLEY. Well, who'd marry me, dyou suppose, if they could get my brains with a full-sized body? No, thank you. I shall take jolly good care to keep Joey out of this until Hypatia is past praying for.

Johnny and Lord Summerhays return through the pavilion from their stroll.

TARLETON. Welcome! welcome! Why have you stayed away so long?

LORD SUMMERHAYS [*shaking hands*] Yes: I should have come sooner. But I'm still rather lost in England. [*Johnny takes his hat and hangs it up beside his own*]. Thank you. [*Johnny returns to his swing and his novel. Lord Summerhays comes to the writing table*]. The fact is that as Ive nothing to do, I never have time to go anywhere. [*He sits down next Mrs Tarleton*].

TARLETON [*following him and sitting down on his left*] Paradox, paradox. Good. Paradoxes are the only truths. Read Chesterton. But theres lots for you to do here. You have a genius for government. You learnt your job out there in Jinghiskahn. Well, we want to be governed here in England. Govern us.

LORD SUMMERHAYS. Ah yes, my friend; but in Jinghiskahn you have to govern the right way. If you dont, you go under and come home. Here everything has to be done the wrong way, to suit governors who understand nothing but partridge shooting (our English native princes, in fact) and voters who dont know what theyre voting about. I dont understand these democratic games; and I'm afraid I'm too old to learn. What can I do but sit in the window of my club, which consists mostly of retired Indian Civil servants? We look on at the muddle and the folly and amateurishness; and we ask each other where a single fortnight of it would have landed us.

TARLETON. Very true. Still, Democracy's all right, you know. Read Mill. Read Jefferson.

LORD SUMMERHAYS. Yes. Democracy reads well; but it doesnt act well, like some people's plays. No, no, my friend Tarleton: to make Democracy work, you need an aristocratic democracy. To make Aristocracy work, you need a democratic aristocracy. Youve got neither, and theres an end of it.

TARLETON. Still, you know, the superman may come. The superman's an idea. I believe in ideas. Read Whatshisname.

LORD SUMMERHAYS. Reading is a dangerous amusement, Tarleton. I wish I could persuade your free library people of that.

TARLETON. Why man, it's the beginning of education.

LORD SUMMERHAYS. On the contrary, it's the end of it. How can you dare teach a man to read until youve taught him everything else first?

JOHNNY [intercepting his father's reply by coming out of the swing and taking the floor] Leave it at that. Thats good sense. Anybody on for a game of tennis?

BENTLEY. Oh, lets have some more improving conversation. Wouldnt you rather, Johnny?

JOHNNY. If you ask me, no.

TARLETON. Johnny: you dont cultivate your mind. You dont read.

JOHNNY [*coming between his mother and Lord Summerhays, book in hand*] Yes I do. I bet you what you like that, page for page, I read more than you, though I dont talk about it so much. Only, I dont read the same books. I like a book with a plot in it. You like a book with nothing in it but some idea that the chap that writes it keeps worrying, like a cat chasing its own tail. I can stand a little of it, just as I can stand watching the cat for two minutes, say, when Ive nothing better to do. But a man soon gets fed up with that sort of thing. The fact is, you look on an author as a sort of god. *I* look on him as a man that I pay to do a certain thing for me. I pay him to amuse me and to take me out of myself and make me forget.

TARLETON. No. Wrong principle. You want to remember. Read Kipling. "Lest we forget."

JOHNNY. If Kipling wants to remember, let him remember. If he had to run Tarleton's Underwear, he'd be jolly glad to forget. As he has a much softer job, and wants to keep himself before the public, his cry is, "Dont you forget the sort of things I'm rather clever at writing about." Well, I dont blame him: it's his business: I should do the same in his place. But what he wants and what I want are two different things. I want to forget; and I pay another man to make me forget. If I buy a book or go to the theatre, I want to forget the shop and forget myself from the moment I go in to the moment I come out. Thats what I pay my money for. And if I find that the author's simply getting at me the whole time, I consider that he's obtained my money under false pretences. I'm not a morbid crank: I'm a natural man; and, as such, I dont like being got at. If a man in my employment did it, I should sack him. If a member of my club did it, I should cut him. If he went too far with it, I should bring his conduct before the committee. I might even punch his head, if it came to that. Well, who and what is an author that he should be privileged to take liberties that are not allowed to other men?

MRS TARLETON. You see, John! What have I always told you? Johnny has as much to say for himself as anybody when he likes.

JOHNNY. I'm no fool, mother, whatever some people may fancy. I dont set up to have as many ideas as the governor; but what ideas I have are consecutive, at all events. I can think as well as talk.

BENTLEY [to Tarleton, chuckling] Had you there, old man, hadnt he? You are rather all over the shop with your ideas, aint you?

JOHNNY [handsomely] I'm not saying anything against you, governor. But I do say that the time has come for sane, healthy, unpretending men like me to make a stand against this conspiracy of the writing and talking and artistic lot to put us in the back row. It isnt a fact that we're inferior to them: it's a put-up job; and it's they that have put the job up. It's we that run the country for them; and all the thanks we get is to be told we're Philistines and vulgar tradesmen and sordid city men and so forth, and that theyre all angels of light and leading. The time has come to assert ourselves and put a stop to their stuck-up nonsense. Perhaps if we had nothing better to do than talking or writing, we could do it better than they. Anyhow, theyre the failures and refuse of business (hardly a man of them that didnt begin in an office) and we're the successes of it. Thank God I havnt failed yet at anything; and I dont believe I should fail at literature if it would pay me to turn my hand to it.

BENTLEY. Hear, hear!

MRS TARLETON. Fancy you writing a book, Johnny! Do you think he could, Lord Summerhays?

LORD SUMMERHAYS. Why not? As a matter of fact all the really prosperous authors I have met since my return to England have been very like him.

TARLETON [*again impressed*] Thats an idea. Thats a new idea. I believe I ought to have made Johnny an author. Ive never said so before for fear of hurting his feelings, because, after all, the lad cant help it; but Ive never thought Johnny worth tuppence as a man of business.

JOHNNY [*sarcastic*] Oh! You think youve always kept that to yourself, do you, Governor? I know your opinion of me as well as you know it yourself. It takes one man of business to appreciate another; and you arnt, and you never have been, a real man of business. I know where Tarleton's would have been three or four times if it hadnt been for me. [*With a snort and a nod to emphasize the implied warning, he retreats to the Turkish bath, and lolls against it with an air of good-humored indifference*].

TARLETON. Well, who denies it? Youre quite right, my boy. I dont mind confessing to you all that the circumstances that condemned me to keep a shop are the biggest tragedy in modern life. I ought to have been a writer. I'm essentially a man of ideas. When I was a young man I sometimes used to pray that I might fail, so that I should be justified in giving up business and doing something: something first-class. But it was no good: I couldnt fail. I said to myself that if I could only once go to my Chickabiddy here and shew her a chartered accountant's statement proving that I'd made £20 less than last year, I could ask her to let me chance Johnny's and Hypatia's future by going into literature. But it was no good. First it was £250 more than last year. Then it was £700. Then it was £2000. Then I saw it was no use: Prometheus was chained to his rock: read Shelley: read Mrs Browning. Well, well, it was not to be. [*He rises solemnly*]. Lord Summerhays: I ask you to excuse me for a few moments. There are times when a man needs to meditate in solitude on his destiny. A chord is touched; and he sees the drama of his life as a spectator sees a play. Laugh if you feel inclined: no man sees the comic side of it more than I. In the theatre of life everyone may be amused except the actor. [*Brightening*] There is an idea in this: an idea for a picture. What a pity young Bentley is not a painter! Tarleton meditating on his destiny. Not in a toga. Not in the trappings of the tragedian or the philosopher. In plain coat and trousers: a man like any other man. And beneath that coat and trousers a human soul. Tarleton's Underwear! [*He goes out gravely into the vestibule*].

MRS TARLETON [*fondly*] I suppose it's a wife's partiality, Lord Summerhays; but I do think John is really great. I'm sure he was meant to be a king. My father looked down on John, because he was a rate collector and John kept a shop. It hurt his pride to have to borrow money so often from John; and he used to console himself by saying, "After all, he's only a linendraper." But at last one day he said to me, "John is a king."

BENTLEY. How much did he borrow on that occasion?

LORD SUMMERHAYS [*sharply*] Bentley!

MRS TARLETON. Oh, dont scold the child: he'd have to say something like that if it was to be his last word on earth. Besides, he's quite right: my poor father had asked for his usual five pounds; and John gave him a hundred in his big way. Just like a king.

LORD SUMMERHAYS. Not at all. I had five kings to manage in Jinghiskahn; and I think you do your husband some injustice, Mrs Tarleton. They pretended to like me because I kept their brothers from murdering them; but I didnt like them. And I like Tarleton.

MRS TARLETON. Everybody does. I really must go and make the cook do him a Welsh rabbit. He expects one on special occasions. [*She goes to the inner door*]. Johnny: when he comes back ask him where we're to put that new Turkish bath. Turkish baths are his latest. [*She goes out*].

JOHNNY [*coming forward again*] Now that the governor has given himself away, and the old lady's gone, I'll tell you something, Lord Summerhays. If you study men whove made an enormous pile in business without being keen on money, youll find that they all have a slate off. The governor's a wonderful man; but he's not quite all there, you know. If you notice, he's different from me; and whatever my failings may be, I'm a sane man. Erratic: thats what he is. And the danger is that some day he'll give the whole show away.

LORD SUMMERHAYS. Giving the show away is a method like any other method. Keeping it to yourself is only another method. I should keep an open mind about it.

JOHNNY. Has it ever occurred to you that a man with an open mind must be a bit of a scoundrel? If you ask me, I like a man who makes up his mind once for all as to whats right and whats wrong and then sticks to it. At all events you know where to have him.

LORD SUMMERHAYS. That may not be his object.

BENTLEY. He may want to have you old chap.

JOHNNY. Well, let him. If a member of my club wants to steal my umbrella, he knows where to find it. If a man put up for the club who had an open mind on the subject of property in umbrellas, I should blackball him. An open mind is all very well in clever talky-talky; but in conduct and in business give me solid ground.

LORD SUMMERHAYS. Yes: the quicksands make life difficult. Still, there they are. It's no use pretending theyre rocks.

JOHNNY. I dont know. You can draw a line and make other chaps toe it. Thats what I call morality.

LORD SUMMERHAYS. Very true. But you dont make any progress when youre toeing a line.

HYPATIA [*suddenly, as if she could bear no more of it*] Bentley: do go and play tennis with Johnny. You must take exercise.

LORD SUMMERHAYS. Do, my boy, do. [*To Johnny*] Take him out and make him skip about.

BENTLEY [*rising reluctantly*] I promised you two inches more round my chest this summer. I tried exercises with an indiarubber expander; but I wasnt strong enough: instead of my expanding it, it crumpled me up. Come along, Johnny.

JOHNNY. Do you no end of good, young chap. [*He goes out with Bentley through the pavilion*].

Hypatia throws aside her work with an enormous sigh of relief.

LORD SUMMERHAYS. At last!

HYPATIA. At last. Oh, if I might only have a holiday in an asylum for the dumb. How I envy the animals! They cant talk. If Johnny could only put back his ears or wag his tail instead of laying down the law, how much better it would be! We should know when

[175]

he was cross and when he was pleased; and thats all we know now, with all his talk. It never stops: talk, talk, talk, talk. Thats my life. All the day I listen to mamma talking; at dinner I listen to papa talking; and when papa stops for breath I listen to Johnny talking.

LORD SUMMERHAYS. You make me feel very guilty. I talk too, I'm afraid.

HYPATIA. Oh, I dont mind that, because your talk is a novelty. But it must have been dreadful for your daughters.

LORD SUMMERHAYS. I suppose so.

HYPATIA. If parents would only realize how they bore their children! Three or four times in the last half hour Ive been on the point of screaming.

LORD SUMMERHAYS. Were we very dull?

HYPATIA. Not at all: you were very clever. Thats whats so hard to bear, because it makes it so difficult to avoid listening. You see, I'm young; and I do so want something to happen. My mother tells me that when I'm her age, I shall be only too glad that nothing's happened; but I'm not her age; so what good is that to me? Theres my father in the garden, meditating on his destiny. All very well for him: he's had a destiny to meditate on; but I havnt had any destiny yet. Everything's happened to him: nothing's happened to me. Thats why this unending talk is so maddeningly uninteresting to me.

LORD SUMMERHAYS. It would be worse if we sat in silence.

HYPATIA. No it wouldnt. If you all sat in silence, as if you were waiting for something to happen, then there would be hope even if nothing did happen. But this eternal cackle, cackle, cackle about things in general is only fit for old, old, OLD people. I suppose it means something to them: theyve had their fling. All I listen for is some sign of it ending in something; but just when it seems to be coming to a point, Johnny or papa just starts another hare; and it all begins over again; and I realize that it's never going to lead anywhere and never going to stop. Thats when I want to scream. I wonder how you can stand it.

LORD SUMMERHAYS. Well, I'm old and garrulous myself, you see. Besides, I'm not here of my own free will, exactly. I came because you ordered me to come.

HYPATIA. Didnt you want to come?

LORD SUMMERHAYS. My dear: after thirty years of managing other people's business, men lose the habit of considering what they want or dont want.

HYPATIA. Oh, dont begin to talk about what men do, and about thirty years experience. If you cant get off that subject, youd better send for Johnny and papa and begin it all over again.

LORD SUMMERHAYS. I'm sorry. I beg your pardon.

HYPATIA. I asked you, didnt you want to come?

LORD SUMMERHAYS. I did not stop to consider whether I wanted or not, because when I read your letter I knew I had to come.

HYPATIA. Why?

LORD SUMMERHAYS. Oh come, Miss Tarleton! Really! Really! Dont force me to call you a blackmailer to your face. You have me in your power; and I do what you tell me very obediently. Dont ask me to pretend I do it of my own free will.

HYPATIA. I dont know what a blackmailer is. I havnt even that much experience.

LORD SUMMERHAYS. A blackmailer, my dear young lady, is a person who knows a disgraceful secret in the life of another person, and extorts money from that other person by threatening to make his secret public unless the money is paid.

HYPATIA. I havnt asked you for money.

LORD SUMMERHAYS. No; but you asked me to come down here and talk to you; and you mentioned casually that if I didnt youd have nobody to talk about me to but Bentley. That was a threat, was it not?

HYPATIA. Well, I wanted you to come.

LORD SUMMERHAYS. In spite of my age and my unfortunate talkativeness?

HYPATIA. I like talking to you. I can let myself go with you. I can say things to you I cant say to other people.

LORD SUMMERHAYS. I wonder why?

HYPATIA. Well, you are the only really clever, grown-up, high-class, experienced man I know who has given himself away to me by making an utter fool of himself with me. You cant wrap yourself up in your toga after that. You cant give yourself airs with me.

LORD SUMMERHAYS. You mean you can tell Bentley about me if I do.

HYPATIA. Even if there wasnt any Bentley: even if you didnt care (and I really dont see why you should care so much) still, we never could be on conventional terms with one another again. Besides, Ive got a feeling for you: almost a ghastly sort of love for you.

LORD SUMMERHAYS [shrinking] I beg you—no, please.

HYPATIA. Oh, it's nothing at all flattering; and, of course, nothing wrong, as I suppose youd call it.

LORD SUMMERHAYS. Please believe that I know that. When men of my age—

HYPATIA [impatiently] Oh, do talk about yourself when you mean yourself, and not about men of your age.

LORD SUMMERHAYS. I'll put it as bluntly as I can. When, as you say, I made an utter fool of myself, believe me, I made a poetic fool of myself. I was seduced, not by appetites which, thank Heaven, Ive long outlived: not even by the desire of second childhood for a child companion, but by the innocent impulse to place the delicacy and wisdom and spirituality of my age at the affectionate service of your youth for a few years, at the end of which you would be a grown, strong, formed—widow. Alas, my dear, the delicacy of age reckoned, as usual, without the derision and cruelty of youth. You told me that you didnt want to be an old man's nurse, and that you didnt want to have undersized children like Bentley. It served me right: I dont reproach you: I was an old fool. But how you can imagine, after that, that I can suspect you of the smallest feeling for me except the inevitable feeling of early youth for late age, or imagine that I have any feeling for you except one of shrinking humiliation, I cant understand.

HYPATIA. I dont blame you for falling in love with me. I shall be grateful to you all my life for it, because that was the first time that anything really interesting happened to me.

LORD SUMMERHAYS. Do you mean to tell me that nothing of that kind had ever happened before? that no man had ever—

HYPATIA. Oh, lots. Thats part of the routine of life here: the very dullest part of it. The young man who comes a-courting is as familiar an incident in my life as coffee for breakfast. Of course, he's too much of a gentleman to misbehave himself; and I'm too much of a lady to let him; and he's shy and sheepish; and I'm correct and self-possessed; and at last, when I can bear it no longer, I either frighten him off or give him a chance of proposing, just to see how he'll do it, and refuse him because he does it in the same silly way as all the rest. You dont call that an event in one's life, do you? With you it was different. I should as soon have expected the North Pole to fall in love with me as you. You know I'm only a linendraper's daughter when all's said. I was afraid of you: you, a great man! a lord! and older than my father. And then, what a situation it was! Just think of it! I was engaged to your son; and you knew nothing about it. He was afraid to tell you: he brought you down here because he thought if he could throw us together I could get round you because I was such a ripping girl. We arranged it all: he and I. We got Papa and Mamma and Johnny out of the way splendidly; and then Bentley took himself off, and left us—you and me!— to take a walk through the heather and admire the scenery of Hindhead. You never dreamt that it was all a plan: that what made me so nice was the way I was playing up to my destiny as the sweet girl that was to make your boy happy. And then! and then! [*She rises to dance and clap her hands in her glee*].

LORD SUMMERHAYS [*shuddering*] Stop, stop. Can no woman understand a man's delicacy?

HYPATIA [*revelling in the recollection*] And then—ha, ha!—you proposed. You! A father! For your son's girl!

LORD SUMMERHAYS. Stop, I tell you. Dont profane what you dont understand.

HYPATIA. That was something happening at last with a vengeance. It was splendid. It was my first peep behind the scenes. If I'd been seventeen I should have fallen in love with you. Even as it is, I feel quite differently towards you from what I do towards other old men. So [*offering her hand*] you may kiss my hand if that will be any fun for you.

LORD SUMMERHAYS [*rising and recoiling to the table,*

deeply revolted] No, no, no. How dare you? [*She laughs mischievously*]. How callous youth is! How coarse! How cynical! How ruthlessly cruel!

HYPATIA. Stuff! It's only that youre tired of a great many things Ive never tried.

LORD SUMMERHAYS. It's not alone that. Ive not forgotten the brutality of my own boyhood. But do try to learn, glorious young beast that you are, that age is squeamish, sentimental, fastidious. If you cant understand my holier feelings, at least you know the bodily infirmities of the old. You know that I darent eat all the rich things you gobble up at every meal; that I cant bear the noise and racket and clatter that affect you no more than they affect a stone. Well, my soul is like that too. Spare it: be gentle with it [*he involuntarily puts out his hands to plead: she takes them with a laugh*]. If you could possibly think of me as half an angel and half an invalid, we should get on much better together.

HYPATIA. We get on very well, I think. Nobody else ever called me a glorious young beast. I like that. Glorious young beast expresses exactly what I like to be.

LORD SUMMERHAYS [*extricating his hands and sitting down*] Where on earth did you get these morbid tastes? You seem to have been well brought up in a normal, healthy, respectable, middle-class family. Yet you go on like the most unwholesome product of the rankest Bohemianism.

HYPATIA. Thats just it. I'm fed up with—

LORD SUMMERHAYS. Horrible expression. Dont.

HYPATIA. Oh, I daresay it's vulgar; but theres no other word for it. I'm fed up with nice things: with respectability, with propriety! When a woman has nothing to do, money and respectability mean that

[181]

nothing is ever allowed to happen to her. I dont want to be good; and I dont want to be bad: I just dont want to be bothered about either good or bad: I want to be an active verb.

LORD SUMMERHAYS. An active verb? Oh, I see. An active verb signifies to be, to do, or to suffer.

HYPATIA. Just so: how clever of you! I want to be; I want to do; and I'm game to suffer it if costs that. But stick here doing nothing but being good and nice and ladylike I simply wont. Stay down here with us for a week; and I'll shew you what it means: shew it to you going on day after day, year after year, lifetime after lifetime.

LORD SUMMERHAYS. Shew me what?

HYPATIA. Girls withering into ladies. Ladies withering into old maids. Nursing old women. Running errands for old men. Good for nothing else at last. Oh, you cant imagine the fiendish selfishness of the old people and the maudlin sacrifice of the young. It's more unbearable than any poverty: more horrible than any regular-right-down wickedness. Oh, home! home! parents! family! duty! how I loathe them! How I'd like to see them all blown to bits! The poor escape. The wicked escape. Well, I cant be poor: we're rolling in money: it's no use pretending we're not. But I can be wicked; and I'm quite prepared to be.

LORD SUMMERHAYS. You think that easy?

HYPATIA. Well, isnt it? Being a man, you ought to know.

LORD SUMMERHAYS. It requires some natural talent, which can no doubt be cultivated. It's not really easy to be anything out of the common.

HYPATIA. Anyhow, I mean to make a fight for living.

LORD SUMMERHAYS. Living your own life, I believe the Suffragist phrase is.

HYPATIA. Living any life. Living, instead of withering without even a gardener to snip you off when youre rotten.

LORD SUMMERHAYS. Ive lived an active life; but Ive withered all the same.

HYPATIA. No: youve worn out: that quite different. And youve some life in you yet or you wouldnt have fallen in love with me. You can never imagine how delighted I was to find that instead of being the correct sort of big panjandrum you were supposed to be, you were really an old rip like papa.

LORD SUMMERHAYS. No, no: not about your father: I really cant bear it. And if you must say these terrible things: these heart-wounding shameful things, at least find something prettier to call me than an old rip.

HYPATIA. Well, what would you call a man proposing to a girl who might be—

LORD SUMMERHAYS. His daughter: yes, I know.

HYPATIA. I was going to say his granddaughter.

LORD SUMMERHAYS. You always have one more blow to get in.

HYPATIA. Youre too sensitive. Did you ever make mud pies when you were a kid—beg pardon: a child.

LORD SUMMERHAYS. I hope not.

HYPATIA. It's a dirty job; but Johnny and I were vulgar enough to like it. I like young people because theyre not too afraid of dirt to live. Ive grown out of the mud pies; but I like slang; and I like bustling you up by saying thing that shock you; and I'd rather put up with swearing and smoking than with dull respectability; and there are lots of things that would just shrivel you up that I think rather jolly. Now!

LORD SUMMERHAYS. Ive not the slightest doubt of it. Dont insist.

HYPATIA. It's not your ideal, is it?

LORD SUMMERHAYS. No.

HYPATIA. Shall I tell you why? Your ideal is an old woman. I daresay she's got a young face; but she's an old woman. Old, old, old. Squeamish. Cant stand up to things. Cant enjoy things: not real things. Always on the shrink.

LORD SUMMERHAYS. On the shrink! Detestable expression.

HYPATIA. Bah! you cant stand even a little thing like that. What good are you? Oh, what good are you?

LORD SUMMERHAYS. Dont ask me. I dont know. I dont know.

Tarleton returns from the vestibule. Hypatia sits down demurely.

HYPATIA. Well, papa: have you meditated on your destiny?

TARLETON [*puzzled*] What? Oh! my destiny. Gad, I forgot all about it: Jock started a rabbit and put it clean out of my head. Besides, why should I give way to morbid introspection? Its a sign of madness. Read Lombroso. [*To Lord Summerhays*] Well, Summerhays, has my little girl been entertaining you?

LORD SUMMERHAYS. Yes. She is a wonderful entertainer.

TARLETON. I think my idea of bringing up a young girl has been rather a success. Dont you listen to this, Patsy: it might make you conceited. She's never been treated like a child. I always said the same thing to her mother. Let her read what she likes. Let her do what she likes. Let her go where she likes. Eh, Patsy?

HYPATIA. Oh yes, if there had only been anything for me to do, any place for me to go, anything I wanted to read.

TARLETON. There, you see! She's not satisfied.

Restless. Wants things to happen. Wants adventures to drop out of the sky.

HYPATIA [*gathering up her work*] If youre going to talk about me and my education, I'm off.

TARLETON. Well, well, off with you. [*To Lord Summerhays*] She's active, like me. She actually wanted me to put her into the shop.

HYPATIA. Well, they tell me that the girls there have adventures sometimes. [*She goes out through the inner door*].

TARLETON. She had me there, though she doesnt know it, poor innocent lamb! Public scandal exaggerates enormously, of course; but moralize as you will, superabundant vitality is a physical fact that cant be talked away. [*He sits down between the writing table and the sideboard*]. Difficult question this, of bringing up children. Between ourselves, it has beaten me. I never was so surprised in my life as when I came to know Johnny as a man of business and found out what he was really like. How did you manage with your sons?

LORD SUMMERHAYS. Well, I really hadnt time to be a father: thats the plain truth of the matter. Their poor dear mother did the usual thing while they were with us. Then of course Eton, Oxford, the usual routine of their class. I saw very little of them, and thought very little about them: how could I? with a whole province on my hands. They and I are—acquaintances. Not, perhaps, quite ordinary acquaintances: theres a sort of—er—I should almost call it a sort of remorse about the way we shake hands (when we do shake hands) which means, I suppose, that we're sorry we dont care more for one another; and I'm afraid we dont meet oftener than we can help. We put each other too much out of countenance. It's really a very difficult relation. To my mind not altogether a natural one.

TARLETON [*impressed, as usual*] Thats an idea, certainly. I dont think anybody has ever written about that.

LORD SUMMERHAYS. Bentley is the only one who was really my son in any serious sense. He was completely spoilt. When he was sent to a preparatory school he simply yelled until he was sent home. Eton was out of the question; but we managed to tutor him into Oxford. No use: he was sent down. By that time my work was over; and I saw a good deal of him. But I could do nothing with him—except look on. I should have thought your case was quite different. You keep up the middle-class tradition: the day school and the business training instead of the university. I believe in the day school part of it. At all events, you know your own children.

TARLETON. Do we? I'm not so sure of it. Fact is, my dear Summerhays, once childhood is over, once the little animal has got past the stage at which it acquires what you might call a sense of decency, it's all up with the relation between parent and child. You cant get over the fearful shyness of it.

LORD SUMMERHAYS. Shyness?

TARLETON. Yes, shyness. Read Dickens.

LORD SUMMERHAYS [*surprised*] Dickens!! Of all authors, Charles Dickens! Are you serious?

TARLETON. I dont mean his books. Read his letters to his family. Read any man's letters to his children. Theyre not human. Theyre not about himself or themselves. Theyre about hotels, scenery, about the weather, about getting wet and losing the train and what he saw on the road and all that. Not a word about himself. Forced. Shy. Duty letters. All fit to be published: that says everything. I tell you theres a wall ten feet thick and ten miles high between parent and child. I know what I'm talking about. Ive girls in my employment: girls and young men. I had ideas on the subject. I used to go to the parents and tell them not to let their children go out into the world without instruction in the dangers and temptations they were going to be thrown into. What did every one of the mothers say to me? "Oh, sir, how could I speak of such things to my own daughter?" The men said I was quite right; but they didnt do it, any more than I'd been able to do it myself to Johnny. I had to leave books in his way; and I felt just awful when I did it. Believe me, Summerhays, the relation between the young and the old should be an innocent relation. It should be something they could talk about. Well, the relation between parent and child may be an affectionate relation. It may be a useful relation. It may be a necessary relation. But it can never be an innocent relation. Youd die rather than allude to it. Depend on it, in a thousand years itll be considered bad form to know who your father and mother are. Embarrassing. Better hand Bentley over to me. I can look him in the face and talk to him as man to man. You can have Johnny.

LORD SUMMERHAYS. Thank you. Ive lived so long in a country where a man may have fifty sons, who are no more to him than a regiment of soldiers, that I'm afraid Ive lost the English feeling about it.

TARLETON [restless again] You mean Jinghiskahn. Ah yes. Good thing the empire. Educates us. Opens our minds. Knocks the Bible out of us. And civilizes the other chaps.

LORD SUMMERHAYS. Yes: it civilizes them. And it uncivilizes us. Their gain. Our loss. Tarleton, believe me, our loss.

TARLETON. Well, why not? Averages out the human race. Makes the nigger half an Englishman. Makes the Englishman half a nigger.

LORD SUMMERHAYS. Speaking as the unfortunate Englishman in question, I dont like the process. If I had my life to live over again, I'd stay at home and supercivilize myself.

TARLETON. Nonsense! dont be selfish. Think how youve improved the other chaps. Look at the Spanish empire! Bad job for Spain, but splendid for South America. Look at what the Romans did for Britain! They burst up and had to clear out; but think of all they taught us? They were the making of us: I believe there was a Roman camp on Hindhead: I'll shew it to you tomorrow. Thats the good side of Imperialism: it's unselfish. I despise the Little Englanders: theyre always thinking about England. Small-minded. I'm for the Parliament of man, the federation of the world. Read Tennyson. [*He settles down again*]. Then theres the great food question.

LORD SUMMERHAYS [*apprehensively*] Need we go into that this afternoon?

TARLETON. No; but I wish youd tell the Chickabiddy that the Jinghiskahns eat no end of toasted cheese, and that it's the secret of their amazing health and long life!

LORD SUMMERHAYS. Unfortunately they are neither healthy nor long lived. And they dont eat toasted cheese.

TARLETON. There you are! They would be if they ate it. Anyhow, say what you like, provided the moral is a Welsh rabbit for my supper.

LORD SUMMERHAYS. British morality in a nutshell!

TARLETON [*hugely amused*] Yes, Ha ha! Awful hypocrites, aint we?

They are interrupted by excited cries from the grounds.

HYPATIA ⎰ Papa! Mamma! Come out as fast as you
         ⎱ can. Quick Quick.

BENTLEY ⎰ Hello, governor! Come out. An aeroplane.
         ⎱ Look, look.

TARLETON [*starting up*] Aeroplane! Did he say an aeroplane?

LORD SUMMERHAYS. Aeroplane! [*A shadow falls on the pavilion; and some of the glass at the top is shattered and falls on the floor*].

Tarleton and Lord Summerhays rush out through the pavilion into the garden.

HYPATIA ⎰ Take care. Take care of the
         ⎱ chimney.

BENTLEY ⎰ Come this side; it's coming
         ⎱ right where youre standing.

TARLETON ⎰ Hallo! where the devil are
          │ you coming? youll have
          ⎱ my roof off.

LORD SUMMERHAYS ⎰ He's lost control.

MRS TARLETON. Look, look, Hypatia. There are two people in it.

BENTLEY. Theyve cleared it. Well steered!

TARLETON ⎰ Yes; but theyre coming slam
          ⎱ into the greenhouse.

LORD SUMMERHAYS ⎰ Look out for the glass.

MRS TARLETON ⎰ Theyll break all the glass.
              ⎱ Theyll spoil all the grapes.

BENTLEY ⎰ Mind where youre coming.
         │ He'll save it. No: theyre
         ⎱ down.

An appalling crash of breaking glass is heard. Everybody shrieks.

[189]

MRS TARLETON	Oh, are they killed? John: are they killed?
LORD SUMMERHAYS	Are you hurt? Is anything broken? Can you stand?
HYPATIA	Oh, you must be hurt. Are you sure? Shall I get you some water? Or some wine?
TARLETON	Are you all right? Sure you wont have some brandy just to take off the shock.

THE AVIATOR. No, thank you. Quite right. Not a scratch. I assure you I'm all right.

BENTLEY. What luck! And what a smash! You are a lucky chap, I can tell you.

The Aviator and Tarleton come in through the pavilion, followed by Lord Summerhays and Bentley, the Aviator on Tarleton's right. Bentley passes the Aviator and turns to have an admiring look at him. Lord Summerhays overtakes Tarleton less pointedly on the opposite side with the same object.

THE AVIATOR. I'm really very sorry. I'm afraid Ive knocked your vinery into a cocked hat. [*Effusively*] You dont mind, do you?

TARLETON. Not a bit. Come in and have some tea. Stay to dinner. Stay over the week-end. All my life Ive wanted to fly.

THE AVIATOR [*taking off his goggles*] Youre really more than kind.

BENTLEY. Why, it's Joey Percival.

PERCIVAL. Hallo, Ben! That you?

TARLETON. What! The man with three fathers!

PERCIVAL. Oh! has Ben been talking about me?

TARLETON. Consider yourself as one of the family— if you will do me the honor. And your friend too. Wheres your friend?

PERCIVAL. Oh, by the way! before he comes in: let me explain. I dont know him.

TARLETON. Eh?

PERCIVAL. Havnt even looked at him. I'm trying to make a club record with a passenger. The club supplied the passenger. He just got in; and Ive been too busy handling the aeroplane to look at him. I havnt said a word to him; and I cant answer for him socially; but he's an ideal passenger for a flyer. He saved me from a smash.

LORD SUMMERHAYS. I saw it. It was extraordinary. When you were thrown out he held on to the top bar with one hand. You came past him in the air, going straight for the glass. He caught you and turned you off into the flower bed, and then lighted beside you like a bird.

PERCIVAL. How he kept his head I cant imagine. Frankly, *I* didnt.

The Passenger, also begoggled, comes in through the pavilion with Johnny and the two ladies. The Passenger comes between Percival and Tarleton, Mrs Tarleton between Lord Summerhays and her husband, Hypatia between Percival and Bentley, and Johnny to Bentley's right.

TARLETON. Just discussing your prowess, my dear sir. Magnificent. Youll stay to dinner. Youll stay the night. Stay over the week. The Chickabiddy will be delighted.

MRS TARLETON. Wont you take off your goggles and have some tea?

The passenger begins to remove the goggles.

TARLETON. Do. Have a wash. Johnny: take the gentleman to your room: I'll look after Mr Percival. They must—

By this time the passenger has got the goggles off, and

stands revealed as a remarkably good-looking woman.

MRS TARLETON	Well I never!!!	
BENTLEY	[*in a whisper*] Oh, I say!	
JOHNNY	By George!	
LORD SUMMERHAYS	A lady!	*All*
HYPATIA	A woman!	*together.*
TARLETON	[*to Percival*] You never told me—	
PERCIVAL	I hadnt the least idea—	

An embarrassed pause.

PERCIVAL. I assure you if I'd had the faintest notion that my passenger was a lady I shouldnt have left you to shift for yourself in that selfish way.

LORD SUMMERHAYS. The lady seems to have shifted for both very effectually, sir.

PERCIVAL. Saved my life. I admit it most gratefully.

TARLETON. I must apologize, madam, for having offered you the civilities appropriate to the opposite sex. And yet, why opposite? We are all human: males and females of the same species. When the dress is the same the distinction vanishes. I'm proud to receive in my house a lady of evident refinement and distinction. Allow me to introduce myself: Tarleton: John Tarleton (*seeing conjecture in the passenger's eye*) yes, yes: Tarleton's Underwear. My wife, Mrs Tarleton: youll excuse me for having in what I had taken to be a confidence between man and man alluded to her as the Chickabiddy. My daughter Hypatia, who has always wanted some adventure to drop out of the sky, and is now, I hope, satisfied at last. Lord Summerhays: a man known wherever the British flag waves. His son Bentley, engaged to

Hypatia. Mr Joseph Percival, the promising son of three highly intellectual fathers.

HYPATIA [*startled*] Bentley's friend? [*Bentley nods*].

TARLETON [*continuing, to the passenger*] May I now ask to be allowed the pleasure of knowing your name?

THE PASSENGER. My name is Lina Szczepanowska [*pronouncing it Sh-Chepanovska*].

PERCIVAL. Sh—I beg your pardon?

LINA. Szczepanowska.

PERCIVAL [*dubiously*] Thank you.

TARLETON [*very politely*] Would you mind saying it again?

LINA. Say fish.

TARLETON. Fish.

LINA. Say church.

TARLETON. Church.

LINA. Say fish church.

TARLETON [*remonstrating*] But it's not good sense.

LINA [*inexorable*] Say fish church.

TARLETON. Fish church.

LINA. Again.

TARLETON. No, bu—[*resigning himself*] fish church.

LINA. Now say Szczepanowska.

TARLETON. Szczepanowska. Got it, by Gad. [*A sibilant whispering becomes audible: they are all saying Sh-ch to themselves*]. Szczepanowska! Not an English name, is it?

LINA. Polish. I'm a Pole.

TARLETON [*dithyrambically*] Ah yes. What other nation, madame, could have produced your magical personality? Your countrywomen have always appealed to our imagination. Women of Destiny! beautiful! musical! passionate! tragic! You will be at home here: my own temperament is pre-eminently Polish. Wont you sit down?

The group breaks up. Johnny and Bentley hurry to the pavilion and fetch the two wicker chairs. Johnny gives his to Lina. Hypatia and Percival take the chairs at the worktable. Lord Summerhays gives the chair at the vestibule end of the writing table to Mrs Tarleton; and Bentley replaces it with a wicker chair, which Lord Summerhays takes. Johnny remains standing behind the worktable, Bentley behind his father.

MRS TARLETON [*to Lina*] Have some tea now, wont you?

LINA. I never drink tea.

TARLETON [*sitting down at the end of the writing table nearest Lina*] Bad thing to aeroplane on, I should imagine. Too jumpy. Been up much?

LINA. Not in an aeroplane. Ive parachuted; but thats child's play.

MRS TARLETON. But arnt you very foolish to run such a dreadful risk?

LINA. You cant live without running risks.

MRS TARLETON. Oh, what a thing to say! Didnt you know you might have been killed?

LINA. That was why I went up.

HYPATIA. Of course. Cant you understand the fascination of the thing? the novelty! the daring! the sense of something happening!

LINA. Oh no. It's too tame a business for that. I went up for family reasons.

TARLETON. Eh? What? Family reasons?

MRS TARLETON. I hope it wasnt to spite your mother?

PERCIVAL [*quickly*] Or your husband?

LINA. I'm not married. And why should I want to spite my mother?

HYPATIA [*aside to Percival*] That was clever of you, Mr Percival.

PERCIVAL. What?

HYPATIA. To find out.

TARLETON. I'm in a difficulty. I cant understand a lady going up in an aeroplane for family reasons. It's rude to be curious and ask questions; but then it's inhuman to be indifferent, as if you didnt care.

LINA. I'll tell you with pleasure. For the last hundred and fifty years, not a single day has passed without some member of my family risking his life—or her life. It's a point of honor with us to keep up that tradition. Usually several of us do it; but it happens that just at this moment it is being kept up by one of my brothers only. Early this morning I got a telegram from him to say that there had been a fire, and that he could do nothing for the rest of the week. Fortunately I had an invitation from the Aerial League to see this gentleman try to break the passenger record. I appealed to the President of the League to let me save the honor of my family. He arranged it for me.

TARLETON. Oh, I must be dreaming. This is stark raving nonsense.

LINA [quietly] You are quite awake, sir.

JOHNNY. We cant all be dreaming the same thing, governor.

TARLETON. Of course not, you duffer; but then I'm dreaming you as well as the lady.

MRS TARLETON. Dont be silly, John. The lady is only joking, I'm sure. [To Lina] I suppose your luggage is in the aeroplane.

PERCIVAL. Luggage was out of the question. If I stay to dinner I'm afraid I cant change unless youll lend me some clothes.

MRS TARLETON. Do you mean neither of you?

PERCIVAL. I'm afraid so.

MRS TARLETON. Oh well, never mind: Hypatia will lend the lady a gown.

LINA. Thank you: I'm quite comfortable as I am. I am not accustomed to gowns: they hamper me and make me feel ridiculous; so if you dont mind I shall not change.

MRS TARLETON. Well, I'm beginning to think I'm doing a bit of dreaming myself.

HYPATIA [*impatiently*] Oh, it's all right, mamma. Johnny: look after Mr Percival. [*To Lina, rising*] Come with me.

Lina follows her to the inner door. They all rise.

JOHNNY [*to Percival*] I'll shew you.

PERCIVAL. Thank you.

Lina goes out with Hypatia, and Percival with Johnny.

MRS TARLETON. Well, this is a nice thing to happen! And look at the greenhouse! Itll cost thirty pounds to mend it. People have no right to do such things. And you invited them to dinner too! What sort of woman is that to have in our house when you know that all Hindhead will be calling on us to see that aeroplane? Bunny: come with me and help me to get all the people out of the grounds: I declare they came running as if theyd sprung up out of the earth [*she makes for the inner door*].

TARLETON. No: dont you trouble, Chickabiddy: I'll tackle em.

MRS TARLETON. Indeed youll do nothing of the kind: youll stay here quietly with Lord Summerhays. Youd invite them all to dinner. Come, Bunny. [*She goes out, followed by Bentley. Lord Summerhays sits down again*].

TARLETON. Singularly beautiful woman, Summerhays. What do you make of her? She must be a princess. Whats this family of warriors and statesmen that risk their lives every day?

LORD SUMMERHAYS. They are evidently not warriors and statesmen, or they wouldnt do that.

TARLETON. Well, then, what the devil are they?

LORD SUMMERHAYS. I think I know. The last time I saw that lady, she did something I should not have thought possible.

TARLETON. What was that?

LORD SUMMERHAYS. Well, she walked backwards along a taut wire without a balancing pole and turned a somersault in the middle. I remember that her name was Lina, and that the other name was foreign; though I dont recollect it.

TARLETON. Szcz! You couldnt have forgotten that if youd heard it.

LORD SUMMERHAYS. I didnt hear it: I only saw it on a program. But it's clear she's an acrobat. It explains how she saved Percival. And it accounts for her family pride.

TARLETON. An acrobat, eh? Good! good! good! Summerhays: that brings her within reach. Thats better than a princess. I steeled this evergreen heart of mine when I thought she was a princess. Now I shall let it be touched. She is accessible. Good.

LORD SUMMERHAYS. I hope you are not serious. Remember: you have a family. You have a position. You are not in your first youth.

TARLETON. No matter.

Theres magic in the night.
When the heart is young.

My heart is young. Besides, I'm a married man, not a widower like you. A married man can do anything he likes if his wife dont mind. A widower cant be too careful. Not that I would have you think me an unprincipled man or a bad husband. I'm not. But Ive a superabundance of vitality. Read Pepys' Diary.

LORD SUMMERHAYS. The woman is your guest, Tarleton.

TARLETON. Well, is she? A woman I bring into my house is my guest. A woman you bring into my house is my guest. But a woman who drops bang down out of the sky into my greenhouse and smashes every blessed pane of glass in it must take her chance.

LORD SUMMERHAYS. Still, you know that my name must not be associated with any scandal. Youll be careful, wont you?

TARLETON. Oh Lord, yes! Yes, yes, yes, yes, yes. I was only joking, of course.

Mrs Tarleton comes back through the inner door.

MRS TARLETON. Well I never! John: I dont think that young woman's right in her head. Do you know what she's just asked for?

TARLETON. Champagne?

MRS TARLETON. No. She wants a Bible and six oranges.

TARLETON. What?

MRS TARLETON. A Bible and six oranges.

TARLETON. I understand the oranges: she's doing an orange cure of some sort. But what on earth does she want the Bible for?

MRS TARLETON. I'm sure I cant imagine. She cant be right in her head.

LORD SUMMERHAYS. Perhaps she wants to read it.

MRS TARLETON. But why should she? on a weekday at all events. What would you advise me to do, Lord Summerhays?

LORD SUMMERHAYS. Well, is there a Bible in the house?

TARLETON. Stacks of em. Theres the family Bible, and the Doré Bible, and the parallel revised version Bible, and the Doves Press Bible, and Johnny's Bible and Bobby's Bible and Patsy's Bible and the Chicka-biddy's Bible and my Bible; and I daresay the servants could raise a few more between them. Let her have the lot.

MRS TARLETON. Dont talk like that before Lord Summerhays, John.

LORD SUMMERHAYS. It doesnt matter, Mrs Tarleton: in Jinghiskahn it was a punishable offence to expose a Bible for sale. The empire has no religion.

Lina comes in. She has left her cap in Hypatia's room, but has made no other change. She stops just inside the door, holding it open, evidently not intending to stay.

LINA. Oh, Mrs Tarleton, shall I be making myself very troublesome if I ask for a music-stand in my room as well?

TARLETON. Not at all. You can have the piano if you like. Or the gramophone. Have the gramophone?

LINA. No, thank you: no music.

MRS TARLETON [*going towards her*] Do you think it's good for you to eat so many oranges? Arnt you afraid of getting jaundice?

LINA. Not in the least. But billiard balls will do quite as well.

MRS TARLETON. But you cant eat billiard balls, child!

TARLETON. Get em, Chickabiddy. I understand. [*He imitates a juggler tossing up balls*]. Eh?

LINA [*going to him, past his wife*] Just so.

TARLETON. Billiard balls and cues? Plates, knives, and forks? Two paraffin lamps and a hatstand?

LINA. No: that is popular low-class business. In our family we touch nothing but classical work. Anybody can do lamps and hatstands. *I* can do silver bullets. That is really hard. [*She passes on to Lord Summerhays, and looks gravely down at him as he sits by the writing table*].

[199]

MRS TARLETON. Well, I'm sure I dont know what youre talking about; and I only hope you know yourselves. However, you shall have what you want, of course. [*She goes out through the inner door*].

LORD SUMMERHAYS. Will you forgive my curiosity? What is the Bible for?

LINA. To quiet my soul.

LORD SUMMERHAYS [*with a sigh*] Ah yes, yes. It no longer quiets mine, I am sorry to say.

LINA. That is because you do not know how to read it. Put it up before you on a stand; and open it at the Psalms. When you can read them and understand them, quite quietly and happily, and keep six balls in the air all the time, you are in perfect condition; and youll never make a mistake that evening. If you find you cant do that, then go and pray until you can. And be very careful that evening.

LORD SUMMERHAYS. Is that the usual form of test in your profession?

LINA. Nothing that we Szczepanowskis do is usual, my lord.

LORD SUMMERHAYS. Are you all so wonderful?

LINA. It is our profession to be wonderful.

LORD SUMMERHAYS. Do you never condescend to do as common people do? For instance, do you not pray as common people pray?

LINA. Common people do not pray, my lord: they only beg.

LORD SUMMERHAYS. You never ask for anything?

LINA. No.

LORD SUMMERHAYS. Then why do you pray?

LINA. To remind myself that I have a soul.

TARLETON [*walking about*] True. Fine. Good. Beautiful. All this damned materialism: what good is it to anybody? Ive got a soul: dont tell me I havnt. Cut me up and you cant find it. Cut up a steam engine and you cant find the steam. But, by George, it makes the engine go. Say what you will, Summerhays, the divine spark is a fact.

LORD SUMMERHAYS. Have I denied it?

TARLETON. Our whole civilization is a denial of it. Read Walt Whitman.

LORD SUMMERHAYS. I shall go to the billiard room and get the balls for you.

LINA. Thank you.

Lord Summerhays goes out through the vestibule door.

TARLETON [*going to her*] Listen to me. [*She turns quickly*]. What you said just now was beautiful. You touch chords. You appeal to the poetry in a man. You inspire him. Come now! Youre a woman of the world: youre independent: you must have driven lots of men crazy. You know the sort of man I am, dont you? See through me at a glance eh?

LINA. Yes. [*She sits down quietly in the chair Lord Summerhays has just left*].

TARLETON. Good. Well, do you like me? Dont misunderstand me: I'm perfectly aware that youre not going to fall in love at first sight with a ridiculous old shopkeeper. I cant help that ridiculous old shopkeeper. I have to carry him about with me whether I like it or not. I have to pay for his clothes, though I hate the cut of them: especially the waistcoat. I have to look at him in the glass while I'm shaving. I loathe him because he's a living lie. My soul's not like that: it's like yours. I want to make a fool of myself. About you. Will you let me?

LINA [*very calm*] How much will you pay?

TARLETON. Nothing. But I'll throw as many sovereigns as you like into the sea to shew you that I'm in earnest.

LINA. Are those your usual terms?

TARLETON. No. I never made that bid before.

LINA [*producing a dainty little book and preparing to write in it*] What did you say your name was?

TARLETON. John Tarleton. The great John Tarleton of Tarleton's Underwear.

LINA [*writing*] T-a-r-l-e-t-o-n. Er—? [*She looks up at him inquiringly*].

TARLETON [*promptly*] Fifty-eight.

LINA. Thank you. I keep a list of all my offers. I like to know what I'm considered worth.

TARLETON. Let me look.

LINA [*offering the book to him*] It's in Polish.

TARLETON. Thats no good. Is mine the lowest offer?

LINA. No: the highest.

TARLETON. What do most of them come to? Diamonds? Motor cars? Furs? Villa at Monte Carlo?

LINA. Oh yes: all that. And sometimes the devotion of a lifetime.

TARLETON. Fancy that! A young man offering a woman his old age as a temptation!

LINA. By the way, you did not say how long.

TARLETON. Until you get tired of me.

LINA. Or until you get tired of me?

TARLETON. I never get tired. I never go on long enough for that. But when it becomes so grand, so inspiring that I feel that everything must be an anticlimax after that, then I run away.

LINA. Does she let you go without a struggle?

TARLETON. Yes. Glad to get rid of me. When love takes a man as it takes me—when it makes him great—it frightens a woman.

LINA. The lady here is your wife, isnt she? Dont you care for her?

TARLETON. Yes. And mind! she comes first always.

I reserve her dignity even when I sacrifice my own. Youll respect that point of honor, wont you?

LINA. Only a point of honor?

TARLETON [*impulsively*] No, by God! a point of affection as well.

LINA [*smiling, pleased with him*] Shake hands, old pal [*she rises and offers him her hand frankly*]

TARLETON [*giving his hand rather dolefully*] Thanks. That means no, doesnt it?

LINA. It means something that will last longer than yes. I like you. I admit you to my friendship. What a pity you were not trained when you were young! Youd be young still.

TARLETON. I suppose, to an athlete like you, I'm pretty awful, eh?

LINA. Shocking.

TARLETON. Too much crumb. Wrinkles. Yellow patches that wont come off. Short wind. I know. I'm ashamed of myself. I could do nothing on the high rope.

LINA. Oh yes: I could put you in a wheelbarrow and run you along, two hundred feet up.

TARLETON [*shuddering*] Ugh! Well, I'd do even that for you. Read The Master Builder.

LINA. Have you learnt everything from books?

TARLETON. Well, have you learnt everything from the flying trapeze?

LINA. On the flying trapeze there is often another woman; and her life is in your hands every night and your life in hers.

TARLETON. Lina: I'm going to make a fool of myself. I'm going to cry [*he crumples into the nearest chair*].

LINA. Pray instead: dont cry. Why should you cry? Youre not the first Ive said no to.

TARLETON. If you had said yes, should I have been the first then?

LINA. What right have you to ask? Have I asked am *I* the first?

TARLETON. Youre right: a vulgar question. To a man like me, everybody is the first. Life renews itself.

LINA. The youngest child is the sweetest.

TARLETON. Dont probe too deep, Lina. It hurts.

LINA. You must get out of the habit of thinking that these things matter so much. It's linendraperish.

TARLETON. Youre quite right. Ive often said so. All the same, it does matter; for I want to cry. [*He buries his face in his arms on the worktable and sobs*].

LINA [*going to him*] O la la! [*She slaps him vigorously, but not unkindly, on the shoulder*]. Courage, old pal, courage! Have you a gymnasium here?

TARLETON. Theres a trapeze and bars and things in the billiard room.

LINA. Come. You need a few exercises. I'll teach you how to stop crying. [*She takes his arm and leads him off into the vestibule*].

A young man, cheaply dressed and strange in manner, appears in the garden; steals to the pavilion door; and looks in. Seeing that there is nobody, he enters cautiously until he has come far enough to see into the hatstand corner. He draws a revolver, and examines it, apparently to make sure that it is loaded. Then his attention is caught by the Turkish bath. He looks down the lunette, and opens the panels.

HYPATIA [*calling in the garden*] Mr Percival! Mr Percival! Where are you?

The young man makes for the door, but sees Percival coming. He turns and bolts into the Turkish bath, which he closes upon himself just in time to escape being caught by Percival, who runs in through the pavilion, bareheaded. He also, it appears, is in search of a hiding-place; for he stops and turns between the two tables to take a survey of the room; then runs into the corner between the end of the sideboard and the wall. Hypatia, excited, mischievous, her eyes glowing, runs in, precisely on his trail; turns at the same spot; and discovers him just as he makes a dash for the pavilion door. She flies back and intercepts him.

HYPATIA. Aha! Arnt you glad Ive caught you?

PERCIVAL [*illhumoredly turning away from her and coming towards the writing table*] No I'm not. Confound it, what sort of girl are you? What sort of house is this? Must I throw all good manners to the winds?

HYPATIA [*following him*] Do, do, do, do, do. This is the house of a respectable shopkeeper, enormously rich. This is the respectable shopkeeper's daughter, tired of good manners. [*Slipping her left hand into his right*] Come, handsome young man, and play with the respectable shopkeeper's daughter.

PERCIVAL [*withdrawing quickly from her touch*] No, no: dont you know you mustnt go on like this with a perfect stranger?

HYPATIA. Dropped down from the sky. Dont you know that you must always go on like this when you get the chance? You must come to the top of the hill and chase me through the bracken. You may kiss me if you catch me.

PERCIVAL. I shall do nothing of the sort.

HYPATIA. Yes, you will: you cant help yourself. Come along. [*She seizes his sleeve*]. Fool, fool: come along. Dont you want to?

PERCIVAL. No: certainly not. I should never be forgiven if I did it.

HYPATIA. Youll never forgive yourself if you dont.

PERCIVAL. Nonsense. Youre engaged to Ben. Ben's my friend. What do you take me for?

HYPATIA. Ben's old. Ben was born old. Theyre all

old here, except you and me and the man-woman or woman-man or whatever you call her that came with you. They never do anything: they only discuss whether what other people do is right. Come and give them something to discuss.

PERCIVAL. I will do nothing incorrect.

HYPATIA. Oh, dont be afraid, little boy: youll get nothing but a kiss; and I'll fight like the devil to keep you from getting that. But we must play on the hill and race through the heather.

PERCIVAL. Why?

HYPATIA. Because we want to, handsome young man.

PERCIVAL. But if everybody went on in this way—

HYPATIA. How happy! oh how happy the world would be!

PERCIVAL. But the consequences may be serious.

HYPATIA. Nothing is worth doing unless the consequences may be serious. My father says so; and I'm my father's daughter.

PERCIVAL. I'm the son of three fathers. I mistrust these wild impulses.

HYPATIA. Take care. Youre letting the moment slip. I feel the first chill of the wave of prudence. Save me.

PERCIVAL. Really, Miss Tarleton! [*She strikes him across the face*]. Damn you! [*Recovering himself, horrified at his lapse*] I beg your pardon; but since weve both forgotten ourselves, youll please allow me to leave the house [*He turns towards the inner door, having left his cap in the bedroom*].

HYPATIA [*standing in his way*] Are you ashamed of having said "Damn you" to me?

PERCIVAL. I had no right to say it. I'm very much ashamed of it. I have already begged your pardon.

HYPATIA. And youre not ashamed of having said "Really, Miss Tarleton!"?

PERCIVAL. Why should I?

HYPATIA. O man, man! mean, stupid, cowardly, selfish masculine male man! You ought to have been a governess. I was expelled from school for saying that the very next person that said "Really, Miss Tarleton!" to me, I would strike across the face. You were the next.

PERCIVAL. I had no intention of being offensive. Surely there is nothing that can wound any lady in— [*He hesitates, not quite convinced*]. At least—er—I really didnt mean to be disagreeable.

HYPATIA. Liar.

PERCIVAL. Of course if youre going to insult me, I am quite helpless. Youre a woman: you can say what you like.

HYPATIA. And you can only say what you dare. Poor wretch: it isnt much. [*He bites his lip, and sits down, very much annoyed*]. Really, Mr Percival! You sit down in the presence of a lady and leave her standing. [*He rises hastily*]. Ha, ha! Really, Mr Percival! Oh really, really, really, really, really, Mr Percival! How do you like it? Wouldnt you rather I damned you?

PERCIVAL. Miss Tarleton—

HYPATIA [*caressingly*] Hypatia, Joey. Patsy, if you like.

PERCIVAL. Look here: this is no good. You want to do what you like?

HYPATIA. Dont you!

PERCIVAL. No. Ive been too well brought up. Ive argued all through this thing; and I tell you I'm not prepared to cast off the social bond. It's like a corset: it's a support to the figure even if it does squeeze and deform it a bit. I want to be free.

HYPATIA. Well, I'm tempting you to be free.

PERCIVAL. Not at all. Freedom, my good girl, means

[207]

being able to count on how other people will behave. If every man who dislikes me is to throw a handful of mud in my face, and every woman who likes me is to behave like Potiphar's wife, then I shall be a slave: the slave of uncertainty: the slave of fear: the worst of all slaveries. How would you like it if every laborer you met in the road were to make love to you? No. Give me the blessed protection of a good stiff conventionality among thoroughly well-brought-up ladies and gentlemen.

HYPATIA. Another talker! Men like conventions because men made them. I didnt make them: I dont like them: I wont keep them. Now, what will you do?

PERCIVAL. Bolt. [*He runs out through the pavilion*].

HYPATIA. I'll catch you. [*She dashes off in pursuit*].

During this conversation the head of the scandalized man in the Turkish bath has repeatedly risen from the lunette, with a strong expression of moral shock. It vanishes abruptly as the two turn towards it in their flight. At the same moment Tarleton comes back through the vestibule door, exhausted by severe and unaccustomed exercise.

TARLETON [*looking after the flying figures with amazement*] Hallo, Patsy: whats up? Another aeroplane? [*They are far too preoccupied to hear him; and he is left staring after them as they rush away through the garden. He goes to the pavilion door and looks up; but the heavens are empty. His exhaustion disables him from further inquiry. He dabs his brow with his handkerchief and walks stiffly to the nearest convenient support, which happens to be the Turkish bath. He props himself upon it with his elbow, and covers his eyes with his hand for a moment. After a few sighing breaths, he feels a little better, and uncovers his eyes. The man's head rises from the lunette a few inches from his nose. He recoils from*

[208]

the bath with a violent start]. Oh Lord! My brain's gone. [*Calling piteously*] Chickabiddy! [*He staggers down to the writing table*].

THE MAN [*coming out of the bath, pistol in hand*] Another sound; and youre a dead man.

TARLETON [*braced*] Am I! Well, youre a live one: thats one comfort. I thought you were a ghost. [*He sits down, quite undisturbed by the pistol*] Who are you; and what the devil were you doing in my new Turkish bath?

THE MAN [*with tragic intensity*] I am the son of Lucinda Titmus.

TARLETON [*the name conveying nothing to him*] Indeed? And how is he? Quite well, I hope, eh?

THE MAN. She is dead. Dead, my God! and you are alive.

TARLETON [*unimpressed by the tragedy, but sympathetic*] Oh! Lost your mother? Thats sad. I'm sorry. But we cant all have the luck to die before our mothers, and be nursed out of the world by the hands that nursed us into it.

THE MAN. Much you care, damn you!

TARLETON. Oh, dont cut up rough. Face it like a man. You see I didnt know your mother; but Ive no doubt she was an excellent woman.

THE MAN. Not know her! Do you dare to stand there by her open grave and deny that you knew her?

TARLETON [*trying to recollect*] What did you say her name was?

THE MAN. Lucinda Titmus.

TARLETON. Well, I ought to remember a rum name like that if I ever heard it. But I dont. Have you a photograph or anything?

THE MAN. Forgotten even the name of your victim!

TARLETON. Oh! she was my victim, was she?

THE MAN. She was. And you shall see her face again before you die, dead as she is. I have a photograph.

TARLETON. Good.

THE MAN. Ive two photographs.

TARLETON. Still better. Treasure the mother's pictures. Good boy!

THE MAN. One of them as you knew her. The other as she became when you flung her aside, and she withered into an old woman.

TARLETON. She'd have done that anyhow, my lad. We all grow old. Look at me! [*Seeing that the man is embarrassed by his pistol in fumbling for the photographs with his left hand in his breast pocket*] Let me hold the gun for you.

THE MAN [*retreating to the worktable*] Stand back. Do you take me for a fool?

TARLETON. Well, youre a little upset, naturally. It does you credit.

THE MAN. Look here, upon this picture and on this. [*He holds out the two photographs like a hand at cards, and points to them with the pistol*].

TARLETON. Good. Read Shakespear: he has a word for every occasion. [*He takes the photographs, one in each hand, and looks from one to the other, pleased and interested, but without any sign of recognition*] What a pretty girl! Very pretty. I can imagine myself falling in love with her when I was your age. I wasnt a bad-looking young fellow myself in those days. [*Looking at the other*] Curious that we should both have gone the same way.

THE MAN You and she the same way! What do you mean?

TARLETON. Both got stout, I mean.

THE MAN. Would you have had her deny herself food?

TARLETON. No: it wouldnt have been any use. It's constitutional. No matter how little you eat you put on flesh if youre made that way. [*He resumes his study of the earlier photograph*].

THE MAN. Is that all the feeling that rises in you at the sight of the face you once knew so well?

TARLETON [*too much absorbed in the portrait to heed him*] Funny that I cant remember! Let this be a lesson to you, young man. I could go into court tomorrow and swear I never saw that face before in my life if it wasnt for that brooch [*pointing to the photograph*]. Have you got that brooch, by the way? [*The man again resorts to his breast pocket*]. You seem to carry the whole family property in that pocket.

THE MAN [*producing a brooch*] Here it is to prove my bona fides.

TARLETON [*pensively putting the photographs on the table and taking the brooch*] I bought that brooch in Cheapside from a man with a yellow wig and a cast in his left eye. I've never set eyes on him from that day to this. And yet I remember that man; and I cant remember your mother.

THE MAN. Monster! Without conscience! without even memory! You left her to her shame—

TARLETON [*throwing the brooch on the table and rising pepperily*] Come, come, young man! none of that. Respect the romance of your mother's youth. Dont you start throwing stones at her. I dont recall her features just at this moment; but Ive no doubt she was kind to me and we were happy together. If you have a word to say against her, take yourself out of my house and say it elsewhere.

THE MAN. What sort of a joker are you? Are you trying to put me in the wrong, when you have to answer to me for a crime that would make every honest man spit at you as you passed in the street if I were to make it known?

TARLETON. You read a good deal, dont you?

THE MAN. What if I do? What has that to do with your infamy and my mother's doom?

TARLETON. There, you see! Doom! Thats not good sense; but it's literature. Now it happens that I'm a tremendous reader: always was. When I was your age I read books of that sort by the bushel: the Doom sort, you know. It's odd, isnt it, that you and I should be like one another in that respect? Can you account for it in any way?

THE MAN. No. What are you driving at?

TARLETON. Well, do you know who your father was?

THE MAN. I see what you mean now. You dare set up to be my father! Thank heaven Ive not a drop of your vile blood in my veins.

TARLETON [*sitting down again with a shrug*] Well, if you wont be civil, theres no pleasure in talking to you, is there? What do you want? Money?

THE MAN. How dare you insult me?

TARLETON. Well, what do you want?

THE MAN. Justice.

TARLETON. Youre quite sure thats all?

THE MAN. It's enough for me.

TARLETON. A modest sort of demand, isnt it? Nobody ever had it since the world began, fortunately for themselves; but you must have it, must you? Well, youve come to the wrong shop for it; youll get no justice here: we dont keep it. Human nature is what we stock.

THE MAN. Human nature! Debauchery! gluttony! selfishness! robbery of the poor! Is that what you call human nature?

TARLETON. No: thats what you call it. Come, my

lad! Whats the matter with you? You dont look starved; and youve a decent suit of clothes.

THE MAN. Forty-two shillings.

TARLETON. They can do you a very decent suit for forty-two shillings. Have you paid for it?

THE MAN. Do you take me for a thief? And do you suppose I can get credit like you?

TARLETON. Then you were able to lay your hand on forty-two shillings. Judging from your conversational style, I should think you must spend at least a shilling a week on romantic literature.

THE MAN Where would I get a shilling a week to spend on books when I can hardly keep myself decent? I get books at the Free Library.

TARLETON [springing to his feet] What!!!

THE MAN [recoiling before his vehemence] The Free Library. Theres no harm in that.

TARLETON. Ingrate! I supply you with free books; and the use you make of them is to persuade yourself that it's a fine thing to shoot me [He throws himself doggedly back into his chair]. I'll never give another penny to a Free Library.

THE MAN. Youll never give another penny to anything. This is the end: for you and me.

TARLETON. Pooh! Come, come, man! talk business. Whats wrong? Are you out of employment?

THE MAN. No. This is my Saturday afternoon. Dont flatter yourself that I'm a loafer or a criminal. I'm a cashier; and I defy you to say that my cash has ever been a farthing wrong. I've a right to call you to account because my hands are clean.

TARLETON. Well, call away. What have I to account for? Had you a hard time with your mother? Why didnt she ask me for money?

THE MAN. She'd have died first. Besides, who wanted

your money? Do you suppose we lived in the gutter? My father maynt have been in as large a way as you; but he was better connected; and his shop was as respectable as yours.

TARLETON. I suppose your mother brought him a little capital.

THE MAN. I dont know. Whats that got to do with you?

TARLETON. Well, you say she and I knew one another and parted. She must have had something off me then, you know. One doesnt get out of these things for nothing. Hang it, young man: do you suppose Ive no heart? Of course she had her due; and she found a husband with it, and set him up in business with it, and brought you up respectably; so what the devil have you to complain of?

THE MAN. Are women to be ruined with impunity?

TARLETON. I havnt ruined any woman that I'm aware of. Ive been the making of you and your mother.

THE MAN. Oh, I'm a fool to listen to you and argue with you. I came here to kill you and then kill myself.

TARLETON. Begin with yourself, if you dont mind. Ive a good deal of business to do still before I die. Havnt you?

THE MAN. No. Thats just it: Ive no business to do. Do you know what my life is? I spend my days from nine to six—nine hours of daylight and fresh air—in a stuffy little den counting another man's money. Ive an intellect: a mind and brain and a soul; and the use he makes of them is to fix them on his tuppences and his eighteenpences and his two pound seventeen and tenpences and see how much they come to at the end of the day and take care that no one steals them. I enter and enter, and add and add, and take money and give change, and fill cheques and stamp receipts;

and not a penny of that money is my own: not one of
those transactions has the smallest interest for me or
anyone else in the world but him; and even he couldnt
stand it if he had to do it all himself. And I'm envied:
aye, envied for the variety and liveliness of my job,
by the poor devil of a bookkeeper that has to copy all
my entries over again. Fifty thousand entries a year
that poor wretch makes; and not ten out of the fifty
thousand ever has to be referred to again; and when
all the figures are counted up and the balance sheet
made out, the boss isnt a penny the richer than he'd
be if bookkeeping had never been invented. Of all the
damnable waste of human life that ever was invented,
clerking is the very worst.

TARLETON. Why not join the territorials?

THE MAN. Because the boss wont let me. He hasnt
the sense to see that it would pay him to get some
cheap soldiering out of me. How can a man tied to a
desk from nine to six be anything—be even a man,
let alone a soldier? But I'll teach him and you a lesson.
Ive had enough of living a dog's life and despising
myself for it. Ive had enough of being talked down to
by hogs like you, and wearing my life out for a salary
that wouldnt keep you in cigars. Youll never believe
that a clerk's a man until one of us makes an example
of one of you.

TARLETON. Despotism tempered by assassination,
eh?

THE MAN. Yes. Thats what they do in Russia. Well,
a business office is Russia as far as the clerks are
concerned. So dont you take it so coolly. You think
I'm not going to do it; but I am.

TARLETON [rising and facing him] Come, now, as
man to man! It's not my fault that youre poorer than
I am; and it's not your fault that I'm richer than you.

And if you could undo all that passed between me and your mother, you wouldnt undo it; and neither would she. But youre sick of your slavery; and you want to be the hero of a romance and to get into the papers. Eh? A son revenges his mother's shame. Villain weltering in his gore. Mother: look down from heaven and receive your unhappy son's last sigh.

THE MAN. Oh, rot! do you think I read novelettes? And do you suppose I believe such superstitions as heaven? I go to church because the boss told me I'd get the sack if I didnt. Free England! Ha! [*Lina appears at the pavilion door, and comes swiftly and noiselessly forward on seeing the man with a pistol in his hand*].

TARLETON. Youre afraid of getting the sack; but youre not afraid to shoot yourself.

THE MAN. Damn you! youre trying to keep me talking until somebody comes. [*He raises the pistol desperately, but not very resolutely*].

LINA [*at his right elbow*] Somebody has come.

THE MAN [*turning on her*] Stand off. I'll shoot you if you lay a hand on me. I will, by God.

LINA. You cant cover me with that pistol. Try.

He tries, presenting the pistol at her face. She moves round him in the opposite direction to the hands of a clock with a light dancing step. He finds it impossible to cover her with the pistol: she is always too far to his left. Tarleton, behind him, grips his wrist and drags his arm straight up, so that the pistol points to the ceiling. As he tries to turn on his assailant, Lina grips his other wrist.

LINA. Please stop. I cant bear to twist anyone's wrist; but I must if you dont let the pistol go.

THE MAN [*letting Tarleton take it from him*] All right: I'm done. Couldnt even do that job decently. Thats a clerk all over. Very well: send for your damned police and make an end of it. I'm accustomed to prison from nine to six: I daresay I can stand it from six to nine as well.

TARLETON. Dont swear. Thats a lady. [*He throws the pistol on the writing table*].

THE MAN [*looking at Lina in amazement*] Beaten by a female! It needed only this. [*He collapses in the chair near the worktable, and hides his face. They cannot help pitying him*].

LINA. Old pal: dont call the police. Lend him a bicycle and let him get away.

THE MAN. I cant ride a bicycle. I never could afford one. I'm not even that much good.

TARLETON. If I gave you a hundred pound note now to go and have a good spree with, I wonder would you know how to set about it. Do you ever take a holiday?

THE MAN. Take! I got four days last August.

TARLETON. What did you do?

THE MAN. I did a cheap trip to Folkestone. I spent sevenpence on dropping pennies into silly automatic machines and peep-shows of rowdy girls having a jolly time. I spent a penny on the lift and fourpence on refreshments. That cleaned me out. The rest of the time I was so miserable that I was glad to get back to the office. Now you know.

LINA. Come to the gymnasium: I'll teach you how to make a man of yourself. [*The man is about to rise irresolutely, from the mere habit of doing what he is told, when Tarleton stops him*].

TARLETON. Young man: dont. Youve tried to shoot me; but I'm not vindictive. I draw the line at putting a man on the rack. If you want every joint in your body stretched until it's an agony to live—until you have an unnatural feeling that all your muscles are singing and laughing with pain—then go to the gymnasium with that lady. But youll be more comfortable in jail.

LINA [*greatly amused*] Was that why you went away, old pal? Was that the telegram you said you had forgotten to send?

Mrs Tarleton comes in hastily through the inner door.

MRS TARLETON [*on the steps*] Is anything the matter, John? Nurse says she heard you calling me a quarter of an hour ago; and that your voice sounded as if you were ill. [*She comes between Tarleton and the man*]. Is anything the matter?

TARLETON. This is the son of an old friend of mine. Mr—er—Mr Gunner. [*To the man, who rises awkwardly*]. My wife.

MRS TARLETON. Good evening to you.

GUNNER. Er—[*He is too nervous to speak, and makes a shambling bow*].

Bentley looks in at the pavilion door, very peevish, and too preoccupied with his own affairs to pay any attention to those of the company.

BENTLEY. I say: has anybody seen Hypatia? She promised to come out with me; and I cant find her anywhere. And wheres Joey?

GUNNER [*suddenly breaking out aggressively, being incapable of any middle way between submissiveness and violence*] I can tell you where Hypatia is. I can tell you where Joey is. And I say it's a scandal and an infamy. If people only knew what goes on in this so-called respectable house it would be put a stop to. These are the morals of our pious capitalist class! This is your rotten bourgeoisie! This—

MRS TARLETON. Dont you dare use such language in company. I wont allow it.

TARLETON. All right, Chickabiddy: it's not bad language: it's only Socialism.

MRS TARLETON. Well, I wont have any Socialism in my house.

TARLETON [*to Gunner*] You hear what Mrs Tarleton says. Well, in this house everybody does what she says or out they go.

GUNNER. Do you suppose I want to stay? Do you think I would breathe this polluted atmosphere a moment longer than I could help?

BENTLEY [*running forward between Lina and Gunner*] But what did you mean by what you said about Miss Tarleton and Mr Percival, you beastly rotter, you?

GUNNER [*to Tarleton*] Oh! is Hypatia your daughter? And Joey is Mister Percival, is he? One of your set, I suppose. One of the smart set! One of the bridge-playing, eighty-horse-power, week-ender set! One of the johnnies I slave for! Well, Joey has more decency than your daughter, anyhow. The women are the worst. I never believed it til I saw it with my own eyes. Well, it wont last for ever. The writing is on the wall. Rome fell. Babylon fell. Hindhead's turn will come.

MRS TARLETON [*naïvely looking at the wall for the writing*] Whatever are you talking about, young man?

GUNNER. I know what I'm talking about. I went into that Turkish bath a boy: I came out a man.

MRS TARLETON. Good gracious! he's mad. [*To Lina*] Did John make him take a Turkish bath?

LINA. No. He doesnt need Turkish baths: he needs to put on a little flesh. I dont understand what it's all about. I found him trying to shoot Mr Tarleton.

MRS TARLETON [*with a scream*] Oh! and John encouraging him, I'll be bound! Bunny: you go for the police. [*To Gunner*] I'll teach you to come into my house and shoot my husband.

GUNNER. Teach away. I never asked to be let off. I'm ashamed to be free instead of taking my part with the rest. Women—beautiful women of noble birth—are going to prison for their opinions. Girl students in Russia go to the gallows; let themselves be cut in pieces with the knout, or driven through the frozen snows of Siberia, sooner than stand looking on tamely at the world being made a hell for the toiling millions. If you were not all skunks and cowards youd be suffering with them instead of battening here on the plunder of the poor.

MRS TARLETON [*much vexed*] Oh, did you ever hear such silly nonsense? Bunny: go and tell the gardener to send over one of his men to Grayshott for the police.

GUNNER. I'll go with him. I intend to give myself up. I'm going to expose what Ive seen here, no matter what the consequences may be to my miserable self.

TARLETON. Stop. You stay where you are, Ben. Chickabiddy: youve never had the police in. If you had, youd not be in a hurry to have them in again. Now, young man: cut the cackle; and tell us, as short as you can, what did you see?

GUNNER. I cant tell you in the presence of ladies.

MRS TARLETON. Oh, you are tiresome. As if it mattered to anyone what you saw. Me! A married woman that might be your mother. [*To Lina*] And I'm sure youre not particular, if youll excuse my saying so.

TARLETON. Out with it. What did you see?

GUNNER. I saw your daughter with my own eyes—oh well, never mind what I saw.

BENTLEY [*almost crying with anxiety*] You beastly rotter. I'll get Joey to give you such a hiding—

TARLETON. You cant leave it at that, you know. What did you see my daughter doing?

GUNNER. After all, why shouldnt she do it? The Russian students do it. Women should be as free as men. I'm a fool. I'm so full of your bourgeois morality that I let myself be shocked by the application of my own revolutionary principles. If she likes the man why shouldnt she tell him so?

MRS TARLETON. I do wonder at you, John, letting him talk like this before everybody. [*Turning rather tartly to Lina*] Would you mind going away to the drawing room just for a few minutes, Miss Chipenoska. This is a private family matter, if you dont mind.

LINA. I should have gone before, Mrs Tarleton, if there had been anyone to protect Mr Tarleton and the young gentleman. [*She goes out through the inner door*].

GUNNER. There you are! It's all of a piece here. The men effeminate, the women unsexed—

TARLETON. Dont begin again, old chap. Keep it for Trafalgar Square.

HYPATIA'S VOICE OUTSIDE. No, no. [*She breaks off in a stifled half laugh, half scream, and is seen darting across the garden with Percival in hot pursuit. Immediately afterwards she appears again, and runs into the pavilion. Finding it full of people, including a stranger, she stops; but Percival, flushed and reckless, rushes in and seizes her before he, too, realizes that they are not alone. He releases her in confusion*].

Dead silence. They are all afraid to look at one another except Mrs Tarleton, who stares sternly at Hypatia. Hypatia is the first to recover her presence of mind.

HYPATIA. Excuse me rushing in like this. Mr Percival has been chasing me down the hill.

GUNNER. Who chased him up it? Dont be ashamed. Be fearless. Be truthful.

TARLETON. Gunner: will you go to Paris for a fortnight? I'll pay your expenses.

HYPATIA. What do you mean?

GUNNER. There was a silent witness in the Turkish bath.

TARLETON. I found him hiding there. Whatever went on here, he saw and heard. Thats what he means.

PERCIVAL [*sternly approaching Gunner, and speaking with deep but contained indignation*] Am I to understand you as daring to put forward the monstrous and blackguardly lie that this lady behaved improperly in my presence?

GUNNER [*turning white*] You know what I saw and heard.

Hypatia, with a gleam of triumph in her eyes, slips noiselessly into the swing chair, and watches Percival and Gunner, swinging slightly, but otherwise motionless.

PERCIVAL. I hope it is not necessary for me to assure you all that there is not one word of truth—not one grain of substance—in this rascally calumny, which no man with a spark of decent feeling would have uttered even if he had been ignorant enough to believe it. Miss Tarleton's conduct, since I have had the honor of knowing her, has been, I need hardly say, in every respect beyond reproach. [*To Gunner*] As for you, sir, youll have the goodness to come out with me immediately. I have some business with you which cant be settled in Mrs Tarleton's presence or in her house.

GUNNER [*painfully frightened*] Why should I go out with you?

PERCIVAL. Because I intend that you shall.

GUNNER. I wont be bullied by you. [*Percival makes a threatening step towards him*]. Police! [*He tries to bolt; but Percival seizes him*]. Leave me go, will you? What right have you to lay hands on me?

TARLETON. Let him run for it, Mr Percival. He's very poor company. We shall be well rid of him. Let him go.

PERCIVAL. Not until he has taken back and made the fullest apology for the abominable lie he has told. He shall do that, or he shall defend himself as best he can against the most thorough thrashing I'm capable of giving him. [*Releasing Gunner, but facing him ominously*] Take your choice. Which is it to be?

GUNNER. Give me a fair chance. Go and stick at a desk from nine to six for a month, and let me have your grub and your sport and your lessons in boxing, and I'll fight you fast enough. You know I'm no good or you darent bully me like this.

PERCIVAL. You should have thought of that before you attacked a lady with a dastardly slander. I'm waiting for your decision. I'm rather in a hurry, please.

GUNNER. I never said anything against the lady.

MRS TARLETON {Oh, listen to that!
BENTLEY   {What a liar!
ΠΥΡΑΤΙΑ   {Oh!
TARLETON   {Oh, come!

PERCIVAL. We'll have it in writing, if you dont mind. [*Pointing to the writing table*] Sit down; and take that pen in your hand. [*Gunner looks irresolutely a little way round; then obeys*]. Now write. "I," whatever your name is—

GUNNER [*after a vain attempt*] I cant. My hand's shaking too much. You see it's no use. I'm doing my best. I cant.

PERCIVAL. Mr Summerhays will write it: you can sign it.

BENTLEY [*insolently to Gunner*] Get up. [*Gunner obeys; and Bentley, shouldering him aside towards Percival, takes his place and prepares to write*].

PERCIVAL. Whats your name?

GUNNER. John Brown.

TARLETON. Oh come! Couldnt you make it Horace Smith? or Algernon Robinson?

GUNNER [*agitatedly*] But my name is John Brown. There are really John Browns. How can I help it if my name's a common one?

BENTLEY. Shew us a letter addressed to you.

GUNNER. How can I? I never get any letters: I'm only a clerk. I can shew you J. B. on my handkerchief. [*He takes out a not very clean one*].

BENTLEY [*with disgust*] Oh, put it up again. Let it go at John Brown.

PERCIVAL. Where do you live?

GUNNER. 4 Chesterfield Parade, Kentish Town, N.W.

PERCIVAL [*dictating*] I, John Brown, of 4 Chesterfield Parade, Kentish Town, do hereby voluntarily confess that on the 31st May 1909 I—[*To Tarleton*] What did he do exactly?

TARLETON [*dictating*]—I trespassed on the land of John Tarleton at Hindhead, and effected an unlawful entry into his house, where I secreted myself in a portable Turkish bath—

BENTLEY. Go slow, old man. Just a moment. "Turkish bath"—yes?

TARLETON [*continuing*]—with a pistol, with which I threatened to take the life of the said John Tarleton—

MRS TARLETON. Oh, John! You might have been killed.

TARLETON. —and was prevented from doing so only by the timely arrival of the celebrated Miss Lina Szczepanowska.

MRS TARLETON. Is she celebrated? [*Apologetically*] I never dreamt—

BENTLEY. Look here: I'm awfully sorry; but I cant spell Szczepanowska.

PERCIVAL. I think it's S, z, c, z—Better say the Polish lady.

BENTLEY [*writing*] "the Polish lady"?

TARLETON [*to Percival*] Now it's your turn.

PERCIVAL [*dictating*] I further confess that I was guilty of uttering an abominable calumny concerning

[224]

Miss Hypatia Tarleton, for which there was not a shred of foundation.

Impressive silence whilst Bentley writes.

BENTLEY. "foundation"?

PERCIVAL. I apologize most humbly to the lady and her family for my conduct—[*he waits for Bentley to write*].

BENTLEY. "conduct"?

PERCIVAL. —and I promise Mr Tarleton not to repeat it, and to amend my life—

BENTLEY. "amend my life"?

PERCIVAL. —and to do what in me lies to prove worthy of his kindness in giving me another chance—

BENTLEY. "another chance"?

PERCIVAL. —and refraining from delivering me up to the punishment I so richly deserve.

BENTLEY. "richly deserve."

PERCIVAL [*to Hypatia*] Does that satisfy you, Miss Tarleton?

HYPATIA. Yes: that will teach him to tell lies next time.

BENTLEY [*rising to make place for Gunner and handing him the pen*] You mean it will teach him to tell the truth next time.

TARLETON. Ahem! Do you, Patsy?

PERCIVAL. Be good enough to sign. [*Gunner sits down helplessly and dips the pen in the ink*]. I hope what you are signing is no mere form of words to you, and that you not only say you are sorry, but that you are sorry.

Lord Summerhays and Johnny come in through the pavilion door.

MRS TARLETON. Stop. Mr Percival: I think, on Hypatia's account, Lord Summerhays ought to be told about this.

Lord Summerhays, wondering what the matter is,

comes forward between Percival and Bentley. Johnny stops beside Hypatia.

PERCIVAL. Certainly.

TARLETON [*uneasily*] Take my advice and cut it short. Get rid of him.

MRS TARLETON. Hypatia ought to have her character cleared.

TARLETON. You let well alone, Chickabiddy. Most of our characters will bear a little careful dusting; but they wont bear scouring. Patsy is jolly well out of it. What does it matter, anyhow?

PERCIVAL. Mr Tarleton: we have already said either too much or not enough. Lord Summerhays: will you be kind enough to witness the declaration this man has just signed?

GUNNER. I havnt yet. Am I to sign now?

PERCIVAL. Of course. [*Gunner, who is now incapable of doing anything on his own initiative, signs*]. Now stand up and read your declaration to this gentleman. [*Gunner makes a vague movement and looks stupidly round. Percival adds peremptorily*] Now, please.

GUNNER [*rising apprehensively and reading without punctuation in a hardly audible voice, like a very sick man*] I John Brown of 4 Chesterfield Parade Kentish Town do hereby voluntarily confess that on the 31st May 1909 I trespassed on the land of John Tarleton at Hindhead and effected an unlawful entry into his house where I secreted myself in a portable Turkish bath with a pistol with which I threatened to take the life of the said John Tarleton and was prevented from doing so only by the timely arrival of the Polish lady I further confess that I was guilty of uttering an abominable calumny concerning Miss Hypatia Tarleton for which there was not a shred of foundation I apologize most humbly to the lady and her family for my conduct and I promise Mr Tarleton not to repeat it and to amend my life and to do what in me lies to prove worthy of his kindness in giving me another chance and refraining from delivering me up to the punishment I so richly deserve.

A short and painful silence follows. Then Percival speaks.

PERCIVAL. Do you consider that sufficient, Lord Summerhays?

LORD SUMMERHAYS. Oh quite, quite.

PERCIVAL [*to Hypatia*] Lord Summerhays would probably like to hear you say that you are satisfied, Miss Tarleton.

HYPATIA [*coming out of the swing, and advancing between Percival and Lord Summerhays*] I must say that you have behaved like a perfect gentleman, Mr Percival.

PERCIVAL [*first bowing to Hypatia, and then turning with cold contempt to Gunner, who is standing helpless*] We need not trouble you any further. [*Gunner turns vaguely towards the pavilion*].

JOHNNY [*with less refined offensiveness, pointing to the pavilion*] Thats your way. The gardener will shew you the shortest way into the road. Go the shortest way.

GUNNER [*oppressed and disconcerted, hardly knows how to get out of the room*] Yes, sir. I—[*He turns again, appealing to Tarleton*] Maynt I have my mother's photographs back again? [*Mrs Tarleton pricks up her ears*].

TARLETON. Eh? What? Oh, the photographs! Yes, yes, yes: take them. [*Gunner takes them from the table, and is creeping away, when Mrs Tarleton puts out her hand and stops him*].

MRS TARLETON. Whats this, John? What were you doing with his mother's photographs?

TARLETON. Nothing, nothing. Never mind, Chicka-biddy: it's all right.

MRS TARLETON [*snatching the photographs from Gunner's irresolute fingers, and recognizing them at a glance*] Lucy Titmus! Oh John, John!

TARLETON [*grimly, to Gunner*] Young man: youre a fool; but youve just put the lid on this job in a masterly manner. I knew you would. I told you all to let well alone. You wouldnt; and now you must take the consequences—or rather *I* must take them.

MRS TARLETON [*maternally*] Are you Lucy's son?

GUNNER. Yes!

MRS TARLETON. And why didnt you come to me? I didnt turn my back on your mother when she came to me in her trouble. Didnt you know that?

GUNNER. No. She never talked to me about anything.

TARLETON. How could she talk to her own son? Shy, Summerhays, shy. Parent and child. Shy. [*He sits down at the end of the writing table nearest the sideboard like a man resigned to anything that fate may have in store for him*].

MRS TARLETON. Then how did you find out?

GUNNER. From her papers after she died.

MRS TARLETON [*shocked*] Is Lucy dead? And I never knew! [*With an effusion of tenderness*] And you here being treated like that, poor orphan, with nobody to take your part! Tear up that foolish paper, child; and sit down and make friends with me.

JOHNNY | Hallo, mother: this is all very well, you know—

PERCIVAL | But may I point out, Mrs Tarleton, that—

BENTLEY | Do you mean that after what he said of—

HYPATIA | Oh, look here, mamma: this is really—

MRS TARLETON. Will you please speak one at a time?

Silence.

PERCIVAL [*in a very gentlemanly manner*] Will you allow me to remind you, Mrs Tarleton, that this man has uttered a most serious and disgraceful falsehood concerning Miss Tarleton and myself?

MRS TARLETON. I dont believe a word of it. If the poor lad was there in the Turkish bath, who has a better right to say what was going on here than he has? You ought to be ashamed of yourself, Patsy: and so ought you too, Mr Percival, for encouraging her. [*Hypatia retreats to the pavilion, and exchanges grimaces with Johnny, shamelessly enjoying Percival's sudden reverse. They know their mother*].

PERCIVAL [*gasping*] Mrs Tarleton: I give you my word of honor—

MRS TARLETON. Oh, go along with you and your word of honor. Do you think I'm a fool? I wonder you can look the lad in the face after bullying him and making him sign those wicked lies; and all the time you carrying on with my daughter before youd been half an hour in my house. Fie, for shame!

PERCIVAL. Lord Summerhays: I appeal to you. Have I done the correct thing or not?

LORD SUMMERHAYS. Youve done your best, Mr Percival. But the correct thing depends for its success on everybody playing the game very strictly. As a single-handed game, it's impossible.

BENTLEY [*suddenly breaking out lamentably*] Jocy: have you taken Hypatia away from me?

LORD SUMMERHAYS [*severely*] Bentley! Bentley! Control yourself, sir.

TARLETON. Come, Mr Percival! the shutters are up on the gentlemanly business. Try the truth.

PERCIVAL. I am in a wretched position. If I tell the truth nobody will believe me.

TARLETON. Oh yes they will. The truth makes everybody believe it.

PERCIVAL. It also makes everybody pretend not to believe it. Mrs Tarleton: youre not playing the game.

MRS TARLETON. I dont think youve behaved at all nicely, Mr Percival.

BENTLEY. I wouldnt have played you such a dirty trick, Joey. [*Struggling with a sob*] You beast.

LORD SUMMERHAYS. Bentley: you must control yourself. Let me say at the same time, Mr Percival, that my son seems to have been mistaken in regarding you either as his friend or as a gentleman.

PERCIVAL. Miss Tarleton: I'm suffering this for your sake. I ask you just to say that I am not to blame. Just that and nothing more.

HYPATIA [*gloating mischievously over his distress*] You chased me through the heather and kissed me. You shouldnt have done that if you were not in earnest.

PERCIVAL. Oh, this is really the limit. [*Turning desperately to Gunner*] Sir: I appeal to you. As a gentleman! as a man of honor! as a man bound to stand by another man! You were in that Turkish bath. You saw how it began. Could any man have behaved more correctly than I did? Is there a shadow of foundation for the accusations brought against me?

GUNNER [*sorely perplexed*] Well, what do you want me to say?

JOHNNY. He has said what he had to say already, hasnt he? Read that paper.

GUNNER. When I tell the truth, you make me go back on it. And now you want me to go back on myself! What is a man to do?

PERCIVAL [*patiently*] Please try to get your mind clear, Mr Brown. I pointed out to you that you could not, as a gentleman, disparage a lady's character. You agree with me, I hope.

GUNNER. Yes: that sounds all right.

PERCIVAL. But youre also bound to tell the truth. Surely youll not deny that.

GUNNER. Who's denying it? I say nothing against it.

PERCIVAL. Of course not. Well, I ask you to tell the truth simply and unaffectedly. Did you witness any improper conduct on my part when you were in the bath?

GUNNER. No, sir.

JOHNNY ⎱ ⎰Then what do you mean by saying that—
HYPATIA ⎬ ⎨Do you mean to say that I—
BENTLEY ⎱ ⎰Oh, you are a rotter. Youre afraid—

TARLETON [rising] Stop. [Silence]. Leave it at that. Enough said. You keep quiet, Johnny. Mr Percival: youre whitewashed. So are you, Patsy. Honors are easy. Lets drop the subject. The next thing to do is to open a subscription to start this young man on a ranch in some far country thats accustomed to be in a disturbed state. He—

MRS TARLETON. Now stop joking the poor lad, John: I wont have it. He's been worried to death between you all [To Gunner] Have you had your tea?

GUNNER. Tea? No: it's too early. I'm all right; only I had no dinner: I didnt think I'd want it. I didnt think I'd be alive.

MRS TARLETON. Oh, what a thing to say! You mustnt talk like that.

JOHNNY. He's out of his mind. He thinks it's past dinner-time.

MRS TARLETON. Oh, youve no sense, Johnny. He calls his lunch his dinner, and has his tea at half-past six. Havnt you, dear?

GUNNER [timidly] Hasnt everybody?

JOHNNY [laughing] Well, by George, thats not bad.

MRS TARLETON. Now dont be rude, Johnny: you

[231]

know I dont like it. [*To Gunner*] A cup of tea will pick you up.

GUNNER. I'd rather not. I'm all right.

TARLETON [*going to the sideboard*] Here! try a mouthful of sloe gin.

GUNNER. No, thanks, I'm a teetotaler. I cant touch alcohol in any form.

TARLETON. Nonsense! This isnt alcohol. Sloe gin. Vegetarian, you know.

GUNNER [*hesitating*] Is it a fruit beverage?

TARLETON. Of course it is. Fruit beverage. Here you are. [*He gives him a glass of sloe gin*].

GUNNER [*going to the sideboard*] Thanks. [*He begins to drink it confidently; but the first mouthful startles and almost chokes him*]. It's rather hot.

TARLETON. Do you good. Dont be afraid of it.

MRS TARLETON [*going to him*] Sip it, dear. Dont be in a hurry. *Gunner sips slowly, each sip making his eyes water.*

JOHNNY [*coming forward into the place left vacant by Gunner's visit to the sideboard*] Well, now that the gentleman has been attended to, I should like to know where we are. It may be a vulgar business habit; but I confess I like to know where I am.

TARLETON. I dont. Wherever you are, youre there anyhow. I tell you again, leave it at that.

BENTLEY. I want to know too. Hypatia's engaged to me.

HYPATIA. Bentley: if you insult me again: if you say another word, I'll leave the house and not enter it until you leave it.

JOHNNY. Put that in your pipe and smoke it, my boy.

BENTLEY [*inarticulate with fury and suppressed tears*] Oh! Beasts! Brutes!

MRS TARLETON. Now dont hurt his feelings, poor little lamb!

LORD SUMMERHAYS [*very sternly*] Bentley: you are not behaving well. You had better leave us until you have recovered yourself.

Bentley goes out in disgrace, but gets no further than half-way to the pavilion door, when, with a wild sob, he throws himself on the floor and begins to yell.

MRS TARLETON	[*running to him*] Oh, poor child, poor child! Dont cry, duckie: he didnt mean it: dont cry.
LORD SUMMER-HAYS	Stop that infernal noise, sir: do you hear? Stop it instantly.
JOHNNY	Thats the game he tried on me. There you are! Now, mother! Now, Patsy! You see for yourselves.
HYPATIA	[*covering her ears*] Oh you little wretch! Stop him, Mr Percival. Kick him.
TARLETON	Steady on, steady on. Easy, Bunny, easy.

LINA [*appearing at the door*] Leave him to me, Mrs Tarleton. [*Clear and authoritative*] Stand clear, please.

She quickly lifts the upper half of Bentley from the ground; dives under him; rises with his body hanging across her shoulders; and runs out with him.

BENTLEY [*in scared, sobered, humble tones as he is borne off*] What are you doing? Let me down. Please, Miss Szczepanowska—[*they pass out of hearing*].

An awestruck silence falls on the company as they speculate on Bentley's fate.

JOHNNY. I wonder what she's going to do with him.

HYPATIA. Spank him, I hope. Spank him hard.

LORD SUMMERHAYS. I hope so, I hope so. Tarleton: I'm beyond measure humiliated and annoyed by my son's behavior in your house. I had better take him home.

TARLETON. Not at all: not at all. Now, Chickabiddy: as Miss Lina has taken away Ben, suppose you take away Mr Brown for a while.

GUNNER [*with unexpected aggressiveness*] My name isnt Brown. [*They stare at him: he meets their stare defiantly, pugnacious with sloe gin; drains the last drop from his glass; throws it on the sideboard; and advances to the writing table*]. My name's Baker: Julius Baker. Mister Baker. If any man doubts it, I'm ready for him.

MRS TARLETON. John: you shouldnt have given him that sloe gin. It's gone to his head.

GUNNER. Dont you think it. Fruit beverages dont go to the head; and what matter if they did? I say nothing to you, maam: I regard you with respect and affection. [*Lachrymosely*] You were very good to my mother: my poor mother! [*Relapsing into his daring mood*] But I say my name's Baker; and I'm not to be treated as a child or made a slave of by any man. Baker is my name. Did you think I was going to give you my real name? Not likely! Not me!

TARLETON. So you thought of John Brown. That was clever of you.

GUNNER. Clever! Yes: we're not all such fools as you think: we clerks. It was the bookkeeper put me up to that. It's the only name that nobody gives as a false name, he said. Clever, eh? I should think so.

MRS TARLETON. Come now, Julius—

GUNNER [*reassuring her gravely*] Dont you be alarmed, maam. I know what is due to you as a lady and to myself as a gentleman. I regard you with respect and affection. If you had been my mother, as you ought to have been, I should have had more chance. But you shall have no cause to be ashamed of me. The strength of a chain is no greater than its weakest link; but the greatness of a poet is the greatness of his greatest moment. Shakespear used to get drunk. Frederick the Great ran away from a battle. But it was what they could rise to, not what they could sink to, that made them great. They werent good always; but they were good on their day. Well, on my day—on my day, mind you—I'm good for something too. I know that Ive made a silly exhibition of myself here. I know I didnt rise to the occasion. I know that if youd been my mother, youd have been ashamed of me. I lost my presence of mind: I was a contemptible coward. But [*slapping himself on the chest*] I'm not the man I was then. This is my day. Ive seen the tenth possessor of a foolish face carried out kicking and screaming by a woman. [*To Percival*] You crowed pretty big over me. You hypnotized me. But when you were put through the fire yourself, you were found wanting. I tell you straight I dont give a damn for you.

MRS TARLETON. No: thats naughty. You shouldnt say that before me.

GUNNER. I would cut my tongue out sooner than say anything vulgar in your presence; for I regard you with respect and affection. I was not swearing. I was affirming my manhood.

MRS TARLETON. What an idea! What puts all these things into your head?

GUNNER. Oh, dont think, because I'm only a clerk, that I'm not one of the intellectuals. I'm a reading man, a thinking man. I read in a book—a high class six shilling book—this precept: Affirm your manhood. It appealed to me. Ive always remembered it. I believe in it. I feel I must do it to recover your respect after my cowardly behavior. Therefore, I affirm it in your presence. I tell that man who insulted me that I dont give a damn for him. And neither I do.

TARLETON. I say, Summerhays: did you have chaps of this sort in Jinghiskahn?

LORD SUMMERHAYS. Oh yes: they exist everywhere: they are a most serious modern problem.

GUNNER. Yes. Youre right. [*Conceitedly*] I'm a problem. And I tell you that when we clerks realize that we're problems! well, look out: thats all.

LORD SUMMERHAYS [*suavely, to Gunner*] You read a great deal, you say?

GUNNER. Ive read more than any man in this room, if the truth were known, I expect. Thats whats going to smash up your Capitalism. The problems are beginning to read. Ha! We're free to do that here in England. What would you do with me in Jinghiskahn if you had me there?

LORD SUMMERHAYS. Well, since you ask me so directly, I'll tell you. I should take advantage of the fact that you have neither sense enough nor strength enough to know how to behave yourself in a difficulty of any sort. I should warn an intelligent and ambitious policeman that you are a troublesome person. The intelligent and ambitious policeman would take an early opportunity of upsetting your temper by ordering you to move on, and treading on your heels until you were provoked into obstructing an officer in the discharge of his duty. Any trifle of that sort would be sufficient to make a man like you lose your self-possession and put yourself in the wrong. You would then be charged and imprisoned until things quieted down.

GUNNER. And you call that justice!

LORD SUMMERHAYS. No. Justice was not my business. I had to govern a province; and I took the necessary steps to maintain order in it. Men are not governed by justice, but by law or persuasion. When they refuse to be governed by law or persuasion, they have to be governed by force or fraud, or both. I used both when law and persuasion failed me. Every ruler of men since the world began has done so, even when he has hated both fraud and force as heartily as I do. It is as well that you should know this, my young friend; so that you may recognize in time that anarchism is a game at which the police can beat you. What have you to say to that?

GUNNER. What have I to say to it! Well, I call it scandalous: thats what I have to say to it.

LORD SUMMERHAYS. Precisely: thats all anybody has to say to it, except the British public, which pretends not to believe it. And now let me ask you a sympathetic personal question. Havnt you a headache?

GUNNER. Well, since you ask me, I have. Ive over-excited myself.

MRS TARLETON. Poor lad! No wonder, after all youve gone through! You want to eat a little and to lie down. You come with me. I want you to tell me about your poor dear mother and about yourself. Come along with me. [*She leads the way to the inner door*].

GUNNER [*following her obediently*] Thank you kindly, madam. [*She goes out. Before passing out after her, he partly closes the door and lingers for a moment to whisper*] Mind: I'm not knuckling down to any man here. I knuckle down to Mrs Tarleton because she's a woman in a thousand. I affirm my manhood all the same. Understand: I dont give a damn for the lot of you. [*He hurries out, rather afraid of the consequences of this defiance, which has provoked Johnny to an impatient movement towards him*].

HYPATIA. Thank goodness he's gone! Oh, what a bore! WHAT a bore!!! Talk! talk! talk!

TARLETON. Patsy: it's no good. We're going to talk. And we're going to talk about you.

JOHNNY. It's no use shirking it, Pat. We'd better know where we are.

LORD SUMMERHAYS. Come, Miss Tarleton. Wont you sit down? I'm very tired of standing. [*Hypatia comes from the pavilion and takes a chair at the worktable. Lord Summerhays takes the opposite chair, on her right. Percival takes the chair Johnny placed for Lina on her arrival. Tarleton sits down at the end of the writing table. Johnny remains standing. Lord Summerhays continues, with a sigh of relief at being seated*] We shall now get the change of subject we are all pining for.

JOHNNY [*puzzled*] Whats that?

LORD SUMMERHAYS. The great question. The question that men and women will spend hours over without complaining. The question that occupies all the novel readers and all the playgoers. The question they never get tired of.

JOHNNY. But what question?

LORD SUMMERHAYS. The question which particular young man some young woman will mate with.

PERCIVAL. As if it mattered!

HYPATIA [*sharply*] Whats that you said?

PERCIVAL. I said: As if it mattered.

HYPATIA. I call that ungentlemanly.

PERCIVAL. Do you care about that? you who are so magnificently unladylike!

JOHNNY. Look here, Mr Percival: youre not supposed to insult my sister.

HYPATIA. Oh, shut up, Johnny. I can take care of myself. Dont you interfere.

JOHNNY. Oh, very well, If you choose to give yourself away like that—to allow a man to call you un-

[238]

ladylike and then to be unladylike, Ive nothing more to say.

HYPATIA. I think Mr Percival is most ungentlemanly; but I wont be protected. I'll not have my affairs interfered with by men on pretence of protecting me. I'm not your baby. If I interfered between you and a woman, you would soon tell me to mind my own business.

TARLETON. Children: dont squabble. Read Dr Watts. Behave yourselves.

JOHNNY. Ive nothing more to say; and as I dont seem to be wanted here, I shall take myself off [*He goes out with affected calm through the pavilion*].

TARLETON. Summerhays: a family is an awful thing, an impossible thing. Cat and dog. Patsy: I'm ashamed of you.

HYPATIA. I'll make it up with Johnny afterwards; but I really cant have him here sticking his clumsy hoof into my affairs.

LORD SUMMERHAYS. The question is, Mr Percival, are you really a gentleman, or are you not?

PERCIVAL. Was Napoleon really a gentleman or was he not? He made the lady get out of the way of the porter and said, "Respect the burden, madam." That was behaving like a very fine gentleman; but he kicked Volney for saying that what France wanted was the Bourbons back again. That was behaving rather like a navvy. Now I, like Napoleon, am not all one piece. On occasion, as you have all seen, I can behave like a gentleman. On occasion, I can behave with a brutal simplicity which Miss Tarleton herself could hardly surpass.

TARLETON. Gentleman or no gentleman, Patsy: what are your intentions?

HYPATIA. My intentions! Surely it's the gentleman who should be asked his intentions.

TARLETON. Come now, Patsy! none of that nonsense. Has Mr Percival said anything to you that I ought to know or that Bentley ought to know? Have you said anything to Mr Percival?

HYPATIA. Mr Percival chased me through the heather and kissed me.

LORD SUMMERHAYS. As a gentleman, Mr Percival, what do you say to that?

PERCIVAL. As a gentleman, I do not kiss and tell. As a mere man: a mere cad, if you like, I say that I did so at Miss Tarleton's own suggestion.

HYPATIA. Beast!

PERCIVAL. I dont deny that I enjoyed it. But I did not initiate it. And I began by running away.

TARLETON. So Patsy can run faster than you, can she?

PERCIVAL. Yes, when she is in pursuit of me. She runs faster and faster. I run slower and slower. And these woods of yours are full of magic. There was a confounded fern owl. Did you ever hear the churr of a fern owl? Did you ever hear it create a sudden silence by ceasing? Did you ever hear it call its mate by striking its wings together twice and whistling that single note that no nightingale can imitate? That is what happened in the woods when I was running away. So I turned; and the pursuer became the pursued.

HYPATIA. I had to fight like a wild cat.

LORD SUMMERHAYS. Please dont tell us this. It's not fit for old people to hear.

TARLETON. Come: how did it end?

HYPATIA. It's not ended yet.

TARLETON. How is it going to end?

HYPATIA. Ask him?

TARLETON. How is it going to end, Mr Percival?

PERCIVAL. I cant afford to marry, Mr Tarleton. Ive only a thousand a year until my father dies. Two people cant possibly live on that.

TARLETON. Oh, cant they? When *I* married, I should have been jolly glad to have felt sure of the quarter of it.

PERCIVAL. No doubt; but I am not a cheap person, Mr Tarleton. I was brought up in a household which cost at least seven or eight times that; and I am in constant money difficulties because I simply dont know how to live on the thousand a year scale. As to ask a woman to share my degrading poverty, it's out of the question. Besides, I'm rather young to marry. I'm only 28.

HYPATIA. Papa: buy the brute for me.

LORD SUMMERHAYS [*shrinking*] My dear Miss Tarleton: dont be so naughty. I know how delightful it is to shock an old man; but there is a point at which it becomes barbarous. Dont. Please dont.

HYPATIA. Shall I tell papa about you?

LORD SUMMERHAYS. Tarleton: I had better tell you that I once asked your daughter to become my widow.

TARLETON [*to Hypatia*] Why didnt you accept him, you young idiot?

LORD SUMMERHAYS. I was too old.

TARLETON. All this has been going on under my nose, I suppose. You run after young men; and old men run after you. And I'm the last person in the world to hear of it.

HYPATIA. How could I tell you?

LORD SUMMERHAYS. Parents and children, Tarleton.

TARLETON. Oh, the gulf that lies between them! the impassable, eternal gulf! And so I'm to buy the brute for you, eh?

HYPATIA. If you please, papa.

TARLETON. Whats the price, Mr Percival?

PERCIVAL. We might do with another fifteen hundred if my father would contribute. But I should like more.

TARLETON. It's purely a question of money with you, is it?

PERCIVAL [*after a moment's consideration*] Practically yes: it turns on that.

TARLETON. I thought you might have some sort of preference for Patsy, you know.

PERCIVAL. Well, but does that matter, do you think? Patsy fascinates me, no doubt. I apparently fascinate Patsy. But, believe me, all that is not worth considering. One of my three fathers (the priest) has married hundreds of couples: couples selected by one another, couples selected by the parents, couples forced to marry one another by circumstances of one kind or another; and he assures me that if marriages were made by putting all the men's names into one sack and the women's names into another, and having them taken out by a blindfolded child like lottery numbers, there would be just as high a percentage of happy marriages as we have here in England. He said Cupid was nothing but the blindfolded child: pretty idea that, I think! I shall have as good a chance with Patsy as with anyone else. Mind: I'm not bigoted about it. I'm not a doctrinaire: not the slave of a theory. You and Lord Summerhays are experienced married men. If you can tell me of any trustworthy method of selecting a wife, I shall be happy to make use of it. I await your suggestions. [*He looks with polite attention to Lord Summerhays, who, having nothing to say, avoids his eye. He looks to Tarleton, who purses his lips glumly and rattles his money in his pockets without a word*].

Apparently neither of you has anything to suggest. Then Patsy will do as well as another, provided the money is forthcoming.

HYPATIA. Oh, you beauty! you beauty!

TARLETON. When I married Patsy's mother, I was in love with her.

PERCIVAL. For the first time?

TARLETON. Yes: for the first time.

PERCIVAL. For the last time?

LORD SUMMERHAYS [revolted] Sir: you are in the presence of his daughter.

HYPATIA. Oh, dont mind me. I dont care. I'm accustomed to papa's adventures.

TARLETON [blushing painfully] Patsy, my child: that was not—not delicate.

HYPATIA. Well, papa, youve never shewn any delicacy in talking to me about my conduct; and I really dont see why I shouldnt talk to you about yours. It's such nonsense! Do you think young people dont know?

LORD SUMMERHAYS. I'm sure they dont feel. Tarleton: this is too horrible, too brutal. If neither of these young people have any—any—any—

PERCIVAL. Shall we say paternal sentimentality? I'm extremely sorry to shock you; but you must remember that Ive been educated to discuss human affairs with three fathers simultaneously. I'm an adult person. Patsy is an adult person. You do not inspire me with veneration. Apparently you do not inspire Patsy with veneration. That may surprise you. It may pain you. I'm sorry. It cant be helped. What about the money?

TARLETON. You dont inspire me with generosity, young man.

HYPATIA [laughing with genuine amusement] He had you there, Joey.

TARLETON. I havent been a bad father to you, Patsy.

HYPATIA. I dont say you have, dear. If only I could persuade you Ive grown up, we should get along perfectly.

TARLETON. Do you remember Bill Burt?

HYPATIA. Why?

TARLETON [to the others] Bill Burt was a laborer here. I was going to sack him for kicking his father. He said his father had kicked him until he was big enough to kick back. Patsy begged him off. I asked that man what it felt like the first time he kicked his father, and found that it was just like kicking any other man. He laughed and said that it was the old man that knew what it felt like. Think of that, Summerhays! think of that!

HYPATIA. I havnt kicked you, papa.

TARLETON. Youve kicked me harder than Bill Burt ever kicked.

LORD SUMMERHAYS. It's no use, Tarleton. Spare yourself. Do you seriously expect these young people, at their age, to sympathize with what this gentleman calls your paternal sentimentality?

TARLETON [wistfully] Is it nothing to you but paternal sentimentality, Patsy?

HYPATIA. Well, I greatly prefer your superabundant vitality, papa.

TARLETON [violently] Hold your tongue, you young devil. The young are all alike: hard, coarse, shallow, cruel, selfish, dirty-minded. You can clear out of my house as soon as you can coax him to take you; and the sooner the better. [To Percival] I think you said your price was fifteen hundred a year. Take it. And I wish you joy of your bargain.

PERCIVAL. If you wish to know who I am—

TARLETON. I dont care a tinker's curse who you are

or what you are. Youre willing to take that girl off my hands for fifteen hundred a year: thats all that concerns me. Tell her who you are if you like: it's her affair, not mine.

HYPATIA. Dont answer him, Joey: it wont last. Lord Summerhays, I'm sorry about Bentley; but Joey's the only man for me.

LORD SUMMERHAYS. It may—

HYPATIA. Please dont say it may break your poor boy's heart. It's much more likely to break yours.

LORD SUMMERHAYS. Oh!

TARLETON [springing to his feet] Leave the room. Do you hear: leave the room.

PERCIVAL. Arnt we getting a little cross? Dont be angry, Mr Tarleton. Read Marcus Aurelius.

TARLETON. Dont you dare make fun of me. Take your aeroplane out of my vinery and yourself out of my house.

PERCIVAL [rising, to Hypatia] I'm afraid I shall have to dine at the Beacon, Patsy.

HYPATIA [rising] Do. I dine with you.

TARLETON. Did you hear me tell you to leave the room?

HYPATIA. I did. [To Percival] You see what living with one's parents means, Joey. It means living in a house where you can be ordered to leave the room. Ive got to obey: it's his house, not mine.

TARLETON. Who pays for it? Go and support yourself as I did if you want to be independent.

HYPATIA. I wanted to and you wouldnt let me. How can I support myself when I'm a prisoner?

TARLETON. Hold your tongue.

HYPATIA. Keep your temper.

PERCIVAL [coming between them] Lord Summerhays: youll join me, I'm sure, in pointing out to both father and daughter that they have now reached that very common stage in family life at which anything but a blow would be an anti-climax. Do you seriously want to beat Patsy, Mr Tarleton?

TARLETON. Yes. I want to thrash the life out of her. If she doesnt get out of my reach, I'll do it. [*He sits down and grasps the writing table to restrain himself*].

HYPATIA [*coolly going to him and leaning with her breast on his writhing shoulders*] Oh, if you want to beat me just to relieve your feelings—just really and truly for the fun of it and the satisfaction of it, beat away. I dont grudge you that.

TARLETON [*almost in hysterics*] I used to think that this sort of thing went on in other families but that it never could happen in ours. And now—[*He is broken with emotion, and continues lamentably*] I cant say the right thing. I cant do the right thing. I dont know what is the right thing. I'm beaten; and she knows it. Summerhays: tell me what to do.

LORD SUMMERHAYS. When my council in Jinghis-kahn reached the point of coming to blows, I used to adjourn the sitting. Let us postpone the discussion. Wait until Monday: we shall have Sunday to quiet down in. Believe me, I'm not making fun of you; but I think theres something in this young gentleman's advice. Read something.

TARLETON. I'll read King Lear.

HYPATIA. Dont. I'm very sorry dear.

TARLETON. Youre not. Youre laughing at me. Serve me right! Parents and children! No man should know his own child. No child should know its own father. Let the family be rooted out of civilization! Let the human race be brought up in institutions!

HYPATIA. Oh yes. How jolly! You and I might be friends then; and Joey could stay to dinner.

TARLETON. Let him stay to dinner. Let him stay to breakfast. Let him spend his life here. Dont you say I drove him out. Dont you say I drove you out.

PERCIVAL. I really have no right to inflict myself on you. Dropping in as I did—

TARLETON. Out of the sky. Ha! Dropping in. The new sport of aviation. You just see a nice house; drop in; scoop up the man's daughter; and off with you again.

Bentley comes back, with his shoulders hanging as if he too had been exercised to the last pitch of fatigue. He is very sad. They stare at him as he gropes to Percival's chair.

BENTLEY. I'm sorry for making a fool of myself. I beg your pardon. Hypatia: I'm awfully sorry; but Ive made up my mind that I'll never marry. [*He sits down in deep depression*].

HYPATIA [*running to him*] How nice of you, Bentley! Of course you guessed I wanted to marry Joey. What did the Polish lady do to you?

BENTLEY [*turning his head away*] I'd rather not speak of her, if you dont mind.

HYPATIA. Youve fallen in love with her. [*She laughs*].

BENTLEY. It's beastly of you to laugh.

LORD SUMMERHAYS. You are not the first to fall today under the lash of that young lady's derision, Bentley.

Lina, her cap on, and her goggles in her hand, comes impetuously through the inner door.

LINA [*on the steps*] Mr Percival: can we get that aeroplane started again? [*She comes down and runs to the pavilion door*]. I must get out of this into the air: right up into the blue.

PERCIVAL. Impossible. The frame's twisted. The petrol has given out: thats what brought us down.

And how can we get a clear run to start with among these woods?

LINA [*swooping back through the middle of the pavilion*] We can straighten the frame. We can buy petrol at the Beacon. With a few laborers we can get her out on to the Portsmouth Road and start her along that.

TARLETON [*rising*] But why do you want to leave us, Miss Szcz?

LINA. Old pal: this is a stuffy house. You seem to think of nothing but making love. All the conversation here is about love-making. All the pictures are about love-making. The eyes of all of you are sheep's eyes. You are steeped in it, soaked in it: the very texts on the walls of your bedrooms are the ones about love. It is disgusting. It is not healthy. Your women are kept idle and dressed up for no other purpose than to be made love to. I have not been here an hour; and already everybody makes love to me as if because I am a woman it were my profession to be made love to. First you, old pal. I forgave you because you were nice about your wife.

HYPATIA. Oh! oh! oh! Oh, papa!

LINA. Then you, Lord Summerhays, come to me; and all you have to say is to ask me not to mention that you made love to me in Vienna two years ago. I forgave you because I thought you were an ambassador; and all ambassadors make love and are very nice and useful to people who travel. Then this young gentleman. He is engaged to this young lady; but no matter for that: he makes love to me because I carry him off in my arms when he cries. All these I bore in silence. But now comes your Johnny and tells me I'm a ripping fine woman, and asks me to marry him. I, Lina Szczepanowska, MARRY him!!!!! I do not mind this boy: he is a child: he loves me: I should

have to give him money and take care of him: that
would be foolish, but honorable. I do not mind you,
old pal: you are what you call an old —ouf? but you
do not offer to buy me: you say until we are tired—
until you are so happy that you dare not ask for more.
That is foolish too, at your age; but it is an adventure:
it is not dishonorable. I do not mind Lord Summerhays: it was in Vienna: they had been toasting him
at a great banquet: he was not sober. That is bad for
the health; but it is not dishonorable. But your
Johnny! Oh, your Johnny! with his marriage. He will
do the straight thing by me. He will give me a home, a
position. He tells me I must know that my present
position is not one for a nice woman. This to me, Lina
Szczepanowska! I am an honest woman: I earn my
living. I am a free woman: I live in my own house. I
am a woman of the world: I have thousands of friends:
every night crowds of people applaud me, delight in
me, buy my picture, pay hard-earned money to see
me. I am strong: I am skilful: I am brave: I am independent: I am unbought: I am all that a woman ought
to be; and in my family there has not been a single
drunkard for four generations. And this Englishman!
this linendraper! he dares to ask me to come and live
with him in this rrrrrrabbit hutch, and take my bread
from his hand, and ask him for pocket money, and
wear soft clothes, and be his woman! his wife! Sooner
that that, I would stoop to the lowest depths of my
profession. I would stuff lions with food and pretend
to tame them. I would deceive honest people's eyes
with conjuring tricks instead of real feats of strength
and skill. I would be a clown and set bad examples of
conduct to little children. I would sink yet lower and
be an actress or an opera singer, imperilling my soul
by the wicked lie of pretending to be somebody else.

All this I would do sooner than take my bread from the hand of a man and make him the master of my body and soul. And so you may tell your Johnny to buy an Englishwoman: he shall not buy Lina Szczepanowska; and I will not stay in the house where such dishonor is offered me. Adieu. [*She turns precipitately to go, but is faced in the pavilion doorway by Johnny, who comes in slowly, his hands in his pockets, meditating deeply*].

JOHNNY [*confidentially to Lina*] You wont mention our little conversation, Miss Shepanoska. It'll do no good; and I'd rather you didnt.

TARLETON. Weve just heard about it, Johnny.

JOHNNY [*shortly, but without ill-temper*] Oh: is that so?

HYPATIA. The cat's out of the bag, Johnny, about everybody. They were all beforehand with you: papa, Lord Summerhays, Bentley and all. Dont you let them laugh at you.

JOHNNY [*a grin slowly overspreading his countenance*] Well, theres no use my pretending to be surprised at you, Governor, is there? I hope you got it as hot as I did. Mind, Miss Shepanoska: it wasnt lost on me. I'm a thinking man. I kept my temper. Youll admit that.

LINA [*frankly*] Oh yes. I do not quarrel. You are what is called a chump; but you are not a bad sort of chump.

JOHNNY. Thank you. Well, if a chump may have an opinion, I should put it at this. You make, I suppose, ten pounds a night off your own bat, Miss Lina?

LINA [*scornfully*] Ten pounds a night! I have made ten pounds a minute.

JOHNNY [*with increased respect*] Have you indeed? I didnt know: youll excuse my mistake, I hope. But the principle is the same. Now I trust you wont be offended at what I'm going to say; but Ive thought about this and watched it in daily experience; and you may take it from me that the moment a woman becomes pecuniarily independent, she gets hold of the wrong end of the stick in moral questions.

LINA. Indeed! And what do you conclude from that, Mister Johnny?

JOHNNY. Well, obviously, that independence for women is wrong and shouldnt be allowed. For their own good, you know. And for the good of morality in general. You agree with me, Lord Summerhays, dont you?

LORD SUMMERHAYS. It's a very moral moral, if I may so express myself.

Mrs Tarleton comes in softly through the inner door.

MRS TARLETON. Dont make too much noise. The lad's asleep.

TARLETON. Chickabiddy: we have some news for you.

JOHNNY [*apprehensively*] Now theres no need, you know, Governor, to worry mother with everything that passes.

MRS TARLETON [*coming to Tarleton*] Whats been going on? Dont you hold anything back from me, John. What have you been doing?

TARLETON. Patsy isnt going to marry Bentley.

MRS TARLETON. Of course not. Is that your great news? I never believed she'd marry him.

TARLETON. Theres something else. Mr Percival here—

MRS TARLETON [*to Percival*] Are you going to marry Patsy?

PERCIVAL [*diplomatically*] Patsy is going to marry me, with your permission.

MRS TARLETON. Oh, she has my permission: she ought to have been married long ago.

HYPATIA. Mother!

TARLETON. Miss Lina here, though she has been so short a time with us, has inspired a good deal of attachment in—I may say in almost all of us. Therefore I hope she'll stay to dinner, and not insist in flying away in that aeroplane.

PERCIVAL. You must stay, Miss Szczepanowska. I cant go up again this evening.

LINA. Ive seen you work it. Do you think I require any help? And Bentley shall come with me as a passenger.

BENTLEY [*terrified*] Go up in an aeroplane! I darent.

LINA. You must learn to dare.

BENTLEY [*pale but heroic*] All right. I'll come.

LORD SUMMER- ⎫ ⎧ No, no, Bentley, impossible. I
HAYS ⎪ ⎪ shall not allow it.
MRS TARLETON ⎬ ⎨ Do you want to kill the child? He
⎭ ⎩ shant go.

BENTLEY. I will. I'll lie down and yell until you let me go. I'm not a coward. I wont be a coward.

LORD SUMMERHAYS. Miss Szczepanowska: my son is very dear to me. I implore you to wait until tomorrow morning.

LINA. There may be a storm tomorrow. And I'll go: storm or no storm. I must risk my life tomorrow.

BENTLEY. I hope there will be a storm.

LINA [*grasping his arm*] You are trembling.

BENTLEY. Yes: it's terror, sheer terror. I can hardly see. I can hardly stand. But I'll go with you.

LINA [*slapping him on the back and knocking a ghastly white smile into his face*] You shall. I like you, my boy. We go tomorrow, together.

BENTLEY. Yes: together: tomorrow.

TARLETON. Well, sufficient unto the day is the evil thereof. Read the old book.

MRS TARLETON. Is there anything else?

TARLETON. Well, I—er [*he addresses Lina, and stops*]. I—er [*he addresses Lord Summerhays, and stops*]. I—er [*he gives it up*]. Well, I suppose—er—I suppose theres nothing more to be said.

HYPATIA [*fervently*] Thank goodness!

Silent Audiences

MR G. B. SHAW'S BAN ON APPLAUSE

(Written statement presented as an
interview, in the *Daily Mail*, London,
28 February 1910)

"Why do you disappoint your first night audiences by
refusing to take a call? You know they are complaining of it," said a representative on Saturday in a
casual conversation with Mr. George Bernard Shaw
concerning his play "Misalliance" at the Repertory
Theatre.

"Well, there is nothing new in it. I never took a call
at the Court Theatre. I have never taken a call since
the days when there was an opposition to be faced and
talked to. All the public honours of a performance are
due to the performers; the author has no business
on the stage. He is not made up for it. And he often
makes his play ridiculous. Fancy delighting the audience with a touching love scene that makes all the
young people believe that the author must be like the
portraits of Byron, and then an elderly buffer like me
trotting out before the curtain and ruining the illusion.

"Besides, that audience the other night nearly
destroyed my play. Of course, they meant well. They
gratified and encouraged us, and we love them for it.
But consider what the wretches did. They actually
added twenty-five minutes to the schedule time of my
play by their constant interruptions—their reckless
bursts of applause and laughter. Why can't they
laugh internally, like old Weller in 'Pickwick'?

JOKES BY THE HANDFUL

"How can any play be decently performed when the actors have to wait for two minutes between every sentence while the audience makes a disturbance? Of course, one likes to see them enjoying themselves; but they lose a great deal by it. They ought to know by this time that I do not dole out solitary jokes. I fling them out by handfuls; so that if you laugh at the first you lose the next six. In the modern drama, too, laughter and tears come together; if you guffaw at a joke, you may profane a deep stroke of pathos."

"But do you expect the audience to sit in silence?"

"They do in Berlin, where my plays are an institution. But I propose to get over the difficulty by enclosing the gallery with thick sound-proof glass and letting the people hear the dialogue by electrophone. Then they can laugh their fill without interrupting the performance; and when they realise that every outburst loses them two minutes of the play they will learn self-restraint.

APPLAUSE AND INTERRUPTION.

"But does not applause hearten up the actors and improve the play?"

"Actors need no such encouragement. They are serious artists doing serious service to the community, and practising a high profession. Bishops preach without applause. Barristers plead without applause. I can write a play without applause: do you think actors cannot act it under the same conditions? Applaud as much as you like when the curtain comes down; and show your sincerity by coming again; but don't interrupt a work of art like the performance of a play any more than you would interrupt a symphony or a church service."

The Repertory Theatre

(An interview, drafted by Shaw, *The Observer*, 12 June 1910)

"*The present season of the Repertory Company at the Duke of York's Theatre will end next Friday.*

"*The new repertory season will follow 'Peter Pan' (after Christmas). Mr. Somerset Maugham will write a special play for the Repertory Theatre, and there will also be works from Mr. Henry Arthur Jones, Mr. Alfred Sutro, Mr. Haddon Chambers, and Mr. Henry James.*

"*Mr. J. M. Barrie will provide a full evening's play.*"

(Extract from Mr. Frohman's announcement, which contains no reference to Mr. Bernard Shaw, Mr. Granville Barker, Mr. John Galsworthy and other dramatists associated with the original plans for the Repertory Theatre.)

This announcement formed the subject yesterday of the following conversation between Mr. Bernard Shaw and a representative of the THE OBSERVER:—

"Of course you have seen the announcement of the programme of the Repertory Theatre for 1911 ?"

"Yes."

"Your name and that of Mr. Granville Barker are conspicuously absent?"

"That is so."

"Does that mean that you are both too much a matter of course to be mentioned; or can it be that you have withdrawn from the scheme after allowing several of your plays to be announced in the preliminary prospectus?"

"It means that Mr. Frohman, having tried a programme of plays by myself, Mr. Granville Barker,

[256]

Mr. Galsworthy, and so forth is going to try again with a programme of plays by other authors."

"Why?"

"You must ask Mr. Frohman."

"Have you not asked Mr. Frohman?"

"I never ask indiscreet questions. Besides, Mr. Frohman is entitled to have his proceedings explained by himself, and not by me. And remember that he is in no way bound to answer such a question at all, because it cannot be answered without such a disclosure not only of his own business affairs, but those of his authors, as no man engaged in a private business enterprise is free to make."

"The public cannot be prevented from inferring that the higher drama does not pay?"

"The public does not know enough about economics to understand what paying means. The higher drama —since you are kind enough to apply that term to my plays and those of Mr. Barker and Mr. Galsworthy— paid at the Court Theatre in the sense that everybody concerned got a living out of it. But if anybody supposes that the higher drama will pay at the rate of from 50 per cent. to 100 per cent. per night, they little know the condition of public taste in this country. Yet as long as such profits are possible in the theatre, plays which require some nursing through a period of public indifference and violent Press hostility before they begin to return a steady humdrum ten to twenty per cent. will be regarded as failures.

"SCRAP YOUR FAILURES."

"Now, the first rule of modern commercial management—a rule which is an absolute necessity of the game—is to cut your failures—meaning the pieces which do not fill the house to the doors—and cut them promptly, no matter how much you have spent on them, scrapping failure after failure until you hit on a success. You must never argue with the public or with the Press. You take your defeats like a man, and you forget all about them when the successes come. But on this method you can have no higher drama at all, for both the Press and the public regard the higher drama as so much nasty medicine. The taste for it has to be laboriously acquired; and even when people like it they have to be told that they like it before they will recognise the fact.

"At the Repertory Theatre there were critics who laughed so much over 'Misalliance' and 'The Madras House' that there was some question of asking them to leave the theatre if they could not control themselves, as they were delaying the performance; yet these very critics informed the public next morning that they had suffered the weariest agonies of boredom, simply because that is the customary thing to write about such plays.

"They write it just as they wear two-inch collars. For the same reason they describe me on all other occasions as one of our leading dramatists and an amazingly brilliant and witty writer, because that, too, is the fashion. As to noticing their own sensations or forming an independent opinion, they are too shy, too sheepish to do anything of the sort. Unfortunately, the prejudice they create, the impression of ignominious failure they set up at each new production, has to be lived down; and the process is much more difficult in a repertory theatre than in a short-run theatre like the Court.

"My 'Getting Married,' which was frantically denounced by the critics, beat them hollow in a week, because it was played every night: but it takes longer when the performances are only occasional.

MR. FROHMAN'S "HEROIC" EXPENDITURE.

"Now, nobody can reasonably ask Mr. Frohman to undertake campaigns for the education of the public and the living down of the wild vituperation of the Press. With his large operations and his heroic scale of expenditure there is no time, no room for such campaigning. You must remember that he is no desperate adventurer in new forms of drama, compelled to produce plays by me and Mr. Barker and our like, or else to go without plays at all. He always has a more lucrative alternative under his hand; and, as everybody who understands modern competitive business knows, he is not really free to lose his opportunities.

"When Messrs. Vedrenne and Barker produced 'John Bull's Other Island' and 'The Voysey Inheritance,' they had no alternative open to them: it was that or nothing. Mr. Frohman will never to the end of his life be without a handful of plays that will produce, for a couple of months at all events, a bigger profit than either of these works within the same period.

"Grasp this fact, and you will understand how it was that though Mr. Barker's play and mine did quite as well as our old Court successes, Mr. Frohman was forced to drop them like hot potatoes the moment he realised what he was up against.

"The catastrophe was a perfectly friendly one. I foretold it; but, as usual, everybody thought I was jesting, and Mr. Frohman was far too sanguine and friendly to admit the possibility of failure until it was forced on him by the hard facts. I urged him to look into the figures of the past enterprises; but you might as well offer figures to Don Quixote. American buoyancy is proof against all figures. What an American wants is adventure, with huge risks and wild possibilities, not the sober, modest certainties of classic art."

THE VALUE OF FAILURE.

"Then, why did you go into the scheme if you foresaw that it would fail?"

"For two reasons. First, I have too much sense to sit twiddling my thumbs when there is work to be done, merely because I do not think it will fulfil all the hopes that are based on it. The season at the Duke of York's was well worth doing. Second, because I shall never be able to persuade English men of business to endow the National Theatre unless I am in a position to say that I have exhausted all the resources of private enterprise. People would not believe that where Messrs. Vedrenne and Barker, at the little Court Theatre, in Sloane-square, had made a modest success, a great commercial manager like Mr. Frohman could not have made a triumphant one. Well, Mr. Frohman did his best, and was knocked out in a week."

"But he announces that he is going on?"

"Yes, with plays by Mr. Barrie, Mr. Henry Arthur Jones, Mr. Somerset Maugham and all the most popular playwrights of the day. What will be the inevitable result? If all the plays are popular successes, they must be run simultaneously at separate theatres. Else all those that draw £20 less than the most popular of them must be scrapped, exactly as 'Misalliance' and 'The Madras House' were scrapped. Is it likely that these authors will consent to take such a chance with my awful example staring them in the face? The scheme is commercially impossible, only Mr. Frohman does not know when he is beaten."

THE DRAMA OF THE TWENTY-FIRST CENTURY.

"Then there will be no more performances of your plays and Mr. Barker's until the National Theatre is an accomplished fact?"

"Bless me, you don't suppose the National Theatre will be a Shaw-Barker theatre, do you? An English National Theatre will venture on its first performance of a play by me, with great misgiving and in the teeth of much opposition, on the occasion of the centenary of my death."

"Then Shaw and Barker are to vanish from the stage?"

"Not at all. We shall presently break out in a new place, and show our friend Frohman how to perform commercial impossibilities. London and its Press may kick against the pricks as hard as it likes; but it has got to come along. It has pulled against us all through, and it is pulling still and will keep on pulling; but it is already out of sight of the ground it was struggling to hold against us in 1904. The struggle has made frightful drafts on our energies; but, after all, what are our energies for? So don't congratulate yourself prematurely: we shall be at you again before you have finished chuckling over this defeat of ours."

"May I conclude that there is a new scheme on hand?"

"Conclude nothing until the curtain has gone up on my next play and Barker's, or until we are both dead. Good morning."

PLAYS AND CONVERSATIONS.

"One more question, Mr. Shaw. Why do you call your plays conversations?"

"Why not?"

"Well, all plays are necessarily conversations, are they not?"

"You are the first person on the London Press who has been intelligent enough to put your finger on that glaring fact. Well, I wanted to find out whether the critics could really tell the difference between a farce and a tragedy, or a melodrama and a high comedy, unless the author told them. I found they couldn't. 'Misalliance' was a specially developed example of high comedy, observing the strictest conditions as to unity of time and place. And the poor critics went about bleating that it was not a play, but only a conversation. They will presently discover that Beethoven's 'Eroica' is not a symphony, but only a musical score. They really are blazing duffers. They walk into my traps every time."

"Yes, Mr. Shaw. Good morning."

Author's Note

(From the programme of the production
by the Macdona Players at the Royal
Court Theatre, London, 17 March 1930)

A word of explanation is needed when presenting a play of contemporary life which though virtually new to the London stage, yet contains such anachronisms as allusions to Russia as it was under the Tsars; treats aeroplanes as marvellous and perilous spectacles at which whole households rush out of doors to gaze;

and represents an elderly lady as scandalised by having to entertain one of her own sex in the costume of an air pilot.

Misalliance was written twenty years ago as a contribution to an attempt made by the late Charles Frohman to establish a repertory theatre in London. It actually reached two or three performances at the Duke of York's Theatre before the attempt collapsed. Frohman was of a sanguine temperament: his successes in the ordinary routine of theatrical management had persuaded him that it needed only his lucky touch to achieve the same financial results with a repertory of highbrow plays. The first week's receipts shattered that illusion; and as action and re-action are equal and opposite, the panic in which he abandoned the enterprise was proportionate to the high spirits in which he had entered on it.

I suppose I must take my share with Sir James Barrie and Mr. Harley Granville-Barker of the responsibility for having lured our late friend into an adventure which obviously could not have turned out as lucrative as he expected. Happily, Mr. Galsworthy's Justice consoled him with *kudos*, and finally rescued him by a triumphant revival of Trelawny of the Wells. Trelawny saved the situation for Frohman; but Mr. Granville-Barker and myself, having each written and produced a full dress play only to have the two extinguished and thrown on our hands as failures, were left in the soup. Mr. Granville-Barker's play, The Madras House, in due time came to its own in a brilliant revival at the Ambassador's Theatre; but Misalliance received its *coup de grace* from an American manager who, believing as American managers are apt to do that he knew exactly what Misalliance needed to make it a great popular success, cut out what he considered the highbrow parts and made the rest unintelligible, with the result that the apparent failure in London became a real and crushing one on the other side of the pond.

And so the play lay derelict as far as the theatre was concerned until Mr. Charles Macdona, who really does know how to run a repertory theatre, and is prepared to live dangerously by doing it, picked it up and experimented with it in the provinces. It immediately showed signs of life, and I have been unable to prevent him from bringing it to a second birth in London. I trust it will not prove a miscarriage, but I cannot deny that much water, and—alas!—a good deal of blood has flowed through the bridges since it was a more or less topical play; and I beg your indulgence for it accordingly.

G. BERNARD SHAW

St. Patrick's Day, 1930.

The Dark Lady of the Sonnets

WITH

Preface

New Prologue

Note to the New York Press

Mr Bernard Shaw and Shakespeare

Mr Bernard Shaw's New Play

" Stratford Must Not Wait"

G. B. S. on the National Theatre

Composition begun 17 June 1910; completed 20 June 1910. First published in German translation, as *Die schwarze Dame der Sonette*, in the *Neue Freie Presse* (Vienna), 25 December 1910. Published in the *English Review* and *Redbook Magazine* (New York), January 1911. First collected in *Misalliance, The Dark Lady of the Sonnets*, and *Fanny's First Play*, 1914. First presented at *His Majesty's Theatre*, London, on 24 November 1910, for two charity matinées in behalf of the Shakespeare Memorial National Theatre.

The Warder   *Hugh B. Tabberer*
William Shakespear   *Harley Granville Barker*
Queen Elizabeth   *Suzanne Sheldon*
Mary Fitton   *Mona Limerick*

Period—The spacious times of Great Elizabeth. Fin de siècle 15–1600

Scene—*The Terrace, Whitehall Palace. Midsummer Night*

Preface

Contents

HOW THE PLAY CAME TO BE WRITTEN

I had better explain why, in this little *pièce d'occasion*, written for a performance in aid of the funds of the project of establishing a National Theatre as a memorial to Shakespear, I have identified the Dark Lady with Mistress Mary Fitton. First, let me say that I do not contend that the Dark Lady was Mary Fitton, because when the case in Mary's favor (or against her, if you please to consider that the Dark Lady was no better than she ought to have been) was complete, a portrait of Mary came to light and turned out to be that of a fair lady, not of a dark one. That settles the question, if the portrait is authentic, which I see no reason to doubt, and the lady's hair undyed, which is perhaps less certain. Shakespear rubbed in the lady's complexion in his sonnets mercilessly; for in his day black hair was as unpopular as red hair was in the early days of Queen Victoria. Any tinge lighter than raven black must be held fatal to the strongest claim to be the Dark Lady. And so, unless it can be shewn that Shakespear's sonnets exasperated Mary Fitton into dyeing her hair and getting painted in false colors, I must give up all pretence that my play is historical. The later suggestion of Mr Acheson that the Dark Lady, far from being a maid of honor, kept a tavern in Oxford, and was the mother of Davenant the poet, is the one I should have adopted had I wished to be up to date. Why, then, did I introduce the Dark Lady as Mistress Fitton?

Well, I had two reasons. The play was not to have been written by me at all, but by Dame Edith Lyttelton; and it was she who suggested a scene of jealousy between Queen Elizabeth and the Dark Lady at the expense of the unfortunate Bard. Now this, if the Dark Lady was a maid of honor, was quite easy. If she were a tavern landlady, it would have strained all probability. So I stuck to Mary Fitton. But I had another and more personal reason. I was, in a manner, present at the birth of the Fitton theory. Its parent and I had become acquainted; and he used to consult me on obscure passages in the sonnets, on which, as far as I can remember, I never succeeded in throwing the faintest light, at a time when nobody else thought my opinion, on that or any other subject, of the slightest importance. I thought it would be friendly to immortalize him, as the silly literary saying is, much as Shakespear immortalized Mr W. H., as he said he would, simply by writing about him.

Let me tell the story formally.

THOMAS TYLER

Throughout the eighties at least, and probably for some years before, the British Museum reading room was used daily by a gentleman of such astonishing and crushing ugliness that no one who had once seen him could ever thereafter forget him. He was of fair complexion, rather golden red than sandy; aged between forty-five and sixty; and dressed in frock coat and tall hat of presentable but never new appearance. His figure was rectangular, waistless, neckless, ankleless, of middle height, looking shortish because, though he was not particularly stout, there was nothing slender about him. His ugliness was not unamiable: it was accidental, external, excrescential. Attached to his face from the left ear to the point of his chin was a monstrous goitre, which hung down to his collar bone, and was very inadequately balanced by a smaller one on his right eyelid. Nature's malice was so overdone in his case that it somehow failed to produce the effect of repulsion it seemed to have aimed at. When you first met Thomas Tyler you could think of nothing else but whether surgery could really do nothing for him. But after a very brief acquaintance you never thought of his disfigurements at all, and talked to him as you might to Romeo or Lovelace; only, so many people, especially women, would not risk the preliminary ordeal, that he remained a man apart and a bachelor all his days. I am not to be frightened or prejudiced by a tumor; and I struck up a cordial acquaintance with him, in the course of which he kept me pretty closely on the track of his work at the Museum, in which I was then, like himself, a daily reader.

He was by profession a man of letters of an uncommercial kind. He was a specialist in pessimism; had made a translation of Ecclesiastes of which eight copies a year were sold; and followed up the pessimism of Shakespear and Swift with keen interest. He delighted in a hideous conception which he called the theory of the cycles, according to which the history of mankind and the universe keeps eternally repeating itself without the slightest variation throughout all eternity; so that he had lived and died and had his goitre before and would live and die and have it again and again and again. He liked to believe that nothing that happened to him was completely novel: he was persuaded that he often had some recollection of its previous occurrence in the last cycle. He hunted out allusions to this favorite theory in his three favorite pessimists. He tried his hand occasionally at deciphering ancient inscriptions, reading them as people seem to read the stars, by discovering bears and bulls and swords and goats where, as it seems to me, no sane human being can see anything but stars higgledy-piggledy. Next to the translation of Ecclesiastes, his *magnum opus* was his work on Shakespear's Sonnets, in which he accepted a previous identification of Mr W. H., the "onlie begetter" of the sonnets, with the Earl of Pembroke (William Herbert), and promulgated his own identification of Mistress Mary Fitton with the Dark Lady. Whether he was right or wrong about the Dark Lady did not matter urgently to me: she might have been Maria Tompkins for all I cared. But Tyler would have it that she was Mary Fitton;

and he tracked Mary down from the first of her marriages in her teens to her tomb in Cheshire, whither he made a pilgrimage and whence returned in triumph with a picture of her statue, and the news that he was convinced she was a dark lady by traces of paint still discernible.

In due course he published his edition of the Sonnets, with the evidence he had collected. He lent me a copy of the book, which I never returned. But I reviewed it in the Pall Mall Gazette on the 7th of January 1886, and thereby let loose the Fitton theory in a wider circle of readers than the book could reach. Then Tyler died, sinking unnoted like a stone in the sea. I observe that Mr Acheson, Mrs Davenant's champion, calls him Reverend. It may very well be that he got his knowledge of Hebrew in reading for the Church; and there was always something of the clergyman or the schoolmaster in his dress and air. Possibly he may actually have been ordained. But he never told me that or anything else about his affairs; and his black pessimism would have shot him violently out of any church at present established in the West. We never talked about affairs: we talked about Shakespear, and the Dark Lady, and Swift, and Koheleth, and the cycles, and the mysterious moments when a feeling came over us that this had happened to us before, and about the forgeries of the Pentateuch which were offered for sale to the British Museum, and about literature and things of the spirit generally. He always came to my desk at the Museum and spoke to me about something or other, no doubt finding that people who were keen on this sort of conversation were rather scarce. He remains a vivid spot of memory in the void of my forgetfulness, a quite considerable and dignified soul in a grotesquely disfigured body.

FRANK HARRIS

To the review in the Pall Mall Gazette I attribute, rightly or wrongly, the introduction of Mary Fitton to Mr Frank Harris. My reason for this is that Mr Harris wrote a play about Shakespear and Mary Fitton; and when I, as a pious duty to Tyler's ghost, reminded the world that it was to Tyler we owed the Fitton theory, Frank Harris, who clearly had not a notion of what had first put Mary into his head, believed, I think, that I had invented Tyler expressly for his discomfiture; for the stress I laid on Tyler's claims must have seemed unaccountable and perhaps malicious on the assumption that he was to me a mere name among the thousands of names in the British Museum catalogue. Therefore I make it clear that I had and have personal reasons for remembering Tyler, and for regarding myself as in some sort charged with the duty of reminding the world of his work. I am sorry for his sake that Mary's portrait is fair, and that Mr W. H. has veered round again from Pembroke to Southampton; but even so his work was not wasted: it is by exhausting all the hypotheses that we reach the verifiable one; and after all, the wrong road always leads somewhere.

Frank Harris's play was written long before mine. I read it in manuscript before the Shakespear Memorial National Theatre was mooted; and if there is anything except the Fitton theory (which is Tyler's property) in my play which is also in Mr Harris's it was I who annexed it from him and not he from me. It does not matter anyhow, because this play of mine is a brief trifle, and full of manifest impossibilities at that; whilst Mr Harris's play is serious both in size, intention, and quality. But there could not in the nature of things be much resemblance, because Frank conceives Shakespear to have been a broken-hearted, melancholy, enormously sentimental person, whereas I am convinced that he was very like myself: in fact, if I had been born in 1556 instead of in 1856, I should have taken to blank verse and given Shakespear a harder run for his money than all the other Elizabethans put together. Yet the success of Frank Harris's book on Shakespear gave me great delight.

To those who know the literary world of London there was a sharp stroke of ironic comedy in the irresistible verdict in its favor. In critical literature there is one prize that is always open to competition, one blue ribbon that always carries the highest critical rank with it. To win, you must write the best book of your generation on Shakespear. It is felt on all sides that to do this a certain fastidious refinement, a delicacy of taste, a correctness of manner and tone, and high academic distinction in addition to the indispensable scholarship and literary reputation, are needed; and men who pretend to these qualifications are constantly looked to with a gentle expectation that presently they will achieve the great feat. Now if there is a man on earth who is the utter contrary of everything that this description implies; whose very existence is an insult to the ideal it realizes; whose eye disparages, whose resonant voice denounces, whose cold shoulder jostles every decency, every delicacy, every amenity, every dignity, every sweet usage of that quiet life of mutual admiration in which perfect Shakespearean appreciation is expected to arise, that man is Frank Harris. Here is one who is extraordinarily qualified, by a range of sympathy and understanding that extends from the ribaldry of a buccaneer to the shyest tenderness of the most sensitive poetry, to be all things to all men, yet whose proud humor it is to be to every man, provided the man is eminent and pretentious, the champion of his enemies. To the Archbishop he is an atheist, to the atheist a Catholic mystic, to the Bismarckian Imperialist an Anacharsis Klootz, to Anacharsis Klootz a Washington, to Mrs Proudie a Don Juan, to Aspasia a John Knox: in short, to everyone his complement rather than his counterpart, his antagonist rather than his fellow-creature. Always provided, however, that the persons thus affronted are respectable persons. Sophie Perovskaia, who perished on the scaffold for blowing Alexander II to fragments, may perhaps have echoed Hamlet's

Oh God, Horatio, what a wounded name—
Things standing thus unknown—I leave behind!

but Frank Harris, in his Sonia, has rescued her from that injustice, and enshrined her among the saints. He has lifted the Chicago anarchists out of their infamy, and shewn that, compared with the Capitalism that killed them, they were heroes and martyrs. He has done this with the most unusual power of conviction. The story, as he tells it, inevitably and irresistibly displaces all the vulgar, mean, purblind, spiteful versions. There is a precise realism and an unsmiling, measured, determined sincerity which gives a strange dignity to the work of one whose fixed practice and ungovernable impulse it is to kick conventional dignity whenever he sees it.

HARRIS "DURCH MITLEID WISSEND"

Frank Harris is everything except a humorist, not, apparently, from stupidity, but because scorn overcomes humor in him. Nobody ever dreamt of reproaching Milton's Lucifer for not seeing the comic side of his fall; and nobody who has read Mr Harris's stories desires to have them lightened by chapters from the hand of Artemus Ward. Yet he knows the taste and the value of humour. He was one of the few men of letters who really appreciated Oscar Wilde, though he did not rally fiercely to Wilde's side until the world deserted Oscar in his ruin. I myself was present at a curious meeting between the two, when Harris, on the eve of the Queensbury trial, prophesied to Wilde with miraculous precision exactly what immediately afterwards happened to him, and warned him to leave the country. It was the first time within my knowledge that such a forecast proved true. Wilde, though under no illusion as to the folly of the quite unselfish suit-at-law he had been persuaded to begin, nevertheless so miscalculated the force of the social vengeance he was unloosing on himself that he fancied it could be stayed by putting up the editor of The Saturday Review (as Mr Harris then was) to declare that he considered Dorian Grey a highly moral book, which it certainly is. When Harris foretold him the truth, Wilde denounced him as a fainthearted friend who was failing him in his hour of need, and left the room in anger. Harris's idiosyncratic power of pity saved him from feeling or shewing the smallest resentment; and events presently proved to Wilde how insanely he had been advised in taking the action, and how accurately Harris had gauged the situation.

The same capacity for pity governs Harris's study of Shakespear, whom, as I have said, he pities too much; but that he is not insensible to humor is shewn not only by his appreciation of Wilde, but by the fact that the group of contributors who made his editorship of The Saturday Review so remarkable, and of whom I speak none the less highly because I happened to be one of them myself, were all, in their various ways, humorists.

"SIDNEY'S SISTER: PEMBROKE'S MOTHER"

And now to return to Shakespear. Though Mr Harris followed Tyler in identifying Mary Fitton as the Dark Lady, and the Earl of Pembroke as the addressee of the other sonnets and the man who made love successfully to Shakespear's mistress, he very characteristically refuses to follow Tyler on one point, though for the life of me I cannot remember whether it was one of the surmises which Tyler published, or only one which he submitted to me to see what I would say about it, just as he used to submit difficult lines from the sonnets.

This surmise was that "Sidney's sister: Pembroke's mother" set Shakespear on to persuade Pembroke to marry, and that this was the explanation of those earlier sonnets which so persistently and unnaturally urged matrimony on Mr W. H. I take this to be one of the brightest of Tyler's ideas, because the persuasions in the sonnets are unaccountable and out of character unless they were offered to please somebody whom Shakespear desired to please, and who took a motherly interest in Pembroke. There is a further temptation in the theory for me. The most charming of all Shakespear's old women, indeed the most charming of all his women, young or old, is the Countess of Rousillon in All's Well That Ends Well. It has a certain individuality among them which suggests a portrait. Mr Harris will have it that all Shakespear's nice old women are drawn from his beloved mother;

[278]

but I see no evidence whatever that Shakespear's mother was a particularly nice woman or that he was particularly fond of her. That she was a simple incarnation of extravagant maternal pride like the mother of Coriolanus in Plutarch, as Mr Harris asserts, I cannot believe: she is quite as likely to have borne her son a grudge for becoming "one of these harlotry players" and disgracing the Ardens. Anyhow, as a conjectural model for the Countess of Rousillon, I prefer that one of whom Jonson wrote

> Sidney's sister: Pembroke's mother:
> Death ere thou has slain another,
> Learned and fair and good as she,
> Time shall throw a dart at thee.

But Frank will not have her at any price, because his ideal Shakespear is rather like a sailor in a melodrama; and a sailor in a melodrama must adore his mother. I do not at all belittle such sailors. They are the emblems of human generosity; but Shakespear was not an emblem; he was a man and the author of Hamlet, who had no illusions about his mother. In weak moments one almost wishes he had.

SHAKESPEAR'S SOCIAL STANDING

On the vexed question of Shakespear's social standing Mr Harris says that Shakespear "had not had the advantage of a middle-class training." I suggest that Shakespear missed this questionable advantage, not because he was socially too low to have attained to it, but because he conceived himself as belonging to the upper class from which our public school boys are now drawn. Let Mr Harris survey for a moment the field of contemporary journalism. He will see there some men who have the very characteristics from which he infers that Shakespear was at a social disadvantage through his lack of middle-class training. They are rowdy, ill-mannered, abusive, mischievous, fond of quoting obscene schoolboy anecdotes, adepts in that sort of blackmail which consists in mercilessly libelling and insulting every writer whose opinions are sufficiently heterodox to make it almost impossible for him to risk perhaps five years of a slender income by an appeal to a prejudiced orthodox jury; and they see nothing in all this cruel blackguardism but an uproariously jolly rag, although they are by no means without genuine literary ability, a love of letters, and even some artistic conscience. But he will find not one of the models of this type (I say nothing of mere imitators of it) below the rank that looks at the middle class, not humbly and enviously from below, but insolently from above. Mr Harris himself notes Shakespear's contempt for the tradesman and mechanic, and his incorrigible addiction to smutty jokes. He does us the public service of sweeping away the familiar plea of the Bardolatrous ignoramus, that Shakespear's coarseness was part of the manners of his time, putting his pen with precision on the one name, Spenser, that is necessary to expose such a libel on Elizabethan decency. There was nothing whatever to prevent Shakespear from being as decent as More was before him, or Bunyan after him, and as self-respecting as Raleigh or Sidney, except the tradition of his class, in which education or statesmanship may no doubt be acquired by those who have a turn for them, but in which insolence, derision, profligacy, obscene jesting, debt contracting, and rowdy mischievousness, give continual scandal to the pious, serious, industrious, solvent bourgeois. No other class is infatuated enough to believe that gentlemen are born and not made by a very elaborate process of culture. Even kings are taught and coached and drilled from their earliest boyhood to play their part. But the man of family (I am convinced that Shakespear took that view of himself) will plunge into society without a lesson in table manners, into politics without a lesson in history, into the city without a lesson in business, and into the army without a lesson in honor.

It has been said, with the object of proving Shakespear a laborer, that he could hardly write his name. Why ? Because he "had not the advantage of a middle-class training." Shakespear himself tells us, through Hamlet, that gentlemen purposely wrote badly lest they should be mistaken for scriveners; but most of them, then as now, wrote badly because they could not write any better. In short, the whole range of Shakespear's foibles: the snobbishness, the naughtiness, the contempt for tradesmen and mechanics, the assumption that witty conversation can only mean smutty conversation, the flunkeyism towards social superiors and insolence towards social inferiors, the easy ways with servants which is seen not only between The Two Gentlemen of Verona and their valets, but in the affection and respect inspired by a great servant like Adam: all these are the characteristics of Eton and Harrow, not of the public elementary or private adventure school. They prove, as everything we know about Shakespeare suggests, that he thought of the Shakespears and Ardens as families of consequence, and regarded himself as a gentleman under a cloud through his father's ill luck in business, and never for a moment as a man of the people. This is at once the explanation of and excuse for his snobbery. He was not a parvenu trying to cover his humble origin with

a purchased coat of arms: he was a gentleman resuming what he conceived to be his natural position
as soon as he gained the means to keep it up.

THIS SIDE IDOLATRY

There is another matter which I think Mr Harris
should ponder. He says that Shakespear was but
"little esteemed by his own generation." He even
describes Jonson's description of his "little Latin
and less Greek" as a sneer, whereas it occurs in an
unmistakeably sincere eulogy of Shakespear, written
after his death, and is clearly meant to heighten the
impression of Shakespear's prodigious natural
endowments by pointing out that they were not due
to scholastic acquirements. Now there is a sense in
which it is true enough that Shakespear was too little
esteemed by his own generation, or, for the matter of
that, by any subsequent generation. The bargees on
the Regent's Canal do not chant Shakespear's verses
as the gondoliers in Venice are said to chant the verses
of Tasso (a practice which was suspended for some
reason during my stay in Venice: at least no gondolier
ever did it in my hearing). Shakespear is no more a
popular author than Rodin is a popular sculptor or
Richard Strauss a popular composer. But Shakespear
was certainly not such a fool as to expect the Toms,
Dicks, and Harrys of his time to be any more interested
in dramatic poetry than Newton, later on, expected
them to be interested in fluxions. And when we come
to the question whether Shakespear missed that
assurance which all great men have had from the
more capable and susceptible members of their
generation that they were great men, Ben Jonson's
evidence disposes of so improbable a notion at once

and for ever. "I loved the man," says Ben, "this side idolatry, as well as any." Now why in the name of common sense should he have made that qualification unless there had been, not only idolatry, but idolatry fulsome enough to irritate Jonson into an express disavowal of it? Jonson, the bricklayer, must have felt sore sometimes when Shakespear spoke and wrote of bricklayers as his inferiors. He must have felt it a little hard that being a better scholar, and perhaps a braver and tougher man physically than Shakespear, he was not so successful or so well liked. But in spite of this he praised Shakespear to the utmost stretch of his powers of eulogy: in fact, notwithstanding his disclaimer, he did not stop "this side idolatry." If, therefore, even Jonson felt himself forced to clear himself of extravagance and absurdity in his appreciation of Shakespear, there must have been many people about who idolized Shakespear as American ladies idolize Paderewski, and who carried Bardolatry, even in the Bard's own time, to an extent that threatened to make his reasonable admirers ridiculous.

SHAKESPEAR'S PESSIMISM

I submit to Mr Harris that by ruling out this idolatry, and its possible effect in making Shakespear think that his public would stand anything from him, he has ruled out a far more plausible explanation of the faults of such a play as Timon of Athens than his theory that Shakespear's passion for the Dark Lady "cankered and took on proud flesh in him, and tortured him to nervous breakdown and madness." In Timon the intellectual bankruptcy is obvious enough: Shakespear tried once too often to make a play out of the cheap pessimism which is thrown into despair by a comparison of actual human nature with theoretical morality, actual law and administration with abstract justice, and so forth. But Shakespear's perception of the fact that all men, judged by the moral standard which they apply to others and by which they justify their punishment of others, are fools and scoundrels, does not date from the Dark Lady complication: he seems to have been born with it. If in The Comedy of Errors and A Midsummer Night's Dream the persons of the drama are not quite so ready for treachery and murder as Laertes and even Hamlet himself (not to mention the procession of ruffians who pass through the latest plays) it is certainly not because they have any more regard for law or religion. There is only one place in Shakespear's plays where the sense of shame is used as a human attribute; and that is where Hamlet is ashamed, not of anything he himself has done, but of his mother's relations with his uncle. This scene is an unnatural one: the son's reproaches to his mother, even the fact of his being able to discuss the subject with her, is more repulsive than her relations with her deceased husband's brother.

Here, too, Shakespear betrays for once his religious sense by making Hamlet, in his agony of shame, declare that his mother's conduct makes "sweet religion a rhapsody of words." But for that passage we might almost suppose that the feeling of Sunday morning in the country which Orlando describes so perfectly in As You Like It was the beginning and end of Shakespear's notion of religion. I say almost, because Isabella in Measure for Measure has religious charm, in spite of the conventional theatrical assumption that female religion means an inhumanly ferocious chastity. But for the most part Shakespear differentiates his heroes from his villains much more by what they do than by what they are. Don Juan in Much Ado is a true villain: a man with a malicious will; but he is too dull a duffer to be of any use in a leading part; and when we come to the great villains like Macbeth, we find, as Mr Harris points out, that they are precisely identical with the heroes: Macbeth is only Hamlet incongruously committing murders and engaging in hand-to-hand combats. And Hamlet, who does not dream of apologizing for the three murders he commits, is always apologizing because he has not yet committed a fourth, and finds, to his great bewilderment, that he does not want to commit it. "It cannot be," he says, "but I am pigeon-livered, and lack gall to make oppression bitter; else, ere this, I should have fatted all the region kites with this slave's offal." Really one is tempted to suspect that when Shylock asks "Hates any man the thing he would not kill?" he is expressing the natural and proper sentiments of the human race as Shakespear understood them, and not the vindictiveness of a stage Jew.

GAIETY OF GENIUS

In view of these facts, it is dangerous to cite Shakespear's pessimism as evidence of the despair of a heart broken by the Dark Lady. There is an irrepressible gaiety of genius which enables it to bear the whole weight of the world's misery without blenching. There is a laugh always ready to avenge its tears of discouragement. In the lines which Mr Harris quotes only to declare that he can make nothing of them, and to condemn them as out of character, Richard III, immediately after pitying himself because

> There is no creature loves me
> And if I die no soul will pity me,

adds, with a grin,

[285]

> Nay, wherefore should they, since that I myself
> Find in myself no pity for myself?

Let me again remind Mr Harris of Oscar Wilde. We all dreaded to read De Profundis: our instinct was to stop our ears, or run away from the wail of a broken, though by no means contrite, heart. But we were throwing away our pity. De Profundis was de profundis indeed: Wilde was too good a dramatist to throw away so powerful an effect; but none the less it was de profundis in excelsis. There was more laughter between the lines of that book than in a thousand farces by men of no genius. Wilde, like Richard and Shakespear, found in himself no pity for himself. There is nothing that marks the born dramatist more unmistakeably than this discovery of comedy in his own misfortunes almost in proportion to the pathos with which the ordinary man announces their tragedy. I cannot for the life of me see the broken heart in Shakespear's latest works. "Hark, hark! the lark at heaven's gate sings" is not the lyric of a broken man; nor is Cloten's comment that if Imogen does not appreciate it, "it is a vice in her ears which horse hairs, and cats' guts, and the voice of unpaved eunuch to boot, can never amend," the sally of a saddened one. Is it not clear that to the last there was in Shakespear an incorrigible divine levity, an inexhaustible joy that derided sorrow? Think of the poor Dark Lady having to stand up to this unbearable power of extracting a grim fun from everything. Mr Harris writes as if Shakespear did all the suffering and the Dark Lady all the cruelty. But why does he not put himself in the Dark Lady's place for a moment as he has put himself so successfully in Shakespear's? Imagine her reading the hundred and thirtieth sonnet!

My mistress' eyes are nothing like the sun;
Coral is far more red than her lips' red;
If snow be white, why then her breasts are dun;
If hairs be wire, black wires grow on her head;
I have seen roses damasked, red and white,
But no such roses see I in her cheeks;
And in some perfumes is there more delight
Than in the breath that from my mistress reeks.
I love to hear her speak; yet well I know
That music hath a far more pleasing sound.
I grant I never saw a goddess go:
My mistress, when she walks, treads on the ground.
   And yet, by heaven, I think my love as rare
   As any she belied with false compare.

Take this as a sample of the sort of compliment from which she was never for a moment safe with Shakespear. Bear in mind that she was not a comedian; that the Elizabethan fashion of treating brunettes as ugly women must have made her rather sore on the subject of her complexion; that no human being, male or female, can conceivably enjoy being chaffed on that point in the fourth couplet about the perfumes; that Shakespear's revulsions, as the sonnet immediately preceding shews, were as violent as his ardors, and were expressed with the realistic power and horror that makes Hamlet say that the heavens got sick when they saw the queen's conduct; and then ask Mr Harris whether any woman could have stood it for long, or have thought the "sugred" compliment worth the cruel wounds, the cleaving of the heart in twain, that seemed to Shakespear as natural and amusing a reaction as the burlesquing of his heroics by Pistol, his sermons by Falstaff, and his poems by Cloten and Touchstone.

JUPITER AND SEMELE

This does not mean that Shakespear was cruel: evidently he was not; but it was not cruelty that made Jupiter reduce Semele to ashes: it was the fact that he could not help being a god nor she help being a mortal. The one thing Shakespear's passion for the Dark Lady was not, was what Mr Harris in one passage calls it: idolatrous. If it had been, she might have been able to stand it. The man who dotes "yet doubts: suspects, yet strongly loves," is tolerable even by a spoilt and tyrannical mistress; but what woman could possibly endure a man who dotes without doubting; who *knows* and who is hugely amused at the absurdity of his infatuation for a woman of whose mortal imperfections not one escapes him: a man always exchanging grins with Yorick's skull, and inviting "my lady" to laugh at the sepulchral humor of the fact that though she paint an inch thick (which the Dark Lady may have done), to Yorick's favor she must come at last. To the Dark Lady he must sometimes have seemed cruel beyond description: an intellectual Caliban. True, a Caliban who could say

Be not afeard: the isle is full of noises,
Sound and sweet airs that give delight and hurt not.
Sometimes a thousand twangling instruments
Will hum about mine ears; and sometimes voices,
That, if I then had waked after long sleep,
Will make me sleep again; and then, in dreaming,
The clouds, methought, would open and shew riches
Ready to drop on me: that when I wak'd
I cried to dream again.

which is very lovely; but the Dark Lady may have had

that vice in her ears which Cloten dreaded: she may not have seen the beauty of it, whereas there can be no doubt at all that of "My mistress' eyes are nothing like the sun," &c., not a word was lost on her.

And is it to be supposed that Shakespear was too stupid or too modest not to see at last that it was a case of Jupiter and Semele? Shakespear was most certainly not modest in that sense. The timid cough of the minor poet was never heard from him.

> Not marble, nor the gilded monuments
> Of princes, shall outlive this powerful rhyme

is only one out of a dozen passages in which he (possibly with a keen sense of the fun of scandalizing the modest coughers) proclaimed his place and his power in "the wide world dreaming of things to come." The Dark Lady most likely thought this side of him insufferably conceited; for there is no reason to suppose that she liked his plays any better than Minna Wagner liked Richard's music dramas: as likely as not, she thought The Spanish Tragedy worth six Hamlets. He was not stupid either: if his class limitations and a profession that cut him off from actual participation in great affairs of State had not confined his opportunities of intellectual and political training to private conversation and to the Mermaid Tavern, he would probably have become one of the ablest men of his time instead of being merely its ablest playwright. One might surmise that Shakespear found out that the Dark Lady's brains could no more keep pace with his than Anne Hathaway's, if there were any evidence that their friendship ceased when he stopped writing sonnets to her. As a matter of fact the consolidation of a passion into an enduring intimacy generally puts an end to sonnets.

That the Dark Lady broke Shakespear's heart, as Mr Harris will have it she did, is an extremely un-Shakespearian hypothesis. "Men have died from time to time, and worms have eaten them; but not for love," says Rosalind. Richard of Gloster, into whom Shakespear put all his own impish superiority to vulgar sentiment, exclaims

And this word "love," which greybeards call divine,
Be resident in men like one another
And not in me: I am myself alone.

Hamlet has not a tear for Ophelia: her death moves him to fierce disgust for the sentimentality of Laertes by her grave; and when he discusses the scene with Horatio immediately after, he utterly forgets her, though he is sorry he forgot himself, and jumps at the proposal of a fencing match to finish the day with. As against this view Mr Harris pleads Romeo, Orsino, and even Antonio; and he does it so penetratingly that he convinces you that Shakespear did betray himself again and again in these characters; but self-betrayal is one thing; and self-portrayal, as in Hamlet and Mercutio, is another. Shakespear never "saw himself," as actors say, in Romeo or Orsino or Antonio. In Mr Harris's own play Shakespear is presented with the most pathetic tenderness. He is tragic, bitter, pitiable, wretched and broken among a robust crowd of Jonsons and Elizabeths; but to me he is not Shakespear because I miss the Shakespearian irony and the Shakespearian gaiety. Take these away and Shakespeare is no longer Shakespear: all the bite, the impetus, the strength, the grim delight in his own power of looking terrible facts in the face with a chuckle, is gone; and you have nothing left but that most depressing of all things: a victim. Now who can think of Shakespear as a man with a grievance? Even in that most thoroughgoing and inspired of all Shakespear's loves: his love of music (which Mr Harris has been the first to appreciate at anything like its value), there is a dash of mockery. "Spit in the hole, man; and tune again." "Divine air! Now is his soul ravished. Is it not strange that sheeps guts should hale the souls out of men's bodies?" "An he had been a dog that should have howled thus, they would have hanged him." There is just as much Shakespear here as in the inevitable quotation about the sweet south and the bank of violets.

I lay stress on this irony of Shakespear's, this impish rejoicing in pessimism, this exultation in what breaks the hearts of common men, not only because it is diagnostic of that immense energy of life which we call genius, but because its omission is the one glaring defect in Mr Harris's otherwise extraordinarily penetrating book. Fortunately, it is an omission that does not disable the book as (in my judgment) it disabled the hero of the play, because Mr Harris left himself out of his play, whereas he pervades his book, mordant, deep-voiced, and with an unconquerable style which is the man.

THE IDOL OF THE BARDOLATERS

There is even an advantage in having a book on Shakespear with the Shakespearian irony left out of account. I do not say that the missing chapter should not be added in the next edition: the hiatus is too great: it leaves the reader too uneasy before this touching picture of a writhing worm substituted for the invulnerable giant. But it is none the less probable that in no other way could Mr Harris have got at his man as he has. For, after all, what is the secret of the hopeless failure of the academic Bardolaters to give us a credible or even interesting Shakespear, and the easy triumph of Mr Harris in giving us both? Simply that Mr Harris has assumed that he was dealing with a man, whilst the others have assumed that they were writing about a god, and have therefore rejected every consideration of fact, tradition, or interpretation, that pointed to any human imperfection in their hero. They thus leave themselves with so little material that they are forced to begin by saying that we know very little about Shakespear. As a matter of fact, with the plays and sonnets in our hands, we know much more about Shakespear than we know about Dickens or Thackeray: the only difficulty is that we deliberately suppress it because it proves that Shakespear was not only very unlike the conception of a god current in Clapham, but was not, according to the same reckoning, even a respectable man. The academic view starts with a Shakespear who was not scurrilous; therefore the verses about "lousy Lucy" cannot have been written by him, and the cognate passages in the plays are either strokes of character-drawing or gags interpolated by the actors. This ideal Shakespear was too well behaved to get drunk; therefore the tradition that his death was hastened by a drinking bout with Jonson and Drayton must be rejected, and the remorse of Cassio treated as a thing observed, not experienced: nay, the disgust of Hamlet at the drinking customs of Denmark is taken to establish Shakespear as the superior of Alexander in self-control, and the greatest of teetotalers.

Now this system of inventing your great man to start with, and then rejecting all the materials that do not fit him, with the ridiculous result that you have to declare that there are no materials at all (with your waste-paper basket full of them), ends in leaving Shakespear with a much worse character than he deserves. For though it does not greatly matter whether he wrote the lousy Lucy lines or not, and does not really matter at all whether he got drunk when he made a night of it with Jonson and Drayton, the sonnets raise an unpleasant question which does matter a good deal; and the refusal of the academic Bardolaters to discuss or even mention this question has had the effect of producing a silent verdict against Shakespear. Mr Harris tackles the question openly, and has no difficulty whatever in convincing us that Shakespear was a man of normal constitution sexually, and was not the victim of that most cruel and pitiable of all the freaks of nature: the freak which transposes the normal aim of the affections. Silence on this point means condemnation; and the condemnation has been general throughout the present generation, though it only needed Mr Harris's fearless handling of the matter to sweep away what is nothing but a morbid and very disagreeable modern fashion. There is always some stock accusation brought against eminent persons. When I was a boy every well-known man was accused of beating his wife. Later on, for some unexplained reason, he was accused of psychopathic derangement. And this fashion is retrospective. The cases of Shakespear and Michel Angelo are cited as proving that every genius of the first magnitude was a sufferer; and both here and in Germany there are circles in which such derangement is grotesquely reverenced as part of the stigmata of heroic powers. All of which is gross nonsense. Unfortunately, in Shakespear's case, prudery, which cannot prevent the accusation from being whispered, does prevent the refutation from being shouted. Mr Harris, the deep-voiced, refuses to be silenced. He dismisses with proper contempt the stupidity which places an outrageous construction on Shakespear's apologies in the sonnets for neglecting that "perfect ceremony" of love which consists in returning calls and making protestations and giving presents and paying the trumpery attentions which men of genius always refuse to bother about, and to which touchy people who have no genius attach so much importance. No reader who had not been tampered with by the psychopathic monomaniacs could ever put any construction but the obvious and innocent one on these passages. But the general vocabulary of the sonnets to Pembroke (or whoever "Mr W. H." really was) is so overcharged according to modern ideas that a reply on the general case is necessary.

SHAKESPEAR'S ALLEGED SYCOPHANCY AND PERVERSION

That reply, which Mr Harris does not hesitate to give, is two-fold: first, that Shakespear was, in his attitude towards earls, a sycophant; and, second, that the normality of Shakespear's sexual constitution is only too well attested by the excessive susceptibility to the normal impulse shewn in the whole mass of his writings. This latter is the really conclusive reply. In the case of Michel Angelo, for instance, one must admit that if his works are set beside those of Titian or Paul Veronese, it is impossible not to be struck by the absence in the Florentine of that susceptibility to feminine charm which pervades the pictures of the Venetians. But, as Mr. Harris points out (though he does not use this particular illustration) Paul Veronese is an anchorite compared to Shakespear. The language of the sonnets addressed to Pembroke, extravagant as it now seems, is the language of compliment and fashion, transfigured no doubt by Shakespear's verbal magic, and hyperbolical, as Shakespear always seems to people who cannot conceive so vividly as he, but still unmistakeable for anything else than the expression of a friendship delicate enough to be wounded, and a manly loyalty deep enough to be outraged. But the language of the sonnets to the Dark Lady is the language of passion: their cruelty shews it. There is no evidence that Shakespear was capable of being unkind in cold blood. But in his revulsions from love, he was bitter, wounding, even ferocious; sparing neither himself nor the unfortunate woman whose only offence was that she had reduced the great man to the common human denominator.

In seizing on these two points Mr Harris has made so sure a stroke, and places his evidence so featly that there is nothing left for me to do but to plead that the second is sounder than the first, which is, I think, marked by the prevalent mistake as to Shakespear's social position, or, if you prefer it, the confusion between his actual social position as a penniless tradesman's son taking to the theatre for a livelihood, and his own conception of himself as a gentleman of good family. I am prepared to contend that though Shakespear was undoubtedly sentimental in his expressions of devotion to Mr W. H. even to a point which nowadays makes both ridiculous, he was not sycophantic if Mr W. H. was really attractive and promising, and Shakespear deeply attached to him. A sycophant does not tell his patron that his fame will survive, not in the renown of his own actions, but in the sonnets of his sycophant. A sycophant, when his patron cuts him out in a love affair, does not tell his patron exactly what he thinks of him. Above all, a sycophant does not write to his patron precisely as he feels on all occasions; and this rare kind of sincerity is all over the sonnets. Shakespear, we are told, was "a very civil gentleman." This must mean that his desire to please people and be liked by them, and his reluctance to hurt their feelings, led him into amiable flattery even when his feelings were not strongly stirred. If this be taken into account along with the fact that Shakespear conceived and expressed all his emotions with a vehemence that sometimes carried him into ludicrous extravagance, making Richard offer his kingdom for a horse and Othello declare of Cassio that

> Had all his hairs been lives, my great revenge
> Had stomach for them all,

we shall see more civility and hyperbole than sycophancy even in the earlier and more coldblooded sonnets.

SHAKESPEAR AND DEMOCRACY

Now take the general case pled against Shakespear as an enemy of democracy by Tolstoy, the late Ernest Crosbie and others, and endorsed by Mr Harris. Will it really stand fire? Mr Harris emphasizes the passages in which Shakespear spoke of mechanics and even of small master tradesmen as base persons whose clothes were greasy, whose breath was rank, and whose political imbecility and caprice moved Coriolanus to say to the Roman Radical who demanded at least "good words" from him

> He that will give good words to thee will flatter
> Beneath abhorring.

But let us be honest. As political sentiments these lines are an abomination to every democrat. But suppose they are not political sentiments! Suppose they are merely a record of observed fact. John Stuart Mill told our British workmen that they were mostly liars. Carlyle told us all that we are mostly fools. Matthew Arnold and Ruskin were more circumstantial and more abusive. Everybody, including the workers themselves, know that they are dirty, drunken, foul-mouthed, ignorant, gluttonous, prejudiced: in short, heirs to the peculiar ills of poverty and slavery, as well as co-heirs with the plutocracy to all the failings of human nature. Even Shelley admitted, 200 years after Shakespear wrote Coriolanus, that universal suffrage was out of the question. Surely the real test, not of Democracy, which was not a live political issue in Shakespear's time, but of impartiality in judging classes, which is what one demands from a great human poet, is not that he should flatter the poor and denounce the rich, but that he should weigh them both in the same balance. Now whoever will read Lear and Measure for Measure will find stamped on his mind such an appalled sense of the danger of dressing man in a little brief authority, such a merciless stripping of the purple from the "poor, bare, forked animal" that calls itself a king and fancies itself a god, that one wonders what was the real nature of the mysterious restraint that kept "Eliza and our James" from teaching Shakespear to be civil to crowned heads, just as one wonders why Tolstoy was allowed to go free when so many less terrible levellers went to the galleys or Siberia. From the mature Shakespear we get no such scenes of village snobbery as that between the stage country gentleman Alexander Iden and the stage Radical Jack Cade. We get the shepherd in As

You Like It, and many honest, brave, human, and loyal servants, beside the inevitable comic ones. Even in the Jingo play, Henry V, we get Bates and Williams drawn with all respect and honor as normal rank and file men. In Julius Caesar, Shakespear went to work with a will when he took his cue from Plutarch in glorifying regicide and transfiguring the republicans. Indeed hero-worshippers have never forgiven him for belittling Caesar and failing to see that side of his assassination which made Goethe denounce it as the most senseless of crimes. Put the play beside the Charles I of Wills, in which Cromwell is written down to a point at which the Jack Cade of Henry VI becomes a hero in comparison; and then believe, if you can, that Shakespear was one of them that "crook the pregnant hinges of the knee where thrift may follow fawning." Think of Rosencrantz, Guildenstern, Osric, the fop who annoyed Hotspur, and a dozen passages concerning such people! If such evidence can prove anything (and Mr Harris relies throughout on such evidence) Shakespear loathed courtiers.

If, on the other hand, Shakespear's characters are mostly members of the leisured classes, the same thing is true of Mr Harris's own plays and mine. Industrial slavery is not compatible with that freedom of adventure, that personal refinement and intellectual culture, that scope of action, which the higher and subtler drama demands. Even Cervantes had finally to drop Don Quixote's troubles with innkeepers demanding to be paid for his food and lodging, and make him as free of economic difficulties as Amadis de Gaul. Hamlet's experiences simply could not have happened to a plumber. A poor man is useful on the stage only as a blind man is: to excite sympathy. The poverty of the apothecary in Romeo and Juliet produces a great effect, and even points the sound moral that a poor man cannot afford to have a conscience; but if all the characters of the play had been as poor as he, it would have been nothing but a melodrama of the sort that the Sicilian players gave us here; and that was not the best that lay in Shakespear's power. When poverty is abolished, and leisure and grace of life become general, the only plays surviving from our epoch which will have any relation to life as it will be lived then will be those in which none of the persons represented are troubled with want of money or wretched drudgery. Our plays of poverty and squalor, now the only ones that are true to the life of the majority of living men, will then be classed with the records of misers and monsters, and read only by historical students of social pathology.

Then consider Shakespear's kings and lords and gentlemen! Would even John Ball or Jeremiah complain that they are flattered? Surely a more mercilessly exposed string of scoundrels never crossed the stage. The very monarch who paralyses a rebel by appealing to the divinity that hedges a king, is a drunken and sensual assassin, and is presently killed contemptuously before our eyes in spite of his hedge of divinity. I could write as convincing a chapter on Shakespear's Dickensian prejudice against the throne and the nobility and gentry in general as Mr Harris or Ernest Crosbie on the other side. I could even go so far as to contend that one of Shakespear's defects is his lack of an intelligent comprehension of feudalism. He had of course no prevision of democratic Collectivism. He was, except in the commonplaces of war and patriotism, a privateer through and through. Nobody in his plays, whether king or citizen, has any civil public business or conception of such a thing, except in the method of appointing constables, to the abuses in which he called attention quite in the vein of the Fabian Society. He was concerned about drunkenness and about the idolatry and hypocrisy of our judicial system; but his implied remedy was personal sobriety and freedom from idolatrous illusion in so far as he had any remedy at all, and did not merely despair of human nature. His first and last word on parliament was "Get thee glass eyes, and, like a scurvy politician, seem to see the thing thou dost not." He had no notion of the feeling with which the land nationalizers of today regard the fact that he was a party to the enclosure of common lands at Wellcome. The explanation is, not a general deficiency in his mind, but the simple fact that in his day what English land needed was individual appropriation and cultivation, and what the English Constitution needed was the incorporation of Whig principles of individual liberty.

SHAKESPEAR AND THE BRITISH PUBLIC

I have rejected Mr Harris's view that Shakespear died broken-hearted of "the pangs of love despised." I have given my reasons for believing that Shakespear died game, and indeed in a state of levity which would have been considered unbecoming in a bishop. But Mr Harris's evidence does prove that Shakespear had a grievance and a very serious one. He might have been jilted by ten dark ladies and been none the worse for it; but his treatment by the British Public was another matter. The idolatry which exasperated Ben Jonson was by no means a popular movement; and, like all such idolatries, it was excited by the magic of Shakespear's art rather than by his views. He was launched on his career as a successful playwright by the Henry VI trilogy, a work of no originality, depth, or subtlety except the originality, depth, and subtlety of the feelings and fancies of the common people. But Shakespear was not satisfied with this. What is the use of being Shakespear if you are not allowed to express any notions but those of Autolycus? Shakespear did not see the world as Autolycus did: he saw it, if not exactly as Ibsen did (for it was not quite the same world), at least with much of Ibsen's power of penetrating its illusions and idolatries, and with all Swift's horror of its cruelty and uncleanliness.

Now it happens to some men with these powers that they are forced to impose their fullest exercise on the world because they cannot produce popular work. Take Wagner and Ibsen for instance! Their earlier works are no doubt much cheaper than their later ones; still, they were not popular when they were written. The alternative of doing popular work was never really open to them: had they stooped they would have picked up less than they snatched from above the people's heads. But Handel and Shakespear were not held to their best in this way. They could turn out anything they were asked for, and even heap up the measure. They reviled the British Public, and never forgave it for ignoring their best work and admiring their splendid commonplaces; but they produced the commonplaces all the same, and made them sound magnificent by mere brute faculty for their art. When Shakespear was forced to write popular plays to save his theatre from ruin, he did it mutinously, calling the plays As *You* Like It, and Much Ado About Nothing. All the same, he did it so well that to this day these two genial vulgarities are the main Shakespearean stock-in-trade of our theatres. Later on Burbage's power and popularity as an actor enabled Shakespear to free himself from the tyranny of the box office, and to express himself more freely in plays consisting largely of monologue to be spoken by a great actor from whom the public would stand a good deal. The history of Shakespear's tragedies has thus been the history of a line long of famous actors, from Burbage and Betterton to Forbes Robertson; and the man of whom we are told that "when he would have said that Richard died, and cried A horse! A horse! he Burbage cried" was the father of nine generations of Shakespearean playgoers, all speaking of Garrick's Richard, and Kean's Othello, and Irving's Shylock, and Forbes Robertson's Hamlet without knowing or caring how much these had to do with Shakespear's Richard and Othello and so forth. And the plays which were written without great and predominant parts, such as Troilus and Cressida, All's Well That Ends Well, and Measure for Measure, have dropped on our stage as dead as the second part of Goethe's Faust or Ibsen's Emperor or Galilean.

Here, then, Shakespear had a real grievance; and though it is a sentimental exaggeration to describe him as a broken-hearted man in the face of the passages of reckless jollity and serenely happy poetry in his latest plays, yet the discovery that his most serious work could reach success only when carried on the back of a very fascinating actor who was enormously overcharging his part, and that the serious plays which did not contain parts big enough to hold the overcharge were left on the shelf, amply accounts for the evident fact that Shakespear did not end his life in a glow of enthusiastic satisfaction with mankind and with the theatre, which is all that Mr Harris can allege in support of his broken-heart theory. But even if Shakespear had had no failures, it was not possible for a man of his powers to observe the political and

moral conduct of his contemporaries without per-
ceiving that they were incapable of dealing with the
problems raised by their own civilization, and that
their attempts to carry out the codes of law and to
practise the religions offered to them by great
prophets and law-givers were and still are so foolish
that we now call for The Superman, virtually a new
species, to rescue the world from mismanagement.
This is the real sorrow of great men; and in the face
of it the notion that when a great man speaks bitterly
or looks melancholy he must be troubled by a disappointment in love seems to me sentimental trifling.

If I have carried the reader with me thus far, he will
find that trivial as this little play of mine is, its sketch
of Shakespear is more complete than its levity suggests. Alas! its appeal for a National Theatre as a
monument to Shakespear failed to touch the very
stupid people who cannot see that a National Theatre
is worth having for the sake of the National Soul. I
had unfortunately represented Shakespear as trea-
suring and using (as I do myself) the jewels of unconsciously musical speech which common people
utter and throw away every day; and this was taken as
a disparagement of Shakespear's "originality." Why
was I born with such contemporaries? Why is
Shakespear made ridiculous by such a posterity?

POSTSCRIPT 1933. The recent death of Frank Harris
has refreshed the interest of the sketch of him in this
preface, especially as he died in the act of finishing a
curious biography of me which has attracted a good
deal of notice, and which is truthful as to its record of
bare facts, though its critical side is badly lamed
through Frank's having lost touch with me before the

end of the nineteenth century, and never reconsidered his estimates in the light of my later exploits.

The appeal for a national theatre with which the play concludes, and for the sake of which it was written, elicited applause but no subscriptions. Two years ago a great Shakespear Memorial Theatre was completed at Stratford-upon-Avon through the efforts of Sir Archibald Flower, replacing the old Shakespear theatre which owed its existence to his family; but Sir Archibald had wasted no time in appealing to Shakespear's countrymen: he had turned to America and received a noble response. The attempt to establish a National Theatre in London to commemorate Shakespear's exploits in that old city, now expanded into a concentration camp much too big for any civic consciousness, was and still is a complete failure, though there is enough money (not English money, of course) available to carry out the project if the Government would provide a site, and the municipality forgo its rates, as foreign Governments and municipalities do.

New Prologue

(Read by Shaw before B.B.C. broadcast
of the play on 22 April 1938. First
published in *The Listener*, 27 April 1938)

This play which you are going to hear is all about Shakespear and Queen Elizabeth; but it is really only an appeal for the Shakespear Memorial National Theatre which we have been trying to make the English nation establish for thirty years past. Dame Edith

Lyttelton invented the play in 1910; I wrote the dialogue; and we had a grand performance at the Haymarket Theatre with Mr. Granville-Barker in the part of Shakespear. But I am not going to talk to you about the National Theatre. Shakespear does this so eloquently in the play, and Queen Elizabeth is so up-to-date with her reply to him, that if I anticipate them I shall spoil their speeches for you. So let me tell you how far the play is historical. It takes place in the old royal place of Whitehall, where Shakespear often acted for the amusement of King James. We have Ben Jonson's word for it. He says it was "on banks of Thames" that Shakespear "did oft delight Eliza and our James".

Now I have my doubts about Eliza. She was a bit of a scholar; but she was a great out-of-doors woman; and when she was not taken up with her queen business she liked riding, hunting, staying in country-houses, dancing, flirting, and ordering the most magnificent dresses ever worn by mortal woman. There is no evidence that she took any interest in the theatre. A stage player was to her at best a nobleman's servant of much less importance to her than his cook, and at worst a rogue and a vagabond. Still, a playwright whose works got printed had to be able to put his stage directions into good Latin; for in Eliza's time playwrights were not so illiterate as they are today. Chapman and Ben Jonson would have died rather than write "he exits" "she exits" "they exit" instead of the good Latin *exit* and *exeunt*. Even Shakespear, who, according to Ben Jonson had "little Latin and less Greek", knew better than that; and so Queen Elizabeth, if she had ever heard of Shakespear, would have allowed him a disreputable sort of middle class professional rank. But my own belief is that she never did hear of him, and that the name Will Shakespear meant absolutely nothing to her. When Dame Edith planned this play, we both thought it was high time to introduce them to one another.

And now, as there is nothing about either Will or Eliza in the title of the play, you may be wondering who on earth the dark lady was. Well, nobody knows; but there *was* a dark lady all the same. Shakespear, in addition to his plays, wrote a batch of 154 sonnets, most of them addressed to a certain young man known as Mr. W. H., who was one of those very attractive people whom we call world's sweethearts. They are mostly film stars nowadays. They are adored equally by men and women because their attraction is one of beauty and charm, and has nothing to do with sex. Shakespear's sonnets to this young gentleman are far more affectionate and admiring than any that he would have addressed to a woman. And the proof of this is that the sonnets to Mr. W. H. are interrupted by some that were addressed to a woman with whom Shakespear had fallen in love. He was furious about it; for Shakespear did not like being captured in this way; especially by a lady for whose character he had no respect, and whose personal appearance was by no means satisfactory; for it happened that she was a black haired beauty; and as Queen Elizabeth had red hair, black hair was very unfashionable. And so the lady is known to us only as Shakespear's dark lady. He was fascinated by her; but he revenged himself by writing savage sonnets, one of which is the most terrible denunciation of that sort of love in existence; and another points out all the lady's defects so mercilessly that she can hardly have been consoled by the concluding lines "And yet, by Heaven, I think my love as rare as any she belied by false compare". It may gratify a woman to be told "I love you". But to be told "*and yet* I love you" after a whole string of insults, is quite another pair of shoes. No wonder the dark lady preferred Mr. W. H. and thereby provoked a first class quarrel between him and Shakespear.

In the play I have assumed that the dark lady was a maid of honor at Elizabeth's court. A friend of mine, the late Thomas Tyler, discovered that one of Elizabeth's maids of honor named Mary Fitton got into scrapes at court by her gallantries. Well, I had to get the dark lady into Whitehall Palace somehow; so let us pretend that she was Mary Fitton.

Whitehall Palace was burnt long before I arrived in London 62 years ago; but it still exists in my imagination; and the place where it stood is now right under my bedroom window. It ought to bear Shakespear's name; but they call it Horseguards Avenue because all the tourists and the country folk and the provincial football fans congregate at the end of it to stare at the two mounted guardsmen in their sentry boxes and cuirasses. Not one of them ever turns round to look at the spot where the sweet swan of Avon upon banks of Thames did oft delight Eliza and our James. I wanted the National Theatre to be there; and when the Government announced their intention of pulling down the old houses which are now all Government offices, with the old-fashioned grates which make more smoke every morning when the charladies arrive than the whole city of Edinburgh, I claimed a place for Shakespear's National Theatre there. But the Government had never heard of Shakespear; and my dream of seeing the National Theatre from my window was shattered by an assurance that when the site was filled up with new offices I should not be able to see anything at all. So we have had to buy a magnificent site in Kensington, which Shakespear knew only as a far-off village.

And now I ask you to imagine the old palace still standing. You may find it hard to imagine it by daylight; but if you imagine it at 11 o'clock at night with everybody gone to bed except the warders on duty it will be as easy as any other dream. As I see it the place is a terrace overlooking the river, with the Queen's apartments on one side, and a gateway on the other. Have you got it? Right; then up goes the curtain.

Fin de siècle 15–1600. *Midsummer night on the terrace of the Palace at Whitehall, overlooking the Thames. The Palace clock chimes four quarters and strikes eleven.*

A Beefeater on guard. A Cloaked Man approaches.

THE BEEFEATER. Stand. Who goes there? Give the word.

THE MAN. Marry! I cannot. I have clean forgotten it.

THE BEEFEATER. Then cannot you pass here. What is your business? Who are you? Are you a true man?

THE MAN. Far from it, Master Warder. I am not the same man two days together: sometimes Adam, sometimes Benvolio, and anon the Ghost.

THE BEEFEATER [*recoiling*] A ghost! Angels and ministers of grace defend us!

THE MAN. Well said, Master Warder. With your leave I will set that down in writing; for I have a very poor and unhappy brain for remembrance. [*He takes out his tablets and writes*]. Methinks this is a good scene, with you on your lonely watch, and I approaching like a ghost in the moonlight. Stare not so amazedly at me; but mark what I say. I keep tryst here tonight with a dark lady. She promised to bribe the warder. I gave her the wherewithal: four tickets for the Globe Theatre.

THE BEEFEATER. Plague on her! She gave me two only.

THE MAN [*detaching a tablet*] My friend: present this tablet, and you will be welcomed at any time when the plays of Will Shakespear are in hand. Bring your wife. Bring your friends. Bring the whole garrison. There is ever plenty of room.

THE BEEFEATER. I care not for these new-fangled plays. No man can understand a word of them. They are all talk. Will you not give me a pass for The Spanish Tragedy?

THE MAN. To see The Spanish Tragedy one pays, my friend. Here are the means. [*He gives him a piece of gold*].

THE BEEFEATER [*overwhelmed*] Gold! Oh, sir, you are a better paymaster than your dark lady.

THE MAN. Women are thrifty, my friend.

THE BEEFEATER. Tis so, sir. And you have to consider that the most open handed of us must een cheapen that which we buy every day. This lady has to make a present to a warder nigh every night of her life.

THE MAN [*turning pale*] I'll not believe it.

THE BEEFEATER. Now you, sir, I dare be sworn, do not have an adventure like this twice in the year.

THE MAN. Villain: wouldst tell me that my dark lady hath ever done thus before? that she maketh occasions to meet other men?

THE BEEFEATER. Now the Lord bless your innocence, sir, do you think you are the only pretty man in the world? A merry lady, sir: a warm bit of stuff. Go to: I'll not see her pass a deceit on a gentleman that hath given me the first piece of gold I ever handled.

THE MAN. Master Warder: is it not a strange thing that we, knowing that all women are false, should be amazed to find our own particular drab no better than the rest?

THE BEEFEATER. Not all, sir. Decent bodies, many of them.

THE MAN [*intolerantly*] No. All false. All. If thou deny it, thou liest.

THE BEEFEATER. You judge too much by the Court, sir. There, indeed, you may say of frailty that its name is woman.

THE MAN [*pulling out his tablets again*] Prithee say that again: that about frailty: the strain of music.

THE BEEFEATER. What strain of music, sir? I'm no musician, God knows.

THE MAN. There is music in your soul: many of your degree have it very notably. [*Writing*] "Frailty: thy name is woman!" [*Repeating it affectionately*] "Thy name is woman."

THE BEEFEATER. Well, sir, it is but four words. Are you a snapper-up of such unconsidered trifles?

THE MAN [*eagerly*] Snapper-up of—[*he gasps*] Oh! Immortal phrase! [*He writes it down*]. This man is a greater than I.

THE BEEFEATER. You have my lord Pembroke's trick, sir.

THE MAN. Like enough: he is my near friend. But what call you his trick?

THE BEEFEATER. Making sonnets by moonlight. And to the same lady too.

THE MAN. No!

THE BEEFEATER. Last night he stood here on your errand, and in your shoes.

THE MAN. Thou, too, Brutus! And I called him friend!

THE BEEFEATER. Tis ever so, sir.

THE MAN. Tis ever so. Twas ever so. [*He turns away, overcome*]. Two Gentlemen of Verona! Judas! Judas!!

THE BEEFEATER. Is he so bad as that, sir?

THE MAN [*recovering his charity and self-possession*] Bad? O no. Human, Master Warder, human. We call one another names when we are offended, as children do. That is all.

THE BEEFEATER. Ay, sir: words, words, words. Mere wind, sir. We fill our bellies with the east wind, sir, as the Scripture hath it. You cannot feed capons so.

THE MAN A good cadence. By your leave [*He makes a note of it*].

THE BEEFEATER. What manner of thing is a cadence, sir? I have not heard of it.

THE MAN. A thing to rule the world with, friend.

THE BEEFEATER. You speak strangely, sir: no offence. But, an't like you, you are a very civil gentleman; and a poor man feels drawn to you, you being, as twere, willing to share your thought with him.

THE MAN. Tis my trade. But alas! the world for the most part will none of my thoughts.

Lamplight streams from the palace door as it opens from within.

THE BEEFEATER. Here comes your lady, sir. I'll to t'other end of my ward. You may een take your time about your business: I shall not return too suddenly unless my sergeant comes prowling round. Tis a fell sergeant, sir: strict in his arrest. Good een, sir; and good luck! [*He goes*].

THE MAN. "Strict in his arrest"! "Fell sergeant"! [*As if tasting a ripe plum*] O-o-o-h! [*He makes a note of them*].

A Cloaked Lady gropes her way from the palace and wanders along the terrace, walking in her sleep.

THE LADY [*rubbing her hands as if washing them*] Out, damned spot. You will mar all with these cosmetics. God made you one face; and you make yourself another. Think of your grave, woman, not ever of being beautified. All the perfumes of Arabia will not whiten this Tudor hand.

THE MAN. "All the perfumes of Arabia"! "Beautified"! "Beautified"! a poem in a single word. Can this be my Mary? [*To the Lady*] Why do you speak in a strange voice, and utter poetry for the first time? Are you ailing? You walk like the dead. Mary! Mary!

THE LADY [*echoing him*] Mary! Mary! Who would have thought that woman to have had so much blood in her! Is it my fault that my counsellors put deeds of blood on me? Fie! If you were women you would have more wit than to stain the floor so foully. Hold not up her head so: the hair is false. I tell you yet again, Mary's buried: she cannot come out of her grave. I fear her not: these cats that dare jump into thrones though they be fit only for men's laps must be put away. Whats done cannot be undone. Out, I say. Fie! a queen, and freckled!

THE MAN [*shaking her arm*] Mary, I say: art asleep?

The Lady wakes; starts, and nearly faints. He catches her on his arm.

THE LADY. Where am I? What art thou?

THE MAN. I cry your mercy. I have mistook your person all this while. Methought you were my Mary: my mistress.

THE LADY [*outraged*] Profane fellow: how do you dare?

THE MAN. Be not wroth with me, lady. My mistress is a marvellous proper woman. But she does not speak so well as you. "All the perfumes of Arabia"! That was well said: spoken with good accent and excellent discretion.

THE LADY. Have I been in speech with you here?

THE MAN. Why, yes, fair lady. Have you forgot it?

THE LADY. I have walked in my sleep.

THE MAN. Walk ever in your sleep, fair one; for then your words drop like honey.

THE LADY [*with cold majesty*] Know you to whom you speak, sir, that you dare express yourself so saucily?

THE MAN [*unabashed*] Not I, not care neither. You are some lady of the Court, belike. To me there are but two sorts of women: those with excellent voices, sweet and low, and cackling hens that cannot make me dream. Your voice has all manner of loveliness in it. Grudge me not a short hour of its music.

THE LADY. Sir: you are overbold. Season your admiration for a while with—

THE MAN [*holding up his hand to stop her*] "Season your admiration for a while—"

THE LADY. Fellow: do you dare mimic me to my face?

THE MAN. Tis music. Can you not hear? When a good musician sings a song, do you not sing it and sing it again till you have caught and fixed its perfect melody? "Season your admiration for a while": God! the history of man's heart is in that one word admiration. Admiration! [*Taking up his tablets*] What was it? "Suspend your admiration for a space—"

THE LADY. A very vile jingle of esses. I said "Season your—

THE MAN [*hastily*] Season: ay, season, season, season. Plague on my memory, my wretched memory! I must een write it down. [*He begins to write, but stops, his memory failing him*]. Yet tell me which was the vile jingle? You said very justly: mine own ear caught it even as my false tongue said it.

THE LADY. You said "for a space." I said "for a while."

THE MAN. "For a while" [*he corrects it*]. Good! [*Ardently*] And now be mine neither for a space nor a while, but for ever.

THE LADY. Odds my life! Are you by chance making love to me, knave?

THE MAN. Nay: tis you who have made the love: I but pour it out at your feet. I cannot but love a lass that sets such store by an apt word. Therefore vouchsafe, divine perfection of a woman—no: I have said that before somewhere; and the wordy garment of my love for you must be fire-new—

THE LADY. You talk too much, sir. Let me warn you: I am more accustomed to be listened to than preached at.

THE MAN. The most are like that that do talk well. But though you spake with the tongues of angels, as indeed you do, yet know that I am the king of words.

THE LADY. A king, ha!

THE MAN. No less. We are poor things, we men and women—

THE LADY. Dare you call me woman?

THE MAN. What nobler name can I tender you? How else can I love you? Yet you may well shrink from the name: have I not said we are but poor things? Yet there is a power that can redeem us.

THE LADY. Gramercy for your sermon, sir. I hope I know my duty.

THE MAN. This is no sermon, but the living truth. The power I speak of is the power of immortal poesy. For know that vile as this world is, and worms as we are, you have but to invest all this vileness with a magical garment of words to transfigure us and uplift our souls til earth flowers into a million heavens.

THE LADY. You spoil your heaven with your million. You are extravagant. Observe some measure in your speech.

THE MAN. You speak now as Ben does.

THE LADY. And who, pray, is Ben?

THE MAN. A learned bricklayer who thinks that the sky is at the top of his ladder, and so takes it on him to rebuke me for flying. I tell you there is no word yet coined and no melody yet sung that is extravagant and majestical enough for the glory that lovely words can reveal. It is heresy to deny it: have you not been taught that in the beginning was the Word? that the Word was with God? nay, that the Word was God?

THE LADY. Beware, fellow, how you presume to speak of holy things. The Queen is the head of the Church.

THE MAN. You are the head of my Church when you speak as you did as first. "All the perfumes of Arabia"! Can the Queen speak thus? They say she playeth well upon the virginals. Let her play so to me; and I'll kiss her hands. But until then, you are my Queen; and I'll kiss those lips that have dropt music on my heart. [*He puts his arms about her*].

THE LADY. Unmeasured impudence! On your life, take your hands from me.

The Dark Lady comes stooping along the terrace behind them like a running thrush. When she sees how they are employed, she rises angrily to her full height, and listens jealously.

THE MAN [*unaware of the Dark Lady*] Then cease to make my hands tremble with the streams of life you pour through them. You hold me as the lodestar holds the iron: I cannot but cling to you. We are lost, you and I: nothing can separate us now.

THE DARK LADY. We shall see that, false lying hound, you and your filthy trull. [*With two vigorous cuffs, she knocks the pair asunder, sending the man, who is unlucky enough to receive a right-handed blow, sprawling on the flags*]. Take that, both of you!

THE CLOAKED LADY [*in towering wrath, throwing off her cloak and turning in outraged majesty on her assailant*] High treason!

THE DARK LADY [*recognizing her and falling on her knees in abject terror*] Will: I am lost: I have struck the Queen.

[316]

THE MAN [*sitting up as majestically as his ignominious posture allows*] Woman: you have struck WILLIAM SHAKESPEAR!!!!!!

QUEEN ELIZABETH [*stupent*] Marry, come up!!! Struck William Shakespear quotha! And who in the name of all the sluts and jades and light-o'-loves and fly-by-nights that infest this palace of mine, may William Shakespear be?

THE DARK LADY. Madam: he is but a player. Oh, I could have my hand cut off—

QUEEN ELIZABETH. Belike you will, mistress. Have you bethought you that I am like to have your head cut off as well?

THE DARK LADY. Will: save me. Oh, save me.

ELIZABETH. Save you! A likely savior, on my royal word! I had thought this fellow at least an esquire; for I had hoped that even the vilest of my ladies would not have dishonoured my Court by wantoning with a baseborn servant.

SHAKESPEAR [*indignantly scrambling to his feet*] Baseborn! I, a Shakespear of Stratford! I, whose mother was an Arden! baseborn! You forget yourself, madam.

ELIZABETH [*furious*] S'blood! do I so? I will teach you—

THE DARK LADY [*rising from her knees and throwing herself between them*] Will: in God's name anger her no further. It is death. Madam: do not listen to him.

SHAKESPEAR. Not were it een to save your life, Mary, not to mention mine own, will I flatter a monarch who forgets what is due to my family. I deny not that my father was brought down to be a poor bankrupt; but twas his gentle blood that was ever too generous for trade. Never did he disown his debts. Tis true he paid them not; but it is an attested truth that he gave bills for them; and twas those bills, in the hands of base hucksters, that were his undoing.

ELIZABETH [*grimly*] The son of your father shall learn his place in the presence of the daughter of Harry the Eighth.

SHAKESPEAR [*swelling with intolerant importance*] Name not that inordinate man in the same breath with Stratford's worthiest alderman. John Shakespear wedded but once: Harry Tudor was married six times. You should blush to utter his name.

THE DARK LADY   Will: for pity's
          crying out together   sake—
ELIZABETH   Insolent dog—

SHAKESPEAR [*cutting them short*] How know you that King Harry was indeed your father?

ELIZABETH   Zounds? Now by—[*she stops to grind her teeth with rage*].
THE DARK LADY She will have me whipped through the streets. Oh God! Oh God!

SHAKESPEAR. Learn to know yourself better, madam. I am an honest gentleman of unquestioned parentage, and have already sent in my demand for the coat-of-arms that is lawfully mine. Can you say as much for yourself?

ELIZABETH [*almost beside herself*] Another word; and I begin with mine own hands the work the hangman shall finish.

SHAKESPEAR. You are no true Tudor: this baggage here has as good a right to your royal seat as you. What maintains you on the throne of England? Is it your renownéd wit? your wisdom that sets at nought the craftiest statesmen of the Christian world? No. Tis the mere chance that might have happened to any milkmaid, the caprice of Nature that made you the most wondrous piece of beauty the age hath seen.

[*Elizabeth's raised fists, on the point of striking him, fall to her side*]. That is what hath brought all men to your feet, and founded your throne on the impregnable rock of your proud heart, a stony island in a sea of desire. There, madam, is some wholesome blunt honest speaking for you. Now do your worst.

ELIZABETH [*with dignity*] Master Shakespear: it is well for you that I am a merciful prince. I make allowance for your rustic ignorance. But remember that there are things which be true, and are yet not seemly to be said (I will not say to a queen; for you will have it that I am none) but to a virgin.

SHAKESPEAR [*bluntly*] It is no fault of mine that you are a virgin madam, albeit tis my misfortune.

THE DARK LADY [*terrified again*] In mercy, madam, hold no further discourse with him. He hath ever some lewd jest on his tongue. You hear how he useth me! calling me baggage and the like to your Majesty's face.

ELIZABETH. As for you, mistress, I have yet to demand what your business is at this hour in this place, and how you come to be so concerned with a player that you strike blindly at your sovereign in your jealousy of him.

THE DARK LADY. Madam: as I live and hope for salvation—

SHAKESPEAR [*sardonically*] Ha!

THE DARK LADY [*angrily*]—ay, I'm as like to be saved as thou that believest naught save some black magic of words and verses—I say, madam, as I am a living woman I came here to break with him forever. Oh, madam, if you would know what misery is, listen to this man that is more than man and less at the same time. He will tie you down to anatomize your very soul: he will wring tears of blood from your humiliation;

and then he will heal the wound with flatteries that no woman can resist.

SHAKESPEAR. Flatteries! [*Kneeling*] Oh, madam, I put my case at your royal feet. I confess to much. I have a rude tongue: I am unmannerly: I blaspheme against the holiness of anointed royalty; but oh, my royal mistress, A M I a flatterer?

ELIZABETH. I absolve you as to that. You are far too plain a dealer to please me. [*He rises gratefully*].

THE DARK LADY. Madam: he is flattering you even as he speaks.

ELIZABETH [*a terrible flash in her eye*] Ha! Is it so?

SHAKESPEAR. Madam: she is jealous; and, heaven help me! not without reason. Oh, you say you are a merciful prince; but that was cruel of you, that hiding of your royal dignity when you found me here. For how can I ever be content with this black-haired, black-eyed, black-avised devil again now that I have looked upon real beauty and real majesty?

THE DARK LADY [*wounded and desperate*] He hath swore to me ten times over that the day shall come in England when black women, for all their foulness, shall be more thought on than fair ones. [*To Shakespear, scolding at him*] Deny it if thou canst. Oh, he is compact of lies and scorns. I am tired of being tossed up to heaven and dragged down to hell at every whim that takes him. I am ashamed to my very soul that I have abased myself to love one that my father would not have deemed fit to hold my stirrup—one that will talk to all the world about me—that will put my love and my shame into his plays and make me blush for myself there—that will write sonnets about me that no man of gentle strain would put his hand to. I am all disordered: I know not what I am saying to your Majesty: I am of all ladies most deject and wretched—

SHAKESPEAR. Ha! At last sorrow hath struck a note of music out of thee. "Of all ladies most deject and wretched." [*He makes a note of it*].

THE DARK LADY. Madam: I implore you give me leave to go. I am distracted with grief and shame. I—

ELIZABETH. Go [*The Dark Lady tries to kiss her hand*]. No more. Go. [*The Dark Lady goes, convulsed*]. You have been cruel to that poor fond wretch, Master Shakespear.

SHAKESPEAR. I am not cruel, madam; but you know the fable of Jupiter and Semele. I could not help my lightnings scorching her.

ELIZABETH. You have an overweening conceit of yourself, sir, that displeases your Queen.

SHAKESPEAR. Oh, madam, can I go about with the modest cough of a minor poet, belittling my inspiration and making the mightiest wonder of your reign a thing of nought? I have said that "not marble nor the gilded monuments of princes shall outlive" the words with which I make the world glorious or foolish at my will. Besides, I would have you think me great enough to grant me a boon.

ELIZABETH. I hope it is a boon that may be asked of a virgin Queen without offence, sir. I mistrust your forwardness; and I bid you remember that I do not suffer persons of your degree (if I may say so without offence to your father the alderman) to presume too far.

SHAKESPEAR. Oh, madam, I shall not forget myself again; though by my life, could I make you a serving wench, neither a queen nor a virgin should you be for so much longer as a flash of lightning might take to cross the river to the Bankside. But since you are a queen and will none of me, nor of Philip of Spain, nor of any other mortal man, I must een contain myself as best I may, and ask you only for a boon of State.

ELIZABETH. A boon of State already! You are becoming a courtier like the rest of them. You lack advancement.

SHAKESPEAR. "Lack advancement." By your Majesty's leave: a queenly phrase. [*He is about to write it down*].

ELIZABETH. [*striking the tablets from his hand*] Your tables begin to anger me, sir. I am not here to write your plays for you.

SHAKESPEAR. You are here to inspire them, madam. For this, among the rest, were you ordained. But the boon I crave is that you do endow a great playhouse, or, if I may make bold to coin a scholarly name for it, a National Theatre, for the better instruction and gracing of your Majesty's subjects.

ELIZABETH. Why, sir, are there not theatres enow on the Bankside and in Blackfriars?

SHAKESPEAR. Madam: these are the adventures of needy and desperate men that must, to save themselves from perishing of want, give the sillier sort of people what they best like; and what they best like, God knows, is not their own betterment and instruction, as we well see by the example of the churches, which must needs compel men to frequent them, though they be open to all without charge. Only when there is a matter of a murder, or a plot, or a pretty youth in petticoats, or some naughty tale of wantonness, will your subjects pay the great cost of good players and their finery, with a little profit to boot. To prove this I will tell you that I have written two noble and excellent plays setting forth the advancement of women of high nature and fruitful industry even as your Majesty is: the one a skilful physician, the other a sister devoted to good works. I have also stole from a book of idle wanton tales two of the most damnable foolishnesses in the world, in the one of which a woman goeth in man's attire and maketh impudent love to her swain, who pleaseth the groundling by overthrowing a wrestler; whilst, in the other, one of the same kidney sheweth her wit by saying endless naughtinesses to a gentleman as lewd as herself. I have writ these to save my friends from penury, yet shewing my scorn for such follies and for them that praise them by calling the one As You Like It, meaning that it is not as *I* like it, and the other Much Ado About Nothing, as it truly is. And now these two filthy pieces drive their nobler fellows from the stage, where indeed I cannot have my lady physician presented at all, she being too honest a woman for the taste of the town. Wherefore I humbly beg your Majesty to give order that a theatre be endowed out of the public revenue for the playing of those pieces of mine which no merchant will touch, seeing that his gain is so much greater with the worse than with the better. Thereby you shall also encourage other men to undertake the writing of plays who do now despise it and leave it wholly to those whose counsels will work little good to your realm. For this writing of plays is a great matter, forming as it does the minds and affections of men in such sort that whatsoever they see done in show on the stage, they will presently be doing in earnest in the world, which is but a larger stage. Of late, as you know, the Church taught the people by means of plays; but the people flocked only to such as were full of superstitious miracles and bloody martyrdoms; and so the Church, which also was just then brought into straits by the policy of your royal father, did abandon and discountenance the art of playing; and thus it fell into the hands of poor players and greedy merchants that had their pockets to look to and not the greatness of this your kingdom. Therefore now must your Majesty take up that good work that your Church hath abandoned, and restore the art of playing to its former use and dignity.

ELIZABETH. Master Shakespear: I will speak of this matter to the Lord Treasurer.

SHAKESPEAR. Then am I undone, madam; for there was never yet a Lord Treasurer that could find a penny for anything over and above the necessary expenses of your government, save for a war or a salary for his own nephew.

ELIZABETH. Master Shakespeare: you speak sooth; yet cannot I in any wise mend it. I dare not offend my unruly Puritans by making so lewd a place as the playhouse a public charge; and there be a thousand things to be done in this London of mine before your poetry can have its penny from the general purse. I tell thee, Master Will, it will be three hundred years and more before my subjects learn that man cannot live by bread alone, but by every word that cometh from the mouth of those whom God inspires. By that time you and I will be dust beneath the feet of the horses, if indeed there be any horses then, and men be still riding instead of flying. Now it may be that by then your works will be dust also.

SHAKESPEAR. They will stand, madam: fear not for that.

ELIZABETH. It may prove so. But of this I am certain (for I know my countrymen) that until every other country in the Christian world, even to barbarian Muscovy and the hamlets of the boorish Germans, have its playhouse at the public charge, England will never adventure. And she will adventure then only because it is her desire to be ever in the fashion, and to do humbly and dutifully whatso she seeth everybody else doing. In the meantime you must content yourself as best you can by the playing of those two pieces which you give out as the most damnable ever writ, but which your countrymen, I warn you, will swear are the best you have ever done. But this I will say, that if I could speak across the ages to our descendants, I should heartily recommend them to fulfil your wish; for the Scottish minstrel hath well said that he that maketh the songs of a nation is mightier than he that maketh its laws; and the same may well be true of plays and interludes. [*The clock chimes the first quarter. The warder returns on his round*]. And now, sir, we are upon the hour when it better beseems a virgin queen to be abed than to converse alone with the naughtiest of her subjects. Ho there! Who keeps ward on the queen's lodgings tonight?

THE WARDER. I do, an't please your majesty.

ELIZABETH. See that you keep it better in future. You have let pass a most dangerous gallant even to the very door of our royal chamber. Lead him forth; and bring me word when he is safely locked out; for I shall scarce dare disrobe until the palace gates are between us.

SHAKESPEAR [*kissing her hand*] My body goes through the gate into the darkness, madam; but my thoughts follow you.

ELIZABETH. How! to my bed!

SHAKESPEAR. No, madam, to your prayers, in which I beg you to remember my theatre.

ELIZABETH. That is my prayer to posterity. Forget not your own to God; and so goodnight, Master Will.

SHAKESPEAR. Goodnight, great Elizabeth. God save the Queen!

ELIZABETH. Amen.

Exeunt severally: she to her chamber: he, in custody of the warder, to the gate nearest Blackfriars.

AYOT ST LAWRENCE, *20th June 1910.*

Note to the New York Press

(Drafted by Shaw, October 1910. In the
Archive of the Shakespeare Memorial
Committee, at the British Drama League)

A new play by Bernard Shaw entitled the Dark Lady
of the Sonnets has been announced for performance
by the National Shakespear Memorial Committee.
It is, however, hardly a play. It is an interlude, lasting
half an hour, in which four characters appear:
Queen Elizabeth, Mary Fitton (the Dark Lady),
Shakespear, and a Beefeater. The theory that the
Dark Lady was Mistress Fitton, first put forward by
the late Thomas Tyler (a learned translator of
Ecclesiastes), and lately popularized by Mr. Frank
Harris, has been adopted in the interlude; and I have
taken the opportunity to explode the notion that "the
man Shakespear", as the Baconians call him, was an
illiterate proletarian—a mistake which took in even so
shrewd a genius as Mark Twain. Shakespear was the
son of a merchant who considered himself a gentleman
and married a woman of good family who considered
herself a lady; and this was at a time when the conception of a middle class did not exist. To class him
with stablemen and casual laborers, and to build up
on that absurdity a theory that he could not have
written Love's Labor Lost is about as sensible as to
class George Washington as a negro and infer that the
President of that name cannot have been really George
Washington but George III.

Mr Bernard Shaw and Shakespeare

(An interview, drafted by Shaw, *The
Observer*, London, 13 November 1910)

Mr. Bernard Shaw was asked yesterday by a representative of THE OBSERVER if he would be good
enough to discuss his new play, "The Dark Lady of
the Sonnets," which is to be presented by the
National Shakespeare Memorial Committee at two
matinées at the Haymarket next week, and to state
his views on Shakespeare, who appears as one of its
four characters.

"I have nothing to say about the interlude itself
beyond what has been already published," Mr.
Bernard Shaw replied. "Shakespeare wrote several
sonnets to a certain dark lady who evidently attracted
him irresistibly; but he was furious with himself and
with her, at finding himself enslaved so completely in
spite of seeing that she was no goddess either physically or mentally. She must have suffered torments
from so terrible a lover; for his sonnets are half
adoration, half insult. Just listen to this:—

> For well thou know'st to my dear doting heart
> Thou art the fairest and most precious jewel;
> Yet in good faith some say that thee behold
> Thy face hath not the power to make love groan.

"At one moment he is reproaching her because
she had black hair and eyes, which in Elizabeth's time
were counted ugly. In the next he is declaring, 'but
now is black beauty's successive heir,'" and scorning
the dark women who paint and dye themselves into
Queen Elizabeth's complexion:—

> For since each hand hath put on Nature's power,
>> Fairing the foul with art's false borrowed face,
> Sweet beauty hath no name, no holy bower,
>> But is profaned, if not lives in disgrace.

"This probably pleased the dark lady; but the next day she would get another sonnet in which she was assured that—

> In nothing art thou black, save in thy deeds.

"There are lines in these sonnets that would make any woman's heart sick with love; but what woman, or man either, could stand this sort of thing:—

> My mistress' eyes are nothing like the sun;
>> Coral is far more red than her lip's red;
> If snow be white, why then her breasts are dun;
>> If hairs be wires, black wires grow on her head.
> I have seen roses damask'd, red and white,
>> But no such roses see I in her cheeks;
> And in some perfumes is there more delight
>> Than in the breath that from my mistress reeks.
> I love to hear her speak; yet well I know
>> That music hath a far more pleasing sound.
> I grant I never saw a goddess go;
>> My mistress, when she walks, treads on the ground.
>> And yet, by heaven, I think my love as rare
>> As any she belied with false compare.

"I think you will agree that if ever a woman paid an unbearably high price for turning the greatest of human heads, it is poor Mary Fitton. And he knew it:—

> Whoever hath her wish, thou hast thy Will.
> And Will to boot and will in overplus.
> More than enough am I that vex thee still.

"More than enough! I should think so. The only English writer who has really grasped this part of Shakespeare's story is Frank Harris; but Frank sympathises with Shakespeare. It is like seeing Semele reduced to ashes and sympathising with Jupiter. And remember that Mistress Fitton, like most of us to-day, may have had no sense, or only a very imperfect one, of the enchanting music of Shakespeare's compliments and adorations; whilst his insults and his allusions to her wiry hair, her 'dun breasts,' and—I really can't repeat the brutality about her breath—were all unmistakable and understandable by the most commonplace intelligence.

"Shakespeare was not an ordinary man, passing from fits of affection to moods of sleepy indifference. He was a man of intense transports and furious revulsions, to both of which he gave expression in words that were as violent and extravagant as they were beautiful and forcible. An ordinary man may yawn in his mistress's face; but he does not strike her to the heart with a terrible description of their love as 'the expense of spirit in a waste of shame,' and as 'past reason hated as a swallowed bait on purpose laid to make the taker mad.'

> All this the world well knows; yet none knows well
> To shun the heaven that leads men to this hell.

says William, wandering away into a general reflection on the psychology of sex and forgetting that he is simply digging the hoofs of his Pegasus into the woman's heart.

"But we must drop this subject or I shall go on for ever about it. Not one in a thousand of the readers of THE OBSERVER knows or cares anything about Shakespeare. He is not a real man to them: he is only a bust in Stratford Church. To me he is one of the few realities England has ever produced.

"I find it impossible to believe in the existence of most of my own contemporaries. I see names in the papers and read speeches; and I suppose there is some feeble spark of life in the people they indicate. But Shakespeare did really live and see and feel and speak in the way that I call living.

MR. BARKER AS SHAKESPEARE

"Is all this in the play? I understood it is to last only half an hour."

"Not so long. All this and a good deal more is behind the play. But let us come down to earth. What do you want to know about the matinée?"

"Anything you are disposed to tell me. Your cast, for instance."

"Granville Barker as Shakespeare. What do you think of that, to begin with?"

"Do you consider him the nearest thing we have?"

"Yes. If Shakespeare were alive he would simply gasp at Barker's superior knowledge and the severity and complication of his dramatic construction. Probably he would prefer my old-fashioned style. But he would not make the mistake about Barker that Greene in his "Groat's Worth of Wit" made about Shakespeare."

"And the Dark Lady?"

"Mona Limerick, of course. The darkest lady on the stage, and the most enigmatic. I am convinced that Mary Fitton was exactly like Mona Limerick."

"That completes the cast, does it?"

"Not at all. You have forgotten that there is a person of some importance called Queen Elizabeth."

"Does she appear in the play?"

[331]

"Good heavens! Of course, she appears in the play—overshadows it from beginning to end. The interlude leads up to the case for a National Theatre. How could that be dealt with in the absence of the woman who represented the nation then? Can you imagine 'the spacious times' without 'great Elizabeth'?"

"True. And who is to play Elizabeth?"

"Suzanne Sheldon. She is not to play Elizabeth, but to be Elizabeth. Wait till you see her."

"Is Mr. Barker to produce the interlude?"

"Nobody produces my plays: that is why they are always so well done. Mr. Barker and I and Miss Sheldon and Miss Limerick will call in one of the greatest stage artists in Europe, Mr. Charles Ricketts; and we will lay our heads together; and the production will be the result of that. We have no time and no money—the National Theatre has only got £100,000 so far, and is sitting on it like the British Treasury—but when those five heads come together the result will be a great production."

"You seem to be in very high spirits, Mr. Shaw?"

"I am not. Another straw, and I should sit down and cry. If you were expected to rehearse a play, and reverse the Osborne judgment, and find out all the weak spots in the Copyright Bill, and get a new volume of plays through the Press, and deliver a political speech at the other side of England, all in one week, you would know the difference between high spirits and the delirium of overwork."

"What is your opinion of the new Advisory Board set up by the Lord Chamberlain to assist him in the Censorship?"

"You think that more important than the National Theatre matinée?"

"But you have told me all about that."

"Not at all. My interlude is only a scrap of it. There will be three other plays. One of them is by Barrie. You have heard of Barrie, haven't you ? He is almost as well known as Shakespeare and myself. There will be two rattling good little plays by George Paston—a woman, as the name George denotes. Let me tell you something. Before you are five years older, three-fourths of our most popular playwrights will be women. It is extraordinary how they have mastered—or mistressed—the stage lately."

"I am still curious about the Advisory Committee ?"

"Do not waste your precious intellectual energies on it: it is foredoomed to failure. The absurdities of the Censorship are in the nature of the institution, and not in the personal shortcomings of the officials. It is true that the Lord Chamberlain knows rather less about books and plays than I do about breeding kangaroos; but if he were the whole forty French Academicians rolled into one, and the Pope and the Prime Minister into the bargain, it would not improve matters one scrap—rather the contrary.

"The two famous K.C.'s, and the two famous actors, and the famous professor of English literature are cleverer than Lord Spencer or even Mr. Redford; but they are not cleverer than the Catholic Churches, Roman and Greek; and you know what a pitiable mess *they* have made of the same job. Good morning."

Mr Bernard Shaw's New Play

(An interview, drafted by Shaw, *Daily Mail*, London, 24 November 1910)

Mr. Bernard Shaw has written a short interlude, entitled "The Dark Lady of the Sonnets," which is to be performed in aid of the Shakespeare Memorial National Theatre at matinées to be given to-day and tomorrow at the Haymarket Theatre.

The scene of the little play is the Terrace of White-hall Palace, on a midsummer night, and two of the four characters that appear in it are Queen Elizabeth and Shakespeare. Shakespeare will be played by Mr. Granville Barker, Queen Elizabeth by Miss Suzanne Sheldon.

"What effect is the general election having on the Shakespeare matinée?" an interviewer asked Mr. Bernard Shaw.

"You mean what effect is the Shakespeare matinée having on the general election?" said Mr. Shaw. "Naturally, it is distracting public attention from it. That cannot be helped. Interesting as Cabinet Ministers are, they are not as interesting as Shakespeare and Queen Elizabeth."

"But we can have your play at any time; and this election will never come again."

"This performance will be unique. Not a soul is being paid for it; and everybody is being put to the most frightful trouble and expense. You can have no idea of the inconvenience we are causing. Think of Mr. Herbert Trench, at the Haymarket, working hard at his revival of 'The Blue Bird,' with all its scenic complications, which are to be more elaborate than ever. In we come on him with our four plays, driving his staff out of their senses. What other manager would suffer as much for the memory of Shakespeare? . . ."

Regarding his play, "The Dark Lady of the Sonnets," Mr. Shaw said: "I am giving you in twenty minutes all that we really know of Shakespeare over and above what he has himself put on the stage. I have always wanted to show the public what Shake-speare was really like. This time, when the critics, from mere force of habit, begin to write the old sentences about my characters being only myself over and over again (a most attractive advertisement to my admirers, by the way), they will suddenly remember that this time my character is Shakespeare, and that the hackneyed insult will become an enormous compliment. Still, I hope they will stick to the old commonplaces about me. If they stopped to think they might detect the anachronisms."

"Are there anachronisms?" Mr. Shaw was asked.

"Bushels of them, but none that matter, and none that can be detected except by people who know pretty closely the order in which Shakespeare wrote his plays. I wish I could write all my plays in Elizabethan English; it is my real native language.

"Don't miss the performance. Remember, you will never have another chance of seeing it with this cast. And it will be a great historic occasion. Don't smile; we shall achieve that National Theatre; and all sorts of traditions will gather about it as the centuries pass. This performance will be the beginning of the tradition. They will read about all of us who threw ourselves into this job on the foundations. Perhaps they will talk about you, too, if you are there; so let me sell you a couple of stalls."

"Stratford Must Not Wait"

(A letter to the Editor of the *Evening Standard*, London, 31 March 1926)

Sir,—I am amazed to find myself represented in your issue of March 25 as disparaging the replacement of the Memorial Theatre at Stratford, and advancing London's claim as against it.

I cannot account for this misunderstanding. I have been feverishly ill; but I really cannot have raved to this extent. As to saying that Stratford is an uninteresting town, I have frequented it so devotedly for many years past that I have come to regard it almost as my birthplace; and Mr. Henry Arthur Jones has publicly appealed to the Mayor to throw me out of it lest I should set up a rival tradition. Stratford at one end of the Cotswolds and Glastonbury at the other are the most fascinating places of pilgrimage in England, and the most lovably English.

Those who have any money to spare for British dramatic art should, for this year at least, concentrate on replacing the burnt-out Memorial Theatre in Stratford. Its ruins are an unbearable disfigurement, all the worse as the old building, though hopeless internally for theatrical purposes, was by no means unpresentable in the copied way of the architecture of the mid-nineteenth century. To leave it a smoky ruin as it now is would be a national disgrace.

Commerical enterprise will not help. It is true that commercial enterprise has its eye on Stratford; but what it proposes is to demolish the famous old Clopton bridge and replace it by a ferro-concrete viaduct which will enable motorists to dash all out across the Avon and off to Birmingham through the tail end of the town without noticing the existence of the most celebrated birthplace in the western world.

Local patriotism does what it can; but the town is too small to carry its giant on its own shoulders. It can cater for the pilgrims, and maintain the pleasant spaciousness of the streets and riverside; but this, and the replacement of the present incongruous town hall with a more suitable one, is as much as it can afford; and more should not be expected from it. Were it not for Mr. Archibald Flower, who has followed his family tradition by adopting Shakespeare, and found him sometimes, I fear, a very expensive and troublesome orphan, the great tradition of the town might have broken its back instead of strengthening it.

The case for a general subscription from the whole English-speaking world is irresistible. When an attempt was made to obtain a general subscription for a National Theatre in London in Shakespeare's name, it was a complete and crushing failure. The "Manchester Guardian," like Mrs. Dombey's relatives, still calls on the committee to make an effort. It is welcome to make an effort itself, and let us see whether it can collect a single sixpence.

The public feels that a National Theatre in London is an affair of State, like the National Gallery or the British Museum, and not a matter for collecting cards. Everyone who has spent a week in Stratford at Festival time will want to help to rebuild the theatre there. Nobody who has spent a week in London will ever dream of sending a subscription to build a National Theatre there. The Metropolitan National Theatre must wait until some Government rises to the occasion, or until a certain fund at present in existence has accumulated to the needed figure. The Stratford National Theatre need not and cannot wait.

There are two other highly deserving theatrical funds. One is the Sadlers Wells project. The other is the rebuilding of the Royal Academy of Dramatic Art on the expiration of the lease of its present inadequate premises a few years hence, for which £25,000 is required. Both of these would be helped instead of hindered by a prompt and generous response to the

Stratford appeal. Neither of them has one-tenth of Stratford's power to call attention to the need for public endowment of dramatic art in this country. Both will profit eventually by Stratford's lead.

I hope it is now clear that I am a warm advocate of the Stratford appeal, and that I am recommending its general support with the fullest knowledge of the local situation, and of all the alternative theatrical channels for public generosity. Stratford, for the moment, comes first.—Yours truly,

G. BERNARD SHAW

G.B.S. on the National Theatre

(*New Theatre*, London, May 1948)

"*A London ramp*" *was the term applied by Ivor Brown, writing in the* OBSERVER *of March* 28 [1948], *to the proposal of Sir Stafford Cripps to promote legislation enabling a future government to spend a million pounds on a National Theatre. We asked Bernard Shaw to comment on Ivor Brown's article, and this is what he wrote:*

The National Theatre is being confused with discussions of the plays to be performed in it. That is not its function; it will not and need not perform any experimental or novel plays any more than Westminster Abbey performs the latest compositions of Britten, Bartok, or Stravinsky. It is needed solely as a monument affirming that Drama ranks with Painting, Books, Education, and Religion as vitally necessary to British civilization. Its direction should carry a title, as the presidency of the Royal Academy does.

It must be in London, not in Southwark. Southwark has a cathedral far more venerable than St. Paul's; but many Londoners do not know that it exists. All Londoners, and all whose native tongue is English, know of St. Paul's as a National Pantheon second only to the Abbey. The National Theatre must have as its neighbours the Imperial Institute, the Natural History Museum, and Albert Hall and Memorial, and be on the same side of the river as the two great churches, the Mansion House, the Bank of England, the British Museum, the National Gallery, the Cathedral, Buckingham Palace, Somerset House, University College and London University. No transpontine building can compete in this metropolitan centrality with even Aldgate pump.

By all means let Southwark, with its magnificent thoroughfares that beat London's hollow, its Dulwich Gallery, its Cathedral and famous St. George's church, its Denmark Hill and Ruskinland build a noble municipal theatre on Bankside, large enough to pay its way with prices from sixpence to half a crown (all seats at least fifteen shillings for one evening and one matinee in each week). Let it build half a dozen such, and finally surpass London as London has surpassed Strand in The Garden. Still it will not be a historic London. And historic London is the only spot on earth where a theatre can be national.

G. BERNARD SHAW

Fanny's First Play:
An Easy Play for a Little Theatre

WITH

Preface

Prologue, 1916

Mr Bernard Shaw on the Critics

The Popularity of "G.B.S."

Letter to the Editor of the Play Pictorial

Composition begun 13 August 1910; completed 5 March 1911. First published in German translation, as *Fannis erstes Stück*, in the *Neue Freie Presse* (Vienna), 16 July–8 October 1911. Published in *Misalliance, The Dark Lady of the Sonnets, and Fanny's First Play*, 1914. First presented at the Little Theatre, London, on 19 April 1911, with the authorship concealed.

The Induction

Footman   *A. E. Filmer*
Cecil Savoyard   *Lewis Sealy*
Count O'Dowda   *Harcourt Williams*
Fanny O'Dowda   *Christine Silver*
Mr Trotter   *Claude King*
Mr Vaughan   *S. Creagh Henry*
Mr Gunn   *Reginald Owen*
Flawner Bannal   *Nigel Playfair*

The Play

Robin Gilbey   *Fewlass Llewellyn*
Maria Gilbey   *Gwynneth Galton*
Juggins the footman   *H. K. Ayliff*
Dora Delaney   *Dorothy Minto*
Amelia Knox   *Cicely Hamilton*
Joseph Knox   *Arnold Lucy*
Margaret Knox   *Lillah McCarthy*
Lieutenant Duvallet   *Raymond Lauzette*
Bobby Gilbey   *Shiel Barry*

Period—1911

The Induction—*The Saloon of Count O'Dowda's Country House in Cambridge. Before the Curtain. Evening*

ACT I *Mr Robin Gilbey's Dining Room, Denmark Hill. Morning*

ACT II *Mr Joseph Knox's Drawing Room in the same Neighborhood. Afternoon*

ACT III *Again in Mr Gilbey's Dining Room. Later the same Afternoon*

Epilogue—*As in the Induction. After the Play*

Preface

Fanny's First Play, being but a potboiler, needs no preface. But its lesson is not, I am sorry to say, unneeded. Mere morality, or the substitution of custom for conscience, was once accounted a shameful and cynical thing: people talked of right and wrong, of honor and dishonor, of sin and grace, of salvation and damnation, not of morality and immorality. The word morality, if we met it in the Bible, would surprise us as much as the word telephone or motor car. Nowadays we do not seem to know that there is any other test of conduct except morality; and the result is that the young had better have their souls awakened by disgrace, capture by the police, and a month's hard labor, than drift along from their cradles to their graves doing what other people do for no other reason than that other people do it, and knowing nothing of good and evil, of courage and cowardice, or indeed anything but how to keep hunger and concupiscence and fashionable dressing within the bounds of good taste except when their excesses can be concealed. Is it any wonder that I am driven to offer to young people in our suburbs the desperate advice: Do something that will get you into trouble? But please do not suppose that I defend a state of things which makes such advice the best that can be given under the circumstances, or that I do not know how difficult it is to find out a way of getting into trouble that will combine loss of respectability with integrity of self-respect and reasonable consideration for other peoples' feelings and interests on every point except their dread of losing their own respectability. But when there's a will there's a way. I hate to see dead people walking about: it is unnatural.

And our respectable middle-class people are all as dead as mutton. Out of the mouth of Mrs Knox I have delivered on them the judgment of her God.

The critics whom I have lampooned in the induction to this play under the names of Trotter, Vaughan, and Gunn will forgive me: in fact Mr Trotter forgave me beforehand, and assisted the make-up by which Mr Claude King so successfully simulated his personal appearance. The critics whom I did not introduce were somewhat hurt, as I should have been myself under the same circumstances; but I had not room for them all; so I can only apologize and assure them that I meant no disrespect.

The concealment of the authorship, if a *secret de Polichinelle* can be said to involve concealment, was a necessary part of the play. In so far as it was effectual, it operated as a measure of relief to those critics and playgoers who are so obsessed by my strained legendary reputation that they approach my plays in a condition which is really one of derangement, and are quite unable to conceive a play of mine as anything but a trap baited with paradoxes, and designed to compass their ethical perversion and intellectual confusion. If it were possible, I should put forward all my plays anonymously, or hire some less disturbing person, as Bacon is said to have hired Shakespear, to father my plays for me.

Prologue

(To be substituted for the Induction when the
Play alone is performed)

[This rhymed prologue, written by Shaw in September 1916, was first performed by the Charles Macdona Company in an abridged version of the play at the Theatre Royal, Birmingham, on 18 September 1916. Shaw was in the audience.]

The Actress who plays the part of Margaret Knox comes before the curtain dressed as Fanny O'Dowda, and addresses the audience.

We're going to act a play. I shall be in it (*Applause*)
Thank you for that applause. But just a minute
Would you mind very much if I explained to you
What wouldnt otherwise be very plain to you:
That is, why—though the play's won worldwide fame—
The author's given it such a funny name!
Fanny's First Play! It's catching. Lots of pence in it.
But at first sight there doesnt seem much sense in it.
But dont make up your minds there isnt any:
It's really Fanny's play; and *I* am Fanny.
I wrote the play. It was my very first.
(I had to write it or I should have burst:
I couldnt help it). Now, from what youve read of it,
You know, perhaps, that all the critics said of it
That, though my first might fairly good be reckoned,
Heaven forbid that I should write a second!
That was a nasty one; they thought it witty;
But I felt nothing for the fools but pity;
For stalls and pit to praise my play united;
And now I'll tell you how I came to write it.

     In childhood's sunny days, I, by an aunt of mine,
     Was taken—prematurely—to the pantomime.

[347]

From that time forth, each evening I would be at her:
"Take me again, dear Auntie, to the theatre":
Twas thus I first on Shakespear's golden page struck.
The natural result was, I got stage struck.
I loved the playhouse: after my first bout of it,
I dared my family to keep me out of it.
I went and went and went, until, alas!
Something most unexpected came to pass.
I loved the actors; copied all their ways;
But oh! I got so tired of the plays.
Always the same—what they call oversexed:
You always know just what is coming next:
The husband and the lover and the wife,
Not one of them a bit like real life.
At first I liked them. All my soul was stored with
    them;
But in a year or so I got quite bored with them.
Just think! in real life what is it touches us?
Stories about ourselves, not about duchesses.
If we all live by honest business, such as is
The backbone of this town, why not insist
On plays that shew at least that we exist,
Instead of these continual appealings
To millionaires, as if we had no feelings!
Why are stage lovers' speeches drowned by coughs?
Because we're tired of their all being toffs.
Though too much business maynt be any fun
It's better anyhow than having none.
Remember good Sam Richardson. Said he,
"I keep my shop, sirs; and my shop keeps me."
You havent read Sam's novels: theyre too long;
But in the love scenes Sam could come out strong.
To me the thing's as plain as a church steeple:
We must have business plays for business people.
As to the titled heroine, I'd banish her;

But when I hinted at it to the manager,
He said "To put the duchess on the shelf,
Just write a play and act in it yourself."

Ladies and gentlemen: I all but kissed him:
In fact I threw a kiss—like that—but missed him.
I wrote the play: Fanny's First, at your service.
Youll see me act in it. Oh, I'm so nervous.
You wont expect me in the first act, will you?
But in the second I shall simply thrrrill you.
The third you must especially attend to.
If you dont like my part, oh, p l e a s e pretend to.
You see, unless you think it rather funny
You wont feel youve had value for your money.
I really must break off: it's downright wrong
Making all this up as I go along;
Besides, Ive got to change. I look too rowdy.
Business folk like their daughter to be dowdy.
I'll make myself so plain, youll all despise me,
I'm sure not one of you will recognize me.
But beauty's nothing: common people love it;
But youre not common people; youre above it.
I knew you were. You all look quite resigned.
Well, since youve been so very v e r y kind,
My poor looks shall not be m u c h diminished.
Thank you for hearing me. (*to the prompter, roughly,
as he retires through the curtain*) Ring up. Ive finished.

⌈ INDUCTION ⌉

The end of a saloon in an old-fashioned country-house (Florence Towers, the property of Count O'Dowda) has been curtained off to form a stage for a private theatrical performance. A footman in grandiose Spanish livery enters before the curtain, on its O.P. side.

FOOTMAN [*announcing*] Mr Cecil Savoyard. [*Cecil Savoyard comes in: a middle-aged man in evening dress and a fur-lined overcoat. He is surprised to find nobody to receive him. So is the Footman*]. Oh, beg pardon, sir: I thought the Count was here. He was when I took up your name. He must have gone through the stage into the library. This way, sir. [*He moves towards the division in the middle of the curtains*].

SAVOYARD. Half a mo. [*The Footman stops*]. When does the play begin? Half-past eight?

FOOTMAN. Nine, sir.

SAVOYARD. Oh, good. Well, will you telephone to my wife at the George that it's not until nine?

FOOTMAN. Right, sir. Mrs Cecil Savoyard, sir?

SAVOYARD. No: Mrs William Tinkler. Dont forget.

THE FOOTMAN. Mrs Tinkler, sir. Right, sir. [*The Count comes in through the curtains*]. Here is the Count, sir. [*Announcing*] Mr Cecil Savoyard, sir. [*He withdraws*].

COUNT O'DOWDA [*A handsome man of fifty, dressed with studied elegance a hundred years out of date, advancing cordially to shake hands with his visitor*] Pray excuse me, Mr Savoyard. I suddenly recollected that all the bookcases in the library were locked—in

[351]

fact theyve never been opened since we came from Venice—and as our literary guests will probably use the library a good deal, I just ran in to unlock everything.

SAVOYARD. Oh, you mean the dramatic critics. M'yes. I suppose theres a smoking room?

THE COUNT. My study is available. An old-fashioned house, you understand. Wont you sit down, Mr Savoyard?

SAVOYARD. Thanks. [*They sit. Savoyard, looking at his host's obsolete costume, continues*] I had no idea you were going to appear in the piece yourself.

THE COUNT. I am not. I wear this costume because— well, perhaps I had better explain the position, if it interests you.

SAVOYARD. Certainly.

THE COUNT. Well, you see, Mr Savoyard, I'm rather a stranger in your world. I am not, I hope, a modern man in any sense of the word. I'm not really an Englishman: my family is Irish: Ive lived all my life in Italy—in Venice mostly—my very title is a foreign one: I am a Count of the Holy Roman Empire.

SAVOYARD. Where's that?

THE COUNT. At present, nowhere, except as a memory and an ideal. [*Savoyard inclines his head respectfully to the ideal*]. But I am by no means an idealogue. I am not content with beautiful dreams: I want beautiful realities.

SAVOYARD. Hear, hear! I'm all with you there— when you can get them.

THE COUNT. Why not get them? The difficulty is not that there are no beautiful realities, Mr Savoyard: the difficulty is that so few of us know them when we see them. We have inherited from the past a vast treasure of beauty—of imperishable masterpieces of poetry, of painting, of sculpture, of architecture, of music, of exquisite fashions in dress, in furniture, in domestic decoration. We can contemplate these treasures. We can reproduce many of them. We can buy a few inimitable originals. We can shut out the nineteenth century—

SAVOYARD [*correcting him*] The twentieth.

THE COUNT. To me the century I shut out will always be the nineteenth century, just as your national anthem will always be God Save the Queen, no matter how many kings may succeed. I found England befouled with industrialism: well, I did what Byron did: I simply refused to live in it. You remember Byron's words: "I am sure my bones would not rest in an English grave, or my clay mix with the earth of that country. I believe the thought would drive me mad on my deathbed could I suppose that any of my friends would be base enough to convey my carcase back to her soil. I would not even feed her worms if I could help it."

SAVOYARD. Did Byron say that?

THE COUNT. He did, sir.

SAVOYARD. It dont sound like him. I saw a good deal of him at one time.

THE COUNT. You! But how is that possible? You are too young.

SAVOYARD. I was quite a lad, of course. But I had a job in the original production of Our Boys.

THE COUNT. My dear sir, not that Byron, Lord Byron, the poet.

SAVOYARD. Oh, I beg your pardon. I thought you were talking of the Byron. So you prefer living abroad?

THE COUNT. I find England ugly and Philistine. Well, I dont live in it. I find modern houses ugly. I dont live in them: I have a palace on the grand canal. I find modern clothes prosaic. I dont wear them, except, of course, in the street. My ears are offended by the Cockney twang: I keep out of hearing of it and speak and listen to Italian. I find Beethoven's music coarse and restless, and Wagner's senseless and detestable. I do not listen to them: I listen to Cimarosa, to Pergolesi, to Gluck and Mozart. Nothing simpler, sir.

SAVOYARD. It's all right when you can afford it.

THE COUNT. Afford it! My dear Savoyard, if you are a man with a sense of beauty you can make an earthly paradise for yourself in Venice on £1500 a year, whilst our wretched vulgar industrial millionaires are spending twenty thousand on the amusements of billiard markers. I assure you I am a poor man according to modern ideas. But I have never had anything less than the very best that life has produced. It is my good fortune to have a beautiful and lovable daughter; and that girl, sir, has never seen an ugly sight or heard an ugly sound that I could spare her; and she has certainly never worn an ugly dress or tasted coarse food or bad wine in her life. She has lived in a palace; and her perambulator was a gondola. Now you know the sort of people we are, Mr Savoyard. You can imagine how we feel here.

SAVOYARD. Rather out of it, eh?

THE COUNT. Out of it, sir! Out of what?

SAVOYARD. Well, out of everything.

THE COUNT. Out of soot and fog and mud and east wind; out of vulgarity and ugliness, hypocrisy and greed, superstition and stupidity. Out of all this, and in the sunshine, in the enchanted region of which great artists alone have had the secret, in the sacred footsteps of Byron, of Shelley, of the Brownings, of Turner and Ruskin. Dont you envy me, Mr Savoyard?

SAVOYARD. Some of us must live in England, you know, just to keep the place going. Besides—though, mind you, I dont say it isnt all right from the high art point of view and all that—three weeks of it would drive me melancholy mad. However, I'm glad you told me, because it explains why it is you dont seem to know your way about much in England. I hope, by the way, that everything has given satisfaction to your daughter.

THE COUNT. She seems quite satisfied. She tells me that the actors you sent down are perfectly suited to their parts, and very nice people to work with. I understand she had some difficulties at the first rehearsals with the gentleman you call the producer, because he hadnt read the play; but the moment he found out what it was all about everything went smoothly.

SAVOYARD. Havnt you seen the rehearsals?

THE COUNT. Oh no. I havnt been allowed even to meet any of the company. All I can tell you is that the hero is a Frenchman [*Savoyard is rather scandalized*]: I asked her not to have an English hero. That is all I know. [*Ruefully*] I havnt been consulted even about the costumes, though there, I think, I could have been some use.

SAVOYARD [*puzzled*] But there arnt any costumes.

THE COUNT [*seriously shocked*] What! No costumes! Do you mean to say it is a modern play?

SAVOYARD. I dont know: I didnt read it. I handed it to Billy Burjoyce—the producer, you know—and left it to him to select the company and so on. But I should have had to order the costumes if there had been any. There wernt.

THE COUNT [*smiling as he recovers from his alarm*] I understand. She has taken the costumes into her own hands. She is an expert in beautiful costumes. I venture to promise you, Mr Savoyard, that what you are about to see will be like a Louis Quatorze ballet painted by Watteau. The heroine will be an exquisite Columbine, her lover a dainty Harlequin, her father a picturesque Pantaloon, and the valet who hoodwinks the father and brings about the happiness of the lovers a grotesque but perfectly tasteful Punchinello or Mascarille or Sganarelle.

SAVOYARD. I see. That makes three men; and the clown and policemen will make five. Thats why you wanted five men in the company.

THE COUNT. My dear sir, you dont suppose I mean that vulgar, ugly, silly, senseless, malicious and destructive thing the harlequinade of a nineteenth century English Christmas pantomime! What was it after all but a stupid attempt to imitate the success made by the genius of Grimaldi a hundred years ago? My daughter does not know of the existence of such a thing. I refer to the graceful and charming fantasies of the Italian and French stages of the seventeenth and eighteenth centuries.

SAVOYARD. Oh, I beg pardon. I quite agree that harlequinades are rot. Theyve been dropped at all smart theatres. But from what Billy Burjoyce told me I got the idea that your daughter knew her way about here, and had seen a lot of plays. He had no idea she'd been away in Venice all the time.

THE COUNT. Oh, she has not been. I should have explained that two years ago my daughter left me to complete her education at Cambridge. Cambridge was my own University; and though of course there were no women there in my time, I felt confident that if the atmosphere of the eighteenth century still existed anywhere in England, it would be at Cambridge. About three months ago she wrote to me and asked whether I wished to give her a present on her next birthday. Of course I said yes; and she then astonished and delighted me by telling me that she had written a play, and that the present she wanted was a private performance of it with real actors and real critics.

SAVOYARD. Yes: thats what staggered me. It was easy enough to engage a company for a private performance: it's done often enough. But the notion of having critics was new. I hardly knew how to set about it. They dont expect private engagements; and so they have no agents. Besides, I didnt know what to offer them. I knew that they were cheaper than actors, because they get long engagements: forty years sometimes; but thats no rule for a single job. Then theres such a lot of them: on first nights they run away with all your stalls: you cant find a decent place for your own mother. It would have cost a fortune to bring the lot.

THE COUNT. Of course I never dreamt of having them all. Only a few first-rate representative men.

SAVOYARD. Just so. All you want is a few sample opinions. Out of a hundred notices you wont find more than four at the outside that say anything different. Well, Ive got just the right four for you. And what do you think it has cost me?

THE COUNT [*shrugging his shoulders*] I cannot guess.

SAVOYARD. Ten guineas, and expenses. I had to give Flawner Bannal ten. He wouldnt come for less; and he asked fifty. I had to give it, because if we hadnt had him we might just as well have had nobody at all.

THE COUNT. But what about the others, if Mr Flannel—

SAVOYARD [*shocked*] Flawner Bannal.

THE COUNT.—if Mr Bannal got the whole ten?

SAVOYARD. Oh, I managed that. As this is a high-class sort of thing, the first man I went for was Trotter.

THE COUNT. Oh indeed. I am very glad you have secured Mr Trotter. I have read his Playful Impressions.

SAVOYARD. Well, I was rather in a funk about him. He's not exactly what I call approachable; and he was a bit stand-off at first. But when I explained and told him your daughter—

THE COUNT [*interrupting in alarm*] You did not say that the play was by her, I hope?

SAVOYARD. No: thats been kept a dead secret. I just said your daughter has asked for a real play with a real author and a real critic and all the rest of it. The moment I mentioned the daughter I had him. He has a daughter of his own. Wouldnt hear of payment! Offered to come just to please her! Quite human. I was surprised.

THE COUNT. Extremely kind of him.

SAVOYARD. Then I went to Vaughan, because he does music as well as the drama; and you said you thought there would be music. I told him Trotter would feel lonely without him; so he promised like a bird. Then I thought youd like one of the latest sort: the chaps that go for the newest things and swear theyre oldfashioned. So I nailed Gilbert Gunn. The four will give you a representative team. By the way [*looking at his watch*] theyll be here presently.

THE COUNT. Before they come, Mr Savoyard, could you give me any hints about them that would help me to make a little conversation with them? I am, as you said, rather out of it in England; and I might unwittingly say something tactless.

SAVOYARD. Well, let me see. As you dont like English people, I dont know that youll get on with Trotter, because he's thoroughly English: never happy except when he's in Paris, and speaks French so unnecessarily well that everybody there spots him as an Englishman the moment he opens his mouth. Very witty and all that. Pretends to turn up his nose at the theatre and says people make too much fuss about art [*the Count is extremely indignant*]. But thats only his modesty, because art is his own line, you understand. Mind you dont chaff him about Aristotle.

THE COUNT. Why should I chaff him about Aristotle?

SAVOYARD. Well, I dont know; but it's one of the recognized ways of chaffing him. However, youll get on with him all right: he's a man of the world and a man of sense. The one youll have to be careful about is Vaughan.

THE COUNT. In what way, may I ask?

SAVOYARD. Well, Vaughan has no sense of humor; and if you joke with him he'll think youre insulting him on purpose. Mind: it's not that he doesnt see a joke: he does; and it hurts him. A comedy scene makes him sore all over: he goes away black and blue, and pitches into the play for all he's worth.

THE COUNT. But surely that is a very serious defect in a man of his profession?

SAVOYARD. Yes it is, and no mistake. But Vaughan is honest, and dont care a brass farthing what he says, or whether it pleases anybody or not; and you must have one man of that sort to say the things that nobody else will say.

THE COUNT. It seems to me to carry the principle of division of labor too far, this keeping of the honesty and the other qualities in separate compartments. What is Mr Gunn's speciality, if I may ask?

SAVOYARD. Gunn is one of the Intellectuals.

THE COUNT. But arnt they all Intellectuals?

SAVOYARD. Lord! no: heaven forbid! You must be careful what you say about that: I shouldnt like anyone to call me an Intellectual: I dont think any Englishman would! They dont count really, you know; but still it's rather the thing to have them. Gunn is one of the young Intellectuals: he writes plays himself. He's useful because he pitches into the older Intellectuals who are standing in his way. But you may take it from me that none of these chaps really matter. Flawner Bannal's your man. Bannal really represents the British playgoer. When he likes a thing, you may take your oath there are a hundred thousand people in London thatll like it if they can only be got to know about it. Besides, Bannal's knowledge of the theatre is an inside knowledge. We know him; and he knows us. He knows the ropes: he knows his way about: he knows what he's talking about.

THE COUNT [*with a little sigh*] Age and experience, I suppose?

SAVOYARD. Age! I should put him at twenty at the very outside, myself. It's not an old man's job after all, is it? Bannal may not ride the literary high horse like Trotter and the rest; but I'd take his opinion before any other in London. He's the man in the street; and thats what you want.

THE COUNT. I am almost sorry you didnt give the gentleman his full terms. I should not have grudged the fifty guineas for a sound opinion. He may feel shabbily treated.

SAVOYARD. Well, let him. It was a bit of side, his asking fifty. After all, what is he? Only a pressman. Jolly good business for him to earn ten guineas: he's done the same job often enough for half a quid, I expect.

Fanny O'Dowda comes precipitately through the

curtains, excited and nervous. A girl of nineteen in a dress synchronous with her father's.

FANNY. Papa, papa, the critics have come. And one of them has a cocked hat and sword like a—[*she notices Savoyard*] Oh, I beg your pardon.

THE COUNT. This is Mr Savoyard, your impresario, my dear.

FANNY [*shaking hands*] How do you do?

SAVOYARD. Pleased to meet you, Miss O'Dowda. The cocked hat is all right. Trotter is a member of the new Academic Committee. He induced them to go in for a uniform like the French Academy; and I asked him to wear it.

THE FOOTMAN [*announcing*] Mr Trotter, Mr Vaughan, Mr Gunn, Mr Flawner Bannal.

The four critics enter. Trotter wears a diplomatic dress, with sword and three-cornered hat. His age is about 50. Vaughan is 40. Gunn is 30. Flawner Bannal is 20 and is quite unlike the others, who can be classed at sight as professional men whilst Bannal is obviously an unemployable of the business class picking up a living by an obtuse courage which gives him cheerfulness, conviviality, and bounce, and is helped out positively by a slight turn for writing, and negatively by a comfortable ignorance and lack of intuition which hides from him all the dangers and disgraces that keep men of finer perception in check. The Count approaches them hospitably.

SAVOYARD. Count O'Dowda, gentlemen. Mr Trotter.

TROTTER [*looking at the Count's costume*] Have I the pleasure of meeting a *confrère*?

THE COUNT. No, sir: I have no right to my costume except the right of a lover of the arts to dress myself handsomely. You are most welcome, Mr Trotter. [*Trotter bows in the French manner*].

SAVOYARD. Mr Vaughan.

THE COUNT. How do you do, Mr Vaughan?

VAUGHAN. Quite well, thanks.

SAVOYARD. Mr. Gunn.

THE COUNT. Delighted to make your acquaintance, Mr Gunn.

GUNN. Very pleased.

SAVOYARD. Mr Flawner Bannal.

THE COUNT. Very kind of you to come, Mr Bannal.

BANNAL. Dont mention it.

THE COUNT. Gentlemen, my daughter. [*They all bow*]. We are very greatly indebted to you, gentlemen, for so kindly indulging her whim. [*The dressing bell sounds. The Count looks at his watch*]. Ah! The dressing bell, gentlemen. As our play begins at nine, I have had to put forward the dinner hour a little. May I shew you to your rooms? [*He goes out, followed by all the men, except Trotter, who, going last, is detained by Fanny*].

FANNY. Mr Trotter: I want to say something to you about this play.

TROTTER. No: thats forbidden. You must not attempt to *souffler* the critic.

FANNY. Oh, I would not for the world try to influence your opinion.

TROTTER. But you do: you are influencing me very shockingly. You invite me to this charming house, where I'm about to enjoy a charming dinner. And just before the dinner I'm taken aside by a charming young lady to be talked to about the play. How can you expect me to be impartial? God forbid that I should set up to be a judge, or do more than record an impression; but my impressions can be influenced; and in this case youre influencing them shamelessly all the time.

FANNY. Dont make me more nervous than I am already, Mr Trotter. If you knew how I feel!

TROTTER. Naturally: your first party: your first appearance in England as hostess. But youre doing it beautifully. Dont be afraid. Every *nuance* is perfect.

FANNY. It's so kind of you to say so, Mr Trotter. But that isnt whats the matter. The truth is, this play is going to give my father a dreadful shock.

TROTTER. Nothing unusual in that, I'm sorry to say. Half the young ladies in London spend their evenings making their fathers take them to plays that are not fit for elderly people to see.

FANNY. Oh, I know all about that; but you cant understand what it means to papa. Youre not so innocent as he is.

TROTTER [*remonstrating*] My dear young lady—

FANNY. I dont mean morally innocent: everybody who reads your articles knows youre as innocent as a lamb.

TROTTER. What!

FANNY. Yes, Mr Trotter: Ive seen a good deal of life since I came to England; and I assure you that to me youre a mere baby: a dear, good, well-meaning, delightful, witty, charming baby; but still just a wee lamb in a world of wolves. Cambridge is not what it was in my father's time.

TROTTER. Well, I must say!

FANNY. Just so. Thats one of our classifications in the Cambridge Fabian Society.

TROTTER. Classifications? I dont understand.

FANNY. We classify our aunts into different sorts. And one of the sorts is the "I must says."

TROTTER. I withdraw "I must say." I substitute "Blame my cats!" No: I substitute "Blame my kittens!" Observe, Miss O'Dowda: kittens. I say again in the teeth of the whole Cambridge Fabian Society, kittens. Impertinent little kittens. Blame

[363]

them. Smack them. I guess what is on your conscience. This play to which you have lured me is one of those in which members of Fabian Societies instruct their grandmothers in the art of milking ducks. And you are afraid it will shock your father. Well, I hope it will. And if he consults me about it I shall recommend him to smack you soundly and pack you off to bed.

FANNY. Thats one of your prettiest literary attitudes, Mr Trotter, but it doesnt take me in. You see, I'm much more conscious of what you really are than you are yourself, because weve discussed you thoroughly at Cambridge; and youve never discussed yourself, have you?

TROTTER. I—

FANNY. Of course you havnt; so you see it's no good Trottering at me.

TROTTER. Trottering!

FANNY. Thats what we call it at Cambridge.

TROTTER. If it were not so obviously a stage *cliché*, I should say Damn Cambridge. As it is, I blame my kittens. And now let me warn you. If youre going to be a charming healthy young English girl, you may coax me. If youre going to be an unsexed Cambridge Fabian virago, I'll treat you as my intellectual equal, as I would treat a man.

FANNY [*adoringly*] But how few men are your intellectual equals, Mr Trotter!

TROTTER. I'm getting the worst of this.

FANNY. On no. Why do you say that?

TROTTER. May I remind you that the dinner-bell will ring presently?

FANNY. What does it matter? We're both ready. I havnt told you yet what I want you to do for me.

TROTTER. Nor have you particularly predisposed me to do it, except out of pure magnanimity. What is it?

FANNY. I dont mind this play shocking my father morally. It's good for him to be shocked morally. It's all that the young can do for the old, to shock them and keep them up to date. But I know that this play will shock him artistically; and that terrifies me. No moral consideration could make a breach between us: he would forgive me for anything of that kind sooner or later; but he never gives way on a point of art. I darent let him know that I love Beethoven and Wagner; and as to Strauss, if he heard three bars of Elektra, it'd part us for ever. Now what I want you to do is this. If he's very angry—if he hates the play, because it's a modern play—will you tell him that it's not my fault; that its style and construction, and so forth, are considered the very highest art nowadays; that the author wrote it in the proper way for repertory theatres of the most superior kind—you know the kind of plays I mean?

TROTTER [emphatically] I think I know the sort of entertainments you mean. But please do not beg a vital question by calling them plays. I dont pretend to be an authority; but I have at least established the fact that these productions, whatever else they may be, are certainly not plays.

FANNY. The authors dont say they are.

TROTTER [warmly] I am aware that one author, who is, I blush to say, a personal friend of mine, resorts freely to the dastardly subterfuge of calling them conversations, discussions, and so forth, with the express object of evading criticism. But I'm not to be disarmed by such tricks. I say they are not plays. Dialogues, if you will. Exhibitions of character, perhaps: especially the character of the author. Fiction, possibly, though a little decent reticence as to introducing actual persons, and thus violating the sanctity of private life, might not be amiss. But plays, no. I say NO. Not plays. If you will not concede this point I cant continue our conversation. I take this seriously. It's a matter of principle. I must ask you. Miss O'Dowda, before we go a step further, Do you or do you not claim that these works are plays?

FANNY. I assure you I dont.

TROTTER. Not in any sense of the word?

FANNY. Not in any sense of the word. I loathe plays.

TROTTER [*disappointed*] That last remark destroys all the value of your admission. You admire these—these theatrical nondescripts? You enjoy them?

FANNY. Dont you?

TROTTER. Of course I do. Do you take me for a fool? Do you suppose I prefer popular melodramas? Have I not written most appreciative notices of them? But I say theyre not plays. Theyre not plays. I cant consent to remain in this house another minute if anything remotely resembling them is to be foisted on me as a play.

FANNY. I fully admit that theyre not plays. I only want you to tell my father that plays are not plays nowadays—not in your sense of the word.

TROTTER. Ah, there you go again! In my sense of the word! You believe that my criticism is merely a personal impression; that—

FANNY. You always said it was.

TROTTER. Pardon me: not on this point. If you had been classically educated—

FANNY. But I have.

TROTTER. Pooh! Cambridge! If you had been educated at Oxford, you would know that the definition of a play has been settled exactly and scientifically for two thousand two hundred and sixty years. When I say that these entertainments are not plays, I dont mean in my sense of the word, but in the sense given to it for all time by the immortal Stagirite.

FANNY. Who is the Stagirite?

TROTTER [*shocked*] You dont know who the Stagirite was!

FANNY. Sorry. Never heard of him.

TROTTER. And this is Cambridge education! Well, my dear young lady, I'm delighted to find theres something you dont know; and I shant spoil you by dispelling an ignorance which, in my opinion, is highly becoming to your age and sex. So we'll leave it at that.

FANNY. But you will promise to tell my father that lots of people write plays just like this one—that I havnt selected it out of mere heartlessness?

TROTTER. I cant possibly tell you what I shall say to your father about the play until Ive seen the play. But I'll tell you what I shall say to him about you. I shall say that youre a very foolish young lady; that youve got into a very questionable set; and that the sooner he takes you away from Cambridge and its Fabian Society, the better.

FANNY. It's so funny to hear you pretending to be a heavy father. In Cambridge we regard you as a *bel esprit*, a wit, an Irresponsible, a Parisian Immoralist, *très chic*.

TROTTER. I!

FANNY. Theres quite a Trotter set.

TROTTER. Well, upon my word!

FANNY. They go in for adventures and call you Aramis.

TROTTER. They wouldnt dare!

FANNY. You always make such delicious fun of the serious people. Your *insouciance*—

TROTTER [*frantic*] Stop talking French to me: it's not

a proper language for a young girl. Great heavens! how is it possible that a few innocent pleasantries should be so frightfully misunderstood? Ive tried all my life to be sincere and simple, to be unassuming and kindly. Ive lived a blameless life. Ive supported the Censorship in the face of ridicule and insult. And now I'm told that I'm a centre of Immoralism! of Modern Minxism! a trifler with the most sacred subjects! a Nietzschean!! perhaps a Shavian!!!

FANNY. Do you mean you are really on the serious side, Mr Trotter?

TROTTER. Of course I'm on the serious side. How dare you ask me such a question?

FANNY. Then why dont you play for it?

TROTTER. I do play for it—short, of course, of making myself ridiculous.

FANNY. What! not make yourself ridiculous for the sake of a good cause! Oh, Mr Trotter! Thats *vieux jeu.*

TROTTER [*shouting at her*] Dont talk French. I will not allow it.

FANNY. But this dread of ridicule is so frightfully out of date. The Cambridge Fabian Society—

TROTTER. I forbid you to mention the Fabian Society to me.

FANNY. Its motto is "You cannot learn to skate without making yourself ridiculous."

TROTTER. Skate! What has that to do with it?

FANNY. Thats not all. It goes on, "The ice of life is slippery."

TROTTER. Ice of life indeed! You should be eating penny ices and enjoying yourself. I wont hear another word.

The Count returns.

THE COUNT. We're all waiting in the drawing room,

[368]

my dear. Have you been detaining Mr Trotter all this time?

TROTTER. I'm so sorry. I must have just a little brush up: I— [*He hurries out*].

THE COUNT. My dear, you should be in the drawing room. You should not have kept him here.

FANNY. I know. Dont scold me: I had something important to say to him.

THE COUNT. I shall ask him to take you in to dinner.

FANNY. Yes, papa. Oh, I hope it will go off well.

THE COUNT. Yes, love, of course it will. Come along.

FANNY. Just one thing, papa, while we're alone. Who was the Stagirite?

THE COUNT. The Stagirite! Do you mean to say you dont know?

FANNY. Havnt the least notion

THE COUNT. The Stagirite was Aristotle. By the way, dont mention him to Mr Trotter.

They go to the dining room.

[ACT I]

In the dining room of a house in Denmark Hill, an elderly lady sits at breakfast reading the newspaper. Her chair is at the end of the oblong dining table furthest from the fire. There is an empty chair at the other end. The fireplace is behind this chair; and the door is next the fireplace, between it and the corner. An armchair stands beside the coal-scuttle. In the middle of the back wall is the sideboard, parallel to the table. The rest of the furniture is mostly dining-room chairs, ranged against the walls, and including a baby rocking chair on the lady's side of the room. The lady is a placid person. Her husband, Mr Robin Gilbey, not at all placid, bursts violently into the room with a letter in his hand.

GILBEY [*grinding his teeth*] This is a nice thing. This is a b—

MRS GILBEY [*cutting him short*] Leave it at that, please. Whatever it is, bad language wont make it better.

GILBEY [*bitterly*] Yes, put me in the wrong as usual. Take your boy's part against me. [*He flings himself into the empty chair opposite her*].

MRS GILBEY. When he does anything right, he's your son. When he does anything wrong he's mine. Have you any news of him?

GILBEY. Ive a good mind not to tell you.

MRS GILBEY. Then dont. I suppose he's been found. Thats a comfort, at all events.

GILBEY. No, he hasnt been found. The boy may be at the bottom of the river for all you care. [*Too agitated to sit quietly, he rises and paces the room distractedly*].

MRS GILBEY. Then what have you got in your hand?

GILBEY. Ive a letter from the Monsignor Grenfell. From New York. Dropping us. Cutting us. [*Turning fiercely on her*] Thats a nice thing, isnt it?

MRS GILBEY. What for?

GILBEY [*flinging away towards his chair*] How do *I* know what for?

MRS GILBEY. What does he say?

GILBEY [*sitting down and grumblingly adjusting his spectacles*] This is what he says. "My dear Mr Gilbey: The news about Bobby had to follow me across the Atlantic: it did not reach me until to-day. I am afraid he is incorrigible. My brother, as you may imagine, feels that this last escapade has gone beyond the bounds; and I think, myself, that Bobby ought to be made to feel that such scrapes involve a certain degree of reprobation." "As you may imagine!" And we know no more about it than the babe unborn.

MRS GILBEY. What else does he say?

GILBEY. "I think my brother must have been just a little to blame himself; so, between ourselves, I shall, with due and impressive formality, forgive Bobby later on; but for the present I think it had better be understood that he is in disgrace, and that we are no longer on visiting terms. As ever, yours sincerely." [*His agitation masters him again*] Thats a nice slap in the face to get from a man in his position! This is what your son has brought on me.

MRS GILBEY. Well, I think it's rather a nice letter. He as good as tells you he's only letting on to be offended for Bobby's good.

GILBEY. Oh, very well: have the letter framed and hang it up over the mantelpiece as a testimonial.

MRS GILBEY. Dont talk nonsense, Rob. You ought to be thankful to know that the boy is alive after his disappearing like that for a nearly a week.

GILBEY. Nearly a week! A fortnight, you mean. Wheres your feelings, woman! It was fourteen days yesterday.

MRS GILBEY. Oh, dont call it fourteen days, Rob, as if the boy was in prison.

GILBEY. How do you know he's not in prison? It's got on my nerves, so that I'd believe even that.

MRS GILBEY. Dont talk silly, Rob. Bobby might get into a scrape like any other lad; but he'd never do anything low.

Juggins, the footman, comes in with a card on a salver. He is a rather low-spirited man of thirty-five or more, of good appearance and address, and iron self-command.

JUGGINS [*presenting the salver to Mr Gilbey*] Lady wishes to see Mr Bobby's parents, sir.

GILBEY [*pointing to Mrs Gilbey*] Theres Mr Bobby's parent. I disown him.

JUGGINS. Yes, sir. [*He presents the salver to Mrs Gilbey*].

MRS GILBEY. You mustnt mind what your master says, Juggins: he doesnt mean it. [*She takes the card and reads it*]. Well, I never!

GILBEY. Whats up now?

MRS GILBEY [*reading*] "Miss D. Delaney. Darling Dora." Just like that—in brackets. What sort of person, Juggins?

GILBEY. Whats her address?

MRS GILBEY. The West Circular Road. Is that a respectable address, Juggins?

JUGGINS. A great many most respectable people live in the West Circular Road, madam; but the address is not a guarantee of respectability.

GILBEY. So it's come to that with him, has it?

MRS GILBEY. Dont jump to conclusions, Rob. How do you know? [*To Juggins*] Is she a lady, Juggins? You know what I mean.

JUGGINS. In the sense in which you are using the word, no, madam.

MRS GILBEY. I'd better try what I can get out of her. [*To Juggins*] Shew her up. You dont mind, do you, Rob?

GILBEY. So long as you dont flounce out and leave me alone with her. [*He rises and plants himself on the hearth-rug*].

Juggins goes out.

MRS GILBEY. I wonder what she wants, Rob?

GILBEY. If she wants money, she shant have it. Not a farthing. A nice thing, everybody seeing her on our doorstep! If it wasnt that she may tell us something about the lad, I'd have Juggins put the hussy into the street.

JUGGINS [*returning and announcing*] Miss Delaney. [*He waits for express orders before placing a chair for this visitor*].

Miss Delaney comes in. She is a young lady of hilarious disposition, very tolerable good looks, and killing clothes. She is so affable and confidential that it is very difficult to keep her at a distance by any process short of flinging her out of the house.

DORA [*plunging at once into privileged intimacy and into the middle of the room*] How d'ye do, both. I'm a friend of Bobby's. He told me all about you once, in a moment of confidence. Of course he never let on who he was at the police court?

GILBEY. Police court?

MRS GILBEY [*looking apprehensively at Juggins*]. Tch—! Juggins: a chair.

[373]

DORA. Oh, Ive let it out, have I! [*Contemplating Juggins approvingly as he places a chair for her between the table and the sideboard*] But he's the right sort: I can see that. [*Buttonholing him*] You wont let on downstairs, old man, will you?

JUGGINS. The family can rely on my absolute discretion. [*He withdraws*].

DORA [*sitting down genteelly*] I dont know what youll say to me: you know I really have no right to come here; but then what was I to do? You know Holy Joe, Bobby's tutor, dont you? But of course you do.

GILBEY [*with dignity*] I know Mr Joseph Grenfell, the brother of Monsignor Grenfell, if it is of him you are speaking.

DORA [*wide-eyed and much amused*] No!!! You dont tell me that old geezer has a brother a Monsignor! And youre Catholics! And I never knew it, though Ive known Bobby ever so long! But of course the last thing you find out about a person is their religion, isnt it?

MRS GILBEY. We're not Catholics. But when the Samuelses got an Archdeacon's son to form their boy's mind, Mr Gilbey thought Bobby ought to have a chance too. And the Monsignor is a customer. Mr Gilbey consulted him about Bobby; and he recommended a brother of his that was more sinned against than sinning.

GILBEY [*on tenterhooks*] She dont want to hear about that, Maria. [*To Dora*] Whats your business?

DORA. I'm afraid it was all my fault.

GILBEY. What was all your fault? I'm half distracted. I dont know what has happened to the boy: he's been lost these fourteen days—

MRS GILBEY. A fortnight, Rob.

GILBEY. —and not a word have we heard of him since.

MRS GILBEY. Dont fuss, Rob.

GILBEY [*yelling*] I will fuss. Youve no feeling. You dont care what becomes of the lad [*He sits down savagely*].

DORA [*soothingly*] Youve been anxious about him. Of course. How thoughtless of me not to begin by telling you he's quite safe. Indeed he's in the safest place in the world, as one may say: safe under lock and key.

GILBEY [*horrified, pitiable*] Oh my—[*his breath fails him*]. Do you mean that when he was in the police court he was in the dock? Oh, Maria! Oh, great Lord! What has he done? What has he got for it? [*Desperate*] Will you tell me or will you see me go mad on my own carpet?

DORA [*sweetly*] Yes, old dear—

MRS GILBEY [*starting at the familiarity*] Well!

DORA [*continuing*] I'll tell you; but dont you worry: he's all right. I came out myself this morning: there was such a crowd! and a band! they thought I was a suffragette: only fancy! You see it was like this. Holy Joe got talking about how he'd been a champion sprinter at college.

MRS GILBEY. A what?

DORA. A sprinter. He said he was the fastest hundred yards runner in England. We were all in the old cowshed that night.

MRS GILBEY. What old cowshed?

GILBEY [*groaning*] Oh, get on. Get on.

DORA. Oh, of course, you wouldnt know. How silly of me! It's a rather go-ahead sort of music hall in Stepney. We call it the old cowshed.

MRS GILBEY. Does Mr Grenfell take Bobby to music halls?

DORA. No: Bobby takes him. But Holy Joe likes it: fairly laps it up like a kitten, poor old dear. Well, Bobby says to me, "Darling—"

MRS GILBEY [*placidly*] Why does he call you darling?

DORA. Oh, everybody calls me darling: it's a sort of name Ive got. Darling Dora, you know. Well, he says, "Darling, if you can get Holy Joe to sprint a hundred yards, I'll stand you that squiffer with the gold keys."

MRS GILBEY. Does he call his tutor Holy Joe to his face?

Gilbey clutches at his hair in his impatience.

DORA. Well, what would he call him? After all, Holy Joe is Holy Joe; and boys will be boys.

MRS GILBEY. Whats a squiffer?

DORA. Oh, of course: excuse my vulgarity: a concertina. Theres one in a shop in Green Street, ivory inlaid, with gold keys and Russia leather bellows; and Bobby knew I hankered after it; but he couldnt afford it, poor lad, though I knew he just longed to give it to me.

GILBEY. Maria: if you keep interrupting with silly questions, I shall go out of my senses. Heres the boy in gaol and me disgraced for ever; and all you care to know is what a squiffer is.

DORA. Well, remember it has gold keys. The man wouldnt take a penny less than £15 for it. It was a presentation one.

GILBEY [*shouting at her*] Wheres my son? Whats happened to my son? Will you tell me that, and stop cackling about your squiffer?

DORA. Oh, aint we impatient! Well, it does you credit, old dear. And you neednt fuss: theres no disgrace. Bobby behaved like a perfect gentleman. Besides, it was all my fault, I'll own it: I took too much champagne. I was not what you might call drunk; but I was bright, and a little beyond myself; and—I'll confess it—I wanted to shew off before Bobby, because he was a bit taken by a woman on the

[376]

stage; and she was pretending to be game for anything. You see youve brought Bobby up too strict; and when he gets loose theres no holding him. He does enjoy life more than any lad I ever met.

GILBEY. Never you mind how he's been brought up: thats my business. Tell me how he's been brought down: thats yours.

MRS GILBEY. Oh, dont be rude to the lady, Rob.

DORA. I'm coming to it, old dear: dont you be so headstrong. Well, it was a beautiful moonlight night; and we couldnt get a cab on the nod; so we started to walk, very jolly, you know: arm in arm, and dancing along, singing and all that. When we came into Jamaica Square, there was a young copper on point duty at the corner. I says to Bob: "Dearie boy: is it a bargain about the squiffer if I make Joe sprint for you?" "Anything you like, darling," says he: "I love you." I put on my best company manners and stepped up to the copper. "If you please, sir," says I, "can you direct me to Carrickmines Square?" I was so genteel, and talked so sweet, that he fell to it like a bird. "I never heard of any such Square in these parts," he says. "Then," says I, "what a very silly little officer you must be!"; and I gave his helmet a chuck behind that knocked it over his eyes, and did a bunk.

MRS GILBEY. Did a what?

DORA. A bunk. Holy Joe did one too all right: he sprinted faster than he ever did in college, I bet, the old dear. He got clean off, too. Just as he was overtaking me half-way down the square, we heard the whistle; and at the sound of it he drew away like a streak of lightning; and that was the last I saw of him. I was copped in the Dock Road myself: rotten luck, wasnt it? I tried the innocent and genteel and all the rest; but Bobby's hat done me in.

[377]

GILBEY. And what happened to the boy?

DORA. Only fancy! he stopped to laugh at the copper! He thought the copper would see the joke, poor lamb. He was arguing about it when the two that took me came along to find out what the whistle was for, and brought me with them. Of course I swore I'd never seen him before in my life; but there he was in my hat and I in his. The cops were very spiteful and laid it on for all they were worth: drunk and disorderly and assaulting the police and all that. I got fourteen days without the option, because you see—well, the fact is, I'd done it before, and been warned. Bobby was a first offender and had the option; but the dear boy had no money left and wouldnt give you away by telling his name; and anyhow he couldnt have brought himself to buy himself off and leave me there; so he's doing his month. Well, it was two forty shillingses; and Ive only twenty-eight shillings in the world. If I pawn my clothes I shant be able to earn any more. So I cant pay the fine and get him out; but if youll stand £3 I'll stand one; and thatll do it. If youd like to be very kind and nice you could pay the lot; but I cant deny that it was my fault; so I wont press you.

GILBEY [heart-broken] My son in gaol!

DORA. Oh, cheer up, old dear: it wont hurt him: look at me after fourteen days of it: I'm all the better for being kept a bit quiet. You mustnt let it prey on your mind.

GILBEY. The disgrace of it will kill me. And it will leave a mark on him to the end of his life.

DORA. Not a bit of it. Dont you be afraid: Ive educated Bobby a bit: he's not the mollycoddle he was when you had him in hand.

MRS GILBEY. Indeed Bobby is not a mollycoddle.

They wanted him to go in for singlestick at the Young Men's Christian Association; but, of course, I couldnt allow that: he might have had his eye knocked out.

GILBEY [*to Dora, angrily*] Listen here, you.

DORA. Oh, aint we cross!

GILBEY. I want none of your gaiety here. This is a respectable household. Youve gone and got my poor innocent boy into trouble. It's the like of you thats the ruin of the like of him.

DORA. So you always say, you old dears. But you know better. Bobby came to me: I didnt come to him.

GILBEY. Would he have gone if you hadnt been there for him to go to? Tell me that. You know why he went to you, I suppose.

DORA [*charitably*] It was dull for him at home, poor lad, wasnt it?

MRS GILBEY. Oh no. I'm at home on first Thursdays. And we have the Knoxes to dinner every Friday. Margaret Knox and Bobby are as good as engaged. Mr Knox is my husband's partner. Mrs Knox is very religious; but she's quite cheerful. We dine with them on Tuesdays. So thats two evenings pleasure every week.

GILBEY [*almost in tears*] We done what we could for the boy. Short of letting him go into temptations of all sorts, he can do what he likes. What more does he want?

DORA. Well, old dear, he wants me and thats about the long and short of it. And I must say youre not very nice to me about it. Ive talked to him like a mother, and tried my best to keep him straight; but I dont deny I like a bit of fun myself; and we both get a bit giddy when we're lighthearted. Him and me is a pair, I'm afraid.

[379]

GILBEY. Dont talk foolishness, girl. How could you and he be a pair, you being what you are, and he brought up as he has been, with the example of a religious woman like Mrs Knox before his eyes? I cant understand how he could bring himself to be seen in the street with you. [*Pitying himself*] I havnt deserved this. Ive done my duty as a father. Ive kept him sheltered. [*Angry with her*] Creatures like you that take advantage of a child's innocence ought to be whipped through the streets.

DORA. Well, whatever I may be, I'm too much the lady to lose my temper; and I dont think Bobby would like me to tell you what I think of you; for when I start giving people a bit of my mind I sometimes use language thats beneath me. But I tell you once for all I must have the money to get Bobby out; and if you wont fork out, I'll hunt up Holy Joe. He might get it off his brother, the Monsignor.

GILBEY. You mind your own concerns. My solicitor will do what is right. I'll not have you paying my son's fine as if you were anything to him.

DORA. Thats right. Youll get him out today, wont you?

GILBEY. It's likely I'd leave my boy in prison, isnt it?

DORA. I'd like to know when theyll let him out.

GILBEY. You would, would you? Youre going to meet him at the prison door.

DORA. Well, dont you think any woman would that had the feelings of a lady?

GILBEY [*bitterly*] Oh yes: I know. Here! I must buy the lad's salvation, I suppose. How much will you take to clear out and let him go?

DORA [*pitying him: quite nice about it*] What good would that do, old dear? There are others, you know.

[380]

GILBEY. Thats true. I must send the boy himself away.

DORA. Where to?

GILBEY. Anywhere, so long as he's out of the reach of you and your like.

DORA. Then I'm afraid youll have to send him out of the world, old dear. I'm sorry for you: I really am, though you mightnt believe it; and I think your feelings do you real credit. But I cant give him up just to let him fall into the hands of people I couldnt trust, can I?

GILBEY [*beside himself, rising*] Wheres the police? Wheres the Government? Wheres the Church? Wheres respectability and right reason? Whats the good of them if I have to stand here and see you put my son in your pocket as if he was a chattel slave, and you hardly out of gaol as a common drunk and disorderly? Whats the world coming to?

DORA. It is a lottery, isnt it, old dear?

Mr Gilbey rushes from the room, distracted.

MRS GILBEY [*unruffled*] Where did you buy that white lace? I want some to match a collaret of my own; and I cant get it at Perry and John's.

DORA. Knagg and Pantle's: one and fourpence. It's machine hand-made.

MRS GILBEY. I never give more than one and tuppence. But I suppose youre extravagant by nature. My sister Martha was just like that. Pay anything she was asked.

DORA. Whats tuppence to you, Mrs Bobby, after all?

MRS GILBEY [*correcting her*] Mrs Gilbey.

DORA. Of course, Mrs Gilbey. I am silly.

MRS GILBEY. Bobby must have looked funny in your hat. Why did you change hats with him?

DORA. I dont know. One does, you know.

MRS GILBEY. I never did. The things people do! I

cant understand them. Bobby never told me he was keeping company with you. His own mother!

DORA [*overcome*] Excuse me: I cant help smiling.

Juggins enters.

JUGGINS. Mr Gilbey has gone to Wormwood Scrubs, madam.

MRS GILBEY. Have you ever been in a police court, Juggins?

JUGGINS. Yes, madam.

MRS GILBEY [*rather shocked*] I hope you had not been exceeding, Juggins.

JUGGINS. Yes, madam, I had. I exceeded the legal limit.

MRS GILBEY. Oh, that! Why do they give a woman a fortnight for wearing a man's hat, and a man a month for wearing hers?

JUGGINS. I didnt know that they did, madam.

MRS GILBEY. It doesnt seem justice, does it, Juggins?

JUGGINS. No, madam.

MRS GILBEY [*to Dora, rising*] Well, goodbye. [*Shaking her hand*] So pleased to have made your acquaintance.

DORA [*standing up*] Dont mention it. I'm sure it's most kind of you to receive me at all.

MRS GILBEY. I must go off now and order lunch. [*She trots to the door*]. What was it you called the concertina?

DORA. A squiffer, dear.

MRS GILBEY [*thoughtfully*] A squiffer, of course. How funny! [*She goes out*].

DORA [*exploding into ecstasies of mirth*] Oh my! isnt she an old love? How do you keep your face straight?

JUGGINS. It is what I am paid for.

DORA [*confidentially*] Listen here, dear boy. Your name isnt Juggins. Nobody's name is Juggins.

JUGGINS. My orders are, Miss Delaney, that you are

not to be here when Mr Gilbey returns from Worm-wood Scrubs.

DORA. That means telling me to mind my own business, doesnt it? Well, I'm off. Tootle Loo, Charlie Darling. [*She kisses her hand to him and goes*].

[ACT II]

On the afternoon of the same day, Mrs Knox is writing notes in her drawing room, at a writing-table which stands against the wall. Anyone placed so as to see Mrs Knox's left profile, will have the door on the right and the window on the left, both further away than Mrs Knox, whose back is presented to an obsolete upright piano at the opposite side of the room. The sofa is near the piano. There is a small table in the middle of the room, with some gilt-edged books and albums on it, and chairs near it.

Mr Knox comes in almost furtively, a troubled man of fifty, thinner, harder, and uglier than his partner, Gilbey, Gilbey being a soft stoutish man with white hair and thin smooth skin, whilst Knox has coarse black hair, and blue jaws which no diligence in shaving can whiten. Mrs Knox is a plain woman, dressed without regard to fashion, with thoughtful eyes and thoughtful ways that make an atmosphere of peace and some solemnity. She is surprised to see her husband at home during business hours.

MRS KNOX. What brings you home at this hour? Have you heard anything?

KNOX. No. Have you?

MRS KNOX. No. Whats the matter?

KNOX [*sitting down on the sofa*] I believe Gilbey has found out.

MRS KNOX. What makes you think that?

KNOX. Well, I dont know: I didnt like to tell you: you have enough to worry you without that; but Gilbey's

[384]

been very queer ever since it happened. I cant keep my mind on business as I ought; and I was depending on him. But he's worse than me. He's not looking after anything; and he keeps out of my way. His manner's not natural. He hasnt asked us to dinner; and he's never said a word about our not asking him to dinner, after all these years when weve dined every week as regular as clockwork. It looks to me as if Gilbey's trying to drop me socially. Well, why should he do that if he hasnt heard?

MRS KNOX. I wonder! Bobby hasnt been near us either: thats what I cant make out.

KNOX. Oh, thats nothing. I told him Margaret was down in Cornwall with her aunt.

MRS KNOX [reproachfully] Jo! [She takes her handkerchief from the writing table and cries a little].

KNOX. Well, I got to tell lies, aint I? You wont. Somebody's got to tell em.

MRS KNOX [putting away her handkerchief] It only ends in our not knowing what to believe. Mrs Gilbey told me Bobby was in Brighton for the sea air. Theres something queer about that. Gilbey would never let the boy loose by himself among the temptations of a gay place like Brighton without his tutor; and I saw the tutor in Kensington High Street the very day she told me.

KNOX. If the Gilbeys have found out, it's all over between Bobby and Margaret, and all over between us and them.

MRS KNOX. It's all over between us and everybody. When a girl runs away from home like that, people know what to think of her and her parents.

KNOX. She had a happy, respectable home—everything—

MRS KNOX [interrupting him] Theres no use going over

it all again, Jo. If a girl hasnt happiness in herself, she wont be happy anywhere. Youd better go back to the shop and try to keep your mind off it.

KNOX [*rising restlessly*] I cant. I keep fancying everybody knows it and is sniggering about it. I'm at peace nowhere but here. It's a comfort to be with you. It's a torment to be with other people.

MRS KNOX [*going to him and drawing her arm through his*] There, Jo, there! I'm sure I'd have you here always if I could. But it cant be. God's work must go on from day to day, no matter what comes. We must face our trouble and bear it.

KNOX [*wandering to the window arm in arm with her*] Just look at the people in the street, going up and down as if nothing had happened. It seems unnatural, as if they all knew and didnt care.

MRS KNOX. If they knew, Jo, there'd be a crowd round the house looking up at us. You shouldnt keep thinking about it.

KNOX. I know I shouldnt. You have your religion, Amelia; and I'm sure I'm glad it comforts you. But it doesnt come to me that way. Ive worked hard to get a position and be respectable. Ive turned many a girl out of the shop for being half an hour late at night; and heres my own daughter gone for a fortnight without word or sign, except a telegram to say she's not dead and that we're not to worry about her.

MRS KNOX [*suddenly pointing to the street*] Jo, look!

KNOX. Margaret! With a man!

MRS KNOX. Run down, Jo, quick, Catch her: save her.

KNOX [*lingering*] She's shaking hands with him: she's coming across to the door.

MRS KNOX [*energetically*] Do as I tell you. Catch the man before he's out of sight.

Knox rushes from the room. Mrs Knox looks anxiously and excitedly from the window. Then she throws up the sash and leans out. Margaret Knox comes in, flustered and annoyed. She is a strong, springy girl of eighteen, with large nostrils, an audacious chin, and a gaily resolute manner, even peremptory on occasions like the present, when she is annoyed.

MARGARET. Mother. Mother.

Mrs Knox draws in her head and confronts her daughter.

MRS KNOX [*sternly*] Well, miss?

MARGARET. Oh, mother, do go out and stop father making a scene in the street. He rushed at him and said "Youre the man who took away my daughter" loud enough for all the people to hear. Everybody stopped. We shall have a crowd round the house. Do do something to stop him.

Knox returns with a good-looking young marine officer.

MARGARET. Oh, Monsieur Duvallet, I'm, so sorry—so ashamed. Mother: this is Monsieur Duvallet, who has been extremely kind to me. Monsieur Duvallet: my mother. [*Duvallet bows*].

KNOX. A Frenchman! It only needed this.

MARGARET [*much annoyed*] Father: do please be commonly civil to a gentleman who has been of the greatest service to me. What will he think of us?

DUVALLET [*debonair*] But it's very natural. I understand Mr Knox's feelings perfectly. [*He speaks English better than Knox, having learnt it on both sides of the Atlantic*].

KNOX. If Ive made any mistake I'm ready to apologize. But I want to know where my daughter has been for the last fortnight.

DUVALLET. She has been, I assure you, in a particularly safe place.

KNOX. Will you tell me what place? I can judge for myself how safe it was.

MARGARET. Holloway Gaol. Was that safe enough?

KNOX AND MRS KNOX. Holloway Gaol!

KNOX. Youve joined the Suffragets!

MARGARET. No. I wish I had. I could have had the same experience in better company. Please sit down, Monsieur Duvallet. [*She sits between the table and the sofa. Mrs Knox, overwhelmed, sits at the other side of the table. Knox remains standing in the middle of the room*].

DUVALLET [*sitting down on the sofa*] It was nothing. An adventure. Nothing.

MARGARET [*obdurately*] Drunk and assaulting the police! Forty shillings or a month!

MRS KNOX. Margaret! Who accused you of such a thing?

MARGARET. The policeman I assaulted.

KNOX. You mean to say that you did it!

MARGARET. I did. I had that satisfaction at all events, I knocked two of his teeth out.

KNOX. And you sit there coolly and tell me this!

MARGARET. Well, where do you want me to sit? Whats the use of saying things like that?

KNOX. My daughter in Holloway Gaol!

MARGARET. All the women in Holloway are some-body's daughters. Really, father, you must make up your mind to it. If you had sat in that cell for fourteen days making up your mind to it, you would under-stand that I'm not in the humor to be gaped at while youre trying to persuade yourself that it can't be real. These things really do happen to real people every day; and you read about them in the papers and think it's all right. Well, theyve happened to me: thats all.

KNOX [*feeble-forcible*] But they shouldnt have happened to you. Dont you know that?

MARGARET. They shouldnt happen to anybody, I suppose. But they do. [*Rising impatiently*] And really I'd rather go out and assault another policeman and go back to Holloway than keep talking round and round it like this. If youre going to turn me out of the house, turn me out: the sooner I go the better.

DUVALLET [*rising quickly*] That is impossible, mademoiselle. Your father has his position to consider. To turn his daughter out of doors would ruin him socially.

KNOX. Oh, youve put her up to that, have you? And where did you come in, may I ask?

DUVALLET. I came in at your invitation—at your amiable insistence, in fact, not at my own. But you need have no anxiety on my account. I was concerned in the regrettable incident which led to your daughter's incarceration. I got a fortnight without the option of a fine on the ridiculous ground that I ought to have struck the policeman with my fist. I should have done so with pleasure had I known; but, as it was, I struck him on the ear with my boot—a magnificent *moulinet*, I must say—and was informed that I had been guilty of an act of cowardice, but that for the sake of the *entente cordiale* I should be dealt with leniently. Yet Miss Knox, who used her fist, got a month, but with the option of a fine. I did not know this until I was released, when my first act was to pay the forty shillings. And here we are.

MRS KNOX. You ought to pay the gentleman the fine, Jo.

KNOX. [*reddening*] Oh, certainly. [*He takes out some money*].

DUVALLET. Oh please! it does not matter. [*Knox*

hands him two sovereigns]. If you insist—[*he pockets them*]. Thank you.

MARGARET. I'm ever so much obliged to you, Monsieur Duvallet.

DUVALLET. Can I be of any further assistance, mademoiselle?

MARGARET. I think you had better leave us to fight it out, if you dont mind.

DUVALLET. Perfectly. Madame [*bow*]—Mademoiselle [*bow*]— Monsieur [*bow*]—[*He goes out*].

MRS KNOX. Dont ring, Jo. See the gentleman out yourself.

Knox hastily sees Duvallet out. Mother and daughter sit looking forlornly at one another without saying a word. Mrs Knox slowly sits down. Margaret follows her example. They look at one another again. Mr Knox returns.

KNOX [*shortly and sternly*] Amelia: this is your job. [*To Margaret*] I leave you to your mother. I shall have my own say in the matter when I hear what you have to say to her. [*He goes out, solemn and offended*].

MARGARET [*with a bitter little laugh*] Just what the Suffraget said to me in Holloway. He throws the job on you.

MRS KNOX [*reproachfully*] Margaret!

MARGARET. You know it's true.

MRS KNOX. Margaret: if youre going to be hardened about it, theres no use my saying anything.

MARGARET. I'm not hardened, mother. But I cant talk nonsense about it. You see, it's all real to me. Ive suffered it. Ive been shoved and bullied. Ive had my arms twisted. Ive been made scream with pain in other ways. Ive been flung into a filthy cell with a lot of other poor wretches as if I were a sack of coals being emptied into a cellar. And the only difference between

me and the others was that I hit back. Yes I did. And I
did worse. I wasnt ladylike. I cursed. I called names.
I heard words that I didnt even know that I knew,
coming out of my mouth just as if somebody else had
spoken them. The policeman repeated them in court.
The magistrate said he could hardly believe it. The
policeman held out his hand with his two teeth in it
that I knocked out. I said it was all right; that I had
heard myself using those words quite distinctly; and
that I had taken the good conduct prize for three years
running at school. The poor old gentleman put me back
for the missionary to find out who I was, and to
ascertain the state of my mind. I wouldnt tell, of
course, for your sakes at home here; and I wouldnt
say I was sorry, or apologize to the policeman, or
compensate him or anything of that sort. I wasnt
sorry. The one thing that gave me any satisfaction was
getting in that smack on his mouth; and I said so. So
the missionary reported that I seemed hardened and
that no doubt I would tell who I was after a day in
prison. Then I was sentenced. So now you see I'm not
a bit the sort of girl you thought me. I'm not a bit the
sort of girl I thought myself. And I dont know what
sort of person you really are, or what sort of person
father really is. I wonder what he would say or do if he
had an angry brute of a policeman twisting his arm
with one hand and rushing him along by the nape of
his neck with the other. He couldnt whirl his leg like
a windmill and knock a policeman down by a glorious
kick on the helmet. Oh, if theyd all fought as we two
fought we'd have beaten them.

MRS KNOX. But how did it all begin?

MARGARET. Oh, I dont know. It was boat-race night,
they said.

MRS KNOX. Boat-race night! But what had you to do

with the boat race? You went to the great Salvation
Festival at the Albert Hall with your aunt. She put
you into the bus that passes the door. What made you
get out of the bus?

MARGARET. I dont know. The meeting got on my
nerves, somehow. It was the singing, I suppose: you
know I love singing a good swinging hymn; and I felt
it was ridiculous to go home in the bus after we had
been singing so wonderfully about climbing up the
golden stairs to heaven. I wanted more music—
more happiness—more life. I wanted some comrade
who felt as I did. I felt exalted: it seemed mean to be
afraid of anything: after all, what could anyone do to
me against my will? I suppose I was a little mad: at all
events, I got out of the bus at Piccadilly Circus, because there was a lot of light and excitement there. I
walked to Leicester Square; and went into a great
theatre.

MRS KNOX [*horrified*] A theatre!

MARGARET. Yes, Lots of other women were going in
alone. I had to pay five shillings.

MRS KNOX [*aghast*] Five shillings!

MARGARET [*apologetically*] It was a lot. It was very
stuffy; and I didnt like the people much, because they
didnt seem to be enjoying themselves; but the stage
was splendid and the music lovely. I saw that Frenchman, Monsieur Duvallet, standing against a barrier,
smoking a cigarette. He seemed quite happy; and he
was nice and sailorlike. I went and stood beside him,
hoping he would speak to me.

MRS KNOX [*gasps*] Margaret!

MARGARET [*continuing*] He did, just as if he had
known me for years. We got on together like old friends.
He asked me would I have some champagne; and I
said it would cost too much, but that I would give

anything for a dance. I longed to join the people on the stage and dance with them: one of them was the most beautiful dancer I ever saw. He told me he had come there to see her, and that when it was over we could go somewhere where there was dancing. So we went to a place where there was a band in a gallery and the floor cleared for dancing. Very few people danced: the women only wanted to shew off their dresses; but we danced and danced until a lot of them joined in. We got quite reckless; and we had champagne after all. I never enjoyed anything so much. But at last it got spoilt by the Oxford and Cambridge students up for the boatrace. They got drunk; and they began to smash things; and the police came in. Then it was quite horrible. The students fought with the police; and the police suddenly got quite brutal, and began to throw everybody downstairs. They attacked the women, who were not doing anything, and treated them just as roughly as they had treated the students. Duvallet got indignant and remonstrated with a policeman, who was shoving a woman though she was going quietly as fast as she could. The policeman flung the woman through the door and then turned on Duvallet. It was then that Duvallet swung his leg like a windmill and knocked the policeman down. And then three policemen rushed at him and carried him out by the arms and legs face downwards. Two more attacked me and gave me a shove to the door. That quite maddened me. I just got in one good bang on the mouth of one of them. All the rest was dreadful. I was rushed through the streets to the police station. They kicked me with their knees; they twisted my arms; they taunted and insulted me; they called me vile names; and I told them what I thought of them, and provoked them to do their worst. Theres one good thing about being hard hurt: it makes you sleep. I slept in that filthy cell with all the other drunks sounder than I should have slept at home. I cant describe how I felt next morning: it was hideous; but the police were quite jolly; and everybody said it was a bit of English fun, and talked about last year's boat-race night when it had been a great deal worse. I was black and blue and sick and wretched. But the strange thing was that I wasnt sorry; and I'm not sorry. And I dont feel that I did anything wrong, really. [*She rises and stretches her arms with a large liberating breath*] Now that it's all over I'm rather proud of it; though I know now that I'm not a lady; but whether thats because we're only shopkeepers, or because nobody's really a lady except when theyre treated like ladies, I dont know. [*She throws herself into a corner of the sofa*].

MRS KNOX [*lost in wonder*] But how could you bring yourself to do it, Margaret? I'm not blaming you: I only want to know. How could you bring yourself to do it?

MARGARET I cant tell you. I dont understand it myself. The prayer meeting set me free, somehow. I should never have done it if it were not for the prayer meeting.

MRS KNOX [*deeply horrified*] Oh, dont say such a thing as that. I know that prayer can set us free; though you could never understand me when I told you so; but it sets us free for good, not for evil.

MARGARET. Then I suppose what I did was not evil; or else I was set free for evil as well as good. As father says, you cant have anything both ways at once. When I was at home and at school I was what you call good; but I wasnt free. And when I got free I was what most people would call not good. But I see no harm in what I did; though I see plenty in what other people did to me.

MRS KNOX. I hope you dont think yourself a heroine of romance.

MARGARET. On no. [*She sits down again at the table*]. I'm a heroine of reality, if you call me a heroine at all. And reality is pretty brutal, pretty filthy, when you come to grips with it. Yet it's glorious all the same. It's so real and satisfactory.

MRS KNOX. I dont like this spirit in you, Margaret. I dont like your talking to me in that tone.

MARGARET. It's no use, mother. I dont care for you and papa any the less; but I shall never get back to the old way of talking again. Ive made a sort of descent into hell—

MRS KNOX. Margaret! Such a word!

MARGARET. You should have heard all the words that were flying round that night. You should mix a little with people who dont know any other words. But when I said that about a descent into hell I was not swearing. I was in earnest, like a preacher.

MRS KNOX. A preacher utters them in a reverent tone of voice.

MARGARET. I know: the tone that shews they dont mean anything real to him. They usent to mean anything real to me. Now hell is as real to me as a turnip; and I suppose I shall always speak of it like that. Anyhow, Ive been there; and it seems to me now that nothing is worth doing but redeeming people from it.

MRS KNOX. They are redeemed already if they choose to believe it.

MARGARET. Whats the use of that if they dont choose to believe it? You dont believe it yourself, or you wouldnt pay policemen to twist their arms. Whats the good of pretending? Thats all our respectability is, pretending, pretending, pretending. Thank heaven Ive had it knocked out of me once for all!

MRS KNOX [*greatly agitated*] Margaret: dont talk like that. I cant bear to hear you talking wickedly. I can bear to hear the children of this world talking vainly and foolishly in the language of this world. But when I hear you justifying your wickedness in the words of grace, it's too horrible: it sounds like the devil making fun of religion. Ive tried to bring you up to learn the happiness of religion. Ive waited for you to find out that happiness is within ourselves and doesnt come from outward pleasures. Ive prayed oftener than you think that you might be enlightened. But if all my hopes and all my prayers are to come to this, that you mix up my very words and thoughts with the promptings of the devil, then I dont know what I shall do: I dont indeed: itll kill me.

MARGARET. You shouldnt have prayed for me to be enlightened if you didnt want me to be enlightened. If the truth were known, I suspect we all want our prayers to be answered only by halves: the agreeable halves. Your prayer didnt get answered by halves, mother. Youve got more than you bargained for in the way of enlightenment. I shall never be the same again. I shall never speak in the old way again. Ive been set free from this silly little hole of a house and all its pretences. I know now that I am stronger than you and papa. I havnt found that happiness of yours that is within yourself; but Ive found strength. For good or evil I am set free; and none of the things that used to hold me can hold me now.

Knox comes back, unable to bear his suspense.

KNOX. How long more are you going to keep me waiting, Amelia? Do you think I'm made of iron? Whats the girl done? What are we going to do?

MRS KNOX. She's beyond my control, Jo, and beyond yours. I cant even pray for her now; for I dont know rightly what to pray for.

KNOX. Dont talk nonsense, woman: is this a time for praying? Does anybody know? Thats what we have to consider now. If only we can keep it dark, I dont care for anything else.

MARGARET. Dont hope for that, father. Mind: I'll tell everybody. It ought to be told. It must be told.

KNOX. Hold your tongue, you young hussy; or go out of my house this instant.

MARGARET. I'm quite ready. [*She takes her hat and turns to the door*].

KNOX [*throwing himself in front of it*] Here! where are you going?

MRS KNOX [*rising*] You mustnt turn her out, Jo! I'll go with her if she goes.

KNOX. Who wants to turn her out? But is she going to ruin us? To let everybody know of her disgrace and shame? To tear me down from the position Ive made for myself and you by forty years hard struggling?

MARGARET. Yes: I'm going to tear it all down. It stands between us and everything. I'll tell everybody.

KNOX. Magsy, my child: dont bring down your father's hairs with sorrow to the grave. Theres only one thing I care about in the world: to keep this dark. I'm your father. I ask you here on my knees—in the dust, so to speak—not to let it out.

MARGARET. I'll tell everybody.

Knox collapses in despair. Mrs Knox tries to pray and cannot. Margaret stands inflexible.

[ACT III]

*Again in the Gilbey's dining room. Afternoon. The
table is not laid: it is draped in its ordinary cloth, with
pen and ink, an exercise-book, and school-books on it.
Bobby Gilbey is in the armchair, crouching over the fire,
reading an illustrated paper. He is a pretty youth, of very
surburban gentility, strong and manly enough by nature,
but untrained and unsatisfactory, his parents having
imagined that domestic restriction is what they call
"bringing up". He has learnt nothing from it except a
habit of evading it by deceit.*

*He gets up to ring the bell; then resumes his crouch.
Juggins answers the bell.*

BOBBY. Juggins.

JUGGINS. Sir?

BOBBY [*morosely sarcastic*] Sir be blowed!

JUGGINS [*cheerfully*] Not at all, sir.

BOBBY. I'm a gaol-bird: youre a respectable man.

JUGGINS. That doesnt matter, sir. Your father pays
me to call you sir; and as I take the money, I keep my
part of the bargain.

BOBBY. Would you call me sir if you wernt paid to do
it?

JUGGINS. No, sir.

BOBBY. Ive been talking to Dora about you.

JUGGINS. Indeed, sir?

BOBBY. Yes, Dora says your name cant be Juggins,
and that you have the manners of a gentleman. I
always thought you hadnt any manners. Anyhow,
your manners are different from the manners of a
gentleman in my set.

[398]

JUGGINS. They would be, sir.

BOBBY. You dont feel disposed to be communicative on the subject of Dora's notion, I suppose.

JUGGINS. No, sir.

BOBBY [*throwing his paper on the floor and lifting his knees over the arm of the chair so as to turn towards the footman*] It was part of your bargain that you were to valet me a bit, wasnt it?

JUGGINS. Yes, sir.

BOBBY. Well, can you tell me the proper way to get out of an engagement to a girl without getting into a row for breach of promise?

JUGGINS. No, sir. You cant get out of an engagement without being sued for breach of promise if the lady wishes to be paid for her disappointment.

BOBBY. But it wouldnt be for her happiness to marry me when I dont really care for her.

JUGGINS. Women dont always marry for happiness, sir. They often marry because they wish to be married women and not old maids.

BOBBY. Then what am I to do?

JUGGINS. Marry her, sir, or take the consequences.

BOBBY [*jumping up*] Well, I wont marry her: thats flat. What would you do if you were in my place?

JUGGINS. I should tell the young lady that I found I couldnt fulfil my engagement.

BOBBY. But youd have to make some excuse, you know. I want to give it a gentlemanly turn: to say I'm not worthy of her, or something like that.

JUGGINS. That is not a gentlemanly turn, sir. Quite the contrary.

BOBBY. I dont see that at all. Do you mean that it's not exactly true?

JUGGINS. Not at all, sir.

BOBBY. I can say that no other girl can ever be to

me what she's been. That would be quite true, because our circumstances have been rather exceptional; and she'll imagine I mean I'm fonder of her than I can ever be of anyone else. You see, Juggins, a gentleman has to think of a girl's feelings.

JUGGINS. If you wish to spare her feelings, sir, you can marry her. If you hurt her feelings by refusing, you had better not try to get credit for considerateness at the same time by pretending to spare them. She wont like it. And it will start an argument, of which you will get the worse.

BOBBY. But, you know, Im not really worthy of her.

JUGGINS. Probably she never supposed you were, sir.

BOBBY. Oh, I say, Juggins, you are a pessimist.

JUGGINS [*preparing to go*] Anything else, sir?

BOBBY [*querulously*] You havnt been much use. [*He wanders disconsolately across the room*]. You generally put me up to the correct way of doing things.

JUGGINS. I assure you, sir, theres no correct way of jilting. It's not correct in itself.

BOBBY [*hopefully*] I'll tell you what. I'll say I cant hold her to an engagement with a man whos been in quod. Thatll do it. [*He seats himself on the table, relieved and confident*].

JUGGINS. Very dangerous, sir. No woman will deny herself the romantic luxury of self-sacrifice and forgiveness when they take the form of doing something agreeable. She's almost sure to say that your misfortune will draw her closer to you.

BOBBY. What a nuisance! I dont know what to do. You know, Juggins, your cool simple-minded way of doing it wouldnt go down in Denmark Hill.

JUGGINS. I daresay not, sir. No doubt youd prefer to make it look like an act of self-sacrifice for her sake on your part, or provoke her to break the engagement herself. Both plans have been tried repeatedly, but never with success, as far as my knowledge goes.

BOBBY. You have a devilish cool way of laying down the law. You know, in my class you have to wrap up things a bit. Denmark Hill isnt Camberwell, you know.

JUGGINS. I have noticed, sir, that Denmark Hill thinks that the higher you go in the social scale, the less sincerity is allowed, and that only tramps and riff-raff are quite sincere. Thats a mistake. Tramps are often shameless; but theyre never sincere. Swells—if I may use that convenient name for the upper classes—play much more with their cards on the table. If you tell the young lady that you want to jilt her, and she calls you a pig, the tone of the transaction may leave much to be desired; but itll be less Camberwellian than if you say youre not worthy.

BOBBY. Oh, I cant make you understand, Juggins. The girl isnt a scullerymaid. I want to do it delicately.

JUGGINS. A mistake, sir, believe me, if you are not a born artist in that line.—Beg pardon, sir, I think I heard the bell. [*He goes out*].

Bobby, much perplexed, shoves his hands into his pockets, and comes off the table, staring disconsolately straight before him; then goes reluctantly to his books, and sits down to write. Juggins returns.

JUGGINS [*announcing*] Miss Knox.

Margaret comes in. Juggins withdraws.

MARGARET. Still grinding away for that Society of Arts examination, Bobby? Youll never pass.

BOBBY [*rising*] No: I was just writing to you.

MARGARET. What about?

BOBBY. Oh, nothing. At least—How are you?

MARGARET [*passing round the other end of the table and putting down on it a copy of Lloyd's Weekly and her purse-bag*] Quite well, thank you. How did you enjoy Brighton?

BOBBY. Brighton! I wasnt at— Oh yes, of course, Oh, pretty well. Is your aunt all right?

MARGARET. My aunt! I suppose so. I havent seen her for a month.

BOBBY. I thought you were down staying with her.

MARGARET. Oh! was that what they told you?

BOBBY. Yes. Why? Wernt you really?

MARGARET. No. Ive something to tell you. Sit down and lets be comfortable.

She sits on the edge of the table. He sits beside her, and puts his arm wearily round her waist.

MARGARET. You neednt do that if you dont like, Bobby. Suppose we get off duty for the day, just to see what it's like.

BOBBY. Off duty? What do you mean?

MARGARET. You know very well what I mean. Bobby: did you ever care one little scrap for me in that sort of way? Dont funk answering: *I* dont care a bit for you—that way.

BOBBY [*removing his arm rather huffily*] I beg your pardon, I'm sure. I thought you did.

MARGARET. Well, did you? Come! Dont be mean. Ive owned up. You can put it all on me if you like, but I dont believe you care any more than I do.

BOBBY. You mean weve been shoved into it rather by the pars and mars.

MARGARET. Yes.

BOBBY. Well, it's not that I dont care for you: in fact, no girl can ever be to me exactly what you are; but weve been brought up so much together that it feels more like brother and sister than—well, than the other thing, doesnt it?

MARGARET. Just so. How did you find out the difference.

BOBBY [*blushing*] Oh, I say!

MARGARET. I found out from a Frenchman.

BOBBY. Oh, I say! [*He comes off the table in his consternation*].

MARGARET. Did you learn it from a Frenchwoman? You know you must have learnt it from somebody.

BOBBY. Not a Frenchwoman. She's quite a nice woman. But she's been rather unfortunate. The daughter of a clergyman.

MARGARET [*startled*] Oh, Bobby! That sort of woman!

BOBBY. What sort of woman?

MARGARET. You dont believe she's really a clergyman's daughter, do you, you silly boy? It's a stock joke.

BOBBY. Do you mean to say you dont believe me?

MARGARET. No: I mean to say I dont believe her.

BOBBY [*curious and interested, resuming his seat on the table beside her*] What do you know about her? What do you know about all this sort of thing?

MARGARET. What sort of thing, Bobby?

BOBBY. Well, about life.

MARGARET. Ive lived a lot since I saw you last. I wasnt at my aunt's. All that time that you were in Brighton, I mean.

BOBBY. I wasnt at Brighton, Meg. I'd better tell you: youre bound to find out sooner or later. [*He begins his confession humbly, avoiding her gaze*]. Meg: it's rather awful: youll think me no end of a beast. Ive been in prison.

MARGARET. You!

BOBBY. Yes, me. For being drunk and assaulting the police.

MARGARET. Do you mean to say that you—oh! this is a letdown for me. [*She comes off the table and drops, disconsolate, into a chair at the end of it furthest from the hearth*].

BOBBY. Of course I couldnt hold you to our engagement after that. I was writing to you to break it off. [*He also descends from the table and makes slowly for the hearth*]. You must think me an utter rotter.

MARGARET. Oh, has everybody been in prison for being drunk and assaulting the police? How long were you in?

BOBBY. A fortnight.

MARGARET. Thats what I was in for.

BOBBY. What are you talking about? In where?

MARGARET. In quod.

BOBBY. But I'm serious: I'm not rotting. Really and truly—

MARGARET. What did you do to the copper?

BOBBY. Nothing, absolutely nothing. He exaggerated grossly. I only laughed at him.

MARGARET [*jumping up, triumphant*] Ive beaten you hollow. I knocked out two of his teeth. Ive got one of them. He sold it to me for ten shillings.

BOBBY. Now please do stop fooling, Meg. I tell you I'm not rotting. [*He sits down in the armchair, rather sulkily*].

MARGARET [*taking up the copy of Lloyd's Weekly and going to him*] And I tell you I'm not either. Look! Heres a report of it. The daily papers are no good; but the Sunday papers are splendid. [*She sits on the arm of the chair*]. See! [*Reading*]: "Hardened at Eighteen. A quietly dressed, respectable-looking girl who refuses her name"—thats me.

BOBBY [*pausing a moment in his perusal*] Do you mean to say that you went on the loose out of pure devilment?

MARGARET. I did no harm. I went to see a lovely

dance. I picked up a nice man and went to have a
dance myself. I cant imagine anything more innocent
and more happy. All the bad part was done by other
people: they did it out of pure devilment if you like.
Anyhow, here we are, two gaol-birds, Bobby, disgraced forever. Isnt it a relief?

BOBBY [*rising stiffly*] But you know, it's not the same
for a girl. A man may do things a woman maynt. [*He
stands on the hearthrug with his back to the fire*].

MARGARET. Are you scandalized, Bobby?

BOBBY. Well, you cant expect me to approve of it,
can you, Meg? I never thought you were that sort of
girl.

MARGARET [*rising indignantly*] I'm not. You mustnt
pretend to think that *I*'m a clergyman's daughter,
Bobby.

BOBBY. I wish you wouldnt chaff about that. Dont
forget the row you got into for letting out that you
admired Juggins [*she turns her back on him quickly*]—a
footman! And what about the Frenchman?

MARGARET [*facing him again*] I know nothing about
the Frenchman except that he's a very nice fellow and
can swing his leg round like the hand of a clock and
knock a policeman down with it. He was in Worm-
wood Scrubs with you. I was in Holloway.

BOBBY. It's all very well to make light of it, Meg; but
this is a bit thick, you know.

MARGARET. Do you feel you couldnt marry a woman
whos been in prison.

BOBBY [*hastily*] No. I never said that. It might even
give a woman a greater claim on a man. Any girl, if
she were thoughtless and a bit on, perhaps, might get
into a scrape. Anyone who really understood her
character could see there was no harm in it. But youre
not the larky sort. At least you usent to be.

MARGARET. I'm not; and I never will be. [*She walks straight up to him*]. I didnt do it for a lark, Bob: I did it out of the very depths of my nature. I did it because I'm that sort of person. I did it in one of my religious fits. I'm hardened at eighteen, as they say. So what about the match, now?

BOBBY. Well, I dont think you can fairly hold me to it, Meg. Of course it would be ridiculous for me to set up to be shocked, or anything of that sort. I cant afford to throw stones at anybody; and I dont pretend to. I can understand a lark; I can forgive a slip; as long as it is understood that it is only a lark or a slip. But to go on the loose on principle; to talk about religion in connection with it; to—to—well, Meg, I do find that a bit thick, I must say. I hope youre not in earnest when you talk that way.

MARGARET. Bobby: youre no good. No good to me, anyhow.

BOBBY [*huffed*] I'm sorry, Miss Knox.

MARGARET. Goodbye, Mr Gilbey. [*She turns on her heel and goes to the other end of the table*]. I suppose you wont introduce me to the clergyman's daughter.

BOBBY. I dont think she'd like it. There are limits, after all. [*He sits down at the table, as if to resume work at his books: a hint to her to go*].

MARGARET [*on her way to the door*] Ring the bell, Bobby; and tell Juggins to shew me out.

BOBBY [*reddening*] I'm not a cad, Meg.

MARGARET [*coming to the table*] Then do something nice to prevent us feeling mean about this afterwards. Youd better kiss me. You neednt ever do it again.

BOBBY. If I'm no good, I dont see what fun it would be for you.

MARGARET. Oh, it'd be no fun. If I wanted what you call fun, I should ask the Frenchman to kiss me—or Juggins.

BOBBY [*rising and retreating to the hearth*] Oh, dont be disgusting, Meg. Dont be low.

MARGARET [*determinedly, preparing to use force*] No, I'll make you kiss me, just to punish you. [*She seizes his wrist; pulls him off his balance; and gets her arm round his neck*].

BOBBY. No. stop. Leave go, will you.

Juggins appears at the door.

JUGGINS. Miss Delaney, sir. [*Dora comes in. Juggins goes out. Margaret hastily releases Bobby, and goes to the other side of the room*].

DORA [*through the door, to the departing Juggins*] Well, you are a Juggins to shew me up when theres company. [*To Margaret and Bobby*] It's all right, dear: all right, old man: I'll wait in Juggins's pantry till youre disengaged.

MARGARET. Dont you know me?

DORA [*coming to the middle of the room and looking at her very attentively*] Why, it's never No. 406!

MARGARET. Yes it is.

DORA. Well, I should never have known you out of the uniform. How did you get out? You were doing a month, wernt you?

MARGARET. My bloke paid the fine the day he got out himself.

DORA. A real gentleman! [*Pointing to Bobby, who is staring open-mouthed*] Look at him! He cant take it in.

BOBBY. I suppose you made her acquaintance in prison, Meg. But when it comes to talking about blokes and all that—well!

MARGARET. Oh, Ive learnt the language; and I like it. It's another barrier broken down.

BOBBY. It's not so much the language, Meg. But I think [*he looks at Dora and stops*].

MARGARET [*suddenly dangerous*] What do you think, Bobby?

[407]

DORA. He thinks you oughtnt to be so free with me, dearie. It does him credit: he always was a gentleman, you know.

MARGARET. Does him credit! To insult you like that! Bobby: say that that wasnt what you meant.

BOBBY. I didnt say it was.

MARGARET. Well, deny that it was.

BOBBY. No. I wouldnt have said it in front of Dora; but I do think it's not quite the same thing my knowing her and you knowing her.

DORA. Of course it isnt, old man. [To Margaret] I'll just trot off and come back in half an hour. You two can make it up together. I'm really not fit company for you, dearie: I couldnt live up to you. [She turns to go].

MARGARET. Stop. Do you believe he could live up to me?

DORA. Well, I'll never say anything to stand between a girl and a respectable marriage, or to stop a decent lad from settling himself. I have a conscience; though I maynt be as particular as some.

MARGARET. You seem to me to be a very decent sort; and Bobby's behaving like a skunk.

BOBBY [much ruffled] Nice language that!

DORA. Well, dearie, men have to do some awfully mean things to keep up their respectability. But you cant blame them for that, can you? Ive met Bobby walking with his mother; and of course he cut me dead. I wont pretend I liked it; but what could he do, poor dear?

MARGARET. And now he wants me to cut you dead to keep him in countenance. Well, I shant: not if my whole family were there. But I'll cut him dead if he doesnt treat you properly. [To Bobby, with a threatening move in his direction] I'll educate you, you young beast.

BOBBY [furious, meeting her half-way] Who are you calling a young beast?

MARGARET. You.

DORA [*peacemaking*] Now, dearies!

BOBBY. If you dont take care, youll get your fat head jolly well clouted.

MARGARET. If you dont take care, the policeman's tooth will be the beginning of a collection.

DORA. Now, loveys, be good.

Bobby, lost to all sense of adult dignity, puts out his tongue at Margaret. Margaret, equally furious, catches his protended countenance a box on the cheek. He hurls himself on her. They wrestle.

BOBBY. Cat! I'll teach you.

MARGARET. Pig! Beast! [*She forces him backwards on the table*]. Now where are you?

DORA [*calling*] Juggins, Juggins. Theyll murder one another.

JUGGINS [*throwing open the door, and announcing*] Monsieur Duvallet.

Duvallet enters. Sudden cessation of hostilities, and dead silence. The combatants separate by the whole width of the room. Juggins withdraws.

DUVALLET. I fear I derange you.

MARGARET. Not at all. Bobby: you really are a beast: Monsieur Duvallet will think I'm always fighting.

DUVALLET. Practising jujitsu or the new Iceland wrestling. Admirable, Miss Knox. The athletic young Englishwoman is an example to all Europe. [*Indicating Bobby*] Your instructor, no doubt. Monsieur—[*he bows*].

BOBBY [*bowing awkwardly*] How d'y' do?

MARGARET [*to Bobby*] I'm so sorry, Bobby: I asked Monsieur Duvallet to call for me here; and I forgot to tell you. [*Introducing*] Monsieur Duvallet: Miss Four hundred and seven. Mr Bobby Gilbey. [*Duvallet bows*]. I really dont know how to explain our relationships. Bobby and I are like brother and sister.

[409]

DUVALLET. Perfectly. I noticed it.

MARGARET. Bobby and Miss—Miss—

DORA. Delaney, dear. [*To Duvallet, bewitchingly*] Darling Dora to real friends.

MARGARET. Bobby and Dora are—are—well, not brother and sister.

DUVALLET [*with redoubled comprehension*] PERfectly.

MARGARET. Bobby has spent the last fortnight in prison. You dont mind, do you?

DUVALLET. No, naturally. *I* have spent the last fortnight in prison.

The conversation drops. Margaret renews it with an effort.

MARGARET. Dora has spent the last fortnight in prison.

DUVALLET. Quite so. I felicitate Mademoiselle on her enlargement.

DORA. *Trop merci*, as they say in Boulogne. No call to be stiff with one another, have we?

Juggins comes in.

JUGGINS. Beg pardon, sir. Mr and Mrs Gilbey are coming up the street.

DORA. Let me absquatulate [*making for the door*].

JUGGINS. If you wish to leave without being seen, you had better step into my pantry and leave afterwards.

DORA. Righto! [*She bursts into song*]

Hide me in the meat safe til the cop goes by.
Hum the dear old music as his step draws nigh.

[*She goes out on tiptoe*].

MARGARET. I wont stay here if she has to hide. I'll keep her company in the pantry. [*She follows Dora*].

BOBBY. Lets all go. We cant have any fun with the Mar here. I say, Juggins: you can give us tea in the pantry, cant you?

JUGGINS. Certainly, sir.

BOBBY. Right. Say nothing to my mother. You dont mind, Mr Doovalley, do you?

DUVALLET. I shall be charmed.

BOBBY. Right you are. Come along. [*At the door*] Oh, by the way, Juggins, fetch down that concertina from my room, will you?

JUGGINS. Yes, sir. [*Bobby goes out. Duvallet follows him to the door*]. You understand, sir, that Miss Knox is a lady absolutely *comme il faut?*

DUVALLET. Perfectly. But the other?

JUGGINS. The other, sir, may be both charitably and accurately described in your native idiom as a daughter of joy.

DUVALLET. It is what I thought. These English domestic interiors are very interesting. [*He goes out, followed by Juggins*].

   Presently Mr and Mrs Gilbey come in. They take their accustomed places: he on the hearthrug, she at the colder end of the table.

MRS GILBEY. Did you smell scent in the hall, Rob?

GILBEY. No, I didnt. And I dont want to smell it. Dont you go looking for trouble, Maria.

MRS GILBEY [*snuffing up the perfumed atmosphere*] She's been here. [*Gilbey rings the bell*]. What are you ringing for? Are you going to ask?

GILBEY. No, I'm not going to ask. Juggins said this morning he wanted to speak to me. If he likes to tell me, let him; but I'm not going to ask; and dont you either. [*Juggins appears at the door*]. You said you wanted to say something to me.

JUGGINS. When it would be convenient to you, sir.

GILBEY. Well, what is it?

MRS GILBEY. Oh, Juggins, we're expecting Mr and Mrs Knox to tea.

GILBEY. He knows that. [*He sits down. Then, to Juggins*] What is it?

JUGGINS [*advancing to the middle of the table*] Would it inconvenience you, sir, if I were to give you a month's notice?

GILBEY [*taken aback*] What! Why? Aint you satisfied?

JUGGINS. Perfectly, sir. It is not that I want to better myself, I assure you.

GILBEY. Well, what do you want to leave for, then? Do you want to worse yourself?

JUGGINS. No, sir. Ive been well treated in your most comfortable establishment; and I should be greatly distressed if you or Mrs Gilbey were to interpret my notice as an expression of dissatisfaction.

GILBEY [*paternally*] Now you listen to me, Juggins. I'm an older man than you. Dont you throw out dirty water til you get in fresh. Dont get too big for your boots. Youre like all servants nowadays: you think youve only to hold up your finger to get the pick of half a dozen jobs. But you wont be treated everywhere as youre treated here. In bed every night before eleven; hardly a ring at the door except on Mrs Gilbey's day once a month; and no other man-servant to interfere with you. It may be a bit quiet perhaps; but youre past the age of adventure. Take my advice: think over it. You suit me; and I'm prepared to make it suit you if youre dissatisfied—in reason, you know.

JUGGINS. I realize my advantages, sir; but Ive private reasons—

GILBEY [*cutting him short angrily and retiring to the hearthrug in dudgeon*] Oh, I know. Very well: go. The sooner the better.

MRS GILBEY. Oh, not until we're suited. He must stay his month.

GILBEY [*sarcastic*] Do you want to lose him his character, Maria? Do you think I dont see what it is? We're prison folk now. Weve been in the police court. [*To Juggins*] Well, I suppose you know your own business best. I take your notice: you can go when your month is up, or sooner, if you like.

JUGGINS. Believe me, sir—

GILBEY. Thats enough: I dont want any excuses. I dont blame you. You can go downstairs now, if youve nothing else to trouble me about.

JUGGINS. I really cant leave it at that, sir. I assure you Ive no objection to young Mr Gilbey's going to prison. You may do six months yourself, sir, and welcome, without a word of remonstrance from me. I'm leaving solely because my brother, who has suffered a bereavement, and feels lonely, begs me to spend a few months with him until he gets over it.

GILBEY. And is he to keep you all that time? or are you to spend your savings in comforting him? Have some sense, man: how can you afford such things?

JUGGINS. My brother can afford to keep me, sir. The truth is, he objects to my being in service.

GILBEY. Is that any reason why you should be dependent on him? Dont do it, Juggins: pay your own way like an honest lad; and dont eat your brother's bread while youre able to earn your own.

JUGGINS. There is sound sense in that, sir. But unfortunately it is a tradition in my family that the younger brothers should spunge to a considerable extent on the eldest.

GILBEY. Then the sooner that tradition is broken the better, my man.

JUGGINS. A Radical sentiment, sir. But an excellent one.

GILBEY. Radical! What do you mean? Dont you

begin to take liberties, Juggins, now that you know we're loth to part with you. Your brother isnt a duke, you know.

JUGGINS. Unfortunately, he is, sir.

GILBEY.⎱ ⎰What!
MRS GILBEY.⎰ *together* ⎱Juggins!

JUGGINS. Excuse me, sir: the bell. [*He goes out*].

GILBEY [*overwhelmed*] Maria: did you understand him to say his brother was a duke?

MRS GILBEY. Fancy his condescending! Perhaps if youd offer to raise his wages and treat him as one of the family, he'd stay.

GILBEY. And have my own servant above me! Not me. What's the world coming to? Heres Bobby and—

JUGGINS [*entering and announcing*] Mr and Mrs Knox.

The Knoxes come in. Juggins takes two chairs from the wall and places them at the table, between the host and hostess. Then he withdraws.

MRS GILBEY [*to Mrs Knox*] How are you, dear?

MRS KNOX. Nicely, thank you. Good evening Mr Gilbey. [*They shake hands; and she takes the chair nearest Mrs Gilbey. Mr Knox takes the other chair*].

GILBEY [*sitting down*] I was just saying, Knox, What is the world coming to?

KNOX [*appealing to his wife*] What was I saying myself only this morning?

MRS KNOX. This is a strange time. I was never one to talk about the end of the world; but look at the things that have happened!

KNOX. Earthquakes!

GILBEY. San Francisco!

MRS GILBEY. Jamaica!

KNOX. Martinique!

GILBEY. Messina!

MRS GILBEY. The plague in China!

MRS KNOX. The floods in France!

GILBEY. My Bobby in Wormwood Scrubs!

KNOX. Margaret in Holloway!

GILBEY. And now my footman tells me his brother's a duke!

KNOX. ⎱No!

MRS KNOX. ⎰Whats that?

GILBEY. Just before he let you in. A duke! Here has everything been respectable from the beginning of the world, as you may say, to the present day; and all of a sudden everything is turned upside down.

MRS KNOX. It's like in the book of Revelations. But I do say that when people have happiness within themselves, all the earthquakes, all the floods, and all the prisons in the world cant make them really unhappy.

KNOX. It isnt alone the curious things that are happening, but the unnatural way people are taking them. Why, theres Margaret been in prison, and she hasnt time to go to all the invitations she's had from people that never asked her before.

GILBEY. I never knew we could live without being respectable.

MRS GILBEY. Oh, Rob, what a thing to say! Who says we're not respectable?

GILBEY. Well, it's not what I call respectable to have your children in and out of jail.

KNOX. Oh, come, Gilbey! we're not tramps because weve had, as it were, an accident.

GILBEY. It's no use, Knox: look it in the face. Did I ever tell you my father drank?

KNOX. No. But I knew it. Simmons told me.

GILBEY. Yes: he never could keep his mouth quiet: he told me your aunt was a kleptomaniac.

MRS KNOX. It wasnt true, Mr Gilbey. She used to

pick up handkerchiefs if she saw them lying about; but you might trust her with untold silver.

GILBEY. My Uncle Phil was a teetotaler. My father used to say to me: Rob, he says, dont you ever have a weakness. If you find one getting a hold on you, make a merit of it, he says. Your Uncle Phil doesnt like spirits; and he makes a merit of it, and is chairman of the Blue Ribbon Committee. I do like spirits; and I make a merit of it, and I'm the King Cockatoo of the Convivial Cockatoos. Never put yourself in the wrong, he says. I used to boast about what a good boy Bobby was. Now I swank about what a dog he is; and it pleases people just as well. What a world it is!

KNOX. It turned my blood cold at first to hear Margaret telling people about Holloway; but it goes down better than her singing used to.

MRS KNOX. I never thought she sang right after all those lessons we paid for.

GILBEY. Lord, Knox, it was lucky you and me got let in together. I tell you straight, if it hadnt been for Bobby's disgrace, I'd have broke up the firm.

KNOX. I shouldnt have blamed you: I'd have done the same only for Margaret. Too much straitlacedness narrows a man's mind. Talking of that, what about those hygienic corset advertisements that Vines & Jackson want us to put in the window? I told Vines they wernt decent and we couldnt shew them in our shop. I was pretty high with him. But what am I to say to him now if he comes and throws this business in our teeth?

GILBEY. Oh, put em in. We may as well go it a bit now.

MRS GILBEY. Youve been going it quite far enough, Rob. [To Mrs Knox] He wont get up in the mornings now: he that was always out of bed at seven to the tick!

[416]

MRS KNOX. You hear that, Jo? [*To Mrs Gilbey*] He's taken to whisky and soda. A pint a week! And the beer the same as before!

KNOX. Oh, dont preach, old girl.

MRS KNOX [*to Mrs Gilbey*] Thats a new name he's got for me. [*To Knox*] I tell you, Jo, this doesnt sit well on you. You may call it preaching if you like; but it's the truth for all that. I say that if youve happiness within yourself, you dont need to seek it outside, spending money on drink and theatres and bad company, and being miserable after all. You can sit at home and be happy; and you can work and be happy. If you have that in you, the spirit will set you free to do what you want and guide you to do right. But if you havnt got it, then youd best be respectable and stick to the ways that are marked out for you; for youve nothing else to keep you straight.

KNOX [*angrily*] And is a man never to have a bit of fun? See whats come of it with your daughter! She was to be content with your happiness that youre always talking about; and how did the spirit guide her? To a month's hard for being drunk and assaulting the police. Did *I* ever assault the police?

MRS KNOX. You wouldnt have the courage. I dont blame the girl.

MRS GILBEY. ⎱Oh, Maria! What are you saying?
GILBEY. ⎰What! And you so pious!

MRS KNOX. She went where the spirit guided her. And what harm there was in it she knew nothing about.

GILBEY. Oh, come, Mrs Knox! Girls are not so innocent as all that.

MRS KNOX. I dont say she was ignorant. But I do say that she didnt know what we know: I mean the way certain temptations get a sudden hold that no goodness nor self-control is any use against. She was saved from that, and had a rough lesson too; and I say it was no earthly protection that did that. But dont think, you two men, that youll be protected if you make what she did an excuse to go and do as youd like to do if it wasnt for the fear of losing your characters. The spirit wont guide you, because it isnt in you; and it never has been: not in either of you.

GILBEY [*with ironic humility*] I'm sure I'm obliged to you for your good opinion, Mrs Knox.

MRS KNOX. Well, I will say for you, Mr Gilbey, that youre better than my man here. He's a bitter hard heathen, is my Jo, God help me! [*She begins to cry quietly*].

KNOX. Now, dont take on like that, Amelia. You know I always gave in to you that you were right about religion. But one of us had to think of other things, or we'd have starved, we and the child.

MRS KNOX. How do you know youd have starved? All the other things might have been added unto you.

GILBEY. Come, Mrs Knox, dont tell me Knox is a sinner. I know better. I'm sure youd be the first to be sorry if anything was to happen to him.

KNOX [*bitterly to his wife*] Youve always had some grudge against me; and nobody but yourself can understand what it is.

MRS KNOX. I wanted a man who had that happiness within himself. You made me think you had it; but it was nothing but being in love with me.

MRS GILBEY. And do you blame him for that?

MRS KNOX. I blame nobody. But let him not think he can walk by his own light. I tell him that if he gives up being respectable he'll go right down to the bottom of the hill. He has no powers inside himself to keep him steady; so let him cling to the powers outside him.

KNOX [*rising angrily*] Who wants to give up being respectable? All this for a pint of whisky that lasted a week! How long would it have lasted Simmons, I wonder?

MRS KNOX [*gently*] Oh, well, say no more, Jo. I wont plague you about it. [*He sits down*]. You never did understand; and you never will. Hardly anybody understands: even Margaret didnt til she went to prison. She does now; and I shall have a companion in the house after all these lonely years.

KNOX [*beginning to cry*] I did all I could to make you happy. I never said a harsh word to you.

GILBEY [*rising indignantly*] What right have you to treat a man like that? an honest respectable husband? as if he were dirt under your feet?

KNOX. Let her alone, Gilbey. [*Gilbey sits down, but mutinously*].

MRS KNOX. Well, you gave me all you could, Jo; and if it wasnt what I wanted, that wasnt your fault. But I'd rather have you as you were than since you took to whisky and soda.

KNOX. I dont want any whisky and soda. I'll take the pledge if you like.

MRS KNOX. No: you shall have your beer because you like it. The whisky was only brag. And if you and me are to remain friends, Mr Gilbey, youll get up tomorrow morning at seven.

GILBEY [*defiantly*] Damme if I will! There!

MRS KNOX [*with gentle pity*] How do you know, Mr Gilbey, what youll do tomorrow morning?

GILBEY. Why shouldnt I know? Are we children not to be let do what we like, and our own sons and daughters kicking their heels all over the place? [*To Knox*] I was never one to interfere between man and wife, Knox; but if Maria started ordering me about like that—

MRS GILBEY. Now dont be naughty, Rob. You know you mustnt set yourself up against religion?

GILBEY. Whos setting himself up against religion?

MRS KNOX. It doesnt matter whether you set yourself up against it or not, Mr Gilbey. If it sets itself up against you, youll have to go the appointed way: it's no use quarrelling about it with me that am as great a sinner as yourself.

GILBEY. Oh, indeed! And who told you I was a sinner?

MRS GILBEY. Now, Rob, you know we are all sinners. What else is religion?

GILBEY. I say nothing against religion. I suppose we're all sinners, in a manner of speaking; but I dont like to have it thrown at me as if I'd really done anything.

MRS GILBEY. Mrs Knox is speaking for your good, Rob.

GILBEY. Well, I dont like to be spoken to for my good. Would anybody like it?

MRS KNOX. Dont take offence where none is meant, Mr Gilbey. Talk about something else. No good ever comes of arguing about such things among the like of us.

KNOX. The like of us! Are you throwing it in our teeth that your people were in the wholesale and thought Knox and Gilbey wasnt good enough for you?

MRS KNOX. No, Jo: you know I'm not. What better were my people than yours, for all their pride? But Ive noticed it all my life: we're ignorant. We dont really know whats right and whats wrong. We're all right as long as things go on the way they always did. We bring our children up just as we were brought up; and we go to church or chapel just as our parents did; and we say what everybody says; and it goes on all right until something out of the way happens: theres a family quarrel, or one of the children goes wrong, or a father takes to drink, or an aunt goes mad, or one of us finds ourselves doing something we never thought we'd want to do. And then you know what happens: complaints and quarrels and huff and offence and bad language and bad temper and regular bewilderment as if Satan possessed us all. We find out then that with all our respectability and piety, weve no real religion and no way of telling right from wrong. Weve nothing but our habits; and when theyre upset, where are we? Just like Peter in the storm trying to walk on the water and finding he couldnt.

MRS GILBEY [*piously*] Aye! He found out, didnt he?

GILBEY [*reverently*] I never denied that youve a great intellect, Mrs Knox—

MRS KNOX. Oh, get along with you, Gilbey, if you begin talking about my intellect. Give us some tea, Maria. Ive said my say; and I'm sure I beg the company's pardon for being so long about it, and so disagreeable.

MRS GILBEY. Ring, Rob. [*Gilbey rings*]. Stop. Juggins will think we're ringing for him.

GILBEY [*appalled*] It's too late. I rang before I thought of it.

MRS GILBEY. Step down and apologize, Rob.

KNOX. Is it him that you said was brother to a—

Juggins comes in with the tea-tray. All rise. He takes the tray to Mrs Gilbey.

GILBEY. I didnt mean to ask you to do this, Mr Juggins. I wasnt thinking when I rang.

MRS GILBEY [*trying to take the tray from him*] Let me, Juggins.

[421]

JUGGINS. Please sit down, madam. Allow me to discharge my duties just as usual, sir. I assure you that is the correct thing.

[*They sit down, ill at ease, whilst he places the tray on the table. He then goes out for the curate*].

KNOX [*lowering his voice*] Is this all right, Gilbey? Anybody may be the son of a duke, you know. Is he legitimate?

GILBEY. Good Lord! I never thought of that.

Juggins returns with the cakes. They regard him with suspicion.

GILBEY [*whispering to Knox*] You ask him.

KNOX [*to Juggins*] Just a word with you, my man. Was your mother married to your father?

JUGGINS. I believe so, sir. I cant say from personal knowledge. It was before my time.

GILBEY. Well but look here you know—[*he hesitates*].

JUGGINS. Yes, sir?

KNOX. I know whatll clinch it, Gilbey. You leave it to me. [*To Juggins*] Was your mother the duchess?

JUGGINS. Yes, sir. Quite correct, sir, I assure you. [*To Mrs Gilbey*] That is the milk, madam. [*She has mistaken the jugs*]. This is the water.

They stare at him in pitiable embarrassment.

MRS KNOX. What did I tell you? Heres something out of the common happening with a servant; and we none of us know how to behave.

JUGGINS. It's quite simple, madam. I'm a footman, and should be treated as a footman. [*He proceeds calmly with his duties, handing round cups of tea as Mrs Knox fills them*].

Shrieks of laughter from below stairs reach the ears of the company.

MRS GILBEY. Whats that noise? Is Master Bobby at home? I heard his laugh.

MRS KNOX. I'm sure I heard Margaret's.

GILBEY. Not a bit of it. It was that woman.

JUGGINS. I can explain, sir. I must ask you to excuse the liberty; but I'm entertaining a small party to tea in my pantry.

MRS GILBEY. But youre not entertaining Master Bobby?

JUGGINS. Yes, madam.

GILBEY. Whos with him?

JUGGINS. Miss Knox, sir.

GILBEY. Miss Knox! Are you sure? Is there anyone else?

JUGGINS. Only a French marine officer, sir, and—er—Miss Delaney. [*He places Gilbey's tea on the table before him*]. The lady that called about Master Bobby, sir.

KNOX. Do you mean to say theyre having a party all to themselves downstairs, and we having a party up here and knowing nothing about it?

JUGGINS. Yes, sir. I have to do a good deal of entertaining in the pantry for Master Bobby, sir.

GILBEY. Well, this is a nice state of things!

KNOX. Whats the meaning of it? What do they do it for?

JUGGINS. To enjoy themselves, sir, I should think.

MRS GILBEY. Enjoy themselves! Did ever anybody hear of such a thing?

GILBEY. Knox's daughter shewn into my pantry!

KNOX. Margaret mixing with a Frenchman and a footman—[*Suddenly realising that the footman is offering him cake*] She doesnt know about—about His Grace, you know.

MRS GILBEY. Perhaps she does. Does she, Mr Juggins?

[423]

JUGGINS. The other lady suspects me, madam. They call me Rudolph, or the Long Lost Heir.

MRS GILBEY. It's a much nicer name than Juggins. I think I'll call you by it, if you dont mind.

JUGGINS. Not at all, madam.

Roars of merriment from below.

GILBEY. Go and tell them to stop laughing. What right have they to make a noise like that?

JUGGINS. I asked them not to laugh so loudly, sir. But the French gentleman always sets them off again.

KNOX. Do you mean to tell me that my daughter laughs at a Frenchman's jokes?

GILBEY. We all know what French jokes are.

JUGGINS. Believe me: you do not, sir. The noise this afternoon has all been because the Frenchman said that the cat had whooping cough.

MRS GILBEY [*laughing heartily*] Well, I never!

GILBEY. Dont be a fool, Maria. Look here, Knox: we cant let this go on. People cant be allowed to behave like this.

KNOX. Just what I say.

A concertina adds its music to the revelry.

MRS GILBEY [*excited*] Thats the squiffer. He's bought it for her.

GILBEY. Well, of all the scandalous—[*Redoubled laughter from below*].

KNOX. I'll put a stop to this. [*He goes out to the landing and shouts*] Margaret! [*Sudden dead silence*]. Margaret, I say!

MARGARET'S VOICE. Yes, father. Shall we all come up? We're dying to.

KNOX. Come up and be ashamed of yourselves, behaving like wild Indians.

DORA'S VOICE [*screaming*] Oh! oh! oh! Dont, Bobby. Now—Oh! [*In headlong flight she dashes into*

*and right across the room, breathless, and slightly
abashed by the company*]. I beg your pardon, Mrs
Gilbey, for coming in like that; but whenever I go
upstairs in front of Bobby, he pretends it's a cat
biting my ankles; and I just must scream.

*Bobby and Margaret enter rather more shyly, but
evidently in high spirits. Bobby places himself near his
father, on the hearthrug, and presently slips down into
the armchair.*

MARGARET. How do you do, Mrs. Gilbey? [*She
puts herself behind her mother*].

*Duvallet comes in behaving himself perfectly. Knox
follows.*

MARGARET. Oh—let me introduce. My friend Lieutenant Duvallet. Mrs. Gilbey. Mr Gilbey.

*Duvallet bows and sits down on Mr Knox's left,
Juggins placing a chair for him.*

DORA. Now, Bobby: introduce me: theres a dear.

BOBBY [*a little nervous about it; but trying to keep up
his spirits*] Miss Delaney: Mr and Mrs Knox. [*Knox,
as he resumes his seat, acknowledges the introduction
suspiciously. Mrs Knox bows gravely, looking keenly at
Dora and taking her measure without prejudice*].

DORA. Pleased to meet you. [*Juggins places the baby
rocking-chair for her on Gilbey's right, opposite the
Knoxes*]. Thank you. [*She sits*]. Bobby's given me the
squiffer. Do you know what theyve been doing downstairs? Youd never guess. Theyve been trying to
teach me table manners. The Lieutenant and Rudolph
say I'm a regular pig. I'm sure I never knew there was
anything wrong with me. But live and learn. [*To
Gilbey*] Eh, old dear?

JUGGINS. Old dear is not correct, Miss Delaney. [*He
retires to the end of the sideboard nearest the door*].

DORA. Oh get out! I must call a man something. He doesnt mind: do you, Charlie?

MRS GILBEY. His name isnt Charlie.

DORA. Excuse me. I call everybody Charlie.

JUGGINS. You mustnt.

DORA. Oh, if I were to mind you, I should have to hold my tongue altogether; and then how sorry youd be! Lord, how I do run on! Dont mind me, Mrs Gilbey.

KNOX. What I want to know is, whats to be the end of this? It's not for me to interfere between you and your son, Gilbey: he knows his own intentions best, no doubt, and perhaps has told them to you. But Ive my daughter to look after; and it's my duty as a parent to have a clear understanding about her. No good is ever done by beating about the bush. I ask Lieutenant—well, I dont speak French; and I cant pronounce the name—

MARGARET. Mr Duvallet, father.

KNOX. I ask Mr Doovalley what his intentions are.

MARGARET. Oh, father: how can you?

DUVALLET. I'm afraid my knowledge of English is not enough to understand. Intentions? How?

MARGARET. He wants to know will you marry me.

MRS GILBEY. ⎫ What a thing to say!
KNOX. ⎬ Silence, miss.
DORA. ⎭ Well, thats straight, aint it?

DUVALLET. But I am married already. I have two daughters.

KNOX [rising, virtuously indignant] You sit there after carrying on with my daughter, and tell me coolly youre married.

MARGARET. Papa: you really must not tell people that they sit there. [He sits down again sulkily].

DUVALLET. Pardon. Carrying on? What does that mean?

MARGARET. It means—

KNOX [*violently*] Hold your tongue, you shameless young hussy. Dont you dare say what it means.

DUVALLET [*shrugging his shoulders*] What does it mean, Rudolph?

MRS KNOX. If it's not proper for her to say, it's not proper for a man to say, either. Mr Doovalley: youre a married man with daughters. Would you let them go about with a stranger, as you are to us, without wanting to know whether he intended to behave honorably?

DUVALLET. Ah, madam, my daughters are French girls. That is very different. It would not be correct for a French girl to go about alone and speak to men as English and American girls do. That is why I so immensely admire the English people. You are so free—so unprejudiced—your women are so brave and frank—their minds are so—how do you say?—wholesome. I intend to have my daughters educated in England. Nowhere else in the world but in England could I have met at a Variety Theatre a charming young lady of perfect respectability, and enjoyed a dance with her at a public dancing saloon. And where else arc women trained to box and knock out the teeth of policemen as a protest against injustice and violence? [*Rising, with immense élan*] Your daughter, madam, is superb. Your country is a model to the rest of Europe. If you were a Frenchman, stifled in prudery, hypocrisy, and the tyranny of the family and the home, you would understand how an enlightened Frenchman admires and envies your freedom, your broadmindedness, and the fact that home life can hardly be said to exist in England. You have made an end of the despotism of the parent; the family council is unknown to you; everywhere in these islands one can enjoy the exhilarating, the soul-liberating spectacle of men quarrelling with their brothers, defying their fathers, refusing to speak to their mothers. In France we are not men: we are only sons—grown-up children. Here one is a human being—an end in himself. Oh, Mrs Knox, if only your military genius were equal to your moral genius—if that conquest of Europe by France which inaugurated the new age after the Revolution had only been an English conquest, how much more enlightened the world would have been now! We, alas, can only fight. France is unconquerable. We impose our narrow ideas, our prejudices, our obsolete institutions, our insufferable pedantry on the world by brute force—by that stupid quality of military heroism which shews how little we have evolved from the savage: nay, from the beast. We can charge like bulls; we can spring on our foes like gamecocks; when we are overpowered by treason, we can die fighting like rats. And we are foolish enough to be proud of it! Why should we be? Does the bull progress? Can you civilize the gamecock? Is there any future for the rat? We never fight intelligently: when we lose battles, it is because we have not sense enough to know when we are beaten. At Waterloo, had we known when we were beaten, we should have retreated; tried another plan; and won the battle. But no: we were too pigheaded to admit that there is anything impossible to a Frenchman: we were quite satisfied when our Marshals had six horses shot under them, and our stupid old grognards died fighting rather than surrender like reasonable beings. Think of your great Wellington: think of his inspiring words, when the lady asked him whether British soldiers ever ran away. "All soldiers run away, madam," he said; "but if there are supports for them to fall back on it does not matter." Think of your illustrious Nelson, always beaten on land, always victorious at sea, where his men could not run away. You are not dazzled and misled by false ideals of patriotic enthusiasm: your honest and sensible statesmen demand for England a two-power standard, even a three-power standard, frankly admitting that it is wise to fight three to one: whilst we, fools and braggarts as we are, declare that every Frenchman is a host in himself, and that when one Frenchman attacks three Englishmen he is guilty of an act of cowardice comparable to that of the man who strikes a woman. It is folly: it is nonsense: a Frenchman is not really stronger than a German, than an Italian, even than an Englishman. Sir: if all Frenchwomen were like your daughter if all Frenchmen had the good sense, the power of seeing things as they really are, the calm judgment, the open mind, the philosophic grasp, the foresight and true courage, which are so natural to you as an Englishman that you are hardly conscious of possessing them, France would become the greatest nation in the world.

MARGARET. Three cheers for old England! [*She shakes hands with him warmly*].

BOBBY. Hurra-a-ay! And so say all of us.

Duvallet, having responded to Margaret's handshake with enthusiasm, kisses Juggins on both cheeks, and sinks into his chair, wiping his perspiring brow.

GILBEY. Well, this sort of talk is above me. Can you make anything out of it, Knox?

KNOX. The long and the short of it seems to be that he cant lawfully marry my daughter, as he ought after going to prison with her.

DORA. I'm ready to marry Bobby, if that will be any satisfaction.

GILBEY. No you dont. Not if I know it.

MRS KNOX. He ought to, Mr. Gilbey.

GILBEY. Well, if thats your religion, Amelia Knox, I want no more of it. Would you invite them to your house if he married her?

MRS KNOX. He ought to marry her whether or no.

BOBBY. I feel I ought to, Mrs Knox.

GILBEY. Hold your tongue. Mind your own business.

BOBBY [*wildly*] If I'm not let marry her, I'll do something downright disgraceful. I'll enlist as a soldier.

JUGGINS [*sternly*] That is not a disgrace, sir.

BOBBY. Not for you, perhaps. But youre only a footman. I'm a gentleman.

MRS GILBEY. Dont dare to speak disrespectfully to Mr Rudolph, Bobby. For shame!

JUGGINS [*coming forward to the middle of the table*] It is not gentlemanly to regard the service of your country as disgraceful. It is gentlemanly to marry the lady you make love to.

GILBEY [*aghast*] My boy is to marry this woman and be a social outcast!

JUGGINS. Your boy and Miss Delaney will be inexorably condemned by respectable society to spend the rest of their days in precisely the sort of company they seem to like best and be most at home in.

KNOX. And my daughter? Whos to marry my daughter?

JUGGINS. Your daughter, sir, will probably marry the man she makes up her mind to marry. She is a lady of very determined character.

KNOX. Yes: if he'd have her with her character gone. But who would? Youre the brother of a duke. Would—

BOBBY.   ⎫ ⎧ Whats that?
MARGARET. ⎪ ⎪ Juggins a duke!
DUVALLET. ⎬ ⎨ *Comment!*
DORA.   ⎭ ⎩ What did I tell you?

KNOX. Yes: the brother of a duke: thats what he is. [*To Juggins*] Well, would you marry her?

JUGGINS. I was about to propose that solution of your problem, Mr. Knox.

MRS GILBEY. ⎫ ⎧ Well, I never!
KNOX.   ⎬ ⎨ D'ye mean it?
MRS KNOX. ⎭ ⎩ Marry Margaret!

JUGGINS [*continuing*] As an idle younger son, unable to support myself, or even to remain in the Guards in competition with the grandsons of American millionaires, I could not have aspired to Miss Knox's hand. But as a sober, honest, and industrious domestic servant, who has, I trust, given satisfaction to his employer [*he bows to Mr Gilbey*] I feel I am a man with a character. It is for Miss Knox to decide.

MARGARET. I got into a frightful row once for admiring you, Rudolph.

JUGGINS. I should have got into an equally frightful row myself, Miss, had I betrayed my admiration for you. I looked forward to those weekly dinners.

MRS KNOX. But why did a gentleman like you stoop to be a footman?

DORA. He stooped to conquer.

MARGARET. Shut up, Dora: I want to hear.

JUGGINS. I will explain; but only Mrs Knox will understand. I once insulted a servant. Rashly; for he was a sincere Christian. He rebuked me for trifling with a girl of his own class. I told him to remember what he was, and to whom he was speaking. He said God would remember. I discharged him on the spot.

GILBEY. Very properly.

[431]

KNOX. What right had he to mention such a thing to you?

MRS GILBEY. What are servants coming to?

MRS KNOX. Did it come true, what he said?

JUGGINS. It stuck like a poisoned arrow. It rankled for months. Then I gave in. I apprenticed myself to an old butler of ours who kept a hotel. He taught me my present business, and got me a place as footman with Mr Gilbey. If ever I meet that man again I shall be able to look him in the face.

MRS KNOX. Margaret: it's not on account of the duke: dukes are vanities. But take my advice; and take him.

MARGARET [*slipping her arm through his*] I have loved Juggins since the first day I beheld him. I felt instinctively he had been in the Guards. May he walk out with me, Mr. Gilbey?

KNOX. Dont be vulgar, girl. Remember your new position. [*To Juggins*] I suppose youre serious about this, Mr—Mr Rudolph?

JUGGINS. I propose, with your permission, to begin keeping company this afternoon, if Mrs. Gilbey can spare me.

GILBEY [*in a gust of envy, to Bobby*] Itll be long enough before youll marry the sister of a duke, you young good-for-nothing.

DORA. Dont fret, old dear. Rudolph will teach me high-class manners. I call it quite a happy ending: dont you, lieutenant?

DUVALLET. In France it would be impossible. But here—ah! [*kissing his hand*] la belle Angleterre!

Before the curtain. The Count, dazed and agitated, hurries to the 4 critics, as they rise, bored and weary, from their seats.

THE COUNT. Gentlemen: do not speak to me. I implore you to withhold your opinion. I am not strong enough to bear it. I could never have believed it. Is this a play? Is this, in any sense of the word, Art? Is it agreeable? Can it conceivably do good to any human being? Is it delicate? Do such people really exist? Excuse me, gentlemen: I speak from a wounded heart. There are private reasons for my discomposure. This play implies obscure, unjust, unkind reproaches and menaces to all of us who are parents.

TROTTER. Pooh! you take it too seriously. After all, the thing has amusing passages. Dismiss the rest as impertinence.

THE COUNT. Mr Trotter: it is easy for you to play the pococurantist. [*Trotter, amazed, repeats the first three syllables in his throat, making a noise like a pheasant*]. You see hundreds of plays every year. But to me, who have never seen anything of this kind before, the effect of this play is terribly disquieting. Sir: if it had been what people call an immoral play, I shouldnt have minded a bit. [*Vaughan is shocked*]. Love beautifies every romance and justifies every audacity. [*Bannal assents gravely*]. But there are reticences which everybody should respect. There are decencies too subtle to be put into words, without which human society would be unbearable. People could not talk to one another as those people talk. No child could speak to its parent: no girl could speak to a youth: no human creature could tear down the veils—[*Appealing to Vaughan, who is on his left flank, with Gunn between them*] Could they, sir?

VAUGHAN. Well, I dont see that.

THE COUNT. You dont see it! dont feel it! [*To Gunn*] Sir: I appeal to you.

GUNN [*with studied weariness*] It seems to me the most ordinary sort of old-fashioned Ibsenite drivel.

THE COUNT [*turning to Trotter, who is on his right, between him and Bannal*] Mr Trotter: will you tell me that you are not amazed, outraged, revolted, wounded in your deepest and holiest feelings by every word of this play, every tone, every implication; that you did not sit there shrinking in every fibre at the thought of what might come next?

TROTTER. Not a bit. Any clever modern girl could turn out that kind of thing by the yard.

THE COUNT. Then, sir, tomorrow I start for Venice, never to return. I must believe what you tell me. I perceive that you are not agitated, not surprised, not concerned; that my own horror (yes, gentlemen, horror—horror of the very soul appears unaccountable to you, ludicrous, absurd, even to you, Mr Trotter, who are little younger than myself. Sir: if young people spoke to me like that, I should die of shame: I could not face it. I must go back. The world has passed me by and left me. Accept the apologies of an elderly and no doubt ridiculous admirer of the art of a bygone day, when there was still some beauty in the world and some delicate grace in family life. But I promised my daughter your opinion; and I must keep my word. Gentlemen: you are the choice and master spirits of this age: you walk through it without bewilderment and face its strange products without dismay. Pray deliver your verdict. Mr Bannal: you know that it is the custom at a Court Martial for the youngest officer present to deliver his judgment first; so that he may not be influenced by the authority of his elders. You are the youngest. What is your opinion of the play?

BANNAL. Well, whos it by?

THE COUNT. That is a secret for the present.

BANNAL. You dont expect me to know what to say about a play when I dont know who the author is, do you?

THE COUNT. Why not?

BANNAL. Why not! Why not!! Suppose you had to write about a play by Pinero and one by Jones! Would you say exactly the same thing about them?

THE COUNT. I presume not.

BANNAL. Then how could you write about them until you knew which was Pinero and which was Jones? Besides, what sort of play is this? thats what I want to know. Is it a comedy or a tragedy? Is it a farce or a melodrama? Is it repertory theatre tosh, or really straight paying stuff?

GUNN. Cant you tell from seeing it?

BANNAL. I can see it all right enough; but how am I to know how to take it? Is it serious, or is it spoof? If the author knows what his play is, let him tell us what it is. If he doesnt, he cant complain if I dont know either. *I*'m not the author.

THE COUNT. But is it a good play, Mr Bannal? Thats a simple question.

BANNAL. Simple enough when you know. If it's by a good author, it's a good play, naturally. That stands to reason. Who is the author? Tell me that; and I'll place the play for you to a hair's breadth.

THE COUNT. I'm sorry I'm not at liberty to divulge the author's name. The author desires that the play should be judged on its merits.

BANNAL. But what merits can it have except the author's merits? Who would you say it's by, Gunn?

GUNN. Well, who do you think? Here you have a rotten old-fashioned domestic melodrama acted by the usual stage puppets. The hero's a naval lieutenant. All melodramatic heroes are naval lieutenants. The heroine gets into trouble by defying the law (if she didnt get into trouble, thered be no drama) and plays for sympathy all the time as hard as she can. Her good old pious mother turns on her cruel father when he's going to put her out of the house, and says she'll go too. Then theres the comic relief: the comic shop-keeper, the comic shopkeeper's wife, the comic footman who turns out to be a duke in disguise, and the young scapegrace who gives the author his excuse for dragging in a fast young woman. All as old and stale as a fried fish shop on a winter morning.

THE COUNT. But—

GUNN [interrupting him] I know what youre going to say, Count. Youre going to say that the whole thing seems to you to be quite new and unusual and original. The naval lieutenant is a Frenchman who cracks up the English and runs down the French: the hackneyed old Shaw touch. The characters are second-rate middle class, instead of being dukes and millionaires. The heroine gets kicked through the mud: real mud. Theres no plot. All the old stage conventions and puppets without the old ingenuity and the old enjoyment. And a feeble air of intellectual pretentiousness kept up all through to persuade you that if the author hasnt written a good play it's because he's too clever to stoop to anything so commonplace. And you three experienced men have sat through all this, and cant tell me who wrote it! Why, the play bears the author's signature in every line.

BANNAL. Who?

GUNN. Granville-Barker, of course. Why, old Gilbey is straight out of The Madras House.

BANNAL. Poor old Barker!

VAUGHAN. Utter nonsense! Cant you see the difference in style?

BANNAL. No.

VAUGHAN [contemptuously] Do you know what style is?

BANNAL. Well, I suppose youd call Trotter's uniform style. But it's not my style—since you ask me.

VAUGHAN. To me it's perfectly plain who wrote that play. To begin with, it's intensely disagreeable. Therefore it's not by Barrie, in spite of the footman, whos cribbed from The Admirable Crichton. He was an earl, you may remember. You notice, too, the author's offensive habit of saying silly things that have no real sense in them when you come to examine them, just to set all the fools in the house giggling. Then what does it all come to? An attempt to expose the supposed hypocrisy of the Puritan middle class in England: people just as good as the author, anyhow. With, of course, the inevitable improper female: the Mrs Tanqueray, Iris, and so forth. Well, if you cant recognize the author of that, youve mistaken your profession: thats all I have to say.

BANNAL. Why are you so down on Pinero? And what about that touch that Gunn spotted? the Frenchman's long speech. I believe it's Shaw.

GUNN. Rubbish!

VAUGHAN. Rot! You may put that idea out of your head, Bannal. Poor as this play is, theres the note of passion in it. You feel somehow that beneath all the assumed levity of that poor waif and stray, she really loves Bobby and will be a good wife to him. Now Ive repeatedly proved that Shaw is physiologically incapable of the note of passion.

BANNAL. Yes, I know. Intellect without emotion. Thats right, I always say that myself. A giant brain, if you ask me; but no heart.

GUNN. Oh, shut up, Bannal. This crude medieval psychology of heart and brain—Shakespear would have called it liver and wits—is really schoolboyish. Surely weve had enough of secondhand Schopenhauer. Even such a played-out old back number as Ibsen would have been ashamed of it. Heart and brain, indeed!

VAUGHAN. You have neither one nor the other, Gunn. Youre dekkadent.

GUNN. Decādent! How I love that early Victorian word!

VAUGHAN. Well, at all events, you cant deny that the characters in this play are quite distinguishable from one another. That proves it's not by Shaw, because all Shaw's characters are himself: mere puppets stuck up to spout Shaw. It's only the actors that make them seem different.

BANNAL. There can be no doubt of that: everybody knows it. But Shaw doesnt write his plays as plays. All he wants to do is to insult everybody all round and set us talking about him.

TROTTER [wearily] And naturally, here we are all talking about him. For heaven's sake, let us change the subject.

VAUGHAN. Still, my articles about Shaw—

GUNN. Oh, stow it, Vaughan. Drop it. What Ive always told you about Shaw is—

BANNAL. There you go, Shaw, Shaw, Shaw! Do chuck it. If you want to know my opinion about Shaw—

TROTTER
VAUGHAN }[*yelling*]{ No, please, we dont.
GUNN Shut your head, Bannal.
Oh do drop it.

The deafened Count puts his fingers in his ears and flies from the centre of the group to its outskirts, behind Vaughan.

BANNAL [*sulkily*] Oh, very well. Sorry I spoke, I'm sure.

TROTTER
VAUGHAN }[*beginning again simultaneously*]{ Shaw—
GUNN Shaw—
Shaw—

They are cut short by the entry of Fanny through the curtains. She is almost in tears.

FANNY [*coming between Trotter and Gunn*] I'm so sorry, gentlemen. And it was such a success when I read it to the Cambridge Fabian Society!

TROTTER. Miss O'Dowda: I was about to tell these gentlemen what I guessed before the curtain rose: that you are the author of the play. [*General amazement and consternation*].

FANNY. And you all think it beastly. You hate it. You think I'm a conceited idiot, and that I shall never be able to write anything decent.

She is almost weeping. A wave of sympathy carries away the critics.

VAUGHAN. No, no. Why, I was just saying that it must have been written by Pinero. Didnt I, Gunn?

FANNY [*enormously flattered*] Really?

TROTTER. I thought Pinero was much too popular for the Cambridge Fabian Society.

FANNY. Oh yes, of course; but still—Oh, did you really say that, Mr Vaughan?

GUNN. I owe you an apology, Miss O'Dowda. I said it was by Barker.

FANNY [*radiant*] Granville-Barker! Oh, you couldnt really have thought it so fine as that.

BANNAL. *I* said Bernard Shaw.

FANNY. Oh, of course it would be a little like Bernard Shaw. The Fabian touch, you know.

BANNAL [*coming to her encouragingly*] A jolly good little play, Miss O'Dowda. Mind: I dont say it's like one of Shakespear's—Hamlet or The Lady of Lyons, you know—but still, a firstrate little bit of work. [*He shakes her hand*].

GUNN [*following Bannal's example*] I also, Miss O'Dowda. Capital. Charming. [*He shakes hands*].

VAUGHAN [*with maudlin solemnity*] Only be true to yourself, Miss O'Dowda. Keep serious. Give up making silly jokes. Sustain the note of passion. And youll do great things.

FANNY. You think I have a future?

TROTTER. You have a past, Miss O'Dowda.

FANNY [*looking apprehensively at her father*] Sh-sh-sh!

THE COUNT. A past! What do you mean, Mr Trotter?

TROTTER [*to Fanny*] You cant deceive me. That bit about the police was real. Youre a Suffraget, Miss O'Dowda. You were on that Deputation.

THE COUNT. Fanny: is this true?

FANNY. It is. I did a month with Lady Constance Lytton; and I'm prouder of it than I ever was of anything or ever shall be again.

TROTTER. Is that any reason why you should stuff naughty plays down my throat?

FANNY. Yes: itll teach you what it feels like to be forcibly fed.

[440]

THE COUNT. She will never return to Venice. I feel now as I felt when the Campanile fell.

Savoyard comes in through the curtains.

SAVOYARD [*to the Count*] Would you mind coming to say a word of congratulation to the company? Theyre rather upset at having had no curtain call.

THE COUNT. Certainly, certainly. I'm afraid Ive been rather remiss. Let us go on the stage, gentlemen.

The curtains are drawn, revealing the last scene of the play and the actors on the stage. The Count, Savoyard, the critics, and Fanny join them, shaking hands and congratulating.

THE COUNT. Whatever we may think of the play, gentlemen, I'm sure you will agree with me that there can be only one opinion about the acting.

THE CRITICS. Hear hear! [*They start the applause*].

AYOT ST LAWRENCE, *March 1911.*

Mr. Bernard Shaw on the Critics

(An interview, drafted by Shaw, *Pall Mall Gazette*,
London, 21 April 1911)

There were many callers at Adelphi-terrace yesterday
making inquiries concerning the authorship of
"Fanny's First Play." Mr. George Bernard Shaw,
however, was not at home.

Late last night, when it might have been supposed
that all interviewers had finished their day's duties, a
representative of the "Pall Mall Gazette" managed,
by a lucky accident, to catch him as he was
returning.

"No," said Mr. Shaw, brushing aside the first
question as to the authorship, "nothing shall ever
induce me to betray the secret of the authorship of
'Fanny's First Play.' The performance last night was
superb; and the audience enjoyed it last night as
much as I did."

"How have the critics taken the scene in which
they are introduced?"

"Well, it is rather hard on the ones that were left
out; but it was impossible to put in everybody. Even
those who were put in complain because their repre-
sentatives did not make up like them, as Mr. King
did so successfully in the case of Mr. Walkley. But the
actors would have only been too delighted if they had
had the same facilities. If the gentlemen whose features
were not reproduced had given sittings and written
their own parts, the same perfection of representation might have been achieved."

"But did Mr. Walkley give sittings and write his
own part?"

"Well, you see, the authorship of the play is a

secret. I must not let the public behind the scenes. All I may tell you is that Mr. Walkley was not among the surprised when his double walked on the stage."

"But the author—"

"Why do you say the author? How do you know there are not half a dozen authors?"

"Is it really worth while to keep up this mystification, Mr. Shaw?"

"There is no mystification. For the competent critic there never was any from the rise of the curtain to its fall. But since the class of work to which 'Fanny's First Play' belongs, and the movement to which the Little Theatre belongs, has suffered so much from the incompetent ones, it is just as well to prove, by mystifying them, that they do not know dramatic chalk from dramatic cheese when it is no longer labelled for them.

"Look at the notices. Is there one critic worth his salt who has the smallest doubt as to the authorship of the play, or who treats it as an open question? Not one. It is the duffers who are mystified. All they know about work of the class that Miss McCarthy is producing is that it bores them and leaves them with a sense of being personally belittled. But whether the belittler is Shaw or Barker or Barrie or Hankin or Lowes Dickinson or Galsworthy, or even Ibsen, not to mention younger men like Ashley Dukes, [Gilbert] Cannan, and [Charles] McEvoy, they have no idea."

"But the public?"

"What on earth does the public care who the play is by? It distinguishes between the plays it enjoys and the plays it does not, not between author and author. There is not a reputation in the world that has more than a fortnight's business in it. After that, the notices and the names and the critics do not count. All the same, I wish the critics were a little more helpful, considering how much depends on even that fortnight when attempts are being made to get the Drama out of its worn-out grooves."

"You think criticism is going from bad to worse?"

"Not at all. There are very good men coming along. I do not know who your critic on the 'Pall Mall Gazette' is, but he is a remarkable man; he not only praises my work, but actually understands and enjoys it. Then there is the 'Manchester Guardian' critic, C. E. Montague. Some points in my plays beat him; but he is a very fine critic.

"Desmond McCarthy has written some of the best criticisms of our day. The successor of myself and Max on the 'Saturday Review' keeps its theatrical column well up to its traditions. Young playwright-critics like Dukes and Cannan carry the Shavian iconoclasm to the point of feeling bound to attack the founder of their faith unmercifully; but their writing is alive and keen. And there are one or two others whose names I cannot recall on the spur of the moment.

"Of course, there are still—there probably always will be—newspapers who class the drama as 'gaiety,' and will entrust dramatic criticism to any habitual dead-head who shows some proficiency at billiards; but the tendency is to recognise the criticism of the theatre as a first-rate job requiring a first-rate man.

"Mr. H. W. Massingham, the editor of 'The Nation,' has taken the dramatic criticism of his paper into his own hands on the retirement of William Archer, and does it so remarkably well that one wonders he ever wasted his time on the dreary work of pretending that reports of the matches of our political parties was political criticism.

"Besides these, all the best men of my own time are still in the field; so I see no reason to croak about the critics. Their pursuit is certainly a soul-destroying one if it is too long persisted in; but, comparing one period with another, the present is not one of the famine septennates of theatrical criticism."

The Popularity of "G.B.S."

(An interview, drafted by Shaw, in *The Observer*, London, 15 October 1911)

"Fanny's First Play" reached its 200th performance at the Little Theatre on Tuesday, and "Man and Superman" is drawing crowds at the Criterion. There seemed every reason to believe that London was taking Mr. Bernard Shaw to its heart; and a representative of THE OBSERVER called on him to offer congratulations.

"I want," he said, "to interview you on your popularity—on the successful run of two of your plays."

"Am I to understand that you regard this state of things as an unprecedented novelty?"

The interviewer became speechless with confusion, and silently took up his hat. There are some things that are unanswerable; and this seemed one of them.

"Sit down," said Mr. Shaw, with reassuring affability. "I am sorry that 'Fanny's First Play' has destroyed the cherished legend that I am an unpopular playwright. But the notion that it is the first 'Charley's Aunt' of the new drama is a mistaken one. What has happened is that for the first time I have allowed a play of mine to run itself to death in the usual commercial fashion. And the worst of it is, it will not die. It goes on like Madame Tussaud's. Neither hot weather nor cold can kill it. But what reason have you to doubt that if I had allowed 'John Bull's Other Island,' or 'You Never Can Tell,' or 'Man and Superman' to run on in the same way at the Court Theatre in the great days of Vedrenne and Barker, they would not have been running still ? They were always taken off, sternly and inexorably, on principle, at the height of their success. The same thing occurred at every revival. We were out against the long run system. But the question you began by asking me shows how impossible it is to knock this into the heads of the people who are supposed to know all about the theatres. Do you remember what my friend, Mr. St. Loe Strachey, said very wittily about the poetic passages in my plays ?"

"I did not know there were any," said the interviewer, hoping to provoke an explosion.

"Mr. St. Loe Strachey knew better," said Mr. Shaw, acknowledging the thrust by a slight grin only. "Well, he said that they were only stuck in to show that Todgers's can do it when it likes."

"I don't see the point," said the interviewer.

"Of course, you don't. No one reads Dickens nowadays, it seems. Read 'Martin Chuzzlewit,' and you will understand. Well, Miss Lillah McCarthy, who is, as you know, in private life Mrs. Granville Barker, said: 'Let us just run Fanny to show 'em that Todgers's can do it when it likes.' And I consented."

"Then you still stick to the limited run system ?"

"Certainly. You see I have refused to allow Mr. Loraine to produce 'Man and Superman' for an unlimited run. I have insisted on a short run."

"What do you call a short run, Mr. Shaw?"

"For 'Man and Superman,' with Mr. Loraine in it, 200 nights. He cannot spend his life playing John Tanner. Other authors want him. In America the thing went on for years until it became a public scandal. Mr. Loraine only saved himself by leaving the country and coming back to England. At the Court Theatre we tried to kill it by playing the impossible third act. As it was, we very nearly killed ourselves and Mr. Loraine, whose Don Juan in the Dream of Hell was the most extraordinary feat performed by an actor in our time. In Germany or Russia Mr. Charles Ricketts would have been carried in triumph through the streets for his wonderful production of that scene: it was the climax of English theatrical art in that direction. I assure you the critics would have admired it very much if we had told them so beforehand. Well, even that failed to shake the popularity of 'Man and Superman.' The people came and sat through all that solid philosophising as if it were as jolly as 'Rococo' or 'The Twelve-Pound Look.' After the 200th night of 'Man and Superman' at the Criterion, Mr. Loraine will put on the whole play, third act and all, beginning at ten in the morning and ending at half-past eleven at night. He will appear flying over the Spanish mountains in his new aeroplane; and Miss Pauline Chase and her party will follow in a dirigible."

"Talking of that, Mr. Shaw, is it true that—"

"No, it isn't," said Mr. Shaw. "Don't be ridiculous. Good morning."

Letter from Shaw to the Editor of the *Play Pictorial*, London, pseudonymously signed, January 1912

Sir,—I understand that your next number will deal with the play which has had such a long and successful run at the Little Theatre, and which is to be transferred to the Kingsway Theatre on the first night of the new year. The time is propitious, in my mind, for some public announcement as to the actual author.

It is obvious to the least informed that Fanny O'Dowda does not stand in that capacity, and that she is being used as a stalking horse by someone who did not wish to be too quickly identified with the satire on the dramatic critics which forms the subject matter of the induction and epilogue.

I distinctly said at the private performance "I believe it's Shaw" and I gave my reasons for that opinion, although Trotter, Vaughan and Gunn expressed themselves differently.

As you well know I write for the *Matutinal Meddler* and represent "the man in the street." We are the biggest publicity medium in the world and if my original notice was somewhat guarded, you as an old *confrère* will understand that it was not policy on my part to put forward, however vaguely, any original view as to the play in question.

Trotter may write with his tongue in his Grecian cheek, and Vaughan with his left hand surreptitiously feeling for the throbbing of an enlarged organ of his anatomy, but I am simply a plain, straight-forward Englishman, with a plain straight-forward duty to multitudinous readers who like to assimilate my opinions with their bacon and eggs, and consequently it has hurt my *amour propre* (as Trotter would say) to see "Fanny's First Play," announced in the advertisements as by Xxxxxxx Xxxx, and underneath it "Bernard Shaw . . . at his best," quoted from the *Daily Graphic*.

We like to be the first in the field with news, and I could easily have made a similar statement, were I not possessed, or obsessed, with the desire to say nothing that should not savour absolutely of sound sense and incontrovertible truth.

Knowing Shaw's fearless nature, I could not conceive he would pen a satiric (at the expense of me and my distinguished colleagues) Induction and Epilogue merely as his *apologia* for writing a Shavian version of a Palais Royale farce, minus its entertaining bustle.

Certainly, I thought Margaret's inimitable explanation of the mental excitement which caused her to follow a great Salvation Festival at the Albert Hall, with a visit to the Promenade of the Empire, and subsequently to a public dancing-room, was quite in Shaw's own daring manner, while, on the other hand, I considered that the long-winded pseudo-Shavian platitudes spoken by the Frenchman in the last act was an audacious imitation of Shaw's rich Hibernian humour.

Again, the argument around Shaw's name in the Epilogue suggested his consummate method of advertisement, and now that the play is being moved to a larger theatre, and therefore, likely to appeal to a much larger constituency, I write to suggest to you that some authoritative pronouncement should be made in your highly-prized magazine.

Yours obediently,
FLAWNER BANNEL [*sic*].

Androcles and the Lion:
A Fable Play

WITH

Androcles and the Lion

A Fable Play

WITH

Preface on the Prospect of Christianity

Prefatory Note

Appendix to the Play

'G.B.S.' on Laughing Audiences

Shaw's 'How I Came Back Above Stairs'

New Writing for the New York Production

Composition begun 2 February 1912; completed 6 February 1912. First published in German translation, as *Androklus und der Löwe*, 1913. Published in *Everybody's Magazine* (New York), September 1914. First English publication in *Androcles and the Lion, Overruled, Pygmalion*, 1916. First presented in German in Hamburg, July 1913. Presented at the St James's Theatre, London, on 1 September 1913.

The Lion   *Edward Sillward*
Androcles   *O. P. Heggie*
Megaera   *Clare Greet*
Centurion   *H. D. Nicholson*
The Captain   *Ben Webster*
Lavinia   *Lillah McCarthy*
Lentulus   *Donald Calthrop*
Metellus   *Hesketh Pearson*
Ferrovius   *Alfred Brydone*
Spintho   *J. F. Outram*
Call Boy   *Neville Gartside*
Retiarius   *J. P. Turnbull*
Secutor   *Allan Jeayes*
Editor of the Gladiators   *Herbert Hewetson*
Menagerie Keeper   *Baliol Holloway*
The Emperor   *Leon Quartermaine*
Slave Driver   *Ralph Hutton*
Also Roman soldiers, Christians, gladiators, slaves.

Period—Second or Third Century A.D.

Prologue—*A Jungle Path*

ACT I *The End of Three Converging Roads to Rome. Evening*

ACT II Scene 1: *Behind the Emperor's Box at the Coliseum*
Scene 2: *The Arena*
Scene 3: *The Same as Scene 1*

Preface on the
Prospects of Christianity

Contents

[455]

WHY NOT GIVE CHRISTIANITY A TRIAL?

The question seems a hopeless one after 2000 years of resolute adherence to the old cry of "Not this man, but Barabbas." Yet it is beginning to look as if Barabbas was a failure, in spite of his strong right hand, his victories, his empires, his millions of money, and his moralities and churches and political constitutions. "This man" has not been a failure yet; for nobody has ever been sane enough to try his way. But he has had one quaint triumph. Barabbas has stolen his name and taken his cross as a standard. There is a sort of compliment in that. There is even a sort of loyalty in it, like that of the brigand who breaks every law and yet claims to be a patriotic subject of the king who makes them. We have always had a curious feeling that though we crucified Christ on a stick, he somehow managed to get hold of the right end of it, and that if we were better men we might try his plan. There have been one or two grotesque attempts at it by inadequate people, such as the Kingdom of God in Munster, which was ended by a crucifixion so much more atrocious than the one on Calvary that the bishop who took the part of Annas went home and died of horror. But responsible people have never made such attempts. The moneyed, respectable, capable world has been steadily anti-Christian and Barabbasque since the

crucifixion; and the specific doctrine of Jesus has not
in all that time been put into political or general
social practice. I am no more a Christian than Pilate
was, or you, gentle reader; and yet, like Pilate, I
greatly prefer Jesus to Annas and Caiaphas; and I am
ready to admit that after contemplating the world and
human nature for nearly sixty years, I see no way out
of the world's misery but the way which would have
been found by Christ's will if he had undertaken the
work of a modern practical statesman.

Pray do not at this early point lose patience with me
and shut the book. I assure you I am as sceptical and
scientific and modern a thinker as you will find anywhere. I grant you I know a great deal more about
economics and politics than Jesus did, and can do
things he could not do. I am by all Barabbasque
standards a person of much better character and
standing, and greater practical sense. I have no
sympathy with vagabonds and talkers who try to
reform society by taking men away from their regular
productive work and making vagabonds and talkers
of them too; and if I had been Pilate I should have
recognized as plainly as he the necessity for suppressing attacks on the existing social order, however
corrupt that order might be, by people with no knowledge of government and no power to construct
political machinery to carry out their views, acting on
the very dangerous delusion that the end of the world
was at hand. I make no defence of such Christians as
Savonarola and John of Leyden: they were scuttling
the ship before they had learned how to build a raft;
and it became necessary to throw them overboard to
save the crew. I say this to set myself right with
respectable society; but I must still insist that if
Jesus could have worked out the practical problems of

a Communist constitution, an admitted obligation to deal with crime without revenge or punishment, and a full assumption by humanity of divine responsibilities, he would have conferred an incalculable benefit on mankind, because these distinctive demands of his are now turning out to be good sense and sound economics.

I say distinctive, because his common humanity and his subjection to time and space (that is, to the Syrian life of his period) involved his belief in many things, true and false, that in no way distinguished him from other Syrians of that time. But such common beliefs do not constitute specific Christianity any more than wearing a beard, working in a carpenter's shop, or believing that the earth is flat and that the stars could drop on it from heaven like hailstones. Christianity interests practical statesmen now because of the doctrines that distinguished Christ from the Jews and the Barabbasques generally, including ourselves.

WHY JESUS MORE THAN ANOTHER?

I do not imply, however, that these doctrines were peculiar to Christ. A doctrine peculiar to one man would be only a craze, unless its comprehension depended on a development of human faculty so rare that only one exceptionally gifted man possessed it. But even in this case it would be useless, because incapable of spreading. Christianity is a step in moral evolution which is independent of any individual preacher. If Jesus had never existed (and that he ever existed in any other sense than that in which Shakespear's Hamlet existed has been vigorously questioned) Tolstoy would have thought and taught and quarrelled with the Greek Church all the same.

Their creed has been fragmentarily practised to a considerable extent in spite of the fact that the laws of all countries treat it, in effect, as criminal. Many of its advocates have been militant atheists. But for some reason the imagination of white mankind has picked out Jesus of Nazareth as *the* Christ, and attributed all the Christian doctrines to him; and as it is the doctrine and not the man that matters, and, as, besides, one symbol is as good as another provided everyone attaches the same meaning to it, I raise, for the moment, no question as to how far the gospels are original, and how far they consist of Greek and Chinese interpolations. The record that Jesus said certain things is not invalidated by a demonstration that Confucius said them before him. Those who claim a literal divine paternity for him cannot be silenced by the discovery that the same claim was made for Alexander and Augustus. And I am not just now concerned with the credibility of the gospels as records of fact; for I am not acting as a detective, but turning our modern lights on to certain ideas and doctrines in them which disentangle themselves from the rest because they are flatly contrary to common practice, common sense, and common belief, and yet have, in the teeth of dogged incredulity and recalcitrance, produced an irresistible impression that Christ, though rejected by his posterity as an unpractical dreamer, and executed by his contemporaries as a dangerous anarchist and blasphemous madman, was greater than his judges.

WAS JESUS A COWARD?

I know quite well that this impression of superiority is not produced on everyone, even of those who profess extreme susceptibility to it. Setting aside the huge

mass of inculcated Christ-worship which has no real
significance because it has no intelligence, there is,
among people who are really free to think for themselves on the subject, a great deal of hearty dislike of
Jesus and of contempt for his failure to save himself
and overcome his enemies by personal bravery and
cunning as Mahomet did. I have heard this feeling
expressed far more impatiently by persons brought up
in England as Christians than by Mahometans, who
are, like their prophet, very civil to Jesus, and allow
him a place in their esteem and veneration at least as
high as we accord to John the Baptist. But this
British bulldog contempt is founded on a complete
misconception of his reasons for submitting voluntarily to an ordeal of torment and death. The modern
Secularist is often so determined to regard Jesus as a
man like himself and nothing more, that he slips
unconsciously into the error of assuming that Jesus
shared that view. But it is quite clear from the New
Testament writers (the chief authorities for believing
that Jesus ever existed) that Jesus at the time of his
death believed himself to be the Christ, a divine
personage. It is therefore absurd to criticize his conduct before Pilate as if he were Colonel Roosevelt or
Admiral von Tirpitz or even Mahomet. Whether you
accept his belief in his divinity as fully as Simon
Peter did, or reject it as a delusion which led him to
submit to torture and sacrifice his life without resistance in the conviction that he would presently rise
again in glory, you are equally bound to admit that, far
from behaving like a coward or a sheep, he showed considerable physical fortitude in going through a cruel
ordeal against which he could have defended himself as
effectually as he cleared the money-changers out of
the temple. "Gentle Jesus, meek and mild" is a

snivelling modern invention, with no warrant in the gospels. St Matthew would as soon have thought of applying such adjectives to Judas Maccabeus as to Jesus; and even St Luke, who makes Jesus polite and gracious, does not make him meek. The picture of him as an English curate of the farcical comedy type, too meek to fight a policeman, and everybody's butt, may be useful in the nursery to soften children; but that such a figure could ever have become a centre of the world's attention is too absurd for discussion: grown men and women may speak kindly of a harmless creature who utters amiable sentiments and is a helpless nincompoop when he is called on to defend them; but they will not follow him, nor do what he tells them, because they do not wish to share his defeat and disgrace.

WAS JESUS A MARTYR?

It is important therefore that we should clear our minds of the notion that Jesus died, as some of us are in the habit of declaring, for his social and political opinions. There have been many martyrs to those opinions; but he was not one of them, nor, as his words shew, did he see any more sense in martyrdom than Galileo did. He was executed by the Jews for the blasphemy of claiming to be a God; and Pilate, to whom this was a mere piece of superstitious nonsense, let them execute him as the cheapest way of keeping them quiet, on the formal plea that he had committed treason against Rome by saying that he was the King of the Jews. He was not falsely accused, nor denied full opportunities of defending himself. The proceedings were quite straightforward and regular; and Pilate, to whom the appeal lay, favored him and despised his judges, and was evidently willing enough to be conciliated. But instead of denying the charge, Jesus repeated the offence. He knew what he was doing: he had alienated numbers of his own disciples and been stoned in the streets for doing it before. He was not lying: he believed literally what he said. The horror of the High Priest was perfectly natural: he was a Primate confronted with a heterodox street preacher uttering what seemed to him an appalling and impudent blasphemy. The fact that the blasphemy was to Jesus a simple statement of fact, and that it has since been accepted as such by all western nations, does not invalidate the proceedings, nor give us the right to regard Annas and Caiaphas as worse men than the Archbishop of Canterbury and the Head Master of Eton. If Jesus had been indicted in a modern court, he would have been examined by two doctors; found to be obsessed by a delusion; declared incapable of pleading; and sent to an asylum: that is the whole difference. But please note that when a man is charged before a modern tribunal (to take a case that happened the other day) of having asserted and maintained that he was an officer returned from the front to receive the Victoria Cross at the hands of the King, although he was in fact a mechanic, nobody thinks of treating him as afflicted with a delusion. He is punished for false pretences, because his assertion is credible and therefore misleading. Just so, the claim to divinity made by Jesus was to the High Priest, who looked forward to the coming of a Messiah, one that might conceivably have been true, and might therefore have misled the people in a very dangerous way. That was why he treated Jesus as an impostor and a blasphemer where we should have treated him as a madman.

THE GOSPELS WITHOUT PREJUDICE

All this will become clear if we read the gospels without prejudice. When I was young it was impossible to read them without fantastic confusion of thought. The confusion was so utterly confounded that it was called the proper spirit to read the Bible in. Jesus was a baby; and he was older than creation. He was a man who could be persecuted, stoned, scourged, and killed; and he was a god, immortal and all-powerful, able to raise the dead and call millions of angels to his aid. It was a sin to doubt either view of him: that is, it was a sin to reason about him; and the end was that you did not reason about him, and read about him only when you were compelled. When you heard the gospel stories read in church, or learnt them from painters and poets, you came out with an impression of their contents that would have astonished a Chinaman who had read the story without prepossession. Even sceptics who were specially on their guard, put the Bible in the dock, and read the gospels with the object of detecting discrepancies in the four narratives to shew that the writers were as subject to error as the writers of yesterday's newspaper.

All this has changed greatly within two generations. Today the Bible is so little read that the language of the Authorized Version is rapidly becoming obsolete; so that even in the United States, where the old tradition of the verbal infallibility of "the book of books" lingers more strongly than anywhere else except perhaps in Ulster, retranslations into modern English have been introduced perforce to save its bare intelligibility. It is quite easy today to find cultivated persons who have never read the New Testament, and on whom therefore it is possible to try the experiment

[465]

of asking them to read the gospels and state what they have gathered as to the history and views and character of Christ.

THE GOSPELS NOW UNINTELLIGIBLE TO NOVICES

But it will not do to read the gospels with a mind furnished only for the reception of, say, a biography of Goethe. You will not make sense of them, nor even be able without impatient weariness to persevere in the task of going steadily through them, unless you know something of the history of the human imagination as applied to religion. Not long ago I asked a writer of distinguished intellectual competence whether he had made a study of the gospels since his childhood. His reply was that he had lately tried, but "found it all such nonsense that I could not stick it." As I do not want to send anyone to the gospels with this result, I had better here give a brief exposition of how much of the history of religion is needed to make the gospels and the conduct and ultimate fate of Jesus intelligible and interesting.

WORLDLINESS OF THE MAJORITY

The first common mistake to get rid of is that mankind consists of a great mass of religious people and a few eccentric atheists. It consists of a huge mass of worldly people, and a small percentage of persons deeply interested in religion and concerned about their own souls and other people's; and this section consists mostly of those who are passionately affirming the established religion and those who are passionately attacking it, the genuine philosophers being very few. Thus you never have a nation of millions of Wesleys and one Tom Paine. You have a million Mr Worldly

Wisemans, one Wesley, with his small congregation, and one Tom Paine, with *his* smaller congregation. The passionately religious are a people apart; and if they were not hopelessly outnumbered by the worldly, they would turn the world upside down, as St Paul was reproached, quite justly, for wanting to do. Few people can number among their personal acquaintances a single atheist or a single Plymouth Brother. Unless a religious turn in ourselves has led us to seek the little Societies to which these rare birds belong, we pass our lives among people who, whatever creeds they may repeat, and in whatever temples they may avouch their respectability and wear their Sunday clothes, have robust consciences, and hunger and thirst, not for righteousness, but for rich feeding and comfort and social position and attractive mates and ease and pleasure and respect and consideration: in short, for love and money. To these people one morality is as good as another provided they are used to it and can put up with its restrictions without unhappiness; and in the maintenance of this morality they will fight and punish and coerce without scruple. They may not be the salt of the earth, these Philistines; but they are the substance of civilization; and they save society from ruin by criminals and conquerors as well as by Savonarolas and Knipperdollings. And as they know, very sensibly, that a little religion is good for children and serves morality, keeping the poor in goodhumor or in awe by promising rewards in heaven or threatening torments in hell, they encourage the religious people up to a certain point: for instance, if Savonarola only tells the ladies of Florence that they ought to tear off their jewels and finery and sacrifice them to God, they offer him a cardinal's hat, and praise him as a saint; but if he induces

them to actually do it, they burn him as a public
nuisance.

RELIGION OF THE MINORITY. SALVATIONISM

The religion of the tolerated religious minority has
always been essentially the same religion: that is why
its changes of name and form have made so little
difference. That is why, also, a nation so civilized as
the English can convert negroes to their faith with
great ease, but cannot convert Mahometans or Jews.
The negro finds in civilized Salvationism an unspeakably more comforting version of his crude creed;
but neither Saracen nor Jew sees any advantage in it
over his own version. The Crusader was surprised to
find the Saracen quite as religious and moral as
himself, and rather more than less civilized. The Latin
Christian has nothing to offer the Greek Christian
that Greek Christianity has not already provided.
They are all, at root, Salvationists.

Let us trace this religion of Salvation from its
beginnings. So many things that man does not himself contrive or desire are always happening: death,
plagues, tempests, blights, floods, sunrise and sunset,
growths and harvests and decay, and Kant's two
wonders of the starry heavens above us and the moral
law within us, that we conclude that somebody must
be doing it all, or that somebody is doing the good
and somebody else doing the evil, or that armies of
invisible persons, beneficent and malevolent, are
doing it; hence you postulate gods and devils, angels
and demons. You propitiate these powers with presents, called sacrifices, and flatteries, called praises.
Then the Kantian moral law within you makes you
conceive your god as a judge; and straightway you try
to corrupt him, also with presents and flatteries. This

seems shocking to us; but our objection to it is quite a recent development: no longer ago than Shakespear's time it was thought quite natural that litigants should give presents to human judges; and the buying off of divine wrath by actual money payments to priests, or, in the reformed churches which discountenance this, by subscriptions to charities and church building and the like, is still in full swing. Its practical disadvantage is that though it makes matters very easy for the rich, it cuts off the poor from all hope of divine favor. And this quickens the moral criticism of the poor to such an extent, that they soon find the moral law within them revolting against the idea of buying off the deity with gold and gifts, though are still quite ready to buy him off with the paper money of praise and professions of repentance. Accordingly, you will find that though a religion may last unchanged for many centuries in primitive communities where the conditions of life leave no room for poverty and riches, and the process of propitiating the supernatural powers is as well within the means of the least of the members as within those of the headman, yet when commercial civilization arrives, and capitalism divides the people into a few rich and a great many so poor that they can barely live, a movement for religious reform will arise among the poor, and will be essentially a movement for cheap or entirely gratuitous salvation.

To understand what the poor mean by propitiation, we must examine for a moment what they mean by justice.

THE DIFFERENCE BETWEEN ATONEMENT AND PUNISHMENT

The primitive idea of justice is partly legalized revenge

and partly expiation by sacrifice. It works out from both sides in the notion that two blacks make a white, and that when a wrong has been done, it should be paid for by an equivalent suffering. It seems to the Philistine majority a matter of course that this compensating suffering should be inflicted on the wrongdoer for the sake of its deterrent effect on other would-be wrongdoers; but a moment's reflection will shew that this utilitarian application corrupts the whole transaction. For example, the shedding of innocent blood cannot be balanced by the shedding of guilty blood. Sacrificing a criminal to propitiate God for the murder of one of his righteous servants is like sacrificing a mangy sheep or an ox with the rinderpest: it calls down divine wrath instead of appeasing it. In doing it we offer God as a sacrifice the gratification of our own revenge and the protection of our own lives without cost to ourselves; and cost to ourselves is the essence of sacrifice and expiation. However much the Philistines have succeeded in confusing these things in practice, they are to the Salvationist sense distinct and even contrary. The Baronet's cousin in Dickens's novel, who, perplexed by the failure of the police to discover the murderer of the baronet's solicitor, said "Far better hang wrong fellow than no fellow," was not only expressing a very common sentiment, but trembling on the brink of the rarer Salvationist opinion that it is much better to hang the wrong fellow: that, in fact, the wrong fellow is the right fellow to hang.

The point is a cardinal one, because until we grasp it not only does historical Christianity remain unintelligible to us, but those who do not care a rap about historical Christianity may be led into the mistake of supposing that if we discard revenge, and treat murderers exactly as God treated Cain: that is, exempt them from punishment by putting a brand on them as unworthy to be sacrificed, and let them face the world as best they can with that brand on them, we should get rid both of punishment and sacrifice. It would not at all follow: on the contrary, the feeling that there must be an expiation of the murder might quite possibly lead to our putting some innocent person—the more innocent the better—to a cruel death to balance the account with divine justice.

SALVATION AT FIRST A CLASS PRIVILEGE; AND THE REMEDY

Thus, even when the poor decide that the method of purchasing salvation by offering rams and goats or bringing gold to the altar must be wrong because they cannot afford it, we still do not feel "saved" without a sacrifice and a victim. In vain do we try to substitute mystical rites that cost nothing, such as circumcision, or, as a substitute for that, baptism. Our sense of justice still demands an expiation, a sacrifice, a sufferer for our sins. And this leaves the poor man still in his old difficulty; for if it was impossible for him to procure rams and goats and shekels, how much more impossible is it for him to find a neighbor who will voluntarily suffer for his sins: one who will say cheerfully "You have committed a murder. Well, never mind: I am willing to be hanged for it in your stead"?

Our imagination must come to our rescue. Why not, instead of driving ourselves to despair by insisting on a separate atonement by a separate redeemer for every sin, have one great atonement and one great redeemer to compound for the sins of the world once for all? Nothing easier, nothing cheaper. The yoke is easy, the burden light. All you have to do when the redeemer is once found (or invented by the imagination) is to believe in the efficacy of the transaction, and you are saved. The rams and goats cease to bleed; the altars which ask for expensive gifts and continually renewed sacrifices are torn down; and the Church of the single redeemer and the single atonement rises on the ruins of the old temples, and becomes a single Church of the Christ.

RETROSPECTIVE ATONEMENT; AND THE EXPECTATION OF THE REDEEMER

But this does not happen at once. Between the old costly religion of the rich and the new gratuitous religion of the poor there comes an interregnum in which the redeemer, though conceived by the human imagination, is not yet found. He is awaited and expected under the names of the Christ, the Messiah, Baldur the Beautiful, or what not; but he has not yet come. Yet the sinners are not therefore in despair. It is true that they cannot say, as we say, "The Christ has come, and has redeemed us"; but they can say "The Christ will come, and will redeem us," which, as the atonement is conceived as retrospective, is equally consoling. There are periods when nations are seething with this expectation and crying aloud with prophecy of the Redeemer through their poets. To feel that atmosphere we have only to take up the Bible and read Isaiah at one end of such a period and Luke and John at the other.

COMPLETION OF THE SCHEME BY LUTHER AND CALVIN

We now see our religion as a quaint but quite intelligible evolution from crude attempts to propitiate

the destructive forces of Nature among savages to a
subtle theology with a costly ritual of sacrifice possible
only to the rich as a luxury, and finally to the religion
of Luther and Calvin. And it must be said for the
earlier forms that they involved very real sacrifices.
The sacrifice was not always vicarious, and is not yet
universally so. In India men pay with their own skins,
torturing themselves hideously to attain holiness. In
the west, saints amazed the world with their austerities
and self-scourgings and confessions and vigils. But
Luther delivered us from all that. His reformation was
a triumph of imagination and a triumph of cheapness.
It brought you complete salvation and asked you for
nothing but faith. Luther did not know what he was
doing in the scientific sociological way in which we
know it; but his instinct served him better than knowledge could have done; for it was instinct rather than
theological casuistry that made him hold so resolutely
to Justification by Faith as the trump card by which
he should beat the Pope, or, as he would have put it,
the sign in which he should conquer. He may be said
to have abolished the charge for admission to heaven.
Paul had advocated this; but Luther and Calvin did it.

JOHN BARLEYCORN

There is yet another page in the history of religion
which must be conned and digested before the career
of Jesus can be fully understood. People who can
read long books will find it in Frazer's Golden Bough.
Simpler folk will find it in the peasant's song of John
Barleycorn, now made accessible to our drawing
room amateurs in the admirable collections of Somer-
setshire Folk Songs by Mr Cecil Sharp. From Frazer's

magnum opus you will learn how the same primitive logic which makes the Englishman believe today that by eating a beefsteak he can acquire the strength and courage of the bull, and to hold that belief in the face of the most ignominious defeats by vegetarian wrestlers and racers and bicyclists, led the first men who conceived God as capable of incarnation to believe that they could acquire a spark of his divinity by eating his flesh and drinking his blood. And from the song of John Barleycorn you may learn how the miracle of the seed, the growth, and the harvest, still the most wonderful of all the miracles and as inexplicable as ever, taught the primitive husbandman, and, as we must now affirm, taught him quite rightly, that God is in the seed, and that God is immortal. And thus it became the test of Godhead that nothing that you could do to it could kill it, and that when you buried it, it would rise again in renewed life and beauty and give mankind eternal life on condition that it was eaten and drunk, and again slain and buried, to rise again for ever and ever. You may, and indeed must, use John Barleycorn "right barbarouslee," cutting him "off at knee" with your scythes, scourging him with your flails, burying him in the earth; and he will not resist you nor reproach you, but will rise again in golden beauty amidst a great burst of sunshine and bird music, and save you and renew your life. And from the interweaving of these two traditions with the craving for the Redeemer, you at last get the conviction that when the Redeemer comes he will be immortal; he will give us his body to eat and his blood to drink; and he will prove his divinity by suffering a barbarous death without resistance or reproach, and rise from the dead and return to the earth in glory as the giver of life eternal.

LOOKING FOR THE END OF THE WORLD

Yet another persistent belief has beset the imagination of the religious ever since religion spread among the poor, or, rather, ever since commercial civilization produced a hopelessly poor class cut off from enjoyment in this world. That belief is that the end of this world is at hand, and that it will presently pass away and be replaced by a kingdom of happiness, justice, and bliss in which the rich and the oppressors and the unjust shall have no share. We are all familiar with this expectation: many of us cherish some pious relative who sees in every great calamity a sign of the approaching end. Warning pamphlets are in constant circulation: advertisements are put in the papers and paid for by those who are convinced, and who are horrified at the indifference of the irreligious to the approaching doom. And revivalist preachers, now as in the days of John the Baptist, seldom fail to warn their flocks to watch and pray, as the great day will steal upon them like a thief in the night, and cannot be long deferred in a world so wicked. This belief also associates itself with Barleycorn's second coming; so that the two events become identified at last.

There is the other and more artificial side of this belief, on which it is an inculcated dread. The ruler who appeals to the prospect of heaven to console the poor and keep them from insurrection also curbs the vicious by threatening them with hell. In the Koran we find Mahomet driven more and more to this expedient of government; and experience confirms his evident belief that it is impossible to govern without it in certain phases of civilization. We shall see later on that it gives a powerful attraction to the belief in a Redeemer, since it adds to remorse of conscience, which hardened men bear very lightly, a definite dread of hideous and eternal torture.

THE HONOR OF DIVINE PARENTAGE

One more tradition must be noted. The consummation of praise for a king is to declare that he is the son of no earthly father, but of a god. His mother goes into the temple of Apollo, and Apollo comes to her in the shape of a serpent, or the like. The Roman emperors, following the example of Augustus, claimed the title of God. Illogically, such divine kings insist a good deal on their royal human ancestors. Alexander, claiming to be the son of Apollo, is equally determined to be the son of Philip. As the gospels stand, St Matthew and St Luke give genealogies (the two are different) establishing the descent of Jesus through Joseph from the royal house of David, and yet declare that not Joseph but the Holy Ghost was the father of Jesus. It is therefore now held that the story of the Holy Ghost is a later interpolation borrowed from the Greek and Roman imperial tradition. But experience shews that simultaneous faith in the descent from David and the conception by the Holy Ghost is possible. Such double beliefs are entertained by the human mind without uneasiness or consciousness of the contradiction involved. Many instances might be given: a familiar one to my generation being that of the Tichborne claimant, whose attempt to pass himself off as a baronet was supported by an association of laborers on the ground that the Tichborne family, in resisting it, were trying to do a laborer out of his rights. It is quite possible that Matthew and Luke may have been unconscious of the contradiction: indeed the interpolation theory does not remove the difficulty, as the interpolators themselves must have been unconscious of it. A better ground for suspecting interpolation is that St Paul knew nothing of the divine birth, and taught that Jesus came into the world at his birth as the son of Joseph, but rose from the dead after three days as the son of God. Here again, few notice the discrepancy: the three views are accepted simultaneously without intellectual discomfort. We can provisionally entertain half a dozen contradictory versions of an event if we feel either that it does not greatly matter, or that there is a category attainable in which the contradictions are reconciled.

But that is not the present point. All that need be noted here is that the legend of divine birth was sure to be attached sooner or later to very eminent persons in Roman imperial times, and that modern theologians, far from discrediting it, have very logic ally affirmed the miraculous conception not only of Jesus but of his mother.

With no more scholarly equipment than a knowledge of these habits of the human imagination, anyone may now read the four gospels without bewilderment, and without the contemptuous incredulity which spoils the temper of many modern atheists, or the senseless credulity which sometimes makes pious people force us to shove them aside in emergencies as impracticable lunatics when they ask us to meet violence and injustice with dumb submission in the belief that the strange demeanor of Jesus before Pilate was meant as an example of normal human conduct. Let us admit that without the proper clues the gospels are, to a modern educated person, nonsensical and incredible, whilst the apostles are unreadable. But with the clues, they are fairly plain sailing. Jesus becomes an intelligible and consistent person. His reasons for going "like a lamb to the slaughter" instead of saving himself as Mahomet did, become quite clear. The narrative becomes as credible as any other historical narrative of its period.

MATTHEW

THE ANNUNCIATION: THE MASSACRE:
THE FLIGHT

Let us begin with the gospel of Matthew, bearing in mind that it does not profess to be the evidence of an eyewitness. It is a chronicle, founded, like other chronicles, on such evidence and records as the chronicler could get hold of. The only one of the evangelists who professes to give first-hand evidence as an eyewitness naturally takes care to say so; and the fact that Matthew makes no such pretension, and writes throughout as a chronicler, makes it clear that he is telling the story of Jesus as Holinshed told the story of Macbeth, except that, for a reason to be given later on, he must have collected his material and completed his book within the lifetime of persons contemporary with Jesus. Allowance must also be made for the fact that the gospel is written in the Greek language, whilst the first-hand traditions and the actual utterances of Jesus must have been in Aramaic, the dialect of Palestine. These distinctions are important, as you will find if you read Holinshed or Froissart and then read Benvenuto Cellini. You do not blame Holinshed or Froissart for believing and repeating the things they had read or been told, though you cannot always believe these things yourself. But when Cellini tells you that he saw this or did that, and you find it impossible to believe him, you lose patience with him, and are disposed to doubt everything in his autobiography. Do not forget, then, that Matthew is Holinshed and not Benvenuto. The very first pages of his narrative will put your attitude to the test.

Matthew tells us that the mother of Jesus was betrothed to a man of royal pedigree named Joseph, who was rich enough to live in a house in Bethlehem to which kings could bring gifts of gold without provoking any comment. An angel announces to Joseph that Jesus is the son of the Holy Ghost, and that he must not accuse her of infidelity because of her bearing a son of which he is not the father; but this episode disappears from the subsequent narrative: there is no record of its having been told to Jesus, nor any indication of his having any knowledge of it. The narrative, in fact, proceeds in all respects as if the annunciation formed no part of it.

Herod the Tetrarch, believing that a child has been born who will destroy him, orders all the male children to be slaughtered; and Jesus escapes by the flight of his parents into Egypt, whence they return to Nazareth when the danger is over. Here it is necessary to anticipate a little by saying that none of the other evangelists accepts this story, as none of them except John, who throws over Matthew altogether, shares his craze for treating history and biography as mere records of the fulfilment of ancient Jewish prophecies. This craze no doubt led him to seek for some legend bearing out Hosea's "Out of Egypt have I called my son," and Jeremiah's Rachel weeping for her children: in fact, he says so. Nothing that interests us nowadays turns on the credibility of the massacre of the innocents and the flight into Egypt. We may forget them, and proceed to the important part of the narrative, which skips at once to the manhood of Jesus.

JOHN THE BAPTIST

At this moment, a Salvationist prophet named John is stirring the people very strongly. John has declared that the rite of circumcision is insufficient as a dedication of the individual to God, and has substituted the rite of baptism. To us, who are accustomed to baptism as a matter of course, and to whom circumcision is a rather ridiculous foreign practice of no consequence, the sensational effect of such a heresy as this on the Jews is not apparent: it seems to us as natural that John should have baptized people as that the rector of our village should do so. But, as St Paul found to his cost later on, the discarding of circumcision for baptism was to the Jews as startling a heresy as the discarding of transubstantiation in the Mass was to the Catholics of the XVI century.

JESUS JOINS THE BAPTISTS

Jesus entered as a man of thirty (Luke says) into the religious life of his time by going to John the Baptist and demanding baptism from him, much as certain well-to-do young gentlemen forty years ago "joined the Socialists." As far as established Jewry was concerned, he burnt his boats by this action, and cut himself off from the routine of wealth, respectability, and orthodoxy. He then began preaching John's gospel, which, apart from the heresy of baptism, the value of which lay in its bringing the Gentiles (that is, the uncircumcized) within the pale of salvation, was a call to the people to repent of their sins, as the kingdom of heaven was at hand. Luke adds that he also preached the communism of charity; told the surveyors of taxes not to over-assess the taxpayers;

and advised soldiers to be content with their wages and not to be violent or lay false accusations. There is no record of John going beyond this.

THE SAVAGE JOHN AND THE CIVILIZED JESUS

Jesus went beyond it very rapidly, according to Matthew. Though, like John, he became an itinerant preacher, he departed widely from John's manner of life. John went into the wilderness, not into the synagogues; and his baptismal font was the river Jordan. He was an ascetic, clothed in skins and living on locusts and wild honey, practising a savage austerity. He courted martyrdom, and met it at the hands of Herod. Jesus saw no merit either in asceticism or martyrdom. In contrast to John he was essentially a highly-civilized, cultivated person. According to Luke, he pointed out the contrast himself, chaffing the Jews for complaining that John must be possessed by the devil because he was a teetotaller and vegetarian, whilst, because Jesus was neither one nor the other, they reviled him as a gluttonous man and a wine-bibber, the friend of the officials and their mistresses. He told straitlaced disciples that they would have trouble enough from other people without making any for themselves, and that they should avoid martyrdom and enjoy themselves whilst they had the chance. "When they persecute you in the city," he says, "flee into the next." He preaches in the synagogues and in the open air indifferently, just as they come. He repeatedly says, "I desire mercy and not sacrifice," meaning evidently to clear himself of the inveterate superstition that suffering is gratifying to God. "Be not, as the Pharisees, of a sad countenance," he says. He is convivial, feasting with Roman officials and sinners. He is careless of his person, and is remonstrated with for not washing his hands before sitting down to table. The followers of John the Baptist, who fast, and who expect to find the Christians greater ascetics than themselves, are disappointed at finding that Jesus and his twelve friends do not fast; and Jesus tells them that they should rejoice in him instead of being melancholy. He is jocular, and tells them they will all have as much fasting as they want soon enough, whether they like it or not. He is not afraid of disease, and dines with a leper. A woman, apparently to protect him against infection, pours a costly unguent on his head, and is rebuked because what it cost might have been given to the poor. He pooh-poohs that lowspirited view, and says, as he said when he was reproached for not fasting, that the poor are always there to be helped, but that he is not there to be anointed always, implying that you should never lose a chance of being happy when there is so much misery in the world. He breaks the Sabbath; is impatient of conventionality when it is uncomfortable or obstructive; and outrages the feelings of the Jews by breaches of it. He is apt to accuse people who feel that way of hypocrisy. Like the later Samuel Butler, he regards disease as a department of sin, and on curing a lame man, says "Thy sins are forgiven" instead of "Arise and walk," subsequently maintaining, when the Scribes reproach him for assuming power to forgive sin as well as to cure disease, that the two come to the same thing. He has no modest affectations, and claims to be greater than Solomon or Jonah. When reproached, as Bunyan was, for resorting to the art of fiction when teaching in parables, he justifies himself on the ground that art is the only way in which the people can be taught. He is, in short, what we should call an artist and a Bohemian in his manner of life.

JESUS NOT A PROSELYTIST

A point of considerable practical importance today is that he expressly repudiates the idea that forms of religion, once rooted, can be weeded out and replanted with the flowers of a foreign faith. "If you try to root up the tares you will root up the wheat as well." Our proselytizing missionary enterprises are thus flatly contrary to his advice; and their results appear to bear him out in his view that if you convert a man brought up in another creed, you inevitably demoralize him. He acts on this view himself, and does not convert his disciples from Judaism to Christianity. To this day a Christian would be in religion a Jew initiated by baptism instead of circumcision, and accepting Jesus as the Messiah, and his teachings as of higher authority than those of Moses, but for the action of the Jewish priests, who, to save Jewry from being submerged in the rising flood of Christianity after the capture of Jerusalem and the destruction of the Temple, set up what was practically a new religious order, with new Scriptures and elaborate new observances, and to their list of the accursed added one Jeschu, a bastard magician, whose comic rogueries brought him to a bad end like Punch or Til Eulenspiegel: an invention which cost them dear when the Christians got the upper hand of them politically. The Jew as Jesus, himself a Jew, knew him never dreamt of such things, and could follow Jesus without ceasing to be a Jew.

THE TEACHINGS OF JESUS

So much for his personal life and temperament. His public career as a popular preacher carries him equally far beyond John the Baptist. He lays no stress on baptism or vows, and preaches conduct incessantly. He advocates communism, the widening of the private family with its cramping ties into the great family of mankind under the fatherhood of God, the abandonment of revenge and punishment, the counteracting of evil by good instead of by a hostile evil, and an organic conception of society in which you are not an independent individual but a member of society, your neighbor being another member, and each of you members one of another, as two fingers on a hand, the obvious conclusion being that unless you love your neighbor as yourself and he reciprocates you will both be the worse for it. He conveys all this with extraordinary charm, and entertains his hearers with fables (parables) to illustrate them. He has no synagogue or regular congregation, but travels from place to place with twelve men whom he has called from their work as he passed, and who have abandoned it to follow him.

THE MIRACLES

He has certain abnormal powers by which he can perform miracles. He is ashamed of these powers, but, being extremely compassionate, cannot refuse to exercise them when afflicted people beg him to cure them, when multitudes of people are hungry, and when his disciples are terrified by storms on the lakes. He asks for no reward, but begs the people not to mention these powers of his. There are two obvious reasons for his dislike of being known as a worker of miracles. One is the natural objection of all men who possess such powers, but have far more important business in the world than to exhibit them, to be regarded primarily as charlatans, besides being pestered to give exhibitions to satisfy curiosity. The other is that his view of the effect of miracles upon his mission is exactly that taken later on by Rousseau. He perceives that they will discredit him and divert attention from his doctrine by raising an entirely irrelevant issue between his disciples and his opponents.

Possibly my readers may not have studied Rousseau's Letters Written From The Mountain, which may be regarded as the classic work on miracles as credentials of divine mission. Rousseau shews, as Jesus foresaw, that the miracles are the main obstacle to the acceptance of Christianity, because their incredibility (if they were not incredible they would not be miracles) makes people sceptical as to the whole narrative, credible enough in the main, in which they occur, and suspicious of the doctrine with which they are thus associated. "Get rid of the miracles," said Rousseau, "and the whole world will fall at the feet of Jesus Christ." He points out that miracles offered as evidence of divinity, and failing to convince, make divinity ridiculous. He says, in effect, there is nothing in making a lame man walk: thousands of lame men have been cured and have walked without any miracle. Bring me a man with only one leg and make another grow instantaneously on him before my eyes, and I will be really impressed; but mere cures of ailments that have often been cured before are quite useless as evidence of anything else than desire to help and power to cure.

Jesus, according to Matthew, agreed so entirely with Rousseau, and felt the danger so strongly, that when people who were not ill or in trouble came to him and asked him to exercise his powers as a sign of his mission, he was irritated beyond measure, and refused with an indignation which they, not seeing Rousseau's point, must have thought very unreasonable. To be called "an evil and adulterous generation" merely for asking a miracle worker to give an exhibition of his powers, is rather a startling experience. Mahomet, by the way, also lost his temper when people asked him to perform miracles. But Mahomet expressly disclaimed any unusual powers; whereas it is clear from Matthew's story that Jesus (unfortunately for himself, as he thought) had some powers of healing. It is also obvious that the exercise of such powers would give rise to wild tales of magical feats which would expose their hero to condemnation as an impostor among people whose good opinion was of great consequence to the movement started by his mission.

But the deepest annoyance arising from the miracles would be the irrelevance of the issue raised by them. Jesus's teaching has nothing to do with miracles. If his mission had been simply to demonstrate a new method of restoring lost eyesight, the miracle of curing the blind would have been entirely relevant. But to say "You should love your enemies; and to convince you of this I will now proceed to cure this gentleman of cataract" would have been, to a man of Jesus's intelligence, the proposition of an idiot. If it could be proved today that not one of the miracles of Jesus actually occurred, that proof would not invalidate a single one of his didactic utterances; and conversely, if it could be proved that not only did the miracles actually occur, but that he had wrought a thousand other miracles a thousand times more wonderful, not a jot of weight would be added to his doctrine. And yet the intellectual energy of sceptics and divines has been wasted for generations in arguing about the miracles on the assumption that Christianity is at stake in the controversy as to whether the stories of Matthew are false or true. According to Matthew himself, Jesus must have known this only too well; for wherever he went he was assailed with a clamor for miracles, though his doctrine created bewilderment.

So much for the miracles! Matthew tells us further, that Jesus declared that his doctrines would be attacked by Church and State, and that the common multitude were the salt of the earth and the light of the world. His disciples, in their relations with the political and ecclesiastical organizations, would be as sheep among wolves.

MATTHEW IMPUTES BIGOTRY TO JESUS

Matthew, like most biographers, strives to identify the opinions and prejudices of his hero with his own. Although he describes Jesus as tolerant even to carelessness, he draws the line at the Gentile, and represents Jesus as a bigoted Jew who regards his mission as addressed exclusively to "the lost sheep of the house of Israel." When a woman of Canaan begged Jesus to cure her daughter, he first refused to speak to her, and then told her brutally that "It is not meet to take the children's bread and cast it to the dogs." But when the woman said, "Truth, Lord; yet the dogs eat of the crumbs which fall from their master's table," she melted the Jew out of him and made Christ a Christian. To the woman whom he had just called a dog he said, "O woman, great is thy faith: be it unto thee even as thou wilt." This is somehow one of the most touching stories in the gospel; perhaps because the woman rebukes the prophet by a touch of his own finest quality. It is certainly out of character; but as the sins of good men are always out of character, it is not safe to reject the story as invented in the interest of Matthew's determination that Jesus shall have nothing to do with the Gentiles. At all events, there the story is; and it is by no means the only instance in which Matthew reports Jesus, in spite of the charm of his preaching, as extremely uncivil in private intercourse.

THE GREAT CHANGE

So far the history is that of a man sane and interesting apart from his special gifts as orator, healer, and prophet. But a startling change occurs. One day, after the disciples have discouraged him for a long time by their misunderstandings of his mission, and their speculations as to whether he is one of the old prophets come again, and if so, which, his disciple Peter suddenly solves the problem by exclaiming, "Thou art the Christ, the son of the living God." At this Jesus is extraordinarily pleased and excited. He declares that Peter has had a revelation straight from God. He makes a pun on Peter's name, and declares him the founder of his Church. And he accepts his destiny as a god by announcing that he will be killed when he goes to Jerusalem; for if he is really the Christ, it is a necessary part of his legendary destiny that he shall be slain. Peter, not understanding this, rebukes him for what seems mere craven melancholy; and Jesus turns fiercely on him and cries, "Get thee behind me, Satan."

Jesus now becomes obsessed with a conviction of his divinity, and talks about it continually to his disciples, though he forbids them to mention it to others. They begin to dispute among themselves as to the position they shall occupy in heaven when his kingdom is established. He rebukes them strenuously for this, and repeats his teaching that greatness means service and not domination; but he himself, always instinctively somewhat haughty, now becomes arrogant, dictatorial, and even abusive, never replying to his critics without an insulting epithet, and even cursing a fig-tree which disappoints him when he goes to it for fruit. He assumes all the traditions of the folk-lore gods, and announces that, like John Barleycorn, he will be barbarously slain and buried, but will rise from the earth and return to life. He attaches to himself the immemorial tribal ceremony of eating the god, by blessing bread and wine and handing them to his disciples with the words "This is my body: this is my blood." He forgets his own teaching and threatens eternal fire and eternal punishment. He announces, in addition to his Barleycorn resurrection, that he will come to the world a second time in glory and establish his kingdom on earth. He fears that this may lead to the appearance of impostors claiming to be himself, and declares explicitly and repeatedly that no matter what wonders these impostors may perform, his own coming will be unmistakeable, as the stars will fall from heaven, and trumpets be blown by angels. Further he declares that this will take place during the lifetime of persons then present.

JERUSALEM AND THE MYSTICAL SACRIFICE

In this new frame of mind he at last enters Jerusalem amid great popular curiosity; drives the money-changers and sacrifice sellers out of the temple in a riot; refuses to interest himself in the beauties and wonders of the temple building on the ground that presently not a stone of it shall be left on another; reviles the high priests and elders in intolerable terms; and is arrested by night in a garden to avoid a popular disturbance. He makes no resistance, being persuaded that it is part of his destiny as a god to be murdered and to rise again. One of his followers shews fight, and cuts off the ear of one of his captors. Jesus rebukes him, but does not attempt to heal the wound, though he declares that if he wished to resist he could easily summon twelve million angels to his aid. He is taken before the high priest and by him handed over to the Roman governor, who is puzzled by his silent refusal to defend himself in any way, or to contradict his accusers or their witnesses, Pilate having naturally no idea that the prisoner conceives himself as going through an inevitable process of torment, death, and burial as a prelude to resurrection. Before the high priest he has also been silent except that when the priest asks him is he the Christ, the Son of God, he replies that they shall all see the Son of Man sitting at the right hand of power, and coming on the clouds of heaven. He maintains this attitude with frightful fortitude whilst they scourge him, mock him, torment him, and finally crucify him between two thieves. His prolonged agony of thirst and pain on the cross at last breaks his spirit, and he dies with a cry of "My God: why has Thou forsaken me ?"

NOT THIS MAN BUT BARABBAS

Meanwhile he has been definitely rejected by the people as well as by the priests. Pilate, pitying him, and unable to make out exactly what he has done (the blasphemy that has horrified the high priest does not move the Roman), tries to get him off by reminding the people that they have, by custom, the right to have a prisoner released at that time, and suggests that he should release Jesus. But they insist on his releasing a prisoner named Barabbas instead, and on having Jesus crucified. Matthew gives no clue to the popularity of Barabbas, describing him simply as "a notable prisoner." The later gospels make it clear, very significantly, that his offence was sedition and insurrection; that he was an advocate of physical force; and that he had killed his man. The choice of Barabbas thus appears as a popular choice of the militant advocate of physical force as against the unresisting advocate of mercy.

THE RESURRECTION

Matthew then tells how after three days an angel opened the family vault of one Joseph, a rich man of Arimathea, who had buried Jesus in it, whereupon Jesus rose and returned from Jerusalem to Galilee and resumed his preaching with his disciples, assuring them that he would now be with them to the end of the world.

At that point the narrative abruptly stops. The story has no ending.

DATE OF MATTHEW'S NARRATIVE

One effect of the promise of Jesus to come again in glory during the lifetime of some of his hearers is to date the gospel without the aid of any scholarship. It must have been written during the lifetime of Jesus's contemporaries: that is, whilst it was still possible for the promise of his Second Coming to be fulfilled. The death of the last person who had been alive when Jesus said "There be some of them that stand here that shall in no wise taste death til they see the Son of Man coming in his kingdom" destroyed the last possibility of the promised Second Coming, and bore out the incredulity of Pilate and the Jews. And as Matthew writes as one believing in that Second Coming, and in fact left his story unfinished to be ended by it, he must have produced his gospel within a lifetime of the crucifixion. Also, he must have believed that reading books would be one of the pleasures of the kingdom of heaven on earth.

CLASS TYPE OF MATTHEW'S JESUS

One more circumstance must be noted as gathered from Matthew. Though he begins his story in such a way as to suggest that Jesus belonged to the privileged classes, he mentions later on that when Jesus attempted to preach in his own country, and had no success there, the people said, "Is not this the carpenter's son?" But Jesus's manner throughout is that of an aristocrat, or at the very least the son of a rich bourgeois, and by no means a lowly-minded one at that. We must be careful therefore to conceive Joseph, not as a modern proletarian carpenter working for weekly wages, but as a master craftsman of royal descent. John the Baptist may have been a Keir Hardie; but the Jesus of Matthew is of the Ruskin-Morris class.

This haughty characterization is so marked that if we had no other documents concerning Jesus than the gospel of Matthew, we should not feel as we do about him. We should have been much less loth to say, "There is a man here who was sane until Peter hailed

him as the Christ, and who then became a mono-
maniac." We should have pointed out that his delusion
is a very common delusion among the insane, and that
such insanity is quite consistent with the retention of
the argumentative cunning and penetration which
Jesus displayed in Jerusalem after his delusion had
taken complete hold of him. We should feel horrified
at the scourging and mocking and crucifixion just as
we should if Ruskin had been treated in that way when
he also went mad, instead of being cared for as an
invalid. And we should have had no clear perception
of any special significance in his way of calling the
Son of God the Son of Man. We should have noticed
that he was a Communist; that he regarded much of
what we call law and order as machinery for robbing
the poor under legal forms; that he thought domestic
ties a snare for the soul; that he agreed with the
proverb "The nearer the Church, the farther from
God"; that he saw very plainly that the masters of
the community should be its servants and not its
oppressors and parasites; and that though he did not
tell us not to fight our enemies, he did tell us to love
them, and warned us that they who draw the sword
shall perish by the sword. All this shews a great
power of seeing through vulgar illusions, and a
capacity for a higher morality than has yet been
established in any civilized community; but it does
not place Jesus above Confucius or Plato, not to
mention more modern philosophers and moralists.

MARK

THE WOMEN DISCIPLES AND THE ASCENSION

Let us see whether we can get anything more out
of Mark, whose gospel, by the way, is supposed to be

older than Matthew's. Mark is brief; and it does not take long to discover that he adds nothing to Matthew except the ending of the story by Christ's ascension into heaven, and the news that many women had come with Jesus to Jerusalem, including Mary Magdalene, out of whom he had cast seven devils. On the other hand Mark says nothing about the birth of Jesus, and does not touch his career until his adult baptism by John. He apparently regards Jesus as a native of Nazareth, as John does, and not of Bethlehem, as Matthew and Luke do, Bethlehem being the city of David, from whom Jesus is said by Matthew and Luke to be descended. He describes John's doctrine as "Baptism of repentance unto remission of sins": that is, a form of Salvationism. He tells us that Jesus went into the synagogues and taught, not as the Scribes but as one having authority: that is, we infer, he preaches his own doctrine as an original moralist instead of repeating what the books say. He describes the miracle of Jesus reaching the boat by walking across the sea, but says nothing about Peter trying to do the same. Mark sees what he relates more vividly than Matthew, and gives touches of detail that bring the event more clearly before the reader. He says, for instance, that when Jesus walked on the waves to the boat, he was passing it by when the disciples called out to him. He seems to feel that Jesus's treatment of the woman of Canaan requires some apology, and therefore says that she was a Greek of Syrophenician race, which probably excused any incivility to her in Mark's eyes. He represents the father of the boy whom Jesus cured of epilepsy after the transfiguration as a sceptic who says "Lord, I believe: help thou mine unbelief." He tells the story of the widow's mite, omitted by Matthew. He explains that Barabbas was "lying bound with them that made insurrection, men who in the insurrection had committed murder." Joseph of Arimathea, who buried Jesus in his own tomb, and who is described by Matthew as a disciple, is described by Mark as "one who also himself was looking for the kingdom of God," which suggests that he was an independent seeker. Mark earns our gratitude by making no mention of the old prophecies, and thereby not only saves time, but avoids the absurd implication that Christ was merely going through a predetermined ritual, like the works of a clock, instead of living. Finally Mark reports Christ as saying, after his resurrection, that those who believe in him will be saved and those who do not, damned; but it is impossible to discover whether he means anything by a state of damnation beyond a state of error. The paleographers regard this passage as tacked on by a later scribe.

On the whole Mark leaves the modern reader where Matthew left him.

LUKE

LUKE THE LITERARY ARTIST

When we come to Luke, we come to a later story-teller, and one with a stronger natural gift for his art. Before you have read twenty lines of Luke's gospel you are aware that you have passed from the chronicler writing for the sake of recording important facts, to the artist, telling the story for the sake of telling it. At the very outset he achieves the most charming idyll in the Bible: the story of Mary crowded out of the inn into the stable and laying her newly-born son in the manger, and of the shepherds abiding in the field keeping watch over their flocks by night, and how the angel of the Lord came upon them, and the glory of the Lord shone around them, and suddenly there was with the angel a multitude of the heavenly host. These shepherds go to the stable and take the place of the kings in Matthew's chronicle. So completely has this story conquered and fascinated our imagination that most of us suppose all the gospels to contain it; but it is Luke's story and his alone: none of the others have the smallest hint of it.

THE CHARM OF LUKE'S NARRATIVE

Luke gives the charm of sentimental romance to every incident. The Annunciation, as described by Matthew, is made to Joseph, and is simply a warning to him not to divorce his wife for misconduct. In Luke's gospel it is made to Mary herself, at much greater length, with a sense of the ecstasy of the bride of the Holy Ghost. Jesus is refined and softened almost out of recognition: the stern peremptory disciple of John the Baptist, who never addresses a Pharisee or a Scribe without an insulting epithet, becomes a considerate, gentle, sociable, almost urbane person; and the Chauvinist Jew becomes a pro-Gentile who is thrown out of the synagogue in his own town for reminding the congregation that the prophets had sometimes preferred Gentiles to Jews. In fact they try to throw him down from a sort of Tarpeian rock which they use for executions; but he makes his way through them and escapes: the only suggestion of a feat of arms on his part in the gospels. There is not a word of the Syrophenician woman. At the end he is calmly superior to his sufferings; delivers an address on his way to execution with unruffled composure;

does not despair on the cross; and dies with perfect
dignity, commending his spirit to God, after praying
for the forgiveness of his persecutors on the ground
that "They know not what they do." According to
Matthew, it is part of the bitterness of his death that
even the thieves who are crucified with him revile him.
According to Luke, only one of them does this; and he
is rebuked by the other, who begs Jesus to remember
him when he comes into his kingdom. To which Jesus
replies, "This day shalt thou be with me in Paradise,"
implying that he will spend the three days of his death
there. In short, every device is used to get rid of the
ruthless horror of the Matthew chronicle, and to
relieve the strain of the Passion by touching episodes,
and by representing Christ as superior to human
suffering. It is Luke's Jesus who has won our hearts.

THE TOUCH OF PARISIAN ROMANCE

Luke's romantic shrinking from unpleasantness,
and his sentimentality, are illustrated by his version of
the woman with the ointment. Matthew and Mark
describe it as taking place in the house of Simon the
Leper, where it is objected to as a waste of money. In
Luke's version the leper becomes a rich Pharisee; the
woman becomes a Dame aux Camellias; and nothing
is said about money and the poor. The woman washes
the feet of Jesus with her tears and dries them with her
hair; and he is reproached for suffering a sinful
woman to touch him. It is almost an adaptation of the
unromantic Matthew to the Parisian stage. There is a
distinct attempt to increase the feminine interest all
through. The slight lead given by Mark is taken up
and developed. More is said about Jesus's mother and
her feelings. Christ's following of women, just

mentioned by Mark to account for their presence at his tomb, is introduced earlier; and some of the women are named; so that we are introduced to Joanna the wife of Chuza, Herod's steward, and Susanna. There is the quaint little domestic episode between Mary and Martha. There is the parable of the Prodigal Son, appealing to the indulgence romance has always shewn to Charles Surface and Des Grieux. Women follow Jesus to the cross; and he makes them a speech beginning "Daughters of Jerusalem." Slight as these changes may seem, they make a great change in the atmosphere. The Christ of Matthew could never have become what is vulgarly called a woman's hero (though the truth is that the popular demand for sentiment, as far as it is not simply human, is more manly than womanly); but the Christ of Luke has made possible those pictures which now hang in many ladies' chambers, in which Jesus is represented exactly as he is represented in the Lourdes cinematograph, by a handsome actor. The only touch of realism which Luke does not instinctively suppress for the sake of producing this kind of amenity is the reproach addressed to Jesus for sitting down to table without washing his hands; and that is retained because an interesting discourse hangs on it.

WAITING FOR THE MESSIAH

Another new feature in Luke's story is that it begins in a world in which everyone is expecting the advent of the Christ. In Matthew and Mark, Jesus comes into a normal Philistine world like our own of today. Not until the Baptist foretells that one greater than himself shall come after him does the old Jewish hope of a Messiah begin to stir again; and as Jesus begins as a disciple of John, and is baptized by him, nobody connects him with that hope until Peter has the sudden inspiration which produces so startling an effect on Jesus. But in Luke's gospel men's minds, and especially women's minds, are full of eager expectation of a Christ not only before the birth of Jesus, but before the birth of John the Baptist, the event with which Luke begins his story. Whilst Jesus and John are still in their mothers' wombs, John leaps at the approach of Jesus when the two mothers visit one another. At the circumcision of Jesus pious men and women hail the infant as the Christ.

The Baptist himself is not convinced; for at quite a late period in his former disciple's career he sends two young men to ask Jesus is he really the Christ. This is noteworthy because Jesus immediately gives them a deliberate exhibition of miracles, and bids them tell John what they have seen, and ask him what he thinks *now*. This is in complete contradiction to what I have called the Rousseau view of miracles as inferred from Matthew. Luke shews all a romancer's thoughtlessness about miracles: he regards them as "signs": that is, as proof of the divinity of the person performing them, and not merely of thaumaturgic powers. He revels in miracles just as he revels in parables: they make such capital stories. He cannot allow the calling of Peter, James, and John from their boats to pass without a comic miraculous overdraft of fishes, with the net sinking the boats and provoking Peter to exclaim, "Depart from me; for I am a sinful man, O Lord," which should probably be translated, "I want no more of your miracles: natural fishing is good enough for my boats."

There are some other novelties in Luke's version. Pilate sends Jesus to Herod, who happens to be in

Jerusalem just then, because Herod had expressed
some curiosity about him; but nothing comes of it:
the prisoner will not speak to him. When Jesus is ill
received in a Samaritan village James and John propose to call down fire from heaven and destroy it; and
Jesus replies that he is come not to destroy lives but to
save them. The bias of Jesus against lawyers is em-
phasized, and also his resolution not to admit that he is
more bound to his relatives than to strangers. He
snubs a woman who blesses his mother. As this is
contrary to the traditions of sentimental romance,
Luke would presumably have avoided it had he not
become persuaded that the brotherhood of Man and
the Fatherhood of God are superior even to sentimental considerations. The story of the lawyer asking
what are the two chief commandments is changed by
making Jesus put the question to the lawyer instead
of answering it.

As to doctrine, Luke is only clear when his feelings
are touched. His logic is weak; for some of the sayings
of Jesus are pieced together wrongly, as anyone who
has read them in the right order and context in
Matthew will discover at once. He does not make
anything new out of Christ's mission, and, like the
other evangelists, thinks that the whole point of it is
that Jesus was the long expected Christ, and that he
will presently come back to earth and establish his
kingdom, having duly died and risen again after three
days. Yet Luke not only records the teaching as to
communism and the discarding of hate, which have,
of course, nothing to do with the Second Coming, but
quotes one very remarkable saying which is not compatible with it, which is, that people must not go
about asking where the kingdom of heaven is, and
saying "Lo, here!" and "Lo, there!" because the

[500]

kingdom of heaven is within them. But Luke has no sense that this belongs to a quite different order of thought to his Christianity, and retains undisturbed his view of the kingdom as a locality as definite as Jerusalem or Madagascar.

JOHN

A NEW STORY AND A NEW CHARACTER

The gospel of John is a surprise after the others. Matthew, Mark and Luke describe the same events in the same order (the variations in Luke are negligible), and their gospels are therefore called the synoptic gospels. They tell substantially the same story of a wandering preacher who at the end of his life came to Jerusalem. John describes a preacher who spent practically his whole adult life in the capital, with occasional visits to the provinces. His circumstantial account of the calling of Peter and the sons of Zebedee is quite different from the others; and he says nothing about their being fishermen. He says expressly that Jesus, though baptized by John, did not himself practise baptism, and that his disciples did. Christ's agonized appeal against his doom in the garden of Gethsemane becomes a cold-blooded suggestion made in the temple at a much earlier period. Jesus argues much more; complains a good deal of the unreasonableness and dislike with which he is met; is by no means silent before Caiaphas and Pilate; lays much greater stress on his resurrection and on the eating of his body (losing all his disciples except the twelve in consequence); says many apparently contradictory and nonsensical things to which no ordinary reader can now find any clue; and gives the impression

of an educated, not to say sophisticated mystic, different
both in character and schooling from the simple and
downright preacher of Matthew and Mark, and the
urbane easy-minded charmer of Luke. Indeed, the
Jews say of him "How knoweth this man letters,
having never learnt ?"

JOHN THE IMMORTAL EYE-WITNESS

John, moreover, claims to be not only a chronicler
but a witness. He declares that he is "the disciple
whom Jesus loved," and that he actually leaned on the
bosom of Jesus at the last supper and asked in a
whisper which of them it was that should betray him.
Jesus whispered that he would give a sop to the traitor,
and thereupon handed one to Judas, who ate it and
immediately became possessed by the devil. This is
more natural than the other accounts, in which Jesus
openly indicates Judas without eliciting any protest
or exciting any comment. It also implies that Jesus
deliberately bewitched Judas in order to bring about
his own betrayal. Later on John claims that Jesus said
to Peter "If I will that John tarry til I come, what is
that to thee ?"; and John, with a rather obvious mock
modesty, adds that he must not claim to be immortal,
as the disciples concluded; for Christ did not use that
expression, but merely remarked "If I will that he
tarry til I come." No other evangelist claims personal
intimacy with Christ, or even pretends to be his
contemporary (there is no ground for identifying
Matthew the publican with Matthew the Evangelist);
and John is the only evangelist whose account of
Christ's career and character is hopelessly irrecaoncil-
able with Matthew's. He is almost as bad as Matthew,
by the way, in his repeated explanations of Christ's

actions as having no other purpose than to fulfil the old prophecies. The impression is more unpleasant, because, as John, unlike Matthew, is educated, subtle, and obsessed with artificial intellectual mystifications, the discovery that he is stupid or superficial in so simple a matter strikes one with distrust and dislike, in spite of his great literary charm, a good example of which is his transfiguration of the harsh episode of the Syrophenician woman into the pleasant story of the woman of Samaria. This perhaps is why his claim to be John the disciple, or to be a contemporary of Christ or even of any survivor of Christ's generation, has been disputed, and finally, it seems, disallowed. But I repeat, I take no note here of the disputes of experts as to the date of the gospels, not because I am not acquainted with them, but because, as the earliest codices are Greek manuscripts of the fourth century A.D., and the Syrian ones are translations from the Greek, the paleographic expert has no difficulty in arriving at whatever conclusion happens to suit his beliefs or disbeliefs; and he never succeeds in convincing the other experts except when they believe or disbelieve exactly as he does. Hence I conclude that the dates of the original narratives cannot be ascertained, and that we must make the best of the evangelists' own accounts of themselves. There is, as we have seen, a very marked difference between them, leaving no doubt that we are dealing with four authors of well-marked diversity; but they all end in an attitude of expectancy of the Second Coming which they agree in declaring Jesus to have positively and unequivocally promised within the lifetime of his contemporaries. Any believer compiling a gospel after the last of these contemporaries had passed away, would either reject and omit the tradition of that

promise on the ground that since it was not fulfilled,
and could never now be fulfilled, it could not have
been made, or else have had to confess to the Jews,
who were the keenest critics of the Christians, that
Jesus was either an impostor or the victim of a delusion. Now all the evangelists except Matthew expressly
declare themselves to be believers; and Matthew's
narrative is obviously not that of a sceptic. I therefore
assume as a matter of common sense that, interpolations apart, the gospels are derived from narratives
written in the first century A.D. I include John,
because though it may be claimed that he hedged his
position by claiming that Christ, who specially loved
him, endowed him with a miraculous life until the
Second Coming, the conclusion being that John is alive
at this moment, I cannot believe that a literary forger
could hope to save the situation by so outrageous a
pretension. Also, John's narrative is in many passages
nearer to the realities of public life than the simple
chronicle of Matthew or the sentimental romance of
Luke. This may be because John was obviously more
a man of the world than the others, and knew, as
mere chroniclers and romancers never know, what
actually happens away from books and desks. But it
may also be because he saw and heard what happened
instead of collecting traditions about it. The paleographers and daters of first quotations may say what
they please: John's claim to give evidence as an eye-
witness whilst the others are only compiling history is
supported by a certain verisimilitude which appeals to
me as one who has preached a new doctrine and
argued about it, as well as written stories. This verisimilitude may be dramatic art backed by knowledge
of public life; but even at that we must not forget that
the best dramatic art is the operation of a divinatory

instinct for truth. Be that as it may, John was certainly not the man to believe in the Second Coming and yet give a date for it after that date had passed. There is really no escape from the conclusion that the originals of all the gospels date from the period within which there was still a possibility of the Second Coming occurring at the promised time.

THE PECULIAR THEOLOGY OF JESUS

In spite of the suspicions roused by John's idiosyncrasies, his narrative is of enormous importance to those who go to the gospels for a credible modern religion. For it is John who adds to the other records such sayings as that "I and my father are one"; that "God is a spirit"; that the aim of Jesus is not only that the people should have life, but that they should have it "more abundantly" (a distinction much needed by people who think a man is either alive or dead, and never consider the important question how much alive he is); and that men should bear in mind what they were told in the 82nd Psalm: that they are gods, and are responsible for the doing of the mercy and justice of God. The Jews stoned him for saying these things, and, when he remonstrated with them for stupidly stoning one who had done nothing to them but good works, replied "For a good work we stone thee not; but for blasphemy, because that thou, being a man, makest thyself God." He insists (referring to the 82nd Psalm) that if it is part of their own religion that they are gods on the assurance of God himself, it cannot be blasphemy for him, whom the Father sanctified and sent into the world, to say "I am the son of God." But they will not have this at any price; and he has to escape from their fury. Here the point is obscured by the distinction made by Jesus between himself and other men. He says, in effect, "If you are gods, then, *a fortiori*, I am a god." John makes him say this, just as he makes him say "I am the light of the world." But Matthew makes him say to the people "Ye are the light of the world." John has no grip of the significance of these scraps which he has picked up: he is far more interested in a notion of his own that men can escape death and do even more extraordinary things than Christ himself: in fact, he actually represents Jesus as promising this explicitly, and is finally led into the audacious hint that he, John, is himself immortal in the flesh. Still, he does not miss the significant sayings altogether. However inconsistent they may be with the doctrine he is consciously driving at, they appeal to some sub-intellectual instinct in him that makes him stick them in, like a child sticking tinsel stars on the robe of a toy angel.

John does not mention the ascension; and the end of his narrative leaves Christ restored to life, and appearing from time to time among his disciples. It is on one of these occasions that John describes the miraculous draught of fishes which Luke places at the other end of Christ's career, at the call of the sons of Zebedee.

JOHN AGREED AS TO THE TRIAL AND CRUCIFIXION

Although John, following his practice of shewing Jesus's skill as a debater, makes him play a less passive part at his trial, he still gives substantially the same account of it as all the rest. And the question that would occur to any modern reader never occurs to him, any more than it occurred to Matthew, Mark,

or Luke. That question is. Why on earth did not
Jesus defend himself, and make the people rescue him
from the High Priest? He was so popular that they
were unable to prevent him driving the money-
changers out of the temple, or to arrest him for it.
When they did arrest him afterwards, they had to do
it at night in a garden. He could have argued with
them as he had often done in the temple, and justified
himself both to the Jewish law and to Caesar. And he
had physical force at his command to back up his
arguments: all that was needed was a speech to rally
his followers; and he was not gagged. The reply of the
evangelists would have been that all these inquiries
are idle, because if Jesus had wished to escape, he
could have saved himself all that trouble by doing
what John describes him as doing: that is, casting his
captors to the earth by an exertion of his miraculous
power. If you asked John why he let them get up
again and torment and execute him, John would have
replied that it was part of the destiny of God to be
slain and buried and to rise again, and that to have
avoided this destiny would have been to repudiate his
Godhead. And that is the only apparent explanation.
Whether you believe with the evangelists that Christ
could have rescued himself by a miracle, or, as a modern Secularist, point out that he could have defended
himself effectually, the fact remains that according to
all the narratives he did not do so. He had to die like a
god, not to save himself "like one of the princes." [1]

---

[1] Jesus himself had referred to that psalm (LXXXII) in which
men who have judged unjustly and accepted the persons of the
wicked (including by anticipation practically all the white inhabitants of the British Isles and the North American continent,
to mention no other places) are condemned in the words, "I have
said, ye are gods; and all of ye are children of the Most High;
but ye shall die like men, and fall like one of the princes."

The consensus on this point is important, because it proves the absolute sincerity of Jesus's declaration that he was a god. No impostor would have accepted such dreadful consequences without an effort to save himself. No impostor would have been nerved to endure them by the conviction that he would rise from the grave and live again after three days. If we accept the story at all, we must believe this, and believe also that his promise to return in glory and establish his kingdom on earth within the lifetime of men then living, was one which he believed that he could, and indeed must fulfil. Two evangelists declare that in his last agony he despaired, and reproached God for forsaking him. The other two represent him as dying in unshaken conviction and charity with the simple remark that the ordeal was finished. But all four testify that his faith was not deceived, and that he actually rose again after three days. And I think it unreasonable to doubt that all four wrote their narratives in full faith that the other promise would be fulfilled too, and that they themselves might live to witness the Second Coming.

CREDIBILITY OF THE GOSPELS

It will be noted by the older among my readers, who are sure to be obsessed more or less by elderly wrangles as to whether the gospels are credible as matter-of-fact narratives, that I have hardly raised this question, and have accepted the credible and incredible with equal complacency. I have done this because credibility is a subjective condition, as the evolution of religious belief clearly shews. Belief is not dependent on evidence and reason. There is as much evidence that the miracles occurred as that the battle of Waterloo occurred, or that a large body of Russian troops passed through England in 1914 to take part in the war on the western front. The reasons for believing in the murder of Pompey are the same as the reasons for believing in the raising of Lazarus. Both have been believed and doubted by men of equal intelligence. Miracles, in the sense of phenomena we cannot explain, surround us on every hand: life itself is the miracle of miracles. Miracles in the sense of events that violate the normal course of our experience are vouched for every day: the flourishing Church of Christ Scientist is founded on a multitude of such miracles. Nobody believes all the miracles: everybody believes some of them. I cannot tell why men who will not believe that Jesus ever existed yet believe firmly that Shakespear was Bacon. I cannot tell why people who believe that angels appeared and fought on our side at the battle of Mons, and who believe that miracles occur quite frequently at Lourdes, nevertheless boggle at the miracle of the liquefaction of the blood of St Januarius, and reject it as a trick of priestcraft. I cannot tell why people who will not believe Matthew's story of three kings bringing costly gifts to the cradle of Jesus, believe Luke's story of the shepherds and the stable. I cannot tell why people, brought up to believe the Bible in the old literal way as an infallible record and revelation, and rejecting that view later on, begin by rejecting the Old Testament, and give up the belief in a brimstone hell before they give up (if they ever do) the belief in a heaven of harps, crowns, and thrones. I cannot tell why people who will not believe in baptism on any terms believe in vaccination with the cruel fanaticism of inquisitors. I am convinced that if a dozen sceptics were to draw up in parallel columns a list of the events narrated in the gospels which they consider credible and incredible respectively, their lists would be different in several particulars. Belief is literally a matter of taste.

FASHIONS IN BELIEF

Now matters of taste are mostly also matters of fashion. We are conscious of a difference between medieval fashions in belief and modern fashions. For instance, though we are more credulous than men were in the Middle Ages, and entertain such crowds of fortune-tellers, magicians, miracle workers, agents of communication with the dead, discoverers of the elixir of life, transmuters of metals, and healers of all sorts, as the Middle Ages never dreamed of as possible, yet we will not take our miracles in the form that convinced the Middle Ages. Arithmetical numbers appealed to the Middle Ages just as they do to us, because they are difficult to deal with, and because the greatest masters of numbers, the Newtons and Leibnitzes, rank among the greatest men. But there are fashions in numbers too. The Middle Ages took a fancy to some familiar number like seven; and because it was an odd number, and the world was made in seven days, and there are seven stars in Charles's Wain, and for a dozen other reasons, they were ready to believe anything that had a seven or a seven times seven in it. Seven deadly sins, seven swords of sorrow in the heart of the Virgin, seven champions of Christendom, seemed obvious and reasonable things to believe in simply because they were seven. To us, on the contrary, the number seven is the stamp of superstition. We will believe in nothing less than millions. A medieval doctor gained his patient's confidence by telling him that his vitals were being devoured by seven worms. Such a diagnosis would ruin a modern physician. The modern physician tells his patient that he is ill because every drop of his blood is swarming with a million microbes; and the patient believes him abjectly and instantly. Had a bishop told William the Conqueror that the sun was seventy-seven miles distant from the earth, William would have believed him not only out of respect for the Church, but because he would have felt that seventy-seven miles was the proper distance. The Kaiser, knowing just as little about it as the Conqueror, would send that bishop to an asylum. Yet he (I presume) unhesitatingly accepts the estimate of ninety-two and nine-tenths millions of miles, or whatever the latest big figure may be.

CREDIBILITY AND TRUTH

And here I must remind you that our credulity is not to be measured by the truth of the things we believe. When men believed that the earth was flat, they were not credulous: they were using their common sense, and, if asked to prove that the earth was flat, would have said simply, "Look at it." Those who refuse to believe that it is round are exercising a wholesome scepticism. The modern man who believes that the earth is round is grossly credulous. Flat Earth men drive him to fury by confuting him with the greatest ease when he tries to argue about it. Confront him with a theory that the earth is cylindrical, or annular, or hour-glass shaped, and he is lost. The thing he believes may be true, but that is not why he believes it; he believes it because in some mysterious way it appeals to his imagination. If you ask him why he believes that the sun is ninety-odd million miles off, either he will have to confess that he doesnt know, or he will say that Newton proved it. But he has not read the treatise in which Newton proved it, and does not even know that it was written in Latin. If you press an Ulster Protestant as to why he regards Newton as an infallible authority, and St Thomas Aquinas or the Pope as superstitious liars whom, after his death, he will have the pleasure of watching from his place in heaven whilst they roast in eternal flame, or if you ask me why I take into serious consideration Colonel Sir Almroth Wright's estimates of the number of streptococci contained in a given volume of serum whilst I can only laugh at the earlier estimates of the number of angels that can be accommodated on the point of a needle, no reasonable reply is possible except that somehow sevens and angels are out of fashion, and billions and streptococci are all the rage. I simply cannot tell you why Bacon, Montaigne, and Cervantes had a quite different fashion of credulity and incredulity from the Venerable Bede and Piers Plowman and the divine doctors of the Aquinas-Aristotle school, who were certainly no stupider, and had the same facts before them. Still less can I explain why, if we assume that these leaders of thought had all reasoned out their beliefs, their authority seemed conclusive to one generation and blasphemous to another, neither generation having followed the reasoning or gone into the facts of the matter for itself at all.

It is therefore idle to begin disputing with the reader as to what he should believe in the gospels and what he should disbelieve. He will believe what he can, and disbelieve what he must. If he draws any lines at all, they will be quite arbitrary ones. St John tells us that when Jesus explicitly claimed divine honors by the sacrament of his body and blood, so many of his disciples left him that their number was reduced to twelve. Many modern readers will not hold out so long: they will give in at the first miracle. Others will discriminate. They will accept the healing miracles, and reject the feeding of the multitude. To some the walking on the water will be a legendary exaggeration of a swim, ending in an ordinary rescue of Peter; and the raising of Lazarus will be only a similar glorification of a commonplace feat of artificial respiration, whilst others will scoff at it as a planned imposture in which Lazarus acted as a confederate. Between the rejection of the stories as wholly fabulous and the acceptance of them as the evangelists themselves mean them to be accepted, there will be many shades of belief and disbelief, of sympathy and derision. It is not a question of being a Christian or not. A Mahometan Arab will accept literally and without question parts of the narrative which an English Archbishop has to reject or explain away; and many Theosophists and lovers of the wisdom of India, who never enter a Christian Church except as sightseers, will revel in parts of John's gospel which mean nothing to a pious matter-of-fact Bradford manufacturer. Every reader takes from the Bible what he can get. In submitting a précis of the gospel narratives I have not implied any estimate either of their credibility or of their truth. I have simply informed him or reminded him, as the case may be, of what those narratives tell us about their hero.

CHRISTIAN ICONOLATRY AND THE PERIL
OF THE ICONOCLAST

I must now abandon this attitude, and make a serious draft on the reader's attention by facing the question whether, if and when the medieval and Methodist will-to-believe the Salvationist and miraculous side of the gospel narratives fails us, as it plainly has failed the leaders of modern thought, there will be anything left of the mission of Jesus: whether, in short, we may not throw the gospels into the waste-paper basket, or put them away on the fiction shelf of our libraries. I venture to reply that we shall be, on the contrary, in the position of the man in Bunyan's riddle who found that "the more he threw away, the more he had." We get rid, to begin with, of the idola-trous or iconographic worship of Christ. By this I mean literally that worship which is given to pictures and statues of him, and to finished and unalterable stories about him. The test of the prevalence of this is that if you speak or write of Jesus as a real live person, or even as a still active God, such worshippers are more horrified than Don Juan was when the statue stepped from its pedestal and came to supper with him. You may deny the divinity of Jesus; you may doubt whether he ever existed; you may reject Christianity for Judaism, Mahometanism, Shintoism, or Fire Worship; and the iconolaters, placidly con-temptuous, will only classify you as a freethinker or a heathen. But if you venture to wonder how Christ would have looked if he had shaved and had his hair cut, or what size in shoes he took, or whether he swore when he stood on a nail in the carpenter's shop, or could not button his robe when he was in a hurry, or whether he laughed over the repartees by which he baffled the priests when they tried to trap him into sedition and blasphemy, or even if you tell any part of his story in the vivid terms of modern colloquial slang, you will produce an extraordinary dismay and horror among the iconolaters. You will have made the picture come out of its frame, the statue descend from its pedestal, the story become real, with all the incalculable consequences that may flow from this terrifying miracle. It is at such moments that you realize that the iconolaters have never for a moment conceived Christ as a real person who meant what he said, as a fact, as a force like electricity, only needing the invention of suitable political machinery to be applied to the affairs of mankind with revolutionary effect.

Thus it is not disbelief that is dangerous in our society. It is belief. The moment it strikes you (as it may any day) that Christ is not the lifeless harmless image he has hitherto been to you, but a rallying centre for revolutionary influences which all established States and Churches fight, you must look to yourselves; for you have brought the image to life; and the mob may not be able to bear that horror.

THE ALTERNATIVE TO BARABBAS

But mobs must be faced if civilization is to be saved. It did not need the present war to shew that neither the iconographic Christ nor the Christ of St Paul has succeeded in effecting the salvation of human society. Whilst I write, the Turks are said to be massacring the Armenian Christians on an unprecedented scale; but Europe is not in a position to remonstrate; for her Christians are slaying one another by every device which civilization has put within their reach as busily as they are slaying the Turks. Barabbas is triumphant everywhere; and the final use he makes of his triumph is to lead us all to suicide with heroic gestures and resounding lies. Now those who, like myself, see the Barabbasque social organization as a failure, and are convinced that the Life Force (or whatever you choose to call it) cannot be finally beaten by any failure, and will even supersede humanity by evolving a higher species if we cannot master the problems raised by the multiplication of our own numbers, have always known that Jesus had a real message, and have felt the fascination of his character and doctrine. Not that we should nowadays dream of claiming any supernatural authority for him, much less the technical authority which attaches to an educated modern philosopher and jurist. But when, having entirely got rid of Salvationist Christianity, and even contracted a prejudice against Jesus on the score of his involuntary connection with it, we engage on a purely scientific study of economics, criminology, and biology, and find that our practical conclusions are virtually those of Jesus, we are distinctly pleased and encouraged to find that we were doing him an injustice, and that the nimbus that surrounds his head in the pictures may be interpreted some day as a light of science rather than a declaration of sentiment or a label of idolatry.

The doctrines in which Jesus is thus confirmed are, roughly, the following:

1. The kingdom of heaven is within you. You are the son of God; and God is the son of man. God is a spirit, to be worshipped in spirit and in truth, and not an elderly gentleman to be bribed and begged from. We are members one of another; so that you cannot injure or help your neighbor without injuring or helping yourself. God is your father: you are here to do God's work; and you and your father are one.

2. Get rid of property by throwing it into the common stock. Dissociate your work entirely from money payments. If you let a child starve you are letting God starve. Get rid of all anxiety about tomorrow's dinner

and clothes, because you cannot serve two masters: God and Mammon.

3. Get rid of judges and punishment and revenge. Love your neighbor as yourself, he being a part of yourself. And love your enemies: they are your neighbors.

4. Get rid of your family entanglements. Every mother you meet is as much your mother as the woman who bore you. Every man you meet is as much your brother as the man she bore after you. Dont waste your time at family funerals grieving for your relatives: attend to life, not to death: there are as good fish in the sea as ever came out of it, and better. In the kingdom of heaven, which, as aforesaid, is within you, there is no marriage nor giving in marriage, because you cannot devote your life to two divinities: God and the person you are married to.

Now these are very interesting propositions; and they become more interesting every day, as experience and science drive us more and more to consider them favorably. In considering them, we shall waste our time unless we give them a reasonable construction. We must assume that the man who saw his way through such a mass of popular passion and illusion as stands between us and a sense of the value of such teaching was quite aware of all the objections that occur to an average stockbroker in the first five minutes. It is true that the world is governed to a considerable extent by the considerations that occur to stockbrokers in the first five minutes; but as the result is that the world is so badly governed that those who know the truth can hardly bear to live in it, an objection from an average stockbroker constitutes in itself a *prima facie* case for any social reform.

[517]

THE REDUCTION TO MODERN PRACTICE
OF CHRISTIANITY

All the same, we must reduce the ethical counsels and proposals of Jesus to modern practice if they are to be of any use to us. If we ask our stockbroker to act simply as Jesus advised his disciples to act, he will reply, very justly, "You are advising me to become a tramp." If we urge a rich man to sell all that he has and give it to the poor, he will inform us that such an operation is impossible. If he sells his shares and his lands, their purchaser will continue all those activities which oppress the poor. If all the rich men take the advice simultaneously the shares will fall to zero and the lands be unsaleable. If one man sells out and throws the money into the slums, the only result will be to add himself and his dependants to the list of the poor, and to do no good to the poor beyond giving a chance few of them a drunken spree. We must therefore bear in mind that whereas, in the time of Jesus, and in the ages which grew darker and darker after his death until the darkness, after a brief false dawn in the Reformation and the Renascence, culminated in the commercial night of the nineteenth century, it was believed that you could not make men good by Act of Parliament, we now know that you cannot make them good in any other way, and that a man who is better than his fellows is a nuisance. The rich man must sell up not only himself but his whole class; and that can be done only through the Chancellor of the Exchequer. The disciple cannot have his bread without money until there is bread for everybody without money; and that requires an elaborate municipal organization of the food supply, rate supported. Being members one of another means One Man One Vote, and One Woman One Vote, and universal suffrage and equal incomes and all sorts of modern political measures. Even in Syria in the time of Jesus his teachings could not possibly have been realized by a series of independent explosions of personal righteousness on the part of the separate units of the population. Jerusalem could not have done what even a village community cannot do, and what Robinson Crusoe himself could not have done if his conscience, and the stern compulsion of Nature, had not imposed a common rule on the half dozen Robinson Crusoes who struggled within him for not wholly compatible satisfactions. And what cannot be done in Jerusalem or Juan Fernandez cannot be done in London, New York, Paris, and Berlin.

In short, Christianity, good or bad, right or wrong, must perforce be left out of the question in human affairs until it is made practically applicable to them by complicated political devices; and to pretend that a field preacher under the governorship of Pontius Pilate, or even Pontius Pilate himself in council with all the wisdom of Rome, could have worked out applications of Christianity or any other system of morals for the twentieth century, is to shelve the subject much more effectually than Nero and all its other persecutors ever succeeded in doing. Personal righteousness, and the view that you cannot make people moral by Act of Parliament, is, in fact, the favorite defensive resort of the people who, consciously or subconsciously, are quite determined not to have their property meddled with by Jesus or any other reformer.

MODERN COMMUNISM

Now let us see what modern experience and sociology have to say to the suggestion of Jesus that

you should get rid of your property by throwing it
into the common stock. One can hear the Pharisees of
Jerusalem and Chorazin and Bethsaida saying, "My
good fellow, if you were to divide up the wealth of
Judea equally today, before the end of the year you
would have rich and poor, poverty and affluence, just
as you have today; for there will always be the idle and
the industrious, the thrifty and the wasteful, the
drunken and the sober; and, as you yourself have very
justly observed, the poor we shall have always with
us." And we can hear the reply, "Woe unto you,
liars and hypocrites; for ye have this very day divided
up the wealth of the country yourselves, as must be
done every day (for man liveth not otherwise than
from hand to mouth, nor can fish and eggs endure for
ever); and ye have divided it unjustly; also ye have
said that my reproach to you for having the poor
always with you was a law unto you that this evil
should persist and stink in the nostrils of God to all
eternity; wherefore I think that Lazarus will yet see
you beside Dives in hell." Modern Capitalism has
made short work of the primitive pleas for inequality.
The Pharisees themselves have organized communism
in capital. Joint stock is the order of the day. An
attempt to return to individual properties as the basis
of our production would smash civilization more
completely than ten revolutions. You cannot get the
fields tilled today until the farmer becomes a co-
operator. Take the shareholder to his railway, and ask
him to point out to you the particular length of rail,
the particular seat in the railway carriage, the particular lever in the engine that is his very own and nobody elses; and he will shun you as a madman, very
wisely. And if, like Ananias and Sapphira, you try
to hold back your little shop or what not from the
common stock, represented by the Trust, or Combine,

or Kartel, the Trust will presently freeze you out and rope you in and finally strike you dead industrially as thoroughly as St Peter himself. There is no longer any practical question open as to Communism in production: the struggle today is over the distribution of the product: that is, over the daily dividing-up which is the first necessity of organized society.

REDISTRIBUTION

Now it needs no Christ to convince anybody today that our system of distribution is wildly and monstrously wrong. We have million-dollar babies side by side with paupers worn out by a long life of unremitted drudgery. One person in every five dies in a workhouse, a public hospital, or a madhouse. In cities like London the proportion is very nearly one in two. Naturally so outrageous a distribution has to be effected by violence pure and simple. If you demur, you are sold up. If you resist the selling up you are bludgeoned and imprisoned, the process being euphemistically called the maintenance of law and order. Iniquity can go no further. By this time nobody who knows the figures of the distribution defends them. The most bigoted British Conservative hesitates to say that his king should be much poorer than Mr Rockefeller, or to proclaim the moral superiority of prostitution to needlework on the ground that it pays better. The need for a drastic redistribution of income in all civilized countries is now as obvious and as generally admitted as the need for sanitation.

SHALL HE WHO MAKES, OWN?

It is when we come to the question of the proportions in which we are to redistribute that controversy begins. We are bewildered by an absurdly unpractical notion that in some way a man's income should be given to him, not to enable him to live, but as a sort of Sunday School Prize for good behavior. And this folly is complicated by a less ridiculous but quite as unpractical belief that it is possible to assign to each person the exact portion of the national income that he or she has produced. To a child it seems that the blacksmith has made a horse-shoe, and that therefore the horse-shoe is his. But the blacksmith knows that the horse-shoe does not belong solely to him, but to his landlord, to the rate collector and taxgatherer, to the men from whom he bought the iron and anvil and the coals, leaving only a scrap of its value for himself; and this scrap he has to exchange with the butcher and baker and the clothier for the things that he really appropriates as living tissue or its wrappings, paying for all of them more than their cost; for these fellow traders of his have also their landlords and money-lenders to satisfy. If, then, such simple and direct village examples of apparent individual production turn out on a moment's examination to be the products of an elaborate social organization what is to be said of such products as dreadnoughts, factory-made pins and needles, and steel pens? If God takes the dreadnought in one hand and a steel pen in the other, and asks Job who made them, and to whom they should belong by maker's right, Job must scratch his puzzled head with a potsherd and be dumb, unless indeed it strikes him that God is the ultimate maker, and that all we have a right to do with the product is to feed his lambs.

LABOR TIME

So maker's right as an alternative to taking the advice of Jesus would not work. In practice nothing was possible in that direction but to pay a worker by labor time: so much an hour or day or week or year. But how much? When that question came up, the only answer was "as little as he can be starved into accepting," with the ridiculous results already mentioned, and the additional anomaly that the largest share went to the people who did not work at all, and the least to those who worked hardest. In England nine-tenths of the wealth goes into the pockets of one-tenth of the population.

THE DREAM OF DISTRIBUTION ACCORDING
TO MERIT

Against this comes the protest of the Sunday School theorists "Why not distribute according to merit?" Here one imagines Jesus, whose smile has been broadening down the ages as attempt after attempt to escape from his teaching has led to deeper and deeper disaster, laughing outright. Was ever so idiotic a project mooted as the estimation of virtue in money? The London School of Economics is, we must suppose, to set examination papers with such questions as "Taking the money value of the virtues of Jesus as 100, and of Judas Iscariot as zero, give the correct figures for, respectively, Pontius Pilate, the proprietor of the Gadarene swine, the widow who put her mite in the poor-box, Mr Horatio Bottomley, Shakespear, Mr Jack Johnson, Sir Isaac Newton, Palestrina, Offenbach, Sir Thomas Lipton, Mr Paul Cinquevalli, your family doctor, Florence Nightingale, Mrs Siddons, your charwoman, the Archbishop of Canterbury, and the common hangman." Or "The late Mr Barney Barnato received as his lawful income three thousand times as much money as an

English agricultural laborer of good general character. Name the principal virtues in which Mr Barnato exceeded the laborer three thousandfold; and give in figures the loss sustained by civilization when Mr Barnato was driven to despair and suicide by the reduction of his multiple to one thousand." The Sunday School idea, with its principle "to each the income he deserves," is really too silly for discussion. Hamlet disposed of it three hundred years ago. "Use every man after his deserts, and who shall scape whipping?" Jesus remains unshaken as the practical man; and we stand exposed as the fools, the blunderers, the unpractical visionaries. The moment you try to reduce the Sunday School idea to figures you find that it brings you back to the hopeless plan of paying for a man's time; and your examination paper will read "The time of Jesus was worth nothing (he complained that the foxes had holes and the birds of the air nests whilst he had not a place to lay his head). Dr Crippen's time was worth, say, three hundred and fifty pounds a year. Criticize this arrangement; and, if you dispute its justice, state in pounds, dollars, francs and marks, what their relative time wages ought to have been." Your answer may be that the question is in extremely bad taste and that you decline to answer it. But you cannot object to being asked how many minutes of a bookmaker's time are worth two hours of an astronomer's?

VITAL DISTRIBUTION

In the end you are forced to ask the question you should have asked at the beginning. What do you give a man an income for? Obviously to keep him alive. Since it is evident that the first condition on which he

can be kept alive without enslaving somebody else is
that he shall produce an equivalent for what it costs
to keep him alive, we may quite rationally compel
him to abstain from idling by whatever means we
employ to compel him to abstain from murder, arson,
forgery, or any other crime. The one supremely
foolish thing to do with him is to do nothing: that is
to be as idle, lazy, and heartless in dealing with him as
he is in dealing with us. Even if we provided work for
him instead of basing, as we do, our whole industrial
system on successive competitive waves of overwork
with their ensuing troughs of unemployment, we
should still sternly deny him the alternative of not
doing it; for the result must be that he will become
poor and make his children poor if he has any; and
poor people are cancers in the commonwealth, costing
far more than if they were handsomely pensioned off
as incurables. Jesus had more sense than to propose
anything of the sort. He said to his disciples, in
effect, "Do your work for love; and let the other
people lodge and feed and clothe you for love." Or,
as we should put it nowadays, "for nothing." All
human experience and all natural uncommercialized
human aspiration point to this as the right path. The
Greeks said, "First secure an independent income;
and then practise virtue." We all strive towards an
independent income. We all know as well as Jesus did
that if we have to take thought for the morrow as to
whether there shall be anything to eat or drink it will
be impossible for us to think of nobler things, or live
a higher life than that of a mole, whose life is from
beginning to end a frenzied pursuit of food. Until the
community is organized in such a way that the fear of
bodily want is forgotten as completely as the fear of
wolves already is in civilized capitals, we shall never
have a decent social life. Indeed the whole attraction

of our present arrangement lies in the fact that it does relieve a handful of us from this fear; but as the relief is effected stupidly and wickedly by making the favored handful parasitic on the rest, they are smitten with the degeneracy which seems to be the inevitable biological penalty of complete parasitism. They corrupt culture and statecraft instead of contributing to them, their excessive leisure being as mischievous as the excessive toil of the laborers. Anyhow, the moral is clear. The two main problems of organized society: how to produce subsistence enough for all its members, and how to prevent the theft of that subsistence by idlers, should be carefully dissociated; for the triumphant solution of the first by our inventors and chemists has been offset by the disastrous failure of our rulers to solve the other. Optimism on this point is only wilful blindness: we all have the hard fact of the failure before us. The only people who cling to the lazy delusion that it is possible to find a just distribution that will work automatically are those who postulate some revolutionary change like land nationalization, which by itself would obviously only force into greater urgency the problem of how to distribute the product of the land among all the individuals in the community.

EQUAL DISTRIBUTION

When that problem is at last faced, the question of the proportion in which the national income shall be distributed can have only one answer. All our shares must be equal. It has always been so: it always will be so. It is true that the incomes of robbers vary considerably from individual to individual; and the variation is reflected in the incomes of their parasites.

The commercialization of certain exceptional talents has also produced exceptional incomes, direct and derivative. Persons who live on rent of land and capital are economically, though not legally, in the category of robbers, and have grotesquely different incomes. But in the huge mass of mankind variation of income from individual to individual is unknown, because it is ridiculously impracticable. As a device for persuading a carpenter that a judge is a creature of superior nature to himself, to be deferred and submitted to even to the death, we may give a carpenter a hundred pounds a year and a judge five thousand; but the wage for one carpenter is the wage for all the carpenters: the salary for one judge is the salary for all the judges.

THE CAPTAIN AND THE CABIN BOY

Nothing, therefore, is really in question, or ever has been, but the differences between class incomes. Already there is economic equality between captains, and economic equality between cabin boys. What is at issue still is whether there shall be economic equality between captains and cabin boys. What would Jesus have said? Presumably he would have said that if your only object is to produce a captain and a cabin boy for the purpose of transferring you from Liverpool to New York, or to manœuvre a fleet and carry powder from the magazine to the gun, then you need give no more than a shilling to the cabin boy for every pound you give to the more expensively trained captain. But if in addition to this you desire to allow the two human souls which are inseparable from the captain and the cabin boy, and which alone differentiate them from the donkey-engine, to develop all their possibilities, then you may find the cabin boy costing rather more than the captain, because cabin boy's work does not do so much for the soul as captain's work. Consequently you will have to give him at least as much as the captain unless you definitely wish him to be a lower creature, in which case the sooner you are hanged as an abortionist the better. That is the fundamental argument.

THE POLITICAL AND BIOLOGICAL OBJECTIONS TO INEQUALITY

But there are other reasons for objecting to class stratification of income which have heaped themselves up since the time of Jesus. In politics it defeats every form of government except that of a necessarily corrupt oligarchy. Democracy in the most democratic modern republics: France and the United States for example, is an imposture and a delusion. It reduces justice and law to a farce: law becomes merely an instrument for keeping the poor in subjection; and accused workmen are tried, not by a jury of their peers, but by conspiracies of their exploiters. The press is the press of the rich and the curse of the poor: it becomes dangerous to teach men to read. The priest becomes the mere complement of the policeman in the machinery by which the countryhouse oppresses the village. Worst of all, marriage becomes a class affair: the infinite variety of choice which nature offers to the young in search of a mate is narrowed to a handful of persons of similar income; and beauty and health become the dreams of artists and the advertisements of quacks instead of the normal conditions of life. Society is not only divided but actually destroyed in all directions by inequality of income between classes: such stability as it has is due to the huge blocks of people between whom there is equality of income.

JESUS AS ECONOMIST

It seems therefore that we must begin by holding the right to an income as sacred and equal, just as we now begin by holding the right to life as sacred and equal. Indeed the one right is only a restatement of the other. To hang me for cutting a dock laborer's throat after making much of me for leaving him to starve when I do not happen to have a ship for him to unload is idiotic; for as he does far less mischief with his throat cut than when he is starving, a rational society would esteem the cutthroat more highly than the capitalist. The thing has become so obvious, and the evil so unendurable, that if our attempt at civilization is not to perish like all the previous ones, we shall have to organize our society in such a way as to be able to say to every person in the land, "Take no thought, saying What shall we eat? or What shall we drink? or Wherewithal shall we be clothed?" We shall then no longer have a race of men whose hearts are in their pockets and safes and at their bankers. As Jesus said, where your treasure is, there will your heart be also. That was why he recommended that money should cease to be a treasure, and that we should take steps to make ourselves utterly reckless of it, setting our minds free for higher uses. In other words, that we should all be gentlemen and take care of our country because our country takes care of us, instead of the commercialized cads we are, doing everything and anything for money, and selling our souls and bodies by the pound and the inch after wasting half the day haggling over the price. Decidedly, whether you think Jesus was God or not, you must admit that he was a first-rate political economist.

JESUS AS BIOLOGIST

He was also, as we now see, a first-rate biologist. It took a century and a half of evolutionary preachers, from Buffon and Goethe to Butler and Bergson, to convince us that we and our father are one; that as the kingdom of heaven is within us we need not go about looking for it and crying Lo here! and Lo there!; that God is not a picture of a pompous person in white robes in the family Bible, but a spirit; that it is through this spirit that we evolve towards greater abundance of life; that we are the lamps in which the light of the world burns: that, in short, we are gods though we die like men. All that is today sound biology and psychology; and the efforts of Natural Selectionists like Weismann to reduce evolution to mere automatism have not touched the doctrine of Jesus, though they have made short work of the theologians who conceived God as a magnate keeping men and angels as Lord Rothschild keeps buffaloes and emus at Tring.

MONEY THE MIDWIFE OF SCIENTIFIC COMMUNISM

It may be asked here by some simple-minded reader why we should not resort to crude Communism as the disciples were told to do. This would be quite practicable in a village where production was limited to the supply of the primitive wants which nature imposes on all human beings alike. We know that people need bread and boots without waiting for them to come and ask for these things and offer to pay for them. But when civilization advances to the point at which articles are produced that no man absolutely needs and that only some men fancy or can use, it is necessary that individuals should be able to have things made to their order and at their own cost. It is safe to provide bread for everybody because everybody wants and eats bread; but it would be absurd to provide microscopes and trombones, pet snakes and polo mallets, alembics and test tubes for everybody, as nine-tenths of them would be wasted; and the nine-tenths of the population who do not use such things would object to their being provided at all. We have in the invaluable instrument called money a means of enabling every individual to order and pay for the particular things he desires over and above the things he must consume in order to remain alive, plus the things the State insists on his having and using whether he wants to or not: for example, clothes, sanitary arrangements, armies and navies. In large communities, where even the most eccentric demands for manufactured articles average themselves out until they can be foreseen within a negligible margin of error, direct communism (Take what you want without payment, as the people do in Morris's News From Nowhere) will, after a little experience, be found not only practicable but highly economical to an extent that now seems impossible. The sportsmen, the musicians, the physicists, the biologists will get their apparatus for the asking as easily as their bread, or, as at present, their paving, street lighting, and bridges; and the deaf man will not object to contribute to communal flutes when the musician has to contribute to communal ear trumpets. There are cases (for example, radium) in which the demand may be limited to the merest handful of laboratory workers, and in which nevertheless the whole community must pay because the price is beyond the means of any individual worker. But even when the utmost allowance is made for extensions of communism that now seem fabulous, there will still remain for a long time to come regions of supply and demand in which men will need and use money or individual credit, and for which, therefore, they must have individual incomes. Foreign travel is an obvious instance. We are so far from even national communism still, that we shall probably have considerable developments of local communism before it becomes possible for a Manchester man to go up to London for a day without taking any money with him. The modern practical form of the communism of Jesus is therefore, for the present, equal distribution of the surplus of the national income that is not absorbed by simple communism.

JUDGE NOT

In dealing with crime and the family, modern thought and experience have thrown no fresh light on the views of Jesus. When Swift had occasion to illustrate the corruption of our civilization by making a catalogue of the types of scoundrels it produces, he always gave judges a conspicuous place alongside of them they judged. And he seems to have done this not as a restatement of the doctrine of Jesus, but as the outcome of his own observation and judgement. One of Mr Gilbert Chesterton's stories has for its hero a judge who, whilst trying a criminal case, is so overwhelmed by the absurdity of his position and the wickedness of the things it forces him to do, that he throws off the ermine there and then, and goes out into the world to live the life of an honest man instead of that of a cruel idol. There has also been a propaganda of a soulless stupidity called Determinism, representing man as a dead object driven hither and thither by his environment, antecedents, circumstances, and so forth, which nevertheless does remind us that there are limits to the number of cubits an individual can add to his stature morally or physically, and that it is silly as well as cruel to torment a man five feet high for not being able to pluck fruit that is within the reach of men of average height. I have known a case of an unfortunate child being beaten for not being able to tell the time after receiving an elaborate explanation of the figures on a clock dial, the fact being that she was short-sighted and could not see them. This is a typical illustration of the absurdities and cruelties into which we are led by counter-stupidity to Determinism: the doctrine of Free Will. The notion that people can be good if they like, and that you should give them a powerful additional motive for goodness by tormenting them when they do evil, would soon reduce itself to absurdity if its application were not kept within the limits which nature sets to the self-control of most of us. Nobody supposes that a man with no ear for music or no mathematical faculty could be compelled on pain of death, however cruelly inflicted, to hum all the themes of Beethoven's symphonies or to complete Newton's work on fluxions.

LIMITS TO FREE WILL

Consequently such of our laws as are not merely the intimidations by which tyrannies are maintained under pretext of law, can be obeyed through the exercise of a quite common degree of reasoning power and self-control. Most men and women can endure the ordinary annoyances and disappointments of life without committing murderous assaults. They conclude therefore that any person can refrain from such assaults if he or she chooses to, and proceed to reinforce self-control by threats of severe punishment. But in this they are mistaken. There are people, some of them possessing considerable powers of mind and body, who can no more restrain the fury into which a trifling mishap throws them than a dog can restrain himself from snapping if he is suddenly and painfully pinched. People fling knives and lighted paraffin lamps at one another in a dispute over a dinner-table. Men who have suffered several long sentences of penal servitude for murderous assaults will, the very day after they are released, seize their wives and cast them under drays at an irritating word. We have not only people who cannot resist an opportunity of stealing for the sake of satisfying their wants, but even people who have a specific mania for stealing, and do it when they are in no need of the things they steal. Burglary fascinates some men as sailoring fascinates some boys. Among respectable people how many are there who can be restrained by the warnings of their doctors and the lessons of experience from eating and drinking more than is good for them? It is true that between self-controlled people and ungovernable people there is a narrow margin of moral malingerers who can be made to behave themselves by the fear of consequences; but it is not worth while maintaining an abominable system of malicious, deliberate, costly and degrading ill-treatment of criminals for the sake of these marginal cases. For practical dealing with crime, Determinism or Predestination is quite a good working rule. People without self-control enough for social purposes may be killed, or may be kept in asylums with a view to studying their condition and ascertaining whether it is curable. To torture them and give ourselves virtuous airs at their expense is ridiculous and barbarous; and the desire to do it is vindictive and cruel. And though vindictiveness and cruelty are at least human qualities when they are frankly proclaimed and indulged, they are loathsome when they assume the robes of Justice. Which, I take it, is why Shakespear's Isabella gave such a dressing-down to Judge Angelo, and why Swift reserved the hottest corner of his hell for judges. Also, of course, why Jesus said "Judge not that ye be not judged" and "If any man hear my words and believe not, I judge him not" because "he hath one that judgeth him"; namely, the Father who is one with him.

When we are robbed we generally appeal to the criminal law, not considering that if the criminal law were effective we should not have been robbed. That convicts us of vengeance.

I need not elaborate the argument further. I have dealt with it sufficiently elsewhere. I have only to point out that we have been judging and punishing ever since Jesus told us not to; and I defy anyone to make out a convincing case for believing that the world has been any better than it would have been if there had never been a judge, a prison, or a gallows in it all that time. We have simply added the misery of punishment to the misery of crime, and the cruelty of the judge to the cruelty of the criminal. We have taken the bad man, and made him worse by torture and degradation, incidentally making ourselves worse in the process. It does not seem very sensible, does it? It would have been far easier to kill him as kindly as possible, or to label him and leave him to his conscience, or to treat him as an invalid or a lunatic is now treated (it is only of late years, by the way, that madmen have been delivered from the whip, the chain, and the cage); and this, I presume, is the form in which the teaching of Jesus could have been put into practice.

JESUS ON MARRIAGE AND THE FAMILY

When we come to marriage and the family, we find Jesus making the same objection to that individual appropriation of human beings which is the essence of matrimony as to the individual appropriation of wealth. A married man, he said, will try to please his wife, and a married woman to please her husband, instead of doing the work of God. This is another version of "Where your treasure is, there will your heart be also." Eighteen hundred years later we find a very different person from Jesus, Talleyrand to wit, saying the same thing. A married man with a family, said Talleyrand, will do anything for money. Now this, though not a scientifically precise statement, is true enough to be a moral objection to marriage. As long as a man has a right to risk his life or his livelihood for his ideas he needs only courage and conviction to make his integrity unassailable. But he forfeits that right when he marries. It took a revolution to rescue Wagner from his Court appointment at Dresden; and his wife never forgave him for being glad and feeling free when he lost it and threw her back into poverty. Millet might have gone on painting pot-boiling nudes to the end of his life if his wife had not been of a heroic turn herself. Women, for the sake of their children and parents, submit to slaveries and prostitutions that no unattached woman would endure.

This was the beginning and the end of the objection of Jesus to marriage and family ties, and the explanation of his conception of heaven as a place where there should be neither marrying nor giving in marriage. Now there is no reason to suppose that when he said this he did not mean it. He did not, as St Paul did afterwards in his name, propose celibacy as a rule of life; for he was not a fool, nor, when he denounced marriage, had he yet come to believe, as St Paul did, that the end of the world was at hand and there was therefore no more need to replenish the earth. He must have meant that the race should be continued without dividing with women and men the allegiance the individual owes to God within him. This raises the practical problem of how we are to secure the spiritual freedom and integrity of the priest and the nun without their barrenness and uncompleted experience. Luther the priest did not solve the problem by marrying a nun: he only testified in the most convincing and practical way to the fact that celibacy was a worse failure than marriage.

WHY JESUS DID NOT MARRY

To all appearance the problem oppresses only a few exceptional people. Thoroughly conventional women married to thoroughly conventional men should not be conscious of any restriction: the chain not only leaves them free to do whatever they want to do, but greatly facilitates their doing it. To them an attack on marriage is not a blow struck in defence of their freedom but at their rights and privileges. One would expect that they would not only demur vehemently to the teachings of Jesus in this matter, but object strongly to his not having been a married man himself. Even those who regard him as a god descended from his throne in heaven to take on humanity for a time might reasonably declare that the assumption of humanity must have been incomplete at its most vital point if he were a celibate. But the facts are flatly contrary. The mere thought of Jesus as a married man is felt to be blasphemous by the most conventional believers; and even those of us to whom Jesus is no supernatural personage, but a prophet only as Mahomet was a prophet, feel that there was something more dignified in the bachelordom of Jesus than in the spectacle of Mahomet lying distracted on the floor of his harem whilst his wives stormed and squabbled and henpecked round him. We are not surprised that Jesus called the sons of Zebedee to follow him, he did not call their father, and that the disciples, like Jesus himself, were all men without family entanglements. It is evident from his impatience when people excused themselves from following him because of their family funerals, or when they assumed that his first duty was to his mother, that he had found family ties and domestic affections in his way at every turn, and had become persuaded at last that no man could follow his inner light until he was free from their compulsion. The absence of any protest against this tempts us to declare that on this question of marriage there are no conventional people; and that everyone of us is at heart a good Christian sexually.

INCONSISTENCY OF THE SEX INSTINCT

But the question is not so simple as that. Sex is an exceedingly subtle and complicated instinct; and the mass of mankind neither know nor care much about freedom of conscience, which is what Jesus was

thinking about, and are concerned almost to obsession
with sex, as to which Jesus said nothing. In our sexual
natures we are torn by an irresistible attraction and an
overwhelming repugnance and disgust. We have two
tyrannous physical passions: concupiscence and
chastity. We become mad in pursuit of sex: we
become equally mad in the persecution of that
pursuit. Unless we gratify our desire the race is lost:
unless we restrain it we destroy ourselves. We are thus
led to devise marriage institutions which will at the
same time secure opportunities for the gratification of
sex and raise up innumerable obstacles to it; which
will sanctify it and brand it as infamous; which will
identify it with virtue and with sin simultaneously.
Obviously it is useless to look for any consistency in
such institutions; and it is only by continual reform
and readjustment, and by a considerable elasticity in
their enforcement, that a tolerable result can be arrived
at. I need not repeat here the long and elaborate examination of them that I prefixed to my play entitled
Getting Married. Here I am concerned only with
the views of Jesus on the question; and it is necessary,
in order to understand the attitude of the world
towards them, that we should not attribute the general
approval of the decision of Jesus to remain unmarried
as an endorsement of his views. We are simply in a
state of confusion on the subject; but it is part of the
confusion that we should conclude that Jesus was a
celibate, and shrink even from the idea that his birth
was a natural one, yet cling with ferocity to the
sacredness of the institution which provides a refuge
from celibacy.

FOR BETTER OR WORSE

Jesus, however, did not express a complicated view

of marriage. His objection to it was quite simple, as we have seen. He perceived that nobody could live the higher life unless money and sexual love were obtainable without sacrificing it; and he saw that the effect of marriage as it existed among the Jews (and as it still exists among ourselves) was to make the couples sacrifice every higher consideration until they had fed and pleased one another. The worst of it is that this dangerous preposterousness in marriage, instead of improving as the general conduct of married couples improves, becomes much worse. The selfish man to whom his wife is nothing but a slave, the selfish woman to whom her husband is nothing but a scapegoat and a breadwinner, are not held back from spiritual or any other adventures by fear of their effect on the welfare of their mates. Their wives do not make recreants and cowards of them: their husbands do not chain them to the cradle and the cooking range when their feet should be beautiful on the mountains. It is precisely as people become more kindly, more conscientious, more ready to shoulder the heavier part of the burden (which means that the strong shall give way to the weak and the slow hold back the swift), that marriage becomes an intolerable obstacle to individual evolution. And that is why the revolt against marriage of which Jesus was an exponent always recurs when civilization raises the standard of marital duty and affection, and at the same time produces a greater need for individual freedom in pursuit of a higher evolution.

THE REMEDY

This, fortunately, is only one side of marriage; and the question arises, can it not be eliminated? The reply is reassuring: of course it can. There is no mortal reason in the nature of things why a married couple should be economically dependent on one another. The Communism advocated by Jesus, which we have seen to be entirely practicable, and indeed inevitable if our civilization is to be saved from collapse, gets rid of that difficulty completely. And with the economic dependence will go the force of the outrageous claims that derive their real sanction from the economic pressure behind them. When a man allows his wife to turn him from the best work he is capable of doing, and to sell his soul at the highest commercial prices obtainable; when he allows her to entangle him in a social routine that is wearisome and debilitating to him, or tie him to her apron strings when he needs that occasional solitude which is one of the most sacred of human rights, he does so because he has no right to impose eccentric standards of expenditure and unsocial habits on her, and because these conditions have produced by their pressure so general a custom of chaining wedded couples to one another that married people are coarsely derided when their partners break the chain. And when a woman is condemned by her parents to wait in genteel idleness and uselessness for a husband when all her healthy social instincts call her to acquire a profession and work, it is again her economic dependence on them that makes their tyranny effective.

THE CASE FOR MARRIAGE

Thus, though it would be too much to say that everything that is obnoxious in marriage and family life will be cured by Communism, yet it can be said that it will cure what Jesus objected to in these institutions. He made no comprehensive study of them: he only expressed his own grievance with an overwhelming sense that it is a grievance so deep that all the considerations on the other side are as dust in the balance. Obviously there are such considerations, and very weighty ones too. When Talleyrand said that a married man with a family is capable of anything, he meant anything evil; but an optimist may declare, with equal half truth, that a married man is capable of anything good; that marriage turns vagabonds into steady citizens; and that men and women will, for love of their mates and children, practise virtues that unattached individuals are incapable of. It is true that too much of this domestic virtue is self-denial, which is not a virtue at all; but then the following of the inner light at all costs is largely self-indulgence, which is just as suicidal, just as weak, just as cowardly as self-denial. Ibsen, who takes us into the matter far more resolutely than Jesus, is unable to find any golden rule: both Brand and Peer Gynt come to a bad end; and though Brand does not do as much mischief as Peer, the mischief he does do is of extraordinary ntensity.

CELIBACY NO REMEDY

We must, I think, regard the protest of Jesus against marriage and family ties as the claim of a particular kind of individual to be free from them because they hamper his own work intolerably. When he said that if we are to follow him in the sense of taking up his work we must give up our family ties, he was simply stating a fact; and to this day the Roman Catholic priest, the Buddhist lama, and the fakirs of all the eastern denominations accept the saying. It is also accepted by the physically enterprising, the explorers, the restlessly energetic of all kinds: in short, by the adventurous. The greatest sacrifice in marriage is the sacrifice of the adventurous attitude towards life: the being settled. Those who are born tired may crave for settlement; but to fresher and stronger spirits it is a form of suicide.

Now to say of any institution that it is incompatible with both the contemplative and adventurous life is to disgrace it so vitally that all the moralizings of all the Deans and Chapters cannot reconcile our souls to its slavery. The unmarried Jesus and the unmarried Beethoven, the unmarried Joan of Arc, Clare, Teresa, Florence Nightingale seem as they should be; and the saying that there is always something ridiculous about a married philosopher becomes inevitable. And yet the celibate is still more ridiculous than the married man: the priest, in accepting the alternative of celibacy, disables himself; and the best priests are those who have been men of this world before they became men of the world to come. But as the taking of vows does not annul an existing marriage, and a married man cannot become a priest, we are again confronted with the absurdity that the best priest is a reformed rake. Thus does marriage, itself intolerable, thrust us upon intolerable alternatives. The practical solution is to make the individual economically independent of marriage and the family, and to make marriage as easily dissoluble as any other partnership: in other words, to accept the conclusions to which experience is slowly driving both our sociologists and our legislators. This will not instantly cure all the evils of marriage, nor root up at one stroke its detestable tradition of property in human bodies. But it will leave Nature free to effect a cure; and in free soil the root may wither and perish.

This disposes of all the opinions and teachings of

Jesus which are still matters of controversy. They are all in line with the best modern thought. He told us what we have to do; and we have had to find the way to do it. Most of us are still, as most were in his own time, extremely recalcitrant, and are being forced along that way by painful pressure of circumstances, protesting at every step that nothing will induce us to go; that it is a ridiculous way, a disgraceful way, a socialistic way, an atheistic way, an immoral way, and that the vanguard ought to be ashamed of themselves and must be made to turn back at once. But they find that they have to follow the vanguard all the same if their lives are to be worth living.

AFTER THE CRUCIFIXION

Let us now return to the New Testament narrative; for what happened after the disappearance of Jesus is instructive. Unfortunately, the crucifixion was a complete political success. I remember that when I described it in these terms once before, I greatly shocked a most respectable newspaper in my native town, the Dublin Daily Express, because my journalistic phrase shewed that I was treating it as an ordinary event like Home Rule or the Insurance Act: that is (though this did not occur to the editor), as a real event which had really happened, instead of a portion of the Church service. I can only repeat, assuming as I am that it *was* a real event and did actually happen, that it was as complete a success as any in history. Christianity as a specific doctrine was slain with Jesus, suddenly and utterly. He was hardly cold in his grave, or high in his heaven (as you please), before the apostles dragged the tradition of him down to the level of the thing it has remained ever since.

And that thing the intelligent heathen may study, if they would be instructed in it by modern books, in Samuel Butler's novel, The Way of All Flesh.

THE VINDICTIVE MIRACLES AND THE STONING OF STEPHEN

Take, for example, the miracles. Of Jesus alone of all the Christian miracle workers there is no record, except in certain gospels that all men reject, of a malicious or destructive miracle. A barren fig-tree was the only victim of his anger. Every one of his miracles on sentient subjects was an act of kindness. John declares that he healed the wound of the man whose ear was cut off (by Peter, John says) at the arrest in the garden. One of the first things the apostles did with their miraculous power was to strike dead a wretched man and his wife who had defrauded them by holding back some money from the common stock. They struck people blind or dead without remorse, judging because they had been judged. They healed the sick and raised the dead apparently in a spirit of pure display and advertisement. Their doctrine did not contain a ray of that light which reveals Jesus as one of the redeemers of men from folly and error. They cancelled him, and went back straight to John the Baptist and his formula of securing remission of sins by repentance and the rite of baptism (being born again of water and the spirit). Peter's first harangue softens us by the human touch of its exordium, which was a quaint assurance to his hearers that they must believe him to be sober because it was too early in the day to get drunk; but of Jesus he had nothing to say except that he was the Christ foretold by the prophets as coming from the seed of David, and that they must believe this and be baptized. To this the other apostles added incessant denunciations of the Jews for having crucified him, and threats of the destruction that would overtake them if they did not repent: that is, if they did not join the sect which the apostles were now forming. A quite intolerable young speaker named Stephen delivered an oration to the council, in which he first inflicted on them a tedious sketch of the history of Israel, with which they were presumably as well acquainted as he, and then reviled them in the most insulting terms as "stiffnecked and uncircumcized." Finally, after boring and annoying them to the utmost bearable extremity, he looked up and declared that he saw the heavens open, and Christ standing on the right hand of God. This was too much: they threw him out of the city and stoned him to death. It was a severe way of suppressing a tactless and conceited bore; but it was pardonable and human in comparison to the slaughter of poor Ananias and Sapphira.

PAUL

Suddenly a man of genius, Paul, violently anti-Christian, enters on the scene, holding the clothes of the men who are stoning Stephen. He persecutes the Christians with great vigor, a sport which he combines with the business of a tentmaker. This temperamental hatred of Jesus, whom he has never seen, is a patho-logical symptom of that particular sort of conscience and nervous constitution which brings its victims under the tyranny of two delirious terrors: the terror of sin and the terror of death, which may be called also the terror of sex and the terror of life. Now Jesus, with his healthy conscience on his higher plane, was free from these terrors. He consorted freely with sinners, and was never concerned for a moment, as far as we know, about whether his conduct was sinful or not; so that he has forced us to accept him as the man without sin. Even if we reckon his last days as the days of his delusion, he none the less gave a fairly convincing exhibition of superiority to the fear of death. This must have both fascinated and horrified Paul, or Saul, as he was first called. The horror accounts for his fierce persecution of the Christians. The fascination accounts for the strangest of his fancies: the fancy for attaching the name of Jesus Christ to the great idea which flashed upon him on the road to Damascus, the idea that he could not only make a religion of his two terrors, but that the movement started by Jesus offered him the nucleus for his new Church. It was a monstrous idea; and the shock of it, as he afterwards declared, struck him blind for days. He heard Jesus calling to him from the clouds, "Why persecute me?" His natural hatred of the teacher for whom Sin and Death had no terrors turned into a wild personal worship of him which has the ghastliness of a beautiful thing seen in a false light.

The chronicler of the Acts of the Apostles sees nothing of the significance of this. The great danger of conversion in all ages has been that when the religion of the high mind is offered to the lower mind, the lower mind, feeling its fascination without understanding it, and being incapable of rising to it, drags it down to its level by degrading it. Years ago I said that the conversion of a savage to Christianity is the conversion of Christianity to savagery. The conversion of Paul was no conversion at all: it was Paul who converted the religion that had raised one man above sin and death into a religion that delivered millions of men so completely into their dominion that their own common nature became a horror to them, and the religious life became a denial of life. Paul had no intention of surrendering either his Judaism or his Roman citizenship to the new moral world (as Robert Owen called it) of Communism and Jesuism. Just as in our own time Karl Marx, not content to take political economy as he found it, insisted on rebuilding it from the bottom upwards in his own way, and thereby gave a new lease of life to the errors it was just outgrowing, so Paul reconstructed the old Salvationism from which Jesus had vainly tried to redeem him, and produced a fantastic theology which is still the most amazing thing of the kind known to us. Being intellectually an inveterate Roman Rationalist, always discarding the irrational real thing for the unreal but ratiocinable postulate, he began by discarding Man as he is, and substituted a postulate which he called Adam. And when he was asked, as he surely must have been in a world not wholly mad, what had become of the natural man, he replied "Adam *is* the natural man." This was confusing to simpletons, because according to tradition Adam was certainly the name of the natural man as created in the garden of Eden. It was as if a preacher of our own time had described as typically British Frankenstein's monster, and called him Smith, and somebody, on demanding what about the man in the street, had been told "Smith *is* the man in the street." The thing happens often enough; for indeed the world is full of these Adams and Smiths and men in the street and average sensual men and economic men and womanly women and what not, all of them imaginary Atlases carrying imaginary worlds on their unsubstantial shoulders.

The Eden story provided Adam with a sin: the "original sin" for which we are all damned. Baldly stated, this seems ridiculous; nevertheless it corresponds to something actually existent not only in Paul's consciousness but in our own. The original sin was not the eating of the forbidden fruit, but the consciousness of sin which the fruit produced. The moment Adam and Eve tasted the apple they found themselves ashamed of their sexual relation, which until then had seemed quite innocent to them; and there is no getting over the hard fact that this shame, or state of sin, has persisted to this day, and is one of the strongest of our instincts. Thus Paul's postulate of Adam as the natural man was pragmatically true: it worked. But the weakness of Pragmatism is that most theories will work if you put your back into making them work, provided they have some point of contact with human nature. Hedonism will pass the pragmatic test as well as Stoicism. Up to a certain point every social principle that is not absolutely idiotic works: Autocracy works in Russia and Democracy in America; Atheism works in France, Polytheism in India, Monotheism throughout Islam, and Pragmatism, or No-ism, in England. Paul's fantastic conception of the damned Adam, represented by Bunyan as a pilgrim with a great burden of sins on his back, corresponded to the fundamental condition of evolution, which is, that life, including human life, is continually evolving, and must therefore be continually ashamed of itself and its present and past. Bunyan's pilgrim wants to get rid of his bundle of sins; but he also wants to reach "yonder shining light"; and when at last his bundle falls off him into the sepulchre of Christ, his pilgrimage is still unfinished and his hardest trials still ahead of him. His conscience remains uneasy; "original sin" still torments him; and his adventure with Giant Despair, who throws him into the dungeon of Doubting Castle, from which he escapes by the use of a skeleton key, is more terrible than any he met whilst the bundle was still on his back. Thus Bunyan's allegory of human nature breaks through the Pauline theology at a hundred points. His theological allegory, The Holy War, with its troops of Election Doubters, and its cavalry of "those that rode Reformadoes," is, as a whole, absurd, impossible, and, except in passages where the artistic old Adam momentarily got the better of the Salvationist theologian, hardly readable.

Paul's theory of original sin was to some extent idiosyncratic. He tells us definitely that he finds himself quite well able to avoid the sinfulness of sex by practising celibacy; but he recognizes, rather contemptuously, that in this respect he is not as other men are, and says that they had better marry than burn, thus admitting that though marriage may lead to placing the desire to please wife or husband before the desire to please God, yet preoccupation with unsatisfied desire may be even more ungodly than preoccupation with domestic affection. This view of the case inevitably led him to insist that a wife should be rather a slave than a partner, her real function being, not to engage a man's love and loyalty, but on the contrary to release them for God by relieving the man of all preoccupation with sex just as in her capacity of housekeeper and cook she relieves his preoccupation with hunger by the simple expedient of satisfying his appetite. This slavery also justifies itself pragmatically by working effectively; but it has made Paul the eternal enemy of Woman. Incidentally it has led to many foolish surmises about Paul's personal character and circumstances, by people so enslaved by sex that a celibate appears to them a sort of monster. They forget that not only whole priesthoods, official and unofficial, from Paul to Carlyle and Ruskin, have defied the tyranny of sex, but immense numbers of ordinary citizens of both sexes have, either voluntarily or under pressure of circumstances easily surmountable, saved their energies for less primitive activities.

Howbeit, Paul succeeded in stealing the image of Christ crucified for the figure-head of his Salvationist vessel, with its Adam posing as the natural man, its doctrine of original sin, and its damnation avoidable only by faith in the sacrifice of the cross. In fact, no sooner had Jesus knocked over the dragon of superstition than Paul boldly set it on its legs again in the name of Jesus.

THE CONFUSION OF CHRISTENDOM

Now it is evident that two religions having such contrary effects on mankind should not be confused as they are under a common name. There is not one word of Pauline Christianity in the characteristic utterances of Jesus. When Saul watched the clothes of the men who stoned Stephen, he was not acting upon beliefs which Paul renounced. There is no record of Christ's having said to any man: "Go and sin as much as you like: you can put it all on me." He said "Sin no more," and insisted that he was putting up the standard of conduct, not debasing it, and that the righteousness of the Christian must exceed that of the Scribe and Pharisee. The notion that he was shedding his blood in order that every petty cheat and adulterator and libertine might wallow in it and come out whiter than snow, cannot be imputed to him on his own authority. "I come as an infallible patent medicine for bad consciences" is not one of the sayings in the gospels. If Jesus could have been consulted on Bunyan's allegory as to that business of the burden of sin dropping from the pilgrim's back when he caught sight of the cross, we must infer from his teaching that he would have told Bunyan in forcible terms that he had never made a greater mistake in his life, and that the business of a Christ was to make self-satisfied sinners feel the burden of their sins and stop committing them instead of assuring them that they could not help it, as it was all Adam's fault, but that it did not matter as long as they were credulous and friendly about himself. Even when he believed himself to be a god, he did not regard himself as a scapegoat. He was to take away the sins of the world by good government, by justice and mercy, by setting the welfare of little children above the pride of princes, by casting all the quackeries and idolatries which now usurp and malversate the power of God into what our local authorities quaintly call the dust destructor, and by riding on the clouds of heaven in glory instead of in a thousand-guinea motor car. That was delirious, if you like; but it was the delirium of a free soul, not of a shame-bound one like Paul's. There has really never been a more monstrous imposition perpetrated than the imposition of the limitations of Paul's soul upon the soul of Jesus.

THE SECRET OF PAUL'S SUCCESS

Paul must soon have found that his followers had gained peace of mind and victory over death and sin at the cost of all moral responsibility; for he did his best to reintroduce it by making good conduct the test of sincere belief, and insisting that sincere belief was necessary to salvation. But as his system was rooted in the plain fact that as what he called sin includes sex and is therefore an ineradicable part of human nature (why else should Christ have had to atone for the sin of all future generations?) it was impossible for him to declare that sin, even in its wickedest extremity, could forfeit the sinner's salvation if he repented and believed. And to this day Pauline Christianity is, and owes its enormous vogue to being, a premium on sin. Its consequences have had to be held in check by the worldlywise majority through a violently anti-Christian system of criminal law and stern morality. But of course the main restraint is human nature, which has good impulses as well as bad ones, and refrains from theft and murder and cruelty, even when it is taught that it can commit them all at the expense of Christ and go happily to heaven afterwards, simply because it does not always want to murder or rob or torture.

It is now easy to understand why the Christianity of Jesus failed completely to establish itself politically and socially, and was easily suppressed by the police and the Church, whilst Paulinism overran the whole western civilized world, which was at that time the Roman Empire, and was adopted by it as its official faith, the old avenging gods falling helplessly before the new Redeemer. It still retains, as we may see in Africa, its power of bringing to simple people a message of hope and consolation that no other religion offers. But this enchantment is produced by its spurious association with the personal charm of Jesus, and exists only for untrained minds. In the hands of a logical Frenchman like Calvin, pushing it to its utmost conclusions, and devising "institutes" for hardheaded adult Scots and literal Swiss, it becomes the most infernal of fatalisms; and the lives of civilized children are blighted by its logic whilst negro picca-ninnies are rejoicing in its legends.

PAUL'S QUALITIES

Paul, however, did not get his great reputation by mere imposition and reaction. It is only in comparison with Jesus (to whom many prefer him) that he appears common and conceited. Though in The Acts he is only a vulgar revivalist, he comes out in his own epistles as a genuine poet, though by flashes only. He is no more a Christian than Jesus was a Baptist: he is a disciple of Jesus only as Jesus was a disciple of John. He does nothing that Jesus would have done, and says nothing that Jesus would have said, though much, like the famous ode to charity, that he would have admired. He is more Jewish than the Jews, more Roman than the Romans, proud both ways, full of startling confessions and self-revelations that would not surprise us if they were slipped into the pages of Nietzsche, tormented by an intellectual conscience that demanded an argued case even at the cost of sophistry, with all sorts of fine qualities and occasional illuminations, but always hopelessly in the toils of Sin, Death, and Logic, which had no power over Jesus. As we have seen, it was by introducing this bondage and terror of his into the Christian doctrine that he adapted it to the Church and State systems which Jesus transcended, and made it practicable by destroying the specifically Jesuist side of it. He would have been quite in his place in any modern Protestant State; and he, not Jesus, is the true head and founder of our Reformed Church, as Peter is of the Roman Church. The followers of Paul and Peter made Christendom, whilst the Nazarenes were wiped out.

THE ACTS OF THE APOSTLES

Here we may return to the narrative called The
Acts of the Apostles, which we left at the point where
the stoning of Stephen was followed by the introduction of Paul. The author of The Acts, though a
good story-teller, like Luke, was (herein also like
Luke) much weaker in power of thought than in
imaginative literary art. Hence we find Luke credited
with the authorship of The Acts by people who like
stories and have no aptitude for theology, whilst the
book itself is denounced as spurious by Pauline
theologians because Paul, and indeed all the apostles,
are represented in it as very commonplace revivalists,
interesting us by their adventures more than by any
qualities of mind or character. Indeed, but for the
epistles, we should have a very poor opinion of the
apostles. Paul in particular is described as setting a
fashion which has remained in continual use to this
day. Whenever he addresses an audience, he dwells
with great zest on his misdeeds before his pseudo
conversion, with the effect of throwing into stronger
relief his present state of blessedness; and he tells the
story of that conversion over and over again, ending
with exhortations to the hearers to come and be saved,
and threats of the wrath that will overtake them if they
refuse. At any revival meeting today the same thing
may be heard, followed by the same conversions.
This is natural enough; but it is totally unlike the
preaching of Jesus, who never talked about his
personal history, and never "worked up" an audience
to hysteria. It aims at a purely nervous effect; it
brings no enlightenment; the most ignorant man has
only to become intoxicated with his own vanity, and
mistake his self-satisfaction for the Holy Ghost, to

become qualified as an apostle; and it has absolutely nothing to do with the characteristic doctrines of Jesus. The Holy Ghost may be at work all round producing wonders of art and science, and strengthening men to endure all sorts of martyrdoms for the enlargement of knowledge, and the enrichment and intensification of life ("that ye may have life more abundantly"); but the apostles, as described in The Acts, take no part in the struggle except as persecutors and revilers. To this day, when their successors get the upper hand, as in Geneva (Knox's "perfect city of Christ") and in Scotland and Ulster, every spiritual activity but moneymaking and churchgoing is stamped out; heretics are ruthlessly persecuted; and such pleasures as money can purchase are suppressed so that its possessors are compelled to go on making money because there is nothing else to do. And the compensation for all this privation is partly an insane conceit of being the elect of God, with a reserved seat in heaven, and partly, since even the most infatuated idiot cannot spend his life admiring himself, the less innocent excitement of punishing other people for not admiring him and the nosing out of the sins of the people who, being intelligent enough to be incapable of mere dull self-righteousness, and highly susceptible to the beauty and interest of the real workings of the Holy Ghost, try to live more rational and abundant lives. The abominable amusement of terrifying children with threats of hell is another of these diversions, and perhaps the vilest and most mischievous of them. The net result is that the imitators of the apostles, whether they are called Holy Willies or Stigginses in derision, or, in admiration, Puritans or saints, are, outside their own congregations, and to a considerable extent inside them, heartily detested. Now nobody detests Jesus, though many who have been tormented in their childhood in his name include him in their general loathing of everything connected with the word religion; whilst others, who know him only by misrepresentation as a sentimental pacifist and an ascetic, include him in their general dislike of that type of character. In the same way a student who has had to "get up" Shakespear as a college subject may hate Shakespear; and people who dislike the theatre may include Molière in that dislike without ever having read a line of his or witnessed one of his plays; but nobody with any knowledge of Shakespear or Molière could possibly detest them, or read without pity and horror a description of their being insulted, tortured, and killed. And the same is true of Jesus. But it requires the most strenuous effort of conscience to refrain from crying "Serve him right" when we read of the stoning of Stephen; and nobody has ever cared twopence about the martyrdom of Peter: many better men have died worse deaths: for example, honest Hugh Latimer, who was burned by us, was worth fifty Stephens and a dozen Peters. One feels at last that when Jesus called Peter from his boat, he spoiled an honest fisherman, and made nothing better out of the wreck than a salvation monger.

THE CONTROVERSIES ON BAPTISM AND TRANSUBSTANTIATION

Meanwhile the inevitable effect of dropping the peculiar doctrines of Jesus and going back to John the Baptist, was to make it much easier to convert Gentiles than Jews; and it was by following the line of least resistance that Paul became the apostle to the Gentiles. The Jews had their own rite of initiation:

the rite of circumcision; and they were fiercely jealous for it, because it marked them as the chosen people of God, and set them apart from the Gentiles, who were simply the uncircumcized. When Paul, finding that baptism made way faster among the Gentiles than among the Jews, as it enabled them to plead that they too were sanctified by a rite of later and higher authority than the Mosaic rite, he was compelled to admit that circumcision did not matter; and this, to the Jews, was an intolerable blasphemy. To Gentiles like ourselves, a good deal of the Epistle to the Romans is now tedious to unreadableness because it consists of a hopeless attempt by Paul to evade the conclusion that if a man were baptized it did not matter a rap whether he was circumcized or not. Paul claims circumcision as an excellent thing in its way for a Jew; but if it has no efficacy towards salvation, and if salvation is the one thing needful—and Paul was committed to both propositions—his pleas in mitigation only made the Jews more determined to stone him.

Thus from the very beginning of apostolic Christianity, it was hampered by a dispute as to whether salvation was to be attained by a surgical operation or by a sprinkling of water: mere rites on which Jesus would not have wasted twenty words. Later on, when the new sect conquered the Gentile west, where the dispute had no practical application, the other ceremony—that of eating the god—produced a still more disastrous dispute, in which a difference of belief, not as to the obligation to perform the ceremony, but as to whether it was a symbolic or a real ingestion of divine substance, produced persecution, slaughter, hatred, and everything that Jesus loathed, on a monstrous scale.

But long before that, the superstitions which had fastened on the new faith made trouble. The parthenogenetic birth of Christ, simple enough at first as a popular miracle, was not left so simple by the theologians. They began to ask of what substance Christ was made in the womb of the virgin. When the Trinity was added to the faith the question arose, was the virgin the mother of God or only the mother of Jesus? Arian schisms and Nestorian schisms arose on these questions; and the leaders of the resultant agitations rancorously deposed one another and excommunicated one another according to their luck in enlisting the emperors on their side. In the IV century they began to burn one another for differences of opinion in such matters. In the VIII century Charlemagne made Christianity compulsory by killing those who refused to embrace it; and though this made an end of the voluntary character of conversion, Charlemagne may claim to be the first Christian who put men to death for any point of doctrine that really mattered. From his time onward the history of Christian controversy reeks with blood and fire, torture and warfare. The Crusades, the persecutions in Albi and elsewhere, the Inquisition, the "wars of religion" which followed the Reformation, all presented themselves as Christian phenomena; but who can doubt that they would have been repudiated with horror by Jesus? Our own notion that the massacre of St Bartholomew's was an outrage on Christianity, whilst the campaigns of Gustavus Adolphus, and even of Frederick the Great, were a defence of it, is as absurd as the opposite notion that Frederick was Antichrist, and Torquemada and Ignatius Loyola men after the very heart of Jesus. Neither they nor their exploits had anything to do with him. It is probable that

Archbishop Laud and John Wesley died equally persuaded that he in whose name they had made themselves famous on earth would receive them in Heaven with open arms. George Fox the Quaker would have had ten times their chance; and yet Fox made rather a miserable business of life.

Nevertheless all these perversions of the doctrine of Jesus derived their moral force from his credit, and so had to keep his gospel alive. When the Protestants translated the Bible into the vernacular and let it loose among the people, they did an extremely dangerous thing, as the mischief which followed proves; but they incidentally let loose the sayings of Jesus in open competition with the sayings of Paul and Koheleth and David and Solomon and the authors of Job and the Pentateuch; and, as we have seen, Jesus seems to be the winning name. The glaring contradiction between his teaching and the practice of all the States and all the Churches is no longer hidden. And it may be that though nineteen centuries have passed since Jesus was born (the date of his birth is now quaintly given as 7 B.C., though some contend for 100 B.C.), and though his Church has not yet been founded nor his political system tried, the bankruptcy of all the other systems when audited by our vital statistics, which give us a final test for all political systems, is driving us hard into accepting him, not as a scapegoat, but as one who was much less of a fool in practical matters than we have hitherto all thought him.

THE ALTERNATIVE CHRISTS

Let us now clear up the situation a little. The New Testament tells two stories for two different sorts of readers. One is the old story of the achievement of our salvation by the sacrifice and atonement of a divine personage who was barbarously slain and rose again on the third day: the story as it was accepted by the apostles. And in this story the political, economic and moral views of the Christ have no importance: the atonement is everything; and we are saved by our faith in it, and not by works or opinions (other than that particular opinion) bearing on practical affairs.

The other is the story of a prophet who, after expressing several very interesting opinions as to practical conduct, both personal and political, which are now of pressing importance, and instructing his disciples to carry them out in their daily life, lost his head; believed himself to be a crude legendary form of god; and under that delusion courted and suffered a cruel execution in the belief that he would rise from the dead and come in glory to reign over a regenerated world. In this form, the political, economic, and moral opinions of Jesus, as guides to conduct, are interesting and important: the rest is mere psychopathy and superstition. The accounts of the resurrection, the parthenogenetic birth, and the more incredible miracles are rejected as inventions; and such episodes as the conversation with the devil are classed with similar conversations recorded of St Dunstan, Luther, Bunyan, Swedenborg, and Blake.

CREDULITY NO CRITERION

This arbitrary acceptance and rejection of parts of the gospel is not peculiar to the Secularist view. We have seen Luke and John reject Matthew's story of the massacre of the innocents and the flight into Egypt without ceremony. The notion that Matthew's manuscript is a literal and infallible record of facts, not

subject to the errors that beset all earthly chroniclers,
would have made John stare, being as it is a comparatively modern fancy of intellectually untrained
people who keep the Bible on the same shelf with
Napoleon's Book of Fate, Old Moore's Almanack, and
handbooks of therapeutic herbalism. You may be a
fanatical Salvationist and reject more miracle stories
than Huxley did; and you may utterly repudiate Jesus
as the Savior and yet cite him as a historical witness to
the possession by men of the most marvellous thau-
maturgical powers. "Christ Scientist" and Jesus the
Mahatma are preached by people whom Peter would
have struck dead as worse infidels than Simon Magus;
and the Atonement is preached by Baptist and Congregationalist ministers whose views of the miracles
are those of Ingersoll and Bradlaugh. Luther, who
made a clean sweep of all the saints with their million
miracles, and reduced the Blessed Virgin herself to the
status of an idol, concentrated Salvationism to a point
at which the most execrable murderer who believes in
it when the rope is round his neck, flies straight to the
arms of Jesus, whilst Tom Paine and Shelley fall into
the bottomless pit to burn there to all eternity. And
sceptical physicists like Sir William Crookes demonstrate by laboratory experiments that "mediums"
like Dunglas Home can make the pointer of a spring-
balance go round without touching the weight suspended from it.

BELIEF IN PERSONAL IMMORTALITY
NO CRITERION

Nor is belief in individual immortality any criterion.
Theosophists, rejecting vicarious atonement so sternly
that they insist that the smallest of our sins brings its

Karma, also insist on individual immortality and metempsychosis in order to provide an unlimited field for Karma to be worked out by the unredeemed sinner. The belief in the prolongation of individual life beyond the grave is far more real and vivid among table-rapping Spiritualists than among conventional Christians. The notion that those who reject the Christian (or any other) scheme of salvation by atonement must reject also belief in personal immortality and in miracles is as baseless as the notion that if a man is an atheist he will steal your watch.

I could multiply these instances to weariness. The main difference that set Gladstone and Huxley by the ears is not one between belief in supernatural persons or miraculous events and the sternest view of such belief as a breach of intellectual integrity: it is the difference between belief in the efficacy of the crucifixion as an infallible cure for guilt, and a congenital incapacity for believing this, or (the same thing) desiring to believe it.

THE SECULAR VIEW NATURAL, NOT RATIONAL, THEREFORE INEVITABLE

It must therefore be taken as a flat fundamental modern fact, whether we like it or not, that whilst many of us cannot believe that Jesus got his curious grip of our souls by mere sentimentality, neither can we believe that he was John Barleycorn. The more our reason and study lead us to believe that Jesus was talking the most penetrating good sense when he preached Communism; when he declared that the reality behind the popular belief in God was a creative spirit in ourselves called by him the Heavenly Father and by us Evolution, Élan Vital, Life Force and other names; when he protested against the claims of marriage and the family to appropriate that high part of our energy that was meant for the service of his Father, the more impossible it becomes for us to believe that he was talking equally good sense when he so suddenly announced that he was himself a visible concrete God; that his flesh and blood were miraculous food for us; that he must be tortured and slain in the traditional manner and would rise from the dead after three days; and that at his Second Coming the stars would fall from heaven and he become king of an earthly paradise. But it is easy and reasonable to believe that an over-wrought preacher at last went mad as Swift and Ruskin and Nietzsche went mad. Every asylum has in it a patient suffering from the delusion that he is a god, yet otherwise sane enough. These patients do not nowadays declare that they will be barbarously slain and will rise from the dead, because they have lost that tradition of the destiny of godhead; but they claim everything appertaining to divinity that is within their knowledge.

Thus the gospels as memoirs and suggestive statements of sociological and biological doctrine, highly relevant to modern civilization, though ending in the history of a psychopathic delusion, are quite credible, intelligible, and interesting to modern thinkers. In any other light they are neither credible, intelligible, nor interesting except to people upon whom the delusion imposes.

"THE HIGHER CRITICISM"

Historical research and paleographic criticism will no doubt continue their demonstrations that the New Testament, like the Old, seldom tells a single story or expounds a single doctrine, and gives us often an accretion and conglomeration of widely discrete and even unrelated traditions and doctrines. But these disintegrations, though technically interesting to scholars, and gratifying or exasperating, as the case may be, to people who are merely defending or attacking the paper fortifications of the infallibility of the Bible, have hardly anything to do with the purpose of these pages. I have mentioned the fact that most of the authorities are now agreed (for the moment) that the date of the birth of Jesus may be placed at about 7 B.C.; but they do not therefore date their letters 1923, nor, I presume, do they expect me to do so. What I am engaged in is a criticism (in the Kantian sense) of an established body of belief which has become an actual part of the mental fabric of my readers; and I should be the most exasperating of triflers and pedants if I were to digress into a criticism of some other belief or nobelief which my readers might conceivably profess if they were erudite Scriptural paleographers and historians, in which case, by the way, they would have to change their views so frequently that the gospel they received in their childhood would dominate them after all by its superior persistency. The chaos of mere facts in which the Sermon on the Mount and the Ode to Charity suggest nothing but disputes as to whether they are interpolations or not, in which Jesus becomes nothing but a name suspected of belonging to ten different prophets or executed persons, in which Paul is only the man who could not possibly have written the epistles attributed to him, in which Chinese sages, Greek philosophers, Latin authors, and writers of ancient anonymous inscriptions are thrown at our heads as the sources of this or that scrap of the Bible, is neither a religion nor a criticism of religion: one does not offer the fact that a good deal of the medieval building in Peterborough Cathedral was found to be flagrant jerry-building as a criticism of the Dean's sermons. For good or evil, we have made a synthesis out of the literature we call the Bible; and though the discovery that there is a good deal of jerry-building in the Bible is interesting in its way, because everything about the Bible is interesting, it does not alter the synthesis very materially even for the paleographers, and does not alter it at all for those who know no more about modern paleography than Archbishop Ussher did. I have therefore indicated little more of the discoveries than Archbishop Ussher might have guessed for himself if he had read the Bible without prepossessions.

For the rest, I have taken the synthesis as it really lives and works in men. After all, a synthesis is what you want: it is the case you have to judge brought to an apprehensible issue for you. Even if you have little more respect for synthetic biography than for synthetic rubber, synthetic milk, and the still un-achieved synthetic protoplasm which is to enable us to make different sorts of men as a pastrycook makes different sorts of tarts, the practical issue still lies as plainly before you as before the most credulous votaries of what pontificates as the Higher Criticism.

THE PERILS OF SALVATIONISM

The secular view of Jesus is powerfully reinforced by the increase in our day of the number of people who have had the means of educating and training themselves to the point at which they are not afraid to look facts in the face, even such terrifying facts as sin and death. The result is greater sternness in modern thought. The conviction is spreading that to encourage a man to believe that though his sins be as scarlet he can be made whiter than snow by an easy exercise of self-conceit, is to encourage him to be a rascal. It did not work so badly when you could also conscientiously assure him that if he let himself be caught napping in the matter of faith by death, a red-hot hell would roast him alive to all eternity. In those days a sudden death—the most enviable of all deaths—was regarded as the most frightful calamity. It was classed with plague, pestilence, and famine, battle and murder, in our prayers. But belief in that hell is fast vanishing. All the leaders of thought have lost it; and even for the rank and file it has fled to those parts of Ireland and Scotland which are still in the seventeenth century. Even there, it is tacitly reserved for the other fellow.

THE IMPORTANCE OF HELL IN THE SALVATION SCHEME

The seriousness of throwing over hell whilst still clinging to the Atonement is obvious. If there is no punishment for sin there can be no self-forgiveness for it. If Christ paid our score, and if there is no hell and therefore no chance of our getting into trouble by forgetting the obligation, then we can be as wicked as we like with impunity inside the secular law, even from self-reproach which becomes mere ingratitude to the Savior. On the other hand, if Christ did not pay our score, it still stands against us; and such debts make us extremely uncomfortable. The drive of evolution, which we call conscience and honor, seizes on such slips, and shames us to the dust for being so low in the scale as to be capable of them. The "saved" thief experiences an ecstatic happiness which can never come to the honest atheist: he is tempted to steal again to repeat the glorious sensation. But if the atheist steals he has no such happiness. He is a thief and knows that he is a thief. Nothing can rub that off him. He may try to soothe his shame by some sort of restitution or equivalent act of benevolence; but that does not alter the fact that he did steal; and his conscience will not be easy until he has conquered his will to steal and changed himself into an honest man by developing that divine spark within him which Jesus insisted on as the everyday reality of what the atheist denies.

Now though the state of the believers in the Atonement may thus be the happier, it is most certainly not more desirable from the point of view of the community. The fact that a believer is happier than a sceptic is no more to the point than the fact that a drunken man is happier than a sober one. The happiness of credulity is a cheap and dangerous quality of happiness, and by no means a necessity of life. Whether Socrates got as much happiness out of life as Wesley is an unanswerable question; but a nation of Socrateses would be much safer and happier than a nation of Wesleys; and its individuals would be higher in the evolutionary scale. At all events it is in the Socratic man and not in the Wesleyan that our hope lies now.

THE RIGHT TO REFUSE ATONEMENT

Consequently, even if it were mentally possible for all of us to believe in the Atonement, we should have to cry off it, as we evidently have a right to do. Every man to whom salvation is offered has an inalienable natural right to say "No, thank you: I prefer to retain my full moral responsibility: it is not good for me to be able to load a scapegoat with my sins: I should be less careful how I committed them if I knew they would cost me nothing." Then, too, there is the attitude of Ibsen: that iron moralist to whom the whole scheme of salvation was only an ignoble attempt to cheat God; to get into heaven without paying the price. To be let off, to beg for and accept eternal life as a present instead of earning it, would be mean enough even if we accepted the contempt of the Power on whose pity we were trading; but to bargain for a crown of glory as well! that was too much for Ibsen: it provoked him to exclaim, "Your God is an old man whom you cheat," and to lash the deadened conscience of the nineteenth century back to life with a whip of scorpions.

THE TEACHING OF CHRISTIANITY

And there I must leave the matter to such choice as your nature allows you. The honest teacher who has to make known to a novice the facts about Christianity cannot in any essential regard, I think, put the facts otherwise than as I have put them. If children are to be delivered from the proselytizing atheist on the one hand, and the proselytizing nun in the convent school on the other, with all the other proselytizers that lie between them, they must not be burdened with idle controversies as to whether there was ever such a person as Jesus or not. When Hume said that Joshua's campaigns were impossible, Whately did not wrangle about it: he proved, on the same lines, that the campaigns of Napoleon were impossible. Only fictitious characters will stand Hume's sort of examination: nothing will ever make Edward the Confessor and St Louis as real to us as Don Quixote and Mr Pickwick. We must cut the controversy short by declaring that there is the same evidence for the existence of Jesus as for that of any other person of his time; and the fact that you may not believe everything Matthew tells you no more disproves the existence of Jesus than the fact that you do not believe everything Macaulay tells you disproves the existence of William III. The gospel narratives in the main give you a biography which is quite credible and accountable on purely secular grounds when you have trimmed off everything that Hume or Grimm or Rousseau or Huxley or any modern bishop could reject as fanciful. Without going further than this, you can become a follower of Jesus just as you can become a follower of Confucius or Lao Tse, and may therefore call yourself a Jesuist, or even a Christian, if you hold, as the strictest Secularist quite legitimately may, that all prophets are inspired, and all men with a mission, Christs.

The teacher of Christianity has then to make known to the child, first the song of John Barleycorn, with the fields and seasons as witness to its eternal truth. Then, as the child's mind matures, it can learn, as historical and psychological phenomena, the tradition of the scapegoat, the Redeemer, the Atonement, the Resurrection, the Second Coming, and how, in a world saturated with this tradition, Jesus has been largely accepted as the long expected and often prophesied Redeemer, the Messiah, *the* Christ. It is open to the child also to accept him. If the child is built like Gladstone, he will accept Jesus as his Savior, and Peter and John the Baptist as the Savior's revealer and forerunner respectively. If he is built like Huxley, he will take the secular view, in spite of all that a pious family can do to prevent him. The important thing now is that the Gladstones and Huxleys should

no longer waste their time irrelevantly and ridiculously
wrangling about the Gadarene swine, and that they
should make up their minds as to the soundness of the
secular doctrines of Jesus; for it is about these that
they may come to blows in our own time.

CHRISTIANITY AND THE EMPIRE

Finally, let us ask why it is that the old superstitions have so suddenly lost countenance that
although, to the utter disgrace of the nation's leaders
and rulers, the laws by which persecutors can destroy
or gag all freedom of thought and speech in these
matters are still unrepealed and ready to the hand
of our bigots and fanatics (quite recently a respectable
shopkeeper was convicted of "blasphemy" for saying
that if a modern girl accounted for an illicit pregnancy
by saying she had conceived of the Holy Ghost, we
should know what to think: a remark which would
never have occurred to him had he been properly
taught how the story was grafted on the gospel), yet
somehow they are used only against poor men, and
that only in a half-hearted way. When we consider
that from the time when the first scholar ventured to
whisper as a professional secret that the Pentateuch
could not possibly have been written by Moses to the
time within my own recollection when Bishop
Colenso, for saying the same thing openly, was in-
hibited from preaching and actually excommunicated,
eight centuries elapsed (the point at issue, though
technically interesting to paleographers and historians,
having no more bearing on human welfare than the
controversy as to whether uncial or cursive is the
older form of writing); yet now, within fifty years of
Colenso's heresy, there is not a Churchman of any

authority living, or an educated layman, who could without ridicule declare that Moses wrote the Pentateuch as Pascal wrote his Thoughts or D'Aubigny his History of the Reformation, or that St Jerome wrote the passage about the three witnesses in the Vulgate, or that there are less than three different accounts of the creation jumbled together in the book of Genesis. Now the maddest Progressive will hardly contend that our growth in wisdom and liberality has been greater in the last half century than in the sixteen half centuries preceding: indeed it would be easier to sustain the thesis that the last fifty years have witnessed a distinct reaction from Victorian Liberalism to Collectivism which has perceptibly strengthened the State Churches. Yet the fact remains that whereas Byron's Cain, published a century ago, is a leading case on the point that there is no copyright in a blasphemous book, the Salvation Army might now include it among its publications without shocking anyone.

I suggest that the causes which have produced this sudden clearing of the air include the transformation of many modern States, notably the old self-contained French Republic and the tight little Island of Britain, into empires which overflow the frontiers of all the Churches. In India, for example, there are less than four million Christians out of a population of three hundred and sixteen and a half millions. The King of England is the defender of the faith; but what faith is now *the* faith? The inhabitants of this island would, within the memory of persons still living, have claimed that their faith is surely *the* faith of God, and that all others are heathen. But we islanders are only forty-five millions; and if we count ourselves all as Christians, there are still seventy-seven and a quarter

million Mahometans in the Empire. Add to these the
Hindoos and Buddhists, Sikhs and Jains, whom I was
taught in my childhood, by way of religious instruction, to regard as gross idolaters consigned to eternal
perdition, but whose faith I can now be punished for
disparaging by a provocative word, and you have a
total of over three hundred and forty-two and a
quarter million heretics to swamp our forty-five
million Britons, of whom, by the way, only six
thousand call themselves distinctively "disciples of
Christ," the rest being members of the Church of
England and other denominations whose discipleship
is less emphatically affirmed. In short, the Englishman of today, instead of being, like the forefathers
whose ideas he clings to, a subject of a State practically
wholly Christian, is now crowded, and indeed considerably overcrowded, into a corner of an Empire in
which the Christians are a mere eleven per cent of the
population; so that the Nonconformist who allows his
umbrella stand to be sold up rather than pay rates
towards the support of a Church of England school,
finds himself paying taxes not only to endow the
Church of Rome in Malta, but to send Christians to
prison for the blasphemy of offering Bibles for sale in
the streets of Khartoum.

Turn to France, a country ten times more insular
in its pre-occupation with its own language, its own
history, its own character, than we, who have always
been explorers and colonizers and grumblers. This
once self-centred nation is forty millions strong. The
total population of the French Republic is about one
hundred and fourteen millions. The French are not in
our hopeless Christian minority of eleven per cent;
but they are in a minority of thirty-five per cent,
which is fairly conclusive. And, being a more logical
people than we, they have officially abandoned

Christianity and declared that the French State has no specific religion.

Neither has the British State, though it does not say so. No doubt there are many innocent people in England who take Charlemagne's view, and would, as a matter of course, offer our eighty-nine per cent of "pagans, I regret to say" the alternative of death or Christianity but for a vague impression that those lost ones are all being converted gradually by the missionaries. But no statesman can entertain such ludicrously parochial delusions. No English king or French president can possibly govern on the assumption that the theology of Peter and Paul, Luther and Calvin, has any objective validity, or that the Christ is more than the Buddha, or Jehovah more than Krishna, or Jesus more or less human than Mahomet or Zoroaster or Confucius. He is actually compelled, in so far as he makes laws against blasphemy at all, to treat all the religions, including Christianity, as blasphemous when paraded before people who are not accustomed to them and do not want them. And even that is a concession to a mischievous intolerance which an empire should use its control of education to eradicate.

On the other hand, Governments cannot really divest themselves of religion, or even of dogma. When Jesus said that people should not only live but live more abundantly, he was dogmatizing; and many Pessimist sages, including Shakespear, whose hero begged his friend to refrain from suicide in the words "Absent thee from felicity awhile," would say dogmatizing very perniciously. Indeed many preachers and saints declare, some of them in the name of Jesus himself, that this world is a vale of tears, and that our lives had better be passed in sorrow and even in torment, as a preparation for a better life to come.

Make these sad people comfortable; and they baffle you by putting on hair shirts.

None the less, Governments must proceed on dogmatic assumptions, whether they call them dogmas or not; and they must clearly be assumptions common enough to stamp those who reject them as eccentrics or lunatics. And the greater and more heterogeneous the population the commoner the assumptions must be. A Trappist monastery can be conducted on assumptions which would in twenty-four hours provoke the village at its gates to insurrection. That is because the monastery selects its people; and if a Trappist does not like it he can leave it. But a subject of the British Empire or the French Republic is not selected; and if he does not like it he must lump it; for emigration is practicable only within narrow limits, and seldom provides an effective remedy, all civilizations being now much alike.

To anyone capable of comprehending government at all it must be evident without argument that the set of fundamental assumptions drawn up in the thirty-nine articles or in the Westminster Confession are wildly impossible as political constitutions for modern empires. A personal profession of them by any person disposed to take such professions seriously would practically disqualify him for high imperial office. A Calvinist Viceroy of India and a Particular Baptist Secretary of State for Foreign Affairs would wreck the empire. The Stuarts wrecked even the tight little island which was the nucleus of the empire by their Scottish logic and theological dogma; and it may be sustained very plausibly that the alleged aptitude of the English for self-government, which is contradicted by every chapter of their history, is really only an incurable inaptitude for theology, and indeed for co-ordinated thought in any direction, which makes them equally impatient of systematic despotism and systematic good government: their history being that of a badly governed and accidentally free people (comparatively). Thus our success in colonizing, as far as it has not been produced by exterminating the natives, has been due to our indifference to the salvation of our subjects. Ireland is the exception which proves the rule; for Ireland, the standing instance of the inability of the English to colonize without extermination of natives, is also the one country under British rule in which the conquerors and colonizers proceeded on the assumption that their business was to establish Protestantism as well as to make money and thereby secure at least the lives of the unfortunate inhabitants out of whose labor it could be made. At this moment Ulster is refusing to accept fellow-citizenship with the other Irish provinces because the south believes in St Peter and Bossuet, and the north in St Paul and Calvin. Imagine the effect of trying to govern India or Egypt from Belfast or from the Vatican!

The position is perhaps graver for France than for England, because the sixty-five per cent of French subjects who are neither French nor Christian nor Modernist includes some thirty millions of negroes who are susceptible, and indeed highly susceptible, of conversion to those salvationist forms of pseudo-Christianity which have produced all the persecutions and religious wars of the last fifteen hundred years. When the late explorer Sir Henry Stanley told me of the emotional grip which Christianity had over the Baganda tribes, and read me their letters, which were exactly like medieval letters in their literal faith and ever-present piety, I said "Can these men handle a rifle?" To which Stanley replied with some scorn "Of course they can, as well as any white man." Now at this moment (1915) a vast European war is being waged, in which the French are using Senegalese soldiers. I ask the French Government, which, like our own Government, is deliberately leaving the religious instruction of these negroes in the hands of missions of Petrine Catholics and Pauline Calvinists, whether they have considered the possibility of a new series of crusades, by ardent African Salvationists, to rescue Paris from the grip of the modern scientific "infidel," and to raise the cry of "Back to the Apostles: back to Charlemagne!"

We are more fortunate in that an overwhelming majority of our subjects are Hindoos, Mahometans, and Buddhists: that is, they have, as a prophylactic against salvationist Christianity, highly civilized religions of their own. Mahometanism, which Napoleon at the end of his career classed as perhaps the best popular religion for modern political use, might in some respects have arisen as a reformed Christianity if Mahomet had had to deal with a population of seventeenth-century Christians instead of Arabs who worshipped stones. As it is, men do not reject Mahomet for Calvin; and to offer a Hindoo so crude a theology as ours in exchange for his own, or our Jewish canonical literature as an improvement on Hindoo scripture, is to offer old lamps for older ones in a market where the oldest lamps, like old furniture in England, are the most highly valued.

Yet, I repeat, government is impossible without a religion: that is, without a body of common assumptions. The open mind never acts: when we have done our utmost to arrive at a reasonable conclusion, we still, when we can reason and investigate no more, must close our minds for the moment with a snap, and act dogmatically on our conclusions. The man who waits to make an entirely reasonable will dies intestate. A man so reasonable as to have an open mind about theft and murder, or about the need for food and reproduction, might just as well be a fool and a scoundrel for any use he could be as a legislator or a State official. The modern pseudo-democratic statesman, who says that he is only in power to carry out the will of the people, and moves only as the cat jumps, is clearly a political and intellectual brigand. The rule of the negative man who has no convictions means in practice the rule of the positive mob. Freedom of conscience as Cromwell used the phrase is an excellent thing; nevertheless if any man had proposed to give effect to freedom of conscience as to cannibalism in England, Cromwell would have laid him by the heels almost as promptly as he would have laid a Roman Catholic, though in Fiji at the same moment he would have supported heartily the freedom of conscience of a vegetarian who disparaged the sacred diet of Long Pig.

Here then comes in the importance of the repudiation by Jesus of proselytism. His rule "Dont pull up the tares: sow the wheat: if you try to pull up the tares you will pull up the wheat with it" is the only possible rule for a statesman governing a modern empire, or a voter supporting such a statesman. There is nothing in the teaching of Jesus that cannot be assented to by a Brahman, a Mahometan, a Buddhist or a Jew, without any question of their conversion to Christianity. In some ways it is easier to reconcile a Mahometan to Jesus than a British parson, because the idea of a professional priest is unfamiliar and even monstrous to a Mahometan (the tourist who persists in asking who is the dean of St Sophia puzzles beyond words the sacristan who lends him a huge pair of slippers); and Jesus never suggested that his disciples should separate themselves from the laity: he picked them up by the wayside, where any man or woman might follow him. For priests he had not a civil word; and they shewed their sense of his hostility by getting him killed as soon as possible. He was, in short, a thoroughgoing anti-Clerical. And though, as we have seen, it is only by political means that his doctrine can be put into practice, he not only never suggested a sectarian theocracy as a form of government, and would certainly have prophesied the downfall of the late President Kruger if he had survived to his time, but, when challenged, he refused to teach his disciples not to pay tribute to Caesar, admitting that Caesar, who presumably had the kingdom of heaven within him as much as any disciple, had his place in the scheme of things. Indeed the apostles made this an excuse for carrying subservience to the State to a pitch of idolatry that ended in the theory of the divine right of kings, and provoked men to cut king's heads off to restore some sense of proportion in the matter. Jesus certainly did not consider the overthrow of the Roman empire or the substitution of a new ecclesiastical organization for the Jewish Church or for the priesthood of the Roman gods as part of his program. He said that God was better than Mammon; but he never said that Tweedledum was better than Tweedledee; and that is why it is now possible for British citizens and statesmen to follow Jesus, though they cannot possibly follow either Tweedledum or Tweedledee without bringing the empire down with a crash on their heads. And at that I must leave it.

LONDON, *December 1915*

Prefatory Note

(From the programme of the St James's Theatre,
London, 1 September 1913)

The version of the old story of Androcles and the
Lion to be played to-night at the St. James's Theatre
is not hampered by a pedantic retention of the details
as given by Aulus Gellius. His Androcles was called
Androclus, and Androclus was neither a Greek nor a
tailor nor a Christian, but a Roman slave who ran
away from the cruelties of his master and was later on
captured and condemned to be devoured by wild
beasts in the arena. But it happened that during his
flight he had taken refuge in a cave; and into this
cave came a lion who had a thorn in his paw which
Androclus extracted. It was to this very lion that
Androclus was afterwards thrown in the arena; and
the lion, instead of eating him, caressed him. The
story figured in natural histories like those of Aelian
and was found to please children, in whose story
books it has appeared ever since. Nobody believes it;
though everybody believes much more improbable
stories. It would be incredible of some lions just as
the action of Androclus would be incredible of some
men. But there are lions and lions, just as there are
men and men. The author of the present version has
petted a full-grown lion and had his advances received
with much more cordiality than he could expect from
most St. Bernard dogs. He conceives the lion of
Androclus to have been just such a fearless and amiable
creature. He conceives Androclus as having that fellow
feeling for animals which it becomes the most highly
evolved of animals to have (Man is your real king of
beasts) and which enables some men to handle bees

without being stung and snakes without being bitten. Given such a pair, there is nothing incredible in the story except the theatrical coincidence of the meeting of the two in the arena. Such coincidences are privileged on the stage, and are the special delight of this particular author. And really, when one considers how many men met lions in the arena from first to last, it is not too much to ask you to believe that just for once they turned out to be old friends.

If the author is asked why he has made Androcles a Christian, he can only ask why not. St. Francis preached to the birds as to his "little brothers"; and St. Francis was a Christian. St. Anthony preached to the fishes, who probably understood at least as much of his sermon as a modern fashionable congregation would have done; and St. Anthony was a Christian. Depend on it, Androcles had that root of the religious matter in him which made all religions free to him except the religion of hunting and killing. That is, the religion of the English country house.

But the twentieth-century Christian need not regard the Christianity of the early Christian martyrs as having much to do with his safe and eminently respectable Sunday profession of faith. Christians in those days were neither safe nor respectable. What is more, some of the most eminent Christians were by no means fond of the average Christians of their time. The author once asked an old Owenite Socialist why he had given up Socialism. He replied that after preaching it for some years he had noticed that it seemed to have a very bad effect on the moral character of those who gave themselves up to its propaganda. The same may be said of all persecuted creeds. A doctrine may be true and important, and its persecutors may be altogether in the wrong; but this makes the position of the man who is persecuted for propagating it all the more morbid. One sane man in a lunatic asylum can no more keep his normal health and temper than one lunatic in a *conseil de prud-hommes*. Add to this consideration the fact that all movements which attack the existing state of society attract both the people who are not good enough for the world and the people for whom the world is not good enough; so that the saint is always embarrassed by finding that the dynamiter and the assassin, the thief and the libertine, make common cause with him; and you will not be surprised to learn, if you do not know it already, that early Christians like Saint Augustine have a good many stories to tell of Christians who thoroughly deserved their evil reputation. The character of Spintho in the present play is by no means a malicious invention of the author's. Indeed had he gone on to exhibit Spintho as having taken the precaution to marry an orthodox Roman in order to shirk the Christian obligation to practise Communism, and as ostentatiously giving the lady black eyes to show how his conjugal duties revolted his ascetic nature, there would have been warrant for that too, and worse, in the records of the Fathers of the Church.

In representing a Roman centurion and a Roman captain (a pure invention) as corresponding to a British sergeant and a British company officer, some violence may or may not have been done to the petty accuracies of military history. Centurions were much chaffed in Rome as being mostly thick-booted vulgar persons, whacking their men with vinewood cudgels, and out of place in refined society; and the nearest thing to a modern captain as far as rank was concerned was probably not much more of a patrician. The patrician soldier was not a professional soldier: he commanded armies or adorned Senates or governed provinces as part of the natural pursuits of a patrician. But the relation of patrician officer to plebeian routineer existed as it exists to-day; and whether my captain should have been called something else, or my Centurion a Decurion, does not trouble me any more than the old controversy as to whether the audience turned their thumbs up or down when they wanted a defeated gladiator slain.

In short, if you demand my authorities for this and that, I must reply that only those who have never hunted up the authorities as I have believe that there is any authority who is not contradicted flatly by some other authority. Marshal Junot, reproached for having no respect for ancestry, said that he was an ancestor himself. In the same spirit I point out that the authorities on the story of Androcles and on the history of the early Christian martyrs are the people who have written about them; and now that I, too, have written about them, I take my place as the latest authority on the subject and ask you to respect me accordingly.

G. B. S.

Overture: forest sounds, roaring of lions, Christian hymn faintly.

A jungle path. A lion's roar, a melancholy suffering roar, comes from the jungle. It is repeated nearer. The lion limps from the jungle on three legs, holding up his right forepaw, in which a huge thorn sticks. He sits down and contemplates it. He licks it. He shakes it. He tries to extract it by scraping it along the ground, and hurts himself worse. He roars piteously. He licks it again. Tears drop from his eyes. He limps painfully off the path and lies down under the trees, exhausted with pain. Heaving a long sigh, like wind in a trombone, he goes to sleep.

Androcles and his wife Megaera come along the path. He is a small, thin, ridiculous little man who might be any age from thirty to fifty-five. He has sandy hair, watery compassionate blue eyes, sensitive nostrils, and a very presentable forehead; but his good points go no further: his arms and legs and back, though wiry of their kind, look shrivelled and starved. He carries a big bundle, is very poorly clad, and seems tired and hungry.

His wife is a rather handsome pampered slattern, well fed and in the prime of life. She has nothing to carry, and has a stout stick to help her along.

MEGAERA [*suddenly throwing down her stick*] I wont go another step.

ANDROCLES [*pleading wearily*] Oh, not again, dear. Whats the good of stopping every two miles and saying you wont go another step? We must get on to the next village before night. There are wild beasts in this wood: lions, they say.

MEGAERA. I dont believe a word of it. You are always threatening me with wild beasts to make me walk the very soul out of my body when I can hardly drag one foot before another. We havnt seen a single lion yet.

ANDROCLES. Well, dear, do you want to see one?

MEGAERA [*tearing the bundle from his back*] You cruel brute, you dont care how tired I am, or what becomes of me [*she throws the bundle on the ground*]: always thinking of yourself. Self! self! self! always yourself! [*She sits down on the bundle*].

ANDROCLES [*sitting down sadly on the ground with his elbows on his knees and his head in his hands*] We all have to think of ourselves occasionally, dear.

MEGAERA. A man ought to think of his wife sometimes.

ANDROCLES. He cant always help it, dear. You make me think of you a good deal. Not that I blame you.

MEGAERA. Blame me! I should think not indeed. Is it my fault that I'm married to you?

ANDROCLES. No dear: that is my fault.

MEGAERA. Thats a nice thing to say to me. Arnt you happy with me?

ANDROCLES. I dont complain, my love.

MEGAERA. You ought to be ashamed of yourself.

ANDROCLES. I am, my dear.

MEGAERA. Youre not: you glory in it.

ANDROCLES. In what, darling?

MEGAERA. In everything. In making me a slave, and making yourself a laughing-stock. It's not fair. You get me the name of being a shrew with your meek ways, always talking as if butter wouldnt melt in your mouth. And just because I look a big strong woman, and because I'm goodhearted and a bit hasty, and because youre always driving me to do things I'm sorry for afterwards, people say "Poor man: what a life his wife leads him!" Oh, if they only knew! And you think I dont know. But I do, I do, [*screaming*] I do.

ANDROCLES. Yes, my dear: I know you do.

MEGAERA. Then why dont you treat me properly and be a good husband to me?

ANDROCLES. What can I do, my dear?

MEGAERA. What can you do! You can return to your duty, and come back to your home and your friends, and sacrifice to the gods as all respectable people do, instead of having us hunted out of house and home for being dirty disreputable blaspheming atheists.

ANDROCLES. I'm not an atheist dear: I am a Christian.

MEGAERA. Well, isnt that the same thing, only ten times worse? Everybody knows that the Christians are the very lowest of the low.

ANDROCLES. Just like us, dear.

MEGAERA. Speak for yourself. Dont you dare to compare me to common people. My father owned his own public-house; and sorrowful was the day for me when you first came drinking in our bar.

ANDROCLES. I confess I was addicted to it, dear. But I gave it up when I became a Christian.

MEGAERA. Youd much better have remained a drunkard. I can forgive a man being addicted to drink: it's only natural; and I dont deny I like a drop myself sometimes. What I cant stand is your being addicted to Christianity. And whats worse again, your being addicted to animals. How is any woman to keep her house clean when you bring in every stray cat and lost cur and lame duck in the whole countryside? You took the bread out of my mouth to feed them: you know you did: dont attempt to deny it.

ANDROCLES. Only when they were hungry and you were getting too stout, dearie.

MEGAERA. Yes: insult me, do. [*Rising*] Oh! I wont bear it another moment. You used to sit and talk to those dumb brute beasts for hours, when you hadnt a word for me.

ANDROCLES. They never answered back, darling. [*He rises and again shoulders the bundle*].

MEGAERA. Well, if youre fonder of animals than of your own wife, you can live with them here in the jungle. Ive had enough of them and enough of you. I'm going back. I'm going home.

ANDROCLES [*barring the way back*] No, dearie: dont take on like that. We cant go back. Weve sold everything: we should starve; and I should be sent to Rome and thrown to the lions—

MEGAERA. Serve you right! I wish the lions joy of you. [*Screaming*] Are you going to get out of my way and let me go home?

ANDROCLES. No, dear—

MEGAERA. Then I'll make my way through the forest; and when I'm eaten by the wild beasts youll know what a wife youve lost. [*She dashes into the jungle and nearly falls over the sleeping lion*]. Oh! Oh! Andy! Andy! [*She totters back and collapses into the arms of Androcles, who, crushed by her weight, falls on his bundle*].

ANDROCLES [*extracting himself from beneath her and slapping her hands in great anxiety*] What is it, my precious, my pet? Whats the matter? [*He raises her head. Speechless with terror, she points in the direction of the sleeping lion. He steals cautiously towards the spot indicated by Megaera. She rises with an effort and totters after him*].

MEGAERA. No, Andy: youll be killed. Come back.

The lion utters a long snoring sigh. Androcles sees the lion, and recoils fainting into the arms of Megaera, who falls back on the bundle. They roll apart and lie staring in terror at one another. The lion is heard groaning heavily in the jungle.

ANDROCLES [*whispering*] Did you see? A lion.

MEGAERA. [*despairing*] The gods have sent him to punish us because youre a Christian. Take me away, Andy. Save me.

ANDROCLES [*rising*] Meggy: theres one chance for you. Itll take him pretty nigh twenty minutes to eat me (I'm rather stringy and tough) and you can escape in less time than that.

MEGAERA. Oh, dont talk about eating. [*The lion rises with a great groan and limps towards them*]. Oh! [*She faints*]

ANDROCLES [*quaking, but keeping between the lion and Megaera*] Dont you come near my wife, do you hear? [*The lion groans. Androcles can hardly stand for trembling*]. Meggy: run. Run for your life. If I take my eye off him, it's all up. [*The lion holds up his wounded paw and flaps it piteously before Androcles*]. Oh, he's lame, poor old chap! He's got a thorn in his paw. A frightfully big thorn. [*Full of sympathy*] Oh, poor old man! Did um get an awful thorn into um's tootsums wootsums? Has it made um too sick to eat a nice little Christian man for um's breakfast? Oh, a nice little Christian man will get um's thorn out for um; and then um shall eat the nice Christian man and the nice Christian man's nice big tender wifey pifey. [*The lion responds by moans of self-pity*]. Yes, yes, yes, yes, yes. Now, now [*taking the paw in this hand*], um is not to bite and not to scratch, not even if it hurts a very very little. Now make velvet paws. Thats right. [*He pulls gingerly at the thorn. The lion, with an angry yell of pain, jerks back his paw so abruptly that Andro-cles is thrown on his back*]. Steadeee! Oh, did the nasty cruel little Christian man hurt the sore paw? [*The lion moans assentingly but apologetically*]. Well, one more little pull and it will be all over. Just one little, little leetle pull; and then um will live happily ever after. [*He gives the thorn another pull. The lion roars and snaps his jaws with a terrifying clash*]. Oh, mustnt frighten um's good kind doctor, um's affectionate nursey. That didnt hurt at all: not a bit. Just one more. Just to shew how the brave big lion can bear pain, not like the little crybaby Christian man. Oopsh! [*The thorn comes out. The lion yells with pain and shakes his paw wildly*]. Thats it. [*Holding up the thorn*]. Now it's out. Now lick um's paw to take away the nasty inflammation, See? [*He licks his own hand. The lion nods intelligently and licks his paw industriously*]. Clever little liony-piony! Understands um's dear old friend Andy Wandy. [*The lion licks his face*]. Yes, kissums Andy Wandy. [*The lion wagging his tail violently, rises on his hind legs, and embraces Androcles, who makes a wry face and cries*] Velvet paws! Velvet paws! [*The lion draws in his claws*]. Thats right. [*He embraces the lion, who finally takes the end of his tail in one paw, places that tight round Androcles' waist, resting it on his hip. Androcles takes the other paw in his hand, stretches out his arm, and the two waltz rapturously round and round and finally away through the jungle*].

MEGAERA [*who has revived during the waltz*] Oh, you coward, you havnt danced with me for years; and now you go off dancing with a great brute beast that you havnt known for ten minutes and that wants to eat your own wife. Coward. Coward! Coward! [*She rushes off after them into the jungle*].

[ACT I]

Evening. The end of three converging roads to Rome. Three triumphal arches span them where they debouch on a square at the gate of the city. Looking north through the arches one can see the campagna threaded by the three long dusty tracks. On the east and west sides of the square are long stone benches. An old beggar sits on the east side, his bowl at his feet.

Through the eastern arch a squad of Roman soldiers tramps along escorting a batch of Christian prisoners of both sexes and all ages, among them one Lavinia, a good-looking resolute young woman, apparently of higher social standing than her fellow-prisoners. A centurion, carrying his vinewood cudgel, trudges alongside the squad, on its right, in command of it. All are tired and dusty; but the soldiers are dogged and indifferent, the Christians lighthearted and determined to treat their hardships as a joke and encourage one another.

A bugle is heard far behind on the road, where the rest of the cohort is following.

CENTURION [*stopping*] Halt! Orders from the Captain. [*They halt and wait*]. Now then, you Christians, none of your larks. The captain's coming. Mind you behave yourselves. No singing. Look respectful. Look serious, if youre capable of it. See that big building over there! Thats the Coliseum. Thats where youll be thrown to the lions or set to fight the gladiators presently. Think of that; and itll help you to behave properly before the captain. [*The Captain arrives*]. Attention! Salute! [*The soldiers salute*].

A CHRISTIAN [*cheerfully*] God bless you, Captain!

THE CENTURION [*scandalized*] Silence!

The Captain, a patrician, handsome, about thirty-five, very cold and distinguished, very superior and authoritative, steps up on a stone seat at the west side of the square, behind the centurion, so as to dominate the others more effectually.

THE CAPTAIN. Centurion.

THE CENTURION [*standing at attention and saluting*] Sir?

THE CAPTAIN [*speaking stiffly and officially*] You will remind your men, Centurion, that we are now entering Rome. You will instruct them that once inside the gates of Rome they are in the presence of the Emperor. You will make them understand that the lax discipline of the march cannot be permitted here. You will instruct them to shave every day, not every week. You will impress on them particularly that there must be an end to the profanity and blasphemy of singing Christian hymns on the march. I have to reprimand you, Centurion, for not only allowing this, but actually doing it yourself.

THE CENTURION [*apologetic*] The men march better, Captain.

THE CAPTAIN. No doubt. For that reason an exception is made in the case of the march called Onward Christian Soldiers. This may be sung, except when marching through the forum or within hearing of the Emperor's palace; but the words must be altered to "Throw them to the Lions."

The Christians burst into shrieks of uncontrollable laughter, to the great scandal of the Centurion.

CENTURION. Silence! Silen-n-n-n-nce! Wheres your behavior? Is that the way to listen to an officer? [*To the Captain*] Thats what we have to put up with from these Christians every day, sir. Theyre always laughing and joking something scandalous. Theyve no religion: thats how it is.

LAVINIA. But I think the Captain meant us to laugh, Centurion. It was so funny.

CENTURION. Youll find out how funny it is when youre thrown to the lions tomorrow. [*To the Captain, who looks displeased*] Beg pardon, Sir. [*To the Christians*] Silennnnce!

THE CAPTAIN. You are to instruct your men that all intimacy with Christian prisoners must now cease. The men have fallen into habits of dependence upon the prisoners, especially the female prisoners, for cooking, repairs to uniforms, writing letters, and advice in their private affairs. In a Roman soldier such dependence is inadmissible. Let me see no more of it whilst we are in the city. Further, your orders are that in addressing Christian prisoners, the manners and tone of your men must express abhorrence and contempt. Any shortcomings in this respect will be regarded as a breach of discipline. [*He turns to the prisoners*] Prisoners.

CENTURION[*fiercely*] Prisonerrrrrs! Tention! Silence!

THE CAPTAIN. I call your attention, prisoners, to the fact that you may be called on to appear in the Imperial Circus at any time from tomorrow onwards according to the requirements of the managers. I may inform you that as there is a shortage of Christians just now, you may expect to be called on very soon.

LAVINIA. What will they do to us, Captain?

CENTURION. Silence!

THE CAPTAIN. The women will be conducted into the arena with the wild beasts of the Imperial Menagerie, and will suffer the consequences. The men, if of an age to bear arms, will be given weapons to defend themselves, if they choose, against the Imperial Gladiators.

LAVINIA. Captain: is there no hope that this cruel persecution—

CENTURION [*shocked*] Silence! Hold your tongue, there. Persecution, indeed!

THE CAPTAIN [*unmoved and somewhat sardonic*] Persecution is not a term applicable to the acts of the Emperor. The Emperor is the Defender of the Faith. In throwing you to the lions he will be upholding the interests of religion in Rome. If you were to throw him to the lions, that would no doubt be persecution.

The Christians again laugh heartily.

CENTURION [*horrified*] Silence, I tell you! Keep silence there. Did anyone ever hear the like of this?

LAVINIA. Captain: there will be nobody to appreciate your jokes when we are gone.

THE CAPTAIN [*unshaken in his official delivery*] I call the attention of the female prisoner Lavinia to the fact that as the Emperor is a divine personage, her imputation of cruelty is not only treason, but sacrilege. I point out to her further that there is no foundation for the charge, as the Emperor does not desire that any prisoner should suffer; nor can any Christian be harmed save through his or her own obstinacy. All that is necessary is to sacrifice to the gods: a simple and convenient ceremony effected by dropping a pinch of incense on the altar, after which the prisoner is at once set free. Under such circumstances you have only your own perverse folly to blame if you suffer. I suggest to you that if you cannot burn a morsel of incense as a matter of conviction, you might at least do so as a matter of good taste, to avoid shocking the religious convictions of your fellow citizens. I am aware that these considerations do not weigh with Christians; but it is my duty to call your attention to them in order that you may have no ground for complaining of your treatment, or of accusing the Emperor of cruelty when he is shewing you the most signal clemency. Looked at from this point of view, every Christian who has perished in the arena has really committed suicide.

LAVINIA. Captain: your jokes are too grim. Do not think it is easy for us to die. Our faith makes life far stronger and more wonderful in us than when we walked in darkness and had nothing to live for. Death is harder for us than for you: the martyr's agony is as bitter as his triumph is glorious.

THE CAPTAIN [*rather troubled, addressing her personally and gravely*] A martyr, Lavinia, is a fool. Your death will prove nothing.

LAVINIA. Then why kill me?

THE CAPTAIN. I mean that truth, if there be any truth, needs no martyrs.

LAVINIA. No; but my faith, like your sword, needs testing. Can you test your sword except by staking your life on it?

THE CAPTAIN [*suddenly resuming his official tone*] I call the attention of the female prisoner to the fact that Christians are not allowed to draw the Emperor's officers into arguments and put questions to them for which the military regulations provide no answer. [*The Christians titter*].

LAVINIA. Captain: how can you?

THE CAPTAIN. I call the female prisoner's attention specially to the fact that four comfortable homes have been offered her by officers of this regiment, of which she can have her choice the moment she chooses to sacrifice as all wellbred Roman ladies do. I have no more to say to the prisoners.

CENTURION. Dismiss! But stay where you are.

THE CAPTAIN. Centurion: you will remain here with

your men in charge of the prisoners until the arrival
of three Christian prisoners in the custody of a cohort
of the tenth legion. Among these prisoners you will
particularly identify an armorer named Ferrovius, of
dangerous character and great personal strength, and a
Greek tailor reputed to be a sorcerer, by name
Androcles. You will add the three to your charge here
and march them all to the Coliseum, where you will
deliver them into the custody of the master of the
gladiators and take his receipt, countersigned by the
keeper of the beasts and the acting manager. You
understand your instructions?

CENTURION. Yes, sir.

THE CAPTAIN. Dismiss. [*He throws off his air of
parade, and descends from his perch. The Centurion seats
himself on it and prepares for a nap, whilst his men stand
at ease. The Christians sit down on the west side of the
square, glad to rest. Lavinia alone remains standing to
speak to the Captain*].

LAVINIA. Captain: is this man who is to join us the
famous Ferrovius, who has made such wonderful
conversions in the northern cities?

THE CAPTAIN. Yes. We are warned that he has the
strength of an elephant and the temper of a mad bull.
Also that he is stark mad. Not a model Christian, it
would seem.

LAVINIA. You need not fear him if he is a Christian,
Captain.

THE CAPTAIN [*coldly*] I shall not fear him in any case,
Lavinia.

LAVINIA [*her eyes dancing*] How brave of you, Captain!

THE CAPTAIN. You are right: it was a silly thing to
say [*In a lower tone, humane and urgent*] Lavinia: do
Christians know how to love?

LAVINIA [*composedly*] Yes, Captain: they love even
their enemies.

THE CAPTAIN. Is that easy?

LAVINIA. Very easy, Captain, when their enemies are as handsome as you.

THE CAPTAIN. Lavinia: you are laughing at me.

LAVINIA. At you, Captain! Impossible.

THE CAPTAIN. Then you are flirting with me, which is worse. Dont be foolish.

LAVINIA. But such a very handsome captain.

THE CAPTAIN. Incorrigible! [*Urgently*] Listen to me. The men in that audience tomorrow will be the vilest of voluptuaries: men in whom the only passion excited by a beautiful woman is a lust to see her tortured and torn shrieking limb from limb. It is a crime to gratify that passion. It is offering yourself for violation by the whole rabble of the streets and the riff-raff of the court at the same time. Why will you not choose rather a kindly love and an honorable alliance?

LAVINIA. They cannot violate my soul. I alone can do that by sacrificing to false gods.

THE CAPTAIN. Sacrifice then to the true God. What does his name matter? We call him Jupiter. The Greeks call him Zeus. Call him what you will as you drop the incense on the altar flame: He will understand.

LAVINIA. No. I couldnt. That is the strange thing, Captain, that a little pinch of incense should make all that difference. Religion is such a great thing that when I meet really religious people we are friends at once, no matter what name we give to the divine will that made us and moves us. Oh, do you think that I, a woman, would quarrel with you for sacrificing to a woman god like Diana, if Diana meant to you what Christ means to me? No: we should kneel side by side before her altar like two children. But when men

who believe neither in my god nor in their own—men
who do not know the meaning of the word religion—
when these men drag me to the foot of an iron statue
that has become the symbol of the terror and darkness
through which they walk, of their cruelty and greed,
of their hatred of God and their oppression of man—
when they ask me to pledge my soul before the people
that this hideous idol is God, and that all this wickedness and falsehood is divine truth, I cannot do it, not if
they could put a thousand cruel deaths on me. I tell
you, it is physically impossible. Listen, Captain: did
you ever try to catch a mouse in your hand? Once
there was a dear little mouse that used to come out
and play on my table as I was reading. I wanted to
take him in my hand and caress him; and sometimes
he got among my books so that he could not escape
me when I stretched out my hand. And I did stretch
out my hand; but it always came back in spite of me. I
was not afraid of him in my heart; but my hand refused: it is not in the nature of my hand to touch a
mouse. Well, Captain, if I took a pinch of incense in
my hand and stretched it out over the altar fire, my
hand would come back. My body would be true to my
faith even if you could corrupt my mind. And all the
time I should believe more in Diana than my persecutors have ever believed in anything. Can you understand that?

THE CAPTAIN [*simply*] Yes: I understand that. But my
hand would not come back. The hand that holds the
sword has been trained not to come back from anything but victory.

LAVINIA. Not even from death?

THE CAPTAIN. Least of all from death.

LAVINIA. Then I must not come back from death
either. A woman has to be braver than a soldier.

THE CAPTAIN. Prouder, you mean.

LAVINIA [*startled*] Prouder! You call our courage pride!

THE CAPTAIN. There is no such thing as courage: there is only pride. You Christians are the proudest devils on earth.

LAVINIA [*hurt*] Pray God then my pride may never become a false pride. [*She turns away as if she did not wish to continue the conversation, but softens and says to him with a smile*] Thank you for trying to save me.

THE CAPTAIN. I knew it was no use; but one tries in spite of one's knowledge.

LAVINIA. Something stirs, even in the iron breast of a Roman soldier?

THE CAPTAIN. It will soon be iron again. I have seen many women die, and forgotten them in a week.

LAVINIA. Remember me for a fortnight, handsome Captain. I shall be watching you, perhaps.

THE CAPTAIN. From the skies? Do not deceive yourself, Lavinia. There is no future for you beyond the grave.

LAVINIA. What does that matter? Do you think I am only running away from the terrors of life into the comfort of heaven? If there were no future, or if the future were one of torment, I should have to go just the same. The hand of God is upon me.

THE CAPTAIN. Yes: when all is said, we are both patricians, Lavinia, and must die for our beliefs. Farewell. [*He offers her his hand. She takes it and presses it. He walks away, trim and calm. She looks after him for a moment, and cries a little as he disappears through the eastern arch. A trumpet-call is heard from the road through the western arch*].

CENTURION [*waking up and rising*] Cohort of the tenth with prisoners. Two file out with me to receive them.

[*He goes out through the western arch, followed by four soldiers in two files*].

Lentulus and Metellus come into the square from the west side with a little retinue of servants. Both are young courtiers, dressed in the extremity of fashion. Lentulus is slender, fair-haired, epicene. Metellus is manly, compactly built, olive skinned, not a talker.

LENTULUS. Christians, by Jove! Lets chaff them.

METELLUS. Awful brutes. If you knew as much about them as I do you wouldnt want to chaff them. Leave them to the lions.

LENTULUS [*indicating Lavinia, who is still looking towards the arches after the Captain*] That woman's got a figure. [*He walks past her, staring at her invitingly; but she is preoccupied and is not conscious of him*]. Do you turn the other cheek when they kiss you?

LAVINIA [*starting*] What?

LENTULUS. Do you turn the other cheek when they kiss you, fascinating Christian?

LAVINIA. Dont be foolish. [*To Metellus, who has remained on her right, so that she is between them*] Please dont let your friend behave like a cad before the soldiers. How are they to respect and obey patricians if they see them behaving like street boys? [*Sharply to Lentulus*] Pull yourself together, man. Hold your head up. Keep the corners of your mouth firm; and treat me respectfully. What do you take me for?

LENTULUS [*irresolutely*] Look here, you know: I— you—I—

LAVINIA. Stuff! Go about your business. [*She turns decisively away and sits down with her comrades, leaving him disconcerted*].

METELLUS. You didnt get much out of that. I told you they were brutes.

LENTULUS. Plucky little filly! I suppose she thinks I

care. [*With an air of indifference he strolls with Metellus to the east side of the square, where they stand watching the return of the Centurion through the western arch with his men, escorting three prisoners: Ferrovius, Androcles, and Spintho. Ferrovius is a powerful, choleric man in the prime of life, with large nostrils, staring eyes, and a thick neck: a man whose sensibilities are keen and violent to the verge of madness. Spintho is a debauchee, the wreck of a good-looking man gone hopelessly to the bad. Androcles is overwhelmed with grief, and is restraining his tears with great difficulty*].

THE CENTURION [*to Lavinia*] Here are some pals for you. This little bit is Ferrovius that you talk so much about. [*Ferrovius turns on him threateningly. The Centurion holds up his left forefinger in admonition*]. Now remember that youre a Christian, and that youve got to return good for evil. [*Ferrovius controls himself convulsively; moves away from temptation to the east side near Lentulus; clasps his hands in silent prayer; and throws himself on his knees*]. Thats the way to manage them eh! This fine fellow [*indicating Androcles, who comes to his left, and makes Lavinia a heart-broken salutation*] is a sorcerer. A Greek tailor, he is. A real sorcerer, too: no mistake about it. The tenth marches with a leopard at the head of the column. He made a pet of the leopard; and now he's crying at being parted from it. [*Androcles sniffs lamentably*]. Aint you, old chap? Well, cheer up, we march with a Billy goat [*Androcles brightens up*] thats killed two leopards and ate a turkey-cock. You can have him for a pet if you like. [*Androcles, quite consoled, goes past the Centurion to Lavinia, and sits down contentedly on the ground on her left*]. This dirty dog [*collaring Spintho*] is a real Christian. He mobs the temples, he does [*at each

accusation he gives the neck of Spintho's tunic a twist];
he goes smashing things mad drunk, he does; he
steals the gold vessels, he does; he assaults the
priestesses, he does—yah! [*He flings Spintho into the
middle of the group of prisoners*]. Youre the sort that
makes duty a pleasure, you are.

SPINTHO [*gasping*] Thats it: strangle me. Kick me.
Beat me. Revile me. Our Lord was beaten and
reviled. Thats my way to heaven. Every martyr goes
to heaven, no matter what he's done. That is so, isnt
it, brother?

CENTURION. Well, if youre going to heaven, *I* dont
want to go there. I wouldnt be seen with you.

LENTULUS. Haw! Good! [*Indicating the kneeling
Ferrovius*]. Is this one of the turn-the-other-cheek
gentlemen, Centurion?

CENTURION. Yes, sir. Lucky for you too, sir, if you
want to take any liberties with him.

LENTULUS [*to Ferrovius*] You turn the other cheek
when youre struck, I'm told.

FERROVIUS [*slowly turning his great eyes on him*] Yes,
by the grace of God, I do, now.

LENTULUS. Not that youre a coward, of course, but
out of pure piety.

FERROVIUS. I fear God more than man; at least I try
to.

LENTULUS. Lets see. [*He strikes him on the cheek.
Androcles makes a wild movement to rise and interfere;
but Lavinia holds him down, watching Ferrovius
intently. Ferrovius, without flinching, turns the other
cheek. Lentulus, rather out of countenance, titters
foolishly, and strikes him again feebly*]. You know, I
should feel ashamed if I let myself be struck like that,
and took it lying down. But then I'm not a Christian:
I'm a man. [*Ferrovius rises impressively and towers*

over him. Lentulus becomes white with terror; and a shade of green flickers in his cheek for a moment].

FERROVIUS [*with the calm of a steam hammer*] I have not always been faithful. The first man who struck me as you have just struck me was a stronger man than you: he hit me harder than I expected. I was tempted and fell; and it was then that I first tasted bitter shame. I never had a happy moment after that until I had knelt and asked his forgiveness by his bedside in the hospital. [*Putting his hands on Lentulus's shoulders with paternal weight*]. But now I have learnt to resist with a strength that is not my own. I am not ashamed now, nor angry.

LENTULUS [*uneasily*] Er—good evening. [*He tries to move away*].

FERROVIUS [*gripping his shoulders*] Oh, do not harden your heart, young man. Come: try for yourself whether our way is not better than yours. I will now strike you on one cheek; and you will turn the other and learn how much better you will feel than if you gave way to the promptings of anger. [*He holds him with one hand and clenches the other fist*].

LENTULUS. Centurion: I call on you to protect me.

CENTURION. You asked for it, sir. It's no business of ours. Youve had two whacks at him. Better pay him a trifle and square it that way.

LENTULUS. Yes, of course. [*To Ferrovius*] It was only a bit of fun, I assure you: I meant no harm. Here [*He proffers a gold coin*].

FERROVIUS [*taking it and throwing it to the old beggar, who snatches it up eagerly, and hobbles off to spend it*] Give all thou hast to the poor. Come, friend: courage! I may hurt your body for a moment; but your soul will rejoice in the victory of the spirit over the flesh. [*He prepares to strike*].

[603]

ANDROCLES. Easy, Ferrovius, easy: you broke the last man's jaw.

Lentulus, with a moan of terror, attempts to fly; but Ferrovius holds him ruthlessly.

FERROVIUS. Yes; but I saved his soul. What matters a broken jaw?

LENTULUS. Dont touch me, do you hear? The law—

FERROVIUS. The law will throw me to the lions tomorrow: what worse could it do were I to slay you? Pray for strength; and it shall be given to you.

LENTULUS. Let me go. Your religion forbids you to strike me.

FERROVIUS. On the contrary, it commands me to strike you. How can you turn the other cheek, if you are not first struck on the one cheek?

LENTULUS [*almost in tears*] But I'm convinced already that what you said is quite right. I apologize for striking you.

FERROVIUS [*greatly pleased*] My son: have I softened your heart? Has the good seed fallen in a fruitful place? Are your feet turning towards a better path?

LENTULUS [*abjectly*] Yes, yes. There is a great deal in what you say.

FERROVIUS [*radiant*] Join us. Come to the lions. Come to suffering and death.

LENTULUS [*falling on his knees and bursting into tears*] Oh, help me. Mother! mother!

FERROVIUS. These tears will water your soul and make it bring forth good fruit, my son. God has greatly blessed my efforts at conversion. Shall I tell you a miracle—yes, a miracle—wrought by me in Cappadocia? A young man—just such a one as you, with golden hair like yours—scoffed at and struck me as you scoffed at and struck me. I sat up all night with that youth wrestling for his soul; and in the morning not only was he a Christian, but his hair was as white as snow. [*Lentulus falls in a dead faint*]. There, there: take him away. The spirit has over-wrought him, poor lad. Carry him gently to his house; and leave the rest to heaven.

CENTURION. Take him home. [*The servants, intimidated, hastily carry him out. Metellus is about to follow when Ferrovius lays his hand on his shoulder*].

FERROVIUS. You are his friend, young man. You will see that he is taken safely home.

METELLUS [*with awestruck civility*] Certainly, sir. I shall do whatever you think best. Most happy to have made your acquaintance, I'm sure. You may depend on me. Good evening, sir.

FERROVIUS [*with unction*] The blessing of heaven upon you and him.

Metellus follows Lentulus. The Centurion returns to his seat to resume his interrupted nap. The deepest awe has settled on the spectators. Ferrovius, with a long sigh of happiness, goes to Lavinia, and offers her his hand.

LAVINIA [*taking it*] So that is how you convert people, Ferrovius.

FERROVIUS. Yes: there has been a blessing on my work in spite of my unworthiness and my backslidings—all through my wicked, devilish temper. This man—

ANDROCLES [*hastily*] Dont slap me on the back, brother. She knows you mean me.

FERROVIUS. How I wish I were weak like our brother here! for then I should perhaps be meek and gentle like him. And yet there seems to be a special providence that makes my trials less than his. I hear tales of the crowd scoffing and casting stones and reviling the brethren; but when I come, all this stops: my influence calms the passion of the mob: they listen to me in silence; and infidels are often converted by a straight heart-to-heart talk with me. Every day I feel happier, more confident. Every day lightens the load of the great terror.

LAVINIA. The great terror? What is that?

Ferrovius shakes his head and does not answer. He sits down beside her on her left, and buries his face in his hands in gloomy meditation.

ANDROCLES. Well, you see, sister, he's never quite sure of himself. Suppose at the last moment in the arena, with the gladiators there to fight him, one of them was to say anything to annoy him, he might forget himself and lay that gladiator out.

LAVINIA. That would be splendid.

FERROVIUS [*springing up in horror*] What!

ANDROCLES. Oh sister!

FERROVIUS. Splendid to betray my master, like Peter! Splendid to act like any common blackguard in the day of my proving! Woman: you are no Christian. [*He moves away from her to the middle of the square, as if her neighborhood contaminated him*].

LAVINIA [*laughing*] You know, Ferrovius, I am not always a Christian. I dont think anybody is. There are moments when I forget all about it, and something comes out quite naturally, as it did then.

SPINTHO. What does it matter? If you die in the arena, youll be a martyr; and all martyrs go to heaven, no matter what they have done. Thats so, isnt it. Ferrovius?

FERROVIUS. Yes: that is so, if we are faithful to the end.

LAVINIA. I'm not so sure.

SPINTHO. Dont say that. Thats blasphemy. Dont say that, I tell you. We shall be saved, no matter WHAT we do.

LAVINIA. Perhaps you men will all go into heaven

bravely and in triumph, with your heads erect and golden trumpets sounding for you. But I am sure I shall only be allowed to squeeze myself in through a little crack in the gate after a great deal of begging. I am not good always: I have moments only.

SPINTHO. Youre talking nonsense, woman. I tell you, martyrdom pays all scores.

ANDROCLES. Well, let us hope so, brother, for your sake. Youve had a gay time, havnt you? with your raids on the temples. I cant help thinking that heaven will be very dull for a man of your temperament. [*Spintho snarls*]. Dont be angry: I say it only to console you in case you should die in your bed to-night in the natural way. Theres a lot of plague about.

SPINTHO [*rising and running about in abject terror*] I never thought of that. Oh Lord, spare me to be martyred. Oh, what a thought to put into the mind of a brother! Oh, let me be martyred today, now. I shall die in the night and go to hell. Youre a sorcerer: youve put death into my mind. Oh, curse you, curse you! [*He tries to seize Androcles by the throat*].

FERROVIUS [*holding him in a grasp of iron*] Whats this, brother? Anger! Violence! Raising your hand to a brother Christian!

SPINTHO. It's easy for you. Youre strong. Your nerves are all right. But I'm full of disease. [*Ferrovius takes his hand from him with instinctive disgust*]. Ive drunk all my nerves away. I shall have the horrors all night.

ANDROCLES [*sympathetic*] Oh, dont take on so, brother. We're all sinners.

SPINTHO [*snivelling, trying to feel consoled*] Yes: I daresay if the truth were known, youre as bad as I am.

LAVINIA [*contemptuously*] Does that comfort you?

FERROVIUS [*sternly*] Pray, man, pray.

SPINTHO. Whats the good of praying? If we're

martyred we shall go to heaven, shant we, whether we pray or not?

FERROVIUS. Whats that? Not pray! [*Seizing him again*] Pray this instant, you dog, you rotten hound, you slimy snake, you beastly goat, or—

SPINTHO. Yes: beat me: kick me. I forgive you: mind that.

FERROVIUS [*spurning him with loathing*] Yah! [*Spintho reels away and falls in front of Ferrovius*].

ANDROCLES [*reaching out and catching the skirt of Ferrovius's tunic*] Dear brother: if you wouldnt mind —just for my sake—

FERROVIUS. Well?

ANDROCLES. Dont call him by the names of the animals. Weve no right to. Ive had such friends in dogs. A pet snake is the best of company. I was nursed on goat's milk. Is it fair to them to call the like of him a dog or a snake or a goat?

FERROVIUS. I only meant that they have no souls.

ANDROCLES [*anxiously protesting*] Oh, believe me, they have. Just the same as you and me. I really dont think I could consent to go to heaven if I thought there were to be no animals there. Think of what they suffer here.

FERROVIUS. Thats true. Yes: that is just. They will have their share in heaven.

SPINTHO [*who has picked himself up and is sneaking past Ferrovius on his left, sneers derisively*]!!

FERROVIUS [*turning on him fiercely*] Whats that you say?

SPINTHO [*cowering*] Nothing.

FERROVIUS [*clenching his fist*] Do animals go to heaven or not?

SPINTHO. I never said they didnt.

FERROVIUS [*implacable*] Do they or do they not?

SPINTHO. They do: they do. [*Scrambling out of Ferrovius's reach*]. Oh, curse you for frightening me!

A bugle call is heard.

CENTURION [*waking up*] Tention! Form as before. Now then, prisoners: up with you and trot along spry. [*The soldiers fall in. The Christians rise*].

A man with an ox goad comes running through the central arch.

THE OX DRIVER. Here, you soldiers! clear out of the way for the Emperor.

THE CENTURION. Emperor! Where's the Emperor? You aint the Emperor, are you?

THE OX DRIVER. It's the menagerie service. My team of oxen is drawing the new lion to the Coliseum. You clear the road.

CENTURION. What! Go in after you in your dust, with half the town at the heels of you and your lion! Not likely. We go first.

THE OX DRIVER. The menagerie service is the Emperor's personal retinue. You clear out, I tell you.

CENTURION. You tell me, do you? Well, I'll tell you something. If the lion is menagerie service, the lion's dinner is menagerie service too. This [*pointing to the Christians*] is the lion's dinner. So back with you to your bullocks double quick; and learn your place. March. [*The soldiers start*]. Now then, you Christians: step out there.

LAVINIA [*marching*] Come along, the rest of the dinner. I shall be the olives and anchovies.

ANOTHER CHRISTIAN [*laughing*] I shall be the soup.

ANOTHER. I shall be the fish.

ANOTHER. Ferrovius shall be the roast boar.

FERROVIUS [*heavily*] I see the joke. Yes, yes: I shall be the roast boar. Ha! ha! [*He laughs conscientiously and marches out with them*].

ANDROCLES [*following*] I shall be the mince pie. [*Each announcement is received with a louder laugh by all the rest as the joke catches on*].

CENTURION [*scandalized*] Silence! Have some sense of your situation. Is this the way for martyrs to behave? [*To Spintho, who is quaking and loitering*] I know what youll be at that dinner. Youll be the emetic. [*He shoves him rudely along*].

SPINTHO. It's too dreadful: I'm not fit to die.

CENTURION. Fitter than you are to live, you swine.

They pass from the square westward. The oxen, drawing a waggon with a great wooden cage and the lion in it, arrive through the central arch.

⌈ ACT II ⌉

Behind the Emperor's box at the Coliseum, where the performers assemble before entering the arena. In the middle a wide passage leading to the arena descends from the floor level under the imperial box. On both sides of this passage steps ascend to a landing at the back entrance to the box. The landing forms a bridge across the passage. At the entrance to the passage are two bronze mirrors, one on each side.

On the west side of this passage, on the right hand of anyone coming from the box and standing on the bridge, the martyrs are sitting on the steps. Lavinia is seated half-way up, thoughtful, trying to look death in the face. On her left Androcles consoles himself by nursing a cat. Ferrovius stands behind them, his eyes blazing, his figure stiff with intense resolution. At the foot of the steps crouches Spintho, with his head clutched in his hands, full of horror at the approach of martydom.

On the east side of the passage the gladiators are standing and sitting at ease, waiting, like the Christians, for their turn in the arena. One (Retiarius) is a nearly naked man with a net and a trident. Another (Secutor) is in armor with a sword. He carries a helmet with a barred visor. The editor of the gladiators sits on a chair a little apart from them.

The Call Boy enters from the passage.

THE CALL BOY. Number six. Retiarius versus Secutor.

The gladiator with the net picks it up. The gladiator with the helmet puts it on; and the two go into the arena,

[611]

the net thrower taking out a little brush and arranging his hair as he goes, the other tightening his straps and shaking his shoulders loose. Both look at themselves in the mirrors before they enter the passage.

LAVINIA. Will they really kill one another?

SPINTHO. Yes, if the people turn down their thumbs.

THE EDITOR. You know nothing about it. The people indeed! Do you suppose we would kill a man worth perhaps fifty talents to please the riffraff? I should like to catch any of my men at it.

SPINTHO. I thought—

THE EDITOR [*contemptuously*] You thought! Who cares what you think? Youll be killed all right enough.

SPINTHO [*groans and again hides his face*]!!!

LAVINIA. Then is nobody ever killed except us poor Christians?

THE EDITOR. If the vestal virgins turn down their thumbs, thats another matter. Theyre ladies of rank.

LAVINIA. Does the Emperor ever interfere?

THE EDITOR. Oh, yes: he turns his thumb up fast enough if the vestal virgins want to have one of his pet fighting men killed.

ANDROCLES. But dont they ever just only pretend to kill one another? Why shouldnt you pretend to die, and get dragged out as if you were dead; and then get up and go home, like an actor?

THE EDITOR. See here: you want to know too much. There will be no pretending about the new lion: let that be enough for you. He's hungry.

SPINTHO [*groaning with horror*] Oh, Lord! cant you stop talking about it? Isnt it bad enough for us without that?

ANDROCLES. I'm glad he's hungry. Not that I want him to suffer, poor chap! but then he'll enjoy eating me so much more. Theres a cheerful side to everything.

THE EDITOR [*rising and striding over to Androcles*] Here: dont you be obstinate. Come with me and drop the pinch of incense on the altar. Thats all you need do to be let off.

ANDROCLES. No: thank you very much indeed; but I really mustnt.

THE EDITOR. What! Not to save your life?

ANDROCLES. I'd rather not. I couldnt sacrifice to Diana: she's a huntress, you know, and kills things.

THE EDITOR. That dont matter. You can choose your own altar. Sacrifice to Jupiter: he likes animals: he turns himself into an animal when he goes off duty.

ANDROCLES. No: it's very kind of you; but I feel I cant save myself that way.

THE EDITOR. But I dont ask you to do it to save yourself: I ask you to do it to oblige me personally.

ANDROCLES [*scrambling up in the greatest agitation*] Oh, please dont say that. This is dreadful. You mean so kindly by me that it seems quite horrible to disoblige you. If you could arrange for me to sacrifice when theres nobody looking, I shouldnt mind. But I must go into the arena with the rest. My honor, you know.

THE EDITOR. Honor! The honor of a tailor?

ANDROCLES [*apologetically*] Well, perhaps honor is too strong an expression. Still, you know, I couldnt allow the tailors to get a bad name through me.

THE EDITOR. How much will you remember of all that when you smell the beast's breath and see his jaws opening to tear out your throat?

SPINTHO [*rising with a yell of terror*] I cant bear it. Wheres the altar? I'll sacrifice.

FERROVIUS. Dog of an apostate. Iscariot!

SPINTHO. I'll repent afterwards. I fully mean to die in the arena: I'll die a martyr and go to heaven; but not this time, not now, not until my nerves are better. Besides, I'm too young: I want to have just one more good time. [*The gladiators laugh at him*]. Oh, will no one tell me where the altar is? [*He dashes into the passage and vanishes*].

ANDROCLES [*to the Editor, pointing after Spintho*] Brother: I cant do that, not even to oblige you. Dont ask me.

THE EDITOR. Well, if youre determined to die, I cant help you. But I wouldnt be put off by a swine like that.

FERROVIUS. Peace, peace: tempt him not. Get thee behind him, Satan.

THE EDITOR [*flushing with rage*] For two pins I'd take a turn in the arena myself today, and pay you out for daring to talk to me like that.

Ferrovius springs forward.

LAVINIA [*rising quickly and interposing*] Brother, brother: you forget.

FERROVIUS [*curbing himself by a mighty effort*] Oh, my temper, my wicked temper! [*To the Editor, as Lavinia sits down again, reassured*] Forgive me, brother. My heart was full of wrath: I should have been thinking of your dear precious soul.

THE EDITOR. Yah! [*He turns his back on Ferrovius contemptuously, and goes back to his seat*].

FERROVIUS [*continuing*] And I forgot it all: I thought of nothing but offering to fight you with one hand tied behind me.

THE EDITOR [*turning pugnaciously*] What!

FERROVIUS [*on the border line between zeal and ferocity*] Oh, dont give way to pride and wrath, brother. I could do it so easily. I could—

[614]

They are separated by the Menagerie Keeper, who rushes in from the passage, furious.

THE KEEPER. Heres a nice business! Who let that Christian out of here down to the dens when we were changing the lion into the cage next the arena?

THE EDITOR. Nobody let him. He let himself.

THE KEEPER. Well, the lion's ate him.

Consternation. The Christians rise, greatly agitated. The gladiators sit callously, but are highly amused. All speak or cry out or laugh at once. Tumult.

LAVINIA. Oh, poor wretch! FERROVIUS. The apostate has perished. Praise be to God's justice! ANDROCLES. The poor beast was starving. It couldnt help itself. THE CHRISTIANS. What! Ate him! How frightful! How terrible! Without a moment to repent! God be merciful to him, a sinner! Oh, I cant bear to think of it! In the midst of his sin! Horrible, horrible! THE EDITOR. Serve the rotter right! THE GLADIATORS. Just walked into it, he did. He's martyred all right enough. Good old lion! Old Jock doesnt like that: look at his face. Devil a better! The Emperor will laugh when he hears of it. I cant help smiling. Ha ha ha!!!!!

THE KEEPER. Now his appetite's taken off, he wont as much as look at another Christian for a week.

ANDROCLES. Couldnt you have saved him, brother?

THE KEEPER. Saved him! Saved him from a lion that I'd just got mad with hunger! a wild one that came out of the forest not four weeks ago! He bolted him before you could say Balbus.

LAVINIA [*sitting down again*] Poor Spintho! And it wont even count as martyrdom!

THE KEEPER. Serve him right! What call had he to walk down the throat of one of my lions before he was asked?

ANDROCLES. Perhaps the lion wont eat me now.

THE KEEPER. Yes: thats just like a Christian: think only of yourself! What am *I* to do? What am I to say to the Emperor when he sees one of my lions coming into the arena half asleep?

THE EDITOR. Say nothing. Give your old lion some bitters and a morsel of fried fish to wake up his appetite. [*Laughter*].

THE KEEPER. Yes: it's easy for you to talk; but—

THE EDITOR [*scrambling to his feet*] Sh! Attention there! The Emperor. [*The Keeper bolts precipitately into the passage. The gladiators rise smartly and form into line*].

The Emperor enters on the Christians' side, conversing with Metellus, and followed by his suite.

THE GLADIATORS. Hail, Caesar! those about to die salute thee.

CAESAR. Good morrow, friends.

Metellus shakes hands with the Editor, who accepts his condescension with bluff respect.

LAVINIA. Blessing, Caesar, and forgiveness!

CAESAR [*turning in some surprise at the salutation*] There is no forgiveness for Christianity.

LAVINIA. I did not mean that, Caesar. I mean that we forgive you.

METELLUS. An inconceivable liberty! Do you not know, woman, that the Emperor can do no wrong and therefore cannot be forgiven?

LAVINIA. I expect the Emperor knows better. Anyhow, we forgive him.

THE CHRISTIANS. Amen!

CAESAR. Metellus: you see now the disadvantage of too much severity. These people have no hope; therefore they have nothing to restrain them from saying what they like to me. They are almost as

impertinent as the gladiators. Which is the Greek
sorcerer?

ANDROCLES [*humbly touching his forelock*] Me, your
Worship.

CAESAR. My Worship! Good! A new title. Well: what
miracles can you perform?

ANDROCLES. I can cure warts by rubbing them with
my tailor's chalk; and I can live with my wife without
beating her.

CAESAR. Is that all?

ANDROCLES. You dont know her, Caesar, or you
wouldnt say that.

CAESAR. Ah, well, my friend, we shall no doubt
contrive a happy release for you. Which is Ferrovius?

FERROVIUS. I am he.

CAESAR. They tell me you can fight.

FERROVIUS. It is easy to fight. *I* can die, Caesar.

CAESAR. That is still easier, is it not?

FERROVIUS. Not to me, Caesar. Death comes hard to
my flesh; and fighting comes very easy to my spirit
[*beating his breast and lamenting*] Oh, sinner that I am!
[*He throws himself down on the steps, deeply discouraged*].

CAESAR. Metellus: I should like to have this man in
the Pretorian Guard.

METELLUS. *I* should not, Caesar. He looks a spoil-
sport. There are men in whose presence it is impossible
to have any fun: men who are a sort of walking
conscience. He would make us all uncomfortable.

CAESAR. For that reason, perhaps, it might be as well
to have him. An Emperor can hardly have too many
consciences. [*To Ferrovius*] Listen, Ferrovius. [*Ferrovius shakes his head and will not look up*]. You and your
friends shall not be outnumbered today in the arena.
You shall have arms; and there will be no more than

one gladiator to each Christian. If you come out of the arena alive, I will consider favorably any request of yours, and give you a place in the Pretorian Guard. Even if the request be that no questions be asked about your faith I shall perhaps not refuse it.

FERROVIUS. I will not fight. I will die. Better stand with the archangels than with the Pretorian Guard.

CAESAR. I cannot believe that the archangels—whoever they may be—would not prefer to be recruited from the Pretorian Guard. However, as you please. Come: let us see the show.

As the Court ascends the steps, Secutor and Retiarius return from the arena through the passage: Secutor covered with dust and very angry: Retiarius grinning.

SECUTOR. Ha, the Emperor. Now we shall see. Caesar: I ask you whether it is fair for the Retiarius, instead of making a fair throw of his net at me, to swish it along the ground and throw the dust in my eyes, and then catch me when I'm blinded. If the vestals had not turned up their thumbs I should have been a dead man.

CAESAR [*halting on the stair*] There is nothing in the rules against it.

SECUTOR [*indignantly*] Caesar: is it a dirty trick or is it not?

CAESAR. It is a dusty one, my friend. [*Obsequious laughter*]. Be on your guard next time.

SECUTOR. Let him be on his guard. Next time I'll throw my sword at his heels and strangle him with his own net before he can hop off. [*To the Retiarius*] You see if I dont. [*He goes out past the gladiators, sulky and furious*].

CAESAR [*to the chuckling Retiarius*] These tricks are not wise, my friend. The audience likes to see a dead man in all his beauty and splendor. If you smudge his face and spoil his armor they will shew their displeasure by not letting you kill him. And when your turn comes, they will remember it against you and turn their thumbs down.

THE RETIARIUS. Perhaps that is why I did it, Caesar. He bet me ten sesterces that he would vanquish me. If I had had to kill him I should not have had the money.

CAESAR [*indulgent, laughing*] You rogues: there is no end to your tricks. I'll dismiss you all and have elephants to fight. They fight fairly. [*He goes up to his box, and knocks at it. It is opened from within by the Captain, who stands as on parade to let him pass*].

The Call Boy comes from the passage, followed by three attendants carrying respectively a bundle of swords, some helmets, and some breastplates and pieces of armor which they throw down in a heap.

THE CALL BOY. By your leave, Caesar. Number eleven! Gladiators and Christians!

Ferrovius springs up, ready for martyrdom. The other Christians take the summons as best they can, some joyful and brave, some patient and dignified, some tearful and helpless, some embracing one another with emotion. The Call Boy goes back into the passage.

CAESAR [*turning at the door of the box*] The hour has come, Ferrovius. I shall go into my box and see you killed, since you scorn the Pretorian Guard. [*He goes into the box. The Captain shuts the door, remaining inside with the Emperor, Metellus and the rest of the suite disperse to their seats. The Christians, led by Ferrovius, move towards the passage*].

LAVINIA [*to Ferrovius*] Farewell.

THE EDITOR. Steady there. You Christians have got to fight. Here! arm yourselves.

FERROVIUS [*picking up a sword*] I'll die sword in hand

to shew people that I could fight if it were my Master's will, and that I could kill the man who kills me if I chose.

THE EDITOR. Put on that armor.

FERROVIUS. No armor.

THE EDITOR [*bullying him*] Do what youre told. Put on that armor.

FERROVIUS [*gripping the sword and looking dangerous*] I said, No armor.

THE EDITOR. And what am I to say when I am accused of sending a naked man in to fight my men in armor?

FERROVIUS. Say your prayers, brother; and have no fear of the princes of this world.

THE EDITOR. Tsha! You obstinate fool! [*He bites his lips irresolutely, not knowing exactly what to do*].

ANDROCLES [*to Ferrovius*] Farewell, brother, till we meet in the sweet by-and-by.

THE EDITOR [*to Androcles*] You are going too. Take a sword there; and put on any armor you can find to fit you.

ANDROCLES. No, really: I cant fight: I never could: I cant bring myself to dislike anyone enough. I'm to be thrown to the lions with the lady.

THE EDITOR. Then get out of the way and hold your noise. [*Androcles steps aside with cheerful docility*]. Now then! Are you all ready there?

A trumpet is heard from the arena.

FERROVIUS [*starting convulsively*] Heaven give me strength!

THE EDITOR. Aha! That frightens you, does it?

FERROVIUS. Man: there is no terror like the terror of that sound to me. When I hear a trumpet or a drum or the clash of steel or the hum of the catapult as the great stone flies, fire runs through my veins: I feel my blood surge up hot behind my eyes: I must charge: I must strike: I must conquer: Caesar himself will not be safe in his imperial seat if once that spirit gets loose in me. Oh, brothers, pray! exhort me! remind me that if I raise my sword my honor falls and my Master is crucified afresh.

ANDROCLES. Just keep thinking how cruelly you might hurt the poor gladiators.

FERROVIUS. It does not hurt a man to kill him.

LAVINIA. Nothing but faith can save you.

FERROVIUS. Faith! Which faith? There are two faiths. There is our faith. And there is the warrior's faith, the faith in fighting, the faith that sees God in the sword. How if that faith should overwhelm me?

LAVINIA. You will find your real faith in the hour of trial.

FERROVIUS. That is what I fear. I know that I am a fighter. How can I feel sure that I am a Christian?

ANDROCLES. Throw away the sword, brother.

FERROVIUS. I cannot. It cleaves to my hand. I could as easily throw a woman I loved from my arms. [*Starting*] Who spoke that blasphemy? Not I.

LAVINIA. I cant help you, friend. I cant tell you not to save your own life. Something wilful in me wants to see you fight your way into heaven.

FERROVIUS. Ha!

ANDROCLES. But if you are going to give up our faith, brother, why not do it without hurting anybody? Dont fight them. Burn the incense.

FERROVIUS. Burn the incense! Never.

LAVINIA. That is only pride, Ferrovius.

FERROVIUS. Only pride! What is nobler than pride? [*Conscience stricken*] Oh, I'm steeped in sin. I'm proud of my pride.

LAVINIA. They say we Christians are the proudest

devils on earth—that only the weak are meek. Oh, I am worse than you. I ought to send you to death; and I am tempting you.

ANDROCLES. Brother, brother: let them rage and kill: let us be brave and suffer. You must go as a lamb to the slaughter.

FERROVIUS. Aye, aye: that is right. Not as a lamb is slain by the butcher; but as a butcher might let himself be slain by a [*looking at the Editor*] by a silly ram whose head he could fetch off in one twist.

Before the Editor can retort, the Call Boy rushes up through the passage, and the Captain comes from the Emperor's box and descends the steps.

THE CALL BOY. In with you: into the arena. The stage is waiting.

THE CAPTAIN. The Emperor is waiting. [*To the Editor*] What are you dreaming of, man? Send your men in at once.

THE EDITOR. Yes, sir: it's these Christians hanging back.

FERROVIUS [*in a voice of thunder*] Liar!

THE EDITOR [*not heeding him*] March. [*The gladiators told off to fight with the Christians march down the passage*] Follow up there, you.

THE CHRISTIAN MEN AND WOMEN [*as they part*] Be steadfast, brother. Farewell. Hold up the faith, brother. Farewell. Go to glory, dearest. Farewell. Remember: we are praying for you. Farewell. Be strong, brother. Farewell. Dont forget that the divine love and our love surround you. Farewell. Nothing can hurt you: remember that, brother. Farewell. Eternal glory, dearest. Farewell.

THE EDITOR [*out of patience*] Shove them in, there.

The remaining gladiators and the Call Boy make a movement towards them.

FERROVIUS [*interposing*] Touch them, dogs; and we die here, and cheat the heathen of their spectacle. [*To his fellow Christians*] Brothers: the great moment has come. That passage is your hill to Calvary. Mount it bravely, but meekly; and remember! not a word of reproach, not a blow nor a struggle. Go. [*They go out through the passage. He turns to Lavinia*] Farewell.

LAVINIA. You forget: I must follow before you are cold.

FERROVIUS. It is true. Do not envy me because I pass before you to glory. [*He goes through the passage*].

THE EDITOR [*to the Call Boy*] Sickening work, this. Why cant they all be thrown to the lions? It's not a man's job. [*He throws himself moodily into his chair*].

The remaining gladiators go back to their former places indifferently. The Call Boy shrugs his shoulders and squats down at the entrance to the passage, near the Editor.

Lavinia and the Christian women sit down again, wrung with grief, some weeping silently, some praying, some calm and steadfast. Androcles sits down at Lavinia's feet. The Captain stands on the stairs, watching her curiously.

ANDROCLES. I'm glad I havnt to fight. That would really be an awful martyrdom. I am lucky.

LAVINIA [*looking at him with a pang of remorse*] Androcles: burn the incense: youll be forgiven. Let my death atone for both. I feel as if I were killing you.

ANDROCLES. Dont think of me, sister. Think of yourself. That will keep your heart up.

The Captain laughs sardonically.

LAVINIA [*startled: she had forgotten his presence*] Are you there, handsome Captain? Have you come to see me die?

THE CAPTAIN [*coming to her side*] I am on duty with the Emperor, Lavinia.

[623]

LAVINIA. Is it part of your duty to laugh at us?

THE CAPTAIN. No: that is part of my private pleasure. Your friend here is a humorist. I laughed at his telling you to think of yourself to keep up your heart. *I* say, think of yourself and burn the incense.

LAVINIA. He is not a humorist: he was right. You ought to know that, Captain: you have been face to face with death.

THE CAPTAIN. Not with certain death, Lavinia. Only death in battle, which spares more men than death in bed. What you are facing is certain death. You have nothing left now but your faith in this craze of yours: this Christianity. Are your Christian fairy stories any truer than our stories about Jupiter and Diana, in which, I may tell you, I believe no more than the Emperor does, or any educated man in Rome?

LAVINIA. Captain: all that seems nothing to me now. I'll not say that death is a terrible thing; but I will say that it is so real a thing that when it comes close, all the imaginary things—all the stories, as you call them— fade into mere dreams beside that inexorable reality. I know now that I am not dying for stories or dreams. Did you hear of the dreadful thing that happened here while we were waiting?

THE CAPTAIN. I heard that one of your fellows bolted, and ran right into the jaws of the lion. I laughed. I still laugh.

LAVINIA. Then you dont understand what that meant?

THE CAPTAIN. It meant that the lion had a cur for his breakfast.

LAVINIA. It meant more than that, Captain. It meant that a man cannot die for a story and a dream. None of us believed the stories and the dreams more

[624]

devoutly than poor Spintho; but he could not face the great reality. What he would have called my faith has been oozing away minute by minute whilst Ive been sitting here, with death coming nearer and nearer, with reality becoming realler and realler, with stories and dreams fading away into nothing.

THE CAPTAIN. Are you then going to die for nothing?

LAVINIA. Yes: that is the wonderful thing. It is since all the stories and dreams have gone that I have now no doubt at all that I must die for something greater than dreams or stories.

THE CAPTAIN. But for what?

LAVINIA. I dont know. If it were for anything small enough to know, it would be too small to die for. I think I'm going to die for God. Nothing else is real enough to die for.

THE CAPTAIN. What is God?

LAVINIA. When we know that, Captain, we shall be gods ourselves.

THE CAPTAIN. Lavinia: come down to earth. Burn the incense and marry me.

LAVINIA. Handsome Captain: would you marry me if I hauled down the flag in the day of battle and burnt the incense? Sons take after their mothers, you know. Do you want your son to be a coward?

THE CAPTAIN [*strongly moved*] By great Diana, I think I would strangle you if you gave in now.

LAVINIA [*putting her hand on the head of Androcles*] The hand of God is on us three, Captain.

THE CAPTAIN. What nonsense it all is! And what a monstrous thing that you should die for such nonsense, and that I should look on helplessly when my whole soul cries out against it! Die then if you must; but at least I can cut the Emperor's throat and then my own when I see your blood.

The Emperor throws open the door of his box angrily, and appears in wrath on the threshold. The Editor, the Call Boy, and the gladiators spring to their feet.

THE EMPEROR. The Christians will not fight; and your curs cannot get their blood up to attack them. It's all that fellow with the blazing eyes. Send for the whip. [*The Call Boy rushes out on the east side for the whip*]. If that will not move them, bring the hot irons. The man is like a mountain. [*He returns angrily into the box and slams the door*].

The Call Boy returns with a man in a hideous Etruscan mask, carrying a whip. They both rush down the passage into the arena.

LAVINIA [*rising*] Oh, that is unworthy. Can they not kill him without dishonoring him?

ANDROCLES [*scrambling to his feet and running into the middle of the space between the staircases*] It's dreadful. Now *I* want to fight. I cant bear the sight of a whip. The only time I ever hit a man was when he lashed an old horse with a whip. It was terrible: I danced on his face when he was on the ground. He mustnt strike Ferrovius: I'll go into the arena and kill him first. [*He makes a wild dash into the passage. As he does so a great clamor is heard from the arena, ending in wild applause. The gladiators listen and look inquiringly at one another*].

EDITOR. Whats up now?

LAVINIA [*to the Captain*] What has happened, do you think?

THE CAPTAIN. What can happen? They are killing them, I suppose.

ANDROCLES [*running in through the passage, screaming with horror and hiding his eyes*]!!!

LAVINIA. Androcles, Androcles: whats the matter?

ANDROCLES. Oh dont ask me, dont ask me. Something too dreadful. Oh! [*He crouches by her and hides his face in her robe, sobbing*].

THE CALL BOY [*rushing through from the passage as before*] Ropes and hooks there! Ropes and hooks!

THE EDITOR. Well, need you excite yourself about it? [*Another burst of applause*].

Two slaves in Etruscan masks, with ropes and drag hooks, hurry in.

ONE OF THE SLAVES. How many dead?

THE CALL BOY. Six. [*The slave blows a whistle twice; and four more masked slaves rush through into the arena with the same apparatus*] And the basket. Bring the baskets [*The slave whistles three times, and runs through the passage with his companion*].

THE CAPTAIN. Who are the baskets for?

THE CALL BOY. For the whip. He's in pieces. Theyre all in pieces, more or less. [*Lavinia hides her face*].

Two more masked slaves come in with a basket and follow the others into the arena, as the Call Boy turns to the gladiators and exclaims, exhausted] Boys: he's killed the lot.

THE EMPEROR [*again bursting from his box, this time in an ecstasy of delight*] Where is he? Magnificent! He shall have a laurel crown.

Ferrovius, madly waving his bloodstained sword, rushes through the passage in despair, followed by his co-religionists, and by the menagerie keeper, who goes to the gladiators. The gladiators draw their swords nervously].

FERROVIUS. Lost! lost for ever! I have betrayed my Master. Cut off this right hand: it has offended. Ye have swords, my brethren: strike.

LAVINIA. No, no. What have you done, Ferrovius?

FERROVIUS. I know not; but there was blood behind my eyes; and theres blood on my sword. What does that mean?

THE EMPEROR [*enthusiastically, on the landing outside his box*] What does it mean ? It means that you are the greatest man in Rome. It means that you shall have a laurel crown of gold. Superb fighter: I could almost yield you my throne. It is a record for my reign: I shall live in history. Once, in Domitian's time, a Gaul slew three men in the arena and gained his freedom. But when before has one naked man slain six armed men of the bravest and best ? The persecution shall cease: if Christians can fight like this, I shall have none but Christians to fight for me. [*To the Gladiators*] You are ordered to become Christians, you there: do you hear ?

RETIARIUS. It is all one to us, Caesar. Had I been there with my net, the story would have been different.

THE CAPTAIN [*suddenly seizing Lavinia by the wrist and dragging her up the steps to the Emperor*] Caesar: this woman is the sister of Ferrovius. If she is thrown to the lions he will fret. He will lose weight; get out of condition—

THE EMPEROR. The lions ? Nonsense! [*To Lavinia*] Madam: I am proud to have the honour of making your acquaintance. Your brother is the glory of Rome.

LAVINIA. But my friends here. Must they die ?

THE EMPEROR. Die! Certainly not. There has never been the slightest idea of harming them. Ladies and gentlemen: you are all free. Pray go into the front of the house and enjoy the spectacle to which your brother has so splendidly contributed. Captain: oblige me by conducting them to the seats reserved for my personal friends.

THE MENAGERIE KEEPER. Caesar: I must have one Christian for the lion. The people have been promised it; and they will tear the decorations to bits if they are disappointed.

THE EMPEROR. True, true: we must have somebody for the new lion.

FERROVIUS. Throw me to him. Let the apostate perish.

THE EMPEROR. No, no: you would tear him in pieces, my friend; and we cannot afford to throw away lions as if they were mere slaves. But we must have somebody. This is really extremely awkward.

THE MENAGERIE KEEPER. Why not that little Greek chap? He's not a Christian: he's a sorcerer.

THE EMPEROR. The very thing: he will do very well.

THE CALL BOY [*issuing from the passage*] Number twelve. The Christian for the new lion.

ANDROCLES [*rising, and pulling himself sadly together*] Well, it was to be, after all.

LAVINIA. I'll go in his place, Caesar. Ask the Captain whether they do not like best to see a woman torn to pieces. He told me so yesterday.

THE EMPEROR. There is something in that: there is certainly something in that—if only I could feel sure that your brother would not fret.

ANDROCLES. No: I should never have another happy hour. No: on the faith of a Christian and the honor of a tailor, I accept the lot that has fallen on me. If my wife turns up, give her my love and say that my wish was that she should be happy with her next, poor fellow! Caesar: go to your box and see how a tailor can die. Make way for number twelve there. [*He marches out along the passage*].

The vast audience in the amphitheatre now sees the Emperor re-enter his box and take his place as Androcles, desperately frightened, but still marching with piteous devotion, emerges from the other end of the passage, and finds himself at the focus of thousands of eager eyes. The lion's cage, with a heavy portcullis grating, is on his

left. *The Emperor gives a signal. A gong sounds. Androcles shivers at the sound; then falls on his knees and
prays. The grating rises with a clash. The lion bounds
into the arena. He rushes round frisking in his freedom.
He sees Androcles. He stops; rises stiffly by straightening
his legs; stretches out his nose forward and his tail in a
horizontal line behind, like a pointer, and utters an
appalling roar. Androcles crouches and hides his face in
his hands. The lion gathers himself for a spring, swishing
his tail to and fro through the dust in an ecstasy of
anticipation. Androcles throws up his hands in suppli-
cation to heaven. The lion checks at the sight of Androcles's face. He then steals towards him; smells him; arches
his back; purrs like a motor car; finally rubs himself
against Androcles, knocking him over. Androcles,
supporting himself on his wrist, looks affrightedly at the
lion. The lion limps on three paws, holding up the other
as if it was wounded. A flash of recognition lights up the
face of Androcles. He flaps his hand as if it had a
thorn in it, and pretends to pull the thorn out and to
hurt himself. The lion nods repeatedly. Androcles holds
out his hands to the lion, who gives him both paws,
which he shakes with enthusiasm. They embrace
rapturously, finally waltz round the arena amid a
sudden burst of deafening applause, and out through the
passage, the Emperor watching them in breathless
astonishment until they disappear, when he rushes from
his box and descends the steps in frantic excitement.*

THE EMPEROR. My friends, an incredible! an amazing
thing! has happened. I can no longer doubt the truth
of Christianity. [*The Christians press to him joyfully*].
This Christian sorcerer—[*with a yell, he breaks off
as he sees Androcles and the lion emerge from the passage,
waltzing. He bolts wildly up the steps into his box, and
slams the door. All, Christians and gladiators alike, fly*

for their lives, the gladiators bolting into the arena, the others in all directions. The place is emptied with magical suddenness].

ANDROCLES [*naïvely*] Now I wonder why they all run away from us like that. [*The lion, combining a series of yawns, purrs, and roars, achieves something very like a laugh*].

THE EMPEROR [*standing on a chair inside his box and looking over the wall*] Sorcerer: I command you to put that lion to death instantly. It is guilty of high treason. Your conduct is most disgra—[*the lion charges at him up the stairs*] help! [*He disappears. The lion rears against the box; looks over the partition at him; and roars. The Emperor darts out through the door and down to Androcles, pursued by the lion*].

ANDROCLES. Dont run away, sir; he cant help springing if you run [*He seizes the Emperor and gets between him and the lion, who stops at once*]. Dont be afraid of him.

THE EMPEROR. I am not afraid of him. [*The lion crouches, growling. The Emperor clutches Androcles*]. Keep between us.

ANDROCLES. Never be afraid of animals, your worship: thats the great secret. He'll be as gentle as a lamb when he knows that you are his friend. Stand quite still; and smile; and let him smell you all over just to reassure him; for, you see, he's afraid of you; and he must examine you thoroughly before he gives you his confidence. [*To the lion*] Come now, Tommy; and speak nicely to the Emperor, the great good Emperor who has power to have all our heads cut off if we dont behave very very respectfully to him.

The lion utters a fearful roar. The Emperor dashes madly up the steps, across the landing, and down again on the other side, with the lion in hot pursuit. Androcles

*rushes after the lion; overtakes him as he is descending;
and throws himself on his back, trying to use his toes as a
brake. Before he can stop him the lion gets hold of the
trailing end of the Emperor's robe.*

ANDROCLES. Oh bad wicked Tommy, to chase the
Emperor like that! Let go the Emperor's robe at once,
sir: wheres your manners? [*The lion growls and worries
the robe*]. Dont pull it away from him, your worship.
He's only playing. Now I shall be really angry with
you, Tommy, if you dont let go. [*The lion growls
again*]. I'll tell you what it is, sir: he thinks you and I
are not friends.

THE EMPEROR [*trying to undo the clasp of his brooch*]
Friends! You infernal scoundrel [*the lion growls*]—
dont let him go. Curse this brooch! I cant get it loose.

ANDROCLES. We musnt let him lash himself into a
rage. You must shew him that you are my particular
friend—if you will have the condescension. [*He
seizes the Emperor's hands and shakes them cordially*].
Look, Tommy: the nice Emperor is the dearest
friend Andy Wandy has in the whole world: he loves
him like a brother.

THE EMPEROR. You little brute, you damned filthy
little dog of a Greek tailor: I'll have you burnt alive
for daring to touch the divine person of the Emperor.
[*The lion growls*].

ANDROCLES. Oh dont talk like that, sir. He understands every word you say: all animals do: they take
it from the tone of your voice. [*The lion growls and
lashes his tail*]. I think he's going to spring at your
worship. If you wouldnt mind saying something
affectionate. [*The lion roars*].

THE EMPEROR [*shaking Androcles's hand frantically*]
My dearest Mr Androcles, my sweetest friend, my
long lost brother, come to my arms. [*He embraces*

[632]

Androcles]. Oh, what an abominable smell of garlic!

The lion lets go the robe and rolls over on his back, clasping his forepaws over one another coquettishly above his nose.

ANDROCLES. There! You see, your worship, a child might play with him now. See! [*He tickles the lion's belly. The lion wriggles ecstatically*]. Come and pet him.

THE EMPEROR. I must conquer these unkingly terrors. Mind you dont go away from him, though. [*He pats the lion's chest*].

ANDROCLES. Oh, sir, how few men would have the courage to do that!

THE EMPEROR. Yes: it takes a bit of nerve. Let us have the Court in and frighten them. Is he safe, do you think?

ANDROCLES. Quite safe now, sir.

THE EMPEROR [*majestically*] What ho, there! All who are within hearing, return without fear. Caesar has tamed the lion. [*All the fugitives steal cautiously in. The menagerie keeper comes from the passage with other keepers armed with iron bars and tridents*]. Take those things away. I have subdued the beast. [*He places his foot on it*].

FERROVIUS [*timidly approaching the Emperor and looking down with awe on the lion*] It is strange that I, who fear no man, should fear a lion.

THE CAPTAIN. Every man fears something, Ferrovius.

THE EMPEROR. How about the Pretorian Guard now?

FERROVIUS. In my youth I worshipped Mars, the God of War. I turned from him to serve the Christian god; but today the Christian god forsook me; and Mars overcame me and took back his own. The Christian god is not yet. He will come when Mars and I are dust; but meanwhile I must serve the gods that are, not the God that will be. Until then I accept service in the Guard, Caesar.

THE EMPEROR. Very wisely said. All really sensible men agree that the prudent course is to be neither bigoted in our attachment to the old nor rash and unpractical in keeping an open mind for the new, but to make the best of both dispensations.

THE CAPTAIN. What do you say, Lavinia ? Will you too be prudent ?

LAVINIA [on the stairs] No: I'll strive for the coming of the God who is not yet.

THE CAPTAIN. May I come and argue with you occasionally ?

LAVINIA. Yes, handsome Captain: you may. [He kisses her hand].

THE EMPEROR. And now, my friends, though I do not, as you see, fear this lion, yet the strain of his presence is considerable; for none of us can feel quite sure what he will do next.

THE MENAGERIE KEEPER. Caesar: give us this Greek sorcerer to be a slave in the menagerie. He has a way with the beasts.

ANDROCLES [distressed] Not if they are in cages. They should not be kept in cages. They must be all let out.

THE EMPEROR. I give this sorcerer to be a slave to the first man who lays lands on him. [The menagerie keepers and the gladiators rush for Androcles. The lion starts up and faces them. They surge back]. You see how magnanimous we Romans are, Androcles. We suffer you to go in peace.

ANDROCLES. I thank your worship. I thank you all, ladies and gentlemen. Come, Tommy. Whilst we stand together, no cage for you: no slavery for me. [He goes out with the lion, everybody crowding away to give him as wide a berth as possible].

*   *   *   *

In this play I have presented one of the Roman persecutions of the early Christians, not as the conflict of a false theology with a true, but as what all such persecutions essentially are: an attempt to suppress a propaganda that seemed to threaten the interests involved in the established law and order, organized and maintained in the name of religion and justice by politicians who are pure opportunist Have-and-Holders. People who are shewn by their inner light the possibility of a better world based on the demand of the spirit for a nobler and more abundant life, not for themselves at the expense of others, but for everybody, are naturally dreaded and therefore hated by the Have-and-Holders, who keep always in reserve two sure weapons against them. The first is a persecution effected by the provocation, organization, and arming of that herd instinct which makes men abhor all departures from custom, and, by the most cruel punishments and the wildest calumnies, force eccentric people to behave and profess exactly as other people do. The second is by leading the herd to war, which immediately and infallibly makes them forget everything, even their most cherished and hardwon public liberties and private interests, in the irresistible surge of their pugnacity and the tense preoccupation of their terror.

There is no reason to believe that there was anything more in the Roman persecutions than this. The attitude of the Roman Emperor and the officers of his staff toward the opinions at issue were much the same as those of a modern British Home Secretary towards members of the lower middle classes when some pious policeman charges them with Bad Taste, technically called blasphemy: Bad Taste being a violation of Good Taste, which in such matters

practically means Hypocrisy. The Home Secretary and
the judges who try the case are usually far more
sceptical and blasphemous than the poor men whom
they persecute; and their professions of horror at the
blunt utterance of their own opinions are revolting to
those behind the scenes who have any genuine
religious sensibility; but the thing is done because the
governing classes, provided only the law against
blasphemy is not applied to themselves, strongly
approve of such persecution because it enables them
to represent their own privileges as part of the religion
of the country.

Therefore my martyrs are the martyrs of all time,
and my persecutors the persecutors of all time. My
Emperor, who has no sense of the value of common
people's lives, and amuses himself with killing as
carelessly as with sparing, is the sort of monster you
can make of any silly-clever-gentleman by idolizing
him. We are still so easily imposed on by such idols
that one of the leading pastors of the Free Churches in
London denounced my play on the ground that my
persecuting Emperor is a very fine fellow, and the
persecuted Christians ridiculous. From which I
conclude that a popular pulpit may be as perilous to a
man's soul as an imperial throne.

All my articulate Christians, the reader will notice,
have different enthusiasms, which they accept as the
same religion only because it involves them in a
common opposition to the official religion and consequently in a common doom. Androcles is a human-
itarian naturalist, whose views surprise everybody.
Lavinia, a clever and fearless freethinker, shocks the
Pauline Ferrovius, who is comparatively stupid and
conscience ridden. Spintho, the blackguardly debauchee, is presented as one of the typical Christians
of that period on the authority of St Augustine, who

seems to have come to the conclusion at one period of his development that most Christians were what we call wrong uns. No doubt he was to some extent right: I have had occasion often to point out that revolutionary movements attract those who are not good enough for established institutions as well as those who are too good for them.

But the most striking aspect of the play at this moment is the terrible topicality given it by the war. We were at peace when I pointed out, by the mouth of Ferrovius, the path of an honest man who finds out, when the trumpet sounds, that he cannot follow Jesus. Many years earlier, in the Devil's Disciple, I touched the same theme even more definitely, and shewed the minister throwing off his black coat for ever when he discovered, amid the thunder of the captains and the shouting, that he was a born fighter. Great numbers of our clergy have found themselves of late in the position of Ferrovius and Anthony Anderson. They have discovered that they hate not only their enemies but everyone who does not share their hatred, and that they want to fight and to force other people to fight. They have turned their churches into recruiting stations and their vestries into munition workshops. But it has never occurred to them to take off their black coats and say quite simply, "I find in the hour of trial that the Sermon on the Mount is tosh, and that I am not a Christian. I apologize for all the unpatriotic nonsense I have been preaching all these years. Have the goodness to give me a revolver and a commission in a regiment which has for its chaplain a priest of the god Mars: *my* God." Not a bit of it. They have stuck to their livings and served Mars in the name of Christ, to the scandal of all religious mankind. When the Archbishop of York behaved like a gentleman and the Head Master of Eton preached a Christian sermon, and were reviled by the rabble, the Martian parsons encouraged the rabble. For this they made no apologies or excuses, good or bad. They simply indulged their passions, just as they had always indulged their class prejudices and commercial interests, without troubling themselves for a moment as to whether they were Christians or not. They did not protest even when a body calling itself the Anti-German League (not having noticed, apparently, that it had been anticipated by the British Empire, the French Republic, and the Kingdoms of Italy, Japan, and Serbia) actually succeeded in closing a church at Forest Hill in which God was worshipped in the German language. One would have supposed that this grotesque outrage on the commonest decencies of even religion would have provoked a remonstrance from the worldliest bench of bishops. But no: apparently it seemed to the bishops as natural that the House of God should be looted when He allowed German to be spoken in it as that a baker's shop with a German name over the door should be pillaged. Their verdict was, in effect, "Serve God right, for creating the Germans!" The incident would have been impossible in a country where the Church was as powerful as the Church of England, had it had at the same time a spark of catholic as distinguished from tribal religion in it. As it is, the thing occurred; and as far as I have observed, the only people who gasped were the Freethinkers.

Thus we see that even among men who make a profession of religion the great majority are as Martian as the majority of their congregations. The average clergyman is an official who makes his living by christening babies, marrying adults, conducting a ritual, and making the best he can (when he has any conscience about it) of a certain routine of school superintendence, district visiting, and organization of almsgiving, which does not necessarily touch Christianity at any point except the point of the tongue. The exceptional or religious clergyman may be an ardent Pauline salvationist, in which case his more cultivated parishioners dislike him, and say that he ought to have joined the Methodists. Or he may be an artist expressing religious emotion without intellectual definition by means of poetry, music, vestments, and architecture, also producing religious ecstasy by physical expedients, such as fasts and vigils, in which case he is denounced as a Ritualist. Or he may be either a Unitarian Deist like Voltaire or Tom Paine, or the more modern sort of Anglican Theosophist to whom the Holy Ghost is the Élan Vital of Bergson, and the Father and Son are an expression of the fact that our functions and aspects are manifold, and that we are all sons and all either potential or actual parents, in which case he is strongly suspected by the straiter Salvationists of being little better than an Atheist. All these varieties, you see, excite remark. They may be very popular with their congregations; but they are regarded by the average man as the freaks of the Church. The Church, like the society of which it is an organ, is balanced and steadied by the great central Philistine mass above whom theology looms as a highly spoken of and doubtless most important thing, like Greek Tragedy, or classical music, or the higher mathematics, but who are very glad when church is over and they can go home to lunch or dinner, having in fact, for all practical purposes, no reasoned convictions at all, and being equally ready to persecute a poor Freethinker for saying that St James was not infallible, and to send one of the

Peculiar People to prison for being so very peculiar as
to take St James seriously.

In short, a Christian martyr was thrown to the
lions not because he was a Christian, but because he
was a crank: that is, an unusual sort of person. And
multitudes of people, quite as civilized and amiable as
we, crowded to see the lions eat him just as they now
crowd the lion-house in the Zoo at feeding-time, not
because they really cared twopence about Diana or
Christ, or could have given you any intelligent or
correct account of the things Diana and Christ stood
against one another for, but simply because they
wanted to see a curious and exciting spectacle. You,
dear reader, have probably run to see a fire; and if
somebody came in now and told you that a lion was
chasing a man down the street you would rush to the
window. And if anyone were to say that you were as
cruel as the people who let the lion loose on the man,
you would be justly indignant. Now that we may no
longer see a man hanged, we assemble outside the jail
to see the black flag run up. That is our duller method
of enjoying ourselves in the old Roman spirit. And if
the Government decided to throw persons of unpopular or eccentric views to the lions in the Albert
Hall or the Earl's Court stadium tomorrow, can you
doubt that all the seats would be crammed, mostly by
people who could not give you the most superficial
account of the views in question. Much less unlikely
things have happened. It is true that if such a revival
does take place soon, the martyrs will not be members
of heretical religious sects: they will be Peculiars,
Anti-Vivisectionists, Flat-Earth men, scoffers at the
laboratories, or infidels who refuse to kneel down when
a procession of doctors goes by. But the lions will hurt
them just as much, and the spectators will enjoy

themselves just as much, as the Roman lions and
spectators used to do.

It was currently reported in the Berlin newspapers
that when Androcles was first performed in Berlin,
the Crown Prince rose and left the house, unable to
endure the (I hope) very clear and fair exposition of
autocratic Imperialism given by the Roman captain
to his Christian prisoners. No English Imperialist was
intelligent and earnest enough to do the same in
London. If the report is correct, I confirm the logic
of the Crown Prince, and am glad to find myself so
well understood. But I can assure him that the
Empire which served for my model when I wrote
Androcles was, as he is now finding to his cost, much
nearer my home than the German one.

"G.B.S." on Laughing Audiences

("Special Interview," drafted by Shaw,
Pall Mall Gazette, London, 2 September 1913)

Mr. Bernard Shaw, interviewed this afternoon on the subject of the reception of his play at the St James's Theatre, was, for so urbane an author, almost out of temper.

"Will you be good enough," he began, with savage concentration, "to ask the editor of the 'Pall Mall Gazette,' and any other editor whom you may chance to meet on your way back, to stop criticising my plays, and to begin criticising my audiences?

"I am too old to alter my ways even if I wanted to, or if anybody else wanted me to. But audiences can be educated; and they need it.

"Last night the performance began at seven o'clock for the convenience of an ungrateful Press. It could, and should, have ended before twenty minutes to ten. But what actually happened? 'Androcles and the Lion,' timed at rehearsal to occupy seventy minutes, lasted ninety-five.

"How do you account for that extra twenty-five minutes? It was occupied, not by my play, but by a senseless, incontinent, indecent, irritating, ill-mannered, maddening, guffawing and brawling that all but ruined a carefully prepared performance, and sent the audience out of the theatre too worried and demoralised to know that they had themselves to thank for a rowdy evening.

DISGUSTING NOISES

"I ask you how are actors to act? How is a play to have any sense or continuity or rhythm or illusion or

[642]

charm when at the end of every speech, and sometimes three or four times in the course of it, the performer has to stop and wait until the spectators express their appreciation and amusement by making disgusting noises?

"Is it any wonder that the play ceases to be a play, and becomes a Christy Minstrel entertainment, with Bones and Mistah Johnson uttering inconsecutive pleasantries, encouraged by roars of laughter?

"You are going to tell me that people must laugh—that laughter is wholesome and healthy; that people go to the theatre to laugh. You might as well tell me that people must spit; that they must blow their noses; that they must yell when they are excited, and use foul language when they are annoyed. Rubbish!

"People can sit for two hours at a stretch at one of the acts of Wagner's Ring without making a sound loud enough to spoil that silence which is the first condition of real attention on the part of an audience and of complete absorption in the play on the part of the performers.

"In my box at the St James's there were, besides myself, four persons; a famous actress, a well-known surgeon, a young American lady, and a young painter. They were all exceptionally susceptible to dramatic impressions, all much more amused and interested than the brawlers were. Yet they did not make a sound from beginning to end that disturbed either the performers or their neighbours.

"After the play I was congratulated on the noise, which was called the success. The producer was congratulated on it. He accepted the congratulations and informed me privately that if his noisy countrymen would guarantee him a pension of thirty shillings a week he would never enter a theatre again.

A HINT TO BRAWLERS

"I made an attempt to stop this nuisance good-humouredly when it almost ruined the last Kingsway production of 'John Bull's Other Island.' Now I drop the mask of good humour, and beg you to convey my sentiments to the brawlers and guffawers in the most offensive terms your pen can compass, and to beg them to exercise their lungs and seek healthy exercise on Hampstead Heath on Bank holidays, and leave my plays unmolested.

"I have done my best to improve their minds and their manners, only to find that they have neither minds nor manners to improve.

"My one ambition now is to see my plays acted to empty houses. In them there may be no money; but at least there is silence and better acting than the public will ever see until it can admire actors without interrupting them.

DRASTIC WAY WITH AUDIENCES

"I hope you have got all that down. Don't soften it, if you please. Make it as much worse as you can: my patience is exhausted. I should like to finish the run of Androcles by throwing the audience to a real lion—not to Mr. Sillward. Then I could say, with Hamlet, 'the rest is silence.' And silence would be such a rest! Ask for that all over your paper, silence, silence, silence, silence.

"Yes, I mean dead silence. Absolute silence from the rise of the curtain to its fall. You will never get a decent theatre until you get that. I tell you that—I, the man whose plays are dying of too much applause.

"Why do the depressing plays flourish and the lively plays perish? Because the depressing plays are listened to in silence. They get a chance. The others are brawled down, laughed down, murdered with noise.

"I have only one message to the British playgoer, and that is: If you want to enjoy yourself in the theatre, hold your silly noise.

"I do not express myself strongly enough; but you gather my meaning, perhaps. Good morning."

Androcles: How Divines Differ About Shaw

(A letter to the Editor of the *Daily News*, London, 29 September 1913)

Sir,—Wandering in the Cevennes, I come upon a column in "The Daily News" headed as above, containing an utterance by the Rev. Morgan Gibbon, of Stamford Hill Congregational Church, which rather interests me in his state of mind. He is represented by an interviewer as saying (and therefore probably said exactly the reverse) that he emphatically controverts the moral of my Androcles fable, because it ends, like "Major Barbara," in the defeat of Christianity by the man of blood and iron, or, as they put it at the St. James's Theatre, in the defeat of the Christian god by Mars.

Here the interviewer conceives Mr. Morgan Gibbon as demanding, because he is a Christian, that every play shall end with the triumph of Christianity over all its adversaries, without regard to the facts of life. I can imagine Mr. Morgan Gibbon's feelings at finding himself accused of such folly in a newspaper largely read by his congregation; and I, for one, shall refuse to believe that he said anything of the kind until he is removed from his pulpit to an asylum. Indeed, the whole context confirms my incredulity: your interviewer has evidently made the most frightful bosh of an attempt to convey to him the feeling of a Christian minister on the very interesting subject of the success of Christianity.

I should very much like to have Mr. Morgan Gibbon's views from himself in his own words. When I travel about Europe and see Germany studded with colossal images of the Man of Blood and Iron, the latest being also the hugest, and the most irresistibly suggestive of Dagon and Moloch; when I read the recent history of the triumphs of Mars in Tripoli, in Morocco, and the Balkan States; when I see compulsory military service rapidly becoming universal and Mars achieving the miracles of the submarine and the aeroplane in a few years, whilst Christ cannot in as many centuries get rid even of such a blazing abomination as the mixed general workhouse, I really cannot see how any sane man can allege that Christianity has gained an inch since the Crucifixion. If you dramatise the world movement as a struggle between Christ and Mars, Christ is down and out, despised and rejected of men, spat upon, nailed up, laughed to scorn, not even allowed the right not to be kicked when He is down. He is not allowed to say to Mars—though it is true—"Kick away, my friend, crucify me, spit on me, hammer your nails in, laugh at me with what side of your mouth you can, you must nevertheless allow me to point out, first, that you cannot kill me, and, second, that no mess could possibly be worse than the mess you are making of the world."

Now I am not going to say—because I do not know—whether this state of things is desirable or undesirable. Nobody who is not in the literal and Scriptural senses of the two words a damned fool can possibly see Androcles and mistake the direction of my sympathies; but my sympathies may be diseased and sentimental and cowardly. Most men who take the blood and iron pose would say so. But of one thing I am absolutely certain; and that is that nothing but mischief can be done by pretending that Mars and Mercury, Militarism and Commerce, are Christianity, or that the ladies and gentlemen who sit under Mr. Morgan Gibbon in Stamford Hill are Christians living in a Christian country. The simple fact that they are not in prison proves that they are not Christians; and it would be an enormous gain to intellectual clearness and honesty of soul if they would say so. Ferrovius in my play is an honest man. When he finds that when it comes to the point he glories in war, and is proud of his pride, he recognises that his real faith consists in the assumptions on which he acts, and not in the words he repeats when nothing is happening to him. If he had been an Englishman he would have said that the Lord is a Man of War, who came not to send peace on earth, but a sword. And he would have knocked down anyone who said he was not a Christian, or refused to cheer Lord Roberts.

I hope Mr. Morgan Gibbon does not think that I sneer at sacred things or at anything or anybody. A sneer is as unbecoming to the human soul as to the human countenance; and ever since I read as a child in "Pickwick" that Mr. Pickwick tried to sneer for the first time in his life and signally failed, I have understood that no gentleman ever sneers. When I think a thing ridiculous I make fun of it. When I despise it I insult it in the most unmistakably direct terms. I know that the "Globe" newspaper thinks that a brass lectern eagle is a sacred thing, because the "Globe" honestly says so. I know that many people think a harmonium a sacred thing, though not so sacred as an organ. I know that most people do not believe that Christians were really killed in the arena at all, and are shocked at the idea of their being callously called to their deaths as numbered turns in a variety entertainment by a vulgar call-boy, instead of simply being painted by Royal Academicians as being politely led up to heaven by angels with palm branches. And it gives me an extraordinary satisfaction when the shrieks of these poor creatures prove that I have brought them face to face for the first time with the grim reality of persecution and their own daily complicity in it, and perhaps hurt their eyes with a flash of the unbearable radiance of real religion.

G. BERNARD SHAW

A note to
"Androcles and the Lion"
WRITTEN FOR THE NEW YORK PRODUCTION

(Distributed with programme at Wallack's Theatre, New York, 27 January 1915)

The author of "Androcles and the Lion" received one of the worst shocks of his life when an American editor published its text under the heading, "A Comedy." It is not a comedy; it is precisely what the author calls it, a Fable Play: that is, an entertainment for children on an old story from the children's books, which nevertheless contains matter for the most mature wisdom to ponder. In England it proved a

[648]

hard test for the flexibility of the mind of the British playgoer. The genuinely religious people, the scholars, and the serious public generally were impressed and intensely interested. The children were delighted. But the hardened playgoers did not know what to make of it. At first they settled down to a Christmas pantomime, with low comedians and a comic lion, and began to laugh very good-humoredly. Then they suddenly found their teeth set on edge by a scene of the sort of satirical comedy they most dread and dislike: that is, the comedy that satirizes the kind of thing they are accustomed to accept as extremely correct, official and heightened. When the play was produced in Berlin, it was reported that at this point the Crown Prince rose and left the theatre. When it was produced in London at the height of the agitation by the militant woman suffragists, the suffragists present were so excited by the satire on the official point of view that the sensation in the house, which was felt without being clearly understood, almost upset the performance for a moment.

But worse remained behind. No sooner had the old playgoers readjusted themselves, with a disagreeable effort, to the episode of satirical comedy, than they found themselves plunged without a moment's preparation into the deepest realities of religion, the most unbearable of all subjects for the purely theatrical public, as it is the most enthralling for the real national public at which the author always aims. And before the playgoers had recovered from their consternation, or decided whether they ought to be scandalized or not, they were back in pantomime fun again. And so it went on, getting more and more bewildering (always except to the serious people who held the thread) until the fun, the satire, the historical study of manners and character, and the deadly deep earnest, were all on the stage at the same moment, many of the audience being so torn one way by laughter and the other way by horror, besides being quite upset by pure shock, that they did not know where they were, and left the theatre rending their garments (metaphorically) and crying Blasphemy, whilst the deeper people for whom the play was written proclaimed that a great movement in religious drama had been inaugurated.

None of these extravagances are likely to recur now that the first shock is over. But it is still helpful to warn old playgoers that they must not expect "Androcles and the Lion" to fall into any of the classifications to which they are accustomed, and that they will get fun and earnest, history and satire, on the same plate and at the same moment; so that it behooves them to keep on the alert and not confuse these elements. If it should seem to them that the author has himself sometimes confused them—that, for instance, he is satirizing or making fun of the truths of religion—it will be prudent for the scandalized playgoer to consider very carefully whether the truths of religion have not become associated in his mind with the mere circumstances and ceremonials under which religion is professed, which is quite another matter. The lady who said, "Don't be blasphemous" when somebody remarked that the cathedral organ was disgracefully out of tune, was no doubt sincerely reverent; but she was rather mixed as to the things that really are religion and the things that are only associated with it by custom.

The play is probably as true to history as it is in the nature of a good play to be. St. Augustine is the authority for the existence of wretches such as Spintho. Some English critics persisted in describing the emperor as Nero, apparently believing that Nero was the only emperor who persecuted Christians. But he is not Nero, and not any particular emperor; nor is the persecution any particular persecution. None of the characters are monsters: they are just such people as may be found in the United States today, placed in the monstrous circumstances created by the Roman Empire. The emperor's power and artificial divinity are a monstrosity, the persecution is a monstrosity, the gladiatorial sports are a monstrosity, and the hideous aestheticism which makes an artistic study and fancy of the combination of the sports with the persecution is a monstrosity, the moral being that monstrous institutions make monsters of quite ordinary men. The intelligent, cultivated, amiable emperor becomes a cruel fool, and the keen-witted, brave, humane, high charactered, aristocratic captain becomes the inhuman tool of a senseless tyranny, because Roman institutions forced these roles on them. The author tells you here, as so often before, that you must reform society before you can reform yourselves, and that if you had been an imperial Roman you would have done as the Romans did under the empire, respectable Christian and Republican as you now are.

Finally, a word must be said about the prophetic character given to this play by the outbreak of war, which followed it so soon. In Ferrovius you have not only an individual character of a familiar type, but a historic symbol of humanity, captivated by the fascination of the Christian doctrine and passionately embracing it, only to discover at the first blast of the war trumpet that his real god is still Mars, and his Christianity only an admiration, an aspiration, a glimpse of a higher future, after all. Readers of the author's "Common Sense About the War" will remember the passage in which he calls on the Christian churches to close their doors until the war is over, and not to put Mars in the place of Christ on their altars. In this he is obviously holding up the example of Ferrovius in this play, who quite simply and honestly gives up his pretention to Christianity after his sanguinary victory in the arena, and confesses himself a disciple of Mars, whilst retaining his conviction that though "the Christian God is not yet," he will have the last word when all our pseudo-Christians are dust.

It may possibly interest the spectators to know that the scene in which Lavinia describes the effect on her of the approach of death, owes something to an actual experience in which the author found himself confronted for some time with what seemed to be an absolute certainty of death, the means by which he escaped being entirely unforeseen.

G. B. S.

Pygmalion:
A Romance in Five Acts

WITH

Composition begun 7 March 1912; completed early June 1912. First published in German translation, 1913. Published in *Everybody's Magazine* (New York), November 1914, and in *Nash's Magazine*, November-December 1914. First collected in *Androcles and the Lion, Overruled, Pygmalion*, 1916. Revised 1941 for separate printing of *Pygmalion* in Standard Edition text, also incorporating several revised sequences from the film scenario. This revision was followed for the Penguin Books edition later in 1941. First presented in German at the Hofburg Theater, Vienna, on 16 October 1913. First presented in English at His Majesty's Theatre, London, on 11 April 1914.

Clara Eynsford-Hill   *Margaret Bussé*
Mrs Eynsford-Hill   *Carlotta Addison*
A Bystander   *Roy Byford*
Freddy Eynsford-Hill   *Algernon Greig*
Eliza Doolittle   *Mrs Patrick Campbell*
Colonel Pickering   *Philip Merivale*
Henry Higgins   *Herbert Tree*
A Sarcastic Bystander   *Alexander Sarner*
Mrs Pearce   *Geraldine Olliffe*
Alfred Doolittle   *Edmund Gurney*
Mrs Higgins   *Rosamond Mayne-Young*
Parlormaid   *Irene Delisse*

Period—The Present

ACT I *The Portico of St Paul's, Covent Garden. 11.15 p.m.*

ACT II *Professor Higgins's Phonetic Laboratory, Wimpole Street. Next day. 11 a.m.*

ACT III *The Drawing Room in Mrs Higgins's Flat on Chelsea Embankment. Several Months Later. At-Home Day*

ACT IV *The Same as Act 2. Several Months Later. Midnight*

ACT V *The Same as Act 3. The Following Morning*

NOTE FOR TECHNICIANS. A complete representation of the play as printed for the first time in this edition is technically possible only on the cinema screen or on stages furnished with exceptionally elaborate machinery. For ordinary theatrical use the scenes separated by rows of asterisks are to be omitted.

In the dialogue an e upside down indicates the indefinite vowel, sometimes called obscure or neutral, for which, though it is one of the commonest sounds in English speech, our wretched alphabet has no letter.

Preface

As will be seen later on, Pygmalion needs, not a preface, but a sequel, which I have supplied in its due place.

The English have no respect for their language, and will not teach their children to speak it. They cannot spell it because they have nothing to spell it with but an old foreign alphabet of which only the consonants—and not all of them—have any agreed speech value. Consequently no man can teach himself what it should sound like from reading it; and it is impossible for an Englishman to open his mouth without making some other Englishman despise him. Most European languages are now accessible in black and white to foreigners: English and French are not thus accessible even to Englishmen and Frenchmen. The reformer we need most today is an energetic phonetic enthusiast: that is why I have made such a one the hero of a popular play.

There have been heroes of that kind crying in the wilderness for many years past. When I became interested in the subject towards the end of the eighteen-seventies, the illustrious Alexander Melville Bell, the inventor of Visible Speech, had emigrated to Canada, where his son invented the telephone; but Alexander J. Ellis was still a London patriarch, with an impressive head always covered by a velvet skull cap, for which he would apologize to public meetings in a very courtly manner. He and Tito Pagliardini, another phonetic veteran, were men whom it was impossible to dislike. Henry Sweet, then a young man, lacked their sweetness of character: he was about

as conciliatory to conventional mortals as Ibsen or
Samuel Butler. His great ability as a phonetician (he
was, I think, the best of them all at his job) would
have entitled him to high official recognition, and
perhaps enabled him to popularize his subject, but
for his Satanic contempt for all academic dignitaries
and persons in general who thought more of Greek
than of phonetics. Once, in the days when the Imperial Institute rose in South Kensington, and Joseph
Chamberlain was booming the Empire, I induced the
editor of a leading monthly review to commission an
article from Sweet on the imperial importance of his
subject. When it arrived, it contained nothing but a
savagely derisive attack on a professor of language
and literature whose chair Sweet regarded as proper
to a phonetic expert only. The article, being libellous,
had to be returned as impossible; and I had to re-
nounce my dream of dragging its author into the
limelight. When I met him afterwards, for the first
time for many years, I found to my astonishment
that he, who had been a quite tolerably presentable
young man, had actually managed by sheer scorn to
alter his personal appearance until he had become a
sort of walking repudiation of Oxford and all its
traditions. It must have been largely in his own des-
pite that he was squeezed into something called a
Readership of phonetics there. The future of phonetics
rests probably with his pupils, who all swore by him;
but nothing could bring the man himself into any
sort of compliance with the university to which he
nevertheless clung by divine right in an intensely
Oxonian way. I daresay his papers, if he has left any,
include some satires that may be published without
too destructive results fifty years hence. He was, I
believe, not in the least an illnatured man: very much

the opposite, I should say; but he would not suffer fools gladly; and to him all scholars who were not rabid phoneticians were fools.

Those who knew him will recognize in my third act the allusion to the Current Shorthand in which he used to write postcards. It may be acquired from a four and sixpenny manual published by the Clarendon Press. The postcards which Mrs Higgins describes are such as I have received from Sweet. I would decipher a sound which a cockney would represent by *zerr*, and a Frenchman by *seu*, and then write demanding with some heat what on earth it meant. Sweet, with boundless contempt for my stupidity, would reply that it not only meant but obviously was the word Result, as no other word containing that sound, and capable of making sense with the context, existed in any language spoken on earth. That less expert mortals should require fuller indications was beyond Sweet's patience. Therefore, though the whole point of his Current Shorthand is that it can express every sound in the language perfectly, vowels as well as consonants, and that your hand has to make no stroke except the easy and current ones with which you write m, n, and u, l, p, and q, scribbling them at whatever angle comes easiest to you, his unfortunate determination to make this remarkable and quite legible script serve also as a shorthand reduced it in his own practice to the most inscrutable of cryptograms. His true objective was the provision of a full, accurate, legible script for our language; but he was led past that by his contempt for the popular Pitman system of shorthand, which he called the Pitfall system. The triumph of Pitman was a triumph of business organization: there was a weekly paper to persuade you to learn Pitman:

there were cheap textbooks and exercise books and transcripts of speeches for you to copy, and schools where experienced teachers coached you up to the necessary proficiency. Sweet could not organize his market in that fashion. He might as well have been the Sybil who tore up the leaves of prophecy that nobody would attend to. The four and sixpenny manual, mostly in his lithographed handwriting, that was never vulgarly advertized, may perhaps some day be taken up by a syndicate and pushed upon the public as The Times pushed the Encyclopædia Britannica; but until then it will certainly not prevail against Pitman. I have bought three copies of it during my lifetime; and I am informed by the publishers that its cloistered existence is still a steady and healthy one. I actually learned the system two several times; and yet the shorthand in which I am writing these lines is Pitman's. And the reason is, that my secretary cannot transcribe Sweet, having been perforce taught in the schools of Pitman. In America I could use the commercially organized Gregg shorthand, which has taken a hint from Sweet by making its letters writable (current, Sweet would have called them) instead of having to be geometrically drawn like Pitman's; but all these systems, including Sweet's, are spoilt by making them available for verbatim reporting, in which complete and exact spelling and word division are impossible. A complete and exact phonetic script is neither practicable nor necessary for ordinary use; but if we enlarge our alphabet to the Russian size, and make our spelling as phonetic as Spanish, the advance will be prodigious.

Pygmalion Higgins is not a portrait of Sweet, to whom the adventure of Eliza Doolittle would have been impossible; still, as will be seen, there are touches of Sweet in the play. With Higgins's physique and temperament Sweet might have set the Thames on fire. As it was, he impressed himself professionally on Europe to an extent that made his comparative personal obscurity, and the failure of Oxford to do justice to his eminence, a puzzle to foreign specialists in his subject. I do not blame Oxford, because I think Oxford is quite right in demanding a certain social amenity from its nurslings (heaven knows it is not exorbitant in its requirements!); for although I well know how hard it is for a man of genius with a seriously underrated subject to maintain serene and kindly relations with the men who underrate it, and who keep all the best places for less important sub-jects which they profess without originality and sometimes without much capacity for them, still, if he overwhelms them with wrath and disdain, he cannot expect them to heap honors on him.

Of the later generations of phoneticians I know little. Among them towered Robert Bridges, to whom perhaps Higgins may owe his Miltonic sym-pathies, though here again I must disclaim all por-traiture. But if the play makes the public aware that there are such people as phoneticians, and that they are among the most important people in England at present, it will serve its turn.

I wish to boast that Pygmalion has been an ex-tremely successful play, both on stage and screen, all over Europe and North America as well as at home. It is so intensely and deliberately didactic, and its subject is esteemed so dry, that I delight in throw-ing it at the heads of the wiseacres who repeat the parrot cry that art should never be didactic. It goes to prove my contention that great art can never be anything else.

Finally, and for the encouragement of people troubled with accents that cut them off from all high employment, I may add that the change wrought by Professor Higgins in the flower-girl is neither impossible nor uncommon. The modern concierge's daughter who fulfils her ambition by playing the Queen of Spain in Ruy Blas at the Théâtre Français is only one of many thousands of men and women who have sloughed off their native dialects and acquired a new tongue. Our West End shop assistants and domestic servants are bi-lingual. But the thing has to be done scientifically, or the last state of the aspirant may be worse than the first. An honest slum dialect is more tolerable than the attempts of phonetically untaught persons to imitate the plutocracy. Ambitious flower-girls who read this play must not imagine that they can pass themselves off as fine ladies by untutored imitation. They must learn their alphabet over again, and different, from a phonetic expert. Imitation will only make them ridiculous.

Oh, Shaw Again

(Spoken preface to film version of *Pygmalion*,
for American audiences, 1938. *New York Times*,
11 December 1938)

Oh, my American friends, how do you do? Now,
since I've got you all here, might I make a little
speech? Right! I will. Do you mind if I sit down?
I am very old.

Now, it's a delightful thing to sit here, and to think
that although at this moment I'm sitting in London,
I can talk in this way to an American audience. Oh—
stop a minute—I quite forgot to tell you who I am.
I am the author of the film that you are going to see,
but I'm also Bernard Shaw.

Mind you, the Bernard Shaw. Your newspapers
are so full of me that you must have heard about me.
Now you've seen the animal. I hope you like it.

You know, I've suffered a great deal from America
in this matter of motion pictures. For years past
you've been trying to teach me how to make a film.
And I'm going to show you really how it should be
done.

One thing that you've never dreamed of doing is—
when you want to know how to make a film—send
for the author. You'll never send for the author.
You'll send for an electrician when the light goes
wrong. You'll send for a photographic expert when
the camera goes wrong. But when the play goes wrong,
you send for anybody who happens to be about. Of
course, I know it's not your fault. You're not in this
business. Well, that's the sort of thing that they've
been giving me in America, and the result is—my
plays have not been filmed.

[665]

And, then, the American newspapers say that I don't want to have my plays screened and that I've always refused to have them made. I've never refused to have them filmed. I can do a great deal more with them on the screen than I can do on the stage. So don't you believe anything that you hear or read in the newspapers about me and about the film business. I know all about the motion picture business and I'm going to teach you—(I mean, of course, the gentlemen who make the films)—but I'm going to teach them what really a film should be like.

My friend, Mr. Gabriel Pascal, who has made this production, has tried the extraordinary experiment of putting a play on the screen just as the author wrote it and as he wanted it produced.

If you agree with me when you see this film of mine—if you enjoy it, very well. You'll show it in the usual way by coming to see it—each of you—about twenty times. And then, if you do that, there will be other films. I'm thinking of doing an American play that I once wrote called 'The Devil's Disciple.' Probably another play of mine, 'Cæsar and Cleopatra,' you may see that on the film. But the really good thing about it is that when you have seen these on the screen—and if you like them—all the American films will become much more like my films. And that will be a splendid thing for America, and it won't be such a bad thing for me. Although, as you know, I'm pretty near the oldest writer here, and I shan't have much enjoyment of them.

You'll have to make up your mind that you'll lose me presently, and then, Heaven only knows what will become of America. I have to educate all the nations. I have to educate England. Several of the Continental nations require a little education, but America most of all. And I shall die before I've educated America properly. But I'm making a beginning.

Now I think it's time for me to get out of the way. I was asked to say something to you. I'm always glad to say something to you. I was asked to say something very agreeable to you. I've done my best. That's my aged idea of an agreeable speech. But, I'm quite friendly. I think you've always heard that about me; at any rate, it's been written—you ought to.

[ACT I]

London at 11.15 p.m. Torrents of heavy summer rain. Cab whistles blowing frantically in all directions. Pedestrians running for shelter into the portico of St Paul's church (not Wren's cathedral but Inigo Jones's church in Covent Garden vegetable market), among them a lady and her daughter in evening dress. All are peering out gloomily at the rain, except one man with his back turned to the rest, wholly preoccupied with a notebook in which he is writing.

The church clock strikes the first quarter.

THE DAUGHTER [*in the space between the central pillars, close to the one on her left*] I'm getting chilled to the bone. What can Freddy be doing all this time? He's been gone twenty minutes.

THE MOTHER [*on her daughter's right*] Not so long. But he ought to have got us a cab by this.

A BYSTANDER [*on the lady's right*] He wont get no cab not until half-past eleven, missus, when they come back after dropping their theatre fares.

THE MOTHER. But we must have a cab. We cant stand here until half-past eleven. It's too bad.

THE BYSTANDER. Well, it aint my fault, missus.

THE DAUGHTER. If Freddy had a bit of gumption, he would have got one at the theatre door.

THE MOTHER. What could he have done, poor boy?

THE DAUGHTER. Other people got cabs. Why couldnt he?

Freddy rushes in out of the rain from the Southampton Street side, and comes between them closing a dripping umbrella. He is a young man of twenty, in evening dress, very wet round the ankles.

THE DAUGHTER. Well, havnt you got a cab?

FREDDY. Theres not one to be had for love or money.

THE MOTHER. Oh, Freddy, there must be one. You cant have tried.

THE DAUGHTER. It's too tiresome. Do you expect us to go and get one ourselves?

FREDDY. I tell you theyre all engaged. The rain was so sudden: nobody was prepared; and everybody had to take a cab. Ive been to Charing Cross one way and nearly to Ludgate Circus the other; and they were all engaged.

THE MOTHER. Did you try Trafalgar Square?

FREDDY. There wasnt one at Trafalgar Square.

THE DAUGHTER. Did you try?

FREDDY. I tried as far as Charing Cross Station. Did you expect me to walk to Hammersmith?

THE DAUGHTER. You havnt tried at all.

THE MOTHER. You really are very helpless, Freddy. Go again; and dont come back until you have found a cab.

FREDDY. I shall simply get soaked for nothing.

THE DAUGHTER. And what about us? Are we to stay here all night in this draught, with next to nothing on? You selfish pig—

FREDDY. Oh, very well: I'll go, I'll go. [*He opens his umbrella and dashes off Strandwards, but comes into collision with a flower girl who is hurrying in for shelter, knocking her basket out of her hands. A blinding flash of lightning, followed instantly by a rattling peal of thunder, orchestrates the incident*].

THE FLOWER GIRL. Nah then, Freddy: look wh' y' gowin, deah.

FREDDY. Sorry [*he rushes off*].

THE FLOWER GIRL [*picking up her scattered flowers and replacing them in the basket*] Theres menners f' yer! Tə-oo banches o voylets trod into the mad. [*She sits down on the plinth of the column, sorting her flowers, on the lady's right. She is not at all a romantic figure. She is perhaps eighteen, perhaps twenty, hardly older. She wears a little sailor hat of black straw that has long been exposed to the dust and soot of London and has seldom if ever been brushed. Her hair needs washing rather badly: its mousy color can hardly be natural. She wears a shoddy black coat that reaches nearly to her knees and is shaped to her waist. She has a brown skirt with a coarse apron. Her boots are much the worse for wear. She is no doubt as clean as she can afford to be; but compared to the ladies she is very dirty. Her features are no worse than theirs; but their condition leaves something to be desired; and she needs the services of a dentist*].

THE MOTHER. How do you know that my son's name is Freddy, pray?

THE FLOWER GIRL. Ow, eez yə-ooa san, is e? Wal, fewd dan y' də-ooty bawmz a mather should, eed now bettern to spawl a pore gel's flahrzn than ran awy athaht pyin. Will ye-oo py me f'them? [*Here, with apologies, this desperate attempt to represent her dialect without a phonetic alphabet must be abandoned as unintelligible outside London*].

THE DAUGHTER. Do nothing of the sort, mother. The idea!

THE MOTHER. Please allow me, Clara. Have you any pennies?

THE DAUGHTER. No. Ive nothing smaller than sixpence.

THE FLOWER GIRL [*hopefully*] I can give you change for a tanner, kind lady.

THE MOTHER [*to Clara*] Give it to me. [*Clara parts reluctantly*]. Now [*to the girl*] This is for your flowers.

THE FLOWER GIRL. Thank you kindly, lady.

THE DAUGHTER. Make her give you the change. These things are only a penny a bunch.

THE MOTHER. Do hold your tongue, Clara. [*To the girl*] You can keep the change.

THE FLOWER GIRL. Oh, thank you, lady.

THE MOTHER. Now tell me how you know that young gentleman's name.

THE FLOWER GIRL. I didnt.

THE MOTHER. I heard you call him by it. Dont try to deceive me.

THE FLOWER GIRL [*protesting*] Who's trying to deceive you? I called him Freddy or Charlie same as you might yourself if you was talking to a stranger and wished to be pleasant.

THE DAUGHTER. Sixpence thrown away! Really, mamma, you might have spared Freddy that. [*She retreats in disgust behind the pillar*].

An elderly gentleman of the amiable military type rushes into the shelter, and closes a dripping umbrella. He is in the same plight as Freddy, very wet about the ankles. He is in evening dress, with a light overcoat. He takes the place left vacant by the daughter.

THE GENTLEMAN. Phew!

THE MOTHER [*to the gentleman*] Oh sir, is there any sign of its stopping?

THE GENTLEMAN. I'm afraid not. It started worse than ever about two minutes ago [*he goes to the plinth beside the flower girl; puts up his foot on it; and stoops to turn down his trouser ends*].

THE MOTHER. Oh dear! [*She retires sadly and joins her daughter*].

THE FLOWER GIRL [*taking advantage of the military*

gentleman's proximity to establish friendly relations with him] If it's worse, it's a sign it's nearly over. So cheer up, Captain; and buy a flower off a poor girl.

THE GENTLEMAN. I'm sorry. I havnt any change.

THE FLOWER GIRL. I can give you change, Captain.

THE GENTLEMAN. For a sovereign? Ive nothing less.

THE FLOWER GIRL. Garn! Oh do buy a flower off me, Captain. I can change half-a-crown. Take this for tuppence.

THE GENTLEMAN. Now dont be troublesome: theres a good girl. [*Trying his pockets*] I really havnt any change—Stop: heres three hapence, if thats any use to you [*he retreats to the other pillar*].

THE FLOWER GIRL [*disappointed, but thinking three halfpence better than nothing*] Thank you, sir.

THE BYSTANDER [*to the girl*] You be careful: give him a flower for it. Theres a bloke here behind taking down every blessed word youre saying. [*All turn to the man who is taking notes*].

THE FLOWER GIRL [*springing up terrified*] I aint done nothing wrong by speaking to the gentleman. Ive a right to sell flowers if I keep off the kerb. [*Hysterically*] I'm a respectable girl: so help me, I never spoke to him except to ask him to buy a flower off me.

General hubbub, mostly sympathetic to the flower girl, but deprecating her excessive sensibility. Cries of Dont start hollerin. Who's hurting you? Nobody's going to touch you. Whats the good of fussing? Steady on. Easy easy, etc., *come from the elderly staid spectators, who pat her comfortingly. Less patient ones bid her shut her head, or ask her roughly what is wrong with her. A remoter group, not knowing what the matter is, crowd in and increase the noise with question and answer:* Whats the row? What-she do? Where is he?

A tec taking her down. What! him? Yes: him over there: Took money off the gentleman, etc.

THE FLOWER GIRL [*breaking through them to the gentleman, crying wildly*] Oh, sir, dont let him charge me. You dunno what it means to me. Theyll take away my character and drive me on the streets for speaking to gentlemen. They—

THE NOTE TAKER [*coming forward on her right, the rest crowding after him*] There! there! there! there! who's hurting you, you silly girl? What do you take me for?

THE BYSTANDER. It's aw rawt: e's a genleman: look at his bə-oots. [*Explaining to the note taker*] She thought you was a copper's nark, sir.

THE NOTE TAKER [*with quick interest*] Whats a copper's nark?

THE BYSTANDER [*inapt at definition*] It's a—well, it's a copper's nark, as you might say. What else would you call it? A sort of informer.

THE FLOWER GIRL [*still hysterical*] I take my Bible oath I never said a word—

THE NOTE TAKER [*overbearing but good-humored*] Oh, shut up, shut up. Do I look like a policeman?

THE FLOWER GIRL [*far from reassured*] Then what did you take down my words for? How do I know whether you took me down right? You just shew me what youve wrote about me. [*The note taker opens his book and holds it steadily under her nose, though the pressure of the mob trying to read it over his shoulders would upset a weaker man*]. Whats that? That aint proper writing. I cant read that.

THE NOTE TAKER. I can. [*Reads, reproducing her pronunciation exactly*] "Cheer ap, Keptin; n' baw ya flahr orf a pore gel."

THE FLOWER GIRL [*much distressed*] It's because I

[674]

called him Captain. I meant no harm. [*To the gentle-man*] Oh, sir, dont let him lay a charge agen me for a word like that. You—

THE GENTLEMAN. Charge! I make no charge. [*To the note taker*] Really, sir, if you are a detective, you need not begin protecting me against molestation by young women until I ask you. Anybody could see that the girl meant no harm.

THE BYSTANDERS GENERALLY [*demonstrating against police espionage*] Course they could. What business is it of yours? You mind your own affairs. He wants promotion, he does. Taking down people's words! Girl never said a word to him. What harm if she did? Nice thing a girl cant shelter from the rain without being insulted, etc., etc., etc. [*She is conduc-ted by the more sympathetic demonstrators back to her plinth, where she resumes her seat and struggles with her emotion*].

THE BYSTANDER. He aint a tec. He's a blooming busybody: thats what he is. I tell you, look at his bə-oots.

THE NOTE TAKER [*turning on him genially*] And how are all your people down at Selsey?

THE BYSTANDER [*suspiciously*] Who told you my people come from Selsey?

THE NOTE TAKER. Never you mind. They did. [*To the girl*] How do you come to be up so far east? You were born in Lisson Grove.

THE FLOWER GIRL [*appalled*] Oh, what harm is there in my leaving Lisson Grove? It wasnt fit for a pig to live in; and I had to pay four-and-six a week. [*In tears*] Oh, boo—hoo—oo—

THE NOTE TAKER. Live where you like; but stop that noise.

THE GENTLEMAN [*to the girl*] Come, come! he cant

touch you: you have a right to live where you please.

A SARCASTIC BYSTANDER [*thrusting himself between the note taker and the gentleman*] Park Lane, for instance. I'd like to go into the Housing Question with you, I would.

THE FLOWER GIRL [*subsiding into a brooding melancholy over her basket, and talking very low-spiritedly to herself*] I'm a good girl, I am.

THE SARCASTIC BYSTANDER [*not attending to her*] Do you know where *I* come from?

THE NOTE TAKER [*promptly*] Hoxton.

Titterings. Popular interest in the note taker's performance increases.

THE SARCASTIC ONE [*amazed*] Well, who said I didnt? Bly me! you know everything, you do.

THE FLOWER GIRL [*still nursing her sense of injury*] Aint no call to meddle with me, he aint.

THE BYSTANDER [*to her*] Of course he aint. Dont you stand it from him. [*To the note taker*] See here: what call have you to know about people what never offered to meddle with you?

THE FLOWER GIRL. Let him say what he likes. I dont want to have no truck with him.

THE BYSTANDER. You take us for dirt under your feet, dont you? Catch you taking liberties with a gentleman!

THE SARCASTIC BYSTANDER. Yes: tell him where he come from if you want to go fortune-telling.

THE NOTE TAKER. Cheltenham, Harrow, Cambridge, and India.

THE GENTLEMAN. Quite right.

Great laughter. Reaction in the note taker's favor. Exclamations of He knows all about it. Told him proper. Hear him tell the toff where he come from? *etc.*

THE GENTLEMAN. May I ask, sir, do you do this for your living at a music hall?

THE NOTE TAKER. I've thought of that. Perhaps I shall some day.

The rain has stopped; and the persons on the outside of the crowd begin to drop off.

THE FLOWER GIRL [*resenting the reaction*] He's no gentleman, he aint, to interfere with a poor girl.

THE DAUGHTER [*out of patience, pushing her way rudely to the front and displacing the gentleman, who politely retires to the other side of the pillar*] What on earth is Freddy doing? I shall get pneumownia if I stay in this draught any longer.

THE NOTE TAKER [*to himself, hastily making a note of her pronunciation of "monia"*] Earlscourt.

THE DAUGHTER [*violently*] Will you please keep your impertinent remarks to yourself.

THE NOTE TAKER. Did I say that out loud? I didnt mean to. I beg your pardon. Your mother's Epsom, unmistakeably.

THE MOTHER [*advancing between her daughter and the note taker*] How very curious! I was brought up in Largelady Park, near Epsom.

THE NOTE TAKER [*uproariously amused*] Ha! ha! What a devil of a name! Excuse me. [*To the daughter*] You want a cab, do you?

THE DAUGHTER. Dont dare speak to me.

THE MOTHER. Oh please, please, Clara. [*Her daughter repudiates her with an angry shrug and retires haughtily*]. We should be so grateful to you, sir, if you found us a cab. [*The note taker produces a whistle*]. Oh, thank you. [*She joins her daughter*].

The note taker blows a piercing blast.

THE SARCASTIC BYSTANDER. There! I knowed he was a plainclothes copper.

THE BYSTANDER. That aint a police whistle: thats a sporting whistle.

THE FLOWER GIRL [*still preoccupied with her wounded feelings*] He's no right to take away my character. My character is the same to me as any lady's.

THE NOTE TAKER. I dont know whether youve noticed it; but the rain stopped about two minutes ago.

THE BYSTANDER. So it has. Why didnt you say so before? and us losing our time listening to your silliness! [*He walks off towards the Strand*].

THE SARCASTIC BYSTANDER. I can tell where you come from. You come from Anwell. Go back there.

THE NOTE TAKER [*helpfully*] *H*anwell.

THE SARCASTIC BYSTANDER [*affecting great distinction of speech*] Thenk you, teacher. Haw haw! So long [*he touches his hat with mock respect and strolls off*].

THE FLOWER GIRL. Frightening people like that! How would he like it himself?

THE MOTHER. It's quite fine now, Clara. We can walk to a motor bus. Come. [*She gathers her skirts above her ankles and hurries off towards the Strand*].

THE DAUGHTER. But the cab—[*her mother is out of hearing*]. Oh, how tiresome! [*She follows angrily*].

All the rest have gone except the note taker, the gentleman, and the flower girl, who sits arranging her basket, and still pitying herself in murmurs.

THE FLOWER GIRL. Poor girl! Hard enough for her to live without being worrited and chivied.

THE GENTLEMAN [*returning to his former place on the note taker's left*] How do you do it, if I may ask?

THE NOTE TAKER. Simply phonetics. The science of speech. Thats my profession: also my hobby. Happy is the man who can make a living by his hobby! You can spot an Irishman or a Yorkshireman by his brogue. *I* can place any man within six miles. I can place him within two miles in London. Sometimes within two streets.

THE FLOWER GIRL. Ought to be ashamed of himself, unmanly coward!

THE GENTLEMAN. But is there a living in that?

THE NOTE TAKER. Oh yes. Quite a fat one. This is an age of upstarts. Men begin in Kentish Town with £80 a year, and end in Park Lane with a hundred thousand. They want to drop Kentish Town; but they give themselves away every time they open their mouths. Now I can teach them—

THE FLOWER GIRL. Let him mind his own business and leave a poor girl—

THE NOTE TAKER [*explosively*] Woman: cease this detestable boohooing instantly; or else seek the shelter of some other place of worship.

THE FLOWER GIRL [*with feeble defiance*] Ive a right to be here if I like, same as you.

THE NOTE TAKER. A woman who utters such depressing and disgusting sounds has no right to be anywhere—no right to live. Remember that you are a human being with a soul and the divine gift of articulate speech: that your native language is the language of Shakespear and Milton and The Bible; and dont sit there crooning like a bilious pigeon.

THE FLOWER GIRL [*quite overwhelmed, looking up at him in mingled wonder and deprecation without daring to raise her head*] Ah-ah-ah-ow-ow-ow-oo!

THE NOTE TAKER [*whipping out his book*] Heavens! what a sound! [*He writes; then holds out the book and reads, reproducing her vowels exactly*] Ah-ah-ah-ow-ow-ow-oo!

THE FLOWER GIRL [*tickled by the performance, and laughing in spite of herself*] Garn!

THE NOTE TAKER. You see this creature with her kerbstone English: the English that will keep her in the gutter to the end of her days. Well, sir, in three months I could pass that girl off as a duchess at an ambassador's garden party. I could even get her a place as lady's maid or shop assistant, which requires better English.

THE FLOWER GIRL. What's that you say?

THE NOTE TAKER. Yes, you squashed cabbage leaf, you disgrace to the noble architecture of these columns, you incarnate insult to the English language: I could pass you off as the Queen of Sheba. [*To the Gentleman*] Can you believe that?

THE GENTLEMAN. Of course I can. I am myself a student of Indian dialects; and—

THE NOTE TAKER [*eagerly*] Are you? Do you know Colonel Pickering, the author of Spoken Sanscrit?

THE GENTLEMAN. I am Colonel Pickering. Who are you?

THE NOTE TAKER. Henry Higgins, author of Higgins's Universal Alphabet.

PICKERING [*with enthusiasm*] I came from India to meet you.

HIGGINS. I was going to India to meet you.

PICKERING. Where do you live?

HIGGINS. 27A Wimpole Street. Come and see me tomorrow.

PICKERING. I'm at the Carlton. Come with me now and lets have a jaw over some supper.

HIGGINS. Right you are.

THE FLOWER GIRL [*to Pickering, as he passes her*] Buy a flower, kind gentleman. I'm short for my lodging.

PICKERING. I really havnt any change. I'm sorry [*he goes away*].

HIGGINS [*shocked at the girl's mendacity*] Liar. You said you could change half-a-crown.

THE FLOWER GIRL [*rising in desperation*] You ought to be stuffed with nails, you ought. [*Flinging the basket at his feet*] Take the whole blooming basket for sixpence.

The church clock strikes the second quarter.

HIGGINS [*hearing in it the voice of God, rebuking him for his Pharisaic want of charity to the poor girl*] A reminder. [*He raises his hat solemnly; then throws a handful of money into the basket and follows Pickering*].

THE FLOWER GIRL [*picking up a half-crown*] Ah-ow-ooh! [*Picking up a couple of florins*] Aaah-ow-ooh! [*Picking up several coins*] Aaaaaah-ow-ooh! [*Picking up a half-sovereign*] Aaaaaaaaaaaah-ow-ooh!!!

FREDDY [*springing out of a taxicab*] Got one at last. Hallo! [*To the girl*] Where are the two ladies that were here?

THE FLOWER GIRL. They walked to the bus when the rain stopped.

FREDDY. And left me with a cab on my hands! Damnation!

THE FLOWER GIRL [*with grandeur*] Never mind, young man. I'm going home in a taxi. [*She sails off to the cab. The driver puts his hand behind him and holds the door firmly shut against her. Quite understanding his mistrust, she shews him her handful of money*]. A taxi fare aint no object to me, Charlie. [*He grins and opens the door*]. Here. What about the basket?

THE TAXIMAN. Give it here. Tuppence extra.

LIZA. No: I dont want nobody to see it. [*She crushes it into the cab and gets in, continuing the conversation through the window*] Goodbye, Freddy.

FREDDY [*dazedly raising his hat*] Goodbye.

TAXIMAN. Where to?

LIZA. Bucknam Pellis [Buckingham Palace].

TAXIMAN. What d'ye mean—Bucknam Pellis?

LIZA. Dont you know where it is? In the Green Park, where the King lives. Goodbye, Freddy. Dont let me keep you standing there. Goodbye.

FREDDY. Goodbye. [*He goes*].

TAXIMAN. Here? Whats this about Bucknam Pellis? What business have you at Bucknam Pellis?

LIZA. Of course I havnt none. But I wasnt going to let him know that. You drive me home.

TAXIMAN. And wheres home?

LIZA. Angel Court, Drury Lane, next Meiklejohn's oil shop.

TAXIMAN. That sounds more like it, Judy. [*He drives off*].

*　　*　　*　　*　　*

Let us follow the taxi to the entrance to Angel Court, a narrow little archway between two shops, one of them Meiklejohn's oil shop. When it stops there, Eliza gets out, dragging her basket with her.

LIZA. How much?

TAXIMAN [*indicating the taximeter*] Cant you read? A shilling.

LIZA. A shilling for two minutes!!

TAXIMAN. Two minutes or ten: it's all the same.

LIZA. Well, I dont call it right.

TAXIMAN. Ever been in a taxi before?

LIZA [*with dignity*] Hundreds and thousands of times, young man.

TAXIMAN [*laughing at her*] Good for you, Judy. Keep the shilling, darling, with best love from all at home. Good luck! [*He drives off*].

LIZA [*humiliated*] Impidence!

She picks up the basket and trudges up the alley with it to her lodging: a small room with very old wall paper hanging loose in the damp places. A broken pane in the window is mended with paper. A portrait of a popular actor and a fashion plate of ladies' dresses, all wildly beyond poor Eliza's means, both torn from newspapers, are pinned up on the wall. A birdcage hangs in the window; but its tenant died long ago: it remains as a memorial only.

These are the only visible luxuries: the rest is the irreducible minimum of poverty's needs: a wretched bed heaped with all sorts of coverings that have any warmth in them, a draped packing case with a basin and jug on it and a little looking glass over it, a chair and table, the refuse of some suburban kitchen, and an American alarum clock on the shelf above the unused fireplace: the whole lighted with a gas lamp with a penny in the slot meter. Rent: four shillings a week.

Here Eliza, chronically weary, but too excited to go to bed, sits, counting her new riches and dreaming and planning what to do with them, until the gas goes out, when she enjoys for the first time the sensation of being able to put in another penny without grudging it. This prodigal mood does not extinguish her gnawing sense of the need for economy sufficiently to prevent her from calculating that she can dream and plan in bed more cheaply and warmly than sitting up without a fire. So she takes off her shawl and skirt and adds them to the miscellaneous bedclothes. Then she kicks off her shoes and gets into bed without any further change.

Next day at 11 a.m. Higgins's laboratory in Wimpole Street. It is a room on the first floor, looking on the street, and was meant for the drawing room. The double doors are in the middle of the back wall; and persons entering find in the corner to their right two tall file cabinets at right angles to one another against the walls. In this corner stands a flat writing-table, on which are a phonograph, a laryngoscope, a row of tiny organ pipes with a bellows, a set of lamp chimneys for singing flames with burners attached to a gas plug in the wall by an indiarubber tube, several tuning-forks of different sizes, a life-size image of half a human head, shewing in section the vocal organs, and a box containing a supply of wax cylinders for the phonograph.

Further down the room, on the same side, is a fireplace, with a comfortable leather-covered easy-chair at the side of the hearth nearest the door, and a coal-scuttle. There is a clock on the mantel-piece. Between the fireplace and the phonograph table is a stand for newspapers.

On the other side of the central door, to the left of the visitor, is a cabinet of shallow drawers. On it is a telephone and the telephone directory. The corner beyond, and most of the side wall, is occupied by a grand piano, with the keyboard at the end furthest from the door, and a bench for the player extending the full length of the keyboard. On the piano is a dessert dish heaped with fruit and sweets, mostly chocolates.

The middle of the room is clear. Besides the easy-chair, the piano bench, and two chairs at the phonograph table, there is one stray chair. It stands near the fireplace. On the walls, engravings: mostly Piranesis and mezzotint portraits. No paintings.

Pickering is seated at the table, putting down some cards and a tuning-fork which he has been using. Higgins is standing up near him, closing two or three file drawers which are hanging out. He appears in the morning light as a robust, vital, appetizing sort of man of forty or thereabouts, dressed in a professional-looking black frock-coat with a white linen collar and black silk tie. He is of the energetic, scientific type, heartily, even violently interested in everything that can be studied as a scientific subject, and careless about himself and other people, including their feelings. He is, in fact, but for his years and size, rather like a very impetuous baby "taking notice" eagerly and loudly, and requiring almost as much watching to keep him out of unintended mischief. His manner varies from genial bullying when he is in a good humor to stormy petulance when anything goes wrong; but he is so entirely frank and void of malice that he remains likeable even in his least reasonable moments.

HIGGINS [*as he shuts the last drawer*] Well, I think thats the whole show.

PICKERING. It's really amazing. I havnt taken half of it in, you know.

HIGGINS. Would you like to go over any of it again?

PICKERING [*rising and coming to the fireplace, where he plants himself with his back to the fire*] No, thank you: not now. I'm quite done up for this morning.

HIGGINS [*following him, and standing beside him on his left*] Tired of listening to sounds?

PICKERING. Yes. It's a fearful strain. I rather fancied myself because I can pronounce twenty-four distinct vowel sounds; but your hundred and thirty beat me. I cant hear a bit of difference between most of them.

HIGGINS [*chuckling, and going over to the piano to eat sweets*] Oh, that comes with practice. You hear no difference at first; but you keep on listening, and presently you find theyre all as different as A from B. [*Mrs Pearce looks in: she is Higgins's housekeeper*]. Whats the matter?

MRS PEARCE [*hesitating, evidently perplexed*] A young woman asks to see you, sir.

HIGGINS. A young woman! What does she want?

MRS PEARCE. Well, sir, she says youll be glad to see her when you know what she's come about. She's quite a common girl, sir. Very common indeed. I should have sent her away, only I thought perhaps you wanted her to talk into your machines. I hope Ive not done wrong; but really you see such queer people sometimes—youll excuse me, I'm sure, sir—

HIGGINS. Oh, thats all right, Mrs Pearce. Has she an interesting accent?

MRS PEARCE. Oh, something dreadful, sir, really. I dont know how you can take an interest in it.

HIGGINS [*to Pickering*] Lets have her up. Shew her up, Mrs Pearce [*he rushes across to his working table and picks out a cylinder to use on the phonograph*].

MRS PEARCE [*only half resigned to it*] Very well, sir. It's for you to say. [*She goes downstairs*].

HIGGINS. This is rather a bit of luck. I'll shew you how I make records. We'll set her talking; and I'll take it down first in Bell's Visible Speech; then in broad Romic; and then we'll get her on the phonograph so that you can turn her on as often as you like with the written transcript before you.

MRS PEARCE [*returning*] This is the young woman, sir.

The flower girl enters in state. She has a hat with three ostrich feathers, orange, sky-blue, and red. She has a nearly clean apron, and the shoddy coat has been tidied a little. The pathos of this deplorable figure, with its innocent vanity and consequential air, touches Pickering, who has already straightened himself in the presence of Mrs Pearce. But as to Higgins, the only distinction he makes between men and women is that when he is neither bullying nor exclaiming to the heavens against some feather-weight cross, he coaxes women as a child coaxes its nurse when it wants to get anything out of her.

HIGGINS [*brusquely, recognizing her with unconcealed disappointment, and at once, babylike, making an intolerable grievance of it*] Why, this is the girl I jotted down last night. She's no use: Ive got all the records I want of the Lisson Grove lingo; and I'm not going to waste another cylinder on it. [*To the girl*] Be off with you: I dont want you.

THE FLOWER GIRL. Dont you be so saucy. You aint heard what I come for yet. [*To Mrs Pearce, who is waiting at the door for further instructions*] Did you tell him I come in a taxi?

MRS PEARCE. Nonsense, girl! what do you think a gentleman like Mr Higgins cares what you came in?

THE FLOWER GIRL. Oh, we are proud! He aint above giving lessons, not him: I heard him say so. Well, I aint come here to ask for any compliment; and if my money's not good enough I can go elsewhere.

HIGGINS. Good enough for what?

THE FLOWER GIRL. Good enough for ya-oo. Now you know, dont you? I'm come to have lessons, I am. And to pay for em ta-oo: make no mistake.

HIGGINS [*stupent*] Well!!! [*Recovering his breath*

with a gasp] What do you expect me to say to you?

THE FLOWER GIRL. Well, if you was a gentleman, you might ask me to sit down, I think. Dont I tell you I'm bringing you business?

HIGGINS. Pickering: shall we ask this baggage to sit down, or shall we throw her out of the window?

THE FLOWER GIRL [*running away in terror to the piano, where she turns at bay*] Ah-ah-oh-ow-ow-ow-oo! [*Wounded and whimpering*] I wont be called a baggage when Ive offered to pay like any lady.

Motionless, the two men stare at her from the other side of the room, amazed.

PICKERING [*gently*] But what is it you want?

THE FLOWER GIRL. I want to be a lady in a flower shop stead of sellin at the corner of Tottenham Court Road. But they wont take me unless I can talk more genteel. He said he could teach me. Well, here I am ready to pay him—not asking any favor—and he treats me zif I was dirt.

MRS PEARCE. How can you be such a foolish ignorant girl as to think you could afford to pay Mr Higgins?

THE FLOWER GIRL. Why shouldnt I? I know what lessons cost as well as you do; and I'm ready to pay.

HIGGINS. How much?

THE FLOWER GIRL [*coming back to him, triumphant*] Now youre talking! I thought youd come off it when you saw a chance of getting back a bit of what you chucked at me last night. [*Confidentially*] Youd had a drop in, hadnt you?

HIGGINS [*peremptorily*] Sit down.

THE FLOWER GIRL. Oh, if youre going to make a compliment of it—

HIGGINS [*thundering at her*] Sit down.

MRS PEARCE [*severely*] Sit down, girl. Do as youre told.

THE FLOWER GIRL. Ah-ah-ah-ow-ow-oo! [*She stands, half rebellious, half bewildered*].

PICKERING [*very courteous*] Wont you sit down? [*He places the stray chair near the hearthrug between himself and Higgins*].

LIZA [*coyly*] Dont mind if I do. [*She sits down. Pickering returns to the hearthrug*].

HIGGINS. Whats your name?

THE FLOWER GIRL. Liza Doolittle.

HIGGINS [*declaiming gravely*]

      Eliza, Elizabeth, Betsy and Bess,

      They went to the woods to get a bird's nes':

PICKERING. They found a nest with four eggs in it:

HIGGINS.   They took one apiece, and left three in it.

They laugh heartily at their own fun.

LIZA. Oh, dont be silly.

MRS PEARCE [*placing herself behind Eliza's chair*] You mustnt speak to the gentleman like that.

LIZA. Well, why wont he speak sensible to me?

HIGGINS. Come back to business. How much do you propose to pay me for the lessons?

LIZA. Oh, I know whats right. A lady friend of mine gets French lessons for eighteenpence an hour from a real French gentleman. Well, you wouldnt have the face to ask me the same for teaching me my own language as you would for French; so I wont give more than a shilling. Take it or leave it.

HIGGINS [*walking up and down the room, rattling his keys and his cash in his pockets*] You know, Pickering, if you consider a shilling, not as a simple shilling, but as a percentage of this girl's income, it works out as fully equivalent to sixty or seventy guineas from a millionaire.

PICKERING. How so?

HIGGINS. Figure it out. A millionaire has about £150 a day. She earns about half-a-crown.

LIZA [*haughtily*] Who told you I only—

HIGGINS [*continuing*] She offers me two-fifths of her day's income for a lesson. Two-fifths of a millionaire's income for a day would be somewhere about £60. It's handsome. By George, it's enormous! it's the biggest offer I ever had.

LIZA [*rising, terrified*] Sixty pounds! What are you talking about? I never offered you sixty pounds. Where would I get—

HIGGINS. Hold your tongue.

LIZA [*weeping*] But I aint got sixty pounds. Oh—

MRS PEARCE. Dont cry, you silly girl. Sit down. Nobody is going to touch your money.

HIGGINS. Somebody is going to touch you, with a broomstick, if you dont stop snivelling. Sit down.

LIZA [*obeying slowly*] Ah-ah-ah-ow-oo-o! One would think you was my father.

HIGGINS. If I decide to teach you, I'll be worse than two fathers to you. Here [*he offers her his silk handkerchief*]!

LIZA. Whats this for?

HIGGINS. To wipe your eyes. To wipe any part of your face that feels moist. Remember: thats your handkerchief; and thats your sleeve. Dont mistake the one for the other if you wish to become a lady in a shop.

Liza, utterly bewildered, stares helplessly at him.

MRS PEARCE. It's no use talking to her like that, Mr Higgins: she doesnt understand you. Besides, youre quite wrong: she doesnt do it that way at all [*she takes the handkerchief*].

LIZA [*snatching it*] Here! You give me that handkerchief. He gev it to me, not to you.

PICKERING [*laughing*] He did. I think it must be regarded as her property, Mrs Pearce.

MRS PEARCE [*resigning herself*] Serve you right, Mr Higgins.

PICKERING. Higgins: I'm interested. What about the ambassador's garden party? I'll say youre the greatest teacher alive if you make that good. I'll bet you all the expenses of the experiment you cant do it. And I'll pay for the lessons.

LIZA. Oh, you are real good. Thank you, Captain.

HIGGINS [*tempted, looking at her*] It's almost irresistible. She's so deliciously low—so horribly dirty—

LIZA [*protesting extremely*] Ah-ah-ah-ah-ow-ow-oo-oo!!! I aint dirty: I washed my face and hands afore I come, I did.

PICKERING. Youre certainly not going to turn her head with flattery, Higgins.

MRS PEARCE [*uneasy*] Oh, dont say that, sir: theres more ways than one of turning a girl's head; and nobody can do it better than Mr Higgins, though he may not always mean it. I do hope, sir, you wont encourage him to do anything foolish.

HIGGINS [*becoming excited as the idea grows on him*] What is life but a series of inspired follies? The difficulty is to find them to do. Never lose a chance: it doesnt come every day. I shall make a duchess of this draggletailed guttersnipe.

LIZA [*strongly deprecating this view of her*] Ah-ah-ah-ow-ow-oo!

HIGGINS [*carried away*] Yes: in six months—in three if she has a good ear and a quick tongue—I'll take her anywhere and pass her off as anything. We'll start today: now! this moment! Take her away and clean her, Mrs Pearce. Monkey Brand, if it wont come off any other way. Is there a good fire in the kitchen?

MRS PEARCE [*protesting*] Yes; but—

HIGGINS [*storming on*] Take all her clothes off and burn them. Ring up Whiteley or somebody for new ones. Wrap her up in brown paper til they come.

LIZA. Youre no gentleman, youre not, to talk of such things. I'm a good girl, I am; and I know what the like of you are, I do.

HIGGINS. We want none of your Lisson Grove prudery here, young woman. Youve got to learn to behave like a duchess. Take her away, Mrs Pearce. If she gives you any trouble, wallop her.

LIZA [*springing up and running between Pickering and Mrs Pearce for protection*] No! I'll call the police, I will.

MRS PEARCE. But Ive no place to put her.

HIGGINS. Put her in the dustbin.

LIZA. Ah-ah-ah-ow-ow-oo!

PICKERING. Oh come, Higgins! be reasonable.

MRS PEARCE [*resolutely*] You must be reasonable, Mr Higgins: really you must. You cant walk over everybody like this.

Higgins, thus scolded, subsides. The hurricane is succeeded by a zephyr of amiable surprise.

HIGGINS [*with professional exquisiteness of modulation*] *I* walk over everybody! My dear Mrs Pearce, my dear Pickering, I never had the slightest intention of walking over anyone. All I propose is that we should be kind to this poor girl. We must help her to prepare and fit herself for her new station in life. If I did not express myself clearly it was because I did not wish to hurt her delicacy, or yours.

Liza, reassured, steals back to her chair.

MRS PEARCE [*to Pickering*] Well, did you ever hear anything like that, sir?

PICKERING [*laughing heartily*] Never, Mrs Pearce: never.

HIGGINS [*patiently*] Whats the matter?

MRS PEARCE. Well, the matter is, sir, that you cant take a girl up like that as if you were picking up a pebble on the beach.

HIGGINS. Why not?

MRS PEARCE. Why not! But you dont know anything about her. What about her parents? She may be married.

LIZA. Garn!

HIGGINS. There! As the girl very properly says, Garn! Married indeed! Dont you know that a woman of that class looks a worn out drudge of fifty a year after she's married?

LIZA. Whood marry me?

HIGGINS [*suddenly resorting to the most thrillingly beautiful low tones in his best elocutionary style*] By George, Eliza, the streets will be strewn with the bodies of men shooting themselves for your sake before Ive done with you.

MRS PEARCE. Nonsense, sir. You mustnt talk like that to her.

LIZA [*rising and squaring herself determinedly*] I'm going away. He's off his chump, he is. I dont want no balmies teaching me.

HIGGINS [*wounded in his tenderest point by her insensibility to his elocution*] Oh, indeed! I'm mad, am I? Very well, Mrs Pearce: you neednt order the new clothes for her. Throw her out.

LIZA [*whimpering*] Nah-ow. You got no right to touch me.

MRS PEARCE. You see now what comes of being saucy. [*Indicating the door*] This way, please.

LIZA [*almost in tears*] I didnt want no clothes. I wouldnt have taken them [*she throws away the handkerchief*]. I can buy my own clothes.

HIGGINS [*deftly retrieving the handkerchief and intercepting her on her reluctant way to the door*] Youre an ungrateful wicked girl. This is my return for offering to take you out of the gutter and dress you beautifully and make a lady of you.

MRS PEARCE. Stop, Mr Higgins. I wont allow it. It's you that are wicked. Go home to your parents, girl; and tell them to take better care of you.

LIZA. I aint got no parents. They told me I was big enough to earn my own living and turned me out.

MRS PEARCE. Wheres your mother?

LIZA. I aint got no mother. Her that turned me out was my sixth stepmother. But I done without them. And I'm a good girl, I am.

HIGGINS. Very well, then, what on earth is all this fuss about? The girl doesnt belong to anybody—is no use of anybody but me. [*He goes to Mrs Pearce and begins coaxing*]. You can adopt her, Mrs Pearce: I'm sure a daughter would be a great amusement to you. Now dont make any more fuss. Take her downstairs; and—

MRS PEARCE. But whats to become of her? Is she to be paid anything? Do be sensible, sir.

HIGGINS. Oh, pay her whatever is necessary: put it down in the housekeeping book. [*Impatiently*] What on earth will she want with money? She'll have her food and her clothes. She'll only drink if you give her money.

LIZA [*turning on him*] Oh you are a brute. It's a lie: nobody ever saw the sign of liquor on me. [*To Pickering*] Oh, sir: youre a gentleman: dont let him speak to me like that.

PICKERING [*in good-humored remonstrance*] Does it occur to you, Higgins, that the girl has some feelings?

HIGGINS [*looking critically at her*] Oh no, I dont

think so. Not any feelings that we need bother about. [*Cheerily*] Have you, Eliza?

LIZA. I got my feelings same as anyone else.

HIGGINS [*to Pickering, reflectively*] You see the difficulty?

PICKERING. Eh? What difficulty?

HIGGINS. To get her to talk grammar. The mere pronunciation is easy enough.

LIZA. I dont want to talk grammar. I want to talk like a lady in a flower-shop.

MRS PEARCE. Will you please keep to the point, Mr Higgins. I want to know on what terms the girl is to be here. Is she to have any wages? And what is to become of her when youve finished your teaching? You must look ahead a little.

HIGGINS [*impatiently*] Whats to become of her if I leave her in the gutter? Tell me that, Mrs Pearce.

MRS PEARCE. Thats her own business, not yours, Mr Higgins.

HIGGINS. Well, when Ive done with her, we can throw her back into the gutter; and then it will be her own business again; so thats all right.

LIZA. Oh, youve no feeling heart in you: you dont care for nothing but yourself. [*She rises and takes the floor resolutely*]. Here! Ive had enough of this. I'm going [*making for the door*]. You ought to be ashamed of yourself, you ought.

HIGGINS [*snatching a chocolate cream from the piano, his eyes suddenly beginning to twinkle with mischief*] Have some chocolates, Eliza.

LIZA [*halting, tempted*] How do I know what might be in them? Ive heard of girls being drugged by the like of you.

Higgins whips out his penknife; cuts a chocolate in two; puts one half into his mouth and bolts it; and offers her the other half.

HIGGINS. Pledge of good faith, Eliza. I eat one half: you eat the other. [*Liza opens her mouth to retort: he pops the half chocolate into it*]. You shall have boxes of them, barrels of them, every day. You shall live on them. Eh?

LIZA [*who has disposed of the chocolate after being nearly choked by it*] I wouldnt have ate it, only I'm too ladylike to take it out of my mouth.

HIGGINS. Listen, Eliza. I think you said you came in a taxi.

LIZA. Well, what if I did? Ive as good a right to take a taxi as anyone else.

HIGGINS. You have, Eliza; and in future you shall have as many taxis as you want. You shall go up and down and round the town in a taxi every day. Think of that, Eliza.

MRS PEARCE. Mr Higgins: youre tempting the girl. It's not right. She should think of the future.

HIGGINS. At her age! Nonsense! Time enough to think of the future when you havnt any future to think of. No, Eliza: do as this lady does: think of other people's futures; but never think of your own. Think of chocolates, and taxis, and gold, and diamonds.

LIZA. No: I dont want no gold and no diamonds. I'm a good girl, I am. [*She sits down again, with an attempt at dignity*].

HIGGINS. You shall remain so, Eliza, under the care of Mrs Pearce. And you shall marry an officer in the Guards, with a beautiful moustache: the son of a marquis, who will disinherit him for marrying you, but will relent when he sees your beauty and goodness—

PICKERING. Excuse me, Higgins; but I really must interfere. Mrs Pearce is quite right. If this girl is to put herself in your hands for six months for an experiment in teaching, she must understand thoroughly what she's doing.

HIGGINS. How can she? She's incapable of understanding anything. Besides, do any of us understand what we are doing? If we did, would we ever do it?

PICKERING. Very clever, Higgins; but not to the present point. [*To Eliza*] Miss Doolittle—

LIZA [*overwhelmed*] Ah-ah-ow-oo!

HIGGINS. There! Thats all youll get out of Eliza. Ah-ah-ow-oo! No use explaining. As a military man you ought to know that. Give her her orders: thats enough for her. Eliza: you are to live here for the next six months, learning how to speak beautifully, like a lady in a florist's shop. If youre good and do whatever youre told, you shall sleep in a proper bedroom, and have lots to eat, and money to buy chocolates and take rides in taxis. If youre naughty and idle you will sleep in the back kitchen among the black beetles, and be walloped by Mrs Pearce with a broomstick. At the end of six months you shall go to Buckingham Palace in a carriage, beautifully dressed. If the King finds out youre not a lady, you will be taken by the police to the Tower of London, where your head will be cut off as a warning to other presumptuous flower girls. If you are not found out, you shall have a present of seven-and-sixpence to start life with as a lady in a shop. If you refuse this offer you will be a most ungrateful wicked girl; and the angels will weep for you. [*To Pickering*] Now are you satisfied, Pickering? [*To Mrs Pearce*] Can I put it more plainly and fairly, Mrs Pearce?

MRS PEARCE [*patiently*] I think youd better let me speak to the girl properly in private. I dont know that

I can take charge of her or consent to the arrangement at all. Of course I know you dont mean her any harm; but when you get what you call interested in people's accents, you never think or care what may happen to them or you. Come with me, Eliza.

HIGGINS. Thats all right. Thank you, Mrs Pearce. Bundle her off to the bath-room.

LIZA [*rising reluctantly and suspiciously*] Youre a great bully, you are. I wont stay here if I dont like. I wont let nobody wallop me. I never asked to go to Bucknam Palace, I didnt. I was never in trouble with the police, not me. I'm a good girl—

MRS PEARCE. Dont answer back, girl. You dont understand the gentleman. Come with me. [*She leads the way to the door, and holds it open for Eliza*].

LIZA [*as she goes out*] Well, what I say is right. I wont go near the King, not if I'm going to have my head cut off. If I'd known what I was letting myself in for, I wouldnt have come here. I always been a good girl; and I never offered to say a word to him; and I dont owe him nothing; and I dont care; and I wont be put upon; and I have my feelings the same as anyone else—

Mrs Pearce shuts the door; and Eliza's plaints are no longer audible.

* * * * *

Eliza is taken upstairs to the third floor greatly to her surprise; for she expected to be taken down to the scullery. There Mrs Pearce opens a door and takes her into a spare bedroom.

MRS PEARCE. I will have to put you here. This will be your bedroom.

LIZA. O-h, I couldnt sleep here, missus. It's too good for the likes of me. I should be afraid to touch anything. I aint a duchess yet, you know.

MRS PEARCE. You have got to make yourself as clean as the room: then you wont be afraid of it. And you must call me Mrs Pearce, not missus. [*She throws open the door of the dressingroom, now modernized as a bathroom*].

LIZA. Gawd! whats this? Is this where you wash clothes? Funny sort of copper I call it.

MRS PEARCE. It is not a copper. This is where we wash ourselves, Eliza, and where I am going to wash you.

LIZA. You expect me to get into that and wet myself all over! Not me. I should catch my death. I knew a woman did it every Saturday night; and she died of it.

MRS PEARCE. Mr Higgins has the gentlemen's bathroom downstairs; and he has a bath every morning, in cold water.

LIZA. Ugh! He's made of iron, that man.

MRS PEARCE. If you are to sit with him and the Colonel and be taught you will have to do the same. They wont like the smell of you if you dont. But you can have the water as hot as you like. There are two taps: hot and cold.

LIZA [*weeping*] I couldnt. I dursnt. Its not natural: it would kill me. Ive never had a bath in my life: not what youd call a proper one.

MRS PEARCE. Well, dont you want to be clean and sweet and decent, like a lady? You know you cant be a nice girl inside if youre a dirty slut outside.

LIZA. Boohoo!!!!

MRS PEARCE. Now stop crying and go back into your room and take off all your clothes. Then wrap yourself in this [*Taking down a gown from its peg and handing it to her*] and come back to me. I will get the bath ready.

LIZA [*all tears*] I cant. I wont. I'm not used to it. Ive never took off all my clothes before. It's not right: it's not decent.

MRS PEARCE. Nonsense, child. Dont you take off all your clothes every night when you go to bed?

LIZA [*amazed*] No. Why should I? I should catch my death. Of course I take off my skirt.

MRS PEARCE. Do you mean that you sleep in the underclothes you wear in the daytime?

LIZA. What else have I to sleep in?

MRS PEARCE. You will never do that again as long as you live here. I will get you a proper nightdress.

LIZA. Do you mean change into cold things and lie awake shivering half the night? You want to kill me, you do.

MRS PEARCE. I want to change you from a frowzy slut to a clean respectable girl fit to sit with the gentlemen in the study. Are you going to trust me and do what I tell you or be thrown out and sent back to your flower basket?

LIZA. But you dont know what the cold is to me. You dont know how I dread it.

MRS PEARCE. Your bed wont be cold here: I will put a hot water bottle in it. [*Pushing her into the bedroom*] Off with you and undress.

LIZA. Oh, if only I'd a known what a dreadful thing it is to be clean I'd never have come. I didnt know when I was well off. I—[*Mrs Pearce pushes her through the door, but leaves it partly open lest her prisoner should take to flight*].

Mrs Pearce puts on a pair of white rubber sleeves, and fills the bath, mixing hot and cold, and testing the result with the bath thermometer. She perfumes it with a handful of bath salts and adds a palmful of mustard. She then takes a formidable looking long handled scrubbing brush and soaps it profusely with a ball of scented soap.

Eliza comes back with nothing on but the bath gown huddled tightly round her, a piteous spectacle of abject terror.

MRS PEARCE. Now come along. Take that thing off.

LIZA. Oh I couldnt, Mrs Pearce: I rcelly couldnt. I never done such a thing.

MRS PEARCE. Nonsense. Here: step in and tell me whether its hot enough for you.

LIZA. Ah-oo! Ah-oo! It's too hot.

MRS PEARCE [*deftly snatching the gown away and throwing Eliza down on her back*] It wont hurt you. [*She sets to work with the scrubbing brush*].

Eliza's screams are heartrending.

  ★ ★ ★ ★ ★

Meanwhile the Colonel has been having it out with Higgins about Eliza. Pickering has come from the hearth to the chair and seated himself astride of it with his arms on the back to cross-examine him.

PICKERING. Excuse the straight question, Higgins. Are you a man of good character where women are concerned?

HIGGINS [*moodily*] Have you ever met a man of good character where women are concerned?

PICKERING. Yes: very frequently.

HIGGINS [*dogmatically, lifting himself on his hands to the level of the piano, and sitting on it with a bounce*] Well, I havnt. I find that the moment I let a woman make friends with me, she becomes jealous, exacting, suspicious, and a damned nuisance. I find that the moment I let myself make friends with a woman, I become selfish and tyrannical. Women upset everything. When you let them into your life, you find that the woman is driving at one thing and youre driving at another.

PICKERING. At what, for example?

HIGGINS [*coming off the piano restlessly*] Oh, Lord knows! I suppose the woman wants to live her own life; and the man wants to live his; and each tries to drag the other on to the wrong track. One wants to go north and the other south; and the result is that both have to go east, though they both hate the east wind. [*He sits down on the bench at the keyboard*]. So here I am, a confirmed old bachelor, and likely to remain so.

PICKERING [*rising and standing over him gravely*] Come, Higgins! You know what I mean. If I'm to be in this business I shall feel responsible for that girl. I hope it's understood that no advantage is to be taken of her position.

HIGGINS. What! That thing! Sacred, I assure you. [*Rising to explain*] You see, she'll be a pupil; and teaching would be impossible unless pupils were sacred. Ive taught scores of American millionairesses how to speak English: the best looking women in the world. I'm seasoned. They might as well be blocks of wood. *I* might as well be a block of wood. It's—

Mrs Pearce opens the door. She has Eliza's hat in her hand. Pickering retires to the easy-chair at the hearth and sits down.

HIGGINS [*eagerly*] Well, Mrs Pearce: is it all right?

MRS PEARCE [*at the door*] I just wish to trouble you with a word, if I may, Mr Higgins.

HIGGINS. Yes, certainly. Come in. [*She comes forward*]. Dont burn that, Mrs Pearce. I'll keep it as a curiosity. [*He takes the hat*].

MRS PEARCE. Handle it carefully, sir, please. I had to promise her not to burn it; but I had better put it in the oven for a while.

HIGGINS [*putting it down hastily on the piano*] Oh! thank you. Well, what have you to say to me?

PICKERING. Am I in the way?

MRS PEARCE. Not at all, sir. Mr Higgins: will you please be very particular what you say before the girl?

HIGGINS [*sternly*] Of course. I'm always particular about what I say. Why do you say this to me?

MRS PEARCE [*unmoved*] No, sir: youre not at all particular when youve mislaid anything or when you get a little impatient. Now it doesnt matter before me: I'm used to it. But you really must not swear before the girl.

HIGGINS [*indignantly*] *I* swear! [*Most emphatically*] I never swear. I detest the habit. What the devil do you mean?

MRS PEARCE [*stolidly*] Thats what I mean, sir. You swear a great deal too much. I dont mind your damning and blasting, and what the devil and where the devil and who the devil—

HIGGINS. Mrs Pearce: this language from your lips! Really!

MRS PEARCE [*not to be put off*]—but there is a certain word I must ask you not to use. The girl used it herself when she began to enjoy the bath. It begins with the same letter as bath. She knows no better: she learnt it at her mother's knee. But she must not hear it from your lips.

HIGGINS [*loftily*] I cannot charge myself with having ever uttered it, Mrs Pearce. [*She looks at him stead-fastly. He adds, hiding an uneasy conscience with a judicial air*] Except perhaps in a moment of extreme and justifiable excitement.

MRS PEARCE. Only this morning, sir, you applied it to your boots, to the butter, and to the brown bread.

HIGGINS. Oh, that! Mere alliteration, Mrs Pearce, natural to a poet.

MRS PEARCE. Well, sir, whatever you choose to call it, I beg you not to let the girl hear you repeat it.

HIGGINS. Oh, very well, very well. Is that all?

MRS PEARCE. No, sir. We shall have to be very particular with this girl as to personal cleanliness.

HIGGINS. Certainly. Quite right. Most important.

MRS PEARCE. I mean not to be slovenly about her dress or untidy in leaving things about.

HIGGINS [*going to her solemnly*] Just so. I intended to call your attention to that. [*He passes on to Pickering, who is enjoying the conversation immensely*]. It is these little things that matter, Pickering. Take care of the pence and the pounds will take care of themselves is as true of personal habits as of money. [*He comes to anchor on the hearthrug, with the air of a man in an unassailable position*].

MRS PEARCE. Yes, sir. Then might I ask you not to come down to breakfast in your dressing-gown, or at any rate not to use it as a napkin to the extent you do, sir. And if you would be so good as not to eat everything off the same plate, and to remember not to put the porridge saucepan out of your hand on the clean tablecloth, it would be a better example to the girl. You know you nearly choked yourself with a fishbone in the jam only last week.

HIGGINS [*routed from the hearthrug and drifting back to the piano*] I may do these things sometimes in absence of mind; but surely I dont do them habitually. [*Angrily*] By the way: my dressing-gown smells most damnably of benzine.

MRS PEARCE. No doubt it does, Mr Higgins. But if you will wipe your fingers—

HIGGINS [*yelling*] Oh very well, very well: I'll wipe them in my hair in future.

MRS PEARCE. I hope youre not offended, Mr Higgins.

HIGGINS [*shocked at finding himself thought capable of an unamiable sentiment*] Not at all, not at all. Youre quite right, Mrs Pearce: I shall be particularly careful before the girl. Is that all?

MRS PEARCE. No, sir. Might she use some of those Japanese dresses you brought from abroad? I really cant put her back into her old things.

HIGGINS. Certainly. Anything you like. Is that all?

MRS PEARCE. Thank you, sir. Thats all. [*She goes out*].

HIGGINS. You know, Pickering, that woman has the most extraordinary ideas about me. Here I am, a shy, diffident sort of man. Ive never been able to feel really grown-up and tremendous, like other chaps. And yet she's firmly persuaded that I'm an arbitrary over-bearing bossing kind of person. I cant account for it.

Mrs Pearce returns.

MRS PEARCE. If you please, sir, the trouble's beginning already. Theres a dustman downstairs, Alfred Doolittle, wants to see you. He says you have his daughter here.

PICKERING [*rising*] Phew! I say!

HIGGINS [*promptly*] Send the blackguard up.

MRS PEARCE. Oh, very well, sir. [*She goes out*].

PICKERING. He may not be a blackguard, Higgins.

HIGGINS. Nonsense. Of course he's a blackguard.

PICKERING. Whether he is or not, I'm afraid we shall have some trouble with him.

HIGGINS [*confidently*] Oh no: I think not. If theres any trouble he shall have it with me, not I with him. And we are sure to get something interesting out of him.

PICKERING. About the girl?

HIGGINS. No. I mean his dialect.

PICKERING. Oh!

MRS PEARCE [*at the door*] Doolittle, sir. [*She admits Doolittle and retires*].

Alfred Doolittle is an elderly but vigorous dustman, clad in the costume of his profession, including a hat with a back brim covering his neck and shoulders. He has well marked and rather interesting features, and seems equally free from fear and conscience. He has a remarkably expressive voice, the result of a habit of giving vent to his feelings without reserve. His present pose is that of wounded honor and stern resolution.

DOOLITTLE [*at the door, uncertain which of the two gentlemen is his man*] Professor Iggins?

HIGGINS. Here. Good morning. Sit down.

DOOLITTLE. Morning, Governor. [*He sits down magisterially*] I come about a very serious matter, Governor.

HIGGINS [*to Pickering*] Brought up in Hounslow. Mother Welsh, I should think. [*Doolittle opens his mouth, amazed. Higgins continues*] What do you want, Doolittle?

DOOLITTLE [*menacingly*] I want my daughter: thats what I want. See?

HIGGINS. Of course you do. Youre her father, arnt you? You dont suppose anyone else wants her, do you? I'm glad to see you have some spark of family feeling left. She's upstairs. Take her away at once.

DOOLITTLE [*rising, fearfully taken aback*] What!

HIGGINS. Take her away. Do you suppose I'm going to keep your daughter for you?

DOOLITTLE [*remonstrating*] Now, now, look here, Governor. Is this reasonable? Is it fairity to take advantage of a man like this? The girl belongs to me. You got her. Where do I come in? [*He sits down again*].

HIGGINS. Your daughter had the audacity to come to my house and ask me to teach her how to speak properly so that she could get a place in a flower-shop. This gentleman and my housekeeper have been here all the time. [*Bullying him*] How dare you come here and attempt to blackmail me? You sent her here on purpose.

DOOLITTLE [*protesting*] No, Governor.

HIGGINS. You must have. How else could you possibly know that she is here?

DOOLITTLE. Dont take a man up like that, Governor.

HIGGINS. The police shall take you up. This is a plant—a plot to extort money by threats. I shall telephone for the police [*he goes resolutely to the telephone and opens the directory*].

DOOLITTLE. Have I asked you for a brass farthing? I leave it to the gentleman here: have I said a word about money?

HIGGINS [*throwing the book aside and marching down on Doolittle with a poser*] What else did you come for?

DOOLITTLE [*sweetly*] Well, what would a man come for? Be human, Governor.

HIGGINS [*disarmed*] Alfred: did you put her up to it?

DOOLITTLE. So help me, Governor, I never did. I take my Bible oath I aint seen the girl these two months past.

HIGGINS. Then how did you know she was here?

DOOLITTLE ["*most musical, most melancholy*"] I'll tell you, Governor, if youll only let me get a word in. I'm willing to tell you. I'm wanting to tell you. I'm waiting to tell you.

HIGGINS. Pickering: this chap has a certain natural gift of rhetoric. Observe the rhythm of his native woodnotes wild. "I'm willing to tell you: I'm wanting to tell you: I'm waiting to tell you." Sentimental rhetoric! thats the Welsh strain in him. It also accounts for his mendacity and dishonesty.

PICKERING. Oh, please, Higgins: I'm west country

myself. [*To Doolittle*] How did you know the girl was here if you didnt send her?

DOOLITTLE. It was like this, Governor. The girl took a boy in the taxi to give him a jaunt. Son of her landlady, he is. He hung about on the chance of her giving him another ride home. Well, she sent him back for her luggage when she heard you was willing for her to stop here. I met the boy at the corner of Long Acre and Endell Street.

HIGGINS. Public house. Yes?

DOOLITTLE. The poor man's club, Governor: why shouldnt I?

PICKERING. Do let him tell his story, Higgins.

DOOLITTLE. He told me what was up. And I ask you, what was my feelings and my duty as a father? I says to the boy, "You bring me the luggage," I says—

PICKERING. Why didnt you go for it yourself?

DOOLITTLE. Landlady wouldnt have trusted me with it, Governor. She's that kind of woman: you know. I had to give the boy a penny afore he trusted me with it, the little swine. I brought it to her just to oblige you like, and make myself agreeable. Thats all.

HIGGINS. How much luggage?

DOOLITTLE. Musical instrument, Governor. A few pictures, a trifle of jewlery, and a bird-cage. She said she didnt want no clothes. What was I to think from that, Governor? I ask you as a parent what was I to think?

HIGGINS. So you came to rescue her from worse than death, eh?

DOOLITTLE [*appreciatively: relieved at being so well understood*] Just so, Governor. Thats right.

PICKERING. But why did you bring her luggage if you intended to take her away?

DOOLITTLE. Have I said a word about taking her away? Have I now?

HIGGINS [*determinedly*] Youre going to take her away, double quick. [*He crosses to the hearth and rings the bell*].

DOOLITTLE [*rising*] No, Governor. Dont say that. I'm not the man to stand in my girl's light. Heres a career opening for her, as you might say; and—

Mrs Pearce opens the door and awaits orders.

HIGGINS. Mrs Pearce: this is Eliza's father. He has come to take her away. Give her to him. [*He goes back to the piano, with an air of washing his hands of the whole affair*].

DOOLITTLE. No. This is a misunderstanding. Listen here—

MRS PEARCE. He cant take her away, Mr Higgins: how can he? You told me to burn her clothes.

DOOLITTLE. Thats right. I cant carry the girl through the streets like a blooming monkey, can I? I put it to you.

HIGGINS. You have put it to me that you want your daughter. Take your daughter. If she has no clothes go out and buy her some.

DOOLITTLE [*desperate*] Wheres the clothes she come in? Did I burn them or did your missus here?

MRS PEARCE. I am the housekeeper, if you please. I have sent for some clothes for your girl. When they come you can take her away. You can wait in the kitchen. This way, please.

Doolittle, much troubled, accompanies her to the door; then hesitates; finally turns confidentially to Higgins.

DOOLITTLE. Listen here, Governor. You and me is men of the world aint we?

HIGGINS. Oh! Men of the world, are we? Youd better go, Mrs Pearce.

MRS PEARCE. I think so, indeed, sir. [*She goes, with dignity*].

PICKERING. The floor is yours, Mr Doolittle.

DOOLITTLE [*to Pickering*] I thank you, Governor. [*To Higgins, who takes refuge on the piano bench, a little overwhelmed by the proximity of his visitor; for Doolittle has a professional flavour of dust about him*]. Well, the truth is, Ive taken a sort of fancy to you, Governor; and if you want the girl, I'm not so set on having her back home again but what I might be open to an arrangement. Regarded in the light of a young woman, she's a fine handsome girl. As a daughter she's not worth her keep; and so I tell you straight. All I ask is my rights as a father; and youre the last man alive to expect me to let her go for nothing; for I can see youre one of the straight sort, Governor. Well, whats a five-pound note to you? and whats Eliza to me? [*He turns to his chair and sits down judicially*].

PICKERING. I think you ought to know, Doolittle, that Mr Higgins's intentions are entirely honorable.

DOOLITTLE. Course they are, Governor. If I thought they wasn't, I'd ask fifty.

HIGGINS [*revolted*] Do you mean to say that you would sell your daughter for £50?

DOOLITTLE. Not in a general way I wouldnt; but to oblige a gentleman like you I'd do a good deal, I do assure you.

PICKERING. Have you no morals, man?

DOOLITTLE [*unabashed*] Cant afford them, Governor. Neither could you if you was as poor as me. Not that I mean any harm, you know. But if Liza is going to have a bit out of this, why not me too?

HIGGINS [*troubled*] I dont know what to do, Pickering. There can be no question that as a matter of morals it's a positive crime to give this chap a farthing. And yet I feel a sort of rough justice in his claim.

DOOLITTLE. Thats it, Governor. Thats all I say. A father's heart, as it were.

PICKERING. Well, I know the feeling; but really it seems hardly right—

DOOLITTLE. Dont say that, Governor. Dont look at it that way. What am I, Governors both? I ask you, what am I? I'm one of the undeserving poor: thats what I am. Think of what that means to a man. It means that he's up agen middle class morality all the time. If theres anything going, and I put in for a bit of it, it's always the same story: "Youre undeserving; so you cant have it." But my needs is as great as the most deserving widow's that ever got money out of six different charities in one week for the death of the same husband. I dont need less than a deserving man: I need more. I dont eat less hearty than him; and I drink a lot more. I want a bit of amusement, cause I'm a thinking man. I want cheerfulness and a song and a band when I feel low. Well, they charge me just the same for everything as they charge the deserving. What is middle class morality? Just an excuse for never giving me anything. Therefore, I ask you, as two gentlemen, not to play that game on me. I'm playing straight with you. I aint pretending to be deserving. I'm undeserving; and I mean to go on being undeserving. I like it; and thats the truth. Will you take advantage of a man's nature to do him out of the price of his own daughter what he's brought up and fed and clothed by the sweat of his brow until she's growed big enough to be interesting to you two gentlemen? Is five pounds unreasonable? I put it to you; and I leave it to you.

HIGGINS [*rising, and going over to Pickering*]

Pickering: if we were to take this man in hand for three months, he could choose between a seat in the Cabinet and a popular pulpit in Wales.

PICKERING. What do you say to that, Doolittle?

DOOLITTLE. Not me, Governor, thank you kindly. Ive heard all the preachers and all the prime ministers —for I'm a thinking man and game for politics or religion or social reform same as all the other amusements—and I tell you it's a dog's life any way you look at it. Undeserving poverty is my line. Taking one station in society with another, it's—it's—well, it's the only one that has any ginger in it, to my taste.

HIGGINS. I suppose we must give him a fiver.

PICKERING. He'll make a bad use of it, I'm afraid.

DOOLITTLE. Not me, Governor, so help me I wont. Dont you be afraid that I'll save it and spare it and live idle on it. There wont be a penny of it left by Monday: I'll have to go to work same as if I'd never had it. It wont pauperize me, you bet. Just one good spree for myself and the missus, giving pleasure to ourselves and employment to others, and satisfaction to you to think it's not been throwed away. You couldnt spend it better.

HIGGINS [taking out his pocket book and coming between Doolittle and the piano] This is irresistible. Lets give him ten. [He offers two notes to the dustman].

DOOLITTLE. No, Governor. She wouldnt have the heart to spend ten; and perhaps I shouldnt neither. Ten pounds is a lot of money: it makes a man feel prudent like; and then goodbye to happiness. You give me what I ask you, Governor: not a penny more, and not a penny less.

PICKERING. Why dont you marry that missus of yours? I rather draw the line at encouraging that sort of immorality.

DOOLITTLE. Tell her so, Governor: tell her so. *I'm*
willing. It's me that suffers by it. Ive no hold on her.
I got to be agreeable to her. I got to give her presents.
I got to buy her clothes something sinful. I'm a slave
to that woman, Governor, just because I'm not her
lawful husband. And she knows it too. Catch her
marrying me! Take my advice, Governor: marry
Eliza while she's young and dont know no better. If
you dont youll be sorry for it after. If you do, she'll
be sorry for it after; but better her than you, because
youre a man, and she's only a woman and dont know
how to be happy anyhow.

HIGGINS. Pickering: if we listen to this man another
minute, we shall have no convictions left. [*To
Doolittle*] Five pounds I think you said.

DOOLITTLE. Thank you kindly, Governor.

HIGGINS. Youre sure you wont take ten?

DOOLITTLE. Not now. Another time, Governor.

HIGGINS [*handing him a five-pound note*] Here you are.

DOOLITTLE. Thank you, Governor. Good morning.
[*He hurries to the door, anxious to get away with his
booty. When he opens it he is confronted with a dainty
and exquisitely clean young Japanese lady in a simple
blue cotton kimono printed cunningly with small white
jasmine blossoms. Mrs Pearce is with her. He gets out
of her way deferentially and apologizes*]. Beg pardon,
miss.

THE JAPANESE LADY. Garn! Dont you know your
own daughter?

DOOLITTLE	*exclaiming*	Bly me! it's Eliza!
HIGGINS	*simul-*	Whats that? This!
PICKERING	*taneously*	By Jove!

LIZA. Dont I look silly?

HIGGINS. Silly?

MRS PEARCE [*at the door*] Now, Mr Higgins, please

dont say anything to make the girl conceited about herself.

HIGGINS [*conscientiously*] Oh! Quite right, Mrs Pearce. [*To Eliza*] Yes: damned silly.

MRS PEARCE. Please, sir.

HIGGINS [*correcting himself*] I mean extremely silly.

LIZA. I should look all right with my hat on. [*She takes up her hat; puts it on; and walks across the room to the fireplace with a fashionable air*].

HIGGINS. A new fashion, by George! And it ought to look horrible!

DOOLITTLE [*with fatherly pride*] Well, I never thought she'd clean up as good looking as that, Governor. She's a credit to me, aint she?

LIZA. I tell you, it's easy to clean up here. Hot and cold water on tap, just as much as you like, there is. Woolly towels, there is; and a towel horse so hot, it burns your fingers. Soft brushes to scrub yourself, and a wooden bowl of soap smelling like primroses. Now I know why ladies is so clean. Washing's a treat for them. Wish they could see what it is for the like of me!

HIGGINS. I'm glad the bathroom met with your approval.

LIZA. It didnt: not all of it; and I dont care who hears me say it. Mrs Pearce knows.

HIGGINS. What was wrong, Mrs Pearce?

MRS PEARCE [*blandly*] Oh, nothing, sir. It doesnt matter.

LIZA. I had a good mind to break it. I didnt know which way to look. But I hung a towel over it, I did.

HIGGINS. Over what?

MRS PEARCE. Over the looking-glass, sir.

HIGGINS. Doolittle: you have brought your daughter up too strictly.

DOOLITTLE. Me! I never brought her up at all, except to give her a lick of a strap now and again. Dont put it on me, Governor. She aint accustomed to it, you see: thats all. But she'll soon pick up your free-and-easy ways.

LIZA. I'm a good girl, I am; and I wont pick up no free-and-easy ways.

HIGGINS. Eliza: if you say again that youre a good girl, your father shall take you home.

LIZA. Not him. You dont know my father. All he come here for was to touch you for some money to get drunk on.

DOOLITTLE. Well, what else would I want money for? To put into the plate in church, I suppose. [*She puts out her tongue at him. He is so incensed by this that Pickering presently finds it necessary to step between them*]. Dont you give me none of your lip; and dont let me hear you giving this gentleman any of it neither, or youll hear from me about it. See?

HIGGINS. Have you any further advice to give her before you go, Doolittle? Your blessing, for instance.

DOOLITTLE. No, Governor: I aint such a mug as to put up my children to all I know myself. Hard enough to hold them in without that. If you want Eliza's mind improved, Governor, you do it yourself with a strap. So long, gentlemen. [*He turns to go*].

HIGGINS [*impressively*] Stop. Youll come regularly to see your daughter. It's your duty, you know. My brother is a clergyman; and he could help you in your talks with her.

DOOLITTLE [*evasively*] Certainly, I'll come, Governor. Not just this week, because I have a job at a distance. But later on you may depend on me. Afternoon, gentlemen. Afternoon, maam. [*He touches his hat to Mrs Pearce, who disdains the salutation and goes out. He winks at Higgins, thinking him probably a fellow sufferer from Mrs Pearce's difficult disposition, and follows her].*

LIZA. Dont you believe the old liar. He'd as soon you set a bulldog on him as a clergyman. You wont see him again in a hurry.

HIGGINS. I dont want to, Eliza. Do you?

LIZA. Not me. I dont want never to see him again, I dont. He's a disgrace to me, he is, collecting dust, instead of working at his trade.

PICKERING. What is his trade, Eliza?

LIZA. Talking money out of other people's pockets into his own. His proper trade's a navvy; and he works at it sometimes too—for exercise—and earns good money at it. Aint you going to call me Miss Doolittle any more?

PICKERING. I beg your pardon, Miss Doolittle. It was a slip of the tongue.

LIZA. Oh, I dont mind; only it sounded so genteel. I should just like to take a taxi to the corner of Tottenham Court Road and get out there and tell it to wait for me, just to put the girls in their place a bit. I wouldnt speak to them, you know.

PICKERING. Better wait til we get you something really fashionable.

HIGGINS. Besides, you shouldnt cut your old friends now that you have risen in the world. Thats what we call snobbery.

LIZA. You dont call the like of them my friends now, I should hope. Theyve took it out of me often enough with their ridicule when they had the chance; and now I mean to get a bit of my own back. But if I'm to have fashionable clothes, I'll wait. I should like to have some. Mrs Pearce says youre going to give me some to wear in bed at night different to what I wear in the daytime; but it do seem a waste of money when you could get something to shew. Besides, I never could fancy changing into cold things on a winter night.

MRS PEARCE [*coming back*] Now, Eliza. The new things have come for you to try on.

LIZA. Ah-ow-oo-ooh! [*She rushes out*].

MRS PEARCE [*following her*] Oh, dont rush about like that, girl. [*She shuts the door behind her*].

HIGGINS. Pickering: we have taken on a stiff job.

PICKERING [*with conviction*] Higgins: we have.

    ★   ★   ★   ★   ★

There seems to be some curiosity as to what Higgins's lessons to Eliza were like. Well, here is a sample: the first one.

Picture Eliza, in her new clothes, and feeling her inside put out of step by a lunch, dinner, and breakfast of a kind to which it is unaccustomed, seated with Higgins and the Colonel in the study, feeling like a hospital out-patient at a first encounter with the doctors.

Higgins, constitutionally unable to sit still, discomposes her still more by striding restlessly about. But for the reassuring presence and quietude of her friend the Colonel she would run for her life, even back to Drury Lane.

HIGGINS. Say your alphabet.

LIZA. I know my alphabet. Do you think I know nothing? I dont need to be taught like a child.

HIGGINS [*thundering*] Say your alphabet.

PICKERING. Say it, Miss Doolittle. You will understand presently. Do what he tells you; and let him teach you in his own way.

LIZA. Oh well, if you put it like that—Ahyee, bəyee, cəyee, dəyee—

HIGGINS [*with the roar of a wounded lion*] Stop.

Listen to this, Pickering. This is what we pay for as elementary education. This unfortunate animal has been locked up for nine years in school at our expense to teach her to speak and read the language of Shakespear and Milton. And the result is Ahyee, Bə-yee, Cə-yee, Də-yee. [*To Eliza*] Say A, B, C, D.

LIZA [*almost in tears*] But I'm sayin it. Ahyee, Bəyee, Cə-yee—

HIGGINS. Stop. Say a cup of tea.

LIZA. A cappətə-ee.

HIGGINS. Put your tongue forward until it squeezes against the top of your lower teeth. Now say cup.

LIZA. C-c-c—I cant. C-Cup.

PICKERING. Good. Splendid, Miss Doolittle.

HIGGINS. By Jupiter, she's done it at the first shot. Pickering: we shall make a duchess of her. [*To Eliza*] Now do you think you could possibly say tea? Not tə-yee, mind: if you ever say bə-yee cə-yee də-yee again you shall be dragged round the room three times by the hair of your head. [*Fortissimo*] T, T, T, T.

LIZA [*weeping*] I cant hear no difference cep that it sounds more genteel-like when you say it.

HIGGINS. Well, if you can hear that difference, what the devil are you crying for? Pickering: give her a chocolate.

PICKERING. No, no. Never mind crying a little, Miss Doolittle: you are doing very well; and the lessons wont hurt. I promise you I wont let him drag you round the room by your hair.

HIGGINS. Be off with you to Mrs Pearce and tell her about it. Think about it. Try to do it by yourself: and keep your tongue well forward in your mouth instead of trying to roll it up and swallow it. Another lesson at half-past four this afternoon. Away with you.

Eliza, still sobbing, rushes from the room.

And that is the sort of ordeal poor Eliza has to go through for months before we meet her again on her first appearance in London society of the professional class.

It is Mrs Higgins's at-home day. Nobody has yet arrived. Her drawing room, in a flat on Chelsea Embankment, has three windows looking on the river; and the ceiling is not so lofty as it would be in an older house of the same pretension. The windows are open, giving access to a balcony with flowers in pots. If you stand with your face to the windows, you have the fireplace on your left and the door in the right-hand wall close to the corner nearest the windows.

Mrs Higgins was brought up on Morris and Burne Jones; and her room, which is very unlike her son's room in Wimpole Street, is not crowded with furniture and little tables and nicknacks. In the middle of the room there is a big ottoman; and this, with the carpet, the Morris wall-papers, and the Morris chintz window curtains and brocade covers of the ottoman and its cushions, supply all the ornament, and are much too handsome to be hidden by odds and ends of useless things. A few good oil-paintings from the exhibitions in the Grosvenor Gallery thirty years ago (the Burne Jones, not the Whistler side of them) are on the walls. The only landscape is a Cecil Lawson on the scale of a Rubens. There is a portrait of Mrs Higgins as she was when she defied fashion in her youth in one of the beautiful Rossettian costumes which, when caricatured by people who did not understand, led to the absurdities of popular estheticism in the eighteen-seventies.

In the corner diagonally opposite the door Mrs Higgins, now over sixty and long past taking the trouble to dress out of the fashion, sits writing at an elegantly simple writing-table with a bell button within reach of her hand. There is a Chippendale chair further back in the room between her and the window nearest her side. At the other side of the room, further forward, is an Elizabethan chair roughly carved in the taste of Inigo Jones. On the same side a piano in a decorated case. The corner between the fireplace and the window is occupied by a divan cushioned in Morris chintz.

It is between four and five in the afternoon.

The door is opened violently; and Higgins enters with his hat on.

MRS HIGGINS [*dismayed*] Henry! [*Scolding him*] What are you doing here today? It is my at-home day: you promised not to come. [*As he bends to kiss her, she takes his hat off, and presents it to him*].

HIGGINS. Oh bother! [*He throws the hat down on the table*].

MRS HIGGINS. Go home at once.

HIGGINS [*kissing her*] I know, mother. I came on purpose.

MRS HIGGINS. But you mustnt. I'm serious, Henry. You offend all my friends: they stop coming whenever they meet you.

HIGGINS. Nonsense! I know I have no small talk; but people dont mind. [*He sits on the settee*].

MRS HIGGINS. Oh! dont they? Small talk indeed! What about your large talk? Really, dear, you mustnt stay.

HIGGINS. I must. Ive a job for you. A phonetic job.

MRS HIGGINS. No use, dear. I'm sorry; but I cant get round your vowels; and though I like to get pretty postcards in your patent shorthand, I always have to read the copies in ordinary writing you so thoughtfully send me.

HIGGINS. Well, this isnt a phonetic job.

MRS HIGGINS. You said it was.

HIGGINS. Not your part of it. Ive picked up a girl.

MRS HIGGINS. Does that mean that some girl has picked you up?

HIGGINS. Not at all. I dont mean a love affair.

MRS HIGGINS. What a pity!

HIGGINS. Why?

MRS HIGGINS. Well, you never fall in love with anyone under forty-five. When will you discover that there are some rather nice-looking young women about?

HIGGINS. Oh, I cant be bothered with young women. My idea of a lovable woman is somebody as like you as possible. I shall never get into the way of seriously liking young women: some habits lie too deep to be changed. [*Rising abruptly and walking about, jingling his money and his keys in his trouser pockets*] Besides, theyre all idiots.

MRS HIGGINS. Do you know what you would do if you really loved me, Henry?

HIGGINS. Oh bother! What? Marry, I suppose.

MRS HIGGINS. No. Stop fidgeting and take your hands out of your pockets. [*With a gesture of despair, he obeys and sits down again*]. Thats a good boy. Now tell me about the girl.

HIGGINS. She's coming to see you.

MRS HIGGINS. I dont remember asking her.

HIGGINS. You didnt. *I* asked her. If youd known her you wouldnt have asked her.

MRS HIGGINS. Indeed! Why?

HIGGINS. Well, it's like this. She's a common flower girl. I picked her off the kerbstone.

MRS HIGGINS. And invited her to my at-home!

HIGGINS [*rising and coming to her to coax her*] Oh,

thatll be all right. Ive taught her to speak properly; and she has strict orders as to her behavior. She's to keep to two subjects: the weather and everybody's health—Fine day and How do you do, you know—and not to let herself go on things in general. That will be safe.

MRS HIGGINS. Safe! To talk about our health! about our insides! perhaps about our outsides! How could you be so silly, Henry?

HIGGINS [*impatiently*] Well, she must talk about something. [*He controls himself and sits down again*]. Oh, she'll be all right: dont you fuss. Pickering is in it with me. Ive a sort of bet on that I'll pass her off as a duchess in six months. I started on her some months ago; and she's getting on like a house on fire. I shall win my bet. She has a quick ear; and she's been easier to teach than my middle-class pupils because she's had to learn a complete new language. She talks English almost as you talk French.

MRS HIGGINS. Thats satisfactory, at all events.

HIGGINS. Well, it is and it isnt.

MRS HIGGINS. What does that mean?

HIGGINS. You see, Ive got her pronunciation all right; but you have to consider not only how a girl pronounces, but what she pronounces; and that's where—

[*They are interrupted by the parlor-maid, announcing guests.*

THE PARLOR-MAID. Mrs and Miss Eynsford Hill. [*She withdraws*].

HIGGINS. Oh Lord! [*He rises; snatches his hat from the table; and makes for the door; but before he reaches it his mother introduces him*].

Mrs and Miss Eynsford Hill are the mother and daughter who sheltered from the rain in Covent Garden. The mother is well bred, quiet, and has the habitual anxiety of straitened means. The daughter has acquired

*a gay air of being very much at home in society: the
bravado of genteel poverty.*

MRS EYNSFORD HILL [*to Mrs Higgins*] How do you
do? [*They shake hands*].

MISS EYNSFORD HILL. How d'you do? [*She shakes*].

MRS HIGGINS [*introducing*] My son Henry.

MRS EYNSFORD HILL. Your celebrated son! I have
so longed to meet you, Professor Higgins.

HIGGINS [*glumly, making no movement in her direction*]
Delighted. [*He backs against the piano and bows
brusquely*].

MISS EYNSFORD HILL [*going to him with confident
familiarity*] How do you do?

HIGGINS [*staring at her*] Ive seen you before somewhere. I havnt the ghost of a notion where; but Ive
heard your voice. [*Drearily*] It doesnt matter. Youd
better sit down.

MRS HIGGINS. I'm sorry to say that my celebrated
son has no manners. You mustnt mind him.

MISS EYNSFORD HILL [*gaily*] I dont. [*She sits in the
Elizabethan chair*].

MRS EYNSFORD HILL [*a little bewildered*] Not at all.
[*She sits on the ottoman between her daughter and Mrs
Higgins, who has turned her chair away from the
writing-table*].

HIGGINS. Oh, have I been rude? I didnt mean to be.

*He goes to the central window, through which, with
his back to the company, he contemplates the river and
the flowers in Battersea Park on the opposite bank as if
they were a frozen desert.*

The parlor-maid returns, ushering in Pickering.

THE PARLOR-MAID. Colonel Pickering. [*She withdraws*].

PICKERING. How do you do, Mrs Higgins?

MRS HIGGINS. So glad youve come. Do you know

Mrs Eynsford Hill—Miss Eynsford Hill? [*Exchange of bows. The Colonel brings the Chippendale chair a little forward between Mrs Hill and Mrs Higgins, and sits down*].

PICKERING. Has Henry told you what weve come for?

HIGGINS [*over his shoulder*] We were interrupted: damn it!

MRS HIGGINS. Oh Henry, Henry, really!

MRS EYNSFORD HILL [*half rising*] Are we in the way?

MRS HIGGINS [*rising and making her sit down again*] No, no. You couldnt have come more fortunately: we want you to meet a friend of ours.

HIGGINS [*turning hopefully*] Yes, by George! We want two or three people. Youll do as well as anybody else.

The parlor-maid returns, ushering Freddy.

THE PARLOR-MAID. Mr Eynsford Hill.

HIGGINS [*almost audibly, past endurance*] God of Heaven! another of them.

FREDDY [*shaking hands with Mrs Higgins*] Ahdedo?

MRS HIGGINS. Very good of you to come. [*Introducing*] Colonel Pickering.

FREDDY [*bowing*] Ahdedo?

MRS HIGGINS. I dont think you know my son, Professor Higgins.

FREDDY [*going to Higgins*] Ahdedo?

HIGGINS [*looking at him much as if he were a pickpocket*] I'll take my oath Ive met you before somewhere. Where was it?

FREDDY. I dont think so.

HIGGINS [*resignedly*] It dont matter, anyhow. Sit down.

He shakes Freddy's hand, and almost slings him on to

the ottoman with his face to the windows; then comes round to the other side of it.

HIGGINS. Well, here we are, anyhow! [*He sits down on the ottoman next Mrs Eynsford Hill on her left*]. And now what the devil are we going to talk about until Eliza comes?

MRS HIGGINS. Henry: you are the life and soul of the Royal Society's soirées; but really youre rather trying on more commonplace occasions.

HIGGINS. Am I? Very sorry. [*Beaming suddenly*] I suppose I am, you know. [*Uproariously*] Ha, ha!

MISS EYNSFORD HILL [*who considers Higgins quite eligible matrimonially*] I sympathize. *I* havnt any small talk. If people would only be frank and say what they really think!

HIGGINS [*relapsing into gloom*] Lord forbid!

MRS EYNSFORD HILL [*taking up her daughter's cue*] But why?

HIGGINS. What they think they ought to think is bad enough, Lord knows; but what they really think would break up the whole show. Do you suppose it would be really agreeable if I were to come out now with what *I* really think?

MISS EYNSFORD HILL [*gaily*] Is it so very cynical?

HIGGINS. Cynical! Who the dickens said it was cynical? I mean it wouldnt be decent.

MRS EYNSFORD HILL [*seriously*] Oh! I'm sure you dont mean that, Mr Higgins.

HIGGINS. You see, we're all savages, more or less. We're supposed to be civilized and cultured—to know all about poetry and philosophy and art and science, and so on; but how many of us know even the meanings of these names? [*To Miss Hill*] What do you know of poetry? [*To Mrs Hill*] What do you know of science? [*Indicating Freddy*] What does he know of art or science or anything else? What the devil do you imagine I know of philosophy?

MRS HIGGINS [*warningly*] Or of manners, Henry?

THE PARLOR-MAID [*opening the door*] Miss Doolittle. [*She withdraws*].

HIGGINS [*rising hastily and running to Mrs Higgins*] Here she is, mother. [*He stands on tiptoe and makes signs over his mother's head to Eliza to indicate to her which lady is her hostess*].

Eliza, who is exquisitely dressed, produces an impression of such remarkable distinction and beauty as she enters that they all rise, quite fluttered. Guided by Higgins's signals, she comes to Mrs Higgins with studied grace.

LIZA [*speaking with pedantic correctness of pronunciation and great beauty of tone*] How do you do, Mrs Higgins? [*She gasps slightly in making sure of the H in Higgins, but is quite successful*]. Mr Higgins told me I might come.

MRS HIGGINS [*cordially*] Quite right: I'm very glad indeed to see you.

PICKERING. How do you do, Miss Doolittle?

LIZA [*shaking hands with him*] Colonel Pickering, is it not?

MRS EYNSFORD HILL. I feel sure we have met before, Miss Doolittle. I remember your eyes.

LIZA. How do you do? [*She sits down on the ottoman gracefully in the place just left vacant by Higgins*].

MRS EYNSFORD HILL [*introducing*] My daughter Clara.

LIZA. How do you do?

CLARA [*impulsively*] How do you do? [*She sits down on the ottoman beside Eliza, devouring her with her eyes*].

FREDDY [*coming to their side of the ottoman*] Ive certainly had the pleasure.

MRS EYNSFORD HILL [*introducing*] My son Freddy.

LIZA. How do you do?

Freddy bows and sits down in the Elizabethan chair, infatuated.

HIGGINS [*suddenly*] By George, yes: it all comes back to me! [*They stare at him*]. Covent Garden! [*Lamentably*] What a damned thing!

MRS HIGGINS. Henry, please! [*He is about to sit on the edge of the table*] Dont sit on my writing-table: youll break it.

HIGGINS [*sulkily*] Sorry.

He goes to the divan, stumbling into the fender and over the fire-irons on his way; extricating himself with muttered imprecations; and finishing his disastrous journey by throwing himself so impatiently on the divan that he almost breaks it. Mrs Higgins looks at him, but controls herself and says nothing.

A long and painful pause ensues.

MRS HIGGINS [*at last, conversationally*] Will it rain, do you think?

LIZA. The shallow depression in the west of these islands is likely to move slowly in an easterly direction. There are no indications of any great change in the barometrical situation.

FREDDY. Ha! ha! how awfully funny!

LIZA. What is wrong with that, young man? I bet I got it right.

FREDDY. Killing!

MRS EYNSFORD HILL. I'm sure I hope it wont turn cold. Theres so much influenza about. It runs right through our whole family regularly every spring.

LIZA [*darkly*] My aunt died of influenza: so they said.

MRS EYNSFORD HILL [*clicks her tongue sympathetically*]!!!

LIZA [*in the same tragic tone*] But it's my belief they done the old woman in.

MRS HIGGINS [*puzzled*] Done her in?

LIZA. Y-e-e-e-es, Lord love you! Why should she die of influenza? She come through diphtheria right enough the year before. I saw her with my own eyes. Fairly blue with it, she was. They all thought she was dead; but my father he kept ladling gin down her throat til she came to so sudden that she bit the bowl off the spoon.

MRS EYNSFORD HILL [*startled*] Dear me!

LIZA [*piling up the indictment*] What call would a woman with that strength in her have to die of influenza? What become of her new straw hat that should have come to me? Somebody pinched it; and what I say is, them as pinched it done her in.

MRS EYNSFORD HILL. What does doing her in mean?

HIGGINS [*hastily*] Oh, thats the new small talk. To do a person in means to kill them.

MRS EYNSFORD HILL [*to Eliza, horrified*] You surely dont believe that your aunt was killed?

LIZA. Do I not! Them she lived with would have killed her for a hat-pin, let alone a hat.

MRS EYNSFORD HILL. But it cant have been right for your father to pour spirits down her throat like that. It might have killed her.

LIZA. Not her. Gin was mother's milk to her. Besides, he'd poured so much down his own throat that he knew the good of it.

MRS EYNSFORD HILL. Do you mean that he drank?

LIZA. Drank! My word! Something chronic.

MRS EYNSFORD HILL. How dreadful for you!

LIZA. Not a bit. It never did him no harm what I could see. But then he did not keep it up regular. [*Cheerfully*] On the burst, as you might say, from time to time. And always more agreeable when he had a drop in. When he was out of work, my mother used to give him fourpence and tell him to go out and not come back until he'd drunk himself cheerful and loving-like. Theres lots of women has to make their husbands drunk to make them fit to live with. [*Now quite at her ease*] You see, it's like this. If a man has a bit of a conscience, it always takes him when he's sober; and then it makes him low-spirited. A drop of booze just takes that off and makes him happy. [*To Freddy, who is in convulsions of suppressed laughter*] Here! what are you sniggering at?

FREDDY. The new small talk. You do it so awfully well.

LIZA. If I was doing it proper, what was you laughing at? [*To Higgins*] Have I said anything I oughtnt?

MRS HIGGINS [*interposing*] Not at all, Miss Doolittle.

LIZA. Well, thats a mercy, anyhow. [*Expansively*] What I always say is—

HIGGINS [*rising and looking at his watch*] Ahem!

LIZA [*looking round at him; taking the hint; and rising*] Well: I must go. [*They all rise. Freddy goes to the door*]. So pleased to have met you. Goodbye. [*She shakes hands with Mrs Higgins*].

MRS HIGGINS. Goodbye.

LIZA. Goodbye, Colonel Pickering.

PICKERING. Goodbye, Miss Doolittle. [*They shake hands*].

LIZA [*nodding to the others*] Goodbye, all.

FREDDY [*opening the door for her*] Are you walking across the Park, Miss Doolittle? If so—

LIZA [*with perfectly elegant diction*] Walk! Not bloody likely. [*Sensation*]. I am going in a taxi. [*She goes out*].

 Pickering gasps and sits down. Freddy goes out on the balcony to catch another glimpse of Eliza.

MRS EYNSFORD HILL [*suffering from shock*] Well, I really cant get used to the new ways.

CLARA [*throwing herself discontentedly into the Elizabethan chair*] Oh, it's all right, mamma, quite right. People will think we never go anywhere or see anybody if you are so old-fashioned.

MRS EYNSFORD HILL. I daresay I am very old-fashioned; but I do hope you wont begin using that expression, Clara. I have got accustomed to hear you talking about men as rotters, and calling everything filthy and beastly; though I do think it horrible and unladylike. But this last is really too much. Dont you think so, Colonel Pickering?

PICKERING. Dont ask me. Ive been away in India for several years; and manners have changed so much that I sometimes dont know whether I'm at a respectable dinner-table or in a ship's forecastle.

CLARA. It's all a matter of habit. Theres no right or wrong in it. Nobody means anything by it. And it's so quaint, and gives such a smart emphasis to things that are not in themselves very witty. I find the new small talk delightful and quite innocent.

MRS EYNSFORD HILL [*rising*] Well, after that, I think it's time for us to go.

Pickering and Higgins rise.

CLARA [*rising*] Oh yes: we have three at-homes to go to still. Goodbye, Mrs Higgins. Goodbye, Colonel Pickering. Goodbye, Professor Higgins.

HIGGINS [*coming grimly at her from the divan, and accompanying her to the door*] Goodbye. Be sure you try on that small talk at the three at-homes. Dont be nervous about it. Pitch it in strong.

CLARA [*all smiles*] I will. Goodbye. Such nonsense, all this early Victorian prudery!

HIGGINS [*tempting her*] Such damned nonsense!

CLARA. Such bloody nonsense!

MRS EYNSFORD HILL [*convulsively*] Clara!

CLARA. Ha! ha! [*She goes out radiant, conscious of being thoroughly up to date, and is heard descending the stairs in a stream of silvery laughter*].

FREDDY [*to the heavens at large*] Well, I ask you— [*He gives it up, and comes to Mrs Higgins*]. Goodbye.

MRS HIGGINS [*shaking hands*] Goodbye. Would you like to meet Miss Doolittle again?

FREDDY [*eagerly*] Yes, I should, most awfully.

MRS HIGGINS. Well, you know my days.

FREDDY. Yes, Thanks awfully. Goodbye. [*He goes out*].

MRS EYNSFORD HILL. Goodbye, Mr Higgins.

HIGGINS. Goodbye. Goodbye.

MRS EYNSFORD HILL [*to Pickering*] It's no use. I shall never be able to bring myself to use that word.

PICKERING. Dont. It's not compulsory, you know. Youll get on quite well without it.

MRS EYNSFORD HILL. Only, Clara is so down on me if I am not positively reeking with the latest slang. Goodbye.

PICKERING. Goodbye [*They shake hands*].

MRS EYNSFORD HILL [*to Mrs Higgins*] You mustnt mind Clara. [*Pickering, catching from her lowered tone that this is not meant for him to hear, discreetly joins Higgins at the window*]. We're so poor! and she gets so few parties, poor child! She doesnt quite know. [*Mrs Higgins, seeing that her eyes are moist, takes her hand sympathetically and goes with her to the door*]. But the boy is nice. Dont you think so?

MRS HIGGINS. Oh, quite nice. I shall always be delighted to see him.

MRS EYNSFORD HILL. Thank you, dear. Goodbye. [*She goes out*].

HIGGINS [*eagerly*] Well? Is Eliza presentable [*he swoops on his mother and drags her to the ottoman,*] *where she sits down in Eliza's place with her son on her left*] ?

Pickering returns to his chair on her right.

MRS HIGGINS. You silly boy, of course she's not presentable. She's a triumph of your art and of her dressmaker's; but if you suppose for a moment that she doesnt give herself away in every sentence she utters, you must be perfectly cracked about her.

PICKERING. But dont you think something might be done ? I mean something to eliminate the sanguinary element from her conversation.

MRS HIGGINS. Not as long as she is in Henry's hands.

HIGGINS [*aggrieved*] Do you mean that my language is improper ?

MRS HIGGINS. No, dearest: it would be quite proper —say on a canal barge; but it would not be proper for her at a garden party.

HIGGINS [*deeply injured*] Well I must say —

PICKERING [*interrupting him*] Come, Higgins: you must learn to know yourself. I havnt heard such language as yours since we used to review the volunteers in Hyde Park twenty years ago.

HIGGINS [*sulkily*] Oh, well, if you say so, I suppose I dont always talk like a bishop.

MRS HIGGINS [*quieting Henry with a touch*] Colonel Pickering: will you tell me what is the exact state of things in Wimpole Street ?

PICKERING [*cheerfully: as if this completely changed the subject*] Well, I have come to live there with Henry. We work together at my Indian Dialects; and we think it more convenient—

MRS HIGGINS. Quite so. I know all about that: it's an excellent arrangement. But where does this girl live ?

HIGGINS. With us, of course. Where should she live ?

MRS HIGGINS. But on what terms ? Is she a servant ? If not, what is she ?

PICKERING [*slowly*] I think I know what you mean, Mrs Higgins.

HIGGINS. Well, dash me if *I* do! Ive had to work at the girl every day for months to get her to her present pitch. Besides, she's useful. She knows where my things are, and remembers my appointments and so forth.

MRS HIGGINS. How does your housekeeper get on with her ?

HIGGINS. Mrs Pearce ? Oh, she's jolly glad to get so much taken off her hands; for before Eliza came, she used to have to find things and remind me of my appointments. But she's got some silly bee in her bonnet about Eliza. She keeps saying "You dont think, sir": doesnt she, Pick ?

PICKERING. Yes: thats the formula. "You dont think, sir." Thats the end of every conversation about Eliza.

HIGGINS. As if I ever stop thinking about the girl and her confounded vowels and consonants. I'm worn out, thinking about her, and watching her lips and her teeth and her tongue, not to mention her soul, which is the quaintest of the lot.

MRS HIGGINS. You certainly are a pretty pair of babies, playing with your live doll.

HIGGINS. Playing! The hardest job I ever tackled: make no mistake about that, mother. But you have no idea how frightfully interesting it is to take a human being and change her into a quite different human being by creating a new speech for her. It's filling up the deepest gulf that separates class from class and soul from soul.

PICKERING [*drawing his chair closer to Mrs Higgins and bending over to her eagerly*] Yes: it's enormously interesting. I assure you, Mrs Higgins, we take Eliza very seriously. Every week—every day almost—there is some new change. [*Closer again*] We keep records of every stage—dozens of gramophone disks and photographs—

HIGGINS [*assailing her at the other ear*] Yes, by George: it's the most absorbing experiment I ever tackled. She regularly fills our lives up: doesnt she, Pick?

PICKERING. We're always talking Eliza.

HIGGINS. Teaching Eliza.

PICKERING. Dressing Eliza.

MRS HIGGINS. What!

HIGGINS. Inventing new Elizas.

HIGGINS. — You know, she has the most extraordinary quickness of ear:

PICKERING. [*speaking together*] I assure you, my dear Mrs Higgins, that girl

HIGGINS. — just like a parrot. Ive tried her with every

PICKERING. — is a genius. She can play the piano quite beautifully.

HIGGINS. — possible sort of sound that a human being can make

PICKERING. — We have taken her to classical concerts and to music

HIGGINS. — Continental dialects, African dialects, Hottentot

PICKERING. — halls; and it's all the same to her: she plays everything

HIGGINS.		clicks, things it took me years to get hold of; and
PICKERING.	[*speaking together*]	she hears right off when she comes home, whether it's
HIGGINS.		she picks them up like a shot, right away, as if she had
PICKERING.		Beethoven and Brahms or Lehar and Lionel Monckton;
HIGGINS.		been at it all her life.
PICKERING.		though six months ago, she'd never as much as touched a piano—

MRS HIGGINS [*putting her fingers in her ears, as they are by this time shouting one another down with an intolerable noise*] Sh-sh-sh—sh! [*They stop*].

PICKERING. I beg your pardon. [*He draws his chair back apologetically*].

HIGGINS. Sorry. When Pickering starts shouting nobody can get a word in edgeways.

MRS HIGGINS. Be quiet, Henry. Colonel Pickering: dont you realize that when Eliza walked into Wimpole Street, something walked in with her?

PICKERING. Her father did. But Henry soon got rid of him.

MRS HIGGINS. It would have been more to the point if her mother had. But as her mother didnt something else did.

PICKERING. But what?

MRS HIGGINS [*unconsciously dating herself by the word*] A problem.

PICKERING. Oh, I see. The problem of how to pass her off as a lady.

HIGGINS. I'll solve that problem. Ive half solved it already.

MRS HIGGINS. No, you two infinitely stupid male creatures: the problem of what is to be done with her afterwards.

HIGGINS. I dont see anything in that. She can go her own way, with all the advantages I have given her.

MRS HIGGINS. The advantages of that poor woman who was here just now! The manners and habits that disqualify a fine lady from earning her own living without giving her a fine lady's income! Is that what you mean?

PICKERING [*indulgently, being rather bored*] Oh, that will be all right, Mrs Higgins. [*He rises to go*].

HIGGINS [*rising also*] We'll find her some light employment.

PICKERING. She's happy enough. Dont you worry about her. Goodbye. [*He shakes hands as if he were consoling a frightened child, and makes for the door*].

HIGGINS. Anyhow, theres no good bothering now. The thing's done. Goodbye, mother. [*He kisses her, and follows Pickering*].

PICKERING [*turning for a final consolation*] There are plenty of openings. We'll do whats right. Goodbye.

HIGGINS [*to Pickering as they go out together*] Lets take her to the Shakespear exhibition at Earls Court.

PICKERING. Yes: lets. Her remarks will be delicious.

HIGGINS. She'll mimic all the people for us when we get home.

PICKERING. Ripping. [*Both are heard laughing as they go downstairs*].

MRS HIGGINS [*rises with an impatient bounce, and returns to her work at the writing-table. She sweeps a litter of disarranged papers out of her way; snatches a sheet of paper from her stationery case; and tries resolutely to write. At the third line she gives it up; flings down her pen; grips the table angrily and exclaims*] Oh, men! men!! men!!!

*   *   *   *   *

Clearly Eliza will not pass as a duchess yet; and Higgins's bet remains unwon. But the six months are not yet exhausted; and just in time Eliza does actually pass as a princess. For a glimpse of how she did it imagine an Embassy in London one summer evening after dark. The hall door has an awning and a carpet across the sidewalk to the kerb, because a grand reception is in progress. A small crowd is lined up to see the guests arrive.

A Rolls-Royce car drives up. Pickering in evening dress, with medals and orders, alights, and hands out Eliza, in opera cloak, evening dress, diamonds, fan, flowers and all accessories. Higgins follows. The car drives off; and the three go up the steps and into the house, the door opening for them as they approach.

Inside the house they find themselves in a spacious hall from which the grand staircase rises. On the left are the arrangements for the gentlemen's cloaks. The male guests are depositing their hats and wraps there.

On the right is a door leading to the ladies' cloak-room. Ladies are going in cloaked and coming out in splendor. Pickering whispers to Eliza and points out the ladies' room. She goes into it. Higgins and Pickering take off their overcoats and take tickets for them from the attendant.

One of the guests, occupied in the same way, has his back turned. Having taken his ticket, he turns round and reveals himself as an important looking young man with an astonishingly hairy face. He has an enormous moustache, flowing out into luxuriant whiskers. Waves of hair cluster on his brow. His hair is cropped closely at the back, and glows with oil. Otherwise he is very smart. He wears several worthless orders. He is evidently a foreigner, guessable as a whiskered Pandour from Hungary; but in spite of the ferocity of his moustache he is amiable and genially voluble.

Recognizing Higgins, he flings his arms wide apart and approaches him enthusiastically.

WHISKERS. Maestro, maestro [*he embraces Higgins and kisses him on both cheeks*]. You remember me?

HIGGINS. No I dont. Who the devil are you?

WHISKERS. I am your pupil: your first pupil, your best and greatest pupil. I am little Nepommuck, the marvellous boy. I have made your name famous throughout Europe. You teach me phonetic. You cannot forget ME.

HIGGINS. Why dont you shave?

NEPOMMUCK. I have not your imposing appearance, your chin, your brow. Nobody notice me when I shave. Now I am famous: they call me Hairy Faced Dick.

HIGGINS. And what are you doing here among all these swells?

NEPOMMUCK. I am interpreter. I speak 32 languages. I am indispensable at these international parties. You are great cockney specialist: you place a man anywhere in London the moment he open his mouth. I place any man in Europe.

A footman hurries down the grand staircase and comes to Nepommuck.

FOOTMAN. You are wanted upstairs. Her Excellency cannot understand the Greek gentleman.

NEPOMMUCK. Thank you, yes, immediately.

The footman goes and is lost in the crowd.

NEPOMMUCK [*to Higgins*] This Greek diplomatist

pretends he cannot speak nor understand English. He cannot deceive me. He is the son of a Clerkenwell watchmaker. He speaks English so villainously that he dare not utter a word of it without betraying his origin. I help him to pretend; but I make him pay through the nose. I make them all pay. Ha Ha! [*He hurries upstairs*].

PICKERING. Is this fellow really an expert? Can he find out Eliza and blackmail her?

HIGGINS. We shall see. If he finds her out I lose my bet.

Eliza comes from the cloakroom and joins them.

PICKERING. Well, Eliza, now for it. Are you ready?

LIZA. Are you nervous, Colonel?

PICKERING. Frightfully. I feel exactly as I felt before my first battle. It's the first time that frightens.

LIZA. It is not the first time for me, Colonel. I have done this fifty times—hundreds of times—in my little piggery in Angel Court in my day-dreams. I am in a dream now. Promise me not to let Professor Higgins wake me; for if he does I shall forget everything and talk as I used to in Drury Lane.

PICKERING. Not a word, Higgins. [*To Eliza*] Now, ready?

LIZA. Ready.

PICKERING. Go.

They mount the stairs, Higgins last. Pickering whispers to the footman on the first landing.

FIRST LANDING FOOTMAN. Miss Doolittle, Colonel Pickering, Professor Higgins.

SECOND LANDING FOOTMAN. Miss Doolittle, Colonel Pickering, Professor Higgins.

At the top of the staircase the Ambassador and his wife, with Nepommuck at her elbow, are receiving.

HOSTESS [*taking Eliza's hand*] How d'ye do?

HOST [*same play*] How d'ye do? How d'ye do, Pickering?

LIZA [*with a beautiful gravity that awes her hostess*] How do you do? [*She passes on to the drawingroom*].

HOSTESS. Is that your adopted daughter, Colonel Pickering? She will make a sensation.

PICKERING. Most kind of you to invite her for me. [*He passes on*].

HOSTESS [*to Nepommuck*] Find out all about her.

NEPOMMUCK [*bowing*] Excellency—[*he goes into the crowd*].

HOST. How d'ye do, Higgins? You have a rival here tonight. He introduced himself as your pupil. Is he any good?

HIGGINS. He can learn a language in a fortnight—knows dozens of them. A sure mark of a fool. As a phonetician, no good whatever.

HOSTESS. How d'ye do, Professor?

HIGGINS. How do you do? Fearful bore for you this sort of thing. Forgive my part in it. [*He passes on*].

In the drawingroom and its suite of salons the reception is in full swing. Eliza passes through. She is so intent on her ordeal that she walks like a somnambulist in a desert instead of a débutante in a fashionable crowd. They stop talking to look at her, admiring her dress, her jewels, and her strangely attractive self. Some of the younger ones at the back stand on their chairs to see.

The Host and Hostess come in from the staircase and mingle with their guests. Higgins, gloomy and contemptuous of the whole business, comes into the group where they are chatting.

HOSTESS. Ah, here is Professor Higgins: he will tell us. Tell us all about the wonderful young lady, Professor.

HIGGINS [*almost morosely*] What wonderful young lady?

HOSTESS. You know very well. They tell me there has been nothing like her in London since people stood on their chairs to look at Mrs Langtry.

Nepommuck joins the group, full of news.

HOSTESS. Ah, here you are at last, Nepommuck. Have you found out all about the Doolittle lady?

NEPOMMUCK. I have found out all about her. She is a fraud.

HOSTESS. A fraud! Oh no.

NEPOMMUCK. YES, yes. She cannot deceive me. Her name cannot be Doolittle.

HIGGINS. Why?

NEPOMMUCK. Because Doolittle is an English name. And she is not English.

HOSTESS. Oh, nonsense! She speaks English perfectly.

NEPOMMUCK. Too perfectly. Can you shew me any English woman who speaks English as it should be spoken? Only foreigners who have been taught to speak it speak it well.

HOSTESS. Certainly she terrified me by the way she said How d'ye do. I had a schoolmistress who talked like that; and I was mortally afraid of her. But if she is not English what is she?

NEPOMMUCK. Hungarian.

ALL THE REST. Hungarian!

NEPOMMUCK. Hungarian. And of royal blood. I am Hungarian. My blood is royal.

HIGGINS. Did you speak to her in Hungarian?

NEPOMMUCK. I did. She was very clever. She said "Please speak to me in English: I do not understand French." French! She pretends not to know the difference between Hungarian and French. Impossible: she knows both.

HIGGINS. And the blood royal? How did you find that out?

NEPOMMUCK. Instinct, maestro, instinct. Only the Magyar races can produce that air of the divine right, those resolute eyes. She is a princess.

HOST. What do you say, Professor?

HIGGINS. I say an ordinary London girl out of the gutter and taught to speak by an expert. I place her in Drury Lane.

NEPOMMUCK. Ha ha ha! Oh, maestro, maestro, you are mad on the subject of cockney dialects. The London gutter is the whole world for you.

HIGGINS [to the Hostess] What does your Excellency say?

HOSTESS. Oh, of course I agree with Nepommuck. She must be a princess at least.

HOST. Not necessarily legitimate, of course. Morganatic perhaps. But that is undoubtedly her class.

HIGGINS. I stick to my opinion.

HOSTESS. Oh, you are incorrigible.

The group breaks up, leaving Higgins isolated. Pickering joins him.

PICKERING. Where is Eliza? We must keep an eye on her.

Eliza joins them.

LIZA. I dont think I can bear much more. The people all stare so at me. An old lady has just told me that I speak exactly like Queen Victoria. I am sorry if I have lost your bet. I have done my best; but nothing can make me the same as these people.

PICKERING. You have not lost it, my dear. You have won it ten times over.

HIGGINS. Let us get out of this. I have had enough of chattering to these fools.

PICKERING. Eliza is tired; and I am hungry. Let us clear out and have supper somewhere.

[ACT IV]

*The Wimpole Street laboratory. Midnight. Nobody
in the room. The clock on the mantelpiece strikes twelve.
The fire is not alight: it is a summer night.*

*Presently Higgins and Pickering are heard on the
stairs.*

HIGGINS [*calling down to Pickering*] I say, Pick:
lock up, will you? I shant be going out again.

PICKERING. Right. Can Mrs Pearce go to bed? We
dont want anything more, do we?

HIGGINS. Lord, no!

*Eliza opens the door and is seen on the lighted landing
in all the finery in which she has just won Higgins's
bet for him. She comes to the hearth, and switches on the
electric lights there. She is tired: her pallor contrasts
strongly with her dark eyes and hair; and her expression
is almost tragic. She takes off her cloak; puts her fan
and gloves on the piano; and sits down on the bench,
brooding and silent. Higgins, in evening dress, with
overcoat and hat, comes in, carrying a smoking jacket
which he has picked up downstairs. He takes off the
hat and overcoat; throws them carelessly on the newspaper stand; disposes of his coat in the same way;
puts on the smoking jacket; and throws himself wearily
into the easy-chair at the hearth. Pickering, similarly
attired, comes in. He also takes off his hat and overcoat,
and is about to throw them on Higgins's when he
hesitates.*

[744]

PICKERING. I say: Mrs Pearce will row if we leave these things lying about in the drawing room.

HIGGINS. Oh, chuck them over the bannisters into the hall. She'll find them there in the morning and put them away all right. She'll think we were drunk.

PICKERING. We are, slightly. Are there any letters?

HIGGINS. I didnt look. [*Pickering takes the overcoats and hats and goes downstairs. Higgins begins half singing half yawning an air from La Fanciulla del Golden West. Suddenly he stops and exclaims*] I wonder where the devil my slippers are!

Eliza looks at him darkly; then rises suddenly and leaves the room.

Higgins yawns again, and resumes his song.

Pickering returns, with the contents of the letter-box in his hand.

PICKERING. Only circulars, and this coroneted billet-doux for you. [*He throws the circulars into the fender, and posts himself on the hearthrug, with his back to the grate*].

HIGGINS [*glancing at the billet-doux*] Money-lender. [*He throws the letter after the circulars*].

Eliza returns with a pair of large down-at-heel slippers. She places them on the carpet before Higgins, and sits as before without a word.

HIGGINS [*yawning again*] Oh Lord! What an evening! What a crew! What a silly tomfoolery! [*He raises his shoe to unlace it, and catches sight of the slippers. He stops unlacing and looks at them as if they had appeared there of their own accord*]. Oh! theyre there, are they?

PICKERING [*stretching himself*] Well, I feel a bit tired. It's been a long day. The garden party, a dinner party, and the reception! Rather too much of a good thing. But youve won your bet, Higgins. Eliza did the trick, and something to spare, eh?

HIGGINS [*fervently*] Thank God it's over!

Eliza flinches violently; but they take no notice of her; and she recovers herself and sits stonily as before.

PICKERING. Were you nervous at the garden party? *I* was. Eliza didnt seem a bit nervous.

HIGGINS. Oh, she wasnt nervous. I knew she'd be all right. No: it's the strain of putting the job through all these months that has told on me. It was interesting enough at first, while we were at the phonetics; but after that I got deadly sick of it. If I hadnt backed myself to do it I should have chucked the whole thing up two months ago. It was a silly notion: the whole thing has been a bore.

PICKERING. Oh come! the garden party was frightfully exciting. My heart began beating like anything.

HIGGINS. Yes, for the first three minutes. But when I saw we were going to win hands down, I felt like a bear in a cage, hanging about doing nothing. The dinner was worse: sitting gorging there for over an hour, with nobody but a damned fool of a fashionable woman to talk to! I tell you, Pickering, never again for me. No more artificial duchesses. The whole thing has been simple purgatory.

PICKERING. Youve never been broken in properly to the social routine. [*Strolling over to the piano*] I rather enjoy dipping into it occasionally myself: it makes me feel young again. Anyhow, it was a great success: an immense success. I was quite frightened once or twice because Eliza was doing it so well. You see, lots of the real people cant do it at all: theyre such fools that they think style comes by nature to people in their position; and so they never learn. Theres always something professional about doing a thing superlatively well.

HIGGINS. Yes: thats what drives me mad: the silly

people dont know their own silly business. [*Rising*] However, it's over and done with; and now I can go to bed at last without dreading tomorrow.

Eliza's beauty becomes murderous.

PICKERING. I think I shall turn in too. Still, it's been a great occasion: a triumph for you. Goodnight. [*He goes*].

HIGGINS [*following him*] Goodnight. [*Over his shoulder, at the door*] Put out the lights, Eliza; and tell Mrs Pearce not to make coffee for me in the morning: I'll take tea. [*He goes out*].

Eliza tries to control herself and feel indifferent as she rises and walks across to the hearth to switch off the lights. By the time she gets there she is on the point of screaming. She sits down in Higgins's chair and holds on hard to the arms. Finally she gives way and flings herself furiously on the floor, raging.

HIGGINS [*in despairing wrath outside*] What the devil have I done with my slippers? [*He appears at the door*].

LIZA [*snatching up the slippers, and hurling them at him one after the other with all her force*] There are your slippers. And there. Take your slippers; and may you never have a day's luck with them!

HIGGINS [*astounded*] What on earth—! [*He comes to her*]. Whats the matter? Get up. [*He pulls her up*]. Anything wrong?

LIZA [*breathless*] Nothing wrong—with you. Ive won your bet for you, havnt I? Thats enough for you. *I* dont matter, I suppose.

HIGGINS. You won my bet! You! Presumptuous insect! *I* won it. What did you throw those slippers at me for?

LIZA. Because I wanted to smash your face. I'd like to kill you, you selfish brute. Why didnt you leave me where you picked me out of—in the gutter? You thank God it's all over, and that now you can throw me back again there, do you? [*She crisps her fingers frantically*].

HIGGINS [*looking at her in cool wonder*] The creature is nervous, after all.

LIZA [*gives a suffocated scream of fury, and instinctively darts her nails at his face*]!!

HIGGINS [*catching her wrists*] Ah! would you? Claws in, you cat. How dare you shew your temper to me? Sit down and be quiet. [*He throws her roughly into the easy-chair*].

LIZA [*crushed by superior strength and weight*] Whats to become of me? Whats to become of me?

HIGGINS. How the devil do I know whats to become of you? What does it matter what becomes of you?

LIZA. You dont care. I know you dont care. You wouldnt care if I was dead. I'm nothing to you— not so much as them slippers.

HIGGINS [*thundering*] Those slippers.

LIZA [*with bitter submission*] Those slippers. I didnt think it made any difference now.

A pause. Eliza hopeless and crushed. Higgins a little uneasy.

HIGGINS [*in his loftiest manner*] Why have you begun going on like this? May I ask whether you complain of your treatment here?

LIZA. No.

HIGGINS. Has anybody behaved badly to you? Colonel Pickering? Mrs Pearce? Any of the servants?

LIZA. No.

HIGGINS. I presume you dont pretend that *I* have treated you badly?

LIZA. No.

HIGGINS. I am glad to hear it. [*He moderates his*

tone]. Perhaps youre tired after the strain of the day. Will you have a glass of champagne? [*He moves towards the door*].

LIZA. No. [*Recollecting her manners*] Thank you.

HIGGINS [*good-humored again*] This has been coming on you for some days. I suppose it was natural for you to be anxious about the garden party. But thats all over now. [*He pats her kindly on the shoulder. She writhes*]. Theres nothing more to worry about.

LIZA. No. Nothing more for you to worry about. [*She suddenly rises and gets away from him by going to the piano bench, where she sits and hides her face*]. Oh God! I wish I was dead.

HIGGINS [*staring after her in sincere surprise*] Why? In heaven's name, why? [*Reasonably, going to her*] Listen to me, Eliza. All this irritation is purely subjective.

LIZA. I dont understand. I'm too ignorant.

HIGGINS. It's only imagination. Low spirits and nothing else. Nobody's hurting you. Nothing's wrong. You go to bed like a good girl and sleep it off. Have a little cry and say your prayers: that will make you comfortable.

LIZA. I heard your prayers. "Thank God it's all over!"

HIGGINS [*impatiently*] Well, dont you thank God it's all over? Now you are free and can do what you like.

LIZA [*pulling herself together in desperation*] What am I fit for? What have you left me fit for? Where am I to go? What am I to do? Whats to become of me?

HIGGINS [*enlightened, but not at all impressed*] Oh, thats whats worrying you, is it? [*He thrusts his hands into his pockets, and walks about in his usual manner, rattling the contents of his pockets, as if condescending

to a trivial subject out of pure kindness]. I shouldnt
bother about it if I were you. I should imagine you
wont have much difficulty in settling yourself somewhere or other, though I hadnt quite realized that
you were going away. [*She looks quickly at him: he
does not look at her, but examines the dessert stand on
the piano and decides that he will eat an apple*]. You
might marry, you know. [*He bites a large piece out of
the apple and munches it noisily*]. You see, Eliza, all
men are not confirmed old bachelors like me and the
Colonel. Most men are the marrying sort (poor
devils!); and youre not bad-looking: it's quite a
pleasure to look at you sometimes—not now, of
course, because youre crying and looking as ugly as
the very devil; but when youre all right and quite
yourself, youre what I should call attractive. That is,
to the people in the marrying line, you understand.
You go to bed and have a good nice rest; and then get
up and look at yourself in the glass; and you wont feel
so cheap.

Eliza again looks at him, speechless, and does not stir.

*The look is quite lost on him: he eats his apple with a
dreamy expression of happiness, as it is quite a good one.*

HIGGINS [*a genial afterthought occurring to him*] I
daresay my mother could find some chap or other
who would do very well.

LIZA. We were above that at the corner of Tottenham
Court Road.

HIGGINS [*waking up*] What do you mean?

LIZA. I sold flowers. I didnt sell myself. Now youve
made a lady of me I'm not fit to sell anything else. I
wish youd left me where you found me.

HIGGINS [*slinging the core of the apple decisively into
the grate*] Tosh, Eliza. Dont you insult human relations by dragging all this cant about buying and selling

into it. You neednt marry the fellow if your dont like him.

LIZA. What else am I to do?

HIGGINS. Oh, lots of things. What about your old idea of a florist's shop? Pickering could set you up in one: he has lots of money. [*Chuckling*] He'll have to pay for all those togs you have been wearing today; and that, with the hire of the jewellery, will make a big hole in two hundred pounds. Why, six months ago you would have thought it the millennium to have a flower shop of your own. Come! youll be all right. I must clear off to bed: I'm devilish sleepy. By the way, I came down for something: I forget what it was.

LIZA. Your slippers.

HIGGINS. Oh yes, of course. You shied them at me. [*He picks them up, and is going out when she rises and speaks to him*].

LIZA. Before you go, sir—

HIGGINS [*dropping the slippers in his surprise at her calling him Sir*] Eh?

LIZA. Do my clothes belong to me or to Colonel Pickering?

HIGGINS [*coming back into the room as if her question were the very climax of unreason*] What the devil use would they be to Pickering?

LIZA. He might want them for the next girl you pick up to experiment on.

HIGGINS [*shocked and hurt*] Is that the way you feel towards us?

LIZA. I dont want to hear anything more about that. All I want to know is whether anything belongs to me. My own clothes were burnt.

HIGGINS. But what does it matter? Why need you start bothering about that in the middle of the night?

LIZA. I want to know what I may take away with me. I dont want to be accused of stealing.

HIGGINS [*now deeply wounded*] Stealing! You shouldnt have said that, Eliza. That shews a want of feeling.

LIZA. I'm sorry. I'm only a common ignorant girl; and in my station I have to be careful. There cant be any feelings between the like of you and the like of me. Please will you tell me what belongs to me and what doesnt?

HIGGINS [*very sulky*] You may take the whole damned houseful if you like. Except the jewels. Theyre hired. Will that satisfy you? [*He turns on his heel and is about to go in extreme dudgeon*].

LIZA [*drinking in his emotion like nectar, and nagging him to provoke a further supply*] Stop, please. [*She takes off her jewels*]. Will you take these to your room and keep them safe? I dont want to run the risk of their being missing.

HIGGINS [*furious*] Hand them over. [*She puts them into his hands*]. If these belonged to me instead of to the jeweller, I'd ram them down your ungrateful throat. [*He perfunctorily thrusts them into his pockets, unconsciously decorating himself with the protruding ends of the chains*].

LIZA [*taking a ring off*] This ring isnt the jeweller's: it's the one you bought me in Brighton. I dont want it now. [*Higgins dashes the ring violently into the fireplace, and turns on her so threateningly that she crouches over the piano with her hands over her face, and exclaims*] Dont you hit me.

HIGGINS. Hit you! You infamous creature, how dare you accuse me of such a thing? It is you who have hit me. You have wounded me to the heart.

LIZA [*thrilling with hidden joy*] I'm glad. Ive got a little of my own back, anyhow.

HIGGINS [*with dignity, in his finest professional style*]

You have caused me to lose my temper: a thing that has hardly ever happened to me before. I prefer to say nothing more tonight. I am going to bed.

LIZA [*pertly*] Youd better leave a note for Mrs Pearce about the coffee; for she wont be told by me.

HIGGINS [*formally*] Damn Mrs Pearce; and damn the coffee; and damn you; and [*wildly*] damn my own folly in having lavished my hard-earned knowledge and the treasure of my regard and intimacy on a heartless guttersnipe. [*He goes out with impressive decorum, and spoils it by slamming the door savagely*].

Eliza goes down on her knees on the hearthrug to look for the ring. When she finds it she considers for a moment what to do with it. Finally she flings it down on the dessert stand and goes upstairs in a tearing rage.

*   *   *   *   *

The furniture of Eliza's room has been increased by a big wardrobe and a sumptuous dressing-table. She comes in and switches on the electric light. She goes to the wardrobe; opens it; and pulls out a walking dress, a hat, and a pair of shoes, which she throws on the bed. She takes off her evening dress and shoes; then takes a padded hanger from the wardrobe; adjusts it carefully in the evening dress; and hangs it in the wardrobe, which she shuts with a slam. She puts on her walking shoes, her walking dress, and hat. She takes her wrist watch from the dressing-table and fastens it on. She pulls on her gloves; takes her vanity bag; and looks into it to see that her purse is there before hanging it on her wrist. She makes for the door. Every movement expresses her furious resolution.

She takes a last look at herself in the glass.

She suddenly puts out her tongue at herself; then

leaves the room, switching off the electric light at the door.

Meanwhile, in the street outside, Freddy Eynsford Hill, lovelorn, is gazing up at the second floor, in which one of the windows is still lighted.

The light goes out.

FREDDY. Goodnight, darling, darling, darling.

Eliza comes out, giving the door a considerable bang behind her.

LIZA. Whatever are you doing here?

FREDDY. Nothing. I spend most of my nights here. It's the only place where I'm happy. Dont laugh at me, Miss Doolittle.

LIZA. Dont you call me Miss Doolittle, do you hear? Liza's good enough for me. [*She breaks down and grabs him by the shoulders*] Freddy: you dont think I'm a heartless guttersnipe, do you?

FREDDY. Oh no, no, darling: how can you imagine such a thing? You are the loveliest, dearest—

He loses all self-control and smothers her with kisses. She, hungry for comfort, responds. They stand there in one another's arms.

An elderly police constable arrives.

CONSTABLE [*scandalized*] Now then! Now then!! Now then!!!

They release one another hastily.

FREDDY. Sorry, constable. Weve only just become engaged.

They run away.

The constable shakes his head, reflecting on his own courtship and on the vanity of human hopes. He moves off in the opposite direction with slow professional steps.

The flight of the lovers takes them to Cavendish Square. There they halt to consider their next move.

LIZA [*out of breath*] He didnt half give me a fright, that copper. But you answered him proper.

FREDDY. I hope I havent taken you out of your way. Where were you going?

LIZA. To the river.

FREDDY. What for?

LIZA. To make a hole in it.

FREDDY [*horrified*] Eliza, darling. What do you mean? What's the matter?

LIZA. Never mind. It doesnt matter now. There's nobody in the world now but you and me, is there?

FREDDY. Not a soul.

They indulge in another embrace, and are again surprised by a much younger constable.

SECOND CONSTABLE. Now then, you two! What's this? Where do you think you are? Move along here, double quick.

FREDDY. As you say, sir, double quick.

They run away again, and are in Hanover Square before they stop for another conference.

FREDDY. I had no idea the police were so devilishly prudish.

LIZA. It's their business to hunt girls off the streets.

FREDDY. We must go somewhere. We cant wander about the streets all night.

LIZA. Cant we? I think it'd be lovely to wander about for ever.

FREDDY. Oh, darling.

They embrace again, oblivious of the arrival of a crawling taxi. It stops.

TAXIMAN. Can I drive you and the lady anywhere, sir?

They start asunder.

LIZA. Oh, Freddy, a taxi. The very thing.

FREDDY. But, damn it, I've no money.

LIZA. I have plenty. The Colonel thinks you should never go out without ten pounds in your pocket. Listen. We'll drive about all night; and in the morning I'll call on old Mrs Higgins and ask her what I ought to do. I'll tell you all about it in the cab. And the police wont touch us there.

FREDDY. Righto! Ripping. [*To the Taximan*] Wimbledon Common. [*They drive off*].

[ACT V]

Mrs Higgins's drawing room. She is at her writing-table as before. The parlormaid comes in.

THE PARLORMAID [*at the door*] Mr Henry, maam, is downstairs with Colonel Pickering.

MRS HIGGINS. Well, shew them up.

THE PARLORMAID. Theyre using the telephone, maam. Telephoning to the police, I think.

MRS HIGGINS. What!

THE PARLORMAID [*coming further in and lowering her voice*] Mr Henry is in a state, maam. I thought I'd better tell you.

MRS HIGGINS. If you had told me that Mr Henry was not in a state it would have been more surprising. Tell them to come up when theyve finished with the police. I suppose he's lost something.

THE PARLORMAID. Yes, maam [*going*].

MRS HIGGINS. Go upstairs and tell Miss Doolittle that Mr Henry and the Colonel are here. Ask her not to come down til I send for her.

THE PARLORMAID. Yes, maam.

Higgins bursts in. He is, as the parlormaid has said, in a state.

HIGGINS. Look here, mother: heres a confounded thing!

MRS HIGGINS. Yes, dear. Good morning. [*He checks his impatience and kisses her, whilst the parlormaid goes out*]. What is it?

HIGGINS. Eliza's bolted.

[757]

MRS HIGGINS [*calmly continuing her writing*] You must have frightened her.

HIGGINS. Frightened her! nonsense! She was left last night, as usual, to turn out the lights and all that; and instead of going to bed she changed her clothes and went right off: her bed wasnt slept in. She came in a cab for her things before seven this morning; and that fool Mrs Pearce let her have them without telling me a word about it. What am I to do?

MRS HIGGINS. Do without, I'm afraid, Henry. The girl has a perfect right to leave if she chooses.

HIGGINS [*wandering distractedly across the room*] But I cant find anything. I dont know what appointments Ive got. I'm—[*Pickering comes in. Mrs Higgins puts down her pen and turns away from the writing-table*].

PICKERING [*shaking hands*] Good morning, Mrs Higgins. Has Henry told you? [*He sits down on the ottoman*].

HIGGINS. What does that ass of an inspector say? Have you offered a reward?

MRS HIGGINS [*rising in indignant amazement*] You dont mean to say you have set the police after Eliza.

HIGGINS. Of course. What are the police for? What else could we do? [*He sits in the Elizabethan chair*].

PICKERING. The inspector made a lot of difficulties. I really think he suspected us of some improper purpose.

MRS HIGGINS. Well, of course he did. What right have you to go to the police and give the girl's name as if she were a thief, or a lost umbrella, or something? Really! [*She sits down again, deeply vexed*].

HIGGINS. But we want to find her.

PICKERING. We cant let her go like this, you know, Mrs Higgins. What were we to do?

MRS HIGGINS. You have no more sense, either of you, than two children. Why—

The parlormaid comes in and breaks off the conversation.

THE PARLORMAID. Mr Henry: a gentleman wants to see you very particular. He's been sent on from Wimpole Street.

HIGGINS. Oh, bother! I cant see anyone now. Who is it?

THE PARLORMAID. A Mr Doolittle, sir.

PICKERING. Doolittle! Do you mean the dustman?

THE PARLORMAID. Dustman! Oh no, sir: a gentleman.

HIGGINS [*springing up excitedly*] By George, Pick, it's some relative of hers that she's gone to. Somebody we know nothing about. [*To the parlormaid*] Send him up, quick.

THE PARLORMAID. Yes, sir. [*She goes*].

HIGGINS [*eagerly, going to his mother*] Genteel relatives! now we shall hear something. [*He sits down in the Chippendale chair*].

MRS HIGGINS. Do you know any of her people?

PICKERING. Only her father: the fellow we told you about.

THE PARLORMAID [*announcing*] Mr Doolittle. [*She withdraws*].

Doolittle enters. He is resplendently dressed as for a fashionable wedding, and might, in fact, be the bridegroom. A flower in his buttonhole, a dazzling silk hat, and patent leather shoes complete the effect. He is too concerned with the business he has come on to notice Mrs Higgins. He walks straight to Higgins, and accosts him with vehement reproach.

DOOLITTLE [*indicating his own person*] See here! Do you see this? You done this.

HIGGINS. Done what, man?

DOOLITTLE. This, I tell you. Look at it. Look at this hat. Look at this coat.

PICKERING. Has Eliza been buying you clothes?

DOOLITTLE. Eliza! not she. Why would she buy me clothes?

MRS HIGGINS. Good morning, Mr Doolittle. Wont you sit down?

DOOLITTLE [*taken aback as he becomes conscious that he has forgotten his hostess*] Asking your pardon, maam. [*He approaches her and shakes her proffered hand*]. Thank you. [*He sits down on the ottoman, on Pickering's right*]. I am that full of what has happened to me that I cant think of anything else.

HIGGINS. What the dickens has happened to you?

DOOLITTLE. I shouldnt mind if it had only happened to me: anything might happen to anybody and nobody to blame but Providence, as you might say. But this is something that you done to me: yes, you, Enry Iggins.

HIGGINS. Have you found Eliza?

DOOLITTLE. Have you lost her?

HIGGINS. Yes.

DOOLITTLE. You have all the luck, you have. I aint found her; but she'll find me quick enough now after what you done to me.

MRS HIGGINS. But what has my son done to you, Mr Doolittle?

DOOLITTLE. Done to me! Ruined me. Destroyed my happiness. Tied me up and delivered me into the hands of middle class morality.

HIGGINS [*rising intolerantly and standing over Doolittle*] Youre raving. Youre drunk. Youre mad. I gave you five pounds. After that I had two conversations with you, at half-a-crown an hour. Ive never seen you since.

DOOLITTLE. Oh! Drunk am I? Mad am I? Tell me this. Did you or did you not write a letter to an old blighter in America that was giving five millions to found Moral Reform Societies all over the world, and that wanted you to invent a universal language for him?

HIGGINS. What! Ezra D. Wannafeller! He's dead. [*He sits down again carelessly*].

DOOLITTLE. Yes: he's dead; and I'm done for. Now did you or did you not write a letter to him to say that the most original moralist at present in England, to the best of your knowledge, was Alfred Doolittle, a common dustman?

HIGGINS. Oh, after your first visit I remember making some silly joke of the kind.

DOOLITTLE. Ah! you may well call it a silly joke. It put the lid on me right enough. Just give him the chance he wanted to shew that Americans is not like us: that they reckonize and respect merit in every class of life, however humble. Them words is in his blooming will, in which, Henry Higgins, thanks to your silly joking, he leaves me a share in his Pre-digested Cheese Trust worth three thousand a year on condition that I lecture for his Wannafeller Moral Reform World League as often as they ask me up to six times a year.

HIGGINS. The devil he does! Whew! [*Brightening suddenly*] What a lark!

PICKERING. A safe thing for you, Doolittle. They wont ask you twice.

DOOLITTLE. It aint the lecturing I mind. I'll lecture them blue in the face, I will, and not turn a hair. It's making a gentleman of me that I object to. Who asked him to make a gentleman of me? I was happy. I was free. I touched pretty nigh everybody for money when I wanted it, same as I touched you, Enry Iggins. Now I am worrited; tied neck and heels; and everybody touches me for money. It's a fine thing for you, says my solicitor. Is it? says I. You mean it's a good thing for you, I says. When I was a poor man and had a solicitor once when they found a pram in the dust cart, he got me off, and got shut of me and got me shut of him as quick as he could. Same with the doctors: used to shove me out of the hospital before I could hardly stand on my legs, and nothing to pay. Now they finds out that I'm not a healthy man and cant live unless they looks after me twice a day. In the house I'm not let do a hand's turn for myself: somebody else must do it and touch me for it. A year ago I hadnt a relative in the world except two or three that wouldnt speak to me. Now Ive fifty, and not a decent week's wages among the lot of them. I have to live for others and not for myself: thats middle class morality. You talk of losing Eliza. Dont you be anxious: I bet she's on my doorstep by this: she that could support herself easy by selling flowers if I wasnt respectable. And the next one to touch me will be you, Enry Iggins. I'll have to learn to speak middle class language from you, instead of speaking proper English. Thats where youll come in; and I daresay thats what you done it for.

MRS HIGGINS. But, my dear Mr Doolittle, you need not suffer all this if you are really in earnest. Nobody can force you to accept this bequest. You can repudiate it. Isnt that so, Colonel Pickering?

PICKERING. I believe so.

DOOLITTLE [*softening his manner in deference to her sex*] Thats the tragedy of it, maam. It's easy to say chuck it; but I havnt the nerve. Which of us has? We're all intimidated. Intimidated, maam: thats what we are. What is there for me if I chuck it but the workhouse in my old age? I have to dye my hair already to keep my job as a dustman. If I was one of the deserving poor, and had put by a bit, I could chuck it; but then why should I, acause the deserving poor might as well be millionaires for all the happiness they ever has. They dont know what happiness is. But I, as one of the undeserving poor, have nothing between me and the pauper's uniform but this here blasted three thousand a year that shoves me into the middle class. (Excuse the expression, maam; youd use it yourself if you had my provocation.) Theyve got you every way you turn: it's a choice between the Skilly of the workhouse and the Char Bydis of the middle class; and I havnt the nerve for the workhouse. Intimidated: thats what I am. Broke. Bought up. Happier men than me will call for my dust, and touch me for their tip; and I'll look on helpless, and envy them. And thats what your son has brought me to. [*He is overcome by emotion*].

MRS HIGGINS. Well, I'm very glad youre not going to do anything foolish, Mr Doolittle. For this solves the problem of Eliza's future. You can provide for her now.

DOOLITTLE [*with melancholy resignation*] Yes, maam: I'm expected to provide for everyone now, out of three thousand a year.

HIGGINS [*jumping up*] Nonsense! he cant provide for her. He shant provide for her. She doesnt belong to him. I paid him five pounds for her. Doolittle: either youre an honest man or a rogue.

DOOLITTLE [*tolerantly*] A little of both, Henry, like the rest of us: a little of both.

HIGGINS. Well, you took that money for the girl; and you have no right to take her as well.

MRS HIGGINS. Henry: dont be absurd. If you want to know where Eliza is, she is upstairs.

HIGGINS [*amazed*] Upstairs!!! Then I shall jolly soon fetch her downstairs. [*He makes resolutely for the door*].

MRS HIGGINS [*rising and following him*] Be quiet, Henry. Sit down.

HIGGINS. I—

MRS HIGGINS. Sit down, dear; and listen to me.

HIGGINS. Oh very well, very well, very well. [*He throws himself ungraciously on the ottoman, with his face towards the windows*]. But I think you might have told us this half an hour ago.

MRS HIGGINS. Eliza came to me this morning. She told me of the brutal way you two treated her.

HIGGINS [*bounding up again*] What!

PICKERING [*rising also*] My dear Mrs Higgins, she's been telling you stories. We didnt treat her brutally. We hardly said a word to her; and we parted on particularly good terms. [*Turning on Higgins*] Higgins: did you bully her after I went to bed?

HIGGINS. Just the other way about. She threw my slippers in my face. She behaved in the most outrageous way. I never gave her the slightest provocation. The slippers came bang into my face the moment I entered the room—before I had uttered a word. And used perfectly awful language.

PICKERING [*astonished*] But why? What did we do to her?

MRS HIGGINS. I think I know pretty well what you did. The girl is naturally rather affectionate, I think. Isnt she, Mr Doolittle?

DOOLITTLE. Very tender-hearted, maam. Takes after me.

MRS HIGGINS. Just so. She had become attached to

you both. She worked very hard for you, Henry. I dont think you quite realize what anything in the nature of brain work means to a girl of her class. Well, it seems that when the great day of trial came, and she did this wonderful thing for you without making a single mistake, you two sat there and never said a word to her, but talked together of how glad you were that it was all over and how you had been bored with the whole thing. And then you were surprised because she threw your slippers at you! *I* should have thrown the fire-irons at you.

HIGGINS. We said nothing except that we were tired and wanted to go to bed. Did we, Pick?

PICKERING [*shrugging his shoulders*] That was all.

MRS HIGGINS [*ironically*] Quite sure?

PICKERING. Absolutely. Really, that was all.

MRS HIGGINS. You didnt thank her, or pet her, or admire her, or tell her how splendid shc'd been.

HIGGINS [*impatiently*] But she knew all about that. We didnt make speeches to her, if thats what you mean.

PICKERING [*conscience stricken*] Perhaps we were a little inconsiderate. Is she very angry?

MRS HIGGINS [*returning to her place at the writing-table*] Well, I'm afraid she wont go back to Wimpole Street, especially now that Mr Doolittle is able to keep up the position you have thrust on her; but she says she is quite willing to meet you on friendly terms and to let bygones be bygones.

HIGGINS [*furious*] Is she, by George? Ho!

MRS HIGGINS. If you promise to behave yourself, Henry, I'll ask her to come down. If not, go home; for you have taken up quite enough of my time.

HIGGINS. Oh, all right. Very well. Pick: you behave yourself. Let us put on our best Sunday manners for this creature that we picked out of the mud. [*He flings himself sulkily into the Elizabethan chair*].

DOOLITTLE [*remonstrating*] Now, now, Enry Iggins! Have some consideration for my feelings as a middle class man.

MRS HIGGINS. Remember your promise, Henry. [*She presses the bell-button on the writing-table*]. Mr Doolittle: will you be so good as to step out on the balcony for a moment. I dont want Eliza to have the shock of your news until she has made it up with these two gentlemen. Would you mind?

DOOLITTLE. As you wish, lady. Anything to help Henry to keep her off my hands. [*He disappears through the window*].

The parlormaid answers the bell. Pickering sits down in Doolittle's place.

MRS HIGGINS. Ask Miss Doolittle to come down, please.

THE PARLORMAID. Yes, maam. [*She goes out*].

MRS HIGGINS. Now, Henry: be good.

HIGGINS. I am behaving myself perfectly.

PICKERING. He is doing his best, Mrs Higgins.

A pause. Higgins throws back his head; stretches out his legs; and begins to whistle.

MRS HIGGINS. Henry, dearest, you dont look at all nice in that attitude.

HIGGINS [*pulling himself together*] I was not trying to look nice, mother.

MRS HIGGINS. It doesnt matter, dear. I only wanted to make you speak.

HIGGINS. Why?

MRS HIGGINS. Because you cant speak and whistle at the same time.

Higgins groans. Another very trying pause.

[766]

HIGGINS [*springing up, out of patience*] Where the devil is that girl? Are we to wait here all day?

Eliza enters, sunny, self-possessed, and giving a staggeringly convincing exhibition of ease of manner. She carries a little work-basket, and is very much at home. Pickering is too much taken aback to rise.

LIZA. How do you do, Professor Higgins? Are you quite well?

HIGGINS [*choking*] Am I—[*He can say no more*].

LIZA. But of course you are: you are never ill. So glad to see you again, Colonel Pickering. [*He rises hastily; and they shake hands*]. Quite chilly this morning, isnt it? [*She sits down on his left. He sits beside her*].

HIGGINS. Dont you dare try this game on me. I taught it to you; and it doesnt take me in. Get up and come home; and dont be a fool.

Eliza takes a piece of needlework from her basket, and begins to stitch at it, without taking the least notice of this outburst.

MRS HIGGINS. Very nicely put, indeed, Henry. No woman could resist such an invitation.

HIGGINS. You let her alone, mother. Let her speak for herself. You will jolly soon see whether she has an idea that I havnt put into her head or a word that I havnt put into her mouth. I tell you I have created this thing out of the squashed cabbage leaves of Covent Garden; and now she pretends to play the fine lady with me.

MRS HIGGINS [*placidly*] Yes, dear; but youll sit down, wont you?

Higgins sits down again, savagely.

LIZA [*to Pickering, taking no apparent notice of Higgins, and working away deftly*] Will you drop me altogether now that the experiment is over, Colonel Pickering?

PICKERING. Oh dont. You mustnt think of it as an experiment. It shocks me, somehow.

LIZA. Oh, I'm only a squashed cabbage leaf—

PICKERING [*impulsively*] No.

LIZA [*continuing quietly*]—but I owe so much to you that I should be very unhappy if you forgot me.

PICKERING. It's very kind of you to say so, Miss Doolittle.

LIZA. It's not because you paid for my dresses. I know you are generous to everybody with money. But it was from you that I learnt really nice manners; and that is what makes one a lady, isnt it? You see it was so very difficult for me with the example of Professor Higgins always before me. I was brought up to be just like him, unable to control myself, and using bad language on the slightest provocation. And I should never have known that ladies and gentlemen didnt behave like that if you hadnt been there.

HIGGINS. Well!!

PICKERING. Oh, thats only his way, you know. He doesnt mean it.

LIZA. Oh, *I* didnt mean it either, when I was a flower girl. It was only my way. But you see I did it; and thats what makes the difference after all.

PICKERING. No doubt. Still, he taught you to speak; and I couldnt have done that, you know.

LIZA [*trivially*] Of course: that is his profession.

HIGGINS. Damnation!

LIZA [*continuing*] It was just like learning to dance in the fashionable way: there was nothing more than that in it. But do you know what began my real education?

PICKERING. What?

LIZA [*stopping her work for a moment*] Your calling me Miss Doolittle that day when I first came to

Wimpole Street. That was the beginning of self-respect for me. [*She resumes her stitching*]. And there were a hundred little things you never noticed, because they came naturally to you. Things about standing up and taking off your hat and opening doors—

PICKERING. Oh, that was nothing.

LIZA. Yes: things that shewed you thought and felt about me as if I were something better than a scullery-maid; though of course I know you would have been just the same to a scullery-maid if she had been let into the drawing room. You never took off your boots in the dining room when I was there.

PICKERING. You mustnt mind that. Higgins takes off his boots all over the place.

LIZA. I know. I am not blaming him. It is his way, isnt it? But it made such a difference to me that you didnt do it. You see, really and truly, apart from the things anyone can pick up (the dressing and the proper way of speaking, and so on), the difference between a lady and a flower girl is not how she behaves, but how she's treated. I shall always be a flower girl to Professor Higgins, because he always treats me as a flower girl, and always will; but I know I can be a lady to you, because you always treat me as a lady, and always will.

MRS HIGGINS. Please dont grind your teeth, Henry.

PICKERING. Well, this is really very nice of you, Miss Doolittle.

LIZA. I should like you to call me Eliza, now, if you would.

PICKERING. Thank you. Eliza, of course.

LIZA. And I should like Professor Higgins to call me Miss Doolittle.

HIGGINS. I'll see you damned first.

MRS HIGGINS. Henry! Henry!

PICKERING [*laughing*] Why dont you slang back at him? Dont stand it. It would do him a lot of good.

LIZA. I cant. I could have done it once; but now I cant go back to it. You told me, you know, that when a child is brought to a foreign country, it picks up the language in a few weeks, and forgets its own. Well, I am a child in your country. I have forgotten my own language, and can speak nothing but yours. Thats the real break-off with the corner of Tottenham Court Road. Leaving Wimpole Street finishes it.

PICKERING [*much alarmed*] Oh! but youre coming back to Wimpole Street, arnt you? Youll forgive Higgins?

HIGGINS [*rising*] Forgive! Will she, by George! Let her go. Let her find out how she can get on without us. She will relapse into the gutter in three weeks without me at her elbow.

Doolittle appears at the centre window. With a look of dignified reproach at Higgins, he comes slowly and silently to his daughter, who, with her back to the window, is unconscious of his approach.

PICKERING. He's incorrigible, Eliza. You wont relapse, will you?

LIZA. No: not now. Never again. I have learnt my lesson. I dont believe I could utter one of the old sounds if I tried. [*Doolittle touches her on her left shoulder. She drops her work, losing her self-possession utterly at the spectacle of her father's splendor*] A-a-a-a-a-ah-ow-ooh!

HIGGINS [*with a crow of triumph*] Aha! Just so. A-a-a-a-ahowooh! A-a-a-a-ahowooh! A-a-a-a-ahowooh! Victory! Victory! [*He throws himself on the divan, folding his arms, and spraddling arrogantly*].

DOOLITTLE. Can you blame the girl? Dont look at me like that, Eliza. It aint my fault. Ive come into some money.

LIZA. You must have touched a millionaire this time, dad.

DOOLITTLE. I have. But I'm dressed something special today. I'm going to St George's, Hanover Square. Your stepmother is going to marry me.

LIZA [angrily] Youre going to let yourself down to marry that low common woman!

PICKERING [quietly] He ought to, Eliza. [To Doolittle] Why has she changed her mind?

DOOLITTLE [sadly] Intimidated, Governor. Intimidated. Middle class morality claims its victim. Wont you put on your hat, Liza, and come and see me turned off?

LIZA. If the Colonel says I must, I—I'll [almost sobbing] I'll demean myself. And get insulted for my pains, like enough.

DOOLITTLE. Dont be afraid: she never comes to words with anyone now, poor woman! respectability has broke all the spirit out of her.

PICKERING [squeezing Eliza's elbow gently] Be kind to them, Eliza. Make the best of it.

LIZA [forcing a little smile for him through her vexation] Oh well, just to shew theres no ill feeling. I'll be back in a moment. [She goes out].

DOOLITTLE [sitting down beside Pickering] I feel uncommon nervous about the ceremony, Colonel. I wish youd come and see me through it.

PICKERING. But youve been through it before, man. You were married to Eliza's mother.

DOOLITTLE. Who told you that, Colonel?

PICKERING. Well, nobody told me. But I concluded —naturally—

DOOLITTLE. No: that aint the natural way, Colonel: it's only the middle class way. My way was always the undeserving way. But dont say nothing to Eliza. She dont know: I always had a delicacy about telling her.

PICKERING. Quite right. We'll leave it so, if you dont mind.

DOOLITTLE. And youll come to the church, Colonel, and put me through straight?

PICKERING. With pleasure. As far as a bachelor can.

MRS HIGGINS. May I come, Mr Doolittle? I should be very sorry to miss your wedding.

DOOLITTLE. I should indeed be honored by your condescension, maam; and my poor old woman would take it as a tremenjous compliment. She's been very low, thinking of the happy days that are no more.

MRS HIGGINS [*rising*] I'll order the carriage and get ready. [*The men rise, except Higgins*]. I shant be more than fifteen minutes. [*As she goes to the door Eliza comes in, hatted and buttoning her gloves*]. I'm going to the church to see your father married, Eliza. You had better come in the brougham with me. Colonel Pickering can go on with the bridegroom.

Mrs Higgins goes out. Eliza comes to the middle of the room between the centre window and the ottoman. Pickering joins her.

DOOLITTLE. Bridegroom! What a word! It makes a man realize his position, somehow. [*He takes up his hat and goes towards the door*].

PICKERING. Before I go, Eliza, do forgive Higgins and come back to us.

LIZA. I dont think dad would allow me. Would you, dad?

DOOLITTLE [*sad but magnanimous*] They played you

off very cunning, Eliza, them two sportsmen. It if had been only one of them, you could have nailed him. But you see, there was two; and one of them chaperoned the other, as you might say. [*To Pickering*] It was artful of you, Colonel; but I bear no malice: I should have done the same myself. I been the victim of one woman after another all my life; and I dont grudge you two getting the better of Eliza. I shant interfere. It's time for us to go, Colonel. So long, Henry. See you in St George's, Eliza. [*He goes out*].

PICKERING [*coaxing*] Do stay with us, Eliza. [*He follows Doolittle*].

Eliza goes out on the balcony to avoid being alone with Higgins. He rises and joins her there. She immediately comes back into the room and makes for the door; but he goes along the balcony quickly and gets his back to the door before she reaches it.

HIGGINS. Well, Eliza, youve had a bit of your own back, as you call it. Have you had enough? and are you going to be reasonable? Or do you want any more?

LIZA. You want me back only to pick up your slippers and put up with your tempers and fetch and carry for you.

HIGGINS. I havnt said I wanted you back at all.

LIZA. Oh, indeed. Then what are we talking about?

HIGGINS. About you, not about me. If you come back I shall treat you just as I have always treated you. I cant change my nature; and I dont intend to change my manners. My manners are exactly the same as Colonel Pickering's.

LIZA. Thats not true. He treats a flower girl as if she was a duchess.

HIGGINS. And I treat a duchess as if she was a flower girl.

[773]

LIZA. I see. [*She turns away composedly, and sits on the ottoman, facing the window*]. The same to everybody.

HIGGINS. Just so.

LIZA. Like father.

HIGGINS [*grinning, a little taken down*] Without accepting the comparison at all points, Eliza, it's quite true that your father is not a snob, and that he will be quite at home in any station of life to which his eccentric destiny may call him. [*Seriously*] The great secret, Eliza, is not having bad manners or good manners or any other particular sort of manners, but having the same manner for all human souls: in short, behaving as if you were in Heaven, where there are no third-class carriages, and one soul is as good as another.

LIZA. Amen. You are a born preacher.

HIGGINS [*irritated*] The question is not whether I treat you rudely, but whether you ever heard me treat anyone else better.

LIZA [*with sudden sincerity*] I dont care how you treat me. I dont mind your swearing at me. I shouldnt mind a black eye: Ive had one before this. But [*standing up and facing him*] I wont be passed over.

HIGGINS. Then get out of my way; for I wont stop for you. You talk about me as if I were a motor bus.

LIZA. So you are a motor bus: all bounce and go, and no consideration for anyone. But I can do without you: dont think I cant.

HIGGINS. I know you can. I told you you could.

LIZA [*wounded, getting away from him to the other side of the ottoman with her face to the hearth*] I know you did, you brute. You wanted to get rid of me.

HIGGINS. Liar.

LIZA. Thank you. [*She sits down with dignity*].

HIGGINS. You never asked yourself, I suppose, whether *I* could do without you.

LIZA [*earnestly*] Dont you try to get round me. Youll have to do without me.

HIGGINS [*arrogant*] I can do without anybody. I have my own soul: my own spark of divine fire. But [*with sudden humility*] I shall miss you, Eliza. [*He sits down near her on the ottoman*]. I have learnt something from your idiotic notions: I confess that humbly and gratefully. And I have grown accustomed to your voice and appearance. I like them, rather.

LIZA. Well, you have both of them on your gramophone and in your book of photographs. When you feel lonely without me, you can turn the machine on. It's got no feelings to hurt.

HIGGINS. I cant turn your soul on. Leave me those feelings; and you can take away the voice and the face. They are not you.

LIZA. Oh, you are a devil. You can twist the heart in a girl as easy as some could twist her arms to hurt her. Mrs Pearce warned me. Time and again she has wanted to leave you; and you always got round her at the last minute. And you dont care a bit for her. And you dont care a bit for me.

HIGGINS. I care for life, for humanity; and you are a part of it that has come my way and been built into my house. What more can you or anyone ask?

LIZA. I wont care for anybody that doesnt care for me.

HIGGINS. Commercial principles, Eliza. Like [*reproducing her Covent Garden pronunciation with professional exactness*] s'yollin voylets [selling violets], isnt it?

LIZA. Dont sneer at me. It's mean to sneer at me.

HIGGINS. I have never sneered in my life. Sneering doesnt become either the human face or the human soul. I am expressing my righteous contempt for Commercialism. I dont and wont trade in affection. You call me a brute because you couldnt buy a claim on me by fetching my slippers and finding my spectacles. You were a fool: I think a woman fetching a man's slippers is a disgusting sight: did I ever fetch your slippers? I think a good deal more of you for throwing them in my face. No use slaving for me and then saying you want to be cared for: who cares for a slave? If you come back, come back for the sake of good fellowship; for youll get nothing else. Youve had a thousand times as much out of me as I have out of you; and if you dare to set up your little dog's tricks of fetching and carrying slippers against my creation of a Duchess Eliza, I'll slam the door in your silly face.

LIZA. What did you do it for if you didnt care for me?

HIGGINS [*heartily*] Why, because it was my job.

LIZA. You never thought of the trouble it would make for me.

HIGGINS. Would the world ever have been made if its maker had been afraid of making trouble? Making life means making trouble. Theres only one way of escaping trouble; and thats killing things. Cowards, you notice, are always shrieking to have troublesome people killed.

LIZA. I'm no preacher: I dont notice things like that. I notice that you dont notice me.

HIGGINS [*jumping up and walking about intolerantly*] Eliza: youre an idiot. I waste the treasures of my Miltonic mind by spreading them before you. Once for all, understand that I go my way and do my work without caring twopence what happens to either of us. I am not intimidated, like your father and your stepmother. So you can come back or go to the devil: which you please.

LIZA. What am I to come back for?

HIGGINS [*bouncing up on his knees on the ottoman and leaning over it to her*] For the fun of it. Thats why I took you on.

LIZA [*with averted face*] And you may throw me out tomorrow if I dont do everything you want me to?

HIGGINS. Yes; and you may walk out tomorrow if I dont do everything you want me to.

LIZA. And live with my stepmother?

HIGGINS. Yes, or sell flowers.

LIZA. Oh! if I only could go back to my flower basket! I should be independent of both you and father and all the world! Why did you take my independence from me? Why did I give it up? I'm a slave now, for all my fine clothes.

HIGGINS Not a bit. I'll adopt you as my daughter and settle money on you if you like. Or would you rather marry Pickering?

LIZA [*looking fiercely round at him*] I wouldnt marry you if you asked me; and youre nearer my age than what he is.

HIGGINS [*gently*] Than he is: not "than what he is."

LIZA [*losing her temper and rising*] I'll talk as I like. Youre not my teacher now.

HIGGINS [*reflectively*] I dont suppose Pickering would, though. He's as confirmed an old bachelor as I am.

LIZA. Thats not what I want; and dont you think it. Ive always had chaps enough wanting me that way. Freddy Hill writes to me twice and three times a day, sheets and sheets.

HIGGINS [*disagreeably surprised*] Damn his impudence! [*He recoils and finds himself sitting on his heels*].

LIZA. He has a right to if he likes, poor lad. And he does love me.

HIGGINS [*getting off the ottoman*] You have no right to encourage him.

LIZA. Every girl has a right to be loved.

HIGGINS. What! By fools like that?

LIZA. Freddy's not a fool. And if he's weak and poor and wants me, may be he'd make me happier than my betters that bully me and dont want me.

HIGGINS. Can he make anything of you? Thats the point.

LIZA. Perhaps I could make something of him. But I never thought of us making anything of one another; and you never think of anything else. I only want to be natural.

HIGGINS. In short, you want me to be as infatuated about you as Freddy? Is that it?

LIZA. No I dont. Thats not the sort of feeling I want from you. And dont you be too sure of yourself or of me. I could have been a bad girl if I'd liked. Ive seen more of some things than you, for all your learning. Girls like me can drag gentlemen down to make love to them easy enough. And they wish each other dead the next minute.

HIGGINS. Of course they do. Then what in thunder are we quarrelling about?

LIZA [*much troubled*] I want a little kindness. I know I'm a common ignorant girl, and you a book-learned gentleman; but I'm not dirt under your feet. What I done [*correcting herself*] what I did was not for the dresses and the taxis: I did it because we were pleasant together and I come—came—to care for you; not to want you to make love to me, and not forgetting the difference between us, but more friendly like.

HIGGINS. Well, of course. Thats just how I feel. And how Pickering feels. Eliza: youre a fool.

LIZA. Thats not a proper answer to give me [*she sinks on the chair at the writing-table in tears*].

HIGGINS. It's all youll get until you stop being a common idiot. If youre going to be a lady, youll have to give up feeling neglected if the men you know dont spend half their time snivelling over you and the other half giving you black eyes. If you cant stand the coldness of my sort of life, and the strain of it, go back to the gutter. Work til youre more a brute than a human being; and then cuddle and squabble and drink til you fall asleep. Oh, it's a fine life, the life of the gutter. It's real: it's warm: it's violent: you can feel it through the thickest skin: you can taste it and smell it without any training or any work. Not like Science and Literature and Classical Music and Philosophy and Art. You find me cold, unfeeling, selfish, dont you? Very well: be off with you to the sort of people you like. Marry some sentimental hog or other with lots of money, and a thick pair of lips to kiss you with and a thick pair of boots to kick you with. If you cant appreciate what youve got, youd better get what you can appreciate.

LIZA [*desperate*] Oh, you are a cruel tyrant. I cant talk to you: you turn everything against me: I'm always in the wrong. But you know very well all the time that youre nothing but a bully. You know I cant go back to the gutter, as you call it, and that I have no real friends in the world but you and the Colonel. You know well I couldnt bear to live with a low common man after you two; and it's wicked and cruel of you to insult me by pretending I could. You think I must go back to Wimpole Street because I have nowhere else to go but father's. But dont you be too sure that you have me under your feet to be trampled on and talked down. I'll marry Freddy, I will, as soon as I'm able to support him.

HIGGINS [*thunderstruck*] Freddy!!!! that young fool! That poor devil who couldnt get a job as an errand boy even if he had the guts to try for it! Woman: do you not understand that I have made you a consort for a king?

LIZA. Freddy loves me: that makes him king enough for me. I dont want him to work: he wasnt brought up to it as I was. I'll go and be a teacher.

HIGGINS. Whatll you teach, in heaven's name?

LIZA. What you taught me. I'll teach phonetics.

HIGGINS. Ha! ha! ha!

LIZA. I'll offer myself as an assistant to that hairy-faced Hungarian.

HIGGINS [*rising in a fury*] What! That impostor! that humbug! that toadying ignoramus! Teach him my methods! my discoveries! You take one step in his direction and I'll wring your neck. [*He lays hands on her*]. Do you hear?

LIZA [*defiantly non-resistant*] Wring away. What do I care? I knew youd strike me some day. [*He lets her go, stamping with rage at having forgotten himself, and recoils so hastily that he stumbles back into his seat on the ottoman*]. Aha! Now I know how to deal with you. What a fool I was not to think of it before! You cant take away the knowledge you gave me. You said I had a finer ear than you. And I can be civil and kind to people, which is more than you can. Aha! [*Purposely dropping her aitches to annoy him*] Thats done you, Enry Iggins, it az. Now I dont care that [*snapping her fingers*] for your bullying and your big talk. I'll advertize it in the papers that your duchess is only a flower girl that you taught, and that she'll teach anybody to be a duchess just the same in six months for a thousand guineas. Oh, when I think of myself crawling under your feet and being trampled on and called names, when all the time I had only to lift up my finger to be as good as you, I could just kick myself.

HIGGINS [*wondering at her*] You damned impudent slut, you! But it's better than snivelling; better than fetching slippers and finding spectacles, isnt it? [*Rising*] By George, Eliza, I said I'd make a woman of you; and I have. I like you like this.

LIZA. Yes: you turn round and make up to me now that I'm not afraid of you, and can do without you.

HIGGINS. Of course I do, you little fool. Five minutes ago you were like a millstone round my neck. Now youre a tower of strength: a consort battleship. You and I and Pickering will be three old bachelors together instead of only two men and a silly girl.

Mrs Higgins returns, dressed for the wedding. Eliza instantly becomes cool and elegant.

MRS HIGGINS. The carriage is waiting, Eliza. Are you ready?

LIZA. Quite. Is the Professor coming?

MRS HIGGINS. Certainly not. He cant behave himself in church. He makes remarks out loud all the time on the clergyman's pronunciation.

LIZA. Then I shall not see you again, Professor. Goodbye. [*She goes to the door*].

MRS HIGGINS [*coming to Higgins*] Goodbye, dear.

HIGGINS. Goodbye, mother. [*He is about to kiss her, when he recollects something*]. Oh, by the way, Eliza, order a ham and a Stilton cheese, will you? And buy me a pair of reindeer gloves, number eights, and a tie to match that new suit of mine. You can choose the color. [*His cheerful, careless, vigorous voice shews that he is incorrigible*].

LIZA [*disdainfully*] Number eights are too small for you if you want them lined with lamb's wool. You have three new ties that you have forgotten in the drawer of your washstand. Colonel Pickering prefers double Gloucester to Stilton; and you dont notice the difference. I telephoned Mrs Pearce this morning not to forget the ham. What you are to do without me I cannot imagine. [*She sweeps out*].

MRS HIGGINS. I'm afraid youve spoilt that girl, Henry. I should be uneasy about you and her if she were less fond of Colonel Pickering.

HIGGINS. Pickering! Nonsense: she's going to marry Freddy. Ha ha! Freddy! Freddy!! Ha ha ha ha ha!!!!! [*He roars with laughter as the play ends*].

*　　*　　*　　*　　*

The rest of the story need not be shewn in action, and indeed, would hardly need telling if our imaginations were not so enfeebled by their lazy dependence on the ready-mades and reach-me-downs of the ragshop in which Romance keeps its stock of "happy endings" to misfit all stories. Now, the history of Eliza Doolittle, though called a romance because the transfiguration it records seems exceedingly improbable, is common enough. Such transfigurations have been achieved by hundreds of resolutely ambitious young women since Nell Gwynne set them the example by playing queens and fascinating kings in the theatre in which she began by selling oranges. Nevertheless, people in all directions have assumed, for no other reason than that she became the heroine of a romance, that she must have married the hero of it. This is unbearable, not only because her little drama, if acted on such a thoughtless assumption, must be spoiled, but because the true sequel is patent to anyone with a sense of human nature in general, and of feminine instinct in particular.

Eliza, in telling Higgins she would not marry him if he asked her, was not coquetting: she was announcing a well-considered decision. When a bachelor interests, and dominates, and teaches, and becomes important to a spinster, as Higgins with Eliza, she always, if she has character enough to be capable of it, considers very seriously indeed whether she will play for becoming that bachelor's wife, especially if he is so little interested in marriage that a determined and devoted woman might capture him if she set herself resolutely to do it. Her decision will depend a good deal on whether she is really free to choose; and that, again, will depend on her age and income. If she is at the end of her youth, and has no security for her livelihood, she will marry him because she must marry anybody who will provide for her. But at Eliza's age a good-looking girl does not feel that pressure: she feels free to pick and choose. She is therefore guided by her instinct in the matter. Eliza's instinct tells her not to marry Higgins. It does not tell her to give him up. It is not in the slightest doubt as to his remaining one of the strongest personal interests in her life. It would be very sorely strained if there was another woman likely to supplant her with him. But as she feels sure of him on that last point, she has no doubt at all as to her course, and would not have any, even if the difference of twenty years in age, which seems so great to youth, did not exist between them.

As our own instincts are not appealed to by her conclusion, let us see whether we cannot discover some reason in it. When Higgins excused his indifference to young women on the ground that they had an irresistible rival in his mother, he gave the clue to his inveterate old-bachelordom. The case is uncommon only to the extent that remarkable mothers are uncommon. If an imaginative boy has a sufficiently rich mother who has intelligence, personal grace, dignity of character without harshness, and a cultivated sense of the best art of her time to enable her to make her house beautiful, she sets a standard for him against which very few women can struggle, besides effecting for him a disengagement of his affections, his sense of beauty, and his idealism from his specifically sexual impulses. This makes him a standing puzzle to the huge number of uncultivated people who have been brought up in tasteless homes by commonplace or disagreeable parents, and to whom, consequently, literature, painting, sculpture, music, and affectionate personal relations come as modes of sex if they come at all. The word passion means nothing else to them; and that Higgins could have a passion for phonetics and idealize his mother instead of Eliza, would seem to them absurd and unnatural. Nevertheless, when we look round and see that hardly anyone is too ugly or disagreeable to find a wife or a husband if he or she wants one, whilst many old maids and bachelors are above the average in quality and culture, we cannot help suspecting that the disentanglement of sex from the associations with which it is so commonly confused, a disentanglement which persons of genius achieve by sheer intellectual analysis, is sometimes produced or aided by parental fascination.

Now, though Eliza was incapable of thus explaining to herself Higgins's formidable powers of resistance to the charm that prostrated Freddy at the first glance, she was instinctively aware that she could never obtain a complete grip of him, or come between him and his mother (the first necessity of the married woman). To put it shortly, she knew that for some mysterious reason he had not the makings of a married man in him, according to her conception of a husband as one to whom she would be his nearest and fondest and warmest interest. Even had there been no mother-rival, she would still have refused to accept an interest in herself that was secondary to philosophic interests. Had Mrs Higgins died, there would still have been Milton and the Universal Alphabet. Landor's remark that to those who have the greatest power of loving, love is a secondary affair, would not have recommended Landor to Eliza. Put that along with her resentment of Higgins's domineering superiority, and her mistrust of his coaxing cleverness in getting round her and evading her wrath when he had gone too far with his impetuous bullying, and you will see that Eliza's instinct had good grounds for warning her not to marry her Pygmalion.

And now, whom did Eliza marry? For if Higgins was a predestinate old bachelor, she was most certainly not a predestinate old maid. Well, that can be told very shortly to those who have not guessed it from the indications she has herself given them.

Almost immediately after Eliza is stung into proclaiming her considered determination not to marry Higgins, she mentions the fact that young Mr Frederick Eynsford Hill is pouring out his love for her daily through the post. Now Freddy is young, practically twenty years younger than Higgins: he is a gentleman (or, as Eliza would qualify him, a toff), and speaks like one. He is nicely dressed, is treated by the Colonel as an equal, loves her unaffectedly, and is not her master, nor ever likely to dominate her in spite of his advantage of social standing. Eliza has no use for the foolish romantic tradition that all women love to be mastered, if not actually bullied and beaten.

"When you go to women" says Nietzsche "take your whip with you." Sensible despots have never confined that precaution to women: they have taken their whips with them when they have dealt with men, and been slavishly idealized by the men over whom they have flourished the whip much more than by women. No doubt there are slavish women as well as slavish men; and women, like men, admire those that are stronger than themselves. But to admire a strong person and to live under that strong person's thumb are two different things. The weak may not be admired and hero-worshipped; but they are by no means disliked or shunned; and they never seem to have the least difficulty in marrying people who are too good for them. They may fail in emergencies; but life is not one long emergency: it is mostly a string of situations for which no exceptional strength is needed, and with which even rather weak people can cope if they have a stronger partner to help them out. Accordingly, it is a truth everywhere in evidence that strong people, masculine or feminine, not only do not marry stronger people, but do not shew any preference for them in selecting their friends. When a lion meets another with a louder roar "the first lion thinks the last a bore." The man or woman who feels strong enough for two, seeks for every other quality in a partner than strength.

The converse is also true. Weak people want to marry strong people who do not frighten them too much; and this often leads them to make the mistake we describe metaphorically as "biting off more than they can chew." They want too much for too little; and when the bargain is unreasonable beyond all bearing, the union becomes impossible: it ends in the weaker party being either discarded or borne as a cross, which is worse. People who are not only weak, but silly or obtuse as well, are often in these difficulties.

This being the state of human affairs, what is Eliza fairly sure to do when she is placed between Freddy and Higgins? Will she look forward to a lifetime of fetching Higgins's slippers or to a lifetime of Freddy fetching hers? There can be no doubt about the answer. Unless Freddy is biologically repulsive to her, and Higgins biologically attractive to a degree that overwhelms all her other instincts, she will, if she marries either of them, marry Freddy.

And that is just what Eliza did.

Complications ensued; but they were economic, not romantic. Freddy had no money and no occupation. His mother's jointure, a last relic of the opulence of Largelady Park, had enabled her to struggle along in Earlscourt with an air of gentility, but not to procure any serious secondary education for her children, much less give the boy a profession. A clerkship at thirty shillings a week was beneath Freddy's dignity, and extremely distasteful to him besides. His prospects consisted of a hope that if he kept up appearances somebody would do something for him. The something appeared vaguely to his imagination as a private secretaryship or a sinecure of some sort. To his mother it perhaps appeared as a marriage to some lady of means who could not resist her boy's niceness. Fancy her feelings when he married a flower girl who had become disclassed under extraordinary circumstances which were now notorious!

It is true that Eliza's situation did not seem wholly ineligible. Her father, though formerly a dustman, and now fantastically disclassed, had become extremely popular in the smartest society by a social talent which triumphed over every prejudice and every disadvantage. Rejected by the middle class, which he loathed, he had shot up at once into the highest circles by his wit, his dustmanship (which he carried like a banner), and his Nietzschean transcendence of good and evil. At intimate ducal dinners he sat on the right hand of the Duchess; and in country houses he smoked in the pantry and was made much of by the butler when he was not feeding in the dining room and being consulted by cabinet ministers. But he found it almost as hard to do all this on four thousand a year as Mrs Eynsford Hill to live in Earlscourt on an income so pitiably smaller that I have not the heart to disclose its exact figure. He absolutely refused to add the last straw to his burden by contributing to Eliza's support.

Thus Freddy and Eliza, now Mr and Mrs Eynsford Hill, would have spent a penniless honeymoon but for a wedding present of £500 from the Colonel to Eliza. It lasted a long time because Freddy did not know how to spend money, never having had any to spend, and Eliza, socially trained by a pair of old bachelors, wore her clothes as long as they held together and looked pretty, without the least regard to their being many months out of fashion. Still, £500 will not last two young people for ever; and they both knew, and Eliza felt as well, that they must shift for themselves in the end. She could quarter herself on Wimpole Street because it had come to be her home; but she was quite aware that she ought not to quarter Freddy there, and that it would not be good for his character if she did.

Not that the Wimpole Street bachelors objected. When she consulted them, Higgins declined to be bothered about her housing problem when that solution was so simple. Eliza's desire to have Freddy in the

house with her seemed of no more importance than
if she had wanted an extra piece of bedroom furniture.
Pleas as to Freddy's character, and the moral obligation on him to earn his own living, were lost on
Higgins. He denied that Freddy had any character,
and declared that if he tried to do any useful work some
competent person would have the trouble of undoing
it: a procedure involving a net loss to the community,
and great unhappiness to Freddy himself, who was
obviously intended by Nature for such light work as
amusing Eliza, which, Higgins declared, was a
much more useful and honorable occupation than
working in the city. When Eliza referred again to her
project of teaching phonetics, Higgins abated not a
jot of his violent opposition to it. He said she was not
within ten years of being qualified to meddle with his
pet subject; and as it was evident that the Colonel
agreed with him, she felt she could not go against
them in this grave matter, and that she had no right,
without Higgins's consent, to exploit the knowledge
he had given her; for his knowledge seemed to her as
much his private property as his watch: Eliza was no
communist. Besides, she was superstitiously devoted
to them both, more entirely and frankly after her
marriage than before it.

It was the Colonel who finally solved the problem,
which had cost him much perplexed cogitation. He
one day asked Eliza, rather shyly, whether she had
quite given up her notion of keeping a flower shop.
She replied that she had thought of it, but had put
it out of her head, because the Colonel had said, that
day at Mrs Higgins's, that it would never do. The
Colonel confessed that when he said that, he had not
quite recovered from the dazzling impression of the day
before. They broke the matter to Higgins that even-

ing. The sole comment vouchsafed by him very nearly led to a serious quarrel with Eliza. It was to the effect that she would have in Freddy an ideal errand boy.

Freddy himself was next sounded on the subject. He said he had been thinking of a shop himself; though it had presented itself to his pennilessness as a small place in which Eliza should sell tobacco at one counter whilst he sold newspapers at the opposite one. But he agreed that it would be extraordinarily jolly to go early every morning with Eliza to Covent Garden and buy flowers on the scene of their first meeting: a sentiment which earned him many kisses from his wife. He added that he had always been afraid to propose anything of the sort, because Clara would make an awful row about a step that must damage her matrimonial chances, and his mother could not be expected to like it after clinging for so many years to that step of the social ladder on which retail trade is impossible.

This difficulty was removed by an event highly unexpected by Freddy's mother. Clara, in the course of her incursions into those artistic circles which were the highest within her reach, discovered that her conversational qualifications were expected to include a grounding in the novels of Mr H. G. Wells. She borrowed them in various directions so energetically that she swallowed them all within two months. The result was a conversion of a kind quite common today. A modern Acts of the Apostles would fill fifty whole Bibles if anyone were capable of writing it.

Poor Clara, who appeared to Higgins and his mother as a disagreeable and ridiculous person, and to her own mother as in some inexplicable way a social failure, had never seen herself in either light; for, though to some extent ridiculed and mimicked in West Kensington like everybody else there, she was accepted as a rational and normal—or shall we say inevitable?—sort of human being. At worst they called her The Pusher; but to them no more than to herself had it ever occurred that she was pushing the air, and pushing it in a wrong direction. Still, she was not happy. She was growing desperate. Her one asset, the fact that her mother was what the Epsom green-grocer called a carriage lady, had no exchange value, apparently. It had prevented her from getting edu-cated, because the only education she could have afforded was education with the Earlscourt green-grocer's daughter. It had led her to seek the society of her mother's class; and that class simply would not have her, because she was much poorer than the greengrocer, and, far from being able to afford a maid, could not afford even a housemaid, and had to scrape along at home with an illiberally treated general servant. Under such circumstances nothing could give her an air of being a genuine product of Large-lady Park. And yet its tradition made her regard a marriage with anyone within her reach as an un-bearable humiliation. Commercial people and pro-fessional people in a small way were odious to her. She ran after painters and novelists; but she did not charm them; and her bold attempts to pick up and practise artistic and literary talk irritated them. She was, in short, an utter failure, an ignorant, incom-petent, pretentious, unwelcome, penniless, useless little snob; and though she did not admit these disqualifications (for nobody ever faces unpleasant truths of this kind until the possibility of a way out dawns on them) she felt their effects too keenly to be satisfied with her position.

Clara had a startling eyeopener when, on being

suddenly wakened to enthusiasm by a girl of her
own age who dazzled her and produced in her a
gushing desire to take her for a model, and gain her
friendship, she discovered that this exquisite appari-
tion had graduated from the gutter in a few months
time. It shook her so violently, that when Mr H. G.
Wells lifted her on the point of his puissant pen, and
placed her at the angle of view from which the life
she was leading and the society to which she clung
appeared in its true relation to real human needs and
worthy social structure, he effected a conversion and
a conviction of sin comparable to the most sensational
feats of General Booth or Gypsy Smith. Clara's
snobbery went bang. Life suddenly began to move
with her. Without knowing how or why, she began
to make friends and enemies. Some of the acquaintances to whom she had been a tedious or indifferent
or ridiculous affliction, dropped her: others became
cordial. To her amazement she found that some
"quite nice" people were saturated with Wells, and
that this accessibility to ideas was the secret of their
niceness. People she had thought deeply religious,
and had tried to conciliate on that tack with disastrous results, suddenly took an interest in her, and
revealed a hostility to conventional religion which she
had never conceived possible except among the most
desperate characters. They made her read Galsworthy; and Galsworthy exposed the vanity of Largelady Park and finished her. It exasperated her to
think that the dungeon in which she had languished
for so many unhappy years had been unlocked all
the time, and that the impulses she had so carefully
struggled with and stifled for the sake of keeping well
with society, were precisely those by which alone
she could have come into any sort of sincere human

contact. In the radiance of these discoveries, and the
tumult of their reaction, she made a fool of herself
as freely and conspicuously as when she so rashly
adopted Eliza's expletive in Mrs Higgins's drawing
room; for the new-born Wellsian had to find her
bearings almost as ridiculously as a baby; but nobody hates a baby for its ineptitudes, or thinks the
worse of it for trying to eat the matches; and Clara
lost no friends by her follies. They laughed at her to
her face this time; and she had to defend herself and
fight it out as best she could.

When Freddy paid a visit to Earlscourt (which he
never did when he could possibly help it) to make the
desolating announcement that he and his Eliza were
thinking of blackening the Largelady scutcheon by
opening a shop, he found the little household already
convulsed by a prior announcement from Clara that
she also was going to work in an old furniture shop in
Dover Street, which had been started by a fellow
Wellsian. This appointment Clara owed, after all, to
her old social accomplishment of Push. She had made
up her mind that, cost what it might, she would see
Mr Wells in the flesh; and she had achieved her end
at a garden party. She had better luck than so rash
an enterprise deserved. Mr Wells came up to her
expectations. Age had not withered him, nor could
custom stale his infinite variety in half an hour. His
pleasant neatness and compactness, his small hands
and feet, his teeming ready brain, his unaffected
accessibility, and a certain fine apprehensiveness
which stamped him as susceptible from his topmost
hair to his tipmost toe, proved irresistible. Clara
talked of nothing else for weeks and weeks afterwards.
And as she happened to talk to the lady of the furniture shop, and that lady also desired above all things

to know Mr Wells and sell pretty things to him, she offered Clara a job on the chance of achieving that end through her.

And so it came about that Eliza's luck held, and the expected opposition to the flower shop melted away. The shop is in the arcade of a railway station not very far from the Victoria and Albert Museum; and if you live in that neighborhood you may go there any day and buy a buttonhole from Eliza.

Now here is a last opportunity for romance. Would you not like to be assured that the shop was an immense success, thanks to Eliza's charms and her early business experience in Covent Garden? Alas! the truth is the truth: the shop did not pay for a long time, simply because Eliza and her Freddy did not know how to keep it. True, Eliza had not to begin at the very beginning: she knew the names and prices of the cheaper flowers; and her elation was unbounded when she found that Freddy, like all youths educated at cheap, pretentious, and thoroughly inefficient schools, knew a little Latin. It was very little, but enough to make him appear to her a Porson or Bentley, and to put him at his ease with botanical nomenclature. Unfortunately he knew nothing else; and Eliza, though she could count money up to eighteen shillings or so, and had acquired a certain familiarity with the language of Milton from her struggles to qualify herself for winning Higgins's bet, could not write out a bill without utterly disgracing the establishment. Freddy's power of stating in Latin that Balbus built a wall and that Gaul was divided into three parts did not carry with it the slightest knowledge of accounts or business: Colonel Pickering had to explain to him what a cheque book and a bank account meant. And the pair were by no means easily teachable. Freddy backed up Eliza in her obstinate refusal to believe that they could save money by engaging a bookkeeper with some knowledge of the business. How, they argued, could you possibly save money by going to extra expense when you already could not make both ends meet? But the Colonel, after making the ends meet over and over again, at last gently insisted; and Eliza, humbled to the dust by having to beg from him so often, and stung by the uproarious derision of Higgins, to whom the notion of Freddy succeeding at anything was a joke that never palled, grasped the fact that business, like phonetics, has to be learned.

On the piteous spectacle of the pair spending their evenings in shorthand schools and polytechnic classes, learning bookkeeping and typewriting with incipient junior clerks, male and female, from the elementary schools, let me not dwell. There were even classes at the London School of Economics, and a humble personal appeal to the director of that institution to recommend a course bearing on the flower business. He, being a humorist, explained to them the method of the celebrated Dickensian essay on Chinese Metaphysics by the gentleman who read an article on China and an article on Metaphysics and combined the information. He suggested that they should combine the London School with Kew Gardens. Eliza, to whom the procedure of the Dickensian gentleman seemed perfectly correct (as in fact it was) and not in the least funny (which was only her ignorance), took the advice with entire gravity. But the effort that cost her the deepest humiliation was a request to Higgins, whose pet artistic fancy, next to Milton's verse, was caligraphy, and who himself wrote a most beautiful Italian hand, that he would teach her to write. He declared that she was congenitally incapable of forming a single letter worthy of the least of Milton's words; but she persisted; and again he suddenly threw himself into the task of teaching her with a combination of stormy intensity, concentrated patience, and occasional bursts of interesting disquisition on the beauty and nobility, the august mission and destiny, of human handwriting. Eliza ended by acquiring an extremely uncommercial script which was a positive extension of her personal beauty, and spending three times as much on stationery as anyone else because certain qualities and shapes of paper became indispensable to her. She could not even address an envelope in the usual way because it made the margins all wrong.

Their commercial schooldays were a period of disgrace and despair for the young couple. They seemed to be learning nothing about flower shops. At last they gave it up as hopeless, and shook the dust of the shorthand schools, and the polytechnics, and the London School of Economics from their feet for ever. Besides, the business was in some mysterious way beginning to take care of itself. They had somehow forgotten their objections to employing other people. They came to the conclusion that their own way was the best, and that they had really a remarkable talent for business. The Colonel, who had been compelled for some years to keep a sufficient sum on current account at his bankers to make up their deficits, found that the provision was unnecessary: the young people were prospering. It is true that there was not quite fair play between them and their competitors in trade. Their week-ends in the country cost them nothing, and saved them the price of their Sunday dinners; for the motor car was the Colonel's;

and he and Higgins paid the hotel bills. Mr F. Hill,
florist and greengrocer (they soon discovered that
there was money in asparagus; and asparagus led to
other vegetables), had an air which stamped the
business as classy; and in private life he was still
Frederick Eynsford Hill, Esquire. Not that there was
any swank about him: nobody but Eliza knew that
he had been christened Frederick Challoner. Eliza
herself swanked like anything.

That is all. That is how it has turned out. It is
astonishing how much Eliza still manages to meddle
in the housekeeping at Wimpole Street in spite of
the shop and her own family. And it is notable that
though she never nags her husband, and frankly
loves the Colonel as if she were his favorite daughter,
she has never got out of the habit of nagging Higgins
that was established on the fatal night when she won
his bet for him. She snaps his head off on the faintest
provocation, or on none. He no longer dares to tease
her by assuming an abysmal inferiority of Freddy's
mind to his own. He storms and bullies and derides;
but she stands up to him so ruthlessly that the Colonel
has to ask her from time to time to be kinder to
Higgins; and it is the only request of his that brings
a mulish expression into her face. Nothing but some
emergency or calamity great enough to break down
all likes and dislikes, and throw them both back on
their common humanity—and may they be spared
any such trial!—will ever alter this. She knows that
Higgins does not need her, just as her father did not
need her. The very scrupulousness with which he
told her that day that he had become used to having
her there, and dependent on her for all sorts of little
services, and that he should miss her if she went
away (it would never have occurred to Freddy or the

Colonel to say anything of the sort) deepens her inner certainty that she is "no more to him than them slippers"; yet she has a sense, too, that his indifference is deeper than the infatuation of commoner souls. She is immensely interested in him. She has even secret mischievous moments in which she wishes she could get him alone, on a desert island, away from all ties and with nobody else in the world to consider, and just drag him off his pedestal and see him making love like any common man. We all have private imaginations of that sort. But when it comes to business, to the life that she really leads as distinguished from the life of dreams and fancies, she likes Freddy and she likes the Colonel; and she does not like Higgins and Mr Doolittle. Galatea never does quite like Pygmalion: his relation to her is too godlike to be altogether agreeable.

THE END

Mr Shaw's "Literary Morals"

(Statement for *The Observer*, 11 January 1914)

The suggestion of the German papers that I had "Pygmalion" produced in Germany lest I should be detected in plagiarism from Smollett shows an amusing ignorance of English culture. The one place where I should have been absolutely safe from detection is London. The place where detection was most certain is Berlin, where an acquaintance with the masterpieces of English literature is quite common.

I have never read "Peregrine Pickle," and, therefore, did not know until the Berlin correspondent of the "Manchester Guardian" pointed it out, that Smollett had got hold of my plot. He is quite welcome to it.

I may add that if I had read it the result would have been just the same. If I find in a book anything I can make use of, I take it gratefully. My plays are full of pillage of this kind. Shakespeare, Dickens, Conan Doyle, Oscar Wilde, Granville Barker: all is fish that comes to my net. In short, my literary morals are those of Molière and Handel.

Shorthand Fragment, 1914

(Possibly intended to be part of a drafted interview.
British Museum Add. MSS. 50560, f. 181)

Is Pygmalion irresistibly funny?

Not at all. There is nothing in it to force on anyone the alternative of their being uproarious or bursting. I can listen to it without yells of merriment; and I, as the author, ought to be more amused by it than anyone else. It is really a serious play, although it is the romance of a flower girl changed into a lady by a gentleman whom she meets by accident on a wet night when they are both sheltering from the rain under the portico of St Paul's Church in Covent Garden. But there is a serious side to the play in the fate of the girl's father, whose story is really a modern version of the old Don Juan play "Il dissoluto punito." This man is an Immoralist, a lover of wine, women, and song, a flouter of respectability, one whose delight it is to épater le bourgeois. In the old play he is cast into hell by the statue of the man he has murdered. In my play a far more real and terrible fate overtakes him. No: it is not the fate of Oswald in Ibsen's Ghosts, nor of the young man in Brieux's Les Avariés. Nothing like that at all. Something quite simple, quite respectable, quite presentable to the youngest schoolgirl. And yet a frightful retribution. The rest of the play is merely to call public attention to the importance of the study of phonetics, which has always been one of my favorite subjects. Let me tell you one remarkable fact. The translation of the play into Swedish by Mr Hugo Vallentin has been made extremely difficult by the fact, astounding to a Londoner, that in Stockholm all classes speak the same language. That is real civilization. Here the flower girl speaks one language and the duchess another; though the difference is not so great as the duchess thinks, especially if she is a smart duchess. We shall never have a standard English until we have a National Theatre co-operating with a serious Academy of Letters. Not that they will do anything; but people will keep saying that they ought to do something; and that is how things finally get done.

All this sounds very serious.

[End of fragment]

G. B. S., Eliza and the Critics

(Statement for the *Daily News*,
London, 17 April 1914)

I have nothing particular to say about Eliza Doolittle's
language. I have something to say about the comments that have been made on it; but perhaps I had
better not say it. I do not know anything more
ridiculous than the refusal of some newspapers (at
several pages length) to print the word "bloody,"
which is in common use as an expletive by four-fifths
of the English nation, including many highly-educated
persons. Cobden's allusion to "the bloody Times"
has been quoted in print over and over again. It is,
however, a class word. It is natural in the mouth of a
member of the class which uses it,—a class which I,
by the way, want to abolish. Yet this class presses so
hard on us that it forces us at last to adopt its tricks
of speech. First we tried to substitute the word
"blooming." But that was only a frail and temporary
defence against the fascination of the real word. We
had to come nearer with the word "bally." Finally a
little smart clique began to say "bloody"; and at
about the same time the word was used in several
plays. I was not the first to use it on the stage: but I
was the first to see that Mrs. Patrick Campbell could
bring down the house with it, quite inoffensively, by
the very simple artistic stroke of using it naturally and
sincerely.

But as I happen to think the word detestable when
used by a smart, or would-be smart, lady as a piece
of smartness, and as it was evident that without a
strong antidote Mrs Campbell's irresistible utterance
of it would set all smart London bloodying all through

the season, I carefully made another lady follow up Mrs Campbell by repeating the word as a fashionable affectation, with an effect which will, I hope, effectually prevent any occurrence of that folly in real life.

Immediately people complain that the repetition "falls flat." They think that the object was to repeat the success. It was, of course, to produce just the contrast—with its implied warning—that actually was produced, and, incidentally, to emphasise my sympathy with the protest so delicately spoken by Miss Addison in the character of a lady who is really refined: suffering from a daughter who only wishes to be smart.

When the ridiculous sensation about this familiar and quite harmless word is exhausted, as it very soon will be, more attention will be paid to the serious interest of Eliza's phonetics. It will be seen, for instance, that the flower girl's conversation is much more picturesque, much better rhetoric, much more concise, interesting, and arresting than the conversation of the drawing-room, and that the moment she learns to speak beautifully she gains an advantage by the intensity of her experiences and the strength of her feeling about it. When the nine days' wonder about the word "bloody," and the laughter at the superficial fun of the play is over—as I hope it soon will be— the scene in the third act will be more interesting than it is now, not less.

Some critics have remarked that Eliza's nature is not changed by the change in her pronunciation. This is a very interesting criticism. It is a naïve betrayal of the firm belief of the middle-class that it differs from the working-class not only in dress and pronunciation, but in nature. Sancta simplicitas! No nonsense about our being "members one of another" among these gentlemen. "I have my feelings same as anyone else," cries Eliza in the play. "Not like us," reply these gentlemen gravely. "You belong to the lower classes." Don't you think that a better joke than any in the play?

H. Beerbohm Tree: From the Point of View of the Playwright

(First appeared in *Herbert Beerbohm Tree: Some Memories of Him and His Art,* ed. Max Beerbohm, 1920)

A tribute to Tree from the playwright's point of view is a duty of such delicacy that it is quite impossible to be delicate about it at all: one must confess bluntly at the outset that Tree was the despair of authors. His attitude towards a play was one of whole-hearted anxiety to solve the problem of how to make it please and interest the audience.

Now this is the author's business, not the actor's. The function of the actor is to make the audience imagine for the moment that real things are happening to real people. It is for the author to make the result interesting. If he fails, the actor cannot save the play unless it is so flimsy a thing that the actor can force upon it some figure of his own fancy and play the author off the stage. This has been done successfully in several well-known, though very uncommon cases. Robert Macaire and Lord Dundreary were imposed by their actors on plays which did not really contain them. Grimaldi's clown was his own invention. These figures died with their creators, though their ghosts still linger on the stage. Irving's

Shylock was a creation which he thrust successfully upon Shakespear's play; indeed, all Irving's impersonations were changelings. His Hamlet and his Lear were to many people more interesting than Shakespear's Hamlet and Lear; but the two pairs were hardly even related. To the author, Irving was not an actor: he was either a rival or a collaborator who did all the real work. Therefore, he was anathema to master authors, and a godsend to journeymen authors, with the result that he had to confine himself to the works of dead authors who could not interfere with him, and, very occasionally, live authors who were under his thumb because they were unable to command production of their works in other quarters.

Into this tradition of creative acting came Tree as Irving's rival and successor; and he also, with his restless imagination, felt that he needed nothing from an author but a literary scaffold on which to exhibit his own creations. He, too, turned to Shakespear as to a forest out of which such scaffolding could be hewn without remonstrance from the landlord, and to foreign authors who could not interfere with him, their interests being in the hands of adapters who could not stand up against his supremacy in his own theatre. As far as I could discover, the notion that a play could succeed without any further help from the actor than a simple impersonation of his part never occurred to Tree. The author, whether Shakespear or Shaw, was a lame dog to be helped over the stile by the ingenuity and inventiveness of the actor-producer. How to add and subtract, to interpolate and prune, until an effective result was arrived at, was the problem of production as he saw it. Of living authors of eminence the two he came into personal contact with were Brieux and Henry Arthur Jones; and I have reason to believe that their experience of him in no way contradicts my own. With contemporary masters of the stage like Pinero and Carton, in whose works the stage business is an integral part of the play, and the producer, when he is not the author in person, is an executant and not an inventor, Tree had never worked; and when he at last came upon the species in me, and found that, instead of having to discover how to make an effective histrionic entertainment on the basis of such scraps of my dialogue as might prove useful, he had only to fit himself into a jig-saw puzzle cut out by me, and just to act his part as well as he could, he could neither grasp the situation nor resist the impersonal compulsion of arrangements which he had not made, and was driven to accept only by the fact that they were the only ones which would work. But to the very end they bewildered him; and he had to go to the box office to assure himself that the omission of his customary care had not produced disastrous results.

Just before the production of my play we lunched together at the Royal Automobile Club. I said to him: "Have you noticed during the rehearsals that though you and I are no longer young, and have achieved all the success possible in our respective professions, we have been treating one another throughout as beginners?" To this, on reflection, he had to assent, because we actually were, relatively to one another, beginners. I had never had to deal with him professionally before, nor he with me; and he was quite unaccustomed to double harness, whilst I was so accustomed to every extremity of multiple harness, both in politics and in the theatre, that I had been trained to foresee everything and consider everybody. Now if I were to say that Tree foresaw nothing and considered nobody, I should suggest that he was a much less amiable man than he was. Let me therefore say that he never foresaw anything or considered anybody in cold blood. Of the foresight which foresees and faces entirely uninteresting facts, and the consideration which considers entirely uninteresting persons, he had as little as a man can have without being run over in the street. When his feelings were engaged, he was human and even shrewd and tenacious. But you really could not lodge an indifferent fact in his mind. This disability of his was carried to such a degree that he could not remember the passages in a play which did not belong to or bear directly upon his own conception of his own part: even the longest run did not mitigate his surprise when they recurred. Thus he never fell into that commonest fault of the actor: the betrayal to the audience that he knows what his interlocutor is going to say, and is waiting wearily for his cue instead of conversing with him. Tree always seemed to have heard the lines of the other performers for the first time, and even to be a little taken aback by them.

Let me give an extreme instance of this. In Pygmalion the heroine, in a rage, throws the hero's slippers in his face. When we rehearsed this for the first time, I had taken care to have a very soft pair of velvet slippers provided; for I knew that Mrs Patrick Campbell was very dexterous, very strong, and a dead shot. And, sure enough, when we reached this passage, Tree got the slippers well and truly delivered with unerring aim bang in his face. The effect was appalling. He had totally forgotten that there was any such incident in the play; and it seemed to him that Mrs Campbell, suddenly giving way to an impulse of diabolical wrath and hatred, had committed an unprovoked and brutal assault on him. The physical impact was nothing; but the wound to his feelings was terrible. He collapsed on the nearest chair, and left me staring in amazement, whilst the entire personnel of the theatre crowded solicitously round him, explaining that the incident was part of the play, and even exhibiting the prompt-book to prove their words. But his *moral* was so shattered that it took quite a long time, and a good deal of skilful rallying and coaxing from Mrs Campbell, before he was in a condition to resume the rehearsal. The worst of it was that as it was quite evident that he would be just as surprised and wounded next time, Mrs Campbell took care that the slippers should never hit him again, and the incident was consequently one of the least convincing in the performance.

This, and many similar scenes that are told of Tree, will not be believed by experienced men of business. They will say curtly that it is no use trying to stuff them with stories like that: that running a theatre like His Majesty's must have been a big business, and that no man could possibly have done it for so long without being too capable and wide-awake to forget everything that did not amuse or interest him. But they will be quite wrong. Theatrical business is not like other business. A man may enter on the management of a theatre without business habits or knowledge, and at the end of forty years of it know less about business than when he began. The explanation is that a London West-End theatre is always either making such an enormous profit that

the utmost waste caused by unbusinesslike management is not worth considering, or else losing so
much that the strictest economy cannot arrest the
process by a halfpenny in the pound. In an industrial
concern the addition of a penny to the piecework rate
or the hourly time rate of wages, the slowing of a
steam engine by a few revolutions, the retention of a
machine two years out-of-date, or the loss of fifteen
minutes' work in the day by unpunctuality, may make
all the difference between profit and bankruptcy.
The employer is held to rigid conditions by a strin-
gent factory code enforced by a Government inspector on the one hand and by a jealous trade union on
the other. He is the creature of circumstance and the
slave of law, with so little liberty for sentiment and
caprice that he very soon loses not only the habit of
indulging them but even the sense of possessing
them. Not so the manager of a theatre. Tree was
accustomed to make two hundred per cent profit
every day when he was in luck. With such a margin
to play with, it was no more worth his while to
economize or remember uninteresting things than
it was to walk when there was a taxi at his beck.
When his theatre was built for him, the equipment of
its stage, apart from the electric lighting installation,
was exactly what it would have been a hundred years
before, except that there were no grooves for side
wings. If every employee on the premises had come
an hour late every day and had received double
wages, the difference in profit would have been hardly
worth noticing. A theatre is a maddening place to a
thrifty man of business, and an economic paradise
to an artist, because there is practically no limit to
the waste of time and money that may go on, provided
the doors are open every night and the curtain up

half an hour later. But for this necessity, and a few County Council by-laws, an actor-manager would be as unbridled as Nero, without even the Neronian check of a Prætorian Guard to kill him if he went beyond all bearing.

There is no denying that such conditions put a strain on human character that it can seldom sustain without injury. If Tree's caprices, and his likes and dislikes, had not been on the whole amiable, the irresponsibility and power of his position would have made a fiend of him. As it was, they produced the oddest results. He was always attended in the theatre by a retinue of persons with no defined business there, who were yet on the salary list. There was one capable gentleman who could get things done; and I decided to treat him as the stage manager; but until I saw his name in the bill under that heading I never felt sure that he was not some casual acquaintance whom Tree had met in the club or in the street and invited to come in and make himself at home. Tree did not know what a stage manager was, just as he did not know what an author was. He had not even made up his mind any too definitely what an actor was. One moment he would surprise and delight his courtiers (for that is the nearest word I can find for his staff and entourage) by some stroke of kindness and friendliness. The next he would commit some appalling breach of etiquet by utterly ignoring their functions and privileges, when they had any. It was amiable and modest in him not to know his own place, since it was the highest in the theatre; but it was exasperating in him not to know anyone else's. I very soon gave up all expectation of being treated otherwise than as a friend who had dropped in; so, finding myself as free to interfere in the proceedings as anyone else who dropped in would apparently have been, I interfered not only in my proper department but in every other as well; and nobody gainsaid me. One day I interfered to such an extent that Tree was moved to a mildly sarcastic remonstrance. "I seem to have heard or read somewhere," he said, "that plays have actually been produced, and performances given, in this theatre, under its present management, before you came. According to you, that couldnt have happened. How do you account for it?" "I cant account for it," I replied, with the blunt good faith of a desperate man. "I suppose you put a notice in the papers that a performance will take place at half-past eight, and take the money at the doors. Then you *have* to do the play somehow. There is no other way of accounting for it." On two such occasions it seemed so brutal to worry him, and so hopeless to advance matters beyond the preliminary arrangement of the stage business (which I had already done), that I told him quite cordially to put the play through in his own way, and shook the dust of the theatre from my feet. On both occasions I had to yield to urgent appeals from other members of the cast to return and extricate them from a hopeless mess; and on both occasions Tree took leave of me as if it had been very kind of me to look in as I was passing to see his rehearsals, and received me on my return as if it were still more friendly of me to come back and see how he was getting on. I tried once or twice to believe that he was only pulling my leg; but that was incredible: his sincerity and insensibility were only too obvious. Finally, I had to fight my way through to a sort of production in the face of an unresisting, amusing, friendly, but heart-breakingly obstructive principal.

We finally agreed that I should have been an actor and he an author; and he always sent me his books afterwards. As a matter of fact, he had a very marked literary talent, and, even as an amateur, achieved a finish of style and sureness of execution that was not always evident in his acting, especially when, as in the case of Pygmalion, he had to impersonate a sort of man he had never met and of whom he had no conception. He tried hard to induce me to let him play the dustman instead of the Miltonic professor of phonetics; and when he resigned himself to his unnatural task, he set to work to make this disagreeable and incredible person sympathetic in the character of a lover, for which I had left so little room that he was quite baffled until he lit on the happy thought of throwing flowers to Eliza in the very brief interval between the end of the play and the fall of the curtain. If he had not been so amusing, so ingenious, and so entirely well-intentioned he would have driven me crazy. As it was, he made me feel like his grandfather. I should add that he never bore the slightest malice for my air of making the best of a bad job. A few days before his death, when he was incredibly young and sanguine, and made me feel hopelessly old and grumpy, he was discussing a revival of Pygmalion as if it promised to be a renewal of the most delightful experience of our lives. The only reproach he ever addressed to me was for not coming to Pygmalion every night, which he thought the natural duty of an author. I promised to come on the hundredth night, adding rather unkindly that this was equivalent to not coming at all. The hundredth night, however, was reached and survived; and I redeemed my promise, only to find that he had contributed to my second act a stroke of comic business so outrageously irrelevant that I solemnly cursed the whole enterprise, and bade the delinquents farewell for ever.

The fact that Tree could do and be done by thus without bloodshed, although he had all the sensitiveness of his profession, and all the unrestrained impulsiveness of a man who had succeeded in placing himself above discipline from the beginning of his adult life, shews that he was never quite unpardonable; and though this, to the world that knows nothing of the theatre, may seem more of an apology than a tribute, those who know the theatre best will understand its value. It has to be considered, too, that the statement that he did nothing unpardonable does not imply that he did nothing irreparable. Almost all the wrongs and errors of the West-End London theatre are like the wrongs and errors of the battlefield: they cannot be undone. If an actor's or an author's chance is spoilt, it is spoilt for years and perhaps for ever: neither play nor part gets a second chance. I doubt whether there is an actor-manager living who has not done both these wrongs more than once. Tree was no exception; but as the result, like that of the elephant sitting on the hen's eggs, was never intended, it was impossible to bear malice for long. I have seen him try to help a very able Shakespearean actor, and, incidentally, to help Shakespear, through what he thought a tedious scene, by pretending to catch flies, with ruinous consequences to both player and Bard. He put a new complexion on Brieux's La Foi, with effects on the feelings of that illustrious author which I shall not attempt to describe. He meant equally well on both occasions.

And here I come to a source of friction between authors and actor-managers which is worth explaining with some care, as it bears on the general

need in England for a school of physical training for
the arts of public life as distinguished from the sports.
An author who understands acting, and writes for the
actor as a composer writes for an instrument, giving
it the material suitable to its range, tone, character,
agility and mechanism, necessarily assumes a certain
technical accomplishment common to all actors; and
this requires the existence of a school of acting, or at
least a tradition. Now we had no such provision in
the days of Tree's novitiate. He had not inherited
the tradition handed down at rehearsal by Phelps to
Forbes Robertson; nor was there any academic
institution with authority enough to impress a novice
of his calibre. To save others from this disadvantage
he later on founded the Academy of Dramatic Art
in Gower Street, which now supplies the want as
far as an unendowed institution can. But he had to do
without teaching himself. Like Irving, he had to make
a style and technique out of his own personality:
that is, out of his peculiar weaknesses as well as his
peculiar powers. And here he sowed dragons'
teeth between himself and the authors. For no un-
commissioned author can write for an idiosyncratic
style and technique: he knows only the classical one.
He must, like Shakespear, assume an executant who
can perform and sustain certain physical feats of
deportment, and build up vocal climaxes with his
voice through a long crescendo of rhetoric. Further,
he assumes the possession of an English voice and an
English feeling for splendor of language and rhythm
of verse. Such professional skill and national gift are
not accidents of personality: they are more or less
within every Englishman's capacity. By themselves
they will no more make an actor than grammar and
spelling will make an author, or fingering and blowing

a bandsman; but one expects every actor to possess them, just as one expects every author to parse and spell correctly and every bandsman to finger and blow properly.

Tree, like so many of our actors who have picked up their profession on the stage without systematic training, found that he could not produce these stock effects. When they were demanded by the author, he had to find a way round them, and, if possible, an interesting way. Thus he had not only to struggle against his handicap, but to triumph over it by turning it into an advantage. And his handicap was not a light one. Instead of that neutral figure which an actor can turn into anything he pleases, he was tall, and built like nobody else on earth. His Dutch extraction gave him an un-English voice, which, again, was like nobody else's voice and could not be disguised. His feeling for verbal music was entirely non-Miltonic: he had a music of his own; but it was not the music characteristic of English rhetoric; and blank verse, as such, had no charm for him; nor, I suspect, did he credit it with charm for anyone else.

The results were most marked in his Shakespearean work, and would certainly have produced curious scenes at rehearsal had the author been present. No doubt it is an exaggeration to say that the only unforgettable passages in his Shakespearean acting are those of which Tree and not Shakespear was the author. His Wolsey, which was a "straight" performance of high merit and dignity, could be cited to the contrary. But take, for examples, his Richard II and his Malvolio. One of the most moving points in his Richard was made with the assistance of a dog who does not appear among Shakespear's *dramatis*

personae. When the dog—Richard's pet dog—turned
to Bolingbroke and licked his hand, Richard's heart
broke; and he left the stage with a sob. Next to this
came his treatment of the entry of Bolingbroke and
the deposed Richard into London. Shakespear makes
the Duke of York describe it. Nothing could be easier
with a well-trained actor at hand. And nothing could
be more difficult and inconvenient than to bring
horses on the stage and represent it in action. But
this is just what Tree did. One still remembers that
great white horse, and the look of hunted terror with
which Richard turned his head as the crowd hooted
him. It passed in a moment; and it flatly contradicted
Shakespear's description of the saint-like patience of
Richard; but the effect was intense: no one but
Chaliapine has since done so much by a single look
and an appearance for an instant on horseback. Again,
one remembers how Richard walked out of Westminster Hall after his abdication.

Turn now to the scenes in which Shakespear has
given the actor a profusion of rhetoric to declaim.
Take the famous "For God's sake let us sit upon the
ground, and tell sad stories of the death of kings."
My sole recollection of that scene is that when I was
sitting in the stalls listening to it, a paper was passed
to me. I opened it and read: "If you will rise and
move a resolution, I will second it.—Murray Carson."
The late Murray Carson was, above all things, an
elocutionist; and the scene was going for nothing.
Tree was giving Shakespear, at immense trouble
and expense, and with extraordinary executive
cunning, a great deal that Shakespear had not asked
for, and denying him something much simpler that
he did ask for, and set great store by.

As Malvolio, Tree was inspired to provide himself

with four smaller Malvolios, who aped the great chamberlain in dress, in manners, in deportment. He had a magnificent flight of stairs on the stage; and when he was descending it majestically, he slipped and fell with a crash sitting. Mere clowning, you will say; but no: the fall was not the point. Tree, without betraying the smallest discomfiture, raised his eyeglass and surveyed the landscape as if he had sat down on purpose. This, like the four satellite Malvolios, was not only funny but subtle. But when he came to speak those lines with which any old Shakespearean hand can draw a laugh by a simple trick of the voice, Tree made nothing of them, not knowing a game which he had never studied.

Even if our actors came to the stage with complete executive mastery of all the traditions and all the conventions, there would still be a conflict between the actor's tendency to adapt the play to his own personality and the author's desire to adapt the actor's personality to the play. But this would not make any serious trouble between them; for a good part can be played a dozen different ways by a dozen different actors and be none the worse: no author worth his salt attaches a definite and invariable physiognomy to each variety of human character. Every actor must be allowed to apply his own methods to his own playing. But if, as under our system, an actor, instead of laying the foundation of a general technique of speech and action, is driven, by the absence of any school in which he can acquire such a technique, to develop his own personality, and acquire a technique of exploiting that personality which is not applicable to any other purpose, then there will be friction at rehearsals if the author produces his own play, as all authors should. For the actor will inevitably try to force a changeling on the author. He will say, in effect: "I will not play this part that you have written; but I will substitute one of my own which is ever so much better." And it will be useless for the author to assert himself, and say: "You *shall* play the part as I have written it." If he knows his business, he will see that the "will not" of the actor really means "cannot," because the author has written for a classical technique which the actor does not possess and cannot learn in three weeks, or even three years. It is better to let the actor do what he can: indeed, there is no alternative.

What Tree could do was always entertaining in some way or other. But, for better for worse, it was hardly ever what the author meant him to do. His parts were his avatars; and the play had to stand the descent of the deity into it as best it could. Sometimes, as in my case, the author understood the situation and made the best of it. Sometimes, no doubt, the author either did not understand the situation or would not make the best of it. But Tree could not act otherwise than as he did; and his productions represented an output of invention on his part that may have supplied many deficiencies in the plays.

One of his ambitions was to create a Tree Don Quixote. He used to discuss this with me eagerly as a project we might carry out together. "What I see," he said, "is a room full of men in evening dress smoking. Somebody mentions the Don. They begin talking about him. They wonder what he would make of our modern civilization. The back wall vanishes; and there is Piccadilly, with all the buses and cabs coming towards you in a stream of traffic; and with them, in the middle, the long tall figure in armor on the lean horse, amazing, foreign, incongruous, and

yet impressive, right in the centre of the picture."
"That is really a very good idea," I would say. "I
must certainly carry it out. But how could we manage
the buses and things?" "Yes," he would go on, not
listening to me after my first words of approval:
"there you see him going down the mountain-side
in Spain just after dawn, through the mist, you know,
on the horse, and—" "And Calvert as Sancho Panza
on the ass," I would say. That always surprised him.
"Yes," he would say slowly. "Yes. Sancho, of course.
Oh, yes." Though he had quite forgotten Sancho,
yet, switching instantly over to his Falstaff line, he
would begin to consider whether he could not double
the two parts, as he doubled Micawber and Peggotty.
For your true actor is still what he was in the days
of Bottom: he wants to play every part in the
comedy.

But the heart of the matter (which I have been
coming to slowly all this time) is that the cure for the
disease of actor-managership (every author must
take that pathological view of it) is actor-author-
managership: the cure of Molière, who acted his
plays as well as wrote them, and managed his theatre
into the bargain. And yet he lasted fifty-one years.
Richard Wagner was author-composer-conductor-
manager at Bayreuth: a much more arduous combination. Tree should have written his own plays. He
could have done so. He had actually begun to do it
as Shakespear and Molière began, by tinkering other
men's plays. The conflict that raged between him
and me at the rehearsals in his theatre would then
have taken place in his own bosom. He would have
taken a parental pride in other parts beside his own.
He would have come to care for a play as a play, and
to understand that it has powers over the audience

even when it is read by people sitting round a table or performed by wooden marionettes. It would have developed that talent of his that wasted itself in *jeux d'esprit* and epigrams. And it would have given him what he was always craving from authors, and in the nature of the case could never get from them: a perfect projection of the great Tree personality. What did he care for Higgins or Hamlet ? His real objective was his amazing self. That also was Shakespear's objective in Hamlet; but Shakespear was not Tree, and therefore Hamlet could never be to Tree what Hamlet was to Shakespear. For with all his cleverness in the disguises of the actor's dressing room, Tree was no mere character actor. The character actor never dares to appear frankly in his own person: he is the victim of a mortal shyness that agonizes and paralyzes him when his mask is stripped off and his cothurnus snatched from beneath his feet. Tree, on the contrary, broke through all his stage disguises: they were his robes of state; and he was never happier than when he stepped in front of the curtain and spoke in his own immensity to the audience, if not as deep calling unto deep (for the audience could not play up to him as splendidly as that), at least as a monarch to his courtiers.

I trust that in the volume of memoirs collected by his equally famous brother Max, who has asked me to contribute this pen-and-ink sketch, he may find his bard, as Elliston found Charles Lamb. It is my misfortune that I cannot do him justice, because, as author and actor, we two were rivals who regarded one another as usurpers. Happily, no bones were broken in the encounter; and if there is any malice in my description of it, I hope I have explained sufficiently to enable the reader to make the necessary allowance and correction.

G. B. Shaw Defends Eliza Doolittle

(Statement for the *Daily Worker*,
London, 14 January 1939)

DAILY WORKER *readers, through our Postbag, are
making known their views on G. Bernard Shaw's film
version of "Pygmalion," now generally released.
Extracts from their letters were sent to G.B.S. for his
comment. Yesterday we received the following reply:—*

Your correspondents must fight it out among
themselves. As to Mr Thornton, who started the disturbance, he gave himself away as hopelessly middle-
class and monstrously unobservant by assuming that
all "working girls" are exactly alike. He thinks they
are all perfectly ladylike. If he marries his son to a
rag-picker he will find out his mistake.

Eliza knew better when she aspired to be a lady
in a florist's shop and knew that the difficulty was
that she could not speak like one.

Another assumption, made by your more sensible
correspondents, is that I am a satirist, and that
Pygmalion is therefore a satire. I have never written
a satire in my life. I am the particular kind of story-
teller called a playwright.

I draw my characters from life as I see them, usually
choosing the most favourable specimens because the
ordinary ones are not interesting enough. There is
no satire in the business.

The notion that Eliza must have been an extraordinarily clever girl to learn how to speak and dress
presentably is mere ignorance.

When Professor Higgins made his bet that he
would pass off a guttersnipe as a duchess in six

months he knew that there are thousands of women, from parlourmaids and telephone operators to actresses and members of parliament, who speak professionally with an acquired elocution and not as they spoke as children in their homes. They are in fact bilingual.

Your correspondents may draw what morals they please: that is what plays and stories are for; but they must bear in mind that if I were out to plant morals on them instead of producing true pictures of life, my plays would be both dull and dishonest. Doolittle would be exactly like Colonel Pickering and neither of them would be in the least like human beings.

Bernard Shaw Flays Filmdom's 'Illiterates'

(Replies to a questionnaire by Dennison Thornton, *Reynolds News*, London, 22 January 1939)

If we are to believe what the film producers are always telling us about the low intelligence of the average filmgoer, how do you account for the tremendous success everywhere of "Pygmalion," which has been praised as one of the most intelligent films yet made?

Only thoughtless people chatter about the low intelligence of the average filmgoer. There is no such person. There are several classes of public entertainment, including several classes of film. And there are several classes of film director, including some who are so illiterate that they cannot conceive anyone being interested in anything but very crudely presented police and divorce court news, and adventures out of boys' journals.

They are usually ranked as infallible authorities on the suitability of scenarios. These gentlemen have never had any use for me and I cannot pretend that I have any use for them.

Do you think that these filmed versions of your plays will bring about a new type of film—films in which problems of conduct and character of importance to the audience are raised and suggestively discussed?

I don't think "Pygmalion" will bring about anything but the confusion of the idiots who maintain that a good play must make a bad film, and that the musical English of a dramatic poet must be converted into the slang of a Californian bar-tender or it will not be understood in Seattle—where, by the way, they do not speak Californian.

In a note to the stage version of "Pygmalion," you deplored what you called "ready-made, happy endings to misfit all stories." Yet you allowed such a ready-made happy ending to be substituted in the film version of "Pygmalion." Why?

I did not. I cannot conceive a less happy ending to the story of "Pygmalion" than a love affair between the middle-aged, middle-class professor, a confirmed old bachelor with a mother-fixation, and a flower girl of 18. Nothing of the kind was emphasised in my scenario, where I emphasised the escape of Eliza from the tyranny of Higgins by a quite natural love affair with Freddy.

But I cannot at my age undertake studio work: and about 20 directors seem to have turned up there and spent their time trying to sidetrack me and Mr Gabriel Pascal, who does really know chalk from cheese. They devised a scene to give a lovelorn complexion at the end to Mr Leslie Howard: but it is too inconclusive to be worth making a fuss about.

Overruled

WITH

Preface

Extract from Interview, drafted by Shaw,
The Observer, *London, 29 September 1912*

Composition begun 2 July 1912; completed 23
July 1912. First published in German translation, as *Es hat nicht sollen sein*, in the *Neue
Freie Presse* (Vienna), 23 March 1913. Published in the *English Review* and in *Hearst's
Magazine* (New York), May 1913. First collected in *Androcles and the Lion, Overruled,
Pygmalion*, 1916. First presented at the Duke
of York's Theatre, London, 14 October 1912.

Gregory Lunn   *Claude King*
Mrs Juno   *Miriam Lewes*
Sibthorpe Juno   *Adolphus Vane Tempest*
Seraphita Lunn   *Geraldine Olliffe*

Period—A Summer Night

Scene—*A Corner of the Lounge of a Seaside
    Hotel*

Preface

Contents

THE ALLEVIATIONS OF MONOGAMY

This piece is not an argument for or against polygamy. It is a clinical study of how the thing actually
occurs among quite ordinary people, innocent of all
unconventional views concerning it. The enormous
majority of cases in real life are those of people in that
position. Those who deliberately and conscientiously
profess what are oddly called advanced views by those
others who believe them to be retrograde, are often,
and indeed mostly, the last people in the world to
engage in unconventional adventures of any kind,
not only because they have neither time nor disposition for them, but because the friction set up between

the individual and the community by the expression of unusual views of any sort is quite enough hindrance to the heretic without being complicated by personal scandals. Thus the theoretic libertine is usually a person of blameless family life, whilst the practical libertine is mercilessly severe on all other libertines, and excessively conventional in professions of social principle.

What is more, these professions are not hypocritical: they are for the most part quite sincere. The common libertine, like the drunkard, succumbs to a temptation which he does not defend, and against which he warns others with an earnestness proportionate to the intensity of his own remorse. He (or she) may be a liar and a humbug, pretending to be better than the detected libertines, and clamoring for their condign punishment; but this is mere self-defence. No reasonable person expects the burglar to confess his pursuits, or to refrain from joining in the cry of Stop Thief when the police get on the track of another burglar. If society chooses to penalize candor, it has itself to thank if its attack is countered by falsehood. The clamorous virtue of the libertine is therefore no more hypocritical than the plea of Not Guilty which is allowed to every criminal. But one result is that the theorists who write most sincerely and favorably about polygamy know least about it; and the practitioners who know most about it keep their knowledge very jealously to themselves. Which is hardly fair to the practice.

INACCESSIBILITY OF THE FACTS

Also, it is impossible to estimate its prevalence. A practice to which nobody confesses may be both universal and unsuspected, just as a virtue which everybody is expected, under heavy penalties, to claim, may have no existence. It is often assumed—indeed it is the official assumption of the Churches and the divorce courts—that a gentleman and a lady cannot be alone together innocently. And that is manifest blazing nonsense, though many women have been stoned to death in the east, and divorced in the west, on the strength of it. On the other hand, the innocent and conventional people who regard gallant adventures as crimes of so horrible a nature that only the most depraved and desperate characters engage in them or would listen to advances in that direction without raising an alarm with the noisiest indignation, are clearly examples of the fact that most sections of society do not know how the other sections live. Industry is the most effective check on gallantry. Women may, as Napoleon said, be the occupation of the idle man just as men are the preoccupation of the idle woman; but the mass of mankind is too busy and too poor for the long and expensive sieges which the professed libertine lays to virtue. Still, wherever there is idleness or even a reasonable supply of elegant leisure there is a good deal of coquetry and philandering. It is so much pleasanter to dance on the edge of a precipice than to go over it that leisured society is full of people who spend a great part of their lives in flirtation, and conceal nothing but the humiliating secret that they have never gone any further. For there is no pleasing people in the matter of reputation in this department: every insult is a flattery: every testimonial is a disparagement: Joseph is despised and promoted, Potiphar's wife admired and condemned: in short, you are never on solid ground until you get away from the subject altogether. There is a continual and irreconcilable conflict between the natural and conventional sides of the case, between spontaneous human relations between independent men and women on the one hand and the property relation between husband and wife on the other, not to mention the confusion under the common name of love of a generous natural attraction and interest with the murderous jealousy that fastens on and clings to its mate (especially a hated mate) as a tiger fastens on a carcase. And the confusion is natural; for these extremes are the extremes of the same passion; and most cases lie somewhere on the scale between them, and are so complicated by ordinary likes and dislikes, by incidental wounds to vanity or gratifications of it, and by class feeling, that A will be jealous of B and not of C, and will tolerate infidelities on the part of D whilst being furiously angry when they are committed by E.

THE CONVENTION OF JEALOUSY

That jealousy is independent of sex is shewn by its intensity in children, and by the fact that very jealous people are jealous of everybody without regard to relationship or sex, and cannot bear to hear the person they "love" speak favorably of anyone under any circumstances (many women, for instance, are much more jealous of their husbands' mothers and sisters than of unrelated women whom they suspect him of fancying); but it is seldom possible to disentangle the two passions in practice. Besides, jealousy is an inculcated passion, forced by society on people in whom it would not occur spontaneously. In Brieux's Bourgeois aux Champs, the benevolent hero finds himself detested by the neighboring peasants and farmers, not because he preserves game, and sets

[830]

mantraps for poachers, and defends his legal rights
over his land to the extremest point of unsocial savagery, but because, being an amiable and public-spirited
person, he refuses to do all this, and thereby offends
and disparages the sense of property in his neighbors.
The same thing is true of matrimonial jealousy: the
man who does not at least pretend to feel it, and behave
as badly as if he really felt it, is despised and insulted;
and many a man has shot or stabbed a friend or been
shot or stabbed by him in a duel, or disgraced himself
and ruined his own wife in a divorce scandal, against
his conscience, against his instinct, and to the destruction of his home, solely because Society conspired to
drive him to keep its own lower morality in countenance in this miserable and undignified manner.

Morality is confused in such matters. In an elegant
plutocracy, a jealous husband is regarded as a boor.
Among the tradesmen who supply that plutocracy
with its meals, a husband who is not jealous, and
refrains from assailing his rival with his fists, is regarded as a ridiculous, contemptible, and cowardly
cuckold. And the laboring class is divided into the
respectable section which takes the tradesman's view,
and the disreputable section which enjoys the license
of the plutocracy without its money: creeping below
the law as its exemplars prance above it; cutting
down all expenses of respectability and even decency;
and frankly accepting squalor and disrepute as the
price of anarchic self-indulgence. The conflict between Malvolio and Sir Toby, between the marquis
and the bourgeois, the cavalier and the puritan, the
ascetic and the voluptuary, goes on continually, and
goes on not only between class and class and individual
and individual, but in the selfsame breast in a series
of reactions and revulsions in which the irresistible

becomes the unbearable, and the unbearable the irresistible, until none of us can say what our characters really are in this respect.

THE MISSING DATA OF A SCIENTIFIC NATURAL HISTORY OF MARRIAGE

Of one thing I am persuaded: we shall never attain to a reasonably healthy public opinion on sex questions until we offer, as the data for that opinion, our actual conduct and our real thoughts instead of a moral fiction which we agree to call virtuous conduct, and which we then—and here comes in the mischief—pretend is our conduct and our thoughts. If the result were that we all believed one another to be better than we really are, there would be something to be said for it; but the actual result appears to be a monstrous exaggeration of the power and continuity of sexual passion. The whole world shares the fate of Lucrezia Borgia, who, though she seems on investigation to have been quite a suitable wife for a modern British Bishop, has been invested by the popular historical imagination with all the extravagances of a Messalina or a Cenci. Writers of belles lettres who are rash enough to admit that their whole life is not one constant preoccupation with adored members of the opposite sex, and who even countenance La Rochefoucauld's remark that very few people would ever imagine themselves in love if they had never read anything about it, are gravely declared to be abnormal or physically defective by critics of crushing unadventurousness and domestication. French authors of saintly temperament are forced to include in their retinue countesses of ardent complexion with whom they are supposed to live in sin. Sentimental controversies on the subject are endless; but they are useless, because nobody tells the truth. Rousseau did it by an extraordinary effort, aided by a superhuman faculty for human natural history; but the result was curiously disconcerting because, though the facts were so conventionally shocking that people felt that they ought to matter a great deal, they actually mattered very little. And even at that everybody pretends not to believe him.

ARTIFICIAL RETRIBUTION

The worst of this is that busybodies with perhaps rather more than a normal taste for mischief are continually trying to make negligible things matter as much in fact as they do in convention by deliberately inflicting injuries—sometimes atrocious injuries—on the parties concerned. Few people have any knowledge of the savage punishments that are legally inflicted for aberrations and absurdities to which no sanely instructed community would call any attention. We create an artificial morality, and consequently an artificial conscience, by manufacturing disastrous consequences for events which, left to themselves, would do very little harm (sometimes not any) and be forgotten in a few days.

But the artificial morality is not therefore to be condemned off-hand. In many cases it may save mischief instead of making it: for example, though the hanging of a murderer is the duplication of a murder, yet it may be less murderous than leaving the matter to be settled by blood feud or vendetta. As long as human nature insists on revenge, the official organization and satisfaction of revenge by the State may be also its minimization. The mischief begins when the official revenge persists after the passion it satisfies has died out of the race. Stoning a woman to death in the east because she has ventured to marry again after being deserted by her husband may be more merciful than allowing her to be mobbed to death; but the official stoning or burning of an adulteress in the west would be an atrocity, because few of us hate an adulteress to the extent of desiring such a penalty, or of being prepared to take the law into our own hands if it were withheld. Now what applies to this extreme case applies also in due degree to the other cases. Offences in which sex is concerned are often needlessly magnified by penalties, ranging from various forms of social ostracism to long sentences of penal servitude, which would be seen to be monstrously disproportionate to the real feeling against them if the removal of both the penalties and the taboo on their discussion made it possible for us to ascertain their real prevalence and estimation. Fortunately there is one outlet for the truth. We are permitted to discuss in jest what we may not discuss in earnest. A serious comedy about sex is taboo: a farcical comedy is privileged.

THE FAVOURITE SUBJECT OF FARCICAL COMEDY

The little piece which follows this preface accordingly takes the form of a farcical comedy, because it is a contribution to the very extensive dramatic literature which takes as its special department the gallantries of married people. The stage has been preoccupied by such affairs for centuries, not only in the jesting vein of Restoration Comedy and Palais Royal farce, but in the more tragically turned adulteries of the Parisian school which dominated the stage until Ibsen put them out of countenance and relegated them to their proper place as articles of commerce. Their continued vogue in that department maintains the tradition that adultery is the dramatic subject *par excellence*, and indeed that a play that is not about adultery is not a play at all. I was considered a heresiarch of the most extravagant kind when I expressed my opinion, at the outset of my career as a playwright, that adultery is the dullest of themes on the stage, and that from Francesca and Paolo down to the latest guilty couple of the school of Dumas *fils*, the romantic adulterers have all been intolerable bores.

THE PSEUDO SEX PLAY

Later on, I had occasion to point out to the defenders of sex as the proper theme of drama, that though they were right in ranking sex as an intensely interesting subject, they were wrong in assuming that sex is an indispensable motive in popular plays. The plays of Molière are, like the novels of the Victorian epoch or Don Quixote, as nearly sexless as anything not absolutely inhuman can be; and some of Shakespear's plays are sexually on a par with the census: they contain women as well as men, and that is all. This had to be admitted; but it was still assumed that the plays of the nineteenth century Paris school are, in contrast with the sexless masterpieces, saturated with sex; and this I strenuously denied. A play about the convention that a man should fight a duel or come to fisticuffs with his wife's lover if she has one, or the convention that he should strangle her like Othello, or turn her out of the house and never see her or allow her to see her children again, or the convention that she should never be spoken to again by any decent person and should finally drown herself, or the convention that persons involved in scenes of recrimination or confession by these conventions should call each other certain abusive names and describe their conduct as guilty and frail and so on: all these may provide material for very effective plays; but such plays are not dramatic studies of sex: one might as well say that Romeo and Juliet is a dramatic study of pharmacy because the catastrophe is brought about through an apothecary. Duels are not sex; divorce cases are not sex; the Trade Unionism of married women is not sex. Only the most insignificant fraction of the gallantries of married people produce any of the conventional results; and plays occupied wholly with the conventional results are therefore utterly unsatisfying as sex plays, however interesting they may be as plays of intrigue and plot puzzles.

The world is finding this out rapidly. The Sunday papers, which in the days when they appealed almost exclusively to the lower middle class were crammed with police intelligence, and more especially with divorce and murder cases, now lay no stress on them; and police papers which confined themselves entirely to such matters, and were once eagerly read, have perished through the essential dulness of their topics. And yet the interest in sex is stronger than ever: in fact, the literature that has driven out the journalism of the divorce courts is a literature occupied with sex to an extent and with an intimacy and frankness that would have seemed utterly impossible to Thackeray or Dickens if they had been told that the change would complete itself within fifty years of their own time.

ART AND MORALITY

It is ridiculous to say, as inconsiderate amateurs of the
arts do, that art has nothing to do with morality. What
is true is that the artist's business is not that of the
policeman; and that such factitious consequences and
put-up jobs as divorces and executions and the detective operations that lead up to them are no essential
part of life, though, like poisons and buttered slides
and red-hot pokers, they provide material for plenty of
thrilling or amusing stories suited to people who are
incapable of any interest in psychology. But the fine
artist must keep the policeman out of his studies of
sex and studies of crime. It is by clinging nervously to
the policeman that most of the pseudo sex plays convince me that the writers have either never had any
serious personal experience of their ostensible subject,
or else have never conceived it possible that the stage
dare present the phenomena of sex as they appear in
nature.

THE LIMITS OF STAGE PRESENTATION

But the stage presents much more shocking phenomena than those of sex. There is, of course, a sense in
which you cannot present sex on the stage, just as you
cannot present murder. Macbeth must no more really
kill Duncan than he must himself be really slain by
Macduff. But the feelings of a murderer can be expressed in a certain artistic convention; and a carefully
pre-arranged sword exercise can be gone through with
sufficient pretence of earnestness to be accepted by
the willing imaginations of the younger spectators as
a desperate combat.

The tragedy of love has been presented on the stage

in the same way. In Tristan and Isolde, the curtain does not, as in Romeo and Juliet, rise with the lark: the whole night of love is played before the spectators. The lovers do not discuss marriage in an elegantly sentimental way: they utter the visions and feelings that come to lovers at the supreme moments of their love, totally forgetting that there are such things in the world as husbands and lawyers and duelling codes and theories of sin and notions of propriety and all the other irrelevancies which provide hackneyed and bloodless material for our so-called plays of passion.

PRUDERIES OF THE FRENCH STAGE

To all stage presentations there are limits. If Macduff were to stab Macbeth, the spectacle would be intolerable; and even the pretence which we allow on our stage is ridiculously destructive to the illusion of the scene. Yet pugilists and gladiators will actually fight and kill in public without shame, even as a spectacle for money. But no sober couple of lovers of any delicacy could endure to be watched. We in England, accustomed to consider the French stage much more licentious than the British, are always surprised and puzzled when we learn, as we may do any day if we come within reach of such information, that French actors are often scandalized by what they consider the indecency of the English stage, and that French actresses who desire a greater license in appealing to the sexual instincts than the French stage allows them, learn English and establish themselves on the English stage. The German and Russian stages are in the same relation to the French and, perhaps more or less, all the Latin stages. The reason is that, partly from a want of respect for the theatre, partly from a sort of respect for art in general which moves them to accord moral privileges to artists, partly from the very objectionable tradition that the realm of art is Alsatia and the contemplation of works of art a holiday from the burden of virtue, partly because French prudery does not attach itself to the same points of behavior as British prudery, and has a different code of the mentionable and the unmentionable, and for many other reasons, the French tolerate plays which are never performed in England until they have been spoiled by a process of bowdlerization; yet French taste is more fastidious than ours as to the exhibition and treatment on the stage of the physical incidents of sex. On the French stage a kiss is as obvious a convention as the thrust under the arm by which Macduff runs Macbeth through. It is even a purposely unconvincing convention: the actors rather insisting that it shall be impossible for any spectator to mistake a stage kiss for a real one. In England, on the contrary, realism is carried to the point at which nobody except the two performers can perceive that the caress is not genuine. And here the English stage is certainly in the right; for whatever question there arises as to what incidents are proper for representation on the stage or not, my experience as a playgoer leaves me in no doubt that once it is decided to represent an incident, it will be offensive, no matter whether it be a prayer or a kiss, unless it is presented with a convincing appearance of sincerity.

OUR DISILLUSIVE SCENERY

For example, the main objection to the use of illusive scenery (in most modern plays scenery is not illusive: everything visible is as real as in your drawing room

at home) is that it is unconvincing; whilst the imaginary scenery with which the audience transfigures a
platform or tribune like the Elizabethan stage or the
Greek stage used by Sophocles, is quite convincing.
In fact, the more scenery you have the less illusion
you produce. The wise playwright, when he cannot
get absolute reality of presentation, goes to the other
extreme, and aims at atmosphere and suggestion of
mood rather than at direct simulative illusion. The
theatre, as I first knew it, was a place of wings and
flats which destroyed both atmosphere and illusion.
This was tolerated, and even intensely enjoyed, but
not in the least because nothing better was possible;
for all the devices employed in the productions of Mr
Granville Barker or Max Reinhardt or the Moscow
Art Theatre were equally available for Colley Cibber
and Garrick, except the intensity of our artificial light.
When Garrick played Richard III in slashed trunk
hose and plumes, it was not because he believed that
the Plantagenets dressed like that, or because the
costumiers could not have made him a XV century
dress as easily as a nondescript combination of the
state robes of George III with such scraps of older
fashions as seemed to playgoers for some reason to be
romantic. The charm of the theatre in those days was
its makebelieve. It has that charm still, not only for
the amateurs, who are happiest when they are most
unnatural and impossible and absurd, but for audiences as well. I have seen performances of my own
plays which were to me far wilder burlesques than
Sheridan's Critic or Buckingham's Rehearsal; yet
they have produced sincere laughter and tears such
as the most finished metropolitan productions have
failed to elicit. Fielding was entirely right when he
represented Partridge as enjoying intensely the per-

formance of the king in Hamlet because anybody could see that the king was an actor, and resenting Garrick's Hamlet because it might have been a real man. Yet we have only to look at the portraits of Garrick to see that his performances would nowadays seem almost as extravagantly stagey as his costumes. In our day Calvé's intensely real Carmen never pleased the mob as much as the obvious fancy ball masquerading of suburban young ladies in the same character.

HOLDING THE MIRROR UP TO NATURE

Theatrical art begins as the holding up to Nature of a distorting mirror. In this phase it pleases people who are childish enough to believe that they can see what they look like and what they are when they look at a true mirror. Naturally they think that a true mirror can teach them nothing. Only by giving them back some monstrous image can the mirror amuse them or terrify them. It is not until they grow up to the point at which they learn that they know very little about themselves, and that they do not see themselves in a true mirror as other people see them, that they become consumed with curiosity as to what they really are like, and begin to demand that the stage shall be a mirror of such accuracy and intensity of illumination that they shall be able to get glimpses of their real selves in it, and also learn a little how they appear to other people.

For audiences of this highly developed class, sex can no longer be ignored or conventionalized or distorted by the playwright who makes the mirror. The old sentimental extravagances and the old grossnesses are of no further use to him. Don Giovanni and

Zerlina are not gross: Tristan and Isolde are not extravagant or sentimental. They say and do nothing that you cannot bear to hear and see; and yet they give you, the one pair briefly and slightly, and the other fully and deeply, what passes in the minds of lovers. The love depicted may be that of a philosophic adventurer tempting an ignorant country girl, or of a tragically serious poet entangled with a woman of noble capacity in a passion which has become for them the reality of the whole universe. No matter: the thing is dramatized and dramatized directly, not talked about as something that happened before the curtain rose, or that will happen after it falls.

FARCICAL COMEDY SHIRKING ITS SUBJECT

Now if all this can be done in the key of tragedy and philosophic comedy, it can, I have always contended, be done in the key of farcical comedy; and Overruled is a trifling experiment in that manner. Conventional farcical comedies are always finally tedious because the heart of them, the inevitable conjugal infidelity, is always evaded. Even its consequences are evaded. Mr Granville Barker has pointed out rightly that if the third acts of our farcical comedies dared to describe the consequences that would follow from the first and second in real life, they would end as squalid tragedies; and in my opinion they would be greatly improved thereby even as entertainments; for I have never seen a three-act farcical comedy without being bored and tired by the third act, and observing that the rest of the audience were in the same condition, though they were not vigilantly introspective enough to find that out, and were apt to blame one another, especially the husbands and wives, for their crossness.

But it is happily by no means true that conjugal infidelities always produce tragic consequences, or that
they need produce even the unhappiness which they
often do produce. Besides, the more momentous the
consequences, the more interesting become the impulses and imaginations and reasonings, if any, of the
people who disregard them. If I had an opportunity
of conversing with the ghost of an executed murderer,
I have no doubt he would begin to tell me eagerly
about his trial, with the names of the distinguished
ladies and gentlemen who honoured him with their
presence on that occasion, and then about his execution. All of which would bore me exceedingly. I should
say, "My dear sir: such manufactured ceremonies do
not interest me in the least. I know how a man is tried,
and how he is hanged. I should have had you killed
in a much less disgusting, hypocritical, and unfriendly
manner if the matter had been in my hands. What I
want to know about is the murder. How did you feel
when you committed it? Why did you do it? What
did you say to yourself about it? If, like most murderers, you had not been hanged, would you have
committed other murders? Did you really dislike the
victim, or did you want his money, or did you murder a person whom you did not dislike, and from
whose death you had nothing to gain, merely for the
sake of murdering? If so, can you describe the charm
to me? Does it come upon you periodically; or is it
chronic? Has curiosity anything to do with it?" I
would ply him with all manner of questions to find
out what murder is really like; and I should not be
satisfied until I had realized that I, too, might commit
a murder, or else that there is some specific quality
present in a murderer and lacking in me. And, if so,
what that quality is.

In just the same way, I want the unfaithful husband or the unfaithful wife in a farcical comedy not to bother me with their divorce cases or the stratagems they employ to avoid a divorce case, but to tell me how and why married couples are unfaithful. I dont want to hear the lies they tell one another to conceal what they have done, but the truths they tell one another when they have to face what they have done without concealment or excuse. No doubt prudent and considerate people conceal such adventures, when they can, from those who are most likely to be wounded by them; but it is not to be presumed that, when found out, they necessarily disgrace themselves by irritating lies and transparent subterfuges.

My playlet, which I offer as a model to all future writers of farcical comedy, may now, I hope, be read without shock. I may just add that Mr Sibthorpe Juno's view that morality demands, not that we should behave morally (an impossibility to our sinful nature) but that we shall not attempt to defend our immoralities, is a standard view in England, and was advanced in all seriousness by an earnest and distinguished British moralist shortly after the first performance of Overruled. My objection to that aspect of the doctrine of original sin is that no necessary and inevitable operation of human nature can reasonably be regarded as sinful at all, and that a morality which assumes the contrary is an absurd morality, and can be kept in countenance only by hypocrisy. When people were ashamed of sanitary problems, and refused to face them, leaving them to solve themselves clandestinely in dirt and secrecy, the solution arrived at was the Black Death. A similar policy as to sex problems has solved itself by an even worse plague than the Black Death; and the remedy for that is not salvarsan, but sound moral hygiene, the first foundation of which is the discontinuance of our habit of telling not only the comparatively harmless lies that we know we ought not to tell, but the ruinous lies that we foolishly think we ought to tell.

A lady and gentleman are sitting together on a chester-field in a retired corner of the lounge of a seaside hotel. It is a summer night: The French window behind them stands open. The terrace without overlooks a moonlit harbor. The lounge is dark. The chesterfield, upholstered in silver grey, and the two figures on it in evening dress, catch the light from an arc lamp somewhere; but the walls, covered with a dark green paper, are in gloom. There are two stray chairs, one on each side. On the gentleman's right, behind him up near the window, is an unused fireplace. Opposite it on the lady's left is a door. The gentleman is on the lady's right.

The lady is very attractive, with a musical voice and soft appealing manners. She is young: that is, one feels sure that she is under thirty-five and over twenty-four. The gentleman does not look much older. He is rather handsome, and has ventured as far in the direction of poetic dandyism in the arrangement of his hair as any man who is not a professional artist can afford to in England. He is obviously very much in love with the lady, and is, in fact, yielding to an irresistible impulse to throw his arms round her.

THE LADY. Dont—oh dont be horrid. Please, Mr Lunn [*she rises from the lounge and retreats behind it*]! Promise me you wont be horrid.

GREGORY LUNN. I'm not being horrid, Mrs Juno. I'm not going to be horrid. I love you: thats all. I'm extraordinarily happy.

MRS JUNO. You will really be good?

GREGORY. I'll be whatever you wish me to be. I tell you I love you. I love loving you. I dont want to be tired and sorry, as I should be if I were to be horrid.

I dont want you to be tired and sorry. Do come and sit down again.

MRS JUNO [*coming back to her seat*] Youre sure you dont want anything you oughtnt to?

GREGORY. Quite sure. I only want you [*she recoils*]. Dont be alarmed: I like wanting you. As long as I have a want, I have a reason for living. Satisfaction is death.

MRS JUNO. Yes; but the impulse to commit suicide is sometimes irresistible.

GREGORY. Not with you.

MRS JUNO. What!

GREGORY. Oh, it sounds uncomplimentary; but it isnt really. Do you know why half the couples who find themselves situated as we are now behave horridly?

MRS JUNO. Because they cant help it if they let things go too far.

GREGORY. Not a bit of it. It's because they have nothing else to do, and no other way of entertaining each other. You dont know what it is to be alone with a woman who has little beauty and less conversation. What is a man to do? She cant talk interestingly; and if he talks that way himself she doesnt understand him. He cant look at her: if he does, he only finds out that she isnt beautiful. Before the end of five minutes they are both hideously bored. Theres only one thing that can save the situation; and thats what you call being horrid. With a beautiful, witty, kind woman, theres no time for such follies. It's so delightful to look at her, to listen to her voice, to hear all she has to say, that nothing else happens. That is why the woman who is supposed to have a thousand lovers seldom has one; whilst the stupid, graceless animals of women have dozens.

MRS JUNO. I wonder! It's quite true that when one feels in danger one talks like mad to stave it off, even when one doesnt quite want to stave it off.

GREGORY. One never does quite want to stave it off. Danger is delicious. But death isnt. We court the danger; but the real delight is in escaping, after all.

MRS JUNO. I dont think we'll talk about it any more. Danger is all very well when you do escape; but sometimes one doesnt. I tell you frankly I dont feel as safe as you do—if you really do.

GREGORY. But surely you can do as you please without injuring anyone, Mrs Juno. That is the whole secret of your extraordinary charm for me.

MRS JUNO. I dont understand.

GREGORY. Well, I hardly know how to begin to explain. But the root of the matter is that I am what people call a good man.

MRS JUNO. I thought so until you began making love to me.

GREGORY. But you knew I loved you all along.

MRS JUNO. Yes, of course; but I depended on you not to tell me so; because I thought you were good. Your blurting it out spoilt it. And it was wicked besides.

GREGORY. Not at all. You see, it's a great many years since Ive been able to allow myself to fall in love. I know lots of charming women; but the worst of it is, theyre all married. Women dont become charming, to my taste, until theyre fully developed; and by that time, if theyre really nice, theyre snapped up and married. And then, because I am a good man, I have to place a limit to my regard for them. I may be fortunate enough to gain friendship and even very warm affection from them; but my loyalty to their husbands and their hearths and their happiness obliges me to draw a line and not overstep it. Of course I value such affectionate regard very highly indeed. I am surrounded with women who are most dear to me. But every one of them has a post sticking up, if I may put it that way, with the inscription: Trespassers Will Be Prosecuted. How we all loathe that notice! In every lovely garden, in every dell full of primroses, on every fair hillside, we meet that confounded board; and there is always a gamekeeper round the corner. But what is that to the horror of meeting it on every beautiful woman, and knowing that there is a husband round the corner? I have had this accursed board standing between me and every dear and desirable woman until I thought I had lost the power of letting myself fall really and wholeheartedly in love.

MRS JUNO. Wasnt there a widow?

GREGORY. No. Widows are extraordinary scarce in modern society. Husbands live longer than they used to; and even when they do die, their widows have a string of names down for their next.

MRS JUNO. Well, what about the young girls?

GREGORY. Oh, who cares for young girls? Theyre unsympathetic. Theyre beginners. They dont attract me. I'm afraid of them.

MRS JUNO. Thats the correct thing to say to a woman of my age. But it doesnt explain why you seem to have put your scruples in your pocket when you met me.

GREGORY. Surely thats quite clear. I——

MRS JUNO. No: please dont explain. I dont want to know. I take your word for it. Besides, it doesnt matter now. Our voyage is over; and tomorrow I start for the north to my poor father's place.

GREGORY [surprised] Your poor father! I thought he was alive.

MRS JUNO. So he is. What made you think he wasnt?

GREGORY. You said your poor father.

MRS JUNO. Oh, thats a trick of mine. Rather a silly trick, I suppose; but theres something pathetic to me about men: I find myself calling them poor So-and-So when theres nothing whatever the matter with them.

GREGORY [*who has listened in growing alarm*] But—I—is ?—wa— ? Oh Lord!

MRS JUNO. Whats the matter ?

GREGORY. Nothing.

MRS JUNO. Nothing! [*Rising anxiously*] Nonsense: youre ill.

GREGORY. No. It was something about your late husband—

MRS JUNO. My late husband! What do you mean ? [*Clutching him, horror-stricken*] Dont tell me he's dead.

GREGORY [*rising, equally appalled*] Dont tell me he's alive.

MRS JUNO. Oh, dont frighten me like this. Of course he's alive—unless youve heard anything.

GREGORY. The first day we met—on the boat—you spoke to me of your poor dear husband.

MRS JUNO [*releasing him, quite reassured*] Is that all ?

GREGORY. Well, afterwards you called him poor Tops. Always poor Tops, or poor dear Tops. What could I think ?

MRS JUNO [*sitting down again*] I wish you hadnt given me such a shock about him; for I havnt been treating him at all well. Neither have you.

GREGORY [*relapsing into his seat, overwhelmed*] And you mean to tell me youre not a widow!

MRS JUNO. Gracious, no! I'm not in black.

GREGORY. Then I have been behaving like a blackguard! I have broken my promise to my mother. I shall never have an easy conscience again.

MRS JUNO. I'm sorry. I thought you knew.

GREGORY. You thought I was a libertine?

MRS JUNO. No: of course I shouldnt have spoken to you if I had thought that. I thought you liked me, but that you knew, and would be good.

GREGORY [*stretching his hand towards her breasts*] I thought the burden of being good had fallen from my soul at last. I saw nothing there but a bosom to rest on: the bosom of a lovely woman of whom I could dream without guilt. What do I see now?

MRS JUNO. Just what you saw before.

GREGORY [*despairingly*] No, no.

MRS JUNO. What else?

GREGORY. Trespassers Will Be Prosecuted: Trespassers Will Be Prosecuted.

MRS JUNO. They wont if they hold their tongues. Dont be such a coward. My husband wont eat you.

GREGORY. I'm not afraid of your husband. I'm afraid of my conscience.

MRS JUNO [*losing patience*] Well! I dont consider myself at all a badly behaved woman; for nothing has passed between us that was not perfectly nice and friendly; but really! to hear a grown-up man talking about promises to his mother!—

GREGORY [*interrupting her*] Yes, yes: I know all about that. It's not romantic: it's not Don Juan: it's not advanced; but we feel it all the same. It's far deeper in our blood and bones than all the romantic stuff. My father got into a scandal once: that was why my mother made me promise never to make love to a married woman. And now Ive done it I cant feel honest. Dont pretend to despise me or laugh at me. You feel it too. You said just now that your own conscience was uneasy when you thought of your husband. What must it be when you think of my wife?

MRS JUNO [*rising aghast*] Your wife!!! You dont dare

[851]

sit there and tell me coolly that youre a married man!

GREGORY. I never led you to believe I was unmarried.

MRS JUNO. Oh! You never gave me the faintest hint that you had a wife.

GREGORY. I did indeed. I discussed things with you that only married people really understand.

MRS JUNO. Oh!!

GREGORY. I thought it the most delicate way of letting you know.

MRS JUNO. Well, you are a daisy, I must say. I suppose thats vulgar; but really! really!! You and your goodness! However, now weve found one another out theres only one thing to be done. Will you please go?

GREGORY [*rising slowly*] I ought to go.

MRS JUNO. Well, go.

GREGORY. Yes. Er—[*he tries to go*] I—I somehow cant. [*He sits down again helplessly*] My conscience is active: my will is paralyzed. This is really dreadful. Would you mind ringing the bell and asking them to throw me out? You ought to, you know.

MRS JUNO. What! make a scandal in the face of the whole hotel! Certainly not. Dont be a fool.

GREGORY. Yes; but I cant go.

MRS JUNO. Then I can. Goodbye.

GREGORY [*clinging to her hand*] Can you really?

MRS JUNO. Of course I—[*she wavers*] Oh dear! [*They contemplate one another helplessly*]. I cant. [*She sinks on the lounge, hand in hand with him*].

GREGORY. For heaven's sake pull yourself together. It's a question of self-control.

MRS JUNO [*dragging her hand away and retreating to the end of the chesterfield*] No: it's a question of distance. Self-control is all very well two or three yards off, or on a ship, with everybody looking on. Dont come any nearer.

GREGORY. This is a ghastly business. I want to go away; and I cant.

MRS JUNO. I think you ought to go [*he makes an effort; and she adds quickly*] but if you try to I shall grab you round the neck and disgrace myself. I implore you to sit still and be nice.

GREGORY. I implore you to run away. I believe I can trust myself to let you go for your own sake. But it will break my heart.

MRS JUNO. I dont want to break your heart. I cant bear to think of your sitting here alone. I cant bear to think of sitting alone myself somewhere else. It's so senseless—so ridiculous—when we might be so happy. I dont want to be wicked, or coarse. But I like you very much: and I do want to be affectionate and human.

GREGORY. I ought to draw a line.

MRS JUNO. So you shall, dear. Tell me: do you really like me? I dont mean love me: you might love the housemaid—

GREGORY [*vehemently*] No!

MRS JUNO. Oh yes you might; and what does that matter anyhow? Are you really fond of me? Are we friends—comrades? Would you be sorry if I died?

GREGORY [*shrinking*] Oh dont.

MRS JUNO. Or was it the usual aimless man's lark: a mere shipboard flirtation?

GREGORY. Oh no, no: nothing half so bad, so vulgar, so wrong. I assure you I only meant to be agreeable. It grew on me before I noticed it.

MRS JUNO. And you were glad to let it grow?

GREGORY. I let it grow because the board was not up.

MRS JUNO. Bother the board! I am just as fond of Sibthorpe as—

GREGORY. Sibthorpe!

MRS JUNO. Sibthorpe is my husband's Christian name. I oughtnt to call him Tops to you now.

GREGORY [*chuckling*] It sounded like something to drink. But I have no right to laugh at him. My Christian name is Gregory, which sounds like a powder.

MRS JUNO [*chilled*] That is so like a man! I offer you my heart's warmest friendliest feeling; and you think of nothing but a silly joke. A quip like that makes you forget me.

GREGORY. Forget you! Oh, if only I could!

MRS JUNO. If you could, would you?

GREGORY [*burying his shamed face in his hands*] No: I'd die first. Oh, I hate myself.

MRS JUNO. I glory in myself. It's so jolly to be reckless. Can a man be reckless, I wonder?

GREGORY [*straightening himself desperately*] No. I'm not reckless. I know what I'm doing: my conscience is awake. Oh, where is the intoxication of love? the delirium? the madness that makes a man think the world well lost for the woman he adores? I dont think anything of the sort: I see that it's not worth it: I know that it's wrong: I have never in my life been cooler, more businesslike.

MRS JUNO [*opening her arms to him*] But you cant resist me.

GREGORY. I must. I ought. [*Throwing himself into her arms*] Oh my darling, my treasure, we shall be sorry for this.

MRS JUNO. We can forgive ourselves. Could we forgive ourselves if we let this moment slip?

GREGORY. I protest to the last. I'm against this. I have been pushed over a precipice. I'm innocent. This wild joy, this exquisite tenderness, this ascent into heaven can thrill me to the uttermost fibre of my heart [*with a gesture of ecstasy she hides her face on his shoulder*]; but it cant subdue my mind or corrupt my conscience, which still shouts to the skies that I'm not a willing party to this outrageous conduct. I repudiate the bliss with which you are filling me.

MRS JUNO. Never mind your conscience. Tell me how happy you are.

GREGORY. No: I recall you to your duty. But oh, I will give you my life with both hands if you can tell me that you feel for me one millionth part of what I feel for you now.

MRS JUNO. Oh yes, yes. Be satisfied with that. Ask for no more. Let me go.

GREGORY. I cant. I have no will. Something stronger than either of us is in command here. Nothing on earth or in heaven can part us now. You know that, dont you?

MRS JUNO. Oh, dont make me say it. Of course I know. Nothing—not life nor death nor shame nor anything can part us.

A MATTER-OF-FACT MALE VOICE IN THE CORRIDOR. All right. This must be it.

The two recover with a violent start; release one another; and spring back to opposite sides of the lounge.

GREGORY. That did it.

MRS JUNO [*in a thrilling whisper*] Sh-sh-sh! That was my husband's voice.

GREGORY. Impossible: it's only our guilty fancy.

A WOMAN'S VOICE. This is the way to the lounge. I know it.

GREGORY. Great Heaven! we're both mad. Thats my wife's voice.

MRS JUNO. Ridiculous! Oh, we're dreaming it all. We—[*the door opens; and Sibthorpe Juno appears in the roseate glow of the corridor (which happens to be*

[855]

*papered in pink) with Mrs Lunn, like Tannhäuser in
the hill of Venus. He is a fussily energetic little man,
who gives himself an air of gallantry by greasing the
points of his moustaches and dressing very carefully. She
is a tall, imposing, handsome, languid woman, with
flashing dark eyes and long lashes. They make for the
chesterfield, not noticing the two palpitating figures
blotted against the walls in the gloom on either side. The
figures flit away noiselessly through the window and
disappear].*

JUNO [*officiously*] Ah: here we are. [*He leads the way
to the sofa*]. Sit down: I'm sure youre tired. [*She sits*].
Thats right. [*He sits beside her on her left*). Hullo! [*he
rises*] this sofa's quite warm

MRS LUNN [*bored*] Is it? I dont notice it. I expect the
sun's been on it.

JUNO. I felt it quite distinctly: I'm more thinly clad
than you. [*He sits down again, and proceeds, with a sigh
of satisfaction*] What a relief to get off the ship and
have a private room! Thats the worst of a ship.
Youre under observation all the time.

MRS LUNN. But why not?

JUNO. Well, of course theres no reason: at least I
suppose not. But, you know, part of the romance of a
journey is that a man keeps imagining that something
might happen; and he cant do that if there are a lot
of people about and it simply cant happen.

MRS LUNN. Mr Juno: romance is all very well on
board ship; but when your foot touches the soil of
England theres an end of it.

JUNO. No: believe me, thats a foreigner's mistake:
we are the most romantic people in the world, we
English. Why, my very presence here is a romance.

MRS LUNN [*faintly ironical*] Indeed?

JUNO. Yes. Youve guessed, of course, that I'm a
married man.

MRS LUNN. Oh, thats all right. I'm a married woman.

JUNO. Thank Heaven for that! To my English mind, passion is not real passion without guilt. I am a red-blooded man, Mrs Lunn: I cant help it. The tragedy of my life is that I married, when quite young, a woman whom I couldnt help being very fond of. I longed for a guilty passion —for the real thing—the wicked thing; and yet I couldnt care twopence for any other woman when my wife was about. Year after year went by: I felt my youth slipping away without ever having had a romance in my life; for marriage is all very well; but it isnt romance. Theres nothing wrong in it, you see.

MRS LUNN. Poor man! How you must have suffered!

JUNO. No: that was what was so tame about it. I wanted to suffer. You get so sick of being happily married. It's always the happy marriages that break up. At last my wife and I agreed that we ought to take a holiday.

MRS LUNN. Hadnt you holidays every year?

JUNO. Oh, the seaside and so on! Thats not what we meant. We meant a holiday from one another.

MRS LUNN. How very odd!

JUNO. She said it was an excellent idea; that domestic felicity was making us perfectly idiotic; that she wanted a holiday too. So we agreed to go round the world in opposite directions. I started for Suez on the day she sailed for New York.

MRS LUNN [*suddenly becoming attentive*] Thats precisely what Gregory and I did. Now I wonder did he want a holiday from me! What he said was that he wanted the delight of meeting me after a long absence.

JUNO. Could anything be more romantic than that? Would anyone else than an Englishman have thought of it? I daresay my temperament seems tame to your boiling southern blood—

MRS LUNN. My what!

JUNO. Your southern blood. Dont you remember how you told me, that night in the saloon when I sang "Farewell and adieu to you dear Spanish ladies," that you were by birth a lady of Spain? Your splendid Andalusian beauty speaks for itself.

MRS LUNN. Stuff! I was born in Gibraltar. My father was Captain Jenkins. In the artillery.

JUNO [*ardently*] It is climate and not race that determines the temperament. The fiery sun of Spain blazed on your cradle; and it rocked to the roar of British cannon.

MRS LUNN. What eloquence! It reminds me of my husband when he was in love—before we were married. Are you in love?

JUNO. Yes: and with the same woman.

MRS LUNN. Well, of course, I didn't suppose you were in love with two women.

JUNO. I dont think you quite understand. I meant that I am in love with you.

MRS LUNN [*relapsing into deepest boredom*] Oh, that! Men do fall in love with me. They all seem to think me a creature with volcanic passions: I'm sure I dont know why; for all the volcanic women I know are plain little creatures with sandy hair. I dont consider human volcanoes respectable. And I'm so tired of the subject! Our house is always full of women who are in love with my husband and men who are in love with me. We encourage it because it's pleasant to have company.

JUNO. And is your husband as insensible as yourself?

MRS LUNN. Oh, Gregory's not insensible: very far from it; but I am the only woman in the world for him.

JUNO. But you? Are you really as insensible as you say you are?

MRS LUNN. I never said anything of the kind. I'm not at all insensible by nature; but (I dont know whether youve noticed it) I am what people call rather a fine figure of a woman.

JUNO [*passionately*] Noticed it! Oh, Mrs Lunn! Have I been able to notice anything else since we met?

MRS LUNN. There you go, like all the rest of them! I ask you, how do you expect a woman to keep up what you call her sensibility when this sort of thing has happened to her about three times a week ever since she was seventeen? It used to upset me and terrify me at first. Then I got rather a taste for it. It came to a climax with Gregory: that was why I married him. Then it became a mild lark, hardly worth the trouble. After that I found it valuable once or twice as a spinal tonic when I was run down; but now it's an unmitigated bore. I dont mind your declaration: I daresay it gives you a certain pleasure to make it. I quite understand that you adore me; but (if you dont mind) I'd rather you didnt keep on saying so.

JUNO. Is there then no hope for me?

MRS LUNN. Oh, yes. Gregory has an idea that married women keep lists of the men theyll marry if they become widows. I'll put your name down, if that will satisfy you.

JUNO. Is the list a long one?

MRS LUNN. Do you mean the real list? Not the one I shew to Gregory: there are hundreds of names on that; but the little private list that he'd better not see?

JUNO. Oh, will you really put me on that? Say you will.

MRS LUNN. Well, perhaps I will. [*He kisses her hand*]. Now dont begin abusing the privilege.

JUNO. May I call you by your Christian name?

MRS LUNN. No: it's too long. You cant go about calling a woman Seraphita.

JUNO [*ecstatically*] Seraphita!

MRS LUNN. I used to be called Sally at home; but when I married a man named Lunn, of course that became ridiculous. Thats my one little pet joke. Call me Mrs Lunn for short. And change the subject, or I shall go to sleep.

JUNO. I cant change the subject. For me there is no other subject. Why else have you put me on your list?

MRS LUNN. Because youre a solicitor. Gregory's a solicitor. I'm accustomed to my husband being a solicitor and telling me things he oughtnt to tell anybody.

JUNO [*ruefully*] Is that all? Oh, I cant believe that the voice of love has ever thoroughly awakened you.

MRS LUNN. No: it sends me to sleep. [*Juno appeals against this by an amorous demonstration*]. It's no use, Mr Juno: I'm hopelessly respectable: the Jenkinses always were. Dont you realize that unless most women were like that, the world couldnt go on as it does?

JUNO [*darkly*] You think it goes on respectably: but I can tell you as a solicitor—

MRS LUNN. Stuff! of course all the disreputable people who get into trouble go to you, just as all the sick people go to the doctors; but most people never go to a solicitor.

JUNO [*rising, with a growing sense of injury*] Look here, Mrs Lunn: do you think a man's heart is a potato? or a turnip? or a ball of knitting wool? that you can throw it away like this?

MRS LUNN. I dont throw away balls of knitting wool. A man's heart seems to me much like a sponge, it sops up dirty water as well as clean.

JUNO. I have never been treated like this in my life. Here am I, a married man, with a most attractive wife: a wife I adore, and who adores me, and has never as much as looked at any other man since we were married. I come and throw all this at your feet. I! I, a solicitor! braving the risk of your husband putting me into the divorce court and making me a beggar and an outcast! I do this for your sake. And you go on as if I were making no sacrifice: as if I had told you it's a fine evening, or asked you to have a cup of tea. It's not human. It's not right. Love has its rights as well as respectability [*he sits down again, aloof and sulky*].

MRS LUNN. Nonsense! Here! heres a flower [*she gives him one*]. Go and dream over it until you feel hungry. Nothing brings people to their senses like hunger.

JUNO [*contemplating the flower without rapture*] What good's this?

MRS LUNN [*snatching it from him*] Oh! you dont love me a bit.

JUNO. Yes I do. Or at least I did. But I'm an Englishman; and I think you ought to respect the conventions of English life.

MRS LUNN. But I a m respecting them; and youre not.

JUNO. Pardon me. I may be doing wrong; but I'm doing it in a proper and customary manner. You may be doing right; but youre doing it in an unusual and questionable manner. I am not prepared to put up with that. I can stand being badly treated: I'm no baby, and can take care of myself with anybody. And of course I can stand being well treated. But the one thing I cant stand is being unexpectedly treated. It's outside my scheme of life. So come now! youve got to behave naturally and straightforwardly with me. You can leave husband and child, home, friends, and country, for my sake, and come with me to some southern isle—or say South America—where we can be all in all to one another. Or you can tell your husband and let him jolly well punch my head if he can. But I'm damned if I'm going to stand any eccentricity. It's not respectable.

GREGORY [*coming in from the terrace and advancing with dignity to his wife's end of the chesterfield*] Will you have the goodness, sir, in addressing this lady, to keep your temper and refrain from using profane language?

MRS LUNN [*rising, delighted*] Gregory! Darling [*she enfolds him in a copious embrace*]!

JUNO [*rising*] You make love to another man to my face!

MRS LUNN. Why, he's my husband.

JUNO. That takes away the last rag of excuse for such conduct. A nice world it would be if married people were to carry on their endearments before everybody!

GREGORY. This is ridiculous. What the devil business is it of yours what passes between my wife and myself? Youre not her husband, are you?

JUNO. Not at present; but I'm on the list. I'm her prospective husband: youre only her actual one. I'm the anticipation: youre the disappointment.

MRS LUNN. Oh, my Gregory is not a disappointment. [*Fondly*] Are you, dear?

GREGORY. You just wait, my pet. I'll settle this chap for you. [*He disengages himself from her embrace, and faces Juno. She sits down placidly*]. You call me a disappointment, do you? Well, I suppose every husband's a disappointment. What about yourself? Dont try to look like an unmarried man. I happen to know the lady you disappointed. I travelled in the same ship with her; and—

JUNO. And you fell in love with her.

GREGORY [*taken aback*] Who told you that?

JUNO. Aha! you confess it. Well, if you want to know, nobody told me. Everybody falls in love with my wife.

GREGORY. And do you fall in love with everybody's wife?

JUNO. Certainly not. Only with yours.

MRS LUNN. But whats the good of saying that, Mr Juno? I'm married to him; and theres an end of it.

JUNO. Not at all. You can get a divorce.

MRS LUNN. What for?

JUNO. For his misconduct with my wife.

GREGORY [*deeply indignant*] How dare you, sir, asperse the character of that sweet lady? a lady whom I have taken under my protection.

JUNO. Protection!

MRS JUNO [*returning hastily*] Really you must be more careful what you say about me, Mr Lunn.

JUNO. My precious! [*He embraces her*] Pardon this betrayal of feeling; but I've not seen my wife for several weeks; and she is very dear to me.

GREGORY. I call this cheek. Who is making love to his own wife before people now, pray?

MRS LUNN. Wont you introduce me to your wife, Mr Juno?

MRS JUNO. How do you do? [*They shake hands; and Mrs Juno sits down beside Mrs Lunn, on her left*].

MRS LUNN. I'm so glad to find you do credit to Gregory's taste. I'm naturally rather particular about the women he falls in love with.

JUNO [*sternly*] This is no way to take your husband's unfaithfulness. [*To Lunn*] You ought to teach your wife better. Wheres her feelings? It's scandalous.

GREGORY. What about your own conduct, pray?

JUNO. I dont defend it; and theres an end to the matter.

[863]

GREGORY. Well, upon my soul! What difference does your not defending it make?

JUNO. A fundamental difference. To serious people I may appear wicked. I dont defend myself: I am wicked, though not bad at heart. To thoughtless people I may even appear comic. Well, laugh at me: I have given myself away. But Mrs Lunn seems to have no opinion at all about me. She doesnt seem to know whether I'm wicked or comic. She doesnt seem to care. She has no moral sense. I say it's not right. I repeat, I have sinned; and I'm prepared to suffer.

MRS JUNO. Have you really sinned, Tops?

MRS LUNN [*blandly*] I dont remember your sinning. I have a shocking bad memory for trifles; but I think I should remember that—if you mean me.

JUNO [*raging*] Trifles! I have fallen in love with a monster.

GREGORY. Dont you dare call my wife a monster.

MRS JUNO [*rising quickly and coming between them*] Please dont lose your temper, Mr Lunn: I wont have my Tops bullied.

GREGORY. Well, then, let him not brag about sinning with my wife. [*He turns impulsively to his wife; makes her rise; and takes her proudly on his arm*]. What pretension has he to any such honor?

JUNO. I sinned in intention. [*Mrs Juno abandons him and resumes her seat, chilled*]. I'm as guilty as if I had actually sinned. And I insist on being treated as a sinner, and not walked over as if I'd done nothing, by your wife or any other man.

MRS LUNN. Tush! [*She sits down again contemptuously*].

JUNO [*furious*] I wont be belittled.

MRS LUNN [*to Mrs Juno*] I hope youll come and stay with us now that you and Gregory are such friends, Mrs Juno.

JUNO. This insane magnanimity—

MRS LUNN. Dont you think youve said enough, Mr Juno ? This is a matter for two women to settle. Wont you take a stroll on the beach with my Gregory while we talk it over. Gregory is a splendid listener.

JUNO. I dont think any good can come of a conversation between Mr Lunn and myself. We can hardly be expected to improve one another's morals. [*He passes behind the chesterfield to Mrs Lunn's end; seizes a chair; deliberately pushes it between Gregory and Mrs Lunn; and sits down with folded arms, resolved not to budge*].

GREGORY. Oh! Indeed! Oh, all right. If you come to that— [*he crosses to Mrs Juno; plants a chair by her side; and sits down with equal determination*].

JUNO. Now we are both equally guilty.

GREGORY. Pardon me. I'm not guilty.

JUNO. In intention. Dont quibble. You were guilty in intention, as I was.

GREGORY. No. I should rather describe myself as being guilty in fact, but not in intention.

JUNO	*rising and*	What!
MRS JUNO	*exclaiming*	No, really—
MRS LUNN	*simultaneously*	Gregory!

GREGORY. Yes: I maintain that I am responsible for my intentions only, and not for reflex actions over which I have no control. [*Mrs Juno sits down, ashamed*]. I promised my mother that I would never tell a lie, and that I would never make love to a married woman. I never have told a lie—

MRS LUNN [*remonstrating*] Gregory! [*She sits down again*].

GREGORY. I say never. On many occasions I have resorted to prevarication; but on great occasions I have always told the truth. I regard this as a great occasion; and I wont be intimidated into breaking my promise. I solemnly declare that I did not know until this evening that Mrs Juno was married. She will bear me out when I say that from that moment my intentions were strictly and resolutely honorable; though my conduct, which I could not control and am therefore not responsible for, was disgraceful—or would have been had this gentleman not walked in and begun making love to my wife under my very nose.

JUNO [*flinging himself back into his chair*] Well, I like this!

MRS LUNN. Really, darling, theres no use in the pot calling the kettle black.

GREGORY. When you say darling, may I ask which of us you are addressing?

MRS LUNN. I really dont know. I'm getting hopelessly confused.

JUNO. Why dont you let my wife say something? I dont think she ought to be thrust into the background like this.

MRS LUNN. I'm sorry, I'm sure. Please excuse me, dear.

MRS JUNO [*thoughtfully*] I dont know what to say. I must think over it. I have always been rather severe on this sort of thing; but when it came to the point I didnt behave as I thought I should behave. I didnt intend to be wicked; but somehow or other, Nature, or whatever you choose to call it, didnt take much notice of my intentions. [*Gregory instinctively seeks her hand and presses it*]. And I really did think, Tops, that I was the only woman in the world for you.

JUNO [*cheerfully*] Oh, thats all right, my precious. Mrs Lunn thought she was the only woman in the world for him.

GREGORY [*reflectively*] So she is, in a sort of way.

JUNO [*flaring up*] And so is my wife. Dont you set

up to be a better husband than I am; for youre not. Ive owned I'm wrong. You havnt.

MRS LUNN. Are you sorry, Gregory?

GREGORY [*perplexed*] Sorry?

MRS LUNN. Yes, sorry. I think it's time for you to say youre sorry, and to make friends with Mr Juno before we all dine together.

GREGORY. Seraphita: I promised my mother—

MRS JUNO [*involuntarily*] Oh, bother your mother! [*Recovering herself*] I beg your pardon.

GREGORY. A promise is a promise. I cant tell a deliberate lie. I know I ought to be sorry; but the flat fact is that I'm not sorry. I find that in this business, somehow or other, there is a disastrous separation between my moral principles and my conduct.

JUNO. Theres nothing disastrous about it. It doesnt matter about your conduct if your principles are all right.

GREGORY. Bosh! It doesnt matter about your principles if your conduct is all right.

JUNO. But your conduct isnt all right; and my principles are.

GREGORY. Whats the good of your principles being right if they wont work?

JUNO. They will work, sir, if you exercise self-sacrifice.

GREGORY. Oh yes: if, if, if. You know jolly well that self-sacrifice doesnt work either when you really want a thing. How much have you sacrificed yourself, pray?

MRS LUNN. Oh, a great deal, Gregory. Dont be rude. Mr Juno is a very nice man: he has been most attentive to me on the voyage.

GREGORY. And Mrs Juno's a very nice woman. She oughtnt to be; but she is.

JUNO. Why oughtnt she to be a nice woman, pray?

GREGORY. I mean she oughtnt to be nice to me. And

[867]

you oughtnt to be nice to my wife. And your wife oughtnt to like me. And my wife oughtnt to like you. And if they do, they oughtnt to go on liking us. And I oughtnt to like your wife; and you oughtnt to like mine; and if we do, we oughtnt to go on liking them. But we do, all of us. We oughtnt; but we do.

JUNO. But, my dear boy, if we admit we are in the wrong wheres the harm of it? We're not perfect; but as long as we keep the ideal before us—

GREGORY. How?

JUNO. By admitting we're wrong.

MRS LUNN [*springing up, out of patience, and pacing round the lounge intolerably*] Well, really, I must have my dinner. These two men, with their morality, and their promises to their mothers, and their admissions that they were wrong, and their sinning and suffering, and their going on at one another as if it meant anything, or as if it mattered, are getting on my nerves. [*Stooping over the back of the chesterfield to address Mrs Juno*] If you will be so very good, my dear, as to take my sentimental husband off my hands occasionally, I shall be more than obliged to you: I'm sure you can stand more male sentimentality than I can. [*Sweeping away to the fireplace*] I, on my part, will do my best to amuse your excellent husband when you find him tiresome.

JUNO. I call this polyandry.

MRS LUNN. I wish you wouldn't call innocent things by offensive names, Mr Juno. What do you call your own conduct?

JUNO [*rising*] I tell you I have admitted—

GREGORY		Whats the good of keeping on at that?
MRS JUNO	*together*	Oh, not that again, please.
MRS LUNN		Tops: I'll scream if you say that again.

JUNO. Oh, well, if you wont listen to me—! [*He sits down again*].

MRS JUNO. What is the position now exactly? [*Mrs Lunn shrugs her shoulders and gives up the conundrum. Gregory looks at Juno. Juno turns away his head huffily*]. I mean, what are we going to do?

MRS LUNN. What would you advise, Mr Juno?

JUNO. I should advise you to divorce your husband.

MRS LUNN. You want me to drag your wife into court and disgrace her?

JUNO. No: I forgot that. Excuse me; but for the moment I thought I was married to you.

GREGORY. I think we had better let bygones be bygones. [*To Mrs Juno, very tenderly*] You will forgive me, wont you? Why should you let a moment's forgetfulness embitter all our future life?

MRS JUNO. But it's Mrs Lunn who has to forgive you.

GREGORY. Oh, dash it, I forgot. This is getting ridiculous.

MRS LUNN. I'm getting hungry.

MRS JUNO. Do you really mind, Mrs Lunn?

MRS LUNN. My dear Mrs Juno, Gregory is one of those terribly uxorious men who ought to have ten wives. If any really nice woman will take him off my hands for a day or two occasionally, I shall be greatly obliged to her.

GREGORY. Seraphita: you cut me to the soul [*he weeps*].

MRS LUNN. Serve you right! Youd think it quite proper if it cut me to the soul.

MRS JUNO. Am I to take Sibthorpe off your hands too, Mrs Lunn?

JUNO [*rising*] Do you suppose I'll allow this?

MRS JUNO. Youve admitted that youve done wrong, Tops. Whats the use of your allowing or not allowing after that?

[869]

JUNO. I do not admit that I have done wrong. I admit that what I did was wrong.

GREGORY. Can you explain the distinction?

JUNO. It's quite plain to anyone but an imbecile. If you tell me Ive done something wrong you insult me. But if you say that something that I did is wrong you simply raise a question of morals. I tell you flatly if you say I did anything wrong you will have to fight me. In fact I think we ought to fight anyhow. I dont particularly want to; but I feel that England expects us to.

GREGORY. I wont fight. If you beat me my wife would share my humiliation. If I beat you, she would sympathize with you and loathe me for my brutality.

MRS LUNN. Not to mention that as we are human beings and not reindeer or barndoor fowl, if two men presumed to fight for us we couldnt decently ever speak to either of them again.

GREGORY. Besides, neither of us could beat the other, as we neither of us know how to fight. We should only blacken each other's eyes and make fools of ourselves.

JUNO. I dont admit that. Every Englishman can use his fists.

GREGORY. Youre an Englishman. Can you use yours?

JUNO. I presume so: I never tried.

MRS JUNO. You never told me you couldnt fight, Tops. I thought you were an accomplished boxer.

JUNO. My precious: I never gave you any ground for such a belief.

MRS JUNO. You always talked as if it were a matter of course. You spoke with the greatest contempt of men who didnt kick other men downstairs.

JUNO. Well, I cant kick Mr Lunn downstairs. We're on the ground floor.

MRS JUNO. You could throw him into the harbor.

GREGORY. Do you want me to be thrown into the harbor?

MRS JUNO. No: I only want to shew Tops that he's making a ghastly fool of himself.

GREGORY [*rising and prowling disgustedly between the chesterfield and the windows*] We're all making fools of ourselves.

JUNO [*following him*] Well, if we're not to fight, I must insist at least on your never speaking to my wife again.

GREGORY. Does my speaking to your wife do you any harm?

JUNO. No. But it's the proper course to take. [*Emphatically*] We must behave with some sort of decency.

MRS LUNN. And are you never going to speak to me again, Mr Juno?

JUNO. I'm prepared to promise never to do so. I think your husband has a right to demand that. Then if I speak to you after, it will not be his fault. It will be a breach of my promise; and I shall not attempt to defend my conduct.

GREGORY [*facing him*] I shall talk to your wife as often as she'll let me.

MRS JUNO. I have no objection to your speaking to me, Mr Lunn.

JUNO. Then I shall take steps.

GREGORY. What steps?

JUNO. Steps. Measures. Proceedings. Such steps as may seem advisable.

MRS LUNN [*to Mrs Juno*] Can your husband afford a scandal, Mrs Juno?

MRS JUNO. No.

MRS LUNN. Neither can mine.

GREGORY. Mrs Juno: I'm very sorry I let you in for all this. I dont know how it is that we contrive to make feelings like ours, which seem to me to be beautiful and sacred feelings, and which lead to such interesting and exciting adventures, end in vulgar squabbles and degrading scenes.

JUNO. I decline to admit that my conduct has been vulgar or degrading.

GREGORY. I promised—

JUNO. Look here, old chap: I dont say a word against your mother; and I'm sorry she's dead; but really, you know, most women are mothers; and they all die some time or other; yet that doesnt make them infallible authorities on morals, does it?

GREGORY. I was about to say so myself. Let me add that if you do things merely because you think some other fool expects you to do them, and he expects you to do them because he thinks you expect him to expect you to do them, it will end in everybody doing what nobody wants to do, which is in my opinion a silly state of things.

JUNO. Lunn: I love your wife; and thats all about it.

GREGORY. Juno: I love yours. What then?

JUNO. Clearly she must never see you again.

MRS JUNO. Why not?

JUNO. Why not! My love: I'm surprised at you.

MRS JUNO. Am I to speak only to men who dislike me?

JUNO. Yes: I think that is, properly speaking, a married woman's duty.

MRS JUNO. Then I wont do it: thats flat. I like to be liked. I like to be loved. I want everyone round me to love me. I dont want to meet or speak to anyone who doesnt like me.

JUNO. But, my precious, this is the most horrible immorality.

MRS LUNN. I dont intend to give up meeting you, Mr Juno. You amuse me very much. I dont like being loved: it bores me. But I do like to be amused.

JUNO. I hope we shall meet very often. But I hope also we shall not defend our conduct.

MRS JUNO [*rising*] This is unendurable. Weve all been flirting. Need we go on footling about it?

JUNO [*huffily*] I dont know what you call footling—

MRS JUNO [*cutting him short*] You do. Youre footling. Mr Lunn is footling. Cant we admit that we're human and have done with it?

JUNO. I have admitted it all along. I—

MRS JUNO [*almost screaming*] Then stop footling.

The dinner gong sounds.

MRS LUNN [*rising*] Thank heaven! Lets go into dinner. Gregory: take in Mrs Juno.

GREGORY. But surely I ought to take in our guest, and not my own wife.

MRS LUNN. Well, Mrs Juno is not your wife, is she?

GREGORY. Oh, of course: I beg your pardon. I'm hopelessly confused. [*He offers his arm to Mrs Juno, rather apprehensively*].

MRS JUNO. You seem quite afraid of me [*she takes his arm*].

GREGORY. I am. I simply adore you. [*They go out together; and as they pass through the door he turns and says in a ringing voice to the other couple*] I have said to Mrs Juno that I simply adore her [*He takes her out defiantly*].

MRS LUNN [*calling after him*] Yes, dear. She's a darling. [*To Juno*] Now, Sibthorpe.

JUNO [*giving her his arm gallantly*] You have called me Sibthorpe! Thank you. I think Lunn's conduct fully justifies me in allowing you to do it.

MRS LUNN. Yes: I think you may let yourself go now.

JUNO. Seraphita: I worship you beyond expression.

MRS LUNN. Sibthorpe: you amuse me beyond description. Come. [*They go in to dinner together*].

Extract from an Interview
drafted by Shaw
The Observer, London, 29 September 1912

"I suppose I must not try to lead the conversation round to the triple bill at the Duke of York's."

"Why not? There is no secret about it. It is in active rehearsal. There will be three plays by three authors—Barrie, Pinero, Shaw. Let the theatres of Europe produce three better men if they can!"

"What is the name of your play, Mr Shaw?"

"There is no need to tell you: the authors will be recognised by their style: you can't mistake them. Good morning."

"One moment more. Is it true that when the three plays were finished it was found that all three authors had hit on the same subject, and that new plays had to be written?"

"No; because the new ones would have been on the same subject, too. What really happened was that the play that was finished first had a ghost in it, and when the second play arrived it had six ghosts in it. Now, it happens that there is only one ghost in stock at the Duke of York's Theatre; so the author of the six ghosts had to retire for ten minutes and knock off another play. As that is the simple truth of the matter, I may safely tell it to you, because nobody will believe it. Good morning."

Exit Mr Shaw.

The Music-Cure:
A Piece of Utter Nonsense

Composition begun 27 April 1913; completed
21 January 1914. First published in German
translation, as *Eine musikalische Kur*, in *Die
Grosse Katharina: Funf Einakter*, 1919. First
English publication in *Translations and Tom-
fooleries*, 1926. First presented at the Little
Theatre, London, on 28 January 1914.

Lord Reginald Fitzambey   *William Armstrong*
Dr Dawkins   *Frank Randell*
Strega Thundridge   *Madge McIntosh*

Period—The Present

Scene—*A Room in the Fitzcarlton Hotel*

This is not a serious play: it is what is called a Variety Turn for two musicians. It is written for two pianists, but can be adapted to any instruments on which the performers happen to be proficient. At its first performance by Miss Madge McIntosh and Mr William Armstrong the difficulty arose that, though Mr Armstrong was an accomplished pianist, Miss McIntosh's virtuosity was confined to the English concertina. That did just as well.

As a last desperate resort a pianola behind the scenes can be employed; but the result will lack spontaneity.

There is, however, no pressing reason why the thing should be performed at all.

Lord Reginald Fitzambey, a fashionably dressed, rather pretty young man of 22, is prostrate on a sofa in a large hotel drawing room, crying convulsively. His doctor is trying to soothe him. The doctor is about a dozen years his senior; and his ways are the ways of a still youthful man who considers himself in smart society as well as professionally attendant on it.

The drawing room has tall central doors, at present locked. If anyone could enter under these circumstances, he would find on his left a grand piano with the keyboard end towards him, and a smaller door beyond the piano. On his right would be the window, and, further on, the sofa on which the unhappy youth is wallowing, with, close by it, the doctor's chair and a little table accommodating the doctor's hat, a plate, a medicine bottle, a half emptied glass, and a bell call.

THE DOCTOR. Come come! be a man. Now really this is silly. You mustnt give way like this. I tell you nothing's happened to you. Hang it all! it's not the end of the world if you did buy a few shares—

REGINALD [*interrupting him frantically*] I never meant any harm in buying those shares. I am ready to give them up. Oh, I never meant any harm in buying those shares. I never meant any harm in buying those shares. [*Clutching the doctor imploringly*] Wont you believe me, Doctor? I never meant any harm in buying those shares. I never—

THE DOCTOR [*extricating himself and replacing Reginald on the couch, not very gently*] Of course you didnt. I know you didnt.

REGINALD. I never—

THE DOCTOR [*desperate*] Dont go on saying that over

[879]

and over again or you will drive us all as distracted as you are yourself. This is nothing but nerves. Remember that youre in a hotel. Theyll put you out if you make a row.

REGINALD [*tearfully*] But you dont understand. Oh, why wont anybody understand? I never—

THE DOCTOR [*shouting him down*] You never meant any harm in buying those shares. This is the four hundreth time youve said it.

REGINALD [*wildly*] Then why do you keep asking me the same questions over and over again? It's not fair. Ive told you I never meant any harm in—

THE DOCTOR. Yes, yes, yes: I know, I know. You think you made a fool of yourself before that committee. Well, you didnt. You stood up to it for six days with the coolness of an iceberg and the cheerfulness of an idiot. Every member of it had a go at you; and everyone of them, including some of the cleverest cross-examiners in London, fell back baffled before your fatuous self-satisfaction, your impenetrable inability to see any reason why you shouldnt have bought those shares.

REGINALD. But why shouldnt I have bought them? I made no secret of it. When the Prime Minister ragged me about it I offered to sell him the shares for what I gave for them.

THE DOCTOR. Yes, after they had fallen six points. But never mind that. The point for you is that you are an under-secretary in the War Office. You knew that the Army was going to be put on vegetarian diet, and that the British Maccaroni Trust shares would go up with a rush when this became public. And what did you do?

REGINALD. I did what any fellow would have done. I bought all the shares I could afford.

THE DOCTOR. You bought a great many more than you could afford.

REGINALD. But why shouldnt I? Explain it to me. I'm anxious to learn. I meant no harm. I see no harm. Why am I to be badgered because the beastly Opposition papers and all the Opposition rotters on that committee try to make party capital out of it by saying that it was disgraceful? It wasnt disgraceful: it was simple common sense. I'm not a financier; but you cant persuade me that if you happen to know that certain shares are going to rise you shouldnt buy them. It would be flying in the face of Providence not to. And they wouldnt see that. They pretended not to see it. They worried me, and kept asking me the same thing over and over again, and wrote blackguardly articles about me—

THE DOCTOR. And you got the better of them all because you couldnt see their point of view. But what beats me is why you broke down afterwards.

REGINALD. Everyone was against me. I thought the committee a pack of fools; and I as good as told them so. But everyone took their part. The governor said I had disgraced the family name. My brothers said I ought to resign from my clubs. My mother said that all her hopes of marrying me to a rich woman were shattered. And I'd done nothing: absolutely nothing to what other chaps are doing every day.

THE DOCTOR. Well, the long and short of it is that officials mustnt gamble.

REGINALD. But I wasnt gambling. I knew. It isnt gambling if you know that the shares will go up. It's a cert.

THE DOCTOR. Well, all I can tell you is that if you werent a son of the Duke of Dunmow, youd have to resign; and—

REGINALD [*breaking down*] Oh, stop talking to me about it. Let me alone. I cant bear it. I never meant any harm in buying those shares. I never meant any harm—

THE DOCTOR. Sh-sh-sh-sh-sh! There: I shouldnt have started the subject again. Take some of this valerian [*he puts the glass to Reginald's lips*]. Thats right. Now youre better.

REGINALD [*exhausted but calm*] Why does valerian soothe me when it excites cats? Theres a question to reflect on! You know, they ought to have made me a philosopher.

THE DOCTOR. Philosophers are born, not made.

REGINALD. Fine old chestnut, that. Everybody's born, not made.

THE DOCTOR. Youre getting almost clever. I dont like it: youre not yourself today. I wish I could take your mind off your troubles. Suppose you try a little music.

REGINALD. I cant play. My fingers wont obey me. And I cant stand the sound of the piano. I sounded a note this morning; and it made me scream.

THE DOCTOR. But why not get somebody to play to you?

REGINALD. Whom could I get, even if I could bear it? You cant play

THE DOCTOR. Well: I'm not the only person in the world.

REGINALD. If you bring anyone else in here, I shall go mad. I'll throw myself out of the window. I cant bear the idea of music. I dread it, hate it, loathe it.

THE DOCTOR. Thats very serious, you know.

REGINALD. Why is it serious?

THE DOCTOR. Well, what would become of you without your turn for music? You have absolutely no capacity in any other direction.

REGINALD. I'm in Parliament. And I'm an under-secretary.

THE DOCTOR. Thats because your father is a Duke. If you were in a Republic you wouldnt be trusted to clean boots, unless your father was a millionaire. No, Reginald: the day you give up vamping accompaniments and playing the latest ragtimes by ear, youre a lost man socially.

REGINALD [*deprecating*] Oh, I say!

THE DOCTOR [*rising*] However, perhaps it's too soon for you to try the music-cure yet. It was your mother's idea; but I'll call and tell her to wait a day or two. I think she meant to send somebody to play. I must be off now. Look in again later. Meanwhile, sleep as much as you can. Or you might read a little.

REGINALD. What can I read?

THE DOCTOR. Try the Strand Magazine.

REGINALD. But it's so frightfully intellectual. It would overtax my brain.

THE DOCTOR. Oh, well, I suppose it would. Well, sleep. Perhaps I'd better give you something to send you off [*he produces a medicine case*].

REGINALD. Whats this? Veronal?

THE DOCTOR. Dont be alarmed. Only the old-fashioned remedy: opium. Take this [*Reginald takes a pill*]: that will do the trick, I expect. If you find after half an hour that it has only excited you, take another. I'll leave one for you [*he puts one on the plate, and pockets his medicine case*].

REGINALD. Better leave me a lot. I like pills.

THE DOCTOR. Thank you: I'm not treating you with a view to a coroner's inquest. You know, dont you, that opium is a poison?

REGINALD. Yes, opium. But not pills.

THE DOCTOR. Well, Heaven forbid that I, a doctor,

should shake anybody's faith in pills. But I shant leave you enough to kill you. [*He puts on his hat*].

REGINALD. Youll tell them, wont you, not to let anyone in. Really and truly I shall throw myself out of the window if any stranger comes in. I should go out of my mind.

THE DOCTOR. None of us have very far to go to do that, my young friend. Ta ta, for the moment [*he makes for the central doors*].

REGINALD. You cant go out that way. I made my mother lock it and take away the key. I felt sure theyd let somebody in that way if she didnt. Youll have to go the way you came.

THE DOCTOR [*returning*] Right. Now let me see you settle down before I go. I want you to be asleep before I leave the room.

Reginald settles himself to sleep with his face to the back of the sofa. The doctor goes softly to the side door and goes out.

REGINALD [*sitting up wildly and staring affrightedly at the piano*] Doctor! Doctor! Help!!!

THE DOCTOR [*returning hastily*] What is it?

REGINALD [*after another doubtful look at the piano*] Nothing. [*He composes himself to sleep again*].

THE DOCTOR. Nothing! There must have been something or you wouldn't have yelled like that. [*Pulling Reginald over so as to see his face*] Here! what was it?

REGINALD. Well, it's gone.

THE DOCTOR. Whats gone?

REGINALD. The crocodile.

THE DOCTOR. The crocodile!

REGINALD. Yes. It laughed at me, and was going to play the piano with its tail.

THE DOCTOR. Opium in small doses doesnt agree with you, my young friend. [*Taking the spare pill from the plate*] I shall have to give you a second pill.

[884]

REGINALD. But suppose two crocodiles come!

THE DOCTOR. They wont. If anything comes it will be something pretty this time. Thats how opium acts. Anyhow, youll be fast asleep in ten minutes. Here. Take it.

REGINALD [*after taking the pill*] It was awfully silly of me. But you know I really saw the thing.

THE DOCTOR. You neednt trouble about what you see with your eyes shut. [*He turns to the door*].

REGINALD. Would you mind looking under the sofa to make sure the crocodile isnt there?

THE DOCTOR. Why not look yourself? that would be more convincing.

REGINALD. I darent.

THE DOCTOR. You duffer! [*He looks*]. All serene. No crocodile. Now go bye bye. [*He goes out*].

Reginald again composes himself to sleep. Somebody unlocks the central doors. A lovely lady enters with a bouquet in her hand. She looks about her; takes a letter from wherever she carries letters; and starts on a voyage of discovery round the room, checking her observations by the contents of the letter. The piano seems specially satisfactory: she nods as she sees it. Reginald seems also to be quite expected. She does not speak to him. When she is quite satisfied that she is in the right room, she goes to the piano and tantalizes the expectant audience for about two minutes by putting down her flowers on the candle-stand; taking off her gloves and putting them with the flowers; taking off half a dozen diamond rings in the same way; sitting down to the keyboard and finding it too near to the piano, then too far, then too high, then too low: in short, exhausting all the tricks of the professional pianist before she at last strikes the keys and preludes brilliantly. At the sound, Reginald, with a scream, rolls from the sofa and writhes on the carpet in horrible contortions. She stops playing, amazed.

REGINALD. Oh! Oh! Oh! The crocodiles! Stop! Ow! Oh! [*He looks at the piano and sees the lady*] Oh I say!

THE LADY. What on earth do you mean by making that noise when I'm playing? Have you no sense? Have you no manners?

REGINALD [*sitting on the floor*] I'm awfully sorry.

THE LADY. Sorry! Why did you do it?

REGINALD. I thought you were a crocodile.

THE LADY. What a silly thing to say! Do I look like a crocodile?

REGINALD. No.

THE LADY. Do I play like a crocodile!

REGINALD [*cautiously rising and approaching her*] Well, you know, it's so hard to know how a crocodile would play.

THE LADY. Stuff! [*She resumes her playing*].

REGINALD. Please! [*He stops her by shutting the keyboard lid*]. Who let you in?

THE LADY [*rising threateningly*] What is that to you, pray?

REGINALD [*retreating timidly*] It's my room, you know.

THE LADY. It's nothing of the sort. It's the Duchess of Dunmow's room. I know it's the right one, because she gave me the key; and it was the right key.

REGINALD. But what did she do that for? Who are you, if you dont mind my asking?

THE LADY. I do mind your asking. It's no business of yours. However, youd better know to whom you are speaking. I am Strega Thundridge. [*She pronounces it Strayga*].

REGINALD. What! The female Paderewski!

STREGA. Pardon me. I believe Mr Paderewski has been called the male Thundridge; but no gentleman would dream of repeating such offensive vulgarities.

[886]

Will you be good enough to return to your sofa, and hold your tongue, or else leave the room.

REGINALD. But, you know, I am ill.

STREGA. Then go to bed, and send for a doctor. [*She sits down again to the keyboard*].

REGINALD [*falling to his knees*] You mustnt play. You really mustnt. I cant stand it. I shall simply not be myself if you start playing.

STREGA [*raising the lid*] Then I shall start at once.

REGINALD [*running to her on his knees and snatching at her hands*] No, you shant. [*She rises indignantly. He holds on to her hands, but exclaims ecstatically*] Oh, I say, what lovely hands youve got!

STREGA. The idea! [*She hurls him to the carpet*].

REGINALD. [*on the floor staring at her*] You are strong.

STREGA. My strength has been developed by playing left hand octave passages—like this. [*She begins playing Liszt's transcription of Schubert's Erl König*].

REGINALD [*puts his fingers in his ears, but continues to stare at her*].

STREGA [*stopping*] I really cannot play if you keep your ears stopped. It is an insult. Leave the room.

REGINALD. But I tell you it's my room.

STREGA [*rising*] Leave the room, or I will ring your bell and have you put out. [*She goes to the little table, and poises her fingers over the bell call*].

REGINALD [*rushing to her*] No no: somebody will come if you ring; and I shall go distracted if a stranger comes in. [*With a touch of her left hand she sends him reeling. He appeals to her plaintively*] Dont you see that I am ill?

STREGA. I see that you are mentally afflicted. But that doesnt matter to me. The Duchess of Dunmow has engaged me to come to this room and play for two hours.

I never break an engagement, especially a two hundred and fifty guinea one. [*She turns towards the piano*].

REGINALD. But didnt she tell you anything about me?

STREGA [*turning back to him*] She said there would be a foolish young man in the room, but that I was not to mind him. She assured me you were not dangerous except to yourself. [*Collaring him and holding him bent backwards over the piano*]. But I will have no nonsense about not listening. All the world listens when I play. Listen, or go.

REGINALD [*helpless*] But I shall have to sit on the stairs. I darent go into any of the rooms: I should meet people there.

STREGA. You will meet plenty of people on the stairs, young man. They are sitting six on each stair, not counting those who are sitting astride the banisters on the chance of hearing me play.

REGINALD. How dreadful! [*Tearfully*] Youve no right to bully me like this. I'm ill: I cant bear it. I'll throw myself out of the window.

STREGA [*releasing him*] Do. What an advertisement! It will be really kind of you. [*She goes back to the keyboard and sits down to play*].

REGINALD [*crossing to the window*] Youll be sorry you were so unfeeling when you see my mangled body. [*He opens the window; looks out; shuts it hastily, and retreats with a scream*]. Theres a crowd. I darent.

STREGA [*pleased*] Waiting to hear me play [*she preludes softly*].

REGINALD [*ravished*] Oh! I can stand that, you know.

STREGA [*ironically, still preluding*] Thank you.

REGINALD. The fact is, I can play a bit myself.

STREGA [*still preluding*] An amateur, I presume.

REGINALD. I have often been told I could make a living at it if I tried. But of course it wouldnt do for a man in my position to lower himself by becoming a professional.

STREGA [*abruptly ceasing to play*] Tactful, that, I dont think! And what do you play, may I ask?

REGINALD. Oh, all the very best music.

STREGA. For instance?

REGINALD. I wish you belonged to me.

STREGA [*rising outraged*] You young blackguard! How dare you?

REGINALD. You dont understand: it's the name of a tune. Let me play it for you. [*He sits down at the keyboard*] I dont think you believe I can play.

STREGA. Pardon me. I have heard a horse play the harmonium at a music hall. I can believe anything.

REGINALD. Aha! [*He plays*]. Do you like that?

STREGA. What is it? Is it intended for music?

REGINALD. Oh, you beautiful doll

STREGA. Take that [*she knocks him sprawling over the keyboard*]! Beautiful doll indeed!

REGINALD. Oh, I say! Look here: thats the name of the tune too. You seem quite ignorant of the best music. Dont you know Rum Tum Tiddle, and Alexander's Rag Time Band, and Take me back to the Garden of Love, and Everybody likes our Mary.

STREGA. Young man: I have never even heard of these abominations. I am now going to educate you musically. I am going to play Chopin, and Brahms, and Bach, and Schumann, and—

REGINALD [*horrified*] You dont mean classical music?

STREGA. I do [*he bolts through the central doors*].

STREGA [*disgusted*] Pig! [*She sits down at the piano again*].

REGINALD [*rushing back into the room*] I forgot the people on the stairs: crowds of them. Oh, what shall I do! Oh dont, Dont, DONT play classical music to me. Say you wont. Please.

STREGA [*looks at him enigmatically and softly plays a Liebeslieder Waltz*]!!

REGINALD. Oh, I say: thats rather pretty.

STREGA. Like it?

REGINALD. Awfully. Oh, I say, you know: I really do wish you belonged to me. [*Strega suddenly plays a violent Chopin study. He goes into convulsions*]. Oh! Stop! Mercy! Help! Oh please, please!

STREGA [*pausing with her hands raised over the keyboard, ready to pounce on the chords*] Will you ever say that again?

REGINALD. Never. I beg your pardon.

STREGA [*satisfied*] Hm! [*She drops her hands in her lap*].

REGINALD [*wiping his brow*] Oh, that was fearfully classical.

STREGA. You want your back stiffened a little, my young friend. Besides, I really cannot earn two hundred and fifty guineas by playing soothing syrup to you. Now prepare for the worst. I'm going to make a man of you.

REGINALD. How?

STREGA. With Chopin's Polonaise in A Flat. Now. Imagine yourself going into battle. [*He runs away as before*] Goose!

REGINALD [*returning as before*] The crowd is worse than ever. Have you no pity?

STREGA. Come here. Dont imagine yourself going into battle. Imagine that you have just been in a battle; and that you have saved your country by deeds of splendid bravery; and that you are going to dance with beautiful women who are proud of you. Can you imagine that?

REGINALD. Rathe-e-e-errr. Thats how I always do imagine myself.

STREGA. Right. Now listen. [*She plays the first section of the Polonaise. Reginald flinches at first, but gradually braces himself; stiffens; struts; throws up his head and slaps his chest*]. Thats better. What a hero! [*After a difficult passage*]. Takes a bit of doing, that, dearest child. [*Coming to the chords which announce the middle section*] Now for it.

REGINALD [*unable to contain himself*] Oh, this is too glorious. I must have a turn or I shall forget myself.

STREGA. Can you play this? Nothing but this. [*She plays the octave passage in the bass*].

REGINALD. Just riddle tiddle, riddle tiddle, riddle tiddle, riddle tiddle? Nothing but that?

STREGA. Very softly at first. Like the ticking of a watch. Then louder and louder, as you feel my soul swelling.

REGINALD. I understand. Just give me those chords again to buck me up to it. [*She plays the chords again. He plays the octave passages; and they play the middle section as a duet. At the repeat he cries*] Again! again!

STREGA. It's meant to be played again. Now.

They repeat it. At the end of the section she pushes him off the bench on to the floor, and goes on with the Polonaise alone.

REGINALD. Wonderful woman: I have a confession to make, a confidence to impart. Your playing draws it from me. Listen, Strega [*she plays a horrible discord*] I mean Miss Thundridge.

STREGA. Thats better; but I prefer Wonderful Woman.

REGINALD. You are a wonderful woman, you know. Adored one—would you mind my taking a little valerian? I'm so excited [*he takes some*]. A—a—ah! Now I feel that I can speak. Listen to me, goddess. I am not happy. I hate my present existence. I loathe parliament. I am not fit for public affairs. I am condemned to live at home with five coarse and brutal sisters who care for nothing but Alpine climbing, and looping the loop on aeroplanes, and going on deputations, and fighting the police. Do you know what they call me?

STREGA [*playing softly*] What do they call you, dear?
REGINALD. They call me a Clinger. Well, I confess it. I am a Clinger. I am not fit to be thrown unprotected upon the world. I want to be shielded. I want a strong arm to lean on, a dauntless heart to be gathered to and cherished, a breadwinner on whose income I can live without the sordid horrors of having to make money for myself. I am a poor little thing, I know, Strega; but I could make a home for you. I have great taste in carpets and pictures. I can cook like anything. I can play quite nicely after dinner. Though you mightnt think it, I can be quite stern and strongminded with servants. I get on splendidly with children: they never talk over my head as grown-up people do. I have a real genius for home life. And I shouldnt at all mind being tyrannized over a little: in fact, I like it. It saves me the trouble of having to think what to do. Oh, Strega, dont you want a dear little domesticated husband who would have no concern but to please you, no thought outside our home, who would be unspotted and unsoiled by the rude cold world, who would never meddle in politics or annoy you by interfering with your profession? Is there any hope for me?

STREGA [*coming away from the piano*] My child: I am a hard, strong, independent, muscular woman. How can you, with your delicate soft nature, see anything to love in me? I should hurt you, shock you, perhaps —yes: let me confess it—I have a violent temper, and might even, in a transport of rage, beat you.

REGINALD. Oh do, do. Dont laugh at this ridiculous confession; but ever since I was a child I have had only one secret longing, and that was to be mercilessly beaten by a splendid, strong, beautiful woman.

STREGA [*solemnly*] Reginald—I think your mother spoke of you as Reginald?—

REGINALD. Rejjy.

STREGA. I too have a confession to make. I too need some music to speak through. Will you be so good?

REGINALD. Angel. [*He rushes to the piano and plays sympathetically whilst she speaks*].

STREGA. I, too, have had my dream. It has consoled me through the weary hours when I practised scales for eight hours a day. It has pursued me through the applause of admiring thousands in Europe and America. It is a dream of a timid little heart fluttering against mine, of a gentle voice to welcome me home, of a silky moustache to kiss my weary fingers when I return from a Titanic struggle with Tchaikovsky's Concerto in G major, of somebody utterly dependent on me, utterly devoted to me, utterly my own, living only to be cherished and worshipped by me.

REGINALD. But you would be angry sometimes: terrible, splendid, ruthless, violent. You would throw down the thing you loved and trample on it as it clung to your feet.

STREGA. Yes—oh, why do you force me to confess it? —I should beat it to a jelly, and then cast myself in transports of remorse on its quivering frame and smother it with passionate kisses.

REGINALD [*transported*] Let it be me, let it be me.

STREGA. You dare face this terrible destiny?

REGINALD. I embrace it. I adore you. I am wholly yours. Oh, let me cling, cling, cling.

STREGA [*embracing him fiercely*] Nothing shall tear you from my arms now.

REGINALD. Nothing. I am provided for. Oh how happy this will make my mother!

STREGA. Sweet: name the day.

He plays a wedding march. She plays the bass.

AYOT ST LAWRENCE, 21st *January* 1914.

Great Catherine
(Whom Glory Still Adores)

WITH

The Author's Apology for Great Catherine

Composition begun 29 July 1913; completed 13 August 1913. First published in German translation, as *Die Grosse Katharina*, in the *Neue Rundschau* (Berlin), April 1914. Published in *Everybody's Magazine* (New York), February 1915. First English publication in *Heartbreak House, Great Catherine, & Playlets of the War*, 1919. First presented at the Vaudeville Theatre, London, on 18 November 1913.

Prince Patiomkin   *Norman McKinnel*
Varinka   *Miriam Lewes*
Cossack Sergeant   *J. Cooke Beresford*
Captain Edstaston (Light Dragoons)
                          Edmond Breon
Naryshkin (Chamberlain)   *Eugene Mayeur*
Empress Catherine II   *Gertrude Kingston*
Princess Dashkoff   *Annie Hill*
Claire   *Dorothy Massingham*

Period—1776

Scene 1: *Prince Patiomkin's Chancery in the Winter Palace*

Scene 2: *The Empress's Bedchamber*

Scene 3: *A Terrace Garden*

Scene 4: *A Recess in the Grand Ballroom of the Palace*

The Author's Apology for
Great Catherine

Exception has been taken to the title of this seeming
tomfoolery on the ground that the Catherine it represents is not Great Catherine, but the Catherine whose
gallantries provide some of the lightest pages of
modern history. Great Catherine, it is said, was the
Catherine whose diplomacy, whose campaigns and
conquests, whose plans of Liberal reform, whose
correspondence with Grimm and Voltaire enabled
her to cut such a magnificent figure in the eighteenth
century. In reply, I can only confess that Catherine's
diplomacy and her conquests do not interest me. It is
clear to me that neither she nor the statesmen with
whom she played this mischievous kind of political
chess had any notion of the real history of their own
times, or of the real forces that were moulding Europe.
The French Revolution, which made such short work
of Catherine's Voltairean principles, surprised and
scandalized her as much as it surprised and scandalized
any provincial governess in the French chateaux.

The main difference between her and our modern
Liberal Governments was that whereas she talked and
wrote quite intelligently about Liberal principles
before she was frightened into making such talking
and writing a flogging matter, our Liberal ministers
take the name of Liberalism in vain without knowing
or caring enough about its meaning even to talk and
scribble about it, and pass their flogging Bills, and
institute their prosecutions for sedition and blasphemy and so forth, without the faintest suspicion
that such proceedings need any apology from the
Liberal point of view.

It was quite easy for Patiomkin to humbug Catherine as to the condition of Russia by conducting her through sham cities run up for the occasion by scenic artists; but in the little world of European court intrigue and dynastic diplomacy which was the only world she knew she was more than a match for him and for all the rest of her contemporaries. In such intrigue and diplomacy, however, there was no romance, no scientific political interest, nothing that a sane mind can now retain even if it can be persuaded to waste time in reading it up. But Catherine as a woman, with plenty of character and (as we should say) no morals, still fascinates and amuses us as she fascinated and amused her contemporaries. They were great sentimental comedians, these Peters, Elizabeths, and Catherines who played their Tsarships as eccentric character parts, and produced scene after scene of furious harlequinade with the monarch as clown, and of tragic relief in the torture chamber with the monarch as pantomime demon committing real atrocities, not forgetting the indispensable love interest on an enormous and utterly indecorous scale. Catherine kept this vast Guignol Theatre open for nearly half a century, not as a Russian but as a highly domesticated German lady whose household routine was not at all so unlike that of Queen Victoria as might be expected from the difference in their notions of propriety in sexual relations.

In short, if Byron leaves you with an impression that he said very little about Catherine, and that little not what was best worth saying, I beg to correct your impression by assuring you that what Byron said was all there really is to say that is worth saying. His Catherine is my Catherine and everybody's Catherine. The young man who gains her favour is a Spanish nobleman in his version. I have made him an English country gentleman, who gets out of his rather dangerous scrape by simplicity, sincerity, and the courage of these qualities. By this I have given some offence to the many Britons who see themselves as heroes: what they mean by heroes being theatrical snobs of superhuman pretensions which, though quite groundless, are admitted with awe by the rest of the human race. They say I think an Englishman a fool. When I do, they have themselves to thank.

I must not, however, pretend that historical portraiture was the motive of a play that will leave the reader as ignorant of Russian history as he may be now before he has turned the page. Nor is the sketch of Catherine complete even idiosyncratically, leaving her politics out of the question. For example, she wrote bushels of plays. I confess I have not yet read any of them. The truth is, this play grew out of the relations which inevitably exist in the theatre between authors and actors. If the actors have sometimes to use their skill as the author's puppets rather than in full self-expression, the author has sometimes to use his skill as the actors' tailor, fitting them with parts written to display the virtuosity of the performer rather than to solve problems of life, character, or history. Feats of this kind may tickle an author's technical vanity; but he is bound on such occasions to admit that the performer for whom he writes is "the onlie begetter" of his work, which must be regarded critically as an addition to the debt dramatic literature owes to the art of acting and its exponents. Those who have seen Miss Gertrude Kingston play the part of Catherine will have no difficulty in believing that it was her talent rather than mine that brought the play into existence. I once recommended Miss Kingston

professionally to play queens. Now in the modern
drama there were no queens for her to play; and as
to the older literature of our stage, did it not provoke
the veteran actress in Sir Arthur Pinero's Trelawny
of the Wells to declare that, as parts, queens are not
worth a tinker's oath? Miss Kingston's comment on
my suggestion, though more elegantly worded, was
to the same effect; and it ended in my having to make
good my advice by writing Great Catherine. History
provided no other queen capable of standing up to
our joint talents.

In composing such bravura pieces, the author
limits himself only by the range of the virtuoso, which
by definition far transcends the modesty of nature.
If my Russians seem more Muscovite than any
Russian, and my English people more insular than
any Briton, I will not plead, as I honestly might, that
the fiction has yet to be written that can exaggerate
the reality of such subjects; that the apparently outrageous Patiomkin is but a timidly bowdlerized ghost
of the original; and that Captain Edstaston is no more
than a miniature that might hang appropriately on
the walls of nineteen out of twenty English country
houses to this day. An artistic presentment must not
condescend to justify itself by a comparison with
crude nature; and I prefer to admit that in this kind
my *dramatis personae* are, as they should be, of the
stage stagey, challenging the actor to act up to them
or beyond them, if he can. The more heroic the overcharging, the better for the performance.

In dragging the reader thus for a moment behind
the scenes, I am departing from a rule which I have
hitherto imposed on myself so rigidly that I never
permit myself, even in a stage direction, to let slip a
word that could bludgeon the imagination of the

reader by reminding him of the boards and the foot-lights and the sky borders and the rest of the theatrical scaffolding, for which nevertheless I have to plan as carefully as if I were the head carpenter as well as the author. But even at the risk of talking shop, an honest playwright should take at least one opportunity of acknowledging that his art is not only limited by the art of the actor, but often stimulated and developed by it. No sane and skilled author writes plays that present impossibilities to the actor or to the stage engineer. If, as occasionally happens, he asks them to do things that they have never done before and cannot conceive as presentable or possible (as Wagner and Thomas Hardy have done, for example), it is always found that the difficulties are not really insuperable, the author having foreseen unsuspected possibilities both in the actor and in the audience, whose will-to-make-believe can perform the quaintest miracles. Thus may authors advance the arts of acting and of staging plays. But the actor also may enlarge the scope of the drama by dis-playing powers not previously discovered by the author. If the best available actors are only Horatios, the authors will have to leave Hamlet out, and be content with Horatios for heroes. Some of the differ-ence between Shakespear's Orlandos and Bassanios and Bertrams and his Hamlets and Macbeths must have been due not only to his development as a dramatic poet, but to the development of Burbage as an actor. Playwrights do not write for ideal actors when their livelihood is at stake: if they did, they would write parts for heroes with twenty arms like an Indian god. Indeed the actor often influences the author too much; for I can remember a time (I am not implying that it is yet wholly past) when the art of writing a fashionable play had become very largely the art of writing it "round" the personalities of a group of fashionable performers of whom Burbage would certainly have said that their parts needed no acting. Everything has its abuse as well as its use.

It is also to be considered that great plays live longer than great actors, though little plays do not live nearly so long as the worst of their exponents. The consequence is that the great actor, instead of putting pressure on contemporary authors to supply him with heroic parts, falls back on the Shakespearean repertory, and takes what he needs from a dead hand. In the nineteenth century, the careers of Kean, Macready, Barry Sullivan, and Irving, ought to have produced a group of heroic plays comparable in intensity to those of Æschylus, Sophocles, and Euripides; but nothing of the kind happened: these actors played the works of dead authors, or, very occasionally, of live poets who were hardly regular professional playwrights. Sheridan Knowles, Bulwer Lytton, Willis, and Tennyson produced a few glaringly artificial high horses for the great actors of their time; but the playwrights proper, who really kept the theatre going, and were kept going by the theatre, did not cater for the great actors: they could not afford to compete with a bard who was not of an age but for all time, and who had, moreover, the overwhelming attraction for the actor-managers of not charging author's fees. The result was that the playwrights and the great actors ceased to think of themselves as having any concern with one another: Tom Robertson, Ibsen, Pinero, and Barrie might as well have belonged to a different solar system as far as Irving was concerned; and the same was true of their respective predecessors.

Thus was established an evil tradition; but I at least can plead that it does not always hold good. If

Forbes Robertson had not been there to play Caesar, I should not have written Caesar and Cleopatra. If Ellen Terry had never been born, Captain Brass-bound's conversion would never have been effected. The Devil's Disciple, with which I won my *cordon bleu* in America as a pot-boiler, would have had a different sort of hero if Richard Mansfield had been a different sort of actor, though the actual commission to write it came from an English actor, William Terriss, who was assassinated before he recovered from the dismay into which the result of his rash proposal threw him. For it must be said that the actor or actress who inspires or commissions a play as often as not regards it as a Frankenstein's monster, and will none of it. That does not make him or her any the less parental in the fecundity of the playwright.

To an author who has any feeling of his business there is a keen and whimsical joy in divining and revealing a side of an actor's genius overlooked before, and unsuspected even by the actor himself. When I snatched Mr Louis Calvert from Shakespear, and made him wear a frock coat and silk hat on the stage for perhaps the first time in his life, I do not think he expected in the least that his performance would enable me to boast of his Tom Broadbent as a genuine stage classic. Mrs Patrick Campbell was famous before I wrote for her, but not for playing illiterate cockney flowermaidens. And in the case which is provoking me to all these impertinences, I am quite sure that Miss Gertrude Kingston, who first made her reputation as an impersonator of the most delight-fully feather-headed and inconsequent ingenues, thought me more than usually mad when I persuaded her to play the Helen of Euripides, and then launched her on a queenly career as Catherine of Russia.

It is not the whole truth that if we take care of the actors the plays will take care of themselves; nor is it any truer that if we take care of the plays the actors will take care of themselves. There is both give and take in the business. I have seen plays written for actors that made me exclaim, "How oft the sight of means to do ill deeds makes deeds ill done!" But Burbage may have flourished the prompt copy of Hamlet under Shakespear's nose at the tenth rehearsal and cried, "How oft the sight of means to do great deeds makes playwrights great!" I say the tenth because I am convinced that at the first he denounced his part as a rotten one; thought the ghost's speech ridiculously long; and wanted to play the king. Anyhow, whether he had the wit to utter it or not, the boast would have been a valid one. The best conclusion is that every actor should say "If I create the hero in myself, God will send an author to write his part." For in the long run the actors will get the authors, and the authors the actors, they deserve.

1776. Patiomkin in his bureau in the Winter Palace, St Petersburg. Huge palatial apartment: style, Russia in the eighteenth century imitating the Versailles du Roi Soleil. Extravagant luxury. Also dirt and disorder.

Patiomkin, gigantic in stature and build, his face marred by the loss of one eye and a marked squint in the other, sits at the end of a table littered with papers and the remains of three or four successive breakfasts. He has supplies of coffee and brandy at hand sufficient for a party of ten. His coat, encrusted with diamonds, is on the floor. It has fallen off a chair placed near the other end of the table for the convenience of visitors. His court sword, with its attachments, is on the chair. His three-cornered hat, also bejewelled, is on the table. He himself is half dressed in an unfastened shirt and an immense dressing-gown, once gorgeous, now food-splashed and dirty, as it serves him for towel, handkerchief, duster, and every other use to which a textile fabric can be put by a slovenly man. It does not conceal his huge hairy chest, nor his half-buttoned knee breeches, nor his legs. These are partly clad in silk stockings, which he occasionally hitches up to his knees, and presently shakes down to his shins, by his restless movements. His feet are thrust into enormous slippers, worth, with their crust of jewels, several thousand roubles apiece.

Superficially Patiomkin is a violent, brutal barbarian, an upstart despot of the most intolerable and dangerous type, ugly, lazy, and disgusting in his personal habits. Yet ambassadors report him the ablest man in Russia, and the one who can do most with the still abler Empress Catherine II, who is not a Russian but a German, by no means barbarous or intemperate in her personal habits.

*She not only disputes with Frederick the Great the
reputation of being the cleverest monarch in Europe, but
may even put in a very plausible claim to be the cleverest
and most attractive individual alive. Now she not only
tolerates Patiomkin long after she has got over her first
romantic attachment to him, but esteems him highly as a
counsellor and a good friend. His love letters are among
the best on record. He has a wild sense of humor, which
enables him to laugh at himself as well as at everybody
else. In the eyes of the English visitor now about to be
admitted to his presence he may be an outrageous ruffian.
In fact he actually is an outrageous ruffian, in no matter
whose eyes; but the visitor will find out, as everyone else
sooner or later finds out, that he is a man to be reckoned
with even by those who are not intimidated by his temper,
bodily strength, and exalted rank.*

*A pretty young lady, Varinka, his favorite niece, is
lounging on an ottoman between his end of the table and
the door, very sulky and dissatisfied, perhaps because he
is preoccupied with his papers and his brandy bottle, and
she can see nothing of him but his broad back.*

There is a screen behind the ottoman.

An old soldier, a Cossack sergeant, enters.

THE SERGEANT [*softly to the lady, holding the door
handle*] Little darling honey: is his Highness the
prince very busy?

VARINKA. His Highness the prince is very busy. He
is singing out of tune; he is biting his nails; he is
scratching his head; he is hitching up his untidy
stockings; he is making himself disgusting and odious
to everybody; and he is pretending to read state
papers that he does not understand because he is too
lazy and selfish to talk and be companionable.

[906]

PATIOMKIN [*growls; then wipes his nose with his dressing-gown*]! !

VARINKA. Pig. Ugh! [*She curls herself up with a shiver of disgust and retires from the conversation*].

THE SERGEANT [*stealing across to the coat, and picking it up to replace it on the back of the chair*] Little Father: the English captain, so highly recommended to you by Old Fritz of Prussia, by the English ambassador, and by Monsieur Voltaire (whom [*crossing himself*] may God in his infinite mercy damn eternally!), is in the antechamber and desires audience.

PATIOMKIN [*deliberately*] To hell with the English captain; and to hell with Old Fritz of Prussia; and to hell with the English ambassador; and to hell with Monsieur Voltaire; and to hell with you too!

THE SERGEANT. Have mercy on me, Little Father. Your head is bad this morning. You drink too much French brandy and too little good Russian kvass.

PATIOMKIN [*with sudden fury*] Why are visitors of consequence announced by a sergeant? [*Springing at him and seizing him by the throat*] What do you mean by this, you hound? Do you want five thousand blows of the stick? Where is General Volkonsky?

THE SERGEANT [*on his knees*] Little Father: you kicked his Highness downstairs.

PATIOMKIN [*flinging him down and kicking him*] You lie, you dog. You lie.

THE SERGEANT. Little Father: life is hard for the poor. If you say it is a lie, it is a lie. He fell downstairs. I picked him up; and he kicked me. They all kick me when you kick them. God knows that is not just, Little Father!

PATIOMKIN [*laughs ogreishly; then returns to his place at the table, chuckling*]! ! ! !

VARINKA. Savage! Boor! It is a disgrace. No wonder the French sneer at us as barbarians.

THE SERGEANT [*who has crept round the table to the screen, and insinuated himself between Patiomkin's back and Varinka*] Do you think the Prince will see the Captain, little darling?

PATIOMKIN. He will not see any captain. Go to the devil!

THE SERGEANT. Be merciful, Little Father. God knows it is your duty to see him! [*To Varinka*] Intercede for him and for me, beautiful little darling. He has given me a rouble.

PATIOMKIN. Oh, send him in, send him in; and stop pestering me. Am I never to have a moment's peace?

The Sergeant salutes joyfully and hurries out, divining that Patiomkin has intended to see the English captain all along, and has played this comedy of fury and exhausted impatience to conceal his interest in the visitor.

VARINKA. Have you no shame? You refuse to see the most exalted persons. You kick princes and generals downstairs. And then you see an English captain merely because he has given a rouble to that common soldier. It is scandalous.

PATIOMKIN. Darling beloved, I am drunk; but I know what I am doing. I wish to stand well with the English.

VARINKA. And you think you will impress an Englishman by receiving him as you are now, half drunk?

PATIOMKIN [*gravely*] It is true: the English despise men who cannot drink. I must make myself wholly drunk [*he takes a huge draught of brandy*].

VARINKA. Sot!

The Sergeant returns ushering a handsome strongly built young English officer in the uniform of a Light Dragoon. He is evidently on fairly good terms with himself, and very sure of his social position. He crosses the room to the end of the table opposite Patiomkin's, and

awaits the civilities of that statesman with confidence.
The Sergeant remains prudently at the door.

THE SERGEANT [*paternally*] Little Father: this is the
English captain, so well recommended to her sacred
Majesty the Empress. God knows, he needs your
countenance and protec—[*he vanishes precipitately,
seeing that Patiomkin is about to throw a bottle at him.
The Captain contemplates these preliminaries with
astonishment, and with some displeasure, which is not
allayed when Patiomkin, hardly condescending to look
at his visitor, of whom he nevertheless takes stock with
the corner of his one eye, says gruffly*] Well?

EDSTASTON. My name is Edstaston: Captain Edstaston of the Light Dragoons. I have the honor to present
to your Highness this letter from the British ambassador, which will give you all necessary particulars.
[*He hands Patiomkin the letter*].

PATIOMKIN [*tearing it open and glancing at it for
about a second*] What do you want?

EDSTASTON. The letter will explain to your Highness
who I am.

PATIOMKIN. I dont want to know who you are.
What do you want?

EDSTASTON. An audience of the Empress. [*Patiomkin
contemptuously throws the letter aside. Edstaston adds
hotly*] Also some civility, if you please.

PATIOMKIN [*with derision*] Ho!

VARINKA. My uncle is receiving you with unusual
civility, Captain. He has just kicked a general downstairs.

EDSTASTON. A Russian general, madam?

VARINKA. Of course.

EDSTASTON. I must allow myself to say, madam,
that your uncle had better not attempt to kick an
English officer downstairs.

PATIOMKIN. You want me to kick you upstairs: eh?
You want an audience of the Empress.

EDSTASTON. I have said nothing about kicking, sir.
If it comes to that, my boots shall speak for me. Her
Majesty has signified a desire to have news of the
rebellion in America. I have served against the rebels;
and I am instructed to place myself at the disposal of
her Majesty, and to describe the events of the war to
her, as an eye-witness, in a discreet and agreeable
manner.

PATIOMKIN. Psha! I know. You think if she once
sets eyes on your face and your uniform your fortune
is made. You think that if she could stand a man like
me, with only one eye, and a cross eye at that, she
must fall down at your feet at first sight, eh?

EDSTASTON [*shocked and indignant*] I think nothing
of the sort: and I'll trouble you not to repeat it. If I
were a Russian subject and you made such a boast
about my queen, I'd strike you across the face with
my sword. [*Patiomkin, with a yell of fury, rushes at
him*]. Hands off, you swine! [*As Patiomkin, towering
over him, attempts to seize him by the throat, Edstaston,
who is a bit of a wrestler, adroitly backheels him. He
falls, amazed, on his back*].

VARINKA [*rushing out*] Help! Call the guard! The
Englishman is murdering my uncle! Help! Help!

*The guard and the Sergeant rush in. Edstaston draws
a pair of small pistols from his boots, and points one at
the Sergeant and the other at Patiomkin, who is sitting
on the floor, somewhat sobered. The soldiers stand
irresolute.*

EDSTASTON. Stand off. [*To Patiomkin*] Order them
off, if you dont want a bullet through your silly head.

THE SERGEANT. Little Father: tell us what to do. Our
lives are yours; but God knows you are not fit to die.

PATIOMKIN [*absurdly self-possessed*] Get out.

THE SERGEANT. Little Father—

PATIOMKIN [*roaring*] Get out. Get out, all of you. [*They withdraw, much relieved at their escape from the pistol. Patiomkin attempts to rise, and rolls over*]. Here! help me up, will you? Dont you see that I'm drunk and cant get up?

EDSTASTON [*suspiciously*] You want to get hold of me.

PATIOMKIN [*squatting resignedly against the chair on which his clothes hang*] Very well, then: I shall stay where I am, because I'm drunk and youre afraid of me.

EDSTASTON. I'm not afraid of you, damn you!

PATIOMKIN [*ecstatically*] Darling: your lips are the gates of truth. Now listen to me [*He marks off the items of his statement with ridiculous stiff gestures of his head and arms, imitating a puppet*] You are Captain Whathisname; and your uncle is the Earl of Whatdyecallum; and your father is Bishop of Thingummybob; and you are a young man of the highest spr-promise (I told you I was drunk), educated at Cambridge, and got your step as captain in the field at the GLORIOUS battle of Bunker's Hill. Invalided home from America at the request of Aunt Fanny, Lady-in-Waiting to the Queen. All right, eh?

EDSTASTON. How do you know all this?

PATIOMKIN [*crowing fantastically*] In er lerrer, darling, darling, darling, darling. Lerrer you shewed me.

EDSTASTON. But you didnt read it.

PATIOMKIN [*flapping his fingers at him grotesquely*] Only one eye, darling. Cross eye. Sees everything. Read lerrer ince-ince-istastaneously. Kindly give me vinegar borle. Green borle. On'y to sober me. Too drunk to speak proply. If you would be so kind, darling. Green borle. [*Edstaston, still suspicious, shakes his head and keeps his pistols ready*] Reach it myself [*He reaches behind him up to the table and snatches at the green bottle, from which he takes a copious draught. Its effect is appalling. His wry faces and agonized belchings are so heartrending that they almost upset Edstaston. When the victim at last staggers to his feet, he is a pale fragile nobleman, aged and quite sober, extremely dignified in manner and address, though shaken by his recent convulsions*]. Young man: it is not better to be drunk than sober; but it is happier. Goodness is not happiness. That is an epigram. But I have overdone this. I am too sober to be good company. Let me redress the balance. [*He takes a generous draught of brandy, and recovers his geniality*]. Aha! Thats better. And now listen, darling. You must not come to Court with pistols in your boots.

EDSTASTON. I have found them useful.

PATIOMKIN. Nonsense. I'm your friend. You mistook my intention because I was drunk. Now that I am sober—in moderation—I will prove that I am your friend. Have some diamonds. [*Roaring*] Hullo there! Dogs, pigs: hullo!

The Sergeant comes in.

THE SERGEANT. God be praised, Little Father: you are still spared to us.

PATIOMKIN. Tell them to bring some diamonds. Plenty of diamonds. And rubies. Get out. [*He aims a kick at the Sergeant, who flees*]. Put up your pistols, darling. I'll give you a pair with gold handgrips. I am your friend.

EDSTASTON [*replacing the pistols in his boots rather unwillingly*] Your Highness understands that if I am missing, or if anything happens to me, there will be trouble.

PATIOMKIN [*enthusiastically*] Call me darling.

EDSTASTON. It is not the English custom.

PATIOMKIN. You have no hearts, you English! [*Slapping his right breast*] Heart! Heart!

EDSTASTON. Pardon, your Highness: your heart is on the other side.

PATIOMKIN [*surprised and impressed*] Is it? You are learned! You arc a doctor! You English are wonderful! We are barbarians, drunken pigs. Catherine does not know it; but we are. Catherine's a German. But I have given her a Russian heart [*he is about to slap himself again*].

EDSTASTON [*delicately*] The other side, your Highness.

PATIOMKIN [*maudlin*] Darling: a true Russian has a heart on both sides.

The Sergeant enters carrying a goblet filled with precious stones.

PATIOMKIN. Get out. [*He snatches the goblet and kicks the Sergeant out, not maliciously but from habit, indeed not noticing that he does it*]. Darling: have some diamonds. Have a fistful. [*He takes a handful and lets them slip back through his fingers into the goblet, which he then offers to Edstaston*].

EDSTASTON. Thank you: I don't take presents.

PATIOMKIN [*amazed*] You refuse!

EDSTASTON. I thank your Highness; but it is not the custom for English gentlemen to take presents of that kind.

PATIOMKIN. Are you really an Englishman?

EDSTASTON [*bows*]!

PATIOMKIN. You are the first Englishman I ever saw refuse anything he could get. [*He puts the goblet on the table; then turns again to Edstaston*]. Listen darling. You are a wrestler: a splendid wrestler. You threw me on my back like magic, though I could lift you with one hand. Darling: you are a giant, a paladin.

EDSTASTON [*complacently*] We wrestle rather well in my part of England.

PATIOMKIN. I have a Turk who is a wrestler: a prisoner of war. You shall wrestle with him for me. I'll stake a million roubles on you.

EDSTASTON [*incensed*] Damn you! do you take me for a prize-fighter? How dare you make me such a proposal?

PATIOMKIN [*with wounded feeling*] Darling: there is no pleasing you. Dont you like me?

EDSTASTON [*mollified*] Well, in a sort of way I do: though I dont know why I should. But my instructions are that I am to see the Empress; and—

PATIOMKIN. Darling: you shall see the Empress. A glorious woman, the greatest woman in the world. But lemme give you piece 'vice—pah! still drunk. They water my vinegar. [*He shakes himself; clears his throat; and resumes soberly*] If Catherine takes a fancy to you, you may ask for roubles, diamonds, palaces, titles, orders, anything! and you may aspire to everything: field-marshal, admiral, minister, what you please—except Tsar.

EDSTASTON. I tell you I don't want to ask for anything. Do you suppose I am an adventurer and a beggar?

PATIOMKIN [*plaintively*] Why not, darling? *I* was an adventurer. *I* was a beggar.

EDSTASTON. Oh, you!

PATIOMKIN. Well: whats wrong with me?

EDSTASTON. You are a Russian. Thats different.

PATIOMKIN [*effusively*] Darling: I am a man; and you are a man; and Catherine is a woman. Woman reduces us all to the common denominator. [*Chuckling*]. Again an epigram! [*Gravely*] You understand it, I hope. Have you had a college education, darling? *I* have.

EDSTASTON. Certainly. I am a Bachelor of Arts.

PATIOMKIN. It is enough that you are a bachelor, darling: Catherine will supply the arts. Aha! Another epigram? I am in the vein today.

EDSTASTON [*embarrassed and a little offended*] I must ask your Highness to change the subject. As a visitor in Russia, I am the guest of the Empress; and I must tell you plainly that I have neither the right nor the disposition to speak lightly of her Majesty.

PATIOMKIN. You have conscientious scruples?

EDSTASTON. I have the scruples of a gentleman.

PATIOMKIN. In Russia a gentleman has no scruples. In Russia we face facts.

EDSTASTON. In England, sir, a gentleman never faces any facts if they are unpleasant facts.

PATIOMKIN. In real life, darling, all facts are unpleasant. [*Greatly pleased with himself*] Another epigram! Where is my accursed chancellor? these gems should be written down and recorded for posterity. [*He rushes to the table; sits down; and snatches up a pen. Then, recollecting himself,*] But I have not asked you to sit down. [*He rises and goes to the other chair*]. I am a savage: a barbarian. [*He throws the shirt and coat over the table on to the floor and puts his sword on the table*]. Be seated, Captain.

EDSTASTON. Thank you.

They bow to one another ceremoniously. Patiomkin's tendency to grotesque exaggeration costs him his balance: he nearly falls over Edstaston, who rescues him and takes the proffered chair.

PATIOMKIN [*resuming his seat*] By the way, what was the piece of advice I was going to give you?

EDSTASTON. As you did not give it, I dont know. Allow me to add that I have not asked for your advice.

PATIOMKIN. I give it to you unasked, delightful

Englishman. I remember it now. It was this. Don't try to become Tsar of Russia.

EDSTASTON [*in astonishment*] I havnt the slightest intention—

PATIOMKIN. Not now; but you will have: take my word for it. It will strike you as a splendid idea to have conscientious scruples—to desire the blessing of the Church on your union with Catherine.

EDSTASTON [*rising in utter amazement*] My union with Catherine! Youre mad.

PATIOMKIN [*unmoved*] The day you hint at such a thing will be the day of your downfall. Besides, it is not lucky to be Catherine's husband. You know what happened to Peter?

EDSTASTON [*shortly: sitting down again*] I do not wish to discuss it.

PATIOMKIN. You think she murdered him?

EDSTASTON. I know that people have said so.

PATIOMKIN [*thunderously: springing to his feet*] It is a lie: Orloff murdered him. [*Subsiding a little*] He also knocked my eye out; but [*sitting down placidly*] I succeeded him for all that. And [*patting Edstaston's hand very affectionately*] I'm sorry to say, darling, that if you become Tsar, *I* shall murder you.

EDSTASTON [*ironically returning the caress*] Thank you. The occasion will not arise. [*Rising*] I have the honor to wish your Highness good morning.

PATIOMKIN [*jumping up and stopping him on his way to the door*] Tut tut! I'm going to take you to the Empress now, this very instant.

EDSTASTON. In these boots? Impossible! I must change.

PATIOMKIN. Nonsense! You shall come just as you are. You shall shew her your calves later on.

EDSTASTON. But it will take me only half an hour to—

PATIOMKIN. In half an hour it will be too late for the *petit lever*. Come along. Damn it, man, I must oblige the British ambassador, and the French ambassador, and old Fritz, and Monsieur Voltaire and the rest of them. [*He shouts rudely to the door*] Varinka! [*To Edstaston, with tears in his voice*] Varinka shall persuade you: nobody can refuse Varinka anything. My niece. A treasure, I assure you. Beautiful! devoted! fascinating! [*Shouting again*] Varinka: where the devil are you?

VARINKA [*returning*] I'll not be shouted for. You have the voice of a bear, and the manners of a tinker.

PATIOMKIN. Tsh-sh-sh. Little angel Mother: you must behave yourself before the English captain. [*He takes off his dressing gown and throws it over the papers and the breakfasts; picks up his coat; and disappears behind the screen to complete his toilette*].

EDSTASTON. Madam! [*He bows*].

VARINKA [*curtseying*] Monsieur le Capitaine!

EDSTASTON. I must apologize for the disturbance I made, madam.

PATIOMKIN [*behind the screen*] You must not call her madam. You must call her Little Mother, and beautiful darling.

EDSTASTON. My respect for the lady will not permit it.

VARINKA. Respect! How can you respect the niece of a savage?

EDSTASTON [*deprecating*] Oh, madam!

VARINKA. Heaven is my witness, Little English Father, we need someone who is not afraid of him. He is so strong! I hope you will throw him down on the floor, many, many, many, times.

PATIOMKIN [*behind the screen*] Varinka!

VARINKA. Yes?

PATIOMKIN. Go and look through the keyhole of the Imperial bed-chamber; and bring me word whether the Empress is awake yet.

VARINKA. Fi donc! I do not look through keyholes.

PATIOMKIN [*emerging, having arranged his shirt and put on his diamonded coat*] You have been badly brought up, little darling. Would any lady or gentleman walk unannounced into a room without first looking through the keyhole? [*Taking his sword from the table and putting it on*] The great thing in life is to be simple; and the perfectly simple thing is to look through keyholes. Another epigram: the fifth this morning! Where is my fool of a chancellor? Where is Popof?

EDSTASTON [*choking with suppressed laughter*]!!!!

PATIOMKIN [*gratified*] Darling: you appreciate my epigram.

EDSTASTON. Excuse me. Pop off! Ha! ha! I cant help laughing. Whats his real name, by the way, in case I meet him?

VARINKA [*surprised*] His real name? Popof, of course. Why do you laugh, Little Father?

EDSTASTON. How can anyone with a sense of humor help laughing? Pop off! [*He is convulsed*].

VARINKA [*looking at her uncle, taps her forehead significantly*]!!

PATIOMKIN [*aside to Varinka*] No: only English. He will amuse Catherine. [*To Edstaston*] Come! you shall tell the joke to the Empress: she is by way of being a humorist [*he takes him by the arm, and leads him towards the door*].

EDSTASTON [*resisting*] No, really. I am not fit—

PATIOMKIN. Persuade him, Little angel Mother.

VARINKA [*taking his other arm*] Yes, yes, yes, Little English Father: God knows it is your duty to be brave and wait on the Empress. Come.

EDSTASTON. No. I had rather—

PATIOMKIN [*hauling him along*] Come.

VARINKA [*pulling him and coaxing him*] Come, little love: you cant refuse me.

EDSTASTON. But how can I?

PATIOMKIN. Why not? She wont eat you.

VARINKA. She will; but you must come.

EDSTASTON. I assure you—it is quite out of the question—my clothes.

VARINKA. You look perfect.

PATIOMKIN. Come along, darling.

EDSTASTON [*struggling*] Impossible—

VARINKA. Come, come, come.

EDSTASTON. No. Believe me—I dont wish—I—

VARINKA. Carry him, uncle.

PATIOMKIN [*lifting him in his arms like a father carrying a little boy*] Yes: I'll carry you.

EDSTASTON. Dash it all, this is ridiculous!

VARINKA [*seizing his ankles and dancing as he is carried out*] You must come. If you kick you will blacken my eyes.

PATIOMKIN. Come, baby, come.

By this time they have made their way through the door and are out of hearing.

THE SECOND SCENE

The Empress's petit lever. The central doors are closed. Those who enter through them find on their left, on a dais of two broad steps, a magnificent curtained bed. Beyond it a door in the panelling leads to the Empress's cabinet. Near the foot of the bed, in the middle of the room, stands a gilt chair, with the Imperial arms carved and the Imperial monogram embroidered.

The Court is in attendance, standing in two melancholy rows down the side of the room opposite to the bed, solemn, bored, waiting for the Empress to awaken. The Princess Dashkoff, with two ladies, stands a little in front of the line of courtiers, by the Imperial chair. Silence, broken only by the yawns and whispers of the courtiers. Naryshkin, the Chamberlain, stands by the head of the bed.

A loud yawn is heard from behind the curtains.

NARYSHKIN [*holding up a warning hand*] Ssh!

The courtiers hastily cease whispering; dress up their lines; and stiffen. Dead silence. A bell tinkles within the curtains. Naryshkin and the Princess solemnly draw them and reveal the Empress.

Catherine turns over on her back, and stretches herself.

CATHERINE [*yawning*] Heigho—ah—yah—ah—ow—what o'clock is it? [*Her accent is German*].

NARYSHKIN [*formally*] Her Imperial Majesty is awake [*The Court falls on its knees*].

ALL. Good morning to your Majesty.

NARYSHKIN. Half-past ten, Little Mother.

CATHERINE [*sitting up abruptly*] Portztausend! [*Contemplating the kneeling courtiers*] Oh, get up, get up.

[*All rise*]. Your etiquette bores me. I am hardly awake in the morning before it begins. [*Yawning again, and relapsing sleepily against her pillows*] Why do they do it, Naryshkin?

NARYSHKIN. God knows it is not for your sake, Little Mother. But you see if you were not a great queen they would all be nobodies.

CATHERINE [*sitting up*] They make me do it to keep up their own little dignities? So?

NARYSHKIN. Exactly. Also because if they didnt you might have them flogged, dear Little Mother.

CATHERINE [*springing energetically out of bed and seating herself on the edge of it*] Flogged! I! A Liberal Empress! A philosopher! You are a barbarian, Naryshkin. [*She rises and turns to the courtiers*] And then, as if I cared! [*She turns again to Naryshkin*] You should know by this time that I am frank and original in character, like an Englishman. [*She walks about restlessly*]. No: what maddens me about all this ceremony is that I am the only person in Russia who gets no fun out of my being Empress. You all glory in me: you bask in my smiles: you get titles and honors and favors from me: you are dazzled by my crown and my robes: you feel splendid when you have been admitted to my presence; and when I say a gracious word to you, you talk about it to everyone you meet for a week afterwards. But what do *I* get out of it? Nothing. [*She throws herself into the chair. Naryshkin deprecates with a gesture: she hurls an emphatic repetition at him*] Nothing!! I wear a crown until my neck aches: I stand looking majestic until I am ready to drop: I have to smile at ugly old ambassadors and frown and turn my back on young and handsome ones. Nobody gives me anything. When I was only an Archduchess, the English ambassador used to give me money whenever I wanted it—or rather whenever he wanted to get anything out of my sacred predecessor Elizabeth [*the Court bows to the ground*]; but now that I am Empress he never gives me a kopek. When I have headaches and colics I envy the scullerymaids. And you are not a bit grateful to me for all my care of you, my work, my thoughts, my fatigue, my sufferings.

THE PRINCESS DASHKOFF. God knows, Little Mother, we all implore you to give your wonderful brain a rest. That is why you get headaches. Monsieur Voltaire also has headaches. His brain is just like yours.

CATHERINE. Dashkoff: what a liar you are! [*Dashkoff curtsies with impressive dignity*]. And you think you are flattering me! Let me tell you I would not give a rouble to have the brains of all the philosophers in France. What is our business for today?

NARYSHKIN. The new museum, Little Mother. But the model will not be ready until tonight.

CATHERINE [*rising eagerly*] Yes: the museum. An enlightened capital should have a museum. [*She paces the chamber with a deep sense of the importance of the museum*]. It shall be one of the wonders of the world. I must have specimens: specimens, specimens, specimens.

NARYSHKIN. You are in high spirits this morning, Little Mother.

CATHERINE [*with sudden levity*] I am always in high spirits, even when people do not bring me my slippers. [*She runs to the chair and sits down, thrusting her feet out*].

The two ladies rush to her feet, each carrying a slipper. Catherine, about to put her feet into them, is checked by a disturbance in the antechamber.

PATIOMKIN [*carrying Edstaston through the antechamber*] Useless to struggle. Come along, beautiful baby darling. Come to Little Mother. [*He sings*]

March him baby,
Baby, baby,
Lit-tle ba-by bumpkins.

VARINKA [*joining in to the same doggerel in canon, a third above*] March him, baby, etc., etc.

EDSTASTON [*trying to make himself heard*] No, no. This is carrying a joke too far. I must insist. Let me down! Hang it, will you let me down! Confound it! No, no. Stop playing the fool, will you? We dont understand this sort of thing in England. I shall be disgraced. Let me down.

CATHERINE [*meanwhile*] What a horrible noise! Naryshkin: see what it is.

Naryshkin goes to the door.

CATHERINE [*listening*] That is Prince Patiomkin.

NARYSHKIN [*calling from the door*] Little Mother: a stranger.

Catherine plunges into bed again and covers herself up. Patiomkin, followed by Varinka, carries Edstaston in; dumps him down on the foot of the bed; and staggers past it to the cabinet door. Varinka joins the courtiers at the opposite side of the room. Catherine, blazing with wrath, pushes Edstaston off her bed on to the floor; gets out of bed; and turns on Patiomkin with so terrible an expression that all kneel down hastily except Edstaston, who is sprawling on the carpet in angry confusion.

CATHERINE. Patiomkin: how dare you? [*Looking at Edstaston*] What is this?

PATIOMKIN [*on his knees: tearfully*] I don't know. I am drunk. What is this, Varinka?

EDSTASTON [*scrambling to his feet*] Madam: this drunken ruffian—

PATIOMKIN. Thas true. Drungn ruffian. Took dvantage of my being drunk. Said: take me to Lil

angel Mother. Take me to beaufl Empress. Take me
to the grea'st woman on earth. Thas whas he said. I
took him. I was wrong. I am not sober.

CATHERINE. Men have grown sober in Siberia for
less, Prince.

PATIOMKIN. Serve em right! Sgusting habit. Ask
Varinka.

*Catherine turns her face from him to the Court. The
courtiers see that she is trying not to laugh, and know by
experience that she will not succeed. They rise, relieved
and grinning.*

VARINKA. It is true. He drinks like a pig.

PATIOMKIN [*plaintively*] No: not like a pig. Like
prince. Lil Mother made poor Patiomkin prince.
Whas use being prince if I maynt drink?

CATHERINE [*biting her lips*] Go. I am offended.

PATIOMKIN. Dont scold, Ll Mother.

CATHERINE [*imperiously*] Go.

PATIOMKIN [*rising unsteadily*] Yes: go. Go bye bye.
Very sleepy. Berr go bye bye than go Siberia. Go bye
bye in Lil Mother's bed [*he pretends to make an
attempt to get into the bed*].

CATHERINE [*energetically pulling him back*] No, no!
Patiomkin! What are you thinking of? [*He falls like
a log on the floor, apparently dead drunk*].

THE PRINCESS DASHKOFF. Scandalous! An insult
to your Imperial Majesty!

CATHERINE. Dashkoff: you have no sense of humor.
[*She steps down to the floor level and looks indulgently
at Patiomkin. He gurgles brutishly. She has an impulse
of disgust*]. Hog. [*She kicks him as hard as she can*].
Oh! You have broken my toe. Brute. Beast. Dashkoff
is quite right. Do you hear?

PATIOMKIN. If you ask my pi-pinion of Dashkoff,
my pipinion is that Dashkoff is drunk. Poor Patiomkin
go bye bye. [*He relapses into drunken slumbers*].

Some of the courtiers move to carry him away.

CATHERINE [*stopping them*] Let him lie. Let him sleep it off. If he goes out it will be to a tavern and low company for the rest of the day. [*Indulgently*] There! [*She takes a pillow from the bed and puts it under his head; then turns to Edstaston; surveys him with perfect dignity; and asks, in her queenliest manner*] Varinka: who is this gentleman?

VARINKA. A foreign captain: I cannot pronounce his name. I think he is mad. He came to the Prince and said he must see your Majesty. He can talk of nothing else. We could not prevent him.

EDSTASTON [*overwhelmed by this apparent betrayal*] Oh! Madam: I am perfectly sane: I am actually an Englishman. I should never have dreamt of approaching your Majesty without the fullest credentials. I have letters from the English ambassador, from the Prussian ambassador. [*Naïvely*] But everybody assured me that Prince Patiomkin is all-powerful with your Majesty; so I naturally applied to him.

PATIOMKIN [*interrupts the conversation by an agonized wheezing groan, as of a donkey beginning to bray*]!!!!

CATHERINE [*like a fishfag*] Schweig, du Hund. [*Resuming her impressive Royal manner*] Have you never been taught, sir, how a gentleman should enter the presence of a sovereign?

EDSTASTON. Yes, Madam; but I did not enter your presence: I was carried.

CATHERINE. But you say you asked the Prince to carry you.

EDSTASTON. Certainly not, Madam. I protested against it with all my might. I appeal to this lady to confirm me.

VARINKA [*pretending to be indignant*] Yes: you protested. But, all the same, you were very very very

[925]

anxious to see her Imperial Majesty. You blushed when the Prince spoke of her. You threatened to strike him across the face with your sword because you thought he did not speak enthusiastically enough of her. [*To Catherine*] Trust me: he has seen your Imperial Majesty before.

CATHERINE [*to Edstaston*] You have seen us before?

EDSTASTON. At the review, Madam.

VARINKA [*triumphantly*] Aha! I knew it. Your Majesty wore the hussar uniform. He saw how radiant! how splendid! your Majesty looked. Oh! he has dared to admire your Majesty. Such insolence is not to be endured.

EDSTASTON. All Europe is a party to that insolence, Madam.

THE PRINCESS DASHKOFF. All Europe is content to do so at a respectful distance. It is possible to admire her Majesty's policy and her eminence in literature and philosophy without performing acrobatic feats in the Imperial bed.

EDSTASTON. I know nothing about her Majesty's eminence in policy or philosophy: I don't pretend to understand such things. I speak as a practical man. And I never knew that foreigners had any policy: I always thought that policy was Mr Pitt's business.

CATHERINE [*lifting her eyebrows*] So?

VARINKA. What else did you presume to admire her Majesty for, pray?

EDSTASTON [*addled*] Well, I—I—I—that is, I—[*He stammers himself dumb*].

CATHERINE [*after a pitiless silence*] We are waiting for your answer.

EDSTASTON. But I never said I admired your Majesty. The lady has twisted my words.

VARINKA. You dont admire her, then?

[926]

EDSTASTON. Well, I—naturally—of course, I cant deny that the uniform was very becoming—perhaps a little unfeminine—still—

Dead silence. Catherine and the court watch him stonily. He is wretchedly embarrassed.

CATHERINE [*with cold majesty*] Well, sir: is that all you have to say?

EDSTASTON. Surely there is no harm in noticing that er—that er—[*He stops again*].

CATHERINE. Noticing that er—? [*He gazes at her, speechless, like a fascinated rabbit. She repeats fiercely*] That er—?

EDSTASTON [*startled into speech*] Well, that your Majesty was—was—[*Soothingly*] Well, let me put it this way: that it was rather natural for a man to admire your Majesty without being a philosopher.

CATHERINE [*suddenly smiling and extending her hand to him to be kissed*] Courtier!

EDSTASTON [*kissing it*] Not at all. Your Majesty is very good. I have been very awkward; but I did not intend it. I am rather stupid, I am afraid.

CATHERINE. Stupid! By no means. Courage, Captain: we are pleased. [*He falls on his knee. She takes his cheeks in her hands; turns up his face; and adds*] We are greatly pleased. [*She slaps his cheek coquettishly: he bows almost to his knee*]. The *petit lever* is over. [*She turns to go into the cabinet, and stumbles against the supine Patiomkin*]. Ach! [*Edstaston springs to her assistance, seizing Patiomkin's heels and shifting him out of the Empress's path*]. We thank you, Captain.

He bows gallantly, and is rewarded by a very gracious smile. Then Catherine goes into her cabinet, followed by the Princess Dashkoff, who turns at the door to make a deep curtsey to Edstaston.

VARINKA. Happy Little Father! Remember: *I* did this for you. [*She runs after the Empress*].

Edstaston, somewhat dazed, crosses the room to the courtiers, and is received with marked deference, each courtier making him a profound bow or curtsey before withdrawing through the central doors. He returns each obeisance with a nervous jerk, and turns away from it, only to find another courtier bowing at the other side. The process finally reduces him to distraction, as he bumps into one in the act of bowing to another and then has to bow his apologies. But at last they are all gone except Naryshkin.

EDSTASTON. Ouf!

PATIOMKIN [*jumping up vigorously*] You have done it, darling. Superbly! Beautifully!

EDSTASTON [*astonished*] Do you mean to say you are not drunk?

PATIOMKIN. Not dead drunk, darling. Only diplomatically drunk. As a drunken hog, I have done for you in five minutes what I could not have done in five months as a sober man. Your fortune is made. She likes you.

EDSTASTON. The devil she does!

PATIOMKIN. Why? Arnt you delighted?

EDSTASTON. Delighted! Gracious heavens, man, I am engaged to be married.

PATIOMKIN. What matter? She is in England, isnt she?

EDSTASTON. No. She has just arrived in St Petersburg.

THE PRINCESS DASHKOFF [*returning*] Captain Edstaston: the Empress is robed, and commands your presence.

EDSTASTON. Say I was gone before you arrived with the message. [*He hurries out. The other three, too taken aback to stop him, stare after him in the utmost astonishment*].

NARYSHKIN [*turning from the door*] She will have him knouted. He is a dead man.

THE PRINCESS DASHKOFF. But what am *I* to do? I cannot take such an answer to the Empress.

PATIOMKIN. P-P-P-P-P-P-W-W-W-W-W-rrrrrr [*a long puff, turning into a growl*]! [*He spits*]. I must kick somebody.

NARYSHKIN [*flying precipitately through the central doors*] No, no, Please.

THE PRINCESS DASHKOFF [*throwing herself recklessly in front of Patiomkin as he starts in pursuit of the Chamberlain*] Kick me. Disable me. It will be an excuse for not going back to her. Kick me hard.

PATIOMKIN. Yah! [*He flings her on the bed and dashes after Naryshkin*].

THE THIRD SCENE

In a terrace garden overlooking the Neva. Claire, a robust young English lady, is leaning on the river wall. She turns expectantly on hearing the garden gate opened and closed. Edstaston hurries in. With a cry of delight she throws her arms round his neck.

CLAIRE. Darling.

EDSTASTON [*making a wry face*] Dont call me darling.

CLAIRE [*amazed and chilled*] Why?

EDSTASTON. I have been called darling all the morning.

CLAIRE [*with a flash of jealousy*] By whom?

EDSTASTON. By everybody. By the most unutterable swine. And if we do not leave this abominable city now: do you hear? now: I shall be called darling by the Empress.

CLAIRE [*with magnificent snobbery*] She would not dare. Did you tell her you were engaged to me?

EDSTASTON. Of course not.

CLAIRE. Why?

EDSTASTON. Because I didn't particularly want to have you knouted, and to be hanged or sent to Siberia myself.

CLAIRE. What on earth do you mean?

EDSTASTON. Well, the long and short of it is—dont think me a coxcomb, Claire: it is too serious to mince matters—I have seen the Empress; and—

CLAIRE. Well: you wanted to see her.

EDSTASTON. Yes; but the Empress has seen me.

CLAIRE. She has fallen in love with you.

EDSTASTON. How did you know?

CLAIRE. Dearest: as if anyone could help it.

EDSTASTON. Oh, dont make me feel like a fool. But, though it does sound conceited to say it, I flatter myself I'm better looking than Patiomkin and the other hogs she is accustomed to. Anyhow, I darent risk staying.

CLAIRE. What a nuisance! Mamma will be furious at having to pack, and at missing the Court ball this evening.

EDSTASTON. I cant help that. We havnt a moment to lose.

CLAIRE. May I tell her she will be knouted if we stay?

EDSTASTON. Do, dearest.

He kisses her and lets her go, expecting her to run into the house.

CLAIRE [*pausing thoughtfully*] Is she—is she good-looking when you see her close?

EDSTASTON. Not a patch on you, dearest.

CLAIRE [*jealous*] Then you did see her close?

EDSTASTON. Fairly close.

CLAIRE. Indeed! How close? No: thats silly of me: I will tell mamma. [*She is going out when Naryshkin enters with the Sergeant and a squad of soldiers*]. What do you want here?

The Sergeant goes to Edstaston; plumps down on his knees; and takes out a magnificent pair of pistols with gold grips. He proffers them to Edstaston, holding them by the barrels.

NARYSHKIN. Captain Edstaston: his Highness Prince Patiomkin sends you the pistols he promised you.

THE SERGEANT. Take them, Little Father; and do not forget us poor soldiers who have brought them to you; for God knows we get but little to drink

EDSTASTON [*irresolutely*] But I cant take these valuable things. By Jiminy, though, theyre beautiful! Look at them, Claire.

As he is taking the pistols the kneeling Sergeant suddenly drops them; flings himself forward; and embraces Edstaston's hips to prevent him from drawing his own pistols from his boots.

THE SERGEANT. Lay hold of him there. Pin his arms. I have his pistols. [*The soldiers seize Edstaston*].

EDSTASTON. Ah, would you, damn you! [*He drives his knee into the Sergeant's epigastrium, and struggles furiously with his captors*].

THE SERGEANT [*rolling on the ground, gasping and groaning*] Owgh! Murder! Holy Nicholas! Owwwgh!

CLAIRE. Help! help! They are killing Charles. Help!

NARYSHKIN [*seizing her and clapping his hand over her mouth*] Tie him neck and crop. Ten thousand blows of the stick if you let him go. [*Claire twists herself loose; turns on him; and cuffs him furiously*] Yow—ow! Have mercy, Little Mother.

CLAIRE. You wretch! Help! Help! Police! We are being murdered. Help!

The Sergeant, who has risen, comes to Naryshkin's rescue, and grasps Claire's hands, enabling Naryshkin to gag her again. By this time Edstaston and his captors are all rolling on the ground together. They get Edstaston on his back and fasten his wrists together behind his knees. Next they put a broad strap round his ribs. Finally they pass a pole through this breast strap and through the wrist strap and lift him by it, helplessly trussed up, to carry him off. Meanwhile he is by no means suffering in silence.

EDSTASTON [*gasping*] You shall hear more of this. Damn you, will you untie me? I will complain to the ambassador. I will write to the Gazette. England will blow your trumpery little fleet out of the water and sweep your tinpot army into Siberia for this. Will you let me go? Damn you! Curse you! What the devil do you mean by it? I'll—I'll—[*he is carried out of hearing*].

NARYSHKIN [*snatching his hands from Claire's face with a scream, and shaking his finger frantically*] Agh! [*The Sergeant, amazed, lets go her hands*]. She has bitten me, the little vixen.

CLAIRE [*spitting and wiping her mouth disgustedly*] How dare you put your dirty paws on my mouth? Ugh? Psha!

THE SERGEANT. Be merciful, Little angel Mother.

CLAIRE. Do not presume to call me your little angel mother. Where are the police?

NARYSHKIN. We are the police in St Petersburg, little spitfire.

THE SERGEANT. God knows we have no orders to harm you, Little Mother. Our duty is done. You are well and strong; but I shall never be the same man again. He is a mighty and terrible fighter, as stout as a bear. He has broken my sweetbread with his strong knees. God knows poor folk should not be set upon such dangerous adversaries!

CLAIRE. Serve you right! Where have they taken Captain Edstaston to?

NARYSHKIN [*spitefully*] To the Empress, little beauty. He has insulted the Empress. He will receive a hundred and one blows of the knout. [*He laughs and goes out, nursing his bitten finger*].

THE SERGEANT. He will feel only the first twenty; and he will be mercifully dead long before the end, little darling.

CLAIRE [*sustained by an invincible snobbery*] They dare not touch an English officer. I will go to the Empress myself; she cannot know who Captain Edstaston is— who we are.

THE SERGEANT. Do so in the name of the Holy Nicholas, little beauty.

CLAIRE. Dont be impertinent. How can I get admission to the palace?

THE SERGEANT. Everybody goes in and out of the palace, little love.

CLAIRE. But I must get into the Empress's presence. I must speak to her.

THE SERGEANT. You shall, dear Little Mother. You shall give the poor old Sergeant a rouble; and the blessed Nicholas will make your salvation his charge.

CLAIRE [impetuously] I will give you [she is about to say fifty roubles, but checks herself cautiously]—Well: I dont mind giving you two roubles if I can speak to the Empress.

THE SERGEANT [joyfully] I praise Heaven for you, Little Mother. Come. [He leads the way out]. It was the temptation of the devil that led your man to bruise my vitals and deprive me of breath. We must be merciful to one another's faults.

A triangular recess communicating by a heavily curtained arch with the huge ballroom of the palace. The light is subdued by red shades on the candles. In the wall adjoining that pierced by the arch is a door. The only piece of furniture is a very handsome chair on the arch side. In the ballroom they are dancing a polonaise to the music of a brass band.

Naryshkin enters through the door, followed by the soldiers carrying Edstaston, still trussed to the pole. Exhausted and dogged, he makes no sound.

NARYSHKIN Halt. Get that pole clear of the prisoner. [*They dump Edstaston on the floor, and detach the pole. Naryshkin stoops over him and addresses him insultingly*]. Well! are you ready to be tortured? This is the Empress's private torture chamber. Can I do anything to make you quite comfortable? You have only to mention it.

EDSTASTON. Have you any back teeth?

NARYSHKIN [*surprised*] Why?

EDSTASTON. His Majesty King George the Third will send for six of them when the news of this reaches London; so look out, damn your eyes!

NARYSHKIN [*frightened*] Oh, I assure you I am only obeying my orders. Personally I abhor torture, and would save you if I could. But the Empress is proud; and what woman would forgive the slight you put upon her?

EDSTASTON. As I said before: Damn your eyes!

NARYSHKIN [*almost in tears*] Well, it isnt my fault.

[*To the soldiers, insolently*] You know your orders? You remember what you have to do when the Empress gives you the word? [*The soldiers salute in assent*].

Naryshkin passes through the curtains, admitting a blare of music and a strip of brilliant white candle-light from the chandeliers in the ballroom as he does so. The white light vanishes and the music is muffled as the curtains fall together behind him. Presently the band stops abruptly; and Naryshkin comes back through the curtains. He makes a warning gesture to the soldiers, who stand at attention. Then he moves the curtain to allow Catherine to enter. She is in full Imperial regalia, and stops sternly just where she has entered. The soldiers fall on their knees.

CATHERINE. Obey your orders.

The soldiers seize Edstaston, and throw him roughly at the feet of the Empress.

CATHERINE [*looking down coldly on him*] Also [*the German word*] you have put me to the trouble of sending for you twice. You had better have come the first time.

EDSTASTON [*exsufflicate, and pettishly angry*] I havnt come either time. Ive been carried. I call it infernal impudence.

CATHERINE. Take care what you say.

EDSTASTON. No use. I daresay you look very majestic and very handsome; but I cant see you; and I am not intimidated. I am an Englishman; and you can kidnap me; but you cant bully me.

NARYSHKIN. Remember to whom you are speaking.

CATHERINE [*violently, furious at his intrusion*] Remember that dogs should be dumb. [*He shrivels*]. And do you, Captain, remember that famous as I am for my clemency, there are limits to the patience even of an Empress.

EDSTASTON. How is a man to remember anything when he is trussed up in this ridiculous fashion? I can hardly breathe. [*He makes a futile struggle to free himself*]. Here: dont be unkind, your Majesty: tell these fellows to unstrap me. You know you really owe me an apology.

CATHERINE. You think you can escape by appealing, like Prince Patiomkin, to my sense of humor?

EDSTASTON. Sense of humor! Ho! Ha, ha! I like that. Would anybody with a sense of humor make a guy of a man like this, and then expect him to take it seriously? I say: do tell them to loosen these straps.

CATHERINE [*seating herself*] Why should I, pray?

EDSTASTON. Why! Why!! Why, because theyre hurting me.

CATHERINE. People sometimes learn through suffering. Manners, for instance.

EDSTASTON. Oh, well, of course, if youre an ill-natured woman, hurting me on purpose, I have nothing more to say.

CATHERINE. A monarch, sir, has sometimes to employ a necessary and salutary severity—

EDSTASTON [*interrupting her petulantly*] Quack! quack! quack!

CATHERINE. Donnerwetter!

EDSTASTON [*continuing recklessly*] This isnt severity: it's tomfoolery. And if you think it's reforming my character or teaching me anything, youre mistaken. It may be a satisfaction to you; but if it is, all I can say is that it's not an amiable satisfaction.

CATHERINE [*turning suddenly and balefully on Naryshkin*] What are you grinning at?

NARYSHKIN [*falling on his knees in terror*] Be merciful, Little Mother. My heart is in my mouth.

CATHERINE. Your heart and your mouth will be in

two separate parts of your body if you again forget
in whose presence you stand. Go. And take your men
with you. [*Naryshkin crawls to the door. The soldiers
rise*]. Stop. Roll that [*indicating Edstaston*] nearer.
[*The soldiers obey*]. Not so close. Did I ask you for a
footstool? [*She pushes Edstaston away with her foot*].

EDSTASTON [*with a sudden squeal*] Agh!!! I must
really ask your Majesty not to put the point of your
Imperial toe between my ribs. I am ticklesome.

CATHERINE. Indeed? All the more reason for you
to treat me with respect, Captain. [*To the others*] Be-
gone. How many times must I give an order before
it is obeyed?

NARYSHKIN. Little Mother: they have brought some
instruments of torture. Will they be needed?

CATHERINE [*indignantly*] How dare you name such
abominations to a Liberal Empress? You will always
be a savage and a fool, Naryshkin. These relics of
barbarism are buried, thank God, in the grave of
Peter the Great. My methods are more civilized.
[*She extends her toe towards Edstaston's ribs*].

EDSTASTON [*shrieking hysterically*] Yagh! Ah! [*Furiously*] If your Majesty does that again I will write to
the London Gazette.

CATHERINE [*to the soldiers*] Leave us. Quick! do you
hear? Five thousand blows of the stick for the soldier
who is in the room when I speak next [*The soldiers
rush out*]. Naryshkin: are you waiting to be knouted?
[*Naryshkin backs out hastily*].

*Catherine and Edstaston are now alone. Catherine
has in her hand a sceptre or baton of gold. Wrapped
round it is a new pamphlet, in French, entitled L'Homme
aux Quarante Écus. She calmly unrolls this and begins
to read it at her ease as if she were quite alone. Several
seconds elapse in dead silence. She becomes more and*

*more absorbed in the pamphlet, and more and more
amused by it.*

CATHERINE [*greatly pleased by a passage, and turning
over the leaf*] Ausgezeichnet!

EDSTASTON. Ahem!

Silence. Catherine reads on.

CATHERINE. Wie komisch!

EDSTASTON. Ahem! ahem!

Silence.

CATHERINE [*soliloquizing enthusiastically*] What a
wonderful author is Monsieur Voltaire! How lucidly
he exposes the folly of this crazy plan for raising the
entire revenue of the country from a single tax on
land! how he withers it with his irony! how he makes
you laugh whilst he is convincing you! how sure one
feels that the proposal is killed by his wit and economic
penetration: killed never to be mentioned again
among educated people!

EDSTASTON. For Heaven's sake, Madam, do you
intend to leave me tied up like this while you discuss
the blasphemies of that abominable infidel? Agh!!
[*She has again applied her toe*]. Oh! Oo!

CATHERINE [*calmly*] Do I understand you to say that
Monsieur Voltaire is a great philanthropist and a
great philosopher as well as the wittiest man in
Europe?

EDSTASTON. Certainly not. I say that his books ought
to be burnt by the common hangman [*her toe touches
his ribs*]. Yagh! Oh dont. I shall faint. I cant bear it.

CATHERINE. Have you changed your opinion of
Monsieur Voltaire?

EDSTASTON. But you cant expect me as a member
of the Church of England [*she tickles him*]—Agh. Ow!
Oh Lord! he is anything you like. He is a philanthropist, a philosopher, a beauty: he ought to have a

statue, damn him! [*she tickles him*] No! bless him! save him victorious, happy and glorious! Oh, let eternal honors crown his name: Voltaire thrice worthy on the rolls of fame! [*Exhausted*]. Now will you let me up? And look here! I can see your ankles when you tickle me: it's not ladylike.

CATHERINE [*sticking out her toe and admiring it critically*] Is the spectacle so disagreeable?

EDSTASTON. It's agreeable enough; only [*with intense expression*] for heaven's sake dont touch me in the ribs.

CATHERINE [*putting aside the pamphlet*] Captain Edstaston: why did you refuse to come when I sent for you?

EDSTASTON. Madam: I cannot talk tied up like this.

CATHERINE. Do you still admire me as much as you did this morning?

EDSTASTON. How can I possibly tell when I cant see you? Let me get up and look. I cant see anything now except my toes and yours.

CATHERINE. Do you still intend to write to the London Gazette about me?

EDSTASTON. Not if you will loosen these straps. Quick: loosen me. I'm fainting.

CATHERINE. I dont think you are [*tickling him*].

EDSTASTON. Agh! Cat!

CATHERINE. What [*she tickles him again*]!

EDSTASTON [*with a shriek*] No: angel, angel!

CATHERINE [*tenderly*] Geliebter!

EDSTASTON. I dont know a word of German; but that sounded kind. [*Becoming hysterical*] Little Mother, beautiful little darling angel mother: dont be cruel: untie me. Oh, I beg and implore you. Dont be unkind. I shall go mad.

CATHERINE. You are expected to go mad with love when an Empress deigns to interest herself in you.

When an Empress allows you to see her foot you should kiss it. Captain Edstaston: you are a booby.

EDSTASTON [*indignantly*] I am nothing of the kind. I have been mentioned in dispatches as a highly intelligent officer. And let me warn your Majesty that I am not so helpless as you think. The English Ambassador is in that ballroom. A shout from me will bring him to my side; and then where will your Majesty be?

CATHERINE. I should like to see the English Ambassador or anyone else pass through that curtain against my orders. It might be a stone wall ten feet thick. Shout your loudest. Sob. Curse. Scream. Yell [*she tickles him unmercifully*].

EDSTASTON [*frantically*] Ahowyow!!!! Agh! Ooh! Stop! Oh Lord! Ya-a-a-ah! [*A tumult in the ballroom responds to his cries*].

VOICES FROM THE BALLROOM. Stand back. You cannot pass. Hold her back there. The Empress's orders. It is out of the question. No, little darling, not in there. Nobody is allowed in there. You will be sent to Siberia. Dont let her through there, on your life. Drag her back. You will be knouted. It is hopeless, Mademoiselle: you must obey orders. Guard there! Send some men to hold her.

CLAIRE'S VOICE. Let me go. They are torturing Charles in there. I will go. How can you all dance as if nothing was happening? Let me go, I tell you. Let—me—go. [*She dashes through the curtain. No one dares follow her*].

CATHERINE [*rising in wrath*] How dare you?

CLAIRE [*recklessly*] Oh, dare your grandmother! Where is my Charles? What are they doing to him?

EDSTASTON [*shouting*] Claire: loosen these straps, in Heaven's name. Quick.

CLAIRE [*seeing him and throwing herself on her knees*

at his side] Oh, how dare they tie you up like that! [*To Catherine*] You wicked wretch! You Russian savage! [*She pounces on the straps, and begins unbuckling them*].

CATHERINE [*conquering herself with a mighty effort*] Now self-control. Self-control, Catherine. Philosophy. Europe is looking on. [*She forces herself to sit down*].

EDSTASTON. Steady, dearest: it is the Empress. Call her your Imperial Majesty. Call her Star of the North, Little Mother, Little Darling: thats what she likes; but get the straps off.

CLAIRE. Keep quiet, dear: I cannot get them off if you move.

CATHERINE [*calmly*] Keep quite still, Captain [*she tickles him*].

EDSTASTON. Ow! Agh! Ahowyow!

CLAIRE [*stopping dead in the act of unbuckling the straps and turning sick with jealousy as she grasps the situation*] Was that what I thought was your being tortured?

CATHERINE [*urbanely*] That is the favorite torture of Catherine the Second, Mademoiselle. I think the Captain enjoys it very much.

CLAIRE. Then he can have as much more of it as he wants. I am sorry I intruded. [*She rises to go*].

EDSTASTON [*catching her train in his teeth and holding on like a bull-dog*] Dont go. Dont leave me in this horrible state. Loosen me. [*This is what he is saying; but as he says it with the train in his mouth it is not very intelligible*].

CLAIRE. Let go. You are undignified and ridiculous enough yourself without making me ridiculous. [*She snatches her train away*].

EDSTASTON. Ow! Youve nearly pulled my teeth out: youre worse than the Star of the North. [*To Catherine*] Darling Little Mother: you have a kind heart, the kindest in Europe. Have pity. Have mercy. I love you. [*Claire bursts into tears*]. Release me.

CATHERINE. Well, just to shew you how much kinder a Russian savage can be than an English one (though I am sorry to say I am a German) here goes! [*She stoops to loosen the straps*].

CLAIRE [*jealously*] You neednt trouble, thank you. [*She pounces on the straps; and the two set Edstaston free between them*]. Now get up, please; and conduct yourself with some dignity if you are not utterly demoralized.

EDSTASTON. Dignity! Ow! I cant. I'm stiff all over. I shall never be able to stand up again. Oh Lord! how it hurts! [*They seize him by the shoulders and drag him up*]. Yah! Agh! Wow! Oh! Mmmmmm! Oh, Little Angel Mother, dont ever do this to a man again. Knout him; kill him; roast him; baste him; head, hang, and quarter him; but dont tie him up like that and tickle him.

CATHERINE. Your young lady seems still to think that you enjoyed it.

CLAIRE. I know what I think. I will never speak to him again. Your Majesty can keep him, as far as I am concerned.

CATHERINE. I would not deprive you of him for worlds; though really I think he's rather a darling [*she pats his cheek*].

CLAIRE [*snorting*] So I see, indeed.

EDSTASTON. Dont be angry, dearest: in this country everybody's a darling. I'll prove it to you. [*To Catherine*] Will your Majesty be good enough to call Prince Patiomkin?

CATHERINE [*surprised into haughtiness*] Why?

EDSTASTON. To oblige me.

Catherine laughs good-humoredly and goes to the

curtains and opens them. The band strikes up a Redowa.

CATHERINE [*calling imperiously*] Patiomkin! [*The music stops suddenly*] Here! To me! Go on with your music there, you fools. [*The Redowa is resumed*].

The sergeant rushes from the ballroom to relieve the Empress of the curtain. Patiomkin comes in dancing with Varinka.

CATHERINE [*to Patiomkin*] The English captain wants you, little darling.

Catherine resumes her seat as Patiomkin intimates by a grotesque bow that he is at Edstaston's service. Varinka passes behind Edstaston and Claire, and posts herself on Claire's right.

EDSTASTON. Precisely. [*To Claire*] You observe, my love: "little darling." Well, if her Majesty calls him a darling, is it my fault that she calls me one too?

CLAIRE. I dont care: I dont think you ought to have done it. I am very angry and offended.

EDSTASTON. They tied me up, dear. I couldn't help it. I fought for all I was worth.

THE SERGEANT [*at the curtains*] He fought with the strength of lions and bears. God knows I shall carry a broken sweetbread to my grave.

EDSTASTON. You cant mean to throw me over, Claire. [*Urgently*] Claire. Claire.

VARINKA [*in a transport of sympathetic emotion, pleading with clasped hands to Claire*] Oh, sweet little angel lamb, he loves you: it shines in his darling eyes. Pardon him, pardon him.

PATIOMKIN [*rushing from the Empress's side to Claire and falling on his knees to her*] Pardon him, pardon him, little cherub! little wild duck! little star! little glory! little jewel in the crown of heaven!

CLAIRE. This is perfectly ridiculous.

VARINKA [*kneeling to her*] Pardon him, pardon him, little delight, little sleeper in a rosy cradle.

CLAIRE. I'll do anything if youll only let me alone.

THE SERGEANT [*kneeling to her*] Pardon him, pardon him, lest the mighty man bring his whip to you. God knows we all need pardon!

CLAIRE [*at the top of her voice*] I pardon him! I pardon him!

PATIOMKIN [*springing up joyfully and going behind Claire, whom he raises in his arms*] Embrace her, victor of Bunker's Hill. Kiss her till she swoons.

THE SERGEANT. Receive her in the name of the holy Nicholas.

VARINKA. She begs you for a thousand dear little kisses all over her body.

CLAIRE [*vehemently*] I do not. [*Patiomkin throws her into Edstaston's arms*]. Oh! [*The pair, awkward and shamefaced, recoil from one another, and remain utterly inexpressive*].

CATHERINE [*pushing Edstaston towards Claire*] There is no help for it, Captain. This is Russia, not England.

EDSTASTON [*plucking up some geniality, and kissing Claire ceremoniously on the brow*] I have no objection.

VARINKA [*disgusted*] Only one kiss! and on the forehead! Fish. See how I kiss, though it is only my horribly ugly old uncle [*she throws her arms round Patiomkin's neck and covers his face with kisses*].

THE SERGEANT [*moved to tears*] Sainted Nicholas: bless your lambs!

CATHERINE. Do you wonder now that I love Russia as I love no other place on earth?

NARYSHKIN [*appearing at the door*] Majesty: the model for the new museum has arrived.

CATHERINE [*rising eagerly and making for the curtains*] Let us go. I can think of nothing but my museum. [*In the archway she stops and turns to Edstaston, who has hurried to lift the curtain for her*]. Captain: I wish you every happiness that your little angel can bring you. [*For his ear alone*] I could have brought you more: but you did not think so. Farewell.

EDSTASTON [*kissing her hand, which, instead of releasing, he holds caressingly and rather patronizingly in his own*] I feel your Majesty's kindness so much that I really cannot leave you without a word of plain wholesome English advice.

CATHERINE [*snatching her hand away and bounding forward as if he had touched her with a spur*] Advice!!!

PATIOMKIN. Madman: take care!

NARYSHKIN. Advise the Empress!!

THE SERGEANT. Sainted Nicholas!

VARINKA. Hoo hoo! [*a stifled splutter of laughter*].

[*exclaiming simultaneously*].

EDSTASTON [*following the Empress and resuming kindly but judicially*] After all, though your Majesty is of course a great queen, yet when all is said, I am a man; and your Majesty is only a woman.

CATHERINE. Only a wo—[*she chokes*].

EDSTASTON [*continuing*] Believe me, this Russian extravagance will not do. I appreciate as much as any man the warmth of heart that prompts it; but it is overdone: it is hardly in the best taste: it is—really I must say it—it is not proper.

CATHERINE [*ironically, in German*] So!

EDSTASTON. Not that I cannot make allowances. Your Majesty has, I know, been unfortunate in your experience as a married woman—

CATHERINE [*furious*] Alle Wetter!!!

EDSTASTON [*sentimentally*] Dont say that. Dont think of him in that way. After all, he was your husband; and whatever his faults may have been, it is not for you to think unkindly of him.

CATHERINE [*almost bursting*] I shall forget myself.

EDSTASTON. Come! I am sure he really loved you; and you truly loved him.

CATHERINE [*controlling herself with a supreme effort*] No, Catherine. What would Voltaire say?

EDSTASTON. Oh, never mind that vile scoffer. Set an example to Europe, Madam, by doing what I am going to do. Marry again. Marry some good man who will be a strength and support to your old age.

CATHERINE. My old—[*she again becomes speechless*].

EDSTASTON. Yes: we must all grow old, even the handsomest of us.

CATHERINE [*sinking into her chair with a gasp*] Thank you.

EDSTASTON. You will thank me more when you see your little ones round your knee, and your man there by the fireside in the winter evenings—by the way, I forgot that you have no firesides here in spite of the coldness of the climate; so shall I say by the stove?

CATHERINE. Certainly, if you wish. The stove, by all means.

EDSTASTON [*impulsively*] Ah, Madam, abolish the stove: believe me, there is nothing like the good old open grate. Home! duty! happiness! they all mean the same thing; and they all flourish best on the drawing room hearthrug. [*Turning to Claire*] And now, my love, we must not detain the Queen: she is anxious to inspect the model of her museum, to which I am sure we wish every success.

CLAIRE [*coldly*] *I* am not detaining her.

EDSTASTON. Well, goodbye [*wringing Patiomkin's hand*], goo-oo-oodbye, Prince: come and see us if ever you visit England. Spire View, Deepdene, Little Mugford, Devon, will always find me. [*To Varinka, kissing her hand*] Goodbye, Mademoiselle: goodbye, Little Mother, if I may call you that just once. [*Varinka puts up her face to be kissed*]. Eh? No, no, no, no: you dont mean that, you know. Naughty! [*To the Sergeant*] Goodbye, my friend. You will drink our healths with this [*tipping him*].

THE SERGEANT. The blessed Nicholas will multiply your fruits, Little Father.

EDSTASTON. Goodbye, goodbye, goodbye, goodbye, goodbye, goodbye.

He goes out backwards bowing, with Claire curtseying, having been listened to in utter dumbfoundedness by Patiomkin and Naryshkin, in childlike awe by Varinka, and with quite inexpressible feelings by Catherine. When he is out of sight she rises with clenched fists and raises her arm and her closed eyes to Heaven. Patiomkin, rousing himself from his stupor of amazement, springs to her like a tiger, and throws himself at her feet.

PATIOMKIN. What shall I do to him for you? Skin him alive? Cut off his eyelids and stand him in the sun? Tear his tongue out? What shall it be?

CATHERINE [*opening her eyes*] Nothing. But oh, if I could only have had him for my—for my—for my—

PATIOMKIN [*in a growl of jealousy*] For your lover?

CATHERINE [*with an ineffable smile*] No: for my museum.

The Inca of Perusalem:
An Almost Historical Comedietta

Composition begun August 1915; completed before 9 August 1915. Published in *Heartbreak House, Great Catherine, & Playlets of the War*, 1919. First presented at the Repertory Theatre, Birmingham, 7 October 1916.

The Archdeacon *Joseph A. Dodd*
Ermyntrude Roosenhonkers-Pipstein
                    Gertrude Kingston
Hotel Manager *Noel Shammon*
The Princess *Cathleen Orford*
Waiter *William Armstrong*
The Inca of Perusalem *Felix Aylmer*

Period—1916

Prologue: *Before the Curtain*

The Play: *A Hotel Sitting Room*

I must remind the reader that this playlet was written when its principal character, far from being a fallen foe and virtually a prisoner in our victorious hands, was still the Caesar whose legions we were resisting with our hearts in our mouths. Many were so horribly afraid of him that they could not forgive me for not being afraid of him: I seemed to be trifling heartlessly with a deadly peril. I knew better; and I have represented Caesar as knowing better himself. But it was one of the quaintnesses of popular feeling during the war that anyone who breathed the slightest doubt of the absolute perfection of German organization, the Machiavellian depth of German diplomacy, the omniscience of German science, the equipment of every German with a complete philosophy of history, and the consequent hopelessness of overcoming so magnificently accomplished an enemy except by the sacrifice of every recreative activity to incessant and vehement war work, including a heartbreaking mass of fussing and cadging and bluffing that did nothing but waste our energies and tire our resolution, was called a pro-German.

Now that this is all over, and the upshot of the fighting has shewn that we could quite well have afforded to laugh at the doomed Inca, I am in another difficulty. I may be supposed to be hitting Caesar when he is down. That is why I preface the play with this reminder that when it was written he was not down. To make quite sure, I have gone through the proof sheets very carefully, and deleted everything that could possibly be mistaken for a foul blow. I have of course maintained the ancient privilege of comedy to chasten Caesar's foibles by laughing at them, whilst introducing enough obvious and outrageous fiction to relieve both myself and my model from the obligations and responsibilities of sober history and biography. But I should certainly put the play in the fire instead of publishing it if it contained a word against our defeated enemy that I would not have written in 1913.

*The tableau curtains are closed. An English archdeacon
comes through them in a condition of extreme irritation.
He speaks through the curtains to someone behind them.*

THE ARCHDEACON. Once for all, Ermyntrude, I
cannot afford to maintain you in your present extravagance. [*He goes to a flight of steps leading to the
stalls and sits down disconsolately on the top step. A
fashionably dressed lady comes through the curtains and
contemplates him with patient obstinacy. He continues,
grumbling*] An English clergyman's daughter should
be able to live quite respectably and comfortably on
an allowance of £150 a year, wrung with great difficulty from the domestic budget.

ERMYNTRUDE. You are not a common clergyman:
you are an archdeacon.

THE ARCHDEACON [*angrily*] That does not affect
my emoluments to the extent of enabling me to
support a daughter whose extravagance would disgrace a royal personage. [*Scrambling to his feet and
scolding at her*] What do you mean by it, Miss?

ERMYNTRUDE. Oh really, father! Miss! Is that the
way to talk to a widow.

THE ARCHDEACON. Is that the way to talk to a father?
Your marriage was a most disastrous imprudence. It
gave you habits that are absolutely beyond your means
—I mean beyond my means: you have no means.
Why did you not marry Matthews: the best curate I
ever had?

ERMYNTRUDE. I wanted to; and you wouldnt let me.

[953]

You insisted on my marrying Roosenhonkers-Pipstein.

THE ARCHDEACON. I had to do the best for you, my child. Roosenhonkers-Pipstein was a millionaire.

ERMYNTRUDE. How do you know he was a millionaire?

THE ARCHDEACON. He came from America. Of course he was a millionaire. Besides, he proved to my solicitors that he had fifteen million dollars when you married him.

ERMYNTRUDE. His solicitors proved to me that he had sixteen millions when he died. He was a millionaire to the last.

THE ARCHDEACON. O Mammon, Mammon! I am punished now for bowing the knee to him. Is there nothing left of your settlement? Fifty thousand dollars a year it secured to you, as we all thought. Only half the securities could be called speculative. The other half were gilt-edged. What has become of it all?

ERMYNTRUDE. The speculative ones were not paid up; and the gilt-edged ones just paid the calls on them until the whole show burst up.

THE ARCHDEACON. Ermyntrude: what expressions!

ERMYNTRUDE. Oh bother! If you had lost ten thousand a year what expressions would you use, do you think? The long and the short of it is that I cant live in the squalid way you are accustomed to.

THE ARCHDEACON. Squalid!

ERMYNTRUDE. I have formed habits of comfort.

THE ARCHDEACON. Comfort!!

ERMYNTRUDE. Well, elegance if you like. Luxury, if you insist. Call it what you please. A house that costs less than a hundred thousand dollars a year to run is intolerable to me.

THE ARCHDEACON. Then, my dear, you had better

become lady's maid to a princess until you can find another millionaire to marry you.

ERMYNTRUDE. Thats an idea. I will [*She vanishes through the curtains*].

THE ARCHDEACON. What! Come back, Miss. Come back this instant. [*The lights are lowered*]. Oh, very well: I have nothing more to say. [*He descends the steps into the auditorium and makes for the door, grumbling all the time*]. Insane, senseless extravagance! [*Barking*] Worthlessness!! [*Muttering*] I will not bear it any longer. Dresses, hats, furs, gloves, motor rides: one bill after another: money going like water. No restraint, no self-control, no decency. [*Shrieking*] I say, no decency! [*Muttering again*] Nice state of things we are coming to! A pretty world! But I simply will not bear it. She can do as she likes. I wash my hands of her: I am not going to die in the workhouse for any good-for-nothing, undutiful, spendthrift daughter; and the sooner that is understood by everybody the better for all par —[*He is by this time out of hearing in the corridor*].

[THE PLAY]

A hotel sitting room. A table in the centre. On it a telephone. Two chairs at it, opposite one another. Behind it, the door. The fireplace has a mirror in the mantelpiece.

A spinster Princess, hatted and gloved, is ushered in by the Hotel Manager, spruce and artificially bland by professional habit, but treating his customer with a condescending affability which sails very close to the east wind of insolence.

THE MANAGER. I am sorry I am unable to accommodate Your Highness on the first floor.

THE PRINCESS [*very shy and nervous*] Oh please dont mention it. This is quite nice. Very nice. Thank you very much.

THE MANAGER. We could prepare a room in the annexe—

THE PRINCESS. Oh no. This will do very well.

She takes off her gloves and hat; puts them on the table; and sits down.

THE MANAGER. The rooms are quite as good up here. There is less noise; and there is the lift. If Your Highness desires anything, there is the telephone—

THE PRINCESS. Oh, thank you, I dont want anything. The telephone is so difficult: I am not accustomed to it.

THE MANAGER. Can I take any order? Some tea?

THE PRINCESS. Oh, thank you. Yes: I should like some tea, if I might—if it would not be too much trouble.

He goes out. The telephone rings. The Princess starts out of her chair, terrified, and recoils as far as possible from the instrument.

THE PRINCESS. Oh dear! [*It rings again. She looks scared. It rings again. She approaches it timidly. It rings again. She retreats hastily. It rings repeatedly. She runs to it in desperation and puts the receiver to her ear*]. Who is there? What do I do? I am not used to the telephone: I dont know how—What! Oh, I can hear you speaking quite distinctly. [*She sits down, delighted, and settles herself for a conversation*]. How wonderful! What! A lady? Oh! a person. Oh yes: I know. Yes, please, send her up. Have my servants finished their lunch yet? Oh no: please dont disturb them: I'd rather not. It doesnt matter. Thank you. What? Oh yes, it's quite easy. I had no idea—am I to hang it up just as it was? Thank you. [*She hangs it up*].

Ermyntrude enters, presenting a plain and staid appearance in a long straight waterproof with a hood over her head gear. She comes to the end of the table opposite to that at which the Princess is seated.

THE PRINCESS. Excuse me. I have been talking through the telephone; and I heard quite well, though I have never ventured before. Wont you sit down?

ERMYNTRUDE. No, thank you, Your Highness. I am only a lady's maid. I understood you wanted one.

THE PRINCESS. Oh no: you mustnt think I want one. It's so unpatriotic to want anything now, on account of the war, you know. I sent my maid away as a public duty; and now she has married a soldier and is expecting a war baby. But I dont know how to do without her. Ive tried my very best; but somehow it doesn't answer: everybody cheats me; and in the end it isnt any saving. So Ive made up my mind to sell my piano and have a maid. That will be a real saving, because I really dont care a bit for music, though of course one has to pretend to. Dont you think so?

ERMYNTRUDE. Certainly I do, Your Highness. Nothing could be more correct. Saving and self-denial both at once; and an act of kindness to me, as I am out of place.

THE PRINCESS. I'm so glad you see it in that way. Er—you wont mind my asking, will you?—how did you lose your place?

ERMYNTRUDE. The war, Your Highness, the war.

THE PRINCESS. Oh yes, of course. But how—

ERMYNTRUDE [*taking out her handkerchief and shewing signs of grief*] My poor mistress—

THE PRINCESS. Oh please say no more. Dont think about it. So tactless of me to mention it.

ERMYNTRUDE [*mastering her emotion and smiling through her tears*] Your Highness is too good.

THE PRINCESS. Do you think you could be happy with me? I attach such importance to that.

ERMYNTRUDE [*gushing*] Oh, I know I shall.

THE PRINCESS. You must not expect too much. There is my uncle. He is very severe and hasty; and he is my guardian. I once had a maid I liked very much; but he sent her away the very first time.

ERMYNTRUDE. The first time of what. Your Highness?

THE PRINCESS. Oh, something she did. I am sure she had never done it before; and I know she would never have done it again, she was so truly contrite and nice about it.

ERMYNTRUDE. About what, Your Highness?

THE PRINCESS. Well, she wore my jewels and one of my dresses at a rather improper ball with her young man; and my uncle saw her.

ERMYNTRUDE. Then he was at the ball, too, Your Highness?

THE PRINCESS [*struck by the inference*] I suppose he must have been. I wonder! You know, it's very sharp of you to find that out. I hope you are not too sharp.

ERMYNTRUDE. A lady's maid has to be, Your Highness. [*She produces some letters*]. Your Highness wishes to see my testimonials, no doubt. I have one from an Archdeacon. [*She proffers the letters*].

THE PRINCESS [*taking them*] Do archdeacons have maids? How curious!

ERMYNTRUDE. No, Your Highness. They have daughters. I have first-rate testimonials from the Archdeacon and from his daughter.

THE PRINCESS [*reading them*] The daughter says you are in every respect a treasure. The Archdeacon says he would have kept you if he could possibly have afforded it. Most satisfactory, I'm sure.

ERMYNTRUDE. May I regard myself as engaged then, Your Highness?

THE PRINCESS [*alarmed*] Oh, I'm sure I dont know. If you like, of course; but do you think I ought to?

ERMYNTRUDE. Naturally I think Your Highness ought to, most decidedly.

THE PRINCESS. Oh well, if you think that, I daresay youre quite right. Youll excuse my mentioning it, I hope; but what wages—er—?

ERYMNTRUDE. The same as the maid who went to the ball. Your Highness need not make any change.

THE PRINCESS. M'yes. Of course she began with less. But she had such a number of relatives to keep! It was quite heartbreaking: I had to raise her wages again and again.

ERMYNTRUDE. I shall be quite content with what she began on; and I have no relatives dependent on me. And I am willing to wear my own dresses at balls.

THE PRINCESS. I am sure nothing could be fairer than that. My uncle cant object to that: can he?

ERMYNTRUDE. If he does, Your Highness, ask him to speak to me about it. I shall regard it as part of my duties to speak to your uncle about matters of business.

THE PRINCESS. Would you? You must be frightfully courageous.

ERMYNTRUDE. May I regard myself as engaged, Your Highness? I should like to set about my duties immediately.

THE PRINCESS. Oh yes, I think so. Oh certainly. I—

A waiter comes in with the tea. He places the tray on the table.

THE PRINCESS. Oh, thank you.

ERMYNTRUDE [*raising the cover from the tea cake and looking at it*] How long has that been standing at the top of the stairs?

THE PRINCESS [*terrified*] Oh please! It doesnt matter.

THE WAITER. It has not been waiting. Straight from the kitchen, madam, believe me.

ERMYNTRUDE. Send the manager here.

THE WAITER. The manager! What do you want with the manager?

ERMYNTRUDE. He will tell you when I have done with him. How dare you treat Her Highness in this disgraceful manner? What sort of pothouse is this? Where did you learn to speak to persons of quality? Take away your cold tea and cold cake instantly. Give them to the chambermaid you were flirting with whilst Her Highness was waiting. Order some fresh tea at once; and do not presume to bring it yourself: have it brought by a civil waiter who is accustomed to wait on ladies, and not, like you, on commercial travellers.

THE WAITER. Alas, madam, I am not accustomed to wait on anybody. Two years ago I was an eminent medical man. My waiting-room was crowded with the flower of the aristocracy and the higher bourgeoisie from nine to six every day. But the war came; and my patients were ordered to give up their luxuries. They gave up their doctors, but kept their weekend hotels, closing every career to me except the career of a waiter. [*He puts his fingers on the teapot to test its temperature, and automatically takes out his watch with the other hand as if to count the teapot's pulse*]. You are right: the tea is cold: it was made by the wife of a once fashionable architect. The cake is only half toasted: what can you expect from a ruined west-end tailor whose attempt to establish a second-hand business failed last Tuesday week? Have you the heart to complain to the manager? Have we not suffered enough! Are our miseries nev—[*the manager enters*] Oh Lord! here he is. [*The waiter withdraws abjectly, taking the tea tray with him*].

THE MANAGER. Pardon, Your Highness; but I have received an urgent inquiry for rooms from an English family of importance; and I venture to ask you to let me know how long you intend to honor us with your presence.

THE PRINCESS [*rising anxiously*] Oh! am I in the way?

ERMYNTRUDE [*sternly*] Sit down, madam [*The Princess sits down forlornly. Ermyntrude turns imperiously to the Manager*]. Her Highness will require this room for twenty minutes.

THE MANAGER. Twenty minutes!

ERMYNTRUDE. Yes: it will take fully that time to find a proper apartment in a respectable hotel.

THE MANAGER. I do not understand.

ERMYNTRUDE. You understand perfectly. How

dare you offer Her Highness a room on the second floor?

THE MANAGER. But I have explained. The first floor is occupied. At least—

ERMYNTRUDE. Well? At least?

THE MANAGER. It is occupied.

ERMYNTRUDE. Dont you dare tell Her Highness a falsehood. It is not occupied. You are saving it up for the arrival of the five fifteen express, from which you hope to pick up some fat armaments contractor who will drink all the bad champagne in your cellar at 25 francs a bottle, and pay twice over for everything because he is in the same hotel with Her Highness, and can boast of having turned her out of the best rooms.

THE MANAGER. But Her Highness was so gracious. I did not know that her Highness was at all particular.

ERMYNTRUDE. And you take advantage of Her Highness's graciousness. You impose on her with your stories. You give her a room not fit for a dog. You send cold tea to her by a decayed professional person disguised as a waiter. But dont think you can trifle with me. I am a lady's maid; and I know the ladies' maids and valets of all the aristocracies of Europe and all the millionaires of America. When I expose your hotel as the second-rate little hole it is, not a soul above the rank of a curate with a large family will be seen entering it. I shake its dust off my feet. Order the luggage to be taken down at once.

THE MANAGER [appealing to the Princess] Can Your Highness believe this of me? Have I had the misfortune to offend Your Highness?

THE PRINCESS. Oh no. I am quite satisfied. Please—

ERMYNTRUDE. Is Your Highness dissatisfied with me?

THE PRINCESS [intimidated] Oh no: please dont think that. I only meant—

ERMYNTRUDE [*to the Manager*] You hear. Perhaps
you think Her Highness is going to do the work of
teaching you your place herself, instead of leaving it
to her maid.

THE MANAGER. Oh please, mademoiselle. Believe
me: our only wish is to make you perfectly comfortable. But in consequence of the war, all royal personages now practise a rigid economy, and desire us to
treat them like their poorest subjects.

THE PRINCESS. Oh yes. You are quite right—

ERMYNTRUDE [*interrupting*] There! Her Highness
forgives you; but dont do it again. Now go downstairs,
my good man, and get that suite on the first floor
ready for us. And send some proper tea. And turn
on the heating apparatus until the temperature in the
rooms is comfortably warm. And have hot water put
in all the bedrooms—

THE MANAGER. There are basins with hot and cold
taps.

ERMYNTRUDE [*scornfully*] Yes: there would be. I
suppose we must put up with that: sinks in our rooms,
and pipes that rattle and bang and guggle all over the
house whenever anyone washes his hands. *I* know.

THE MANAGER [*gallant*] You are hard to please,
mademoiselle.

ERMYNTRUDE. No harder than other people. But
when I'm not pleased I'm not too ladylike to say so.
Thats all the difference. There is nothing more, thank
you.

*The Manager shrugs his shoulders resignedly; makes
a deep bow to the Princess; goes to the door; wafts a kiss
surreptitiously to Ermyntrude; and goes out.*

THE PRINCESS. It's wonderful! How have you the
courage?

ERMYNTRUDE. In Your Highness's service I know

[964]

no fear. Your Highness can leave all unpleasant people to me.

THE PRINCESS. How I wish I could! The most dreadful thing of all I have to go through myself.

ERMYNTRUDE. Dare I ask what it is, Your Highness?

THE PRINCESS. I'm going to be married. I'm to be met here and married to a man I never saw. A boy! A boy who never saw me! One of the sons of the Inca of Perusalem.

ERMYNTRUDE. Indeed? Which son?

THE PRINCESS. I dont know. They havnt settled which. It's a dreadful thing to be a princess: they just marry you to anyone they like. The Inca is to come and look at me, and pick out whichever of his sons he thinks will suit. And then I shall be an alien enemy everywhere except in Perusalem, because the Inca has made war on everybody. And I shall have to pretend that everybody has made war on him. It's too bad.

ERMYNTRUDE. Still, a husband is a husband. I wish I had one.

THE PRINCESS. Oh, how can you say that! I'm afraid youre not a nice woman.

ERMYNTRUDE. Your Highness is provided for. I'm not.

THE PRINCESS. Even if you could bear to let a man touch you, you shouldnt say so.

ERMYNTRUDE. I shall not say so again, Your Highness, except perhaps to the man.

THE PRINCESS. It's too dreadful to think of. I wonder you can be so coarse. I really dont think youll suit. I feel sure now that you know more about men than you should.

ERMYNTRUDE. I am a widow, Your Highness.

THE PRINCESS [overwhelmed] Oh, I BEG your pardon.

[965]

Of course I ought to have known you would not have spoken like that if you were not married. That makes it all right, doesn't it? I'm so sorry.

The Manager returns, white, scared, hardly able to speak.

THE MANAGER. Your Highness: an officer asks to see you on behalf of the Inca of Perusalem.

THE PRINCESS [*rising distractedly*] Oh, I cant, really. Oh, what shall I do?

THE MANAGER. On important business, he says, Your Highness. Captain Duval!

ERMYNTRUDE. Duval! Nonsense! The usual thing. It is the Inca himself, incognito.

THE PRINCESS. Oh, send him away. Oh, I'm so afraid of the Inca. I'm not properly dressed to receive him; and he is so particular: he would order me to stay in my room for a week. Tell him to call tomorrow: say I'm ill in bed. I cant: I wont: I darent: you must get rid of him somehow.

ERMYNTRUDE. Leave him to me, Your Highness.

THE PRINCESS. Youd never dare!

ERMYNTRUDE. I am an Englishwoman, Your Highness, and perfectly capable of tackling ten Incas if necessary. I will arrange the matter. [*To the Manager*] Shew Her Highness to her bedroom; and then shew Captain Duval in here.

THE PRINCESS. Oh, thank you so much. [*She goes to the door. Ermyntrude, noticing that she has left her hat and gloves on the table, runs after her with them*]. Oh, thank you. And oh, please, if I must have one of his sons, I should like a fair one that doesnt shave, with soft hair and a beard. I couldnt bear being kissed by a bristly person. [*She runs out, the Manager bowing as she passes. He follows her*].

Ermyntrude whips off her waterproof; hides it; and

gets herself swiftly into perfect trim at the mirror, before the Manager, with a large jewel case in his hand, returns, ushering in the Inca.

THE MANAGER. Captain Duval.

The Inca, in military uniform, advances with a marked and imposing stage walk; stops; orders the trembling Manager by a gesture to place the jewel case on the table; dismisses him with a frown; touches his helmet graciously to Ermyntrude; and takes off his cloak.

THE INCA. I beg you, madam, to be quite at your ease, and to speak to me without ceremony.

ERMYNTRUDE [*moving haughtily and carelessly to the table*] I hadnt the slightest intention of treating you with ceremony. [*She sits down: a liberty which gives him a perceptible shock*]. I am quite at a loss to imagine why I should treat a perfect stranger named Duval: a captain! almost a subaltern! with the smallest ceremony.

THE INCA. That is true. I had for the moment forgotten my position.

ERMYNTRUDE. It doesnt matter. You may sit down.

THE INCA [*frowning*] What!

ERMYNTRUDE. I said, you . . . may . . . sit . . . down.

THE INCA. Oh [*His moustache droops. He sits down*].

ERMYNTRUDE. What is your business?

THE INCA. I come on behalf of the Inca of Perusalem.

ERMYNTRUDE. The Allerhöchst?

THE INCA. Precisely.

ERMYNTRUDE. I wonder does he feel ridiculous when people call him the Allerhöchst.

THE INCA [*surprised*] Why should he? He is the Allerhöchst.

ERMYNTRUDE. Is he nice looking?

THE INCA. I—er. Er—I. I—er. I am not a good judge.

ERMYNTRUDE. They say he takes himself very seriously.

[967]

THE INCA. Why should he not, madam? Providence has entrusted to his family the care of a mighty empire. He is in a position of half divine, half paternal responsibility towards sixty millions of people, whose duty it is to die for him at the word of command. To take himself otherwise than seriously would be blasphemous. It is a punishable offence—severely punishable—in Perusalem. It is called Incadisparagement.

ERMYNTRUDE. How cheerful! Can he laugh?

THE INCA. Certainly, madam. [*He laughs, harshly and mirthlessly*]. Ha ha! Ha ha ha!

ERMYNTRUDE [*frigidly*] I asked could the Inca laugh. I did not ask could you laugh.

THE INCA. That is true, madam. [*Chuckling*] Devilish amusing that! [*He laughs, genially and sincerely, and becomes a much more agreeable person*]. Pardon me: I am now laughing because I cannot help it. I am amused. The other was merely an imitation: a failure, I admit.

ERMYNTRUDE. You intimated that you had some business?

THE INCA [*producing a very large jewel case, and relapsing into solemnity*] I am instructed by the Allerhöchst to take a careful note of your features and figure, and, if I consider them satisfactory, to present you with this trifling token of His Imperial Majesty's regard. I do consider them satisfactory. Allow me [*he opens the jewel case and presents it*]!

ERMYNTRUDE [*staring at the contents*] What awful taste he must have! I cant wear that.

THE INCA [*reddening*] Take care, madam! This brooch was designed by the Inca himself. Allow me to explain the design. In the centre, the shield of Arminius. The ten surrounding medallions represent the ten castles of His Majesty. The rim is a piece of the telephone cable laid by His Majesty across the Shipskeel canal. The pin is a model in miniature of the sword of Henry the Birdcatcher.

ERMYNTRUDE. Miniature! It must be bigger than the original. My good man, you dont expect me to wear this round my neck: it's as big as a turtle. [*He shuts the case with an angry snap*]. How much did it cost?

THE INCA. For materials and manufacture alone, half a million Perusalem dollars, madam. The Inca's design constitutes it a work of art. As such, it is now worth probably ten million dollars.

ERMYNTRUDE. Give it to me [*she snatches it*]. I'll pawn it and buy something nice with the money.

THE INCA. Impossible, madam. A design by the Inca must not be exhibited for sale in the shop window of a pawnbroker. [*He flings himself into his chair, fuming*].

ERMYNTRUDE. So much the better. The Inca will have to redeem it to save himself from that disgrace; and the poor pawnbroker will get his money back. Nobody would buy it, you know.

THE INCA. May I ask why?

ERMYNTRUDE. Well, look at it! Just look at it! I ask you!

THE INCA [*his moustache drooping ominously*] I am sorry to have to report to the Inca that you have no soul for fine art. [*He rises sulkily*]. The position of daughter-in-law to the Inca is not compatible with the tastes of a pig. [*He attempts to take back the brooch*].

ERMYNTRUDE [*rising and retreating behind her chair with the brooch*] Here! you let that brooch alone. You presented it to me on behalf of the Inca. It is mine. You said my appearance was satisfactory.

THE INCA. Your appearance is not satisfactory. The Inca would not allow his son to marry you if the boy were on a desert island and you were the only other human being on it [*he strides up the room*].

ERMYNTRUDE [*calmly sitting down and replacing the case on the table*] How could he? There would be no clergyman to marry us. It would have to be quite morganatic.

THE INCA [*returning*] Such an expression is out of place in the mouth of a princess aspiring to the highest destiny on earth. You have the morals of a dragoon. [*She receives this with a shriek of laughter. He struggles with his sense of humor*]. At the same time [*he sits down*] there is a certain coarse fun in the idea which compels me to smile [*he turns up his moustache and smiles*].

ERMYNTRUDE. When I marry the Inca's son, Captain, I shall make the Inca order you to cut off that moustache. It is too irresistible. Doesnt it fascinate everyone in Perusalem?

THE INCA [*leaning forward to her energetically*] By all the thunders of Thor, madam, it fascinates the whole world.

ERMYNTRUDE. What I like about you, Captain Duval, is your modesty.

THE INCA [*straightening up suddenly*] Woman: do not be a fool.

ERMYNTRUDE [*indignant*] Well!

THE INCA. You must look facts in the face. This moustache is an exact copy of the Inca's moustache. Well, does the world occupy itself with the Inca's moustache or does it not? Does it ever occupy itself with anything else? If that is the truth, does its recognition constitute the Inca a coxcomb? Other potentates have moustaches; even beards and moustaches. Does the world occupy itself with those beards and moustaches? Do the hawkers in the streets of every capital on the civilized globe sell ingenious cardboard representations of their faces on which, at the pulling of a simple string, the moustaches turn up and down, so—[*he makes his moustache turn up and down several times*]? No! I say No. The Inca's moustache is so watched and studied that it has made his face the political barometer of the whole continent. When that moustache goes up, culture rises with it. Not what you call culture; but Kultur, a word so much more significant that I hardly understand it myself except when I am in specially good form. When it goes down, millions of men perish.

ERMYNTRUDE. You know, if I had a moustache like that, it would turn my head. I should go mad. Are you quite sure the Inca isnt mad?

THE INCA. How can he be mad, madam? What is sanity? The condition of the Inca's mind. What is madness? The condition of the people who disagree with the Inca.

ERMYNTRUDE. Then I am a lunatic because I dont like that ridiculous brooch.

THE INCA. No, madam: you are only an idiot.

ERMYNTRUDE. Thank you.

THE INCA. Mark you: it is not to be expected that you should see eye to eye with the Inca. That would be presumption. It is for you to accept without question or demur the assurance of your Inca that the brooch is a masterpiece.

ERMYNTRUDE. My Inca! Oh, come! I like that. He is not my Inca yet.

THE INCA. He is everybody's Inca, madam. His realm will yet extend to the confines of the habitable earth. It is his divine right; and let those who dispute it look to themselves. Properly speaking, all those who are now trying to shake his world predominance are not at war with him, but in rebellion against him.

ERMYNTRUDE. Well, he started it, you know.

THE INCA. Madam, be just. When the hunters surround the lion, the lion will spring. The Inca had kept the peace for years. Those who attacked him were steeped in blood, black blood, white blood, brown blood, yellow blood, blue blood. The Inca had never shed a drop.

ERMYNTRUDE. He had only talked.

THE INCA. Only talked! Only talked! What is more glorious than talk? Can anyone in the world talk like him? Madam: when he signed the declaration of war, he said to his foolish generals and admirals, "Gentlemen: you will all be sorry for this." And they are. They know now that they had better have relied on the sword of the spirit: in other words, on their Inca's talk, than on their murderous cannons. The world will one day do justice to the Inca as the man who kept the peace with nothing but his tongue and his moustache. While he talked: talked just as I am talking now to you, simply, quietly, sensibly, but GREATLY, there was peace; there was prosperity; Perusalem went from success to success. He has been silenced for a year by the roar of trinitrotoluene and the bluster of fools; and the world is in ruins. What a tragedy! [*He is convulsed with grief*].

ERMYNTRUDE. Captain Duval: I dont want to be unsympathetic; but suppose we get back to business.

THE INCA. Business! What business?

ERMYNTRUDE. Well, my business. You want me to marry one of the Inca's sons: I forget which.

THE INCA. As far as I can recollect the name, it is His Imperial Highness Prince Eitel William Frederick George Franz Josef Alexander Nicholas Victor Emmanuel Albert Theodore Wilson—

ERMYNTRUDE [*interrupting*] Oh, please, please, maynt I have one with a shorter name? What is he called at home?

THE INCA. He is usually called Sonny, madam. [*With great charm of manner*] But you will please understand that the Inca had no desire to pin you to any particular son. There is Chips and Spots and Lulu and Pongo and the Corsair and the Piffler and Jack Johnson the second, all unmarried. At least not seriously married: nothing, in short, that cannot be arranged. They are all at your service.

ERMYNTRUDE. Are they all as clever and charming as their father?

THE INCA [*lifts his eyebrows pityingly, shrugs his shoulders; then, with indulgent paternal contempt*] Excellent lads, madam. Very honest affectionate creatures. I have nothing against them. Pongo imitates farmyard sounds—cock-crowing and that sort of thing—extremely well. Lulu plays Strauss's Sinfonia Domestica on the mouth organ really screamingly. Chips keeps owls and rabbits. Spots motor bicycles. The Corsair commands canal barges and steers them himself. The Piffler writes plays, and paints most abominably. Jack Johnson trims ladies' hats, and boxes with professionals hired for that purpose. He is invariably victorious. Yes: they all have their different little talents. And also, of course, their family resemblances. For example, they all smoke; they all quarrel with one another; and they none of them appreciate their father, who, by the way, is no mean painter, though the Piffler pretends to ridicule his efforts.

ERMYNTRUDE. Quite a large choice, eh?

THE INCA. But very little to choose, believe me. I should not recommend Pongo, because he snores so frightfully that it has been necessary to build him a

[973]

sound-proof bedroom: otherwise the royal family would get no sleep. But any of the others would suit equally well—if you are really bent on marrying one of them.

ERMYNTRUDE. If! What is this! I never wanted to marry one of them. I thought you wanted me to.

THE INCA. I did, madam; but [*confidentially, flattering her*] you are not quite the sort of person I expected you to be; and I doubt whether any of these young degenerates would make you happy. I trust I am not shewing any want of natural feeling when I say that from the point of view of a lively, accomplished, and beautiful woman [*Ermyntrude bows*] they might pall after a time. I suggest that you might prefer the Inca himself.

ERMYNTRUDE. Oh, Captain, how could a humble person like myself be of any interest to a prince who is surrounded with the ablest and most far-reaching intellects in the world?

THE INCA [*explosively*] What on earth are you talking about, madam? Can you name a single man in the entourage of the Inca who is not a born fool?

ERMYNTRUDE. Oh, how can you say that! There is Admiral von Cockpits—

THE INCA [*rising intolerantly and striding about the room*] Von Cockpits! Madam; if Von Cockpits ever goes to heaven, before three weeks are over, the Angel Gabriel will be at war with the man in the moon.

ERMYNTRUDE. But General Von Schinkenburg—

THE INCA. Schinkenburg! I grant you, Schinkenburg has a genius for defending market gardens. Among market gardens he is invincible. But what is the good of that? The world does not consist of market gardens. Turn him loose in pasture and he is lost. The Inca has defeated all these generals again and again at manœuvres; and yet he has to give place to them in the field because he would be blamed for every disaster—accused of sacrificing the country to his vanity. Vanity! Why do they call him vain? Just because he is one of the few men who are not afraid to live. Why do they call themselves brave? Because they have not sense enough to be afraid to die. Within the last year the world has produced millions of heroes. Has it produced more than one Inca? [*He resumes his seat*].

ERMYNTRUDE. Fortunately not, Captain. I'd rather marry Chips.

THE INCA [*making a wry face*] Chips! Oh no: I wouldnt marry Chips.

ERMYNTRUDE. Why?

THE INCA [*whispering the secret*] Chips talks too much about himself.

ERMYNTRUDE. Well, what about Snooks?

THE INCA. Snooks? Who is he? Have I a son named Snooks? There are so many—[*wearily*] so many—that I often forget. [*Casually*] But I wouldnt marry him, anyhow, if I were you.

ERMYNTRUDE. But hasnt any of them inherited the family genius? Surely, if Providence has entrusted them with the care of Perusalem—if they are all descended from Bedrock the Great—

THE INCA [*interrupting her impatiently*] Madam: if you ask me, I consider Bedrock a grossly overrated monarch.

ERMYNTRUDE [*shocked*] Oh, Captain! Take care! Incadisparagement.

THE INCA. I repeat, grossly overrated. Strictly between ourselves, I do not believe all this about Providence entrusting the care of sixty million human beings to the abilities of Chips and the Piffler and

Jack Johnson. I believe in individual genius. That is the Inca's secret. It must be. Why, hang it all, madam, if it were a mere family matter, the Inca's uncle would have been as great a man as the Inca. And—well, everybody knows what the Inca's uncle was.

ERMYNTRUDE. My experience is that the relatives of men of genius are always the greatest duffers imaginable.

THE INCA. Precisely. That is what proves that the Inca is a man of genius. His relatives are duffers.

ERMYNTRUDE. But bless my soul, Captain, if all the Inca's generals are incapables, and all his relatives duffers, Perusalem will be beaten in the war; and then it will become a republic, like France after 1871, and the Inca will be sent to St Helena.

THE INCA [triumphantly] That is just what the Inca is playing for, madam. It is why he consented to the war.

ERMYNTRUDE. What!

THE INCA. Aha! The fools talk of crushing the Inca; but they little know their man. Tell me this. Why did St Helena extinguish Napoleon?

ERMYNTRUDE. I give it up.

THE INCA. Because, madam, with certain rather remarkable qualities, which I should be the last to deny, Napoleon lacked versatility. After all, any fool can be a soldier: we know that only too well in Perusalem, where every fool is a soldier. But the Inca has a thousand other resources. He is an architect. Well, St Helena presents an unlimited field to the architect. He is a painter: need I remind you that St Helena is still without a National Gallery? He is a composer: Napoleon left no symphonies in St Helena. Send the Inca to St Helena, madam, and the world will crowd thither to see his works as they

crowd now to Athens to see the Acropolis, to Madrid
to see the pictures of Velasquez, to Bayreuth to see
the music dramas of that egotistical old rebel Richard
Wagner, who ought to have been shot before he was
forty, as indeed he very nearly was. Take this from
me: hereditary monarchs are played out: the age for
men of genius has come: the career is open to the
talents: before ten years have elapsed every civilized
country from the Carpathians to the Rocky Mountains
will be a Republic.

ERMYNTRUDE. Then goodbye to the Inca.

THE INCA. On the contrary, madam, the Inca will
then have his first real chance. He will be unani-
mously invited by those Republics to return from his
exile and act as Super-president of all the republics.

ERMYNTRUDE. But wont that be a come down for
him? Think of it! after being Inca, to be a mere
President!

THE INCA. Well, why not! An Inca can do nothing.
He is tied hand and foot. A constitutional monarch
is openly called an india-rubber stamp. An emperor is
a puppet. The Inca is not allowed to make a speech:
he is compelled to take up a screed of flatulent twaddle
written by some noodle of a minister and read it aloud.
But look at the American President! He is the Allerhöchst, if you like. No, madam, believe me, there is
nothing like Democracy, American Democracy. Give
the people voting papers: good long voting papers,
American fashion; and while the people are reading
the voting papers the Government does what it likes.

ERMYNTRUDE. What! You too worship before the
statue of Liberty, like the Americans?

THE INCA. Not at all, madam. The Americans do not
worship the statue of Liberty. They have erected it in
the proper place for a statue of Liberty: on its tomb
[he turns down his moustaches].

ERMYNTRUDE [*laughing*] Oh! Youd better not let them hear you say that, Captain.

THE INCA. Quite safe, madam: they would take it as a joke. [*He rises*]. And now, prepare yourself for a surprise. [*She rises*]. A shock. Brace yourself. Steel yourself. And do not be afraid.

ERMYNTRUDE. Whatever on earth can you be going to tell me, Captain?

THE INCA. Madam: I am no captain. I—

ERMYNTRUDE. You are the Inca in disguise.

THE INCA. Good heavens! how do you know that? Who has betrayed me?

ERMYNTRUDE. How could I help divining it, Sir? Who is there in the world like you? Your magnetism—

THE INCA. True; I had forgotten my magnetism. But you know now that beneath the trappings of Imperial Majesty there is a Man: simple, frank, modest, unaffected, colloquial: a sincere friend, a natural human being, a genial comrade, one eminently calculated to make a woman happy. You, on the other hand, are the most charming woman I have ever met. Your conversation is wonderful. I have sat here almost in silence, listening to your shrewd and penetrating account of my character, my motives, if I may say so, my talents. Never has such justice been done me: never have I experienced such perfect sympathy. Will you—I hardly know how to put this—will you be mine?

ERMYNTRUDE. Oh, Sir, you are married.

THE INCA. I am prepared to embrace the Mahometan faith, which allows a man four wives, if you will consent. It will please the Turks. But I had rather you did not mention it to the Inca-ess, if you dont mind.

ERMYNTRUDE. This is really charming of you. But the time has come for me to make a revelation. It is your Imperial Majesty's turn now to brace yourself. To steel yourself. I am not the princess. I am—

THE INCA. The daughter of my old friend Archdeacon Daffodil Donkin, whose sermons are read to me every evening after dinner. I never forget a face.

ERMYNTRUDE. You knew all along!

THE INCA [*bitterly, throwing himself into his chair*] And you supposed that I, who have been condemned to the society of princesses all my wretched life, believed for a moment that any princess that ever walked could have your intelligence!

ERMYNTRUDE. How clever of you, Sir! But you cannot afford to marry me.

THE INCA [*springing up*] Why not?

ERMYNTRUDE. You are too poor. You have to eat war bread. Kings nowadays belong to the poorer classes. The King of England does not even allow himself wine at dinner.

THE INCA [*delighted*] Haw! Ha ha! Haw! haw! [*he is convulsed with laughter, and finally has to relieve his feelings by waltzing half round the room*].

ERMYNTRUDE. You may laugh, Sir; but I really could not live in that style. I am the widow of a millionaire, ruined by your little war.

THE INCA. A millionaire! What are millionaires now, with the world crumbling?

ERMYNTRUDE. Excuse me: mine was a hyphenated millionaire.

THE INCA. A highfalutin millionaire, you mean. [*Chuckling*] Haw! ha ha! really very nearly a pun, that. [*He sits down in her chair*].

ERMYNTRUDE [*revolted, sinking into his chair*] I think it quite the worst pun I ever heard.

THE INCA. The best puns have all been made years ago: nothing remained but to achieve the worst.

[979]

However, madam [*he rises majestically; and she is about to rise also*] No: I prefer a seated audience [*she falls back into her seat at the imperious wave of his hand* So [*he clicks his heels*]. Madam: I recognize my presumption in having sought the honor of your hand. As you say, I cannot afford it. Victorious as I am, I am hopelessly bankrupt; and the worst of it is, I am intelligent enough to know it. And I shall be beaten in consequence, because my most implacable enemy, though only a few months further away from bankruptcy than myself, has not a ray of intelligence, and will go on fighting until civilization is destroyed, unless I, out of sheer pity for the world, condescend to capitulate.

ERMYNTRUDE. The sooner the better, Sir. Many fine young men are dying while you wait.

THE INCA [*flinching painfully*] Why? Why do they do it?

ERMYNTRUDE. Because you make them.

THE INCA. Stuff! How can I? I am only one man; and they are millions. Do you suppose they would really kill each other if they didnt want to, merely for the sake of my beautiful eyes? Do not be deceived by newspaper claptrap, madam. I was swept away by a passion not my own, which imposed itself on me. By myself I am nothing. I dare not walk down the principal street of my own capital in a coat two years old, though the sweeper of that street can wear one ten years old. You talk of death as an unpopular thing. You are wrong: for years I gave them art, literature, science, prosperity, that they might live more abundantly; and they hated me, ridiculed me, caricatured me. Now that I give them death in its frightfullest forms, they are devoted to me. If you doubt me, ask those who for years have begged our taxpayers in vain for a few paltry thousands to spend on Life: on the bodies and minds of the nation's children, on the beauty and healthfulness of its cities, on the honor and comfort of its worn-out workers. They refused; and because they refused, death is let loose on them. They grudged a few hundreds a year for their salvation: they now pay millions a day for their own destruction and damnation. And this they call my doing! Let them say it, if they dare before the judgment-seat at which they and I shall answer at last for what we have left undone no less than for what we have done. [*Pulling himself together suddenly*] Madam: I have the honor to be your most obedient [*he clicks his heels and bows*].

ERMYNTRUDE. Sir! [*she curtsies*].

THE INCA [*turning at the door*] Oh, by the way, there is a princess, isn't there, somewhere on the premises?

ERMYNTRUDE. There is. Shall I fetch her?

THE INCA [*dubious*] Pretty awful, I suppose, eh?

ERMYNTRUDE. About the usual thing.

THE INCA [*sighing*] Ah well! What can one expect? I dont think I need trouble her personally. Will you explain to her about the boys?

ERMYNTRUDE. I am afraid the explanation will fall rather flat without your magnetism.

THE INCA [*returning to her and speaking very humanly*] You are making fun of me. Why does everybody make fun of me? Is it fair?

ERMYNTRUDE [*seriously*] Yes: it is fair. What other defence have we poor common people against your shining armor, your mailed fist, your pomp and parade, your terrible power over us? Are these things fair?

THE INCA. Ah, well, perhaps, perhaps. [*He looks at his watch*]. By the way, there is time for a drive round

[981]

the town and a cup of tea at the Zoo. Quite a bearable band there: it does not play any patriotic airs. I am sorry you will not listen to any more permanent arrangement; but if you would care to come—

ERMYNTRUDE [*eagerly*] Ratherrrrrr. I shall be delighted.

THE INCA [*cautiously*] In the strictest honor, you understand.

ERMYNTRUDE. Dont be afraid. I promise to refuse any incorrect proposals.

THE INCA [*enchanted*] Oh! Charming woman: how well you understand men!

He offers her his arm: they go out together.

O'Flaherty, V.C.:
A Recruiting Pamphlet

WITH

Censorship and Recruiting

Brawling in the Theatre

Composition begun 23 July 1915, but immediately abandoned; re-begun 3 September 1915; completed 14 September 1915. Published in *Hearst's Magazine* (New York), August 1917. First English publication in *Heartbreak House, Great Catherine, & Playlets of the War*, 1919. First presented by Officers of the 40th Squadron, R.F.C., on the Western Front at Treizennes, Belgium, on 17 February 1917, with Robert Loraine as O'Flaherty, supported by a cast of amateurs. First professional performance at the 39th Street Theatre, New York, 21 June 1920, by the Deborah Bierne Irish Players. First presented in England by the Stage Society at the Lyric Theatre, Hammersmith, on 19 December 1920; repeated on 20 December.

Private Dennis O'Flaherty, V.C.   *Arthur Sinclair*
General Sir Pearce Madigan   *Roy Byford*
Mrs O'Flaherty   *Sara Allgood*
Teresa Driscoll   *Nan Fitzgerald*

Period—Summer 1915

Scene—*Outside Sir Pearce Madigan's Country House in Ireland*

It may surprise some people to learn that in 1915 this little play was a recruiting poster in disguise. The British officer seldom likes Irish soldiers; but he always tries to have a certain proportion of them in his battalion, because, partly from a want of common sense which leads them to value their lives less than Englishmen do (lives are really less worth living in a poor country), and partly because even the most cowardly Irishman feels obliged to outdo an Englishman in bravery if possible, and at least to set a perilous pace for him, Irish soldiers give impetus to those military operations which require for their spirited execution more devilment than prudence.

Unfortunately, Irish recruiting was badly bungled in 1915. The Irish were for the most part Roman Catholics and loyal Irishmen, which means that from the English point of view they were heretics and rebels. But they were willing enough to go soldiering on the side of France and see the world outside Ireland, which is a dull place to live in. It was quite easy to enlist them by approaching them from their own point of view. But the War Office insisted on approaching them from the point of view of Dublin Castle. They were discouraged and repulsed by refusals to give commissions to Roman Catholic officers, or to allow distinct Irish units to be formed. To attract them, the walls were covered with placards headed REMEMBER BELGIUM. The folly of asking an Irishman to remember anything when you want him to fight for England was apparent to everyone outside the Castle: FORGET AND FORGIVE would have been more to the point. Remembering Belgium and its broken treaty led Irishmen to remember Limerick and its broken treaty; and the recruiting ended in a rebellion, in suppressing which the British artillery quite unnecessarily reduced the centre of Dublin to ruins, and the British commanders killed their leading prisoners of war in cold blood morning after morning with an effect of long drawn out ferocity. Really it was only the usual childish petulance in which John Bull does things in a week that disgrace him for a century, though he soon recovers his good humor, and cannot understand why the survivors of his wrath do not feel as jolly with him as he does with them. On the smouldering ruins of Dublin the appeals to remember Louvain were presently supplemented by a fresh appeal. IRISHMEN: DO YOU WISH TO HAVE THE HORRORS OF WAR BROUGHT TO YOUR OWN HEARTHS AND HOMES? Dublin laughed sourly.

As for me, I addressed myself quite simply to the business of obtaining recruits. I knew by personal experience and observation what anyone might have inferred from the records of Irish emigration, that all an Irishman's hopes and ambitions turn on his opportunities of getting out of Ireland. Stimulate his loyalty, and he will stay in Ireland and die for her; for, incomprehensible as it seems to an Englishman, Irish patriotism does not take the form of devotion to England and England's king. Appeal to his discontent, his deadly boredom, his thwarted curiosity and desire for change and adventure, and, to escape from Ireland, he will go abroad to risk his life for France, for the Papal States, for secession in America. and even, if no better may be, for England. Knowing that the ignorance and insularity of the Irishman is a danger to himself and to his neighbors, I had no scruple in making that appeal when there was something for him to fight which the whole world had to fight unless it meant to come under the jack boot of the German version of Dublin Castle.

There was another consideration, unmentionable by the recruiting sergeants and war orators, which must nevertheless have helped them powerfully in procuring soldiers by voluntary enlistment. The happy home of the idealist may become common under millennial conditions. It is not common at present. No one will ever know how many men joined the army in 1914 and 1915 to escape from tyrants and taskmasters, termagants and shrews, none of whom are any the less irksome when they happen by ill-luck to be also our fathers, our mothers, our wives, and our children. Even at their amiablest, a holiday from them may be a tempting change for all parties. That is why I did not endow O'Flaherty V.C. with an ideal Irish colleen for his sweetheart, and gave him for his mother a Volumnia of the potato patch rather than an affectionate parent from whom he could not so easily have torn himself away.

I need hardly say that a play thus carefully adapted to its purpose was voted utterly inadmissible; and in due course the British Government, frightened out of its wits for the moment by the rout of the Fifth Army, ordained Irish Conscription, and then did not dare to go through with it. I still think my own line was the more businesslike. But during the war everyone except the soldiers at the front imagined that nothing but an extreme assertion of our most passionate prejudices, without the smallest regard to their effect on others, could win the war. Finally the British blockade won the war; but the wonder is that the British blockhead did not lose it. I suppose the enemy was no wiser. War is not a sharpener of wits; and I am afraid I gave great offence by keeping my head in this matter of Irish recruiting. What can I do but apologize, and publish the play now that it can no longer do any good?

At the door of an Irish country house in a park. Fine summer weather: the summer of 1915. The porch, painted white, projects into the drive; but the door is at the side and the front has a window. The porch faces east; and the door is in the north side of it. On the south side is a tree in which a thrush is singing. Under the window is a garden seat with an iron chair at each end of it.

The last four bars of God Save the King are heard in the distance, followed by three cheers. Then the band strikes up It's a Long Way to Tipperary and recedes until it is out of hearing.

Private O'Flaherty V.C. comes wearily southward along the drive, and falls exhausted into the garden seat. The thrush utters a note of alarm and flies away. The tramp of a horse is heard.

A GENTLEMAN'S VOICE. Tim! Hi! Tim! [*He is heard dismounting*].

A LABORER'S VOICE. Yes, your honor.

THE GENTLEMAN'S VOICE. Take this horse to the stables, will you?

A LABORER'S VOICE. Right, your honor. Yup there. Gwan now. Gwan. [*The horse is led away*].

General Sir Pearce Madigan, an elderly baronet in khaki, beaming with enthusiasm, arrives. O'Flaherty rises and stands at attention.

SIR PEARCE. No, no, O'Flaherty: none of that now. Youre off duty. Remember that though I am a general of forty years service, that little Cross of yours gives you a higher rank in the roll of glory than I can pretend to.

O'FLAHERTY [*relaxing*] I'm thankful to you, Sir

Pearce; but I wouldnt have anyone think that the baronet of my native place would let a common soldier like me sit down in his presence without leave.

SIR PEARCE. Well, youre not a common soldier, O'Flaherty: youre a very uncommon one; and I'm proud to have you for my guest here today.

O'FLAHERTY. Sure I know, sir. You have to put up with a lot from the like of me for the sake of recruiting. All the quality shakes hands with me and says theyre proud to know me, just the way the king said when he pinned the Cross on me. And it's as true as I'm standing here, sir, the queen said to me "I hear you were born on the estate of General Madigan," she says; "and the General himself tells me you were always a fine young fellow." "Bedad, Mam," I says to her, "if the General knew all the rabbits I snared on him, and all the salmon I snatched on him, and all the cows I milked on him, he'd think me the finest ornament for the county jail he ever sent there for poaching."

SIR PEARCE [laughing] Youre welcome to them all, my lad. Come [he makes him sit down again on the garden seat]! sit down and enjoy your holiday [he sits down on one of the iron chairs: the one at the doorless side of the porch].

O'FLAHERTY. Holiday, is it? I'd give five shillings to be back in the trenches for the sake of a little rest and quiet. I never knew what hard work was til I took to recruiting. What with the standing on my legs all day, and the shaking hands, and the making speeches, and—whats worse—the listening to them, and the calling for cheers for king and country, and the saluting the flag til I'm stiff with it, and the listening to them playing God Save the King and Tipperary, and the trying to make my eyes look moist like a man in a picture book, I'm that bet that I hardly get a wink of sleep. I give you my word, Sir Pearce, that I never heard the tune of Tipperary in my life till I came back from Flanders; and already it's drove me to that pitch of tiredness of it that when a poor little innocent slip of a boy in the street the other night drew himself up and saluted and began whistling it at me, I clouted his head for him, God forgive me.

SIR PEARCE [*soothingly*] Yes, yes: I know. I know. One does get fed up with it: Ive been dog tired myself on parade many a time. But still, you know, theres a gratifying side to it, too. After all, he is our king; and it's our own country, isnt it?

O'FLAHERTY. Well, sir, to you that have an estate in it, it would feel like your country. But the divil a perch of it ever I owned. And as to the king, God help him, my mother would have taken the skin off my back if I'd ever let on to have any other king than Parnell.

SIR PEARCE [*rising, painfully shocked*] Your mother! What are you dreaming about, O'Flaherty? A most loyal woman. Always most loyal. Whenever there is an illness in the Royal Family, she asks me every time we meet about the health of the patient as anxiously as if it were yourself, her only son.

O'FLAHERTY. Well, she's my mother; and I wont utter a word agen her. But I'm not saying a word of lie when I tell you that that old woman is the biggest kanatt from here to the cross of Monasterboice. Sure she's the wildest Fenian and rebel, and always has been, that ever taught a poor innocent lad like myself to pray night and morning to St Patrick to clear the English out of Ireland the same as he cleared the snakes. Youll be surprised at my telling you that now, maybe, Sir Pearce?

SIR PEARCE [*unable to keep still, walking away from O'Flaherty*] Surprised! I'm more than surprised, O'Flaherty. I'm overwhelmed. [*Turning and facing him*] Are you—are you joking?

O'FLAHERTY. If youd been brought up by my mother, sir, youd know better than to joke about her. What I'm telling you is the truth; and I wouldnt tell it to you if I could see my way to get out of the fix I'll be in when my mother comes here this day to see her boy in his glory, and she after thinking all the time it was against the English I was fighting.

SIR PEARCE. Do you mean to say you told her such a monstrous falsehood as that you were fighting in the German army?

O'FLAHERTY. I never told her one word that wasnt the truth and nothing but the truth. I told her I was going to fight for the French and for the Russians; and sure who ever heard of the French or the Russians doing anything to the English but fighting them? That was how it was, sir. And sure the poor woman kissed me and went about the house singing in her old cracky voice that the French was on the sea, and theyd be here without delay, and the Orange will decay, says the Shan Van Vocht.

SIR PEARCE [*sitting down again, exhausted by his feelings*] Well, I never could have believed this. Never. What do you suppose will happen when she finds out?

O'FLAHERTY. She mustnt find out. It's not that she'd half kill me, as big as I am and as brave as I am. It's that I'm fond of her, and cant bring myself to break the heart in her. You may think it queer that a man should be fond of his mother, sir, and she having bet him from the time he could feel to the time she was too slow to ketch him; but I'm fond of her; and I'm not ashamed of it. Besides, didnt she win the Cross for me?

SIR PEARCE. Your mother! How?

O'FLAHERTY. By bringing me up to be more afraid of running away than of fighting. I was timid by nature; and when the other boys hurted me, I'd want to run away and cry. But she whaled me for disgracing the blood of the O'Flahertys until I'd have fought the divil himself sooner than face her after funking a fight. That was how I got to know that fighting was easier than it looked, and that the others was as much afeard of me as I was of them, and that if I only held out long enough theyd lose heart and give up. Thats the way I came to be so courageous. I tell you, Sir Pearce, if the German army had been brought up by my mother, the Kaiser would be dining in the banqueting hall at Buckingham Palace this day, and King George polishing his jack boots for him in the scullery.

SIR PEARCE. But I dont like this, O'Flaherty. You cant go on deceiving your mother, you know. It's not right.

O'FLAHERTY. Cant go on deceiving her, cant I? It's little you know what a son's love can do, sir. Did you ever notice what a ready liar I am?

SIR PEARCE. Well, in recruiting a man gets carried away. I stretch it a bit occasionally myself. After all, it's for king and country. But if you wont mind my saying it, O'Flaherty, I think that story about your fighting the Kaiser and the twelve giants of the Prussian guard single-handed would be the better for a little toning down. I dont ask you to drop it, you know; for it's popular, undoubtedly; but still, the truth is the truth. Dont you think it would fetch in almost as many recruits if you reduced the number of guardsmen to six?

O'FLAHERTY. Youre not used to telling lies like I am, sir. I got great practice at home with my mother.

What with saving my skin when I was young and thoughtless, and sparing her feelings when I was old enough to understand them, Ive hardly told my mother the truth twice a year since I was born; and would you have me turn round on her and tell it now; when she's looking to have some peace and quiet in her old age?

SIR PEARCE [*troubled in his conscience*] Well, it's not my affair, of course, O'Flaherty. But hadnt you better talk to Father Quinlan about it?

O'FLAHERTY. Talk to Father Quinlan, is it! Do you know what Father Quinlan says to me this very morning?

SIR PEARCE. Oh, youve seen him already, have you? What did he say?

O'FLAHERTY. He says "You know, dont you" he says "that it's your duty, as a Christian and a good son of the Holy Church, to love your enemies?" he says. "I know it's my juty as a soldier to kill them" I says. "That right, Dinny," he says: "quite right. But" says he "you can kill them and do them a good turn afterwards to shew your love for them" he says; "and it's your duty to have a mass said for the souls of the hundreds of Germans you say you killed" says he; "for many and many of them were Bavarians and good Catholics" he says. "Is it me that must pay for masses for the souls of the Boshes?" I says. "Let the King of England pay for them" I says; "for it was his quarrel and not mine."

SIR PEARCE [*warmly*] It is the quarrel of every honest man and true patriot, O'Flaherty. Your mother must see that as clearly as I do. After all, she is a reasonable, well disposed woman, quite capable of understanding the right and the wrong of the war. Why cant you explain to her what the war is about?

[993]

O'FLAHERTY. Arra, sir, how the divil do I know what the war is about?

SIR PEARCE [*rising again and standing over him*] What! O'Flaherty: do you know what you are saying? You sit there wearing the Victoria Cross for having killed God knows how many Germans; and you tell me you dont know why you did it!

O'FLAHERTY. Asking your pardon, Sir Pearce, I tell you no such thing. I know quite well why I kilt them. I kilt them because I was afeard that, if I didnt, theyd kill me.

SIR PEARCE [*giving it up, and sitting down again*] Yes, yes, of course; but have you no knowledge of the causes of the war? of the interests at stake? of the importance—I may almost say—in fact I will say—the sacred rights for which we are fighting? Dont you read the papers?

O'FLAHERTY. I do when I can get them. Theres not many newsboys crying the evening paper in the trenches. They do say, Sir Pearce, that we shall never beat the Boshes until we make Horatio Bottomley Lord Leftnant of England. Do you think thats true, sir?

SIR PEARCE. Rubbish, man! theres no Lord Lieutenant in England: the king is Lord Lieutenant. It's a simple question of patriotism. Does patriotism mean nothing to you?

O'FLAHERTY. It means different to me than what it would to you, sir. It means England and England's king to you. To me and the like of me, it means talking about the English just the way the English papers talk about the Boshes. And what good has it ever done here in Ireland? It's kept me ignorant because it filled up my mother's mind, and she thought it ought to fill up mine too. It's kept Ireland poor, because instead of trying to better ourselves we thought we was the fine fellows of patriots when we were speaking evil of Englishmen that was as poor as ourselves and maybe as good as ourselves. The Boshes I kilt was more knowledgable men than me: and what better am I now that Ive kilt them? What better is anybody?

SIR PEARCE [*huffed, turning a cold shoulder to him*] I am sorry the terrible experience of this war—the greatest war ever fought—has taught you no better, O'Flaherty.

O'FLAHERTY [*preserving his dignity*] I dont know about its being a great war, sir. It's a big war; but thats not the same thing. Father Quinlan's new church is a big church: you might take the little old chapel out of the middle of it and not miss it. But my mother says there was more true religion in the old chapel. And the war has taught me that may be she was right.

SIR PEARCE [*grunts sulkily*]!!

O'FLAHERTY [*respectfully but doggedly*] And theres another thing it's taught me too, sir, that concerns you and me, if I may make bold to tell it to you.

SIR PEARCE [*still sulkily*] I hope it's nothing you oughtnt to say to me, O'Flaherty.

O'FLAHERTY. It's this, sir: that I'm able to sit here now and talk to you without humbugging you; and thats what not one of your tenants or your tenants' childer ever did to you before in all your long life. It's a true respect I'm shewing you at last, sir. Maybe youd rather have me humbug you and tell you lies as I used, just as the boys here, God help them, would rather have me tell them how I fought the Kaiser, that all the world knows I never saw in my life, than tell them the truth. But I cant take advantage of you the way I used, not even if I seem to be wanting in respect to you and cocked up by winning the Cross.

SIR PEARCE [*touched*] Not at all, O'Flaherty. Not at all.

O'FLAHERTY. Sure whats the Cross to me, barring the little pension it carries? Do you think I dont know that theres hundreds of men as brave as me that never had the luck to get anything for their bravery but a curse from the sergeant, and the blame for the faults of them that ought to have been their betters? Ive learnt more than youd think, sir; for how would a gentleman like you know what a poor ignorant conceited creature I was when I went from here into the wide world as a soldier? What use is all the lying, and pretending, and humbugging, and letting on, when the day comes to you that your comrade is killed in the trench beside you, and you dont as much as look round at him until you trip over his poor body, and then all you say is to ask why the hell the stretcher-bearers dont take it out of the way. Why should I read the papers to be humbugged and lied to by them that had the cunning to stay at home and send me to fight for them? Dont talk to me or to any soldier of the war being right. No war is right; and all the holy water that Father Quinlan ever blessed couldnt make one right. There, sir! Now you know what O'Flaherty v.c. thinks; and youre wiser so than the others that only knows what he done.

SIR PEARCE [*making the best of it, and turning good-humoredly to him again*] Well, what you did was brave and manly, anyhow.

O'FLAHERTY. God knows whether it was or not, better than you nor me, General. I hope He wont be too hard on me for it, anyhow.

SIR PEARCE [*sympathetically*] Oh yes: we all have to

think seriously sometimes, especially when we're a little run down. I'm afraid weve been overworking you a bit over these recruiting meetings. However, we can knock off for the rest of the day; and tomorrow's Sunday. I've had about as much as I can stand myself. [*He looks at his watch*]. It's teatime. I wonder whats keeping your mother.

O'FLAHERTY. It's nicely cocked up the old woman will be, having tea at the same table as you, sir, instead of in the kitchen. She'll be after dressing in the heighth of grandeur; and stop she will at every house on the way to shew herself off and tell them where she's going, and fill the whole parish with spite and envy. But sure, she shouldnt keep you waiting sir.

SIR PEARCE. Oh, thats all right: she must be indulged on an occasion like this. I'm sorry my wife is in London: she'd have been glad to welcome your mother.

O'FLAHERTY. Sure, I know she would, sir. She was always a kind friend to the poor. Little her ladyship knew, God help her, the depth of divilment that was in us: we were like a play to her. You see, sir, she was English: that was how it was. We was to her what the Pathans and Senegalese was to me when I first seen them: I couldnt think, somehow, that they were liars, and thieves, and backbiters, and drunkards, just like ourselves or any other Christians. Oh, her ladyship never knew all that was going on behind her back; how would she? When I was a weeshy child, she gave me the first penny I ever had in my hand; and I wanted to pray for her conversion that night the same as my mother made me pray for yours; and—

SIR PEARCE [*scandalized*] Do you mean to say that your mother made you pray for my conversion?

O'FLAHERTY. Sure and she wouldnt want to see a

gentleman like you going to hell after she nursing your own son and bringing up my sister Annie on the bottle. That was how it was, sir. She'd rob you; and she'd lie to you; and she'd call down all the blessings of God on your head when she was selling you your own three geese that you thought had been ate by the fox the day after youd finished fattening them, sir; and all the time you were like a bit of her own flesh and blood to her. Often has she said she'd live to see you a good Catholic yet, leading victorious armies against the English and wearing the collar of gold that Malachi won from the proud invader. Oh, she's the romantic woman is my mother, and no mistake.

SIR PEARCE [*in great perturbation*] I really cant believe this, O'Flaherty. I could have sworn your mother was as honest a woman as ever breathed.

O'FLAHERTY. And so she is, sir. She's as honest as the day.

SIR PEARCE. Do you call it honest to steal my geese?

O'FLAHERTY. She didnt steal them, sir. It was me that stole them.

SIR PEARCE. Oh! And why the devil did you steal them?

O'FLAHERTY. Sure we needed them, sir. Often and often we had to sell our own geese to pay you the rent to satisfy your needs; and why shouldnt we sell your geese to satisfy ours?

SIR PEARCE. Well, damn me!

O'FLAHERTY [*sweetly*] Sure you had to get what you could out of us; and we had to get what we could out of you. God forgive us both!

SIR PEARCE. Really, O'Flaherty, the war seems to have upset you a little.

O'FLAHERTY. It's set me thinking, sir; and I'm not used to it. It's like the patriotism of the English. They

[998]

never thought of being patriotic until the war broke out; and now the patriotism has took them so sudden and come so strange to them that they run about like frightened chickens, uttering all manner of nonsense. But please God theyll forget all about it when the war's over. Theyre getting tired of it already.

SIR PEARCE. No, no: it has uplifted us all in a wonderful way. The world will never be the same again, O'Flaherty. Not after a war like this.

O'FLAHERTY. So they all say, sir. I see no great differ myself. It's all the fright and the excitement; and when that quiets down theyll go back to their natural divilment and be the same as ever. It's like the vermin: itll wash off after a while.

SIR PEARCE [*rising and planting himself firmly behind the garden seat*] Well, the long and the short of it is, O'Flaherty, I must decline to be a party to any attempt to deceive your mother. I thoroughly disapprove of this feeling against the English, especially at a moment like the present. Even if your mother's political sympathies are really what you represent them to be, I should think that her gratitude to Gladstone ought to cure her of such disloyal prejudices.

O'FLAHERTY [*over his shoulder*] She says Gladstone was an Irishman, sir. What call would he have to meddle with Ireland as he did if he wasnt?

SIR PEARCE. What nonsense! Does she suppose Mr Asquith is an Irishman?

O'FLAHERTY. She wont give him any credit for Home Rule, sir. She says Redmond made him do it. She says you told her so.

SIR PEARCE [*convicted out of his own mouth*] Well, I never meant her to take it up in that ridiculous way. [*He moves to the end of the garden seat on O'Flaherty's left*] I'll give her a good talking to when she comes. I'm not going to stand any of her nonsense.

O'FLAHERTY. It's not a bit of use, sir. She says all the English generals is Irish. She says all the English poets and great men was Irish. She says the English never knew how to read their own books until we taught them. She says we're the lost tribes of the house of Israel and the chosen people of God. She says that the goddess Venus, that was born out of the foam of the sea, came up out of the water in Killiney Bay off Bray Head. She says that Moses built the seven churches, and that Lazarus was buried in Glasnevin.

SIR PEARCE. Bosh! How does she know he was? Did you ever ask her?

O'FLAHERTY. I did, sir, often.

SIR PEARCE. And what did she say?

O'FLAHERTY. She asked me how did I know he wasnt, and fetched me a clout on the side of my head.

SIR PEARCE. But have you never mentioned any famous Englishman to her, and asked her what she had to say about him?

O'FLAHERTY. The only one I could think of was Shakespear, sir; and she says he was born in Cork.

SIR PEARCE [exhausted] Well, I give it up [he throws himself into the nearest chair]. The woman is—Oh, well! No matter.

O'FLAHERTY [sympathetically] Yes, sir: she's pigheaded and obstinate: theres no doubt about it. She's like the English: they think theres no one like themselves. It's the same with the Germans, though theyre educated and ought to know better. Youll never have a quiet world til you knock the patriotism out of the human race.

SIR PEARCE. Still, we—

O'FLAHERTY. Whisht, sir, for God's sake: here she is.

The General jumps up. Mrs O'Flaherty arrives, and comes between the two men. She is very clean, and care-

*fully dressed in the old fashioned peasant costume: black
silk sunbonnet with a tiara of trimmings, and black cloak.*

O'FLAHERTY [*rising shyly*] Good evening, mother.

MRS O'FLAHERTY [*severely*] You hold your whisht,
and learn behavior while I pay my juty to his honor.
[*To Sir Pearce, heartily*] And how is your honor's
good self? And how is her ladyship and all the young
ladies? Oh, it's right glad we are to see your honor
back again and looking the picture of health.

SIR PEARCE [*forcing a note of extreme geniality*] Thank
you, Mrs O'Flaherty. Well, you see weve brought you
back your son safe and sound. I hope youre proud of
him.

MRS O'FLAHERTY. And indeed and I am, your honor.
It's the brave boy he is; and why wouldnt he be,
brought up on your honor's estate and with you before
his eyes for a pattern of the finest soldier in Ireland?
Come and kiss your old mother, Dinny darlint.
[*O'Flaherty does so sheepishly*]. Thats my own darling
boy. And look at your fine new uniform stained already with the eggs youve been eating and the porter
youve been drinking. [*She takes out her handkerchief;
spits on it; and scrubs his lapel with it*]. Oh, it's the
untidy slovenly one you always were. There! It wont
be seen on the khaki: it's not like the old red coat that
would shew up everything that dribbled down on it.
[*To Sir Pearce*] And they tell me down at the lodge
that her ladyship is staying in London, and that Miss
Agnes is to be married to a fine young nobleman. Oh,
it's your honor that is the lucky and happy father! It
will be bad news for many of the young gentlemen of
the quality round here, sir. Theres lots thought she
was going to marry young Master Lawless.

SIR PEARCE. What! That—that—that bosthoon!

MRS O'FLAHERTY [*hilariously*] Let your honor alone

for finding the right word! A big bosthoon he is indeed, your honor. Oh, to think of the times and times I have said that Miss Agnes would be my lady as her mother was before her! Didnt I, Dinny?

SIR PEARCE. And now, Mrs O'Flaherty, I daresay you have a great deal to say to Dennis that doesnt concern me. I'll just go in and order tea.

MRS O'FLAHERTY. Oh, why would your honor disturb yourself? Sure I can take the boy into the yard.

SIR PEARCE. Not at all. It wont disturb me in the least. And he's too big a boy to be taken into the yard now. He has made a front seat for himself. Eh? [*He goes into the house*].

MRS O'FLAHERTY. Sure he has that, your honor. God bless your honor! [*The General being now out of hearing, she turns threateningly to her son with one of those sudden Irish changes of manner which amaze and scandalize less flexible nations, and exclaims*] And what do you mean, you lying young scald, by telling me you were going to fight agen the English? Did you take me for a fool that couldnt find out, and the papers all full of you shaking hands with the English king at Buckingham Palace?

O'FLAHERTY. I didn't shake hands with him: he shook hands with me. Could I turn on the man in his own house, before his own wife, with his money in my pocket and in yours, and throw his civility back in his face?

MRS O'FLAHERTY. You would take the hand of a tyrant red with the blood of Ireland—

O'FLAHERTY. Arra hold your nonsense, mother: he's not half the tyrant you are, God help him. His hand was cleaner than mine that had the blood of his own relations on it, may be.

MRS O'FLAHERTY [*threateningly*] Is that a way to speak to your mother, you young spalpeen?

O'FLAHERTY [*stoutly*] It is so, if you wont talk sense to me. It's a nice thing for a poor boy to be made much of by kings and queens, and shook hands with by the heighth of his country's nobility in the capital cities of the world, and then to come home and be scolded and insulted by his own mother. I'll fight for who I like; and I'll shake hands with what kings I like; and if your own son is not good enough for you, you can go and look for another. Do you mind me now?

MRS O'FLAHERTY. And was it the Belgians learned you such brazen impudence?

O'FLAHERTY. The Belgians is good men; and the French ought to be more civil to them, let alone their being half murdered by the Boshes.

MRS O'FLAHERTY. Good men is it! Good men! to come over here when they were wounded because it was a Catholic country, and then go to the Protestant Church because it didnt cost them anything, and some of them to never go near a church at all. Thats what you call good men!

O'FLAHERTY. Oh, youre the mighty fine politician, arnt you? Much you know about Belgians or foreign parts or the world youre living in, God help you!

MRS O'FLAHERTY. Why wouldnt I know better than you? Amment I your mother?

O'FLAHERTY. And if you are itself, how can you know what you never seen as well as me that was dug into the continent of Europe for six months, and was buried in the earth of it three times with the shells bursting on the top of me? I tell you I know what I'm about. I have my own reasons for taking part in this great conflict. I'd be ashamed to stay at home and not fight when everybody else is fighting.

MRS O'FLAHERTY. If you wanted to fight, why couldnt you fight in the German army?

O'FLAHERTY. Because they only get a penny a day.

MRS O'FLAHERTY. Well, and if they do itself, isnt there the French army?

O'FLAHERTY. They only get a hapenny a day.

MRS O'FLAHERTY [*much dashed*] Oh murder! They must be a mean lot, Dinny.

O'FLAHERTY [*sarcastic*] Maybe youd have me join the Turkish army, and worship the heathen Mahomet that put a corn in his ear and pretended it was a message from the heavens when the pigeon come to pick it out and eat it. I went where I could get the biggest allowance for you; and little thanks I get for it!

MRS O'FLAHERTY. Allowance, is it! Do you know what the thieving blackguards did on me? They came to me and they says, "Was your son a big eater?" they says. "Oh, he was that" says I: "ten shillings a week wouldnt keep him." Sure I thought the more I said the more theyd give me. "Then" says they, "thats ten shillings a week off your allowance" they says, "because you save that by the king feeding him." "Indeed!" says I: "I suppose if I'd six sons youd stop three pound a week from me, and make out that I ought to pay you money instead of you paying me." "Theres a fallacy in your argument" they says.

O'FLAHERTY. A what?

MRS O'FLAHERTY. A fallacy: thats the word he said. I says to him, "It's a Pharisee I'm thinking you mean, sir; but you can keep your dirty money that your king grudges a poor old widow; and please God the English will be bet yet for the deadly sin of oppressing the poor"; and with that I shut the door in his face.

O'FLAHERTY [*furious*] Do you tell me they knocked ten shillings off you for my keep?

MRS O'FLAHERTY [*soothing him*] No, darlint: they only knocked off half a crown. I put up with it because Ive got the old age pension; and they know very well I'm only sixty-two; so Ive the better of them by half a crown a week anyhow.

O'FLAHERTY. It's a queer way of doing business. If theyd tell you straight out what they was going to give you, you wouldnt mind; but if there was twenty ways of telling the truth and only one way of telling a lie, the Government would find it out. It's in the nature of governments to tell lies.

Teresa Driscoll, a parlor maid, comes from the house.

TERESA. Youre to come up to the drawing room to have your tea, Mrs O'Flaherty.

MRS O'FLAHERTY. Mind you have a sup of good black tea for me in the kitchen afterwards, acushla. That washy drawing room tea will give me the wind if I leave it on my stomach. [*She goes into the house, leaving the two young people alone together*].

O'FLAHERTY. Is that yourself, Tessie? And how are you?

TERESA. Nicely, thank you. And hows yourself?

O'FLAHERTY. Finely, thank God. [*He produces a gold chain*]. Look what Ive brought you, Tessie.

TERESA [*shrinking*] Sure I dont like to touch it, Denny. Did you take it off a dead man?

O'FLAHERTY. No: I took it off a live one; and thankful he was to me to be alive and kept a prisoner in ease and comfort, and me left fighting in peril of my life.

TERESA [*taking it*] Do you think it's real gold, Denny?

O'FLAHERTY. It's real German gold, anyhow.

TERESA. But German silver isnt real, Denny.

O'FLAHERTY [*his face darkening*] Well, it's the best the Bosh could do for me, anyhow.

TERESA. Do you think I might take it to the jeweller next market day and ask him?

[1005]

O'FLAHERTY [*sulkily*] You may take it to the divil if you like.

TERESA. You needn't lose your temper about it. I only thought I'd like to know. The nice fool I'd look if I went about shewing off a chain that turned out to be only brass!

O'FLAHERTY. I think you might say Thank you.

TERESA. Do you? I think you might have said something more to me than "Is that yourself?" You couldnt say less to the postman.

O'FLAHERTY [*his brow clearing*] Oh, is that whats the matter? Here! come and take the taste of the brass out of my mouth. [*He seizes her and kisses her*].

Teresa, without losing her Irish dignity, takes the kiss as appreciatively as a connoisseur might take a glass of wine, and sits down with him on the garden seat.

TERESA [*as he squeezes her waist*] Thank God the priest cant see us here!

O'FLAHERTY. It's little they care for priests in France, alanna.

TERESA. And what had the queen on her, Denny, when she spoke to you in the palace?

O'FLAHERTY. She had a bonnet on without any strings to it. And she had a plakeen of embroidery down her bosom. And she had her waist where it used to be, and not where the other ladies had it. And she had little brooches in her ears, though she hadnt half the jewelry of Mrs Sullivan that keeps the pop-shop in Drumpogue. And she dresses her hair down over her forehead, in a fringe like. And she has an Irish look about her eyebrows. And she didnt know what to say to me, poor woman! and I didnt know what to say to her. God help me!

TERESA. Youll have a pension now with the Cross, wont you, Denny?

O'FLAHERTY. Sixpence three farthings a day.

TERESA. That isnt much.

O'FLAHERTY. I take out the rest in glory.

TERESA. And if youre wounded, youll have a wound pension, wont you?

O'FLAHERTY. I will, please God.

TERESA. Youre going out again, arnt you, Denny?

O'FLAHERTY. I cant help myself. I'd be shot for a deserter if I didnt go; and may be I'll be shot by the Boshes if I do go; so between the two of them I'm nicely fixed up.

MRS O'FLAHERTY [*calling from within the house*] Tessie! Tessie darlint!

TERESA [*disengaging herself from his arm and rising*] I'm wanted for the tea table. Youll have a pension anyhow, Denny, wont you, whether youre wounded or not?

MRS O'FLAHERTY. Come, child, come.

TERESA [*impatiently*] Oh, sure I'm coming. [*She tries to smile at Denny, not very convincingly, and hurries into the house*].

O'FLAHERTY [*alone*] And if I do get a pension itself, the divil a penny of it youll ever have the spending of.

MRS O'FLAHERTY [*as she comes from the porch*] Oh, it's a shame for you to keep the girl from her juties, Dinny. You might get her into trouble.

O'FLAHERTY. Much I care whether she gets into trouble or not! I pity the man that gets her into trouble. He'll get himself into worse.

MRS O'FLAHERTY. Whats that you tell me? Have you been falling out with her, and she a girl with a fortune of ten pounds?

O'FLAHERTY. Let her keep her fortune. I wouldnt touch her with the tongs if she had thousands and millions.

MRS O'FLAHERTY. Oh fie for shame, Dinny! why would you say the like of that of a decent honest girl, and one of the Driscolls too?

O'FLAHERTY. Why wouldnt I say it? She's thinking of nothing but to get me out there again to be wounded so that she may spend my pension, bad scran to her!

MRS O'FLAHERTY. Why, whats come over you, child, at all at all?

O'FLAHERTY. Knowledge and wisdom has come over me with pain and fear and trouble. Ive been made a fool of and imposed upon all my life. I thought that covetous sthreal in there was a walking angel; and now if ever I marry at all I'll marry a French-woman.

MRS O'FLAHERTY [*fiercely*] Youll not, so; and dont you dar repeat such a thing to me.

O'FLAHERTY. Wont I, faith! Ive been as good as married to a couple of them already.

MRS O'FLAHERTY. The Lord be praised, what wickedness have you been up to, you young black-guard?

O'FLAHERTY. One of them Frenchwomen would cook you a meal twice in the day and all days and every day that Sir Pearce himself might go begging through Ireland for, and never see the like of. I'll have a French wife, I tell you; and when I settle down to be a farmer I'll have a French farm, with a field as big as the continent of Europe that ten of your dirty little fields here wouldnt so much as fill the ditch of.

MRS O'FLAHERTY [*furious*] Then it's a French mother you may go look for; for I'm done with you.

O'FLAHERTY. And it's no great loss youd be if it wasnt for my natural feelings for you; for it's only a silly ignorant old country-woman you are with all your fine talk about Ireland: you that never stepped beyond the few acres of it you were born on!

MRS O'FLAHERTY [*tottering to the garden seat and shewing signs of breaking down*] Dinny darlint, why are you like this to me? Whats happened to you?

O'FLAHERTY [*gloomily*] Whats happened to everybody? thats what I want to know. Whats happened to you that I thought all the world of and was afeard of? Whats happened to Sir Pearce, that I thought was a great general, and that I now see to be no more fit to command an army than an old hen? Whats happened to Tessie, that I was mad to marry a year ago, and that I wouldnt take now with all Ireland for her fortune? I tell you the world's creation is crumbling in ruins about me; and then you come and ask whats happened to me?

MRS O'FLAHERTY [*giving way to wild grief*] Ochone! ochone! my son's turned agen me. Oh, whatll I do at all at all? Oh! oh! oh! oh!

SIR PEARCE [*running out of the house*] Whats this infernal noise? What on earth is the matter?

O'FLAHERTY. Arra hold your whisht, mother. Dont you see his honor?

MRS O'FLAHERTY. Oh, sir, I'm ruined and destroyed. Oh, wont you speak to Dinny, sir; I'm heart scalded with him. He wants to marry a Frenchwoman on me, and to go away and be a foreigner and desert his mother and betray his country. It's mad he is with the roaring of the cannons and he killing the Germans and the Germans killing him, bad cess to them? My boy is taken from me and turned agen me? and who is to take care of me in my old age after all Ive done for him, ochone! ochone!

O'FLAHERTY. Hold your noise, I tell you. Who's going to leave you? I'm going to take you with me. There now: does that satisfy you?

MRS O'FLAHERTY. Is it take me into a strange land among heathens and pagans and savages, and me not knowing a word of their language nor them of mine?

O'FLAHERTY. A good job they dont: may be theyll think youre talking sense.

MRS O'FLAHERTY. Ask me to die out of Ireland, is it? and the angels not to find me when they come for me!

O'FLAHERTY. And would you ask me to live in Ireland where Ive been imposed on and kept in ignorance, and to die where the divil himself wouldnt take me as a gift, let alone the blessed angels? You can come or stay. You can take your old way or take my young way. But stick in this place I will not among a lot of good-for-nothing divils thatll not do a hand's turn but watch the grass growing and build up the stone wall where the cow walked through it. And Sir Horace Plunkett breaking his heart all the time telling them how they might put the land into decent tillage like the French and Belgians.

SIR PEARCE. Yes: he's quite right, you know, Mrs O'Flaherty: quite right there.

MRS O'FLAHERTY. Well, sir, please God the war will last a long time yet: and may be I'll die before it's over and the separation allowance stops.

O'FLAHERTY. Thats all you care about. It's nothing but milch cows we men are for the women, with their separation allowances, ever since the war began, bad luck to them that made it!

TERESA [coming from the porch between the General and Mrs O'Flaherty] Hannah sent me out for to tell you, sir, that the tea will be black and the cake not fit to eat with the cold if yous all dont come at wanst.

MRS O'FLAHERTY [breaking out again] Oh, Tessie darlint, what have you been saying to Dinny at all at all? Oh! oh—

SIR PEARCE [*out of patience*] You cant discuss that here. We shall have Tessie beginning now.

O'FLAHERTY. Thats right, sir: drive them in.

TERESA. I havnt said a word to him. He—

SIR PEARCE. Hold your tongue; and go in and attend to your business at the tea table.

TERESA. But amment I telling your honor that I never said a word to him? He gave me a beautiful gold chain. Here it is to shew your honor thats it's no lie I'm telling you.

SIR PEARCE. Whats this, O'Flaherty? Youve been looting some unfortunate officer.

O'FLAHERTY. No sir: I stole it from him of his own accord.

MRS O'FLAHERTY. Wouldnt your honor tell him that his mother has the first call on it? What would a slip of a girl like that be doing with a gold chain round her neck?

TERESA [*venomously*] Anyhow, I have a neck to put it round and not a hank of wrinkles.

At this unfortunate remark, Mrs O'Flaherty bounds from her seat; and an appalling tempest of wordy wrath breaks out. The remonstrances and commands of the General, and the protests and menaces of O'Flaherty, only increase the hubbub. They are soon all speaking at once at the top of their voices.

MRS O'FLAHERTY [*solo*] You impudent young heifer, how dar you say such a thing to me? [*Teresa retorts furiously; the men interfere; and the solo becomes a quartet, fortissimo*]. Ive a good mind to clout your ears for you to teach you manners. Be ashamed of yourself do; and learn to know who youre speaking to. That I maytnt sin! but I dont know what the good God was thinking about when he made the like of you. Let me not see you casting

sheeps' eyes at my son again. There never was an
O'Flaherty yet that would demean himself by
keeping company with a dirty Driscoll; and if I
see you next or nigh my house I'll put you in the
ditch with a flea in your ear: mind that now.

TERESA. Is it me you offer such a name to, you
foul-mouthed, dirty minded, lying, sloothering old
sow, you? I wouldnt soil my tongue by calling you
in your right name and telling Sir Pearce whats
the common talk of the town about you. You and
your O'Flahertys! setting yourself up agen the
Driscolls that would never lower themselves to be
seen in conversation with you at the fair. You can
keep your ugly stingy lump of a son; for what is he
but a common soldier? and God help the girl that
gets him, say I! So the back of my hand to you,
Mrs O'Flaherty; and that the cat may tear your
ugly old face!

SIR PEARCE. Silence. Tessie: did you hear me
ordering you to go into the house? Mrs O'Flaherty!
[Louder] Mrs O'Flaherty!! Will you just listen to
me one moment? Please [Furiously] Do you hear
me speaking to you, woman? Are you human beings
or are you wild beasts? Stop that noise immediately: do you hear? [Yelling] Are you going to do
what I order you, or are you not? Scandalous!
Disgraceful! This comes of being too familiar with
you, O'Flaherty: shove them into the house. Out
with the whole damned pack of you.

O'FLAHERTY [to the women] Here now: none of
that, none of that. Go easy, I tell you. Hold your
whisht, mother, will you, or youll be sorry for it
after. [To Teresa] Is that the way for a decent young
girl to speak? [Despairingly] Oh, for the Lord's sake,
shut up, will yous? Have yous no respect for your-

selves or your betters? [*Peremptorily*] Let me have no more of it, I tell you. Och! the divil's in the whole crew of you. In with you into the house this very minute and tear one another's eyes out in the kitchen if you like. In with you.

The two men seize the two women, and push them, still violently abusing one another, into the house. Sir Pearce slams the door upon them savagely. Immediately a heavenly silence falls on the summer afternoon. The two sit down out of breath; and for a long time nothing is said. Sir Pearce sits on an iron chair. O'Flaherty sits on the garden seat. The thrush begins to sing melodiously. O'Flaherty cocks his ears, and looks up at it. A smile spreads over his troubled features. Sir Pearce, with a long sigh, takes out his pipe, and begins to fill it.

O'FLAHERTY [*idyllically*] What a discontented sort of an animal a man is, sir! Only a month ago, I was in the quiet of the country out at the front, with not a sound except the birds and the bellow of a cow in the distance as it might be, and the shrapnel making little clouds in the heavens, and the shells whistling, and may be a yell or two when one of us was hit; and would you believe it, sir, I complained of the noise and wanted to have a peaceful hour at home. Well: them two has taught me a lesson. This morning, sir, when I was telling the boys here how I was longing to be back taking my part for king and country with the others, I was lying, as you well knew, sir. Now I can go and say it with a clear conscience. Some likes war's alarums; and some likes home life. Ive tried both, sir; and I'm all for war's alarums now. I always was a quiet lad by natural disposition.

SIR PEARCE. Strictly between ourselves, O'Flaherty, and as one soldier to another [*O'Flaherty salutes, but without stiffening*], do you think we should have got an army without conscription if domestic life had been as happy as people say it is?

O'FLAHERTY. Well, between you and me and the wall, Sir Pearce, I think the less we say about that until the war's over, the better.

He winks at the General. The General strikes a match. The thrush sings. A jay laughs. The conversation drops.

Censorship and Recruiting

(Statement in reply to a report of the suppression of *O'Flaherty V.C.* in Dublin,
Manchester Guardian, 17 November 1915)

The report is extremely inconsiderate because, thanks
to the folly of the London press, the claim which the
Germans have been intelligent enough to make that
I am what is called a pro-German has been very
widely circulated on the Continent, in America, and
even in Morocco. This is not my fault. I can state
an unanswerable case against the Germans, but I
cannot make the English intelligent enough to see that
it is a better case than the kinematograph heroics with
which they hope to impress Europe as well as amuse
themselves.

Now, this silly report will probably be picked up
by the Germans and circulated abroad in the form
of a statement that I have written a play which the
English Government is suppressing because the poet
Shaw has again raised the cry of "Deutschland über
Alles." I therefore appeal to the press, if they must
circulate an unfounded report, at all events to make
it clear that the author has no more desire to discourage recruiting in Ireland than the military
authorities themselves.

The report, moreover, is absurd, because there is
no censorship in Ireland. There are two authorities—
the Castle authorities and the military authorities.
The Castle authorities have not intervened, and
neither I nor the Abbey Street Theatre would think
for a moment of producing a play if the military
authorities felt that it could do the slightest harm to

recruiting or to anything else. As a matter of fact the play, which appeals strongly to the Irishman's spirit of freedom and love of adventure, would, in my opinion, help recruiting rather than otherwise.

But the military authorities will be the judges of this, and there will be no attempt to disregard their wishes should they for any reason prefer that the Abbey Street Theatre should adhere to its original intention to produce the play in America.

Brawling in the Theatre

(Reply to a review on 20 December 1920
by John Francis Hope, *New Age*, London,
13 January 1921)

The NEW AGE has had the rare fortune to secure the services of a critic of the theatre who understands what is happening on the stage technically. He will presently take to writing plays, and be lost to criticism. All the more reason why he should try to reform an abuse from which he will himself suffer horribly when his manifest destiny is accomplished.

In his notice of the performance of "O'Flaherty, V.C." by the Stage Society he complains that Mr Arthur Sinclair "has a trick of waiting for the laugh which breaks up the sense and structure of the play." This is a shocking injustice to one of the finest actors we have. Is it Mr Sinclair's fault that our playgoers will not behave themselves? What is he to do? If he speaks through loud laughter his lines will not be heard; and the sense and structure of the play will be in a worse plight than ever, not to mention that the critics will accuse him of being an amateur who does not know his professional business, which is, to wait during the laugh and make his lines heard afterwards. It is true that by this procedure his acting is murdered, and the play ceases to be a play and becomes a maddening string of detached bids for another laugh. But the audience will have it so; and Mr Sinclair is powerless. His feelings and those of the author may be imagined. I have seen Mr Sinclair and his fellow-artists play in the silence of rehearsal, when even a whisper from anyone is an admitted outrage. If Mr John Francis Hope had enjoyed the same privilege, and then heard them struggling against noisy interruptions at every comma, he would consecrate his pen to the task of teaching the urgent lesson that audiences, whilst the curtain is up should behave much more strictly than little children; for little children should be seen and not heard, whereas audiences should be neither seen nor heard.

Imagine what a first performance of a symphony by Elgar would be if the audience, at every snatch of melody, every harmonic progression, every stroke of instrumentation, every fortissimo or pianissimo that pleased them, were to break into noisy applause, compelling the players to put down their instruments and the conductor his baton until silence was restored! Would the symphony be a symphony under such circumstances? Yet that is what I have to put up with, and what the players who interpret me have to put up with. They have to pretend to like it, and even to try to provoke it lest they should be reproached for its absence. I have been in provincial opera houses in Italy where the wretched tenor is expected to hold on to a high note until the audience yells with appreciation; so that you may see him, when the yell does not come until his wind is nearly exhausted, looking round at the house, half indignant, half imploring it to come to the rescue. I have seen the basso bow six times to his boots in the middle of a phrase because a boy in the gallery shouted "Brava"! But I have never heard an opera so utterly ruined as some of my plays have been ruined by roaring audiences. I give them plays of the right length: they add half an hour to the rehearsal time by their senseless incontinence; lose their trains; and then complain that my plays are too long. The actors are kept paralysed on the stage waiting for the din to cease; and then even so accomplished a critic as Mr Hope accuses me of "pinning them down to the furniture" because he misses the accustomed game of musical chairs which Mr Sinclair, being able to act if only the audience will let him, has no need to play.

I have done what I can to make the public ashamed of this intolerable nuisance, which robs it with violence of so much artistic enjoyment. I have distributed appeals with the programmes. I have stormed in the Press. I have produced some effect for a time. On the first night of "Pygmalion" the audience held out very fairly until the third act, when their collapse was perhaps excusable. At the Court Theatre, and later at the Kingsway, there was the beginning of a tradition that no noise loud enough to interrupt the performance was allowable. But since the war a new generation of playgoers has raised its intolerable guffaw, and made comedy impossible. It is for the critics to educate them. And that cannot be done by blaming the actors. Blame the real culprits, the playgoers. Within my recollection they have been educated quite easily to listen to Wagner's music-dramas without uttering a sound from the first chord of the act until the last, though they had been accustomed to uproarious encoring, to making dead bodies rise and bow, to calling prisoners out of their dungeons into the castle yard to smirk acknowledgments for "Ah, che la morte." If they cannot always repress a chuckle, they can at least refrain from a heehaw. If they will not, then I shall protect myself by writing in the style of "Venice Preserved," and simply not amusing them.

G. B. S.